Get Co...

FEATURES

Content Tagged by Learning Outcomes

Content is tagged to the book's learning outcomes, type of question, and more. Build assignments to help meet specific needs.

Interactive Applications

Connect Management's **Interactive Applications** deliver the chapter's content through an engaging and interactive environment that allows students to apply the theory. Students will receive immediate feedback on how they are progressing.

Get Engaged.

eBooks

Connect Plus includes an eBook that allows instructors to share notes with students. Students can insert and review their own notes, highlight the text, and search for specific information. Using an eBook with Connect Plus gives students a complete digital solution that allows them to access their materials from any computer.

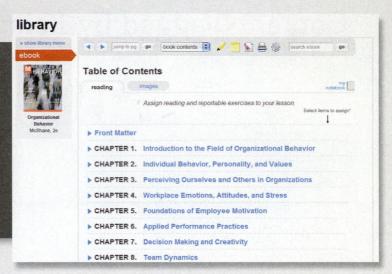

Lecture Capture

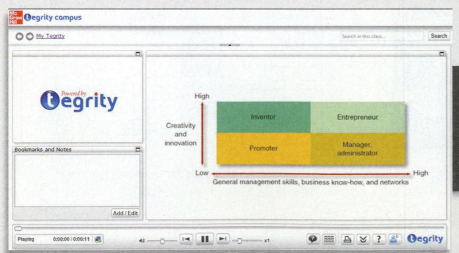

Make classes available anytime, anywhere. With simple, one-click recording, students can search for a word or phrase and be taken to the exact place in the lecture that they need to review.

organizational
behavior 2e

Steven L. McShane
University of Western Australia

Mary Ann Von Glinow
Florida International University

The McGraw-Hill Companies

McGraw-Hill
Irwin

organizational behavior,
second edition

SENIOR VICE PRESIDENT, PRODUCTS & MARKETS   **KURT L. STRAND**

VICE PRESIDENT, GENERAL MANAGER, PRODUCTS & MARKETS   **BRENT GORDON**

VICE PRESIDENT, CONTENT PRODUCTION & TECHNOLOGY SERVICES   **KIMBERLY MERIWETHER DAVID**

MANAGING DIRECTOR   **PAUL DUCHAM**

EXECUTIVE BRAND MANAGER   **MICHAEL ABLASSMEIR**

EXECUTIVE DIRECTOR OF DEVELOPMENT   **ANN TORBERT**

MANAGING DEVELOPMENT EDITOR   **LAURA HURST SPELL**

MARKETING MANAGER   **ELIZABETH TREPKOWSKI**

SENIOR PROJECT MANAGER   **DANA M. PAULEY**

CONTENT PROJECT MANAGER   **MARIANNE L. MUSNI**

SENIOR BUYER   **MICHAEL R. MCCORMICK**

SENIOR DESIGNER   **MATT DIAMOND**

COVER DESIGNER   **KAY LIEBERHERR**

COVER IMAGE   **© GETTY IMAGES**

CONTENT LICENSING SPECIALIST   **BRENDA ROLWES**

PHOTO RESEARCHER   **ALLISON GRIMES**

MEDIA PROJECT MANAGER   **JOYCE J. CHAPPETTO**

TYPEFACE   **10/12 MINION PRO REGULAR**

COMPOSITOR   **APTARA®, INC.**

PRINTER   **QUAD/GRAPHICS**

ORGANIZATIONAL BEHAVIOR

ISBN 978-0-07-802951-6
MHID 0-07-802951-1

Library of Congress Control Number: 2012946888

www.mhhe.com

brief contents

part one
INTRODUCTION
chapter 1 Introduction to the Field of Organizational Behavior 2

part two
INDIVIDUAL BEHAVIOR AND PROCESSES
chapter 2 Individual Behavior, Personality, and Values 22
chapter 3 Perceiving Ourselves and Others in Organizations 44
chapter 4 Workplace Emotions, Attitudes, and Stress 64
chapter 5 Employee Motivation 86
chapter 6 Decision Making and Creativity 110

part three
TEAM PROCESSES
chapter 7 Team Dynamics 130
chapter 8 Communicating in Teams and Organizations 152
chapter 9 Power and Influence in the Workplace 172
chapter 10 Managing Workplace Conflict 192
chapter 11 Leadership in Organizational Settings 212

part four
ORGANIZATIONAL PROCESSES
chapter 12 Designing Organizational Structures 232
chapter 13 Organizational Culture 250
chapter 14 Organizational Change 270

Endnotes 289
Credits 350
Index 352

contents

part one INTRODUCTION

CHAPTER 1 INTRODUCTION TO THE FIELD OF ORGANIZATIONAL BEHAVIOR 2

THE FIELD OF ORGANIZATIONAL BEHAVIOR 4
 Historical Foundations of Organizational Behavior 5
 Why Study Organizational Behavior? 6

PERSPECTIVES OF ORGANIZATIONAL EFFECTIVENESS 7
 Open Systems Perspective 7
 Organizational Learning Perspective 9

HIGH-PERFORMANCE WORK PRACTICES (HPWP) PERSPECTIVE 11
 Stakeholder Perspective 12
 Connecting the Dots: Organizational Effectiveness and Organizational Behavior 14

CONTEMPORARY CHALLENGES FOR ORGANIZATIONS 14
 Globalization 14
 Increasing Workforce Diversity 15
 Emerging Employment Relationships 17

ANCHORS OF ORGANIZATIONAL BEHAVIOR KNOWLEDGE 18
 The Systematic Research Anchor 18
 The Multidisciplinary Anchor 19
 The Contingency Anchor 20
 The Multiple Levels of Analysis Anchor 20

THE JOURNEY BEGINS 20

part two INDIVIDUAL BEHAVIOR AND PROCESSES

CHAPTER 2 INDIVIDUAL BEHAVIOR, PERSONALITY, AND VALUES 22

MARS MODEL OF INDIVIDUAL BEHAVIOR AND PERFORMANCE 24
 Employee Motivation 24
 Ability 25
 Role Perceptions 26
 Situational Factors 26

TYPES OF INDIVIDUAL BEHAVIOR 27
 Task Performance 27
 Organizational Citizenship 27
 Counterproductive Work Behaviors 28
 Joining and Staying with the Organization 28
 Maintaining Work Attendance 28

PERSONALITY IN ORGANIZATIONS 29
  Personality Determinants: Nature versus
  Nurture 30
  Five-Factor Model of Personality 30
  Jungian Personality Theory and the Myers-Briggs
  Type Indicator 32
  Personality Testing in
  Organizations 33

VALUES IN THE WORKPLACE 33
  Types of Values 34
  Values and Individual Behavior 35
  Values Congruence 36

ETHICAL VALUES AND BEHAVIOR 37
  Three Ethical Principles 37
  Moral Intensity, Ethical Sensitivity, Situational
  Influences, and Mindlessness 38
  Supporting Ethical Behavior 39

VALUES ACROSS CULTURES 40
  Individualism and Collectivism 40
  Power Distance 41
  Uncertainty Avoidance 42
  Achievement-Nurturing Orientation 42
  Caveats about Cross-Cultural
  Knowledge 42

  Self-Fulfilling Prophecy 56
  Contingencies of Self-Fulfilling Prophecy 58
  Other Perceptual Effects 58

IMPROVING PERCEPTIONS 59
  Awareness of Perceptual Biases 59
  Improving Self-Awareness 60
  Meaningful Interaction 61

GLOBAL MINDSET: DEVELOPING PERCEPTIONS ACROSS
BORDERS 61
  Developing a Global Mindset 62

CHAPTER 4 WORKPLACE EMOTIONS, ATTITUDES,
               AND STRESS 64

EMOTIONS IN THE WORKPLACE 66
  Types of Emotions 66
  Emotions, Attitudes, and Behavior 67
  Cognitive Dissonance 69
  Emotions and Personality 70

MANAGING EMOTIONS AT WORK 70
  Emotional Display Norms across
  Cultures 71
  Emotional Dissonance 71

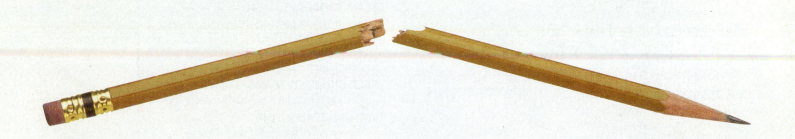

CHAPTER 3 PERCEIVING OURSELVES AND
               OTHERS IN ORGANIZATIONS 44

SELF-CONCEPT: HOW WE PERCEIVE
OURSELVES 46
  Self-Concept Complexity, Consistency,
  and Clarity 46
  Self-Enhancement 47
  Self-Verification 48
  Self-Evaluation 48
  The Social Self 49
  Self-Concept and Organizational
  Behavior 50

PERCEIVING THE WORLD AROUND US 50
  Perceptual Organization and
  Interpretation 52

SPECIFIC PERCEPTUAL PROCESSES AND PROBLEMS 53
  Stereotyping in Organizations 53
  Attribution Theory 55

EMOTIONAL INTELLIGENCE 72
  Assessing and Developing Emotional
  Intelligence at Work 73

JOB SATISFACTION 74
  Job Satisfaction and Work Behavior 75
  Job Satisfaction and Performance 76
  Job Satisfaction and Customer Satisfaction 76
  Job Satisfaction and Business Ethics 77

ORGANIZATIONAL COMMITMENT 77
  Consequences of Affective and Continuance
  Commitment 77
  Building Organizational Commitment 78

WORK-RELATED STRESS AND ITS MANAGEMENT 79
  General Adaptation Syndrome 80
  Consequences of Distress 80
  Stressors: The Causes of Stress 81
  Individual Differences in Stress 82
  Managing Work-Related Stress 83

EVALUATING DECISION OUTCOMES 121
  Escalation of Commitment 121
  Evaluating Decision Outcomes More Effectively 122
CREATIVITY 122
  The Creative Process 123
  Characteristics of Creative People 124
  Organizational Conditions Supporting Creativity 125
  Activities That Encourage Creativity 126
EMPLOYEE INVOLVEMENT IN DECISION MAKING 127
  Benefits of Employee Involvement 127
  Contingencies of Employee Involvement 128

part three   TEAM PROCESSES

CHAPTER 7   TEAM DYNAMICS   130
TEAMS AND INFORMAL GROUPS 132
  Informal Groups 132
ADVANTAGES AND DISADVANTAGES OF TEAMS 133
  The Challenges of Teams 135
A MODEL OF TEAM EFFECTIVENESS 136
  Organizational and Team Environment 136
TEAM DESIGN ELEMENTS 137
  Task Characteristics 137
  Team Size 138
  Team Composition 138
TEAM PROCESSES 140
  Team Development 140
  Team Norms 142
  Team Cohesion 143
  Team Trust 144
SELF-DIRECTED TEAMS 146
  Success Factors for Self-Directed Teams 146
VIRTUAL TEAMS 146
  Success Factors for Virtual Teams 147
TEAM DECISION MAKING 147
  Constraints on Team Decision Making 148
  Team Structures to Improve Decision Making 149

CHAPTER 5   EMPLOYEE MOTIVATION   86
EMPLOYEE ENGAGEMENT 88
EMPLOYEE DRIVES AND NEEDS 89
  Maslow's Needs Hierarchy Theory 90
  Learned Needs Theory 91
  Four-Drive Theory 92
EXPECTANCY THEORY OF MOTIVATION 94
  Expectancy Theory in Practice 95
ORGANIZATIONAL BEHAVIOR MODIFICATION AND SOCIAL
COGNITIVE THEORY 96
  Organizational Behavior Modification 96
  Social Cognitive Theory 97
ORGANIZATIONAL JUSTICE 98
  Equity Theory 98
  Procedural Justice 101
GOAL SETTING AND FEEDBACK 101
  Characteristics of Effective Feedback 102
  Sources of Feedback 103
  Evaluating Goal Setting and Feedback 103
JOB DESIGN PRACTICES 104
  Job Design and Work Efficiency 104
  Job Design and Work Motivation 105
  Job Design Practices That Motivate 108

CHAPTER 6   DECISION MAKING AND
         CREATIVITY   110
RATIONAL CHOICE PARADIGM OF DECISION MAKING 112
  Rational Choice Decision-Making Process 113
  Problems with the Rational Choice Paradigm 113
IDENTIFYING PROBLEMS AND OPPORTUNITIES 114
  Problems with Problem Identification 114
  Identifying Problems and Opportunities More
  Effectively 115
SEARCHING FOR, EVALUATING, AND CHOOSING
ALTERNATIVES 115
  Problems with Goals 116
  Problems with Information Processing 116
  Problems with Maximization 117
  Evaluating Opportunities 118
  Emotions and Making Choices 118
  Intuition and Making Choices 119
  Making Choices More Effectively 120
IMPLEMENTING DECISIONS 121

CHAPTER 8 COMMUNICATING IN TEAMS AND ORGANIZATIONS 152

THE IMPORTANCE OF COMMUNICATION 154

A MODEL OF COMMUNICATION 154
Influences on Effective Encoding and Decoding 155

COMMUNICATION CHANNELS 156
Internet-Based Communication 157
Problems with Email 157
Workplace Communication through Social Media 158
Nonverbal Communication 159

CHOOSING THE BEST COMMUNICATION CHANNEL 160
Social Acceptance 161
Media Richness 161
Communication Channels and Persuasion 163

COMMUNICATION BARRIERS (NOISE) 163
Information Overload 164

CROSS-CULTURAL AND GENDER COMMUNICATION 165
Nonverbal Differences across Cultures 165
Gender Differences in Communication 165

IMPROVING INTERPERSONAL COMMUNICATION 166
Getting Your Message Across 167
Active Listening 167

IMPROVING COMMUNICATION THROUGHOUT THE HIERARCHY 168
Workspace Design 168
Internet-Based Organizational Communication 168
Direct Communication with Top Management 169

COMMUNICATING THROUGH THE GRAPEVINE 169
Grapevine Characteristics 170
Grapevine Benefits and Limitations 171

CHAPTER 9 POWER AND INFLUENCE IN THE WORKPLACE 172

THE MEANING OF POWER 174

SOURCES OF POWER IN ORGANIZATIONS 175
Legitimate Power 175
Reward Power 177
Coercive Power 177
Expert Power 177
Referent Power 178

CONTINGENCIES OF POWER 178
Substitutability 178
Centrality 179
Visibility 179
Discretion 180

THE POWER OF SOCIAL NETWORKS 180
Social Capital and Sources of Power 180
Gaining Power from Social Networks 181

CONSEQUENCES OF POWER 183

INFLUENCING OTHERS 183
Types of Influence Tactics 183
Consequences and Contingencies of Influence Tactics 189

ORGANIZATIONAL POLITICS 190
Minimizing Organizational Politics 190

CHAPTER 10 MANAGING WORKPLACE CONFLICT 192

THE MEANING AND CONSEQUENCES OF CONFLICT 194
Is Conflict Good or Bad? 194
The Emerging View: Constructive and Relationship Conflict 196

CONFLICT PROCESS MODEL 198

STRUCTURAL SOURCES OF CONFLICT IN ORGANIZATIONS 198
Incompatible Goals 199
Differentiation 199
Interdependence 199
Scarce Resources 200
Ambiguous Rules 200
Communication Problems 200

INTERPERSONAL CONFLICT HANDLING STYLES 201
Choosing the Best Conflict Handling Style 202
Cultural and Gender Differences in Conflict Handling Styles 204

STRUCTURAL APPROACHES TO CONFLICT MANAGEMENT 204
Emphasizing Superordinate Goals 204
Reducing Differentiation 204
Improving Communication and Mutual Understanding 205
Reducing Task Interdependence 206
Increasing Resources 206
Clarifying Rules and Procedures 206

THIRD-PARTY CONFLICT RESOLUTION 206
Choosing the Best Third-Party Intervention Strategy 207

RESOLVING CONFLICT THROUGH NEGOTIATION 207
Bargaining Zone Model of Negotiations 207
Strategies for Claiming Value 208
Strategies for Creating Value 209
Situational Influences on Negotiations 210

part four   ORGANIZATIONAL PROCESSES

CHAPTER 12   DESIGNING ORGANIZATIONAL STRUCTURES   232

DIVISION OF LABOR AND COORDINATION   234
Division of Labor   234
Coordinating Work Activities   234

ELEMENTS OF ORGANIZATIONAL STRUCTURE   237
Span of Control   237
Centralization and Decentralization   239
Formalization   239
Mechanistic versus Organic Structures   240

FORMS OF DEPARTMENTALIZATION   241
Simple Structure   241
Functional Structure   241
Divisional Structure   242
Team-Based Structure   244
Matrix Structure   245

CONTINGENCIES OF ORGANIZATIONAL DESIGN   247
External Environment   247
Organizational Size   248
Technology   248
Organizational Strategy   248

CHAPTER 11   LEADERSHIP IN ORGANIZATIONAL SETTINGS   212

WHAT IS LEADERSHIP?   214
Shared Leadership   215

COMPETENCY PERSPECTIVE OF LEADERSHIP   215
Authentic Leadership   217
Competency Perspective Limitations and Practical Implications   218

BEHAVIORAL PERSPECTIVE OF LEADERSHIP   219
Choosing Task- versus People-Oriented Leadership   219
Servant Leadership   219

CONTINGENCY PERSPECTIVE OF LEADERSHIP   220
Path–Goal Theory of Leadership   220
Other Contingency Theories   222
Leadership Substitutes   224

TRANSFORMATIONAL PERSPECTIVE OF LEADERSHIP   225
Transformational versus Transactional Leadership   225
Transformational versus Charismatic Leadership   226
Elements of Transformational Leadership   226
Evaluating the Transformational Leadership Perspective   228

IMPLICIT LEADERSHIP PERSPECTIVE   228
Prototypes of Effective Leaders   229
The Romance of Leadership   229

CROSS-CULTURAL AND GENDER ISSUES IN LEADERSHIP   230
Gender and Leadership   230

CHAPTER 13   ORGANIZATIONAL CULTURE   250

ELEMENTS OF ORGANIZATIONAL CULTURE   252
  Content of Organizational Culture   254
  Organizational Subcultures   255

DECIPHERING ORGANIZATIONAL CULTURE THROUGH
ARTIFACTS   256
  Organizational Stories and Legends   256
  Rituals and Ceremonies   256
  Organizational Language   257
  Physical Structures and Symbols   257

IS ORGANIZATIONAL CULTURE IMPORTANT?   258
  Contingencies of Organizational Culture and
  Effectiveness   259
  Organizational Culture and Business Ethics   260

MERGING ORGANIZATIONAL CULTURES   261
  Bicultural Audit   261
  Strategies for Merging Different Organizational Cultures   262

CHANGING AND STRENGTHENING ORGANIZATIONAL
CULTURE   263
  Actions of Founders and Leaders   263
  Aligning Artifacts   264
  Introducing Culturally Consistent Rewards   264
  Attracting, Selecting, and Socializing Employees   264

ORGANIZATIONAL SOCIALIZATION   265
  Organizational Socialization as a Learning and Adjustment
  Process   266
  Organizational Socialization and Psychological Contracts   266
  Stages of Organizational Socialization   266
  Improving the Socialization Process   268

CROSS-CULTURAL AND ETHICAL ISSUES IN
ORGANIZATIONAL CHANGE   286

ORGANIZATIONAL BEHAVIOR: THE JOURNEY
CONTINUES   287

ENDNOTES   289

CREDITS   350

INDEX   352

CHAPTER 14   ORGANIZATIONAL CHANGE   270

LEWIN'S FORCE FIELD ANALYSIS MODEL   272

UNDERSTANDING RESISTANCE TO CHANGE   273
  Employee Resistance as a Resource for Change   275
  Why Employees Resist Change   275

UNFREEZING, CHANGING, AND REFREEZING   277
  Creating an Urgency for Change   277
  Reducing the Restraining Forces   278
  Refreezing the Desired Conditions   280

LEADERSHIP, COALITIONS, AND PILOT PROJECTS   281
  Transformational Leadership and Change   281
  Coalitions, Social Networks, and Change   281
  Pilot Projects and Diffusion of Change   282

TWO APPROACHES TO ORGANIZATIONAL CHANGE   283
  Action Research Approach   283
  Appreciative Inquiry Approach   284

what's new in the
second edition

Based on feedback from users and reviewers, we undertook an ambitious revision in order to make the book an even more effective teaching and learning tool. Below are the changes we've made for this second edition, broken out by chapter.

OVERALL

- Some topics shifted for better flow, particularly in the first five chapters.
- Dozens of new and revised by-the-numbers and other features.
- Many new real-world examples.
- Updated photos illustrating key concepts throughout.

chapter one
INTRODUCTION TO THE FIELD OF ORGANIZATIONAL BEHAVIOR

Most significantly, the coverage of types of individual behavior was moved to Chapter 2, where it has a more logical link to other topics. We've also further developed the four perspectives of organizational effectiveness, which instructors recognize as the cornerstone of organizational behavior. Updated discussion of contemporary challenges in OB, more details about evidence-based management, and supplemental information about the historical foundations of OB are also included.

chapter two
INDIVIDUAL BEHAVIOR, PERSONALITY, AND VALUES

The coverage of the types of individual behavior now appears after the MARS model of individual behavior, and self-concept has been moved to Chapter 3. Several additional small, yet meaningful changes include new content on presenteeism, role perceptions, situational factors, mindfulness in ethics, the MBTI model, ways that companies support ethical behavior, the relationship between

Big 5 and performance, and problems with cross-cultural knowledge.

chapter three
PERCEIVING OURSELVES AND OTHERS IN ORGANIZATIONS

We've further developed the three self-concept characteristics as well as the four self-concept processes. Self-concept now appears in this chapter due to the logical flow from self-perception (self-concept) to social perception (perceiving others). Behavior modification and social learning (social cognitive) theories have been moved to the motivation chapter (Chapter 5). In addition, the section on global mindset—an important emerging topic that crosses cross-cultural thinking with the perceptual process—has been expanded.

chapter four
WORKPLACE EMOTIONS, ATTITUDES, AND STRESS

This revised chapter fulfills requests for more detail on emotional intelligence. Other expanded and updated topics include cognitive dissonance, emotional labor across cultures, the service profit chain model (job satisfaction and customer service), and individual differences in stress.

chapter five
EMPLOYEE MOTIVATION

This edition includes updated information on employee engagement, further refines discussion of drives and needs, introduces new (and better) exhibits depicting equity theory, presents the SMARTER model of goal setting, and discusses multisource feedback. The chapter also now incorporates condensed coverage of behavior modification and social cognitive theory in the context of learning expectancies in expectancy theory.

chapter six
DECISION MAKING AND CREATIVITY

Coverage of decision heuristic biases has been added, along with updated or refined information on escalation of commitment, stakeholder framing, and the creative process. We've also slightly reorganized some topics to improve the flow.

chapter seven
TEAM DYNAMICS

Chapter revisions include new coverage of the effect of cohesion on performance (and vice versa) and the benefits of brainstorming.

chapter eight
COMMUNICATING IN TEAMS AND ORGANIZATIONS

We've updated the coverage of social media, including a new model on social-media functions in organizational settings. The conceptual foundations of the encoding-decoding process, the importance of communication, social presence effects in communication channels, and gender differences in communication were also revised and updated.

chapter nine
POWER AND INFLUENCE IN THE WORKPLACE

Among the many updates to this chapter, the most important change is the new discussion of social networks, including strong ties, weak ties, network centrality, and structural holes. We've also folded the two forms of information power into their respective sources of power (legitimate and expert). This edition also contains revised and updated information on the dependency model of power, legitimate power and the norm of reciprocity, the consequences of power, and exchange as an influence tactic.

chapter ten
MANAGING WORKPLACE CONFLICT

The most significant change in this chapter is the new section on negotiation. In addition, we've refined the section on the benefits and problems with conflict, as well as the section on structural approaches to managing conflict. This chapter also has some minor reorganization of topics.

chapter eleven
LEADERSHIP IN ORGANIZATIONAL SETTINGS

This edition offers more detailed coverage of shared leadership and servant leadership. Other revised and updated topics include managerial leadership, charismatic leadership, and romance of leadership.

chapter twelve
DESIGNING ORGANIZATIONAL STRUCTURES

The sections on coordination and matrix structures have been updated and revised in this chapter.

chapter thirteen
ORGANIZATIONAL CULTURE

This chapter now introduces psychological contracts and has minor revisions to the topics of organizational socialization.

chapter fourteen
ORGANIZATIONAL CHANGE

We've added new coverage of the role of social networks and viral change in organizational transformations. In addition to various other minor updates, the section on approaches to organizational change was condensed to the two main approaches (action research and appreciative inquiry).

organizational
behavior 2e

Introduction to the Field of
Organizational Behavior

one

Apple, Inc. and Google, Inc. are the two most admired companies in the world, according to *Fortune* magazine's annual list. This is not surprising news to most of us, considering the popularity and innovation of Apple's products and Google's ubiquitous search engine and outpouring of other novel Internet and phone software. What is surprising is that neither company was on anyone's radar screen 15 years ago. Apple was on life support in the late 1990s, barely clinging to a few percentage points of market share in the computer industry. Google wasn't even registered as a company. It was just a computer project by two Stanford PhD students that was quickly outgrowing the dorm room where their equipment was housed. Meanwhile, some firms that were most admired in the late 1990s, such as Dell and Merck, have completely disappeared from the list because they failed to innovate or fell into trouble with ethical misconduct.

Apple and Google are role models of how organizations can succeed in today's turbulent environment. In every sector of the economy, organizations need to be innovative, employ skilled and motivated people who can work in teams, have leaders with foresight and vision, and make decisions that consider the interests of multiple stakeholders. In other words, the best companies succeed through the concepts and practices that we discuss in this book on organizational behavior.

continued on p. 4

LEARNING OBJECTIVES

After studying Chapter 1, you should be able to:

LO1 Define organizational behavior and organizations, and discuss the importance of this field of inquiry.

LO2 Compare and contrast the four current perspectives of organizational effectiveness as well as the early goal attainment perspective.

LO3 Debate the organizational opportunities and challenges of globalization, workforce diversity, and emerging employment relationships.

LO4 Discuss the anchors on which organizational behavior knowledge is based.

continued from p. 3

The purpose of this book is to help you understand what goes on in organizations, including the thoughts and behavior of employees and teams. We examine the factors that make companies effective, improve employee well-being, and drive successful collaboration among coworkers. We look at organizations from numerous and diverse perspectives, from the deepest foundations of employee thoughts and behavior (personality, self-concept, commitment, etc.) to the complex interplay between the organization's structure and culture and its external environment. Along this journey, we emphasize why things happen and what you can do to predict and manage organizational events.

We begin this chapter by introducing you to the field of organizational behavior and why it is important to your career and to organizations. Next, this chapter describes the "ultimate dependent variable" in organizational behavior by presenting the four main perspectives of organizational effectiveness. This is followed by an overview of three challenges facing organizations: globalization, increasing workforce diversity, and emerging employment relationships. We complete this opening chapter by describing four anchors that guide the development of organizational behavior knowledge. ▪

Learning Objective

After reading this section, you should be able to

LO1 Define organizational behavior and organizations, and discuss the importance of this field of inquiry.

THE FIELD OF ORGANIZATIONAL BEHAVIOR

Organizational behavior (OB) is the study of what people think, feel, and do in and around organizations. It looks at employee behavior, decisions, perceptions, and emotional responses. It examines how individuals and teams in organizations relate to each other and to their counterparts in other organizations. OB also encompasses the study of how organizations interact with their external environments, particularly in the context of employee behavior and decisions. OB researchers systematically study these topics at multiple levels of analysis, namely, the individual, team (including interpersonal), and organization.[1]

The definition of organizational behavior begs the question: What are organizations? **Organizations** are groups of people who work interdependently toward some purpose.[2] Notice that organizations are not buildings or government-registered entities. In fact, many organizations exist without either physical walls or government documentation to confer their legal status. Organizations have existed for as long as people have worked together. Massive temples dating back to 3500 BC were constructed through the organized actions of multitudes of people. Craftspeople and merchants in ancient Rome formed guilds, complete with elected managers. More than 1,000 years ago, Chinese factories were producing 125,000 tons of iron each year.[3]

the Chinese philosopher Confucius extolled the virtues of ethics and leadership. In 1776, Adam Smith discussed the benefits of job specialization and division of labor. One hundred years later, German sociologist Max Weber wrote about rational organizations, the work ethic, and charismatic leadership. Soon after, industrial engineer Frederick Winslow Taylor proposed systematic ways to organize work processes and motivate employees through goal setting and rewards.[4]

> ## " A COMPANY IS ONE OF HUMANITY'S MOST AMAZING INVENTIONS. . . . [IT'S] THIS ABSTRACT CONSTRUCT WE'VE INVENTED, AND IT'S INCREDIBLY POWERFUL.
> —STEVE JOBS[5] "

Throughout history, these and other organizations have consisted of people who communicate, coordinate, and collaborate with each other to achieve common objectives. One key feature of organizations is that they are collective entities. They consist of human beings (typically, but not necessarily, employees), and these people interact with each other in an *organized* way. This organized relationship requires some minimal level of communication, coordination, and collaboration to achieve organizational objectives. As such, all organizational members have degrees of interdependence with each other; they accomplish goals by sharing materials, information, or expertise with coworkers.

A second key feature of organizations is that their members have a collective sense of purpose. This collective purpose isn't always well defined or agreed on. Furthermore, although most companies have vision and mission statements, these documents are sometimes out of date or don't describe what employees and leaders try to achieve in reality. Still, imagine an organization without a collective sense of purpose. It would be a collection of people without direction or unifying force. So, whether it's designing smartphones and computers or marketing soft drinks, people working in organizations do have some sense of collective purpose.

Historical Foundations of Organizational Behavior

Organizational behavior emerged as a distinct field around the early 1940s, but organizations have been studied by experts in other fields for many centuries. The Greek philosopher Plato wrote about the essence of leadership. Around the same time,

Foundations of the Organizational Behavior Discipline

Elton Mayo (left), Fritz Roethlisberger (right), and other faculty at Harvard University during the 1930s developed the "human relations" school of thought in which employee attitudes, formal team dynamics, informal groups, and supervisor leadership style strongly influenced employee performance and well-being. These ideas were mostly ignored in earlier organizational research. This human relations view laid the foundation for the field of organizational behavior as we know it today.[6]

From the 1920s to the 1940s, Elton Mayo, Fritz Roethlisberger, and their Harvard University colleagues developed the "human relations" school of management, which emphasized the study of employee attitudes and informal group dynamics in the workplace. Also during that time, political philosopher and social worker Mary Parker Follett advocated new ways of thinking about several OB topics, including constructive conflict, team dynamics, organizational democracy, power, and leadership. In the late 1930s, Chester Barnard wrote insightful views regarding organizational communication, coordination, leadership and authority, organizations as open systems, and team dynamics.[7] This brief historical tour indicates that OB has been around for a long time; it just wasn't organized into a unified discipline until around World War II.

Why Study Organizational Behavior?

Organizational behavior instructors face a challenge: Students who have not yet begun their careers tend to value courses related to specific jobs, such as accounting and marketing.[8] However, OB doesn't have a specific career path—there is no "vice president of OB"—so students sometimes have difficulty recognizing the value that OB knowledge can offer to their future. Meanwhile, students with several years of work experience identify OB as one of the most important courses. Why? Because they have learned through experience that OB *does make a difference* to their career success. OB helps us to make sense of and predict the world in which we live.[9] We use OB theories to question our personal beliefs and assumptions and to adopt more accurate models of workplace behavior. Some experts suggest that OB knowledge even helps us to make sense of what

> " Probably the greatest value of OB knowledge is that it helps us to get things done in organizations. "

goes on in the world, not just what goes on inside organizations.[10]

But probably the greatest value of OB knowledge is that it helps us to get things done in organizations.[11] Everyone in business, government, and not-for-profit firms works with other people, and OB provides the knowledge and tools to interact with others more effectively. Building a high-performance team, motivating coworkers, handling workplace conflicts, influencing your boss, and changing employee behavior are just a few of the areas of knowledge and skills offered in organizational behavior. No matter what career path you choose, you'll find that OB concepts play an important role in performing your job and working more effectively within organizations.

Organizational Behavior Is for Everyone

Organizational behavior is important for anyone who works in organizations, not just for managers. In fact, this book pioneered the notion that OB knowledge is for everyone. Whether you are a geologist, financial analyst, customer service representative, or chief executive officer, you need to understand and apply the many organizational behavior topics discussed in this book. Yes, organizations will continue to have managers, and this book recognizes the relevance of OB knowledge in these vital roles. But this book also recognizes the reality that all employees are increasingly expected to manage themselves and work effectively with each other in the workplace. In the words of one forward-thinking OB writer more than four decades ago: Everyone is a manager.[12]

OB and the Bottom Line

Up to this point, our answer to the question "Why study OB?" has focused on how organizational behavior knowledge benefits you as an individual. However, OB knowledge is just as important for the organization's financial health. Numerous studies have reported that these and other OB practices discussed in this book tend to improve the organization's survival and success.[13] For example, one investigation found that hospitals have lower patient mortality rates when they engage in more OB activities such as training, staff involvement, and employee recognition. Another study found that companies receiving "the best place to work" awards have significantly higher financial and long-term stock market performance. And as we will learn in Chapter 5, employee engagement is associated with significantly higher sales and profitability.

The bottom-line value of organizational behavior is also supported by human capital and investment portfolio studies. For instance, some investment analysts estimate that three-quarters of the value of a typical company comes from its intangible assets, which include the ability to manage and retain employees. "The best companies are the ones that see their human resources as a competitive advantage," concludes a senior portfolio manager at AMP Capital Investors. These investigations suggest that

specific OB characteristics (employee attitudes, work/life balance, performance-based rewards, leadership, employee training and development, etc.) are important "positive screens" for selecting companies with the best long-term stock appreciation.[14]

Learning Objective

After reading this section, you should be able to

LO2 Compare and contrast the four current perspectives of organizational effectiveness as well as the early goal attainment perspective.

PERSPECTIVES OF ORGANIZATIONAL EFFECTIVENESS

We began this chapter by pointing out that Apple and Google have become the two most admired companies in the world. Almost all organizational behavior theories have the implicit or explicit objective of making organizations more effective, and both Apple and Google have applied many of these concepts.[15] **Organizational effectiveness** is considered the "ultimate dependent variable" in organizational behavior.[16] This means that organizational effectiveness is the outcome that most OB theories are ultimately trying to achieve. Many theories use different labels—organizational performance, success, goodness, health, competitiveness, excellence—but they are basically presenting models and recommendations that help organizations to be more effective.

Before describing the four complementary perspectives of organizational effectiveness, we should mention the now discredited "goal attainment" view, which was popular for many years. The goal attainment perspective states that companies are effective when they achieve their stated organizational objectives.[17] According to this definition, Qantas would be an effective organization if it meets or exceeds its annual sales and profit targets. Today, we know this isn't necessarily so. Any leadership team could set corporate goals that are easy to achieve, yet would put the organization out of business. These goals could also be left in the dust by competitors' more aggressive objectives. Worse still, some goals might aim the organization in the wrong direction. Consequently, goal attainment is not part of the organizational effectiveness model in this book.

The best yardstick of organizational effectiveness is a composite of four perspectives: open systems, organizational learning, high-performance work practices, and stakeholders.[18] Organizations are effective when they have a good fit with their external environment, are learning organizations, have efficient and adaptive internal subsystems (i.e. high-performance work practices), and satisfy the needs of key stakeholders. Let's examine each of these perspectives in more detail.

Open Systems Perspective

The **open systems** perspective of organizational effectiveness is one of the earliest and well-entrenched ways of thinking about organizations.[19] Indeed, the other major organizational effectiveness perspectives might be considered detailed extensions of the open systems model. The open systems perspective views organizations as complex organisms that "live" within an external environment, rather like the illustration in Exhibit 1.1. The word *open* describes this permeable relationship, whereas *closed systems* operate without dependence on or interaction with an external environment.

As open systems, organizations depend on the external environment for resources, including raw materials, job applicants, financial resources, information, and equipment. The external environment also consists of rules and expectations, such as laws and cultural norms, that place demands on how organizations should operate. Some environmental resources (e.g., raw materials) are transformed into outputs that are exported to the external environment, whereas other resources (e.g., job applicants, equipment) become subsystems in the transformation process.

Inside the organization are numerous subsystems, such as departments, teams, informal groups, work processes, technological configurations, and other elements. Rather like the Russian matryoshka dolls nested within each other, organizational subsystems are also systems with their own subsystems.[20] For example, the

organizational effectiveness
A broad concept represented by several perspectives, including the organization's fit with the external environment, internal subsystems' configuration for high performance, emphasis on organizational learning, and ability to satisfy the needs of key stakeholders.

open systems
A perspective that holds that organizations depend on the external environment for resources, affect that environment through their output, and consist of internal subsystems that transform inputs to outputs.

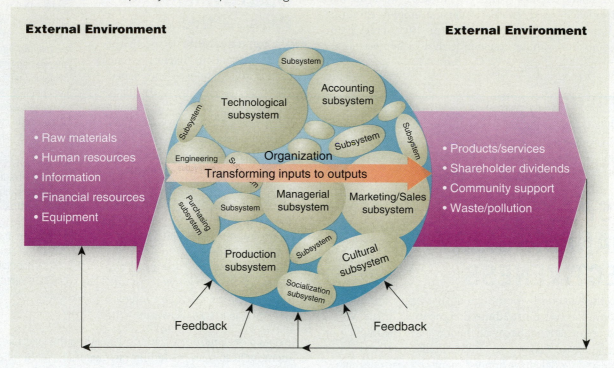

Nordstrom department store in Spokane, Washington, is a subsystem of the Nordstrom chain, but the Spokane store is also a system with its own subsystems of departments, teams, and work processes. An organization's subsystems are organized interdependently so they interact with each other to transform inputs into various outputs. Some outputs (e.g., products, services, community support) may be valued by the external environment, whereas other outputs (e.g., employee layoffs, pollution) are by-products that may have adverse effects on the environment and the organization's relationship with that environment. Throughout this process, organizations receive feedback from the external environment regarding the value of their outputs and the availability of future inputs.

Organization-Environment Fit According to the open systems perspective, organizations are effective when they maintain a good "fit" with their external environment.[21] Good fit exists when the organization puts resources where they are most useful to adapt to and align with the needs of the external environment. For instance, Apple Inc. has good fit with its many external environments—just look at the skyrocketing market share of Apple laptops and iPhones as well as the long lines of people waiting to buy the latest iPad. In contrast, companies with a poor fit with the environment offer the wrong products and operate inappropriately in their environments.

Successful organizations maintain a good fit by anticipating change in the environment and fluidly reconfiguring their subsystems to become more consistent with that environment. To illustrate, food manufacturers have changed their ingredients and production processes to satisfy more health- and environment-conscious consumers. Companies also maintain a good fit by actively managing their external environment. For example, they might try to limit competitor access to critical resources (e.g., gaining exclusive rights), change consumer perceptions and needs (e.g., through marketing), or support legislation that strengthens their position in the marketplace.

The third fit strategy is to move into different environments if the current environment is too challenging. For instance, Nokia started in 1865 as a pulp and paper company. The Finnish company entered the rubber and cable business in the 1920s, moved into electronics in the 1960s, and began producing cell phones a decade later. These strategic choices moved the company decisively into new external environments that seemed to be more appealing for Nokia's long-term survival and success.[22]

Internal Subsystems Effectiveness The open systems perspective considers more than an organization's fit with the external environment. It also defines effectiveness by how well the company operates internally, that is, how well it transforms inputs into outputs. The most common indicator of this internal transformation process is **organizational efficiency** (also called *productivity*), which is the ratio of inputs to outcomes.[23] Companies that produce more goods or services with less labor, materials, and energy are more efficient.

Successful organizations require more than efficient transformation processes, however. They also need to have more *adaptive* and *innovative* transformation processes.[24] Adaptivity makes the organization's transformation process more responsive to changing conditions and customer needs. Innovation enables the company to design work processes that are superior to what competitors can offer. Finally, as organizations grow, there is increased risk that information will get lost, ideas and resources are hoarded, messages are misinterpreted, and rewards are distributed unfairly. Subsystems are also interconnected, so small work practice changes in one subsystem may ripple through the organization and undermine the effectiveness of other subsystems. Consequently, internal subsystems effectiveness calls for well-tuned coordination among subsystems.[25] Employees need to actively communicate with each other and set up workable procedures to minimize these mishaps.

Organizational Learning Perspective

The open-systems perspective has traditionally focused on physical resources that enter the organization and are processed into physical goods (outputs). This was representative of the industrial economy but not the "new economy," where the most valued input as knowledge. The **organizational learning** perspective (also called *knowledge management*) views knowledge as the main driver of competitive advantage. Specifically, organizational learning is founded on the idea that organizational effectiveness depends on the organization's capacity to acquire, share, use, and store valuable knowledge.

Intellectual Capital: The Stock of Organizational Knowledge

The organizational learning perspective views knowledge as a resource, and this stock of knowledge exists in three forms, collectively known as **intellectual capital**.[27] The most commonly-mentioned form of intellectual capital is **human capital**—the knowledge, skills, and abilities that employees carry around in their heads. Human capital has been described as valuable, rare, difficult to imitate, and nonsubstitutable.[28] It is valuable because employees help the organization to discover opportunities and to minimize threats in the external environment. Human capital is rare and difficult to imitate, meaning that talented people are difficult to find and they cannot be cloned like sheep. Finally, human capital is nonsubstitutable because it cannot be easily replaced by technology.

Because of these characteristics, human capital is a competitive advantage as well as a huge risk for most organizations. When key people leave, they take with them some of the most valuable knowledge that makes the company effective. "Innovation is the key to success in this business, and creativity fuels innovation," explains Jim Goodnight, CEO of SAS Institute Inc., a leading statistical software developer in Cary, North Carolina. "As such, 95 percent of my assets drive out the gate every evening. It's my job to maintain a work environment that keeps those people coming back every morning. The creativity they bring to SAS is a competitive advantage for us."[29]

Fortunately, some intellectual capital remains even if every employee did leave the organization. **Structural capital** (also called *organizational capital*) includes the knowledge captured and retained in an organization's systems and structures, such as the documentation of work procedures and the physical layout of the production line.[30] Structural capital also includes the organization's finished products because knowledge can be extracted by taking them apart to discover how they work and are constructed (i.e., reverse engineering).

OB Theory to Practice

Brasilata, the Learning Organization

Brasilata has thrived on organizational learning practices. All 900 employees at the award-winning Brazilian metal can manufacturer are encouraged to think up as many new ideas as possible. After a slow start two decades ago (with only one idea per person each year), the company now receives more than 200,000 ideas each year—an average of more than 220 ideas per employee. Some employee suggestions have sown the seeds of innovative products, such as an award-winning paint can that withstands heavy impact when dropped. Other ideas have dramatically improved productivity. "Innovative action is stimulated by a corporate environment where the communications channels are always open, new ideas are respected and errors tolerated," explains Brasilata CEO Antonio Carlos Alvares Teixeira.[26]

The third form of intellectual capital is **relationship capital**, which is the value derived from an organization's relationships with customers, suppliers, and others who provide added mutual value for the organization. It includes the organization's goodwill, brand image, and combination of relationships that organizational members have with people outside the organization.[31]

Organizational Learning Processes

Organizations nurture their intellectual capital through four organizational learning processes: knowledge acquisition, knowledge sharing, knowledge use, and knowledge storage (see Exhibit 1.2).[32]

- *Knowledge acquisition.* This includes extracting information and ideas from the external environment as well as through insight. One of the fastest and most powerful ways to acquire knowledge is to hire individuals or acquire entire companies (called grafting). Knowledge also enters the organization when employees learn from external sources, such as when a supplier mentions that a competitor is changing its packaging or product design. A third knowledge acquisition strategy is experimentation. Companies receive knowledge through insight as a result of research and other creative processes.

- *Knowledge sharing.* This aspect of organizational learning involves distributing knowledge to others across the organization.

Knowledge sharing is often equated with computer intranets and digital repositories of knowledge. These are relevant, but knowledge sharing mainly occurs through structured and informal communication as well as various forms of learning within the organization, such as observation, experience, training, and practice. For example, Pixar Animation Studios deliberately centralized its cafeteria, mailroom, and restroom facilities so employees would "bump into" and coincidentally share knowledge with people from other areas of the organization rather than just with their own team members.[33]

- *Knowledge use.* Knowledge becomes a competitive advantage when it is applied in ways that add value to the organization and its stakeholders. To do this, employees must realize that the knowledge is available and that they have the freedom to apply that knowledge. This requires an organizational culture that supports creativity and learning. Learning organizations encourage experimentation and open communications, and its leaders recognize mistakes are part of that knowledge use process.

- *Knowledge storage.* Knowledge storage includes any means by which knowledge is held for later retrieval. It is the process that creates organizational memory. Human memory plays a critical role here, as do the many forms of documentation and database systems that exist in organizations. Individual practices and habits hold less explicit (more tacit) knowledge.

Organizational Memory and Unlearning

Corporate leaders need to recognize they are the keepers of an *organizational memory*.[34] This unusual metaphor refers to the storage and preservation of intellectual capital. It includes knowledge that employees possess as well as knowledge embedded in the organization's systems and structures. It includes documents, objects, and anything else that provides meaningful information about how the organization should operate.

How do organizations retain intellectual capital? One way is by keeping knowledgeable employees. Progressive companies achieve this by adapting their employment practices to become more compatible with emerging workforce expectations. A second organizational

▼ **EXHIBIT 1.2** Four Organizational Learning Processes

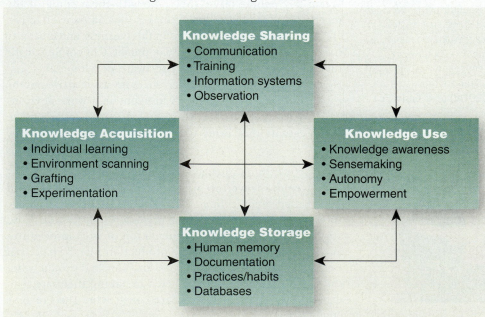

Knowledge Sharing
- Communication
- Training
- Information systems
- Observation

Knowledge Acquisition
- Individual learning
- Environment scanning
- Grafting
- Experimentation

Knowledge Use
- Knowledge awareness
- Sensemaking
- Autonomy
- Empowerment

Knowledge Storage
- Human memory
- Documentation
- Practices/habits
- Databases

memory strategy is to systematically transfer knowledge to other employees. This occurs when newcomers apprentice with skilled employees, thereby acquiring undocumented knowledge. A third strategy is to transfer knowledge into structural capital. This includes bringing out hidden knowledge, organizing it, and putting it in a form that can be available to others. Reliance Industries, India's largest business enterprise, applies this strategy by encouraging employees to document their successes and failures through a special intranet knowledge portal. One of these reports alone provided information that later prevented a costly plant shutdown.[35]

The organizational learning perspective states not only that effective organizations learn, but also that they unlearn routines and patterns of behavior no longer appropriate.[36] Unlearning removes knowledge that no longer adds value and, in fact, may undermine the organization's effectiveness. Some forms of unlearning involve replacing dysfunctional policies, procedures, and routines. Other forms of unlearning erase attitudes, beliefs, and assumptions. For instance, employees rethink the "best way" to perform a task and how to serve clients. Organizational unlearning is particularly important for organizational change, which we discuss in Chapter 14.

HIGH-PERFORMANCE WORK PRACTICES (HPWP) PERSPECTIVE

The open-systems perspective states that successful companies are good at transforming inputs into outputs. However, it does not identify the subsystem characteristics that distinguish effective organizations from others. Consequently, an entire field of research has blossomed around the objective of determining specific "bundles" of organizational practices that offer competitive advantage. This research has had various labels over the years, but it is now most commonly known as **high-performance work practices (HPWP)**.[37]

Similar to organizational learning, the HPWP perspective is founded on the belief that human capital—the knowledge, skills, and abilities employees carry around in their heads—is an important source of competitive advantage for organizations.[38] The distinctive feature of the HPWP perspective is that it tries to identify a specific bundle of systems and structures that generate the most value from this human capital.

Researchers have investigated numerous potential high-performance work practices,

but we will focus on four that are recognized in most studies: employee involvement, job autonomy, competency development, and rewards for performance and competency development.[39] Each of these four work practices individually improves organizational performance, but studies suggests they have a stronger effect when bundled together.[40]

The first two factors—involving employees in decision making and giving them more autonomy over their work activities—tend to strengthen employee motivation as well as improve decision making, organizational responsiveness, and commitment to change. In high-performance workplaces, employee involvement and job autonomy often take the form of self-directed teams (see Chapter 7). The third factor, employee competence development, refers to recruiting, selecting, and training people so employees acquire the most relevant skills, knowledge, values, and other personal characteristics. The fourth high-performance work practice involves linking performance and skill development to various forms of financial and nonfinancial rewards valued by employees.

Why are HPWP practices associated with organizational effectiveness? Early studies were criticized for ignoring this question,[41] but OB experts are now building and testing more theoretical explanations.[42] The first reason is that HPWPs build human capital, which improves performance as employees develop the skills and knowledge to perform the work. A second explanation is that superior human capital may

> " Researchers have identified several high-performance work practices, including involvement, autonomy, rewards, and employee competency development. "

improve the organization's adaptability to rapidly changing environments. Employees respond better when they have a wide skill set to handle diverse tasks as well as confidence to handle unfamiliar situations. A third explanation is that HPWP practices strengthen employee motivation and attitudes toward the employer. They represent the company's investment in and recognition of its workforce, which motivates employees to reciprocate through greater effort in their jobs and assistance to coworkers.

The HPWP perspective is still developing, but it already reveals important information about specific organizational practices that improve the input-output transformation process. Still, this perspective has been criticized for focusing on shareholder and customer needs at the expense of employee well-being.[43] This concern illustrates that the HPWP perspective offers an incomplete picture of organizational effectiveness. The remaining gaps are mostly filled by the stakeholder perspective of organizational effectiveness.

Stakeholder Perspective

The three organizational effectiveness perspectives described so far mainly pay attention to processes and resources, yet they only minimally recognize the importance of relations with **stakeholders**. Stakeholders include anyone with a stake in the company—employees, stockholders, suppliers, labor unions, government, communities, consumer and environmental interest groups, and so on (see Exhibit 1.3). In other words, organizations are more effective when they consider the needs and expectations of any individual, group, or other entity that affects, or is affected by, the organization's objectives and actions. This approach requires organizational leaders and employees to understand, manage, and satisfy the interests of their stakeholders.[44] The stakeholder perspective personalizes the open-systems perspective; it identifies specific people and social entities in the external environment as well as within the organization (the internal environment). It also recognizes that stakeholder relations are dynamic; they can be negotiated and managed, not just taken as a fixed condition.[45]

Understanding, managing, and satisfying the interests of stakeholders is more challenging than it sounds because stakeholders have conflicting interests and organizations don't have the resources to satisfy every stakeholder to the fullest. Therefore, organizational leaders need to decide how much priority to give to each group. One commonly cited factor is to favor stakeholders with the most power.[46] This makes sense when one considers the most powerful stakeholders present the greatest threat and opportunity to the company's survival. Yet stakeholder power should not be the only factor to consider. Ignoring less powerful stakeholders might motivate them to form coalitions or seek government support, which would give them more power. Ignoring smaller stakeholders might also irritate the more powerful stakeholders if ignoring weaker interests violates the norms and standards of society.

▼ **EXHIBIT 1.3** Organizational Stakeholders

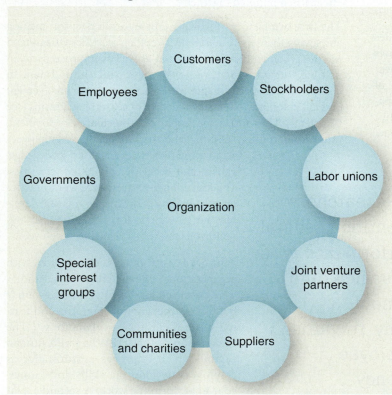

Note: This exhibit does not show the complete set of possible stakeholders.

Values, Ethics, and Corporate Social Responsibility This brings us to one of the key strengths of the stakeholder perspective, namely, that it incorporates values, ethics, and corporate social responsibility into the organizational effectiveness equation.[47] The stakeholder perspective states that to manage the interests of diverse stakeholders, leaders ultimately need to rely on their personal and organizational values for guidance. **Values** are relatively stable, evaluative beliefs that guide our preferences for outcomes or courses of action in a variety of situations.[48] Values help us to know what is right or wrong, or good or bad, in the world. Chapter 2 explains how values anchor our thoughts and to some extent motivate our actions. Although values exist within individuals, groups of people often hold similar values, so we tend to ascribe these *shared values* to the team, department, organization, profession, or entire society. For example, Chapter 13 discusses the importance and dynamics of organizational culture, which includes shared values across the company or within subsystems.

Many companies have adopted the values-driven organization model, whereby employee decisions and behavior are guided by the company's espoused values rather than by expensive and often demoralizing command-and-control management (i.e., top-down decisions with close supervision of employees).[49] Tony Hsieh, CEO of online

stakeholders Individuals, organizations, or other entities that affect, or are affected by, the organization's objectives and actions.

values Relatively stable, evaluative beliefs that guide a person's preferences for outcomes or courses of action in a variety of situations.

ethics The study of moral principles or values that determine whether actions are right or wrong and outcomes are good or bad.

corporate social responsibility (CSR) Organizational activities intended to benefit society and the environment beyond the firm's immediate financial interests or legal obligations.

> ## It's not hard to make decisions when you know what your values are.
>
> —Roy Disney

retailer Zappos, discovered the importance of clarifying the company's values when someone suggested managers need these values to help them make better hiring decisions. After considerable reflection and involvement from staff, Hsieh emailed employees with 10 values. In that email, Hsieh also wrote: "Ideally, we want all 10 values to be reflected in everything we do, including how we interact with each other, how we interact with our customers, and how we interact with our vendors and business partners."[50]

By linking values to organizational effectiveness, the stakeholder perspective also incorporates ethics and corporate social responsibility into the organizational effectiveness equation. In fact, the stakeholder perspective emerged out of earlier writing on ethics and corporate social responsibility. **Ethics** refers to the study of moral principles or values that determine whether actions are right or wrong and outcomes are good or bad. We rely on our ethical values to determine "the right thing to do." Ethical behavior is driven by the moral principles we use to make decisions. These moral principles represent fundamental values. In a recent global survey of MBA students, almost 80 percent felt that a well-run company operates according to its values and code of ethics.[51] Chapter 2 provides more detail about ethical principles and related influences on moral reasoning.

Corporate social responsibility (CSR) consists of organizational activities intended to benefit society and the environment beyond the firm's immediate financial interests or legal obligations.[52] It is the view that companies have a contract with society in which they must serve stakeholders beyond shareholders and customers. In some situations, the interests of the firm's shareholders should be secondary to those of other stakeholders.[53] As part of CSR, many companies have adopted the triple-bottom-line philosophy: They try to support or "earn positive returns" in the economic, social, and environmental spheres of sustainability. Firms that adopt the triple bottom line aim to survive and be profitable in the marketplace (economic), but they also intend to maintain or

improve conditions for society (social) as well as the physical environment.[54] Companies are particularly eager to become "greener," that is, minimize any negative effect they have on the physical environment. This activity ranges from reducing and recycling waste in the production process to using goats to mow the lawn (which is one of the many environmental initiatives at Google).

OB Theory to Practice

MTN Group Goes Green with Y'ello

MTN Group is the largest mobile (cell phone) telecommunications company in Africa and a leader in corporate social responsibility (CSR). Through its award-winning "21 Days of Y'ello Care" program, most of the company's 30,000 employees volunteer for specific CSR events held over three weeks each year. This photo shows MTN employees in Uganda participating in a recent Y'ello Care objective—planting at least 1,000 trees in each of the 21 African and Middle Eastern countries where MTN does business. Y'ello Care themes in previous years included fighting against malaria, reducing traffic accidents, cleaning up the community, and supporting orphanages.[55]

Not everyone agrees that organizations need to cater to a wide variety of stakeholders. More than 30 years ago, economist Milton Friedman pronounced that "there is one and only one social responsibility of business—to use its resources and engage in activities designed to increase its profits."[56] Although few writers take this extreme view today, some point out that companies can benefit other stakeholders only if shareholders receive first priority. But even this position is unpopular with most employees and other stakeholders. "Our company's position on corporate social responsibility and the environment is a significant part of what job candidates find attractive about HBC," acknowledges a senior executive at Hudson's Bay Co., the Canadian department store chain and oldest commercial business in North America.[57] In short, leaders may put their organization at risk if they ignore their broader corporate social responsibility.

Connecting the Dots: Organizational Effectiveness and Organizational Behavior

These four perspectives of organizational effectiveness—open system, organizational learning, high-performance work practices, and stakeholders—provide a roadmap to guide the survival and success of organizations. They also provide a central source of links to the topics discussed throughout this book. The adaptive emphasis of the open systems perspective connects directly to leadership (Chapter 11) and organizational change (Chapter 14). The transformation process aspect of open systems relates to job design (Chapter 5), organizational structure (Chapter 12), and relations between subunits in terms of conflict (Chapter 10) and power and influence (Chapter 9).

The organizational learning perspective highlights the importance of communication (Chapter 8) as well as creativity, employee involvement, and topics in decision making (Chapter 6). The high performance work practices perspective of effectiveness directly casts a spotlight on team dynamics (Chapter 7), employee motivation (Chapter 5), and most individual-level topics (Chapter 2 to Chapter 4). The stakeholder approach has direct relevance to values and ethics (Chapter 2), organizational culture (Chapter 13), and decision making (Chapter 6).

Learning Objective

After reading this section, you should be able to

LO3 Debate the organizational opportunities and challenges of globalization, workforce diversity, and emerging employment relationships.

CONTEMPORARY CHALLENGES FOR ORGANIZATIONS

A message threaded throughout the previous section on organizational effectiveness is that organizations are deeply affected by the external environment. Consequently, they need to anticipate and adjust to environment changes to maintain a good organization-environment fit. The external environment is continuously changing, but some changes over the past decade and in the decade to come are more profound than others. These changes require corporate leaders and all other employees to make personal and organizational adjustments. In this section, we highlight three of the major challenges facing organizations: globalization, increasing workforce diversity, and emerging employment relationships.

Globalization

PricewaterhouseCoopers LLP recently sent Maja Baiocco on a two-year international assignment in Zurich. For Baiocco, an asset management auditor in the accounting firm's office in Toronto, Canada, it was a welcome chance to gain global experience and boost her career. "This company (PwC) is global and opportunities are global, and I know that international experiences are important to expand my experience and open new opportunities for advancement," she says.[59] Maja Baiocco is developing her career in a world of increasing globalization. **Globalization** refers to economic, social, and cultural connectivity with people in

High Expectations

for Corporate Social Responsibility[58]

60% of employed women say that working for a company that prioritizes social and environmental responsibility is very important to them.

31% of managers globally say their companies are currently profiting from sustainable business practices.

38% of employed men say that working for a company that prioritizes social and environmental responsibility is very important to them.

67% of managers globally say that sustainability is critically important to being competitive in today's marketplace

65% of MBA students say they expect to make a positive social or environmental difference in the world through their work.

globalization
Economic, social, and cultural connectivity with people in other parts of the world.

surface-level diversity The observable demographic or physiological differences in people, such as their race, ethnicity, gender, age, and physical disabilities.

deep-level diversity Differences in the psychological characteristics of employees, including personalities, beliefs, values, and attitudes.

other parts of the world. Organizations globalize when they actively participate in other countries and cultures. Although businesses have traded goods across borders for centuries, the degree of globalization today is unprecedented because information technology and transportation systems allow a much more intense level of connectivity and interdependence around the planet.[60]

Globalization offers numerous benefits to organizations in terms of larger markets, lower costs, and greater access to knowledge and innovation. At the same time, there is considerable debate about whether globalization benefits developing nations, and whether it is primarily responsible for increasing work intensification, as well as reducing job security and work/life balance in developed countries.[61] Globalization is now well entrenched, so the most important issue in organizational behavior is how corporate leaders and employees alike can lead and work effectively in this emerging reality.[62]

Throughout this book, we will refer to the effects of globalization on teamwork, diversity, cultural values, organizational structure, leadership, and other themes. Each topic highlights that globalization has brought more complexity to the workplace but also more opportunities and potential benefits for individuals and organizations. Globalization requires additional knowledge and skills that we will also discuss in this book, such as emotional intelligence, a global mind-set, nonverbal communication, and conflict handling.

Increasing Workforce Diversity

Walk into the offices of Verizon Communications and you can quickly see the telecommunications giant values workforce diversity. Women and people of color constitute nearly 60 percent of the company's 195,000-person workforce and nearly half of the company's Board of Directors. African Americans represent 20 percent of Verizon's workforce (compared to 11 percent of the U.S. labor force). More than one-quarter of senior management (vice president and above) positions are held by women. The company also actively supports diversity among its many

suppliers. Verizon's inclusive culture has won awards from numerous organizations and publications representing Hispanic, African American, gay/lesbian, people with disabilities, and other groups. "Verizon incorporates diversity in all that we do," says CEO Ivan Seidenberg. "It's part of our credo to encourage each other to embrace diversity and personal development, not only because it's the right thing to do but also because it's smart business."[63]

Verizon Communications is a model employer and a reflection of the increasing diversity of people living in the United States and in many other countries. The description of Verizon's diversity refers to **surface-level diversity**—the observable demographic and other overt differences in people, such as their race, ethnicity, gender, age, and physical capabilities. Surface-level diversity has changed considerably in the United States over the past few decades. People with non-Caucasian or Hispanic origin represent one-third of the American population, and this is projected to increase substantially over the next few decades. Within the next 50 years, one in four Americans will be Hispanic, 14 percent will be African American, and 8 percent will be of Asian descent. By 2060, people with European non-Hispanic ethnicity will be a minority.[64] Many other countries are also experiencing increasing levels of racial and ethnic diversification.

Diversity also includes differences in the psychological characteristics of employees, including personalities, beliefs, values, and attitudes.[65] We can't directly see this **deep-level diversity**, but it is evident in a person's decisions, statements, and actions. A popular example is the apparent deep-level diversity across generations.[66] Exhibit 1.4 illustrates the distribution of the American workforce by major generational cohort: 37 percent *Baby Boomers* (born from 1946 and 1964), 28 percent *Generation X* (born from 1965 to 1980), and 26 percent *Millennials* (also called *Generation Y*, born after 1980).

Do these generational cohorts have different attitudes and expectations, particularly regarding work? The answer is a qualified yes. Some generational differences are smaller than depicted in the popular press, and some of these differences are due to age, not cohort (i.e., Boomers had many of the same attitudes as Millennials when they were that age).[67] One recent investigation of 23,000 undergraduate college students reported that Millennials expect rapid career advancement regarding promotions and pay increases.[68] These observations are consistent with other studies, which have found that Millennials are more

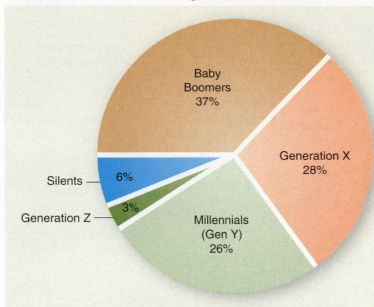

Percentage of United States workforce by age group, based on data from the U.S. Bureau of Labor Statistics. "Silents" represent the generation of employees born before 1946. Generation Z employees are born after 1990, although some sources consider this group part of Millennials.

self-confident, are more narcissistic (self-centered), and have less work centrality (i.e., work is less of a central life interest) when compared to Boomers. Generation-X employees typically average somewhere between these two cohorts.[70]

One large-scale cohort study surveyed the three generational groups when each was in senior high school. The results suggest Millennials have the highest preference for leisure, followed by Gen-Xers and Baby Boomers.[71] Millennials and Gen-Xers also value extrinsic rewards significantly more than Boomers, and Millennials value social interaction significantly less than Boomers or Gen-Xers. Of course, these results don't apply to everyone in each cohort, but they do suggest that deep-level diversity exists across generations.

Consequences of Diversity Diversity presents both opportunities and challenges in organizations.[72] Diversity is an advantage because it provides diverse knowledge. Furthermore, teams with some forms of diversity (particularly occupational diversity) make better decisions on complex problems than teams whose members have similar backgrounds. There is also some evidence that diversity award-winning companies have higher

financial returns, at least in the short run.[73] This is consistent with anecdotal evidence from many corporate leaders, namely that having a diverse workforce improves customer service and creativity. "As a company serving customers around the globe, we greatly value the diverse opinions and experiences that an inclusive and diverse workforce brings to the table," says a Verizon executive.[74]

Is workforce diversity a sound business proposition? The answer is yes, but research indicates that most forms of diversity create challenges as well as offer benefits.[75] Teams with diverse employees usually take longer to perform effectively. Diversity brings numerous communication problems as well as "faultlines" in informal group dynamics. Diversity is also a source of conflict, which can reduce information sharing and, in extreme cases, increase morale problems and turnover.

Aside from the ongoing debate about the productivity and marketing benefits of workforce diversity, companies need to make diversity a priority because surface-level diversity is a moral and legal imperative. Ethically, companies that offer an inclusive workplace are, in essence, making fair and just decisions regarding employment, promotions, rewards, and so on. Fairness is a well-established influence on employee loyalty and satisfaction. In summary, workforce diversity is the new reality and organizations need to adjust to this reality

> Companies that offer an inclusive workplace are, in essence, making fair and just decisions.

both to survive and to experience its potential benefits for organizational success.

work/life balance
The degree to which a person minimizes conflict between work and nonwork demands.

Emerging Employment Relationships

Combine globalization with emerging workforce diversity, then add in recent developments in information technology. The resulting concoction has created incredible changes in employment relationships. A few decades ago, most (although not all) employees in the United States and similar cultures would finish their workday after eight or nine hours and could separate their personal time from the workday. There were no iPhones, Blackberrys, or Internet connections to keep them tethered to work on a 24/7 schedule. Even business travel was more of an exception due to its high cost. Most competitors were located in the same country, so they had similar work practices and labor costs. Today, work hours are longer (although arguably less than 100 years ago), employees experience more work-related stress, and there is growing evidence that family and personal relations are suffering.

Little wonder that one of the most important employment issues over the past decade has been **work/life balance**. Work-life balance occurs when people are able to minimize

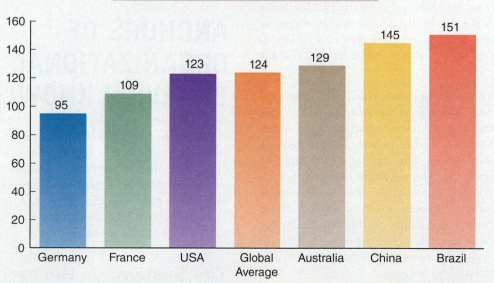

Global Work-Life Balance Index[76]

Germany 95
France 109
USA 123
Global Average 124
Australia 129
China 145
Brazil 151

Figures are based on interviews with more than 16,000 business respondents from the Regus global contacts database in 2012. This shows the Regus work-life balance index for each country listed, as well as globally (includes several countries not shown here). A higher score indicates employees in that country experience better work-life balance. The index is standardized to 100 as the average country score in the first survey (2010).

conflict between their work and nonwork demands.[77] Most employees lack this balance because they spend too many hours each week performing or thinking about their job, whether at the workplace, at home, or on vacation. This focus on work leaves too little time to fulfill nonwork needs and obligations. Our discussion of work-related stress (Chapter 4) will examine work-life balance issues in more detail.

Another employment relationship trend is **virtual work**, whereby employees use information technology to perform their jobs away from the traditional physical workplace. Some virtual work occurs when employees are connected to the office while traveling or at clients' offices. However, the most common form involves working at home rather than commuting to the office (often called *telecommuting* or *teleworking*). Estimates of the number of teleworkers vary from one survey to the next. One estimate is that the number of American employees who work from home at least one day per month has increased from 7.6 million in 2004 to well above 17 million today. This figure will increase substantially over the next few years because the U.S. federal government's new telework legislation requires departments to establish policies and practices that encourage more government employees to work from home one day or more per week.[78]

Telework is already well established in several companies. More than two-thirds of the employees at Agilent Technologies work from home or off-site some or all of the time. Employees at Cisco Systems, the Internet technology company, work from home an average of two days per week. Deloitte LLP has had a telework program for the past 15 years. More than 80 percent of the professional services and accounting firm's 45,000 American employees currently work remotely for at least 20 percent of the workweek.[79]

There has been much study and debate regarding the benefits and risks of virtual work, particularly working from home. The evidence suggests that telework attracts job applicants as well as improves the employee's work/life balance (which reduces stress) and productivity.[80] One recent study of 25,000 IBM employees found that employees who worked at home most of the time could perform 50 hours of work per week before experiencing work/life conflict compared to 46 hours per week for those who worked only at the office. Female telecommuters with children were able to work 40 hours per week, whereas nontelecommuters could only manage 30 hours before feeling work/life balance tension.

Telework also offers environmental benefits. Cisco Systems estimates that telecommuting among its employees worldwide avoids almost 50,000 metric tons of greenhouse gas emission and saves employees $10 million in fuel costs each year. Deloitte saved $30 million in one year due to the reduced office space requirements as more employees worked part of the week from home. Productivity also usually improves with telework in place. One study found that employees allocate 60 percent of the time they would have been commuting to work and use the other 40 percent of that time for personal activities. When a major blizzard shut federal government offices in Washington, DC, 30 percent of employees teleworked, saving the government $30 million per day.[81]

Against these potential benefits, work-at-home employees face a number of real or potential challenges. Family relations may suffer rather than improve if employees lack sufficient space and resources for a home office. Some employees complain of social isolation and reduced promotion opportunities when they work away from the office most of the time.

Telework is clearly better suited to people who are self-motivated, organized, can work effectively with broadband and other technology, and have sufficient fulfillment of social needs elsewhere in their life. Virtual work arrangements are also more successful in organizations that evaluate employees by their performance outcomes rather than face time (i.e. visibility).[82]

Learning Objective

After reading this section, you should be able to

LO4 Discuss the anchors on which organizational behavior knowledge is based.

ANCHORS OF ORGANIZATIONAL BEHAVIOR KNOWLEDGE

Globalization, increasing workforce diversity, and emerging employment relationships are just a few of the trends that challenge organizations and make the field of organizational behavior more relevant than ever before. To understand these and other topics, the field of organizational behavior relies on a set of basic beliefs or knowledge structures (see Exhibit 1.5). These conceptual anchors represent the principles on which OB knowledge is developed and refined.[83]

The Systematic Research Anchor

A key feature of OB knowledge is that it should be based on systematic research, which typically involves forming research questions, systematically collecting data, and testing hypotheses against those data.[84] Systematic research is the foundation for **evidence-based management**, which involves making decisions and taking actions based on this research evidence. Doesn't it make perfect sense, that management practice should be founded on the best available systematic knowledge? Yet many of us who study organizations using systematic methods are amazed at how often corporate leaders embrace fads, consulting models, and their own pet beliefs without bothering to find out if they actually work![85]

There are many reasons why people have difficulty applying evidence-based management. Leaders and other decision makers are bombarded with so many ideas from newspapers, books, consultant reports, and other sources that it is a challenge to figure out which ones are based on good evidence. Another problem is that good OB research is necessarily generic; it is rarely described in the context of a specific problem in a specific organization. Managers therefore have the difficult task of figuring out which theories are relevant to their unique situation.

A third reason why organizational leaders accept fads and other knowledge that lacks sufficient evidence is that consultants and popular book writers are rewarded for marketing their concepts and theories, not for testing to see if they actually work. Indeed, some management concepts have become popular—they are even found in some OB textbooks!—because of heavy marketing, not because of any evidence that they are valid. Finally, as we will learn in Chapter 3, people form perceptions and beliefs quickly and tend to ignore evidence that their beliefs are

OB Theory to Practice

Creating an Evidence-Based Management Organization

1. Stop treating old ideas as if they were brand-new.
2. Be suspicious of "breakthrough" ideas and studies.
3. Celebrate and develop collective brilliance.
4. Emphasize drawbacks as well as virtues.
5. Use success (and failure) stories to illustrate sound practices but not in place of a valid research method.
6. Adopt a neutral stance toward ideologies and theories.

Source: J. Pfeffer and R. I. Sutton, "Evidence-Based Management," *Harvard Business Review* 84, no. 1 (2006), 62–74.

inaccurate. To counter these opposing forces, OB experts have proposed a few simple suggestions to create a more evidence-based organization (see the above OB Theory to Practice feature).

The Multidisciplinary Anchor

Organizational behavior is anchored around the idea that the field should welcome theories and knowledge in other disciplines, not just from its own isolated research base. For instance, psychological research has aided our understanding of individual and interpersonal behavior. Sociologists have contributed to our knowledge of team dynamics, organizational socialization, organizational power, and other aspects of the social system. OB knowledge has also benefited from knowledge in emerging fields such as communications, marketing, and information systems. Borrowing theory from other disciplines is inevitable. Organizations have central roles in society, so they are the subject of many social sciences. Furthermore, organizations consist of people who interact with each other, so there is an inherent intersection between OB and most disciplines that study human beings.

Borrowing theories from other disciplines has helped the field of OB to nurture a diversity of knowledge and perspectives about organizations, but there are a few concerns.[86] One issue is whether OB suffers from a "trade deficit"—importing far more knowledge from other disciplines than is exported to other disciplines. By relying on theories developed in other fields, OB knowledge necessarily lags rather than leads in knowledge production. In contrast, OB-bred theories allow researchers to concentrate on the quality and usefulness of the theory.

Finally, heavy reliance on theories borrowed from other disciplines may leave OB vulnerable to a lack of common identity. The field could potentially become a place for researchers who are raised in and mainly identify with the other disciplines (psychology, sociology, and so on) rather than with organizational

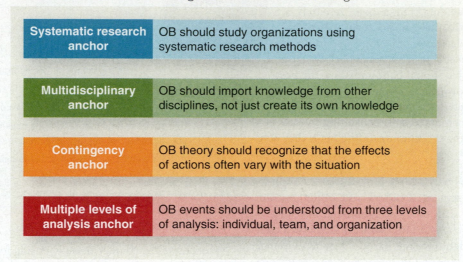

Systematic research anchor	OB should study organizations using systematic research methods
Multidisciplinary anchor	OB should import knowledge from other disciplines, not just create its own knowledge
Contingency anchor	OB theory should recognize that the effects of actions often vary with the situation
Multiple levels of analysis anchor	OB events should be understood from three levels of analysis: individual, team, and organization

behavior. The lack of identification as an "OB scholar" might further challenge the field's ability to develop its own theory and may weaken its focus on practical relevance.

The Contingency Anchor

People and their work environments are complex, and the field of organizational behavior recognizes this by stating that a particular action may have different consequences in different situations. In other words, no single solution is best all of the time.[87] Of course, it would be so much simpler if we could rely on "one best way" theories in which a particular concept or practice has

attributed to them, such as motivation, perceptions, personalities, attitudes, and values. The team level of analysis looks at the way people interact. This includes team dynamics, power, organizational politics, conflict, and leadership. At the organizational level, we focus on how people structure their working relationships and on how organizations interact with their environments.

Although an OB topic is typically pegged into one level of analysis, it usually relates to multiple levels.[89] For instance, communication is located in this book as a team (interpersonal) process, but we also recognize it includes individual and

[**People and their work environments are complex, so a particular action may have different consequences in different situations.**]

the same results in every situation. OB experts do search for simpler theories, but they also remain skeptical about surefire recommendations; an exception is somewhere around the corner. Thus, when faced with a particular problem or opportunity, we need to understand and diagnose the situation and select the strategy most appropriate *under those conditions*.[88]

The Multiple Levels of Analysis Anchor

This textbook divides organizational behavior topics into three levels of analysis: individual, team (including interpersonal), and organization. The individual level includes the characteristics and behaviors of employees as well as the thought processes

organizational processes. Therefore, you should try to think about each OB topic at the individual, team, and organizational levels, not just at one of these levels.

THE JOURNEY BEGINS

This chapter gives you some background about the field of organizational behavior. But it's only the beginning of our journey. Throughout this book, we will challenge you to learn new ways of thinking about how people work in and around organizations. We begin this process in Chapter 2 by presenting a basic model of individual behavior, then introducing over the next few chapters various stable and mercurial characteristics of individuals that relate to elements of the individual behavior model. Next, this book moves to the team level of analysis. We examine a model of team effectiveness and specific features of high-performance teams. We also look at communication, power and influence, conflict, and leadership. Finally, we shift our focus to the organizational level of analysis, where the topics of organizational structure, organizational culture, and organizational change are examined in detail. ■

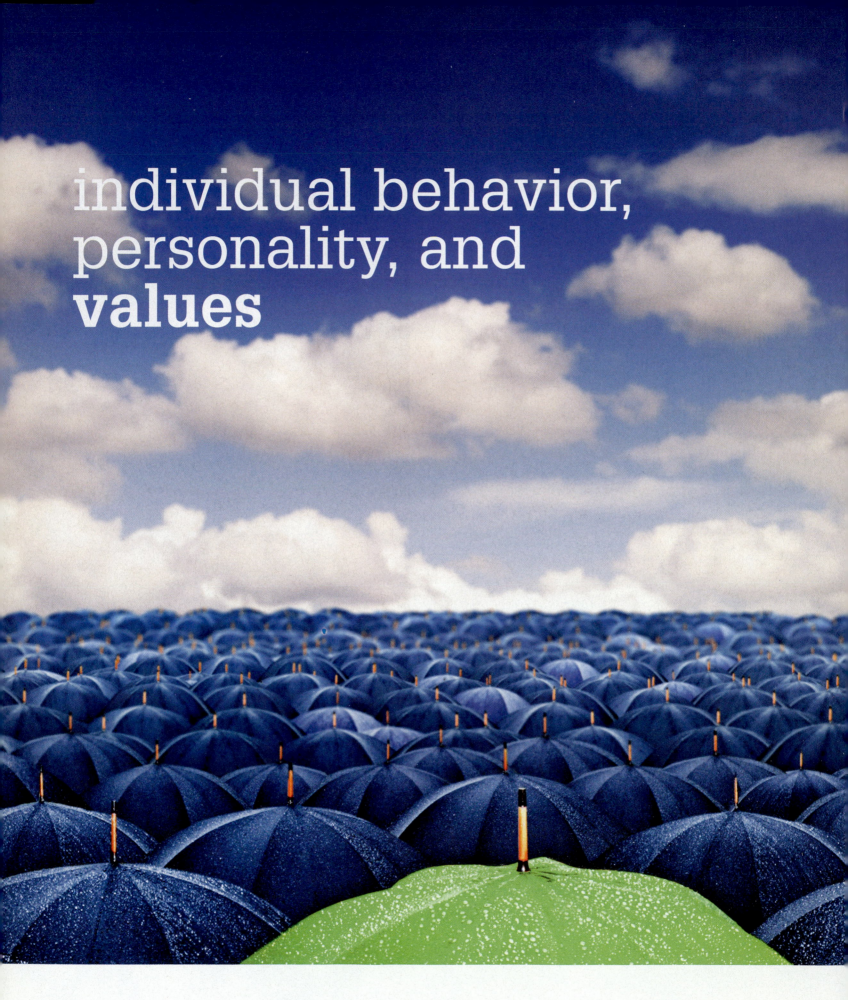

individual behavior,
personality, and
values

Scott Reed joined Chick-fil-A while in high school and soon discovered that the restaurant chain's strong family values were similar to his personal values. "Chick-fil-A's core values line up well with mine," says Reed, who opened a Chick-fil-A franchise in Marietta, Georgia after completing college two decades ago. Reed's two brothers have also worked at the company for several years. His sister, Lauren McGuire, recently joined Chick-fil-A as a franchisee. Values congruence also attracted her to the company: "This is a company that embodies the principles of my heart and soul," says McGuire.[1]

Scott Reed's pride and performance as a Chick-fil-A franchisee illustrates that personal values have a powerful influence on individual attitudes, decisions, and behavior in organizations. This chapter discusses personal values and personality—the two most stable foundations of individual behavior—as well as the factors that influence individual behavior. We begin with the MARS model, which outlines the four direct drivers of individual behavior and results. Next, we review the five types of individual behavior that represent the individual-level dependent variables found in most organizational behavior research. The second half of this chapter presents the topics of personality and values, including ethical and cross-cultural values.

LEARNING OBJECTIVES

After studying Chapter 2, you should be able to:

LO1 Describe the four factors that directly influence individual behavior and performance.

LO2 Summarize the five types of individual behavior in organizations.

LO3 Describe personality and discuss how the "Big Five" personality dimensions and four MBTI types relate to individual behavior in organizations.

LO4 Summarize Schwartz's model of individual values and discuss the conditions under which values influence behavior.

LO5 Describe three ethical principles and discuss four factors that influence ethical behavior.

LO6 Review five values commonly studied across cultures.

After reading this section, you should be able to

LO1 Describe the four factors that directly influence individual behavior and performance.

MARS MODEL OF INDIVIDUAL BEHAVIOR AND PERFORMANCE

For most of the past century, experts have investigated the direct predictors of individual behavior and performance.[2] One of the earliest formulas was *performance = person × situation*, where *person* includes individual characteristics and *situation* represents external influences on the individual's behavior. Another frequently mentioned formula is *performance = ability × motivation*.[3] Sometimes known as the "skill-and-will" model, this formula elaborates two specific characteristics within the person that influence individual performance. Ability, motivation, and situation are by far the most commonly mentioned direct predictors of individual behavior and performance, but in the 1960s researchers identified a fourth key factor: role perceptions (the individual's expected role obligations).[4]

Exhibit 2.1 illustrates these four variables—motivation, ability, role perceptions, and situational factors—which are represented by the acronym *MARS*.[5] All four factors are critical influences on an individual's voluntary behavior and performance; if any one of them is low in a given situation, the employee would perform the task poorly. For example, motivated salespeople with clear role perceptions and sufficient resources (situational factors) will not perform their jobs as well if they lack sales skills and related knowledge (ability). Motivation, ability, and role perceptions are clustered together in the model because they are located within the person. Situational factors are external to the individual but still affect his or her behavior and performance.[6] Let's look at each of these four factors in more detail.

Employee Motivation

Motivation represents the forces within a person that affect his or her direction, intensity, and persistence of voluntary behavior.[7] *Direction* refers to the path along which people steer their effort. People have choices about where they put their effort; they have a sense of what they are trying to achieve and at what level of quality, quantity, and so forth. In other words, motivation is goal directed, not random. People are motivated to arrive at work on time, finish a project a few hours early, or aim for many other targets. The second element of motivation, called *intensity,* is the amount of effort allocated to the goal. Intensity is all about how much people push themselves to complete a task. For example, two employees might be motivated to finish their project a few hours early (direction), but only one of them puts forth enough effort (intensity) to achieve this goal.

▼**EXHIBIT 2.1** MARS Model of Individual Behavior and Results

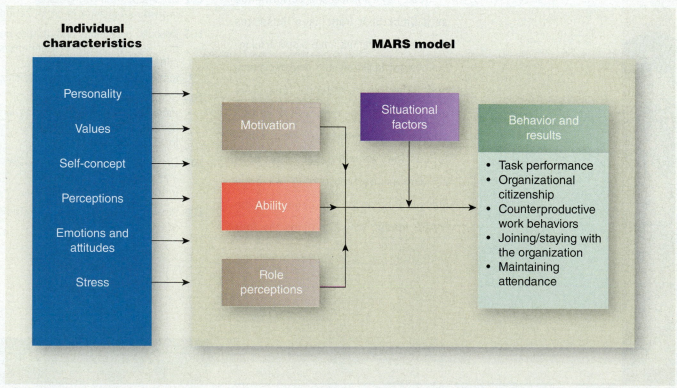

motivation The forces within a person that affect his or her direction, intensity, and persistence of voluntary behavior.

ability The natural aptitudes and learned capabilities required to successfully complete a task.

competencies Skills, knowledge, aptitudes, and other personal characteristics that lead to superior performance.

Finally, motivation involves varying levels of *persistence*, that is, continuing the effort for a certain amount of time. Employees sustain their effort until they reach their goal or give up beforehand. To help remember these three elements of motivation, consider the metaphor of driving a car in which the thrust of the engine is your effort. Direction refers to where you steer the car, intensity is how much you put your foot down on the gas pedal, and persistence is how long you drive toward that destination. Remember, motivation is a force that exists within individuals; it is not their actual behavior. Thus, direction, intensity, and persistence are cognitive (thoughts) and emotional conditions that directly cause us to move.

to identify a list of core competencies for performance in all jobs. For example, one stream of research suggests the most important competencies for job performance are leading/deciding, supporting/cooperating, creating/conceptualizing, adapting/coping, and four others.[10]

The challenge is to match a person's competencies with the job's competency requirements. A good person–job match not only produces higher performance; it also tends to increase the

> "I believe the real difference between success and failure in a corporation can be very often traced to the question of how well the organization brings out the great energies and talents of its people.[8]
> —Thomas J. Watson, Jr. (IBM's second CEO)

Ability

Employee abilities also make a difference in behavior and task performance. **Ability** includes both the natural aptitudes and the learned capabilities required to successfully complete a task. *Aptitudes* are the natural talents that help employees learn specific tasks more quickly and perform them better. There are many physical and mental aptitudes, and they affect our ability to acquire skills. For example, finger dexterity is an aptitude by which individuals learn more quickly and potentially achieve higher performance at picking up and handling small objects with their fingers. Employees with high finger dexterity are not necessarily better than others at first; rather, their learning tends to be faster and performance potential tends to be higher. *Learned capabilities* are the skills and knowledge you currently possess. These capabilities include the physical and mental skills and knowledge you have acquired. Learned capabilities tend to wane over time when not in use.

Aptitudes and learned capabilities are closely related to *competencies,* which has become a frequently used term in business. **Competencies** are a person's characteristics that result in superior performance.[9] These characteristics include knowledge, skills, aptitudes, and behaviors. Some experts extend the meaning of competencies to include personality and values, while others suggest that competencies are action-oriented results of these characteristics, such as serving customers, coping with heavy workloads, and providing creative ideas. Some studies have attempted

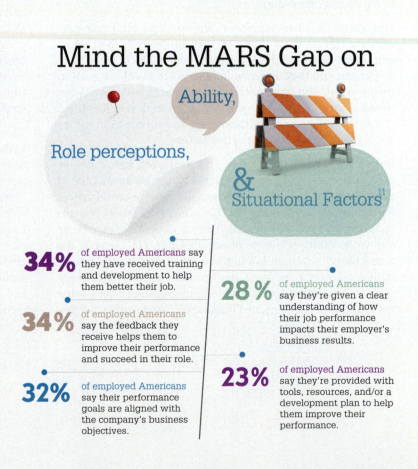

Mind the MARS Gap on

Role perceptions, Ability, & Situational Factors[11]

34% of employed Americans say they have received training and development to help them better their job.

34% of employed Americans say the feedback they receive helps them to improve their performance and succeed in their role.

32% of employed Americans say their performance goals are aligned with the company's business objectives.

28% of employed Americans say they're given a clear understanding of how their job performance impacts their employer's business results.

23% of employed Americans say they're provided with tools, resources, and/or a development plan to help them improve their performance.

employee's well-being. One way to match a person's competencies with the job's task requirements is to select applicants who already demonstrate the required competencies. For example, companies ask applicants to perform work samples, provide references for checking their past performance, and complete various selection tests. A second strategy is to provide training, which has a strong influence on individual performance and organizational effectiveness.[12] The third person–job matching strategy is to redesign the job so employees are given tasks only within their current learned capabilities. For example, a complex task might be simplified—some aspects of the work are transferred to others—so a new employee performs only tasks he or she is currently able to perform. As the employee becomes more competent at these tasks, other tasks are added back into the job.

Role Perceptions

Motivation and ability are important influences on individual behavior and performance, but employees also require accurate **role perceptions** to perform their jobs well. Role perceptions refer to how clearly people understand the job duties (roles) assigned to them or expected of them. These perceptions are critical because they guide the employee's direction of effort and improve coordination with coworkers, suppliers, and other stakeholders. Employees with clearer role perceptions also tend to have higher motivation.

Unfortunately, many employees do not have clear role perceptions. One survey reported that although 76 percent of employees understand the organization's business goals, only 39 percent said they understood how to achieve those goals in their own job. Similarly, when a recent global survey asked what would most improve their performance, employees identified "greater clarity about what the organization needs from me" as the first or second most important factor.[13]

Role clarity exists in three forms. First, employees have clear role perceptions when they understand the specific tasks assigned to them, that is, when they know the specific duties or consequences for which they are accountable. This may seem obvious, but employees are occasionally evaluated on job duties they were never told were within their zone of responsibility. For example, the metro transit system in Washington, DC experienced a serious train derailment a few years ago because the track department staff was not lubricating the tracks. An investigation revealed that the department had lubricated tracks several years earlier, but this work activity stopped after the previous department managers had transferred or retired. The incoming managers did not know about the department's track lubrication duties, so they didn't inform employees that lubricating tracks was part of their job.[14]

The second form of role perceptions refers to how well employees understand the *priority* of their various tasks and performance expectations. This is illustrated in the classic dilemma of prioritizing quantity versus quality, such as how many customers to serve in an hour (quantity) versus how well the employee should serve each customer (quality). It also refers to properly allocating time and resources to various tasks, such as how much time a manager should spend coaching employees each week versus spending time with suppliers and clients. The third form of role perceptions is understanding the *preferred behaviors* or procedures for accomplishing the assigned tasks. This refers to situations in which employees have the knowledge and skills to perform a particular task in more than one way. Employees with clear role perceptions know which of these methods is preferred or required by the organization.

Situational Factors

Employees' behavior and performance also depend on the situation. This statement seems simple enough, but OB experts have been engaged in deep discussion about the meaning of "situation," including its dimensions and relevance to individual behavior.[15] Most of the early writing focused on conditions beyond the employee's immediate control that constrain or facilitate behavior and performance.[16] For example, employees who are motivated, skilled, and know their role obligations will nevertheless perform poorly if they lack time, budget, physical work facilities, and other situational conditions. Some situational constraints—such as consumer preferences and economic conditions—originate from the external environment and, consequently, are beyond the employee's and organization's control.

Along with situational constraints, situational factors also refer to the clarity and consistency of cues the environment provides to employees regarding their role obligations and opportunities.[17] The importance of situational clarity and consistency is illustrated in workplace accidents. Let's say you are motivated, able, and have a clear role obligation to act safely in your job. Even so, you are more likely to have an accident if the work setting does not clearly and consistently communicate a nearby electrical hazard or other safety risk. Your unsafe behavior and accident are affected by the situation, namely the lack of signs and other indicators of the safety risk, or inconsistent placement of these warnings across the workplace.

> [Role clarity exists in three forms: understanding the specific tasks assigned, understanding the *priority* of those tasks, and understanding the *preferred behaviors* to accomplish those tasks.]

Learning Objective

After reading this section, you should be able to

LO2 Summarize the five types of individual behavior in organizations.

TYPES OF INDIVIDUAL BEHAVIOR

The four elements of the MARS model—motivation, ability, role perceptions, and situational factors—affect all voluntary workplace behaviors and performance. There are many varieties of individual behavior, but most can be organized into the five categories described over the next few pages: task performance, organizational citizenship, counterproductive work behaviors, joining and staying with the organization, and maintaining work attendance (Exhibit 2.2).

Task Performance

Task performance refers to goal-directed behaviors under the individual's control that support organizational objectives.[18] Task performance behaviors transform raw materials into goods and services or support and maintain these technical activities. For example, foreign exchange traders at Morgan Stanley make decisions and perform various tasks to buy and sell currencies. Most jobs consist of several tasks. For instance, foreign exchange traders at Morgan Stanley must be able to identify profitable trades, work cooperatively with clients and coworkers in a stressful environment,

assist in training new staff, and work on special telecommunications equipment without error. More generally, tasks might involve working with data, people, or things; working alone or with other people; and degrees of influencing others.[19]

organizational citizenship behaviors (OCBs) Various forms of cooperation and helpfulness to others that support the organization's social and psychological context.

Organizational Citizenship

Few companies would survive if employees performed only their formal job duties. They also need to engage in **organizational citizenship behaviors (OCBs)**—various forms of cooperation and helpfulness to others that support the organization's social and psychological context.[20] In other words, companies excel when employees go the "extra mile" beyond the required job duties. Organizational citizenship behaviors take many forms. Some are directed toward individuals, such as assisting coworkers with their work problems, adjusting your work schedule to accommodate coworkers, showing genuine courtesy toward coworkers, and sharing your work resources (supplies, technology, staff) with coworkers. Other OCBs represent cooperation and helpfulness toward the organization, such

OB Theory to Practice

Walking the Extra Mile

An important shipment of materials had arrived at Customs for Procter & Gamble (P&G) India, but the government shut down all of its offices (including Customs) due to heavy rains. Undeterred by the weather, a P&G plant engineer arranged to transport a customs official from his home to the Customs office and back so the clearance paperwork could be completed. The engineer then arranged for the materials to be delivered to the plant the same day. By going beyond the call of duty, the engineer (with similar behavior by the Customs officer) was able to keep the production lines running.[21]

▼ **EXHIBIT 2.2** Five Types of Individual Behavior in the Workplace

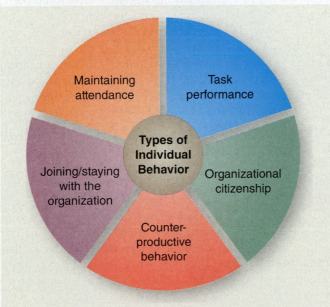

Types of Individual Behavior

- Maintaining attendance
- Task performance
- Organizational citizenship
- Counterproductive behavior
- Joining/staying with the organization

as supporting the company's public image, taking discretionary action to help the organization avoid potential problems, offering ideas beyond those required for your own job, attending voluntary functions that support the organization, and keeping up with new developments in the organization.[22]

Counterproductive Work Behaviors

Organizational behavior is interested in all workplace behaviors, including dysfunctional activities collectively known as **counterproductive work behaviors (CWBs)**. CWBs are voluntary behaviors that have the potential to directly or indirectly harm the organization.[23] Some of the many types of CWBs include harassing coworkers, creating unnecessary conflict, deviating from preferred work methods (e.g., shortcuts that risk work quality), being untruthful, stealing, sabotaging work, avoiding work obligation (tardiness), and wasting resources. CWBs are not minor concerns; research suggests they can substantially undermine the organization's effectiveness.

Joining and Staying with the Organization

Organizations are ultimately people working together, so hiring and retaining talent is a critical requirement in the organization's survival and success. Economic turbulence around the world has generally increased the pool of job applicants and reduced

employee turnover, but employers still face challenges finding qualified applicants for specific job groups. According to one recent report, 59 percent of U.S. companies have difficulty attracting people in some critical skills. This problem is apparent in the health care industry. Some hospitals have closed beds or reduced services due to a lack of nursing staff.[24]

Even when companies are able to hire qualified staff in the face of shortages, they need to ensure that these employees stay with the company. Companies with high turnover suffer because of the high cost of replacing people who leave. More important, as was mentioned in the previous chapter, much of an organization's intellectual capital is the knowledge carried around in employees' heads. When people leave, some of this vital knowledge is lost, often resulting in lower productivity, poorer customer service, and so forth. Some employers attract job applicants and minimize turnover by nurturing an enjoyable work environment.

Maintaining Work Attendance

Along with attracting and retaining employees, organizations need everyone to show up for work at scheduled times. American employees miss an average of approximately 5 days of scheduled work each year, which is lower than in most other countries. For example, one study reported that more than 25 percent of primary and secondary school teachers in India, Uganda, and Indonesia are absent from work on any given workday. The report warned this chronic level of absenteeism undermined the quality of children's education to such an extent that it threatened the economic development of those countries.[26]

Most employees blame the situation for their absenteeism, such as bad weather, transit strike, and family demands (e.g., children or parents require care). However, some people still show up for work because of their strong motivation to be there, whereas others take sick leave even when they are not genuinely unwell. Employees who experience job dissatisfaction or work-related stress are more likely to be absent or late for work because taking time off is a way of temporarily withdrawing from stressful or dissatisfying conditions. Absenteeism is also higher in organizations with generous sick leave because this benefit minimizes the financial loss of taking time away from work. Another factor in absenteeism is the person's values and personality.[27] Finally, studies report absenteeism is higher in teams with strong absence norms, meaning that team members tolerate and even expect coworkers to take time off.[28]

Presenteeism Along with attending work when expected, maintaining work attendance includes staying away from scheduled work when attendance would be dysfunctional for the individual and organization. In fact, OB experts warn that **presenteeism**—attending work when one's capacity to work is significantly diminished by illness, fatigue, personal problems, or other factors—may be more serious than being absent when capable of working.[29] Employees who attend work when

they are unwell or unfit may worsen their own condition and increase coworkers' health risk. These employees are also usually less productive and may reduce coworkers' productivity.

Presenteeism is more common among employees with low job security (such as new and temporary staff), who lack sick leave pay or similar financial buffers, and whose absence would immediately affect many people (i.e., high centrality). Company or team norms about absenteeism also account for presenteeism. Personality also plays a role; some people possess traits that motivate them to show up for work when others would gladly recover at home. Personality is a widely cited predictor of most forms of individual behavior. It is also the most stable personal characteristic, so we introduce this topic next.

Learning Objective

After reading this section, you should be able to

LO3 Describe personality and discuss how the "Big Five" personality dimensions and four MBTI types relate to individual behavior in organizations.

PERSONALITY IN ORGANIZATIONS

While applying for several jobs in the publishing industry, Christina was surprised that three of the positions required applicants to complete a personality test. "One page is a list of characteristics—sentimental, adventurous, attractive, compelling, helpful, etc.—and you check off the ones that best describe what others expect of you," Christina recalls of one test. "The second page is the same list, but you check off the ones that you think truly describe you." Christina didn't hear back from the first company after completing its personality test, so for the second company she completed the personality test "according to a sales personality" because that job was in sales. When writing the personality test at the third firm, she answered questions the way she thought someone would if they were "a good person, but honest" about what they thought. None of the applications resulted in a job offer, leaving Christina wondering what personality profile these companies were seeking and whether her strategy of guessing the best answer on these personality tests was a good idea.[30]

Personality is an important individual characteristic, which explains why several companies try to estimate the personality traits of job applicants and employees. Most of us also think about personality every day in our dealings with others. We use these traits (talkative, risk-oriented, thoughtful, etc.) to simplify our perception of each person and to predict their future behavior. **Personality** is the relatively enduring pattern of thoughts, emotions, and behaviors that characterize a person, along with the psychological processes behind those characteristics.[31] It is, in essence, the bundle of characteristics that make us similar to or different from other people. We estimate an individual's personality by what they say and do, and we infer the person's internal states—including thoughts and emotions—from these observable behaviors.

A basic premise of personality theory is that people have inherent characteristics or traits that can be identified by the consistency or stability of their behavior across time and situations.[32] For example, you probably have some friends who are more talkative than others. You might know some people who like to take risks and others who are risk-averse. This behavior tendency is a key feature of personality theory because it attributes a person's behavior to something within them—the individual's personality—rather than to purely environmental influences.

Of course, people do not act the same way in all situations; in fact, such consistency would be considered abnormal because it indicates a person's insensitivity to social norms, reward systems, and other external conditions.[33] People vary their behavior to suit the situation, even if the behavior is at odds with their personality. For example, talkative people remain relatively quiet in a library where "no talking" rules are explicit and strictly enforced. However, personality differences are still apparent in these situations because talkative people tend to do more talking in libraries relative to how much other people talk in libraries.

> ## WE KNOW WHAT A PERSON THINKS NOT WHEN HE/SHE TELLS US WHAT HE/SHE THINKS, BUT BY HIS/HER ACTIONS.[34]
> —ISAAC BASHEVIS SINGER (AMERICAN AUTHOR)

People typically exhibit a wide range of behaviors, yet within that variety are discernible patterns we refer to as *personality traits*. Traits are broad concepts that allow us to label and understand individual differences. Furthermore, traits predict an individual's behavior far into the future. For example, studies report that an individual's personality in childhood predicts various behaviors and outcomes in adulthood, including educational attainment, employment success, marital relationships, illegal activities, and health-risk behaviors.[35]

Personality Determinants: Nature versus Nurture

What determines an individual's personality? Most experts now agree that personality is shaped by both nature and nurture, although the relative importance of each continues to be debated and studied. *Nature* refers to our genetic or hereditary origins— the genes we inherit from our parents. Studies of identical twins, particularly those separated at birth, reveal that heredity has a very large effect on personality; up to 50 percent of variation in behavior and 30 percent of temperament preferences can be attributed to a person's genetic characteristics.[36] In other words, genetic code not only determines our eye color, skin tone, and physical shape; it also significantly affects our attitudes, decisions, and behavior.

Although personality is heavily influenced by heredity, it is also affected by *nurture*—the person's socialization, life experiences, and other forms of interaction with the environment. An individual's personality development and change occur mainly when people are young; personality stabilizes by the time people reach age 30, although some sources say personality development continues to occur through to age 50.[37]

The main explanation of why personality becomes more stable over time is that we form a clearer and more rigid self-concept as we get older. This increasing clarity of "who we are" serves as an anchor for our behavior because the executive function— the part of the brain that manages goal-directed behavior—tries to keep our behavior consistent with our self-concept.[38] As self-concept becomes clearer and more stable with age, behavior and personality therefore also become more stable and consistent. We discuss self-concept in more detail in the next chapter. The main point here is that personality is not completely determined by heredity; life experiences, particularly early in life, also shape each individual's personality traits.

> "People vary their behavior to suit the situation, even if the behavior is at odds with their personality."

Five-Factor Model of Personality

One of the most important ideas of personality theory is that people possess specific personality traits. Traits such as sociable, depressed, cautious, and talkative represent clusters of thoughts, feelings, and behaviors that allow us to identify, differentiate, and understand people.[39] Hundreds of personality traits have been described over the years, so personality experts have tried to organize them into smaller clusters. The most widely respected clustering of personality traits is the **five-factor model (FFM)**, also known as the "Big Five" personality dimensions. Several decades ago, personality experts identified more than 17,000 words that describe an individual's personality. These words were distilled down to five abstract personality dimensions. Similar results were found in studies of different languages, suggesting that the five-factor model is fairly robust across cultures.[40] These "Big Five" dimensions, represented by the handy acronym *CANOE*, are outlined in Exhibit 2.3 and described below:

- *Conscientiousness.* **Conscientiousness** characterizes people who are organized, dependable, goal-focused,

▼ **EXHIBIT 2.3** Five-Factor Model's Big Five Personality Dimensions

Personality dimension	People with higher scores on this dimension tend to be more:
Conscientiousness	Organized, dependable, goal-focused, thorough, disciplined, methodical, industrious
Agreeableness	Trusting, helpful, good-natured, considerate, tolerant, selfless, generous, flexible
Neuroticism	Anxious, insecure, self-conscious, depressed, temperamental
Openness to experience	Imaginative, creative, unconventional, curious, nonconforming, autonomous, perceptive
Extraversion	Outgoing, talkative, energetic, sociable, assertive

thorough, disciplined, methodical, and industrious. People with low conscientiousness tend to be careless, less thorough, disorganized, and irresponsible.

- *Agreeableness*. This dimension includes the traits of being trusting, helpful, good-natured, considerate, tolerant, selfless, generous, and flexible. Some scholars prefer the label "friendly compliance" for this dimension, with its opposite being "hostile noncompliance." People with low agreeableness tend to be uncooperative and intolerant of others' needs as well as more suspicious and self-focused.

- *Neuroticism*. **Neuroticism** characterizes people who tend to be anxious, insecure, self-conscious, depressed, and temperamental. In contrast, people with low neuroticism (high emotional stability) are poised, secure, and calm.

- *Openness to experience*. This dimension is the most complex and has the least agreement among scholars. It generally refers to the extent to which people are imaginative, creative, unconventional, curious, nonconforming, autonomous, and

ideas. Introverts do not necessarily lack social skills. Rather, they are more inclined to direct their interests to ideas than to social events. Introverts are more comfortable than extraverts at being alone for long periods of time.

These five personality dimensions influence employee motivation and role clarity in various ways.[41] Some experts suggest that agreeableness, conscientiousness, and emotional stability (low neuroticism) cluster around the broad characteristic of "getting along." People with high agreeableness are more sensitive to others (more empathy, less conflict), those with high conscientiousness are more dependable, and those with high emotional stability are more upbeat. Some writers suggest that extraversion also relates to getting along

> " Conscientiousness and emotional stability (low neuroticism) stand out as the personality traits that best predict individual performance in almost every job group. "

aesthetically perceptive. Those who score low on this dimension tend to be more resistant to change, less open to new ideas, and more conventional and fixed in their ways.

- *Extraversion*. **Extraversion** characterizes people who are outgoing, talkative, energetic, sociable, and assertive. The opposite is *introversion*, which characterizes those who are quiet, cautious, and less interactive with others. Extraverts get their energy from the outer world (people and things around them), whereas introverts get their energy from the internal world, such as personal reflection on concepts and

because extraverts are more motivated to interact with others. Openness to experience, extraversion, conscientiousness, and emotional stability cluster around the broad characteristic of "getting ahead." Those with high openness to experience are more eager to try out new ideas, extraverts are more assertive, those with high conscientiousness are more goal-oriented, and those with high emotional stability are more confident in their ability to perform well.

Personality traits reflect an individual's behavior tendencies, so they are fairly good at predicting a number of workplace behaviors and outcomes, even when employee ability and other factors are taken into account. Conscientiousness and emotional stability (low neuroticism) stand out as the personality traits that best predict individual performance in almost every job group.[42] Both are motivational components of personality because they energize a willingness to fulfill work obligations within established rules (conscientiousness) and to allocate resources to accomplish those tasks (emotional stability). Various studies have reported that conscientious employees set higher personal goals for themselves, are more motivated, and have higher performance expectations than do employees with low levels of conscientiousness. They also tend to have higher levels of organizational citizenship and work better in organizations that give employees more freedom than is found in traditional command-and-control workplaces.[43]

The other three personality dimensions predict more specific types of employee behavior and performance.[44] Extraversion is associated with performance in sales and management jobs, where employees must interact with and influence people. Agreeableness is associated with performance in jobs where employees are expected to be cooperative and helpful, such as working in teams, customer relations, and other conflict-handling situations. People high on the openness-to-experience personality dimension tend to be more creative and adaptable to change. Finally, personality influences employee well-being in various ways.[45] Overall, personality influences a person's typical emotional reactions to the job, how well he or she copes with stress, and what career paths would make that person happier.

Jungian Personality Theory and the Myers-Briggs Type Indicator

The five-factor model of personality is the most respected and supported in research, but it is not the most popular in practice. That distinction goes to Jungian personality theory, which is measured through the **Myers-Briggs Type Indicator (MBTI)** (see Exhibit 2.4). Nearly a century ago, Swiss psychiatrist Carl Jung proposed that personality is primarily represented by the individual's preferences regarding perceiving and judging information.[46] Jung explained that perceiving, which involves how people prefer to gather information or perceive the world around them, occurs through two competing orientations: *sensing (S)* and *intuition (N)*. Sensing involves perceiving information directly through the five senses; it relies on an organized structure to acquire factual and preferably quantitative details. Intuition, on the other hand, relies more on insight and subjective experience to see relationships among variables. Sensing types focus on the here and now, whereas intuitive types focus more on future possibilities.

Jung also proposed that judging—how people process information or make decisions based on what they have perceived—consists of two competing processes: *thinking (T)* and *feeling (F)*. People with a thinking orientation rely on rational cause-effect logic and systematic data collection to make decisions. Those with a strong feeling orientation, on the other hand, rely on their emotional responses to the options presented, as well as to how those choices affect others.

Jung noted that along with differing in the four core processes of sensing, intuition, thinking, and feeling, people also differ in their degrees of extraversion-introversion, which was introduced earlier as one of the Big Five personality traits.

Along with measuring the personality traits Jung identified, the MBTI measures Jung's broader categories of *perceiving* and *judging*, which they say represents a person's attitude toward the external world. People with a perceiving orientation are open, curious, and flexible; prefer to adapt spontaneously to events as they unfold; and prefer to keep their options open. Judging types prefer order and structure and want to resolve problems quickly.

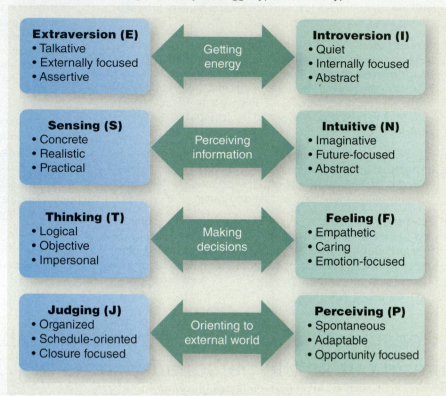

▼ **EXHIBIT 2.4** Jungian and Myers-Briggs Type Indicator Types[47]

Extraversion (E)
• Talkative
• Externally focused
• Assertive

Getting energy

Introversion (I)
• Quiet
• Internally focused
• Abstract

Sensing (S)
• Concrete
• Realistic
• Practical

Perceiving information

Intuitive (N)
• Imaginative
• Future-focused
• Abstract

Thinking (T)
• Logical
• Objective
• Impersonal

Making decisions

Feeling (F)
• Empathetic
• Caring
• Emotion-focused

Judging (J)
• Organized
• Schedule-oriented
• Closure focused

Orienting to external world

Perceiving (P)
• Spontaneous
• Adaptable
• Opportunity focused

The MBTI is one of the most widely used personality tests in work settings as well as in career counseling and executive coaching.[48] Even so, the MBTI and Jung's psychological types model have received uneven support.[49] On the one hand, MBTI seems to improve self-awareness for career development and mutual understanding. It also does a reasonably good job of representing Jung's psychological types. On the other hand, the MBTI poorly predicts job performance and is generally not recommended for employment selection or promotion decisions. For example, although one study found that intuitive types are more common in higher level than lower level management, other research has found no relationship between any MBTI types and effective leadership. One recent large-scale study also reported that the MBTI scores of team members is not useful for predicting the team's development. Finally, the MBTI overlaps with four of the five dimensions of the five-factor personality model, yet it does so less satisfactorily than existing Big Five personality measures.[50]

Personality Testing in Organizations

Personality has become one of the "hot" topics in organizational behavior and gained considerable attention in the workplace. Most often, these tests are applied for personal development, such as career development and team dynamics. For example, many staff at Southwest Airlines post their Myers-Briggs Type Indicator (MBTI) results in their offices. "You can walk by and see someone's four-letter [MBTI type] posted up in their cube," says Southwest's director of leadership development. Southwest began using the MBTI a decade ago to help staff understand and respect coworkers' different personalities and thinking styles. "Behaviors that might have once caused misunderstanding and frustration now are viewed through a different filter," suggests the Southwest Airlines manager.[52]

Personality tests are also being incorporated into the employment selection and promotion decision process. When Amtrak won the contract to operate the Metrolink commuter service in Southern California, for example, it required the previous contractor's train engineers and conductors to complete a Big Five personality inventory as a condition of future employment. Amtrak apparently prefers train crew members with a "focused introverted" personality because employees with these traits are not distracted while operating the train or performing repetitive tasks. A horrendous Metrolink accident claiming two dozen lives occurred two years before Amtrak took over because a train engineer ran a red light while distracted by text messaging.[53]

Personality testing wasn't always this popular in organizations. Less than two decades ago, companies shunned these instruments due to concerns that they do not predict job-related behavior and might unfairly discriminate against visible minorities and other identifiable groups. Personality testing slowly regained acceptance as studies reported that specific traits correlated with specific indicators of job performance (as we described earlier). Today, personality testing flourishes to such an extent that some experts warn we may have gone too far in organizational settings.

OB Theory to Practice

Facebook Personality

Companies spend big dollars on personality tests, yet recent studies have found that job applicants already reveal some of their personality traits through the content of their Facebook pages, blogs, or other personal Web sites. Even the act of blogging or participating in social network sites can indicate specific personality traits. Extraversion, openness to experience, and agreeableness are usually the easiest traits to estimate from the content of online sources, whereas neuroticism is the most difficult.[51]

Learning Objective

After reading this section, you should be able to

LO4 Summarize Schwartz's model of individual values and discuss the conditions under which values influence behavior.

VALUES IN THE WORKPLACE

Colleen Abdoulah developed a strong set of personal values from her parents while she was growing up. For example, Abdoulah recalls her father emphasized that, "No matter how much you earn, you're no better than anyone and they are no better than you." She also learned the importance of having the courage to do the right thing and of forming relationships with people so they feel a sense of ownership. Abdoulah not only practices these values every day, she has instilled them at Wide Open West, the Denver-based Internet, cable, and phone provider where she is CEO to 1,300 employees. "[Our employees] display the courage to do the right thing, serve each other and our customers with humility, and celebrate our learnings and success with grace," says Abdoulah. "Anyone can set values, but we have operationalized our values so that they affect everything we do every day."[54]

Colleen Abdoulah and other successful people often refer to their personal values and the critical events that formed those values earlier in life. *Values*, a concept we introduced in Chapter 1, are stable, evaluative beliefs that guide our preferences for outcomes or courses of action in a variety of situations.[55] They are perceptions about what is good or bad, right or wrong. Values tell us what we "ought" to do. They serve as a moral compass that directs our motivation and, potentially, our decisions and actions.

have minimal conflict with each other (e.g., you can have high agreeableness and high introversion), whereas some values are opposed to other values. For example, someone who values excitement and challenge would have difficulty also valuing stability and moderation. Third, although personality and values are both partly determined by heredity, values are influenced more by socialization whereas personality traits are more innate.

Types of Values

Values come in many forms, and experts on this topic have devoted considerable attention to organizing them into clusters. Several decades ago, social psychologist Milton Rokeach developed two lists of values, distinguishing means (instrumental values) from end goals (terminal values). Although Rokeach's lists are still mentioned in some organizational behavior sources, they were replaced by another model almost two decades ago. The instrumental–terminal values distinction

> # Values serve as a moral compass that directs our motivation and, potentially, our decisions and actions.

People arrange values into a hierarchy of preferences, called a *value system.* Some individuals value new challenges more than they value conformity. Others value generosity more than they value frugality. Each person's unique value system is developed and reinforced through socialization from parents, religious institutions, friends, personal experiences, and the society in which he or she lives. As such, a person's hierarchy of values is stable and long-lasting. For example, one study found that value systems of a sample of adolescents were remarkably similar 20 years later when they were adults.[56]

Notice that our description of values has focused on individuals, whereas executives often describe values as though they belong to the organization. In reality, values exist only within individuals—we call them *personal values.* However, groups of people might hold the same or similar values, so we tend to ascribe these *shared values* to the team, department, organization, profession, or entire society. The values shared by people throughout an organization (*organizational values*) receive fuller discussion in Chapter 13 because they are a key part of corporate culture. The values shared across a society (*cultural values*) receive attention later in this chapter.

Values and personality traits are related to each other, but the two concepts differ in a few ways.[57] The most noticeable distinction is that values are evaluative—they tell us what we *ought* to do—whereas personality traits describe what we naturally *tend* to do. A second distinction is that personality traits

was neither accurate nor useful, and Rokeach overlooked values now included in the current dominant model.

Today, the dominant model of personal values is the one developed and tested by social psychologist Shalom Schwartz and his colleagues.[58] Schwartz's list of 57 values builds on Rokeach's earlier work but does not distinguish instrumental from terminal values. Instead, research has found that human values are organized into the circular model (circumplex) shown in Exhibit 2.5.[59] This model clusters the 57 specific values into 10 broad values categories: universalism, benevolence, tradition, conformity, security, power, achievement, hedonism, stimulation, and self-direction. For example, conformity includes four specific values: politeness, honoring parents, self-discipline, and obedient.

These 10 broad values categories are further clustered into four quadrants. One quadrant, called *openness to change*, refers to the extent to which a person is motivated to pursue innovative ways. This quadrant includes the value categories of self-direction (creativity, independent thought), stimulation (excitement and challenge), and hedonism (pursuit of pleasure, enjoyment, gratification of desires). The opposing quadrant is *conservation*, which is the extent to which a person is motivated to preserve the status quo. The conservation quadrant includes the value categories of conformity (adherence to social norms and expectations), security (safety and stability), and tradition (moderation and preservation of the status quo).

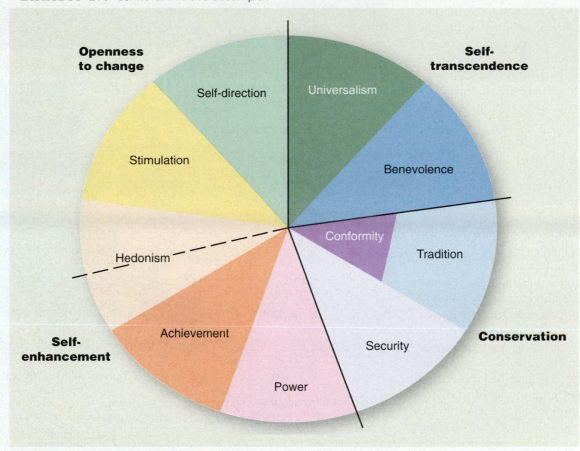

Source: S. H. Schwartz, "Universals in the Content and Structure of Values: Theoretical Advances and Empirical Tests in 20 Countries," *Advances in Experimental Social Psychology* 25 (1992): 1–65; S. H. Schwartz and K. Boehnke, "Evaluating the Structure of Human Values with Confirmatory Factor Analysis," *Journal of Research in Personality* 38, no. 3 (2004); 230–55.

The third quadrant in Schwartz's circumplex model, called *self-enhancement*, refers to how much a person is motivated by self-interest. This quadrant includes the value categories of achievement (pursuit of personal success), power (dominance over others), and hedonism (a values category shared with openness to change). The opposite of self-enhancement is *self-transcendence*, which refers to motivation to promote the welfare of others and nature. Self-transcendence includes the value categories of benevolence (concern for others in one's life) and universalism (concern for the welfare of all people and nature).

Values and Individual Behavior

Personal values guide our decisions and actions to some extent, but this connection isn't always as strong as most people believe. Habitual behavior tends to be consistent with our values, but our everyday conscious

> "The more choices you have, the more your values matter.[60]
>
> —Michael Schrage (MIT Research Fellow, author)"

decisions and actions apply our values much less consistently. The main reason for the "disconnect" between personal values and individual behavior is that values are abstract concepts, so their relevance to specific situations is not obvious much of the time.

Four conditions strengthen the linkage between personal values and behavior.[61] First, we tend to apply our values only when we can think of specific reasons for doing so. In other words, we need logical reasons for applying a specific value in a specific situation. Second, we tend to apply our values when the situation allows or encourages us to do so. Work environments influence our behavior, at least in the short term, so they necessarily encourage or discourage values-consistent behavior. Third, we are more likely to apply values when we actively think about them. This occurs naturally when confronted with situations that obviously violate our values. For example, you become aware that you value security when asked to perform a risky task.

Finally, we act more consistently with our personal values when we are literally reminded of them. In other words, the values–behavior connection is stronger through mindfulness of one's values. This effect was apparent in the following study:[62] Students were given a math test and paid for each correct answer. One group submitted their results to the experimenter for scoring, so they couldn't lie about their results. A second group could lie because they scored the test themselves and told the experimenter their test score. A third group was similar to the second (they scored their own test), but their test included the following statement and they were required to sign their name to that statement: "I understand that this short survey falls under (the university's) honor system." (The university had no such honor system.) The researchers estimated that some students cheated when they scored their own test without the "honor system" statement, whereas no one given the "honor system" form lied about their results. Similar results occurred when, instead of an honor statement, the third group was first asked to recall the Ten Commandments. The message here is that people are more likely to apply their values (honesty, in this case) when explicitly reminded of those values.

Values Congruence

Values tell us what is right or wrong and what we ought to do. This evaluative characteristic affects how comfortable we are with specific organizations and individuals. The key concept here is *values congruence*, which refers to how similar a person's values hierarchy is to the values hierarchy of the organization, a coworker, or another source of comparison. *Person–organization value congruence* occurs when a person's values are similar to the organization's dominant values. This form of values congruence increases (to some extent) the chance that employees will make decisions and act in ways consistent with organizational expectations. It also leads to higher job satisfaction, loyalty, and organizational citizenship as well as lower stress and turnover.[63] "The most difficult but rewarding accomplishment in any career is 'living true' to your values and finding

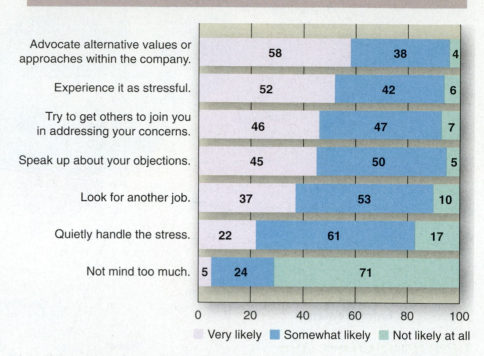

How MBA Students Say They Would React to Personal–Organizational Values Incongruence[64]

	Very likely	Somewhat likely	Not likely at all
Advocate alternative values or approaches within the company.	58	38	4
Experience it as stressful.	52	42	6
Try to get others to join you in addressing your concerns.	46	47	7
Speak up about your objections.	45	50	5
Look for another job.	37	53	10
Quietly handle the stress.	22	61	17
Not mind too much.	5	24	71

Percentage of MBA students who say they would very likely, somewhat likely, or not likely react as stated in situations where their personal values conflict with the organization's values. This sample consists of 1,943 MBA students at 15 top-ranked business schools in the United States, Canada, and Britain. Eighty-three percent predicted they will experience conflict between their personal values and what they are asked to do in business.

companies where you can contribute at the highest level while being your authentic self," says Cynthia Schwalm, a senior executive at Optimer Pharmaceuticals in New York City.[65]

Are organizations the most successful when every employee's personal values are parallel to the company's values? Not at all! While a comfortable degree of values congruence is necessary for the reasons just noted, organizations also benefit from some level of incongruence. Employees with diverse values offer different perspectives, which potentially lead to better decision making. Also, too much congruence can create a "corporate cult" that potentially undermines creativity, organizational flexibility, and business ethics.

A second type of values congruence involves how consistent the values apparent in our actions (enacted values) are with what we say we believe in (espoused values). This *espoused–enacted value congruence* is especially important for people in leadership positions because any obvious gap between espoused and enacted values undermines their perceived integrity, a critical feature of effective leaders. One global survey reported that 55 percent of employees believe senior management behaves consistently with the company's core values.[66] Some companies try to maintain high levels of espoused–enacted values congruence by surveying subordinates and peers about whether the manager's decisions and actions are consistent with the company's espoused values.

A third category, *organization–community values congruence*, refers to the similarity of an organization's dominant values with the prevailing values of the community or society in which it conducts business.[67] An organization headquartered in one country that tries to impose its value system on employees and other stakeholders located in another culture may experience higher employee turnover and have more difficult relations with the communities in which the company operates. Thus, globalization calls for a delicate balancing act: Companies depend on shared values to maintain consistent standards and behaviors, yet they need to operate within the values of different cultures around the world.

Learning Objective

After reading this section, you should be able to

LO5 Describe three ethical principles and discuss four factors that influence ethical behavior.

ETHICAL VALUES AND BEHAVIOR

When asked to identify the most important attribute of a leader, employees mention intelligence, decisiveness, and compassion, but these characteristics don't top the list. Instead, across numerous surveys employees typically choose honesty/ethics as the most important characteristic of effective corporate leaders.[68] Ethics refers to the study of moral principles or values that determine whether actions are right or wrong and outcomes are good or bad (see Chapter 1). People rely on their ethical values to determine "the right thing to do." The importance of ethical corporate conduct is embedded in business school programs and appears regularly in the news, yet surveys report fairly consistent levels of observed wrongdoing in the workplace.

Three Ethical Principles

To better understand business ethics, we need to consider three distinct types of ethical principles: utilitarianism, individual rights, and distributive justice.[69] While your personal values might sway you more toward one principle than the others, all

three should be actively considered to put important ethical issues to the test.

- *Utilitarianism.* This principle advises us to seek the greatest good for the greatest number of people. In other words, we should choose the option that provides the highest degree of satisfaction to those affected. This is sometimes known as a *consequential principle* because it focuses on the consequences of our actions, not on how we achieve those consequences. One problem with utilitarianism is that it is almost impossible to evaluate the benefits or costs of many decisions, particularly when many stakeholders have wide-ranging needs and values. Another problem is that most of us are uncomfortable engaging in behaviors that seem, well, unethical to attain results that are ethical.

- *Individual rights.* This principle reflects the belief that everyone has entitlements that let her or him act in a certain way. Some of the most widely cited rights are freedom of movement, physical security, freedom of speech, fair trial, and freedom from torture. The individual rights principle includes more than legal rights; it also includes human rights that everyone is granted as a moral norm of society. One problem with individual rights is that certain individual rights may conflict with others. The shareholders' right to be informed about corporate activities may ultimately conflict with an executive's right to privacy, for example.

- *Distributive justice.* This principle suggests that people who are similar to each other should receive similar benefits and burdens; those who are dissimilar should receive different

> ## IT TAKES MANY GOOD DEEDS TO BUILD A GOOD REPUTATION AND ONLY ONE BAD ONE TO LOSE IT.
> —BENJAMIN FRANKLIN

benefits and burdens in proportion to their dissimilarity. For example, we expect that two employees who contribute equally in their work should receive similar rewards, whereas those who make a lesser contribution should receive less. A variation of the distributive justice principle says that inequalities are acceptable when they benefit the least well off in society. Thus, employees in risky jobs should be paid more if their work benefits others who are less well off. One problem with the distributive justice principle is that it is difficult to agree on who is "similar" and what factors are "relevant."

Moral Intensity, Ethical Sensitivity, Situational Influences, and Mindlessness

Along with ethical principles and their underlying values, four other factors influence ethical conduct in the workplace: the moral intensity of the issue, the individual's ethical sensitivity, situational factors, and habitual or mindless behavior.[70] **Moral intensity** is the degree to which an issue demands the application of ethical principles. Decisions with high moral intensity

are more important, so the decision maker needs to more carefully apply ethical principles to resolve it. Several factors influence the moral intensity of an issue, including those listed in Exhibit 2.6. Keep in mind that this list represents the factors people tend to think about; some of them might not be considered morally acceptable when people are formally making ethical decisions.[71]

Even if an issue has high moral intensity, some employees might not recognize its ethical importance because they have low **ethical sensitivity**. Ethical sensitivity is a personal characteristic that enables people to recognize the presence of an ethical issue and determine its relative importance.[72] Ethically sensitive people are not necessarily more ethical. Rather, they are more likely to sense whether an issue requires ethical consideration; that is, they can more accurately estimate the moral intensity of the issue. Ethically sensitive people tend to have higher empathy. They also have more information about the specific situation. For example, accountants would be more ethically sensitive regarding the appropriateness of specific accounting procedures than would someone who has not received training in this profession.

▼ **EXHIBIT 2.6** Factors Influencing Perceived Moral Intensity*

Moral Intensity Factor	Moral Intensity Question	Moral Intensity Is Higher When:
Magnitude of consequences	How much harm or benefit will occur to others as a result of this action?	The harm or benefit is larger.
Social consensus	How many other people agree that this action is ethically good or bad?	Many people agree.
Probability of effect	(a) What is the chance this action will actually occur? (b) What is the chance this action will actually cause good or bad consequences?	The probability is higher.
Temporal immediacy	How long after the action will the consequences occur?	The time delay is shorter.
Proximity	How socially, culturally, psychologically, and/or physically close to me are the people affected by this decision?	Those affected are close rather than distant.
Concentration of effect	(a) How many people are affected by this action? (b) Are the people affected by this action easily identifiable as a group?	Many people are affected. Those affected are easily identifiable as a group.

*These are factors people tend to ask themselves about when determining the moral intensity of an issue. Whether some of these questions should be relevant is itself an ethical question.

Source: Based on information in T. J. Jones, "Ethical Decision Making by Individuals in Organizations: An Issue Contingent Model," *Academy of Management Review* 16 (1991): 366–95.

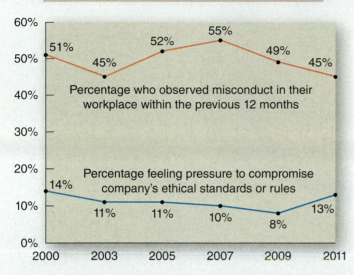

Observing Ethical Misconduct and Under Pressure to Compromise Ethical Standards[73]

Percentage who observed misconduct in their workplace within the previous 12 months

Percentage feeling pressure to compromise company's ethical standards or rules

Percentage of American employees surveyed from 2000 to 2011 (N = 4,800 in 2011 sample) who observed misconduct in their workplace within the previous 12 months and percentage who say they are feeling pressure to compromise their company's ethical standards or rules.

The third important factor explaining why good people engage in unethical decisions and behavior is the situation in which the conduct occurs. Employees say they regularly experience pressure from top management that motivates them to lie to customers, breach regulations, or otherwise act unethically. According to a global survey of managers and human resource managers, the leading cause of unethical corporate behavior is pressure from top management or the board to meet unrealistic deadlines and business objectives.[74] Situational factors do not justify unethical conduct. Rather, we need to be aware of these factors so organizations can reduce their influence in the future.

A final reason why people engage in unethical conduct is that they engage in mindless behavior. In other words, they don't consciously think about whether their actions might be unethical.[75] Earlier in this chapter we said that people are more likely to abide by their values when they are reminded about them. Research suggests that people engage in almost automatic behavior much of the time, so they seldom evaluate whether their actions violate personal values or ethical principles. This mindless behavior is particularly true when (as often happens) employees are located away from the situation where their decisions have an impact (i.e., low moral intensity). Mindless behavior is further supported by implicit assumptions that the company or its key decision makers have high moral standards. Employees quickly dismiss any ethical concerns about their work when they assume their boss

who assigned that work is inherently ethical. For instance, one of the largest cases of accounting fraud occurred because the company's chief financial officer was highly respected in the industry, so employees assumed he was introducing innovative—and legal—accounting procedures. In reality, these activities were extreme forms of accounting fraud.[76]

Supporting Ethical Behavior

Most large and medium-size organizations apply one or more strategies to improve ethical conduct. One of the most basic steps in this direction is a code of ethical conduct—an organization's statement about desired practices, rules of conduct, and philosophy about its relationship to its stakeholders and the environment. Almost all Fortune 500 companies in the United States and the majority of the 500 largest companies in the United Kingdom have ethics codes.[77] These codes are supposed to motivate and guide employee behavior, signal the importance of ethical conduct, and build the firm's trustworthiness to stakeholders. However, critics suggest they do little to reduce unethical conduct. A glaring illustration is that Enron had a well-developed ethics code, yet its senior executives engaged in wholesale wrongdoing, resulting in the energy company's bankruptcy.[78]

Many firms supplement ethics codes with ethics training. Molson Coors developed an award-winning online training program set up as an expedition: Employees must resolve ethics violations at each "camp" as they ascend a mountain. The first few camps present real scenarios with fairly clear ethical violations of the company's ethics code; later camps present much fuzzier dilemmas requiring more careful thought about the company's underlying values.[79]

Some companies also have ways to confidentially communicate wrongdoing, such as an anonymous hotline as well as webpages

OB Theory to Practice

Texas Instruments' Quick Ethics Test[80]

Is the action legal?

Does it comply with our values?

If you do it, will you feel bad?

How will it look in the newspaper?

If you know it's wrong, don't do it!

If you're not sure, ask.

Keep asking until you get an answer.

that employees can use to raise ethical issues or concerns about ethical conduct. A few companies employ ethics ombudspersons who receive information confidentially from employees and proactively investigate possible wrongdoing. Ethics audits are also conducted in some organizations but are more common for evaluation of corporate social responsibility practices.[81]

These additional measures support ethical conduct to some extent, but the most powerful foundation is a set of shared values that reinforce ethical conduct. "If you don't have a culture of ethical decision making to begin with, all the controls and compliance regulations you care to deploy won't necessarily prevent ethical misconduct," warns a senior executive at British communications giant Vodafone. This culture is supported by the ethical conduct and vigilance of corporate leaders. By acting with the highest standards of moral conduct, leaders not only gain support and trust from followers; they role-model the ethical standards that employees are more likely to follow.[82]

Learning Objective

After reading this section, you should be able to

LO6 Review five values commonly studied across cultures.

VALUES ACROSS CULTURES

Sean Billing had been working as director of rooms at Fairmont Hotels in Chicago when he casually asked his boss whether the hotel chain could use his skills and knowledge elsewhere. Soon after, Fairmont assigned Billing to a management position in Kenya, bringing the new properties in the African country up to world-class standards through training and technology without losing the distinctive Kenyan character. Billing jumped at the opportunity, but he also soon discovered the challenge of infusing Fairmont's deep values of customer service, environmentalism, and empowerment into another culture. "It's a little bit of hotel culture shock . . . things are quite different here," admits Billing.[83]

We're Not in Bentonville Anymore![84]

Walmart is established in many countries, but the retailer's capabilities in this globalized world haven't always been up to expectations. In the late 1990s, Walmart established a European beachhead in Germany by opening 85 stores from two acquisitions. The decision may have been astute, if Walmart executives had realized they weren't in the United States anymore. The first CEO of the German operations spoke no German, so he required all direct reports to speak English at all times. The company naively imported the daily morning cheer and required greeters and staff to ask customers, "How are you today?" The morning cheer offended German managers, who felt a loss of their hierarchical position when required to cheer along with frontline employees (who were also somewhat ambivalent to the ritual). The friendly greeting was an affront to German customers because such signs of friendliness are reserved for friends and family. Walmart also banned coworkers from dating each other—yet another sign that Walmart had much to learn about the world beyond America. Less than a decade later, Walmart closed down its German operations, taking a $1 billion loss.

Fairmont Hotels & Resorts operates world-class hotels in several countries and is eager to help Sean Billing and other employees develop and strengthen their cross-cultural competence. People think and act differently across cultures, and these differences are due to unique norms of behavior as well as emphasis on different values.

Individualism and Collectivism

Of the many values studied across cultures, the five summarized in Exhibit 2.7 are by far the most popular. This exhibit also lists countries that have high, medium, or low emphasis on these values. Two seemingly inseparable cross-cultural values are individualism and collectivism. **Individualism** is the extent to which we value independence and personal uniqueness. Highly individualist people value personal freedom, self-sufficiency, control over their own lives, and appreciation of the unique qualities that distinguish them from others. The United States, Chile, Canada, and South Africa are countries that generally exhibit high individualism, whereas Taiwan and Venezuela are countries with low individualism.[85] **Collectivism** is the extent to which we value our duty to groups to which we belong and to group harmony. Highly collectivist people define themselves by their group memberships, emphasize their personal connection to others in their in-groups, and value the goals and well-being of people within those groups.[86] Low collectivism countries include the United States, Japan, and Germany, whereas Israel and Taiwan have relatively high collectivism.

Contrary to popular belief, individualism is not the opposite of collectivism. In fact, an analysis of most previous studies reported that the two concepts are unrelated.[87] For example, cultures that highly value duty to one's group do not necessarily give a low priority to personal freedom and uniqueness. Generally, people across all cultures define themselves by both their uniqueness and their relationship to others. It is an inherent characteristic of everyone's self-concept, which we discuss in the next chapter. Some cultures clearly emphasize uniqueness or group obligations more than others, but both have a place in a person's values and self-concept.

Also note that people in Japan have relatively low collectivism. This is contrary to many cross-cultural books, which claim that

individualism
A cross-cultural value describing the degree to which people in a culture emphasize independence and personal uniqueness.

collectivism
A cross-cultural value describing the degree to which people in a culture emphasize duty to groups to which they belong and to group harmony.

power distance
A cross-cultural value describing the degree to which people in a culture accept unequal distribution of power in a society.

Japan is one of the most collectivist countries on the planet! There are several explanations for the historical misinterpretation, ranging from problems defining and measuring collectivism to erroneous reporting of early cross-cultural research. Whatever the reasons, studies consistently report that people in Japan tend to have relatively low collectivism and moderate individualism (as indicated in Exhibit 2.7).[88]

Power Distance

Power distance refers to the extent to which people accept unequal distribution of power in a society.[89] Those with high power distance accept and value unequal power. They value obedience to authority, are comfortable receiving commands from their superiors without consultation or debate, and prefer to resolve differences through formal procedures rather than directly. In contrast, people with low power distance expect relatively equal power sharing. They view the relationship with their boss as one of interdependence, not dependence;

▼ **EXHIBIT 2.7** Five Cross-Cultural Values

Value	Sample Countries	Representative Beliefs/Behaviors in "High" Cultures
Individualism	High: United States, Chile, Canada, South Africa Medium: Japan, Denmark Low: Taiwan, Venezuela	Defines self more by one's uniqueness; personal goals have priority; decisions have low consideration of effect on others; relationships are viewed as more instrumental and fluid.
Collectivism	High: Israel, Taiwan Medium: India, Denmark Low: United States, Germany, Japan	Defines self more by one's in-group membership; goals of self-sacrifice and harmony have priority; behavior regulated by in-group norms; in-group memberships are viewed as stable with a strong differentiation with out-groups.
Power Distance	High: India, Malaysia Medium: United States, Japan Low: Denmark, Israel	Reluctant to disagree with or contradict the boss; managers are expected and preferred decision makers; perception of dependence (versus interdependence) with the boss.
Uncertainty Avoidance	High: Japan, Belgium, Greece Medium: United States, Norway Low: Denmark, Singapore	Prefer predictable situations; value stable employment, strict laws, and low conflict; dislike deviations from normal behavior.
Achievement Orientation	High: Austria, Japan Medium: United States, Brazil Low: Sweden, Netherlands	Focus on outcomes (versus relationships); decisions based on contribution (equity versus equality); low empathy or showing emotions (versus strong empathy and caring).

Sources: Individualism and collectivism descriptions and results are from the meta-analysis reported in D. Oyserman, H. M. Coon, and M. Kemmelmeier, "Rethinking Individualism and Collectivism: Evaluation of Theoretical Assumptions and Meta-Analyses," *Psychological Bulletin*, 128 (2002): 3–72. The other information is from G. Hofstede, *Culture's Consequences,* 2nd ed. (Thousand Oaks, CA: Sage, 2001).

that is, they believe their boss is also dependent on them, so they expect power sharing and consultation before decisions affecting them are made. People in India and Malaysia tend to have high power distance, whereas people in Denmark and Israel generally have low power distance. Americans collectively have medium-low power distance.

To understand the effect of power distance, consider the experience of a Southeast Asian engineer who immigrated to Canada. In his home country, the engineer generated data analysis reports and submitted them to his supervisor without recommendations. His boss would look at the factual information and make a decision. Including recommendations in those reports would have shown disrespect for the supervisor's higher position, which may have resulted in dismissal. But when the engineer moved to Canada, he was expected to propose recommendations along with the technical data. Excluding recommendations from an engineering report in Canada would be evidence of incompetence, which may result in dismissal. To remain employed, the engineer had to overcome a huge shift in power distance values and expectations.[90]

Uncertainty Avoidance

Uncertainty avoidance is the degree to which people tolerate ambiguity (low uncertainty avoidance) or feel threatened by ambiguity and uncertainty (high uncertainty avoidance). Employees with high uncertainty avoidance value structured situations in which rules of conduct and decision making are clearly documented. They usually prefer direct rather than indirect or ambiguous communications. Uncertainty avoidance tends to be high in Belgium and Greece and very high in Japan. It is generally low in Denmark and Singapore. Americans collectively have medium-low uncertainty avoidance.

Achievement-Nurturing Orientation

Achievement–nurturing orientation reflects a competitive versus cooperative view of relations with other people.[91] People with a high achievement orientation value assertiveness, competitiveness, and materialism. They appreciate people who are tough, and they favor the acquisition of money and material goods. In contrast, people in nurturing-oriented cultures emphasize relationships and the well-being of others. They focus on human interaction and caring rather than competition and personal success. People in Sweden, Norway, and the Netherlands

score very low on achievement orientation (i.e., they have a high nurturing orientation). In contrast, very high achievement orientation scores have been reported in Japan and Austria. The United States places a little above the middle of the range on achievement–nurturing orientation.

Caveats about Cross-Cultural Knowledge

Cross-cultural organizational research has gained considerable attention over the past two decades, likely due to increased globalization and cultural diversity within organizations. Our knowledge of cross-cultural dynamics has blossomed, and many of these findings will be discussed throughout this book, particularly regarding leadership, conflict handling, and influence tactics. However, we also need to raise a few warning flags about cross-cultural knowledge. One problem is that too many studies have relied on small, convenient samples (such as students) to represent an entire culture.[92] The result is that many cross-cultural studies draw conclusions that might not generalize to the cultures they intended to represent.

A second problem is that cross-cultural studies often assume each country has one culture.[93] In reality, many countries (including the United States) have become culturally diverse. As more countries embrace globalization and multiculturalism, it becomes even less appropriate to assume an entire country has one unified culture.

Cultural Diversity within the United States

Studies report that American values vary across regions.[94] Using social indicators rather than surveys, one study found that collectivism is highest across the Southern states, California, and Hawaii; it is lowest among residents in the Mountain, Northwest, and Great Plains states.[95]

A third concern is that cross-cultural research and writing continue to rely on a major study conducted almost four decades ago of 116,000 IBM employees across dozens of countries. That study helped to ignite subsequent cross-cultural research, but its findings are increasingly outdated as values in some cultures have shifted over the years. For example, value systems seem to be converging across Asia as people in these countries interact more frequently with each other and adopt standardized business practices.[96] At least one recent review has recommended that future studies should no longer rely on the IBM study to benchmark values of a particular culture.[97]

perceiving ourselves and others
in organizations

chapter three

Jason Blumer defies anyone's image of an accountant. The president (he prefers Chief Innovation Officer) of a boutique CPA firm in Greenville, South Carolina, usually wears jeans, T-shirts, and flip-flops around the office. He writes a popular blog, is a Twitter maniac, Skypes with clients, and hams it up with distorted photos on his iPad. "There is a new day dawning, and this country better realize we CPAs are now cool, Mac-loving, flip-flop wearing, global-serving, math-hating innovators," says Blumer about his stereotype-busting ways.[1]

Jason Blumer isn't alone in trying to change the perceptions many people hold about accountants. A few accounting associations have launched ad campaigns depicting accountants as active, contemporary, and innovative. These campaigns try to correct misperceptions about members of the accounting profession and, in particular, to attract qualified candidates to this field. As long as accountants are perceived as boring, monotonous, cautious, and unromantic (as various studies have reported), then some potential applicants will decide that this professional does not fit their self-concept.

This chapter investigates the related topics of self-concept (how we perceive ourselves) and social perception (how we perceive others). We begin by studying the three characteristics of an individual's self-concept as well as the four self-concept processes. Next, we focus on perceptions in organizational settings, including several specific perceptual processes such as stereotyping, attribution, and self-fulfilling prophecy. We then identify potentially effective ways to improve perceptions, including practices similar to corporate volunteering. The final section of this chapter reviews the main elements of global mindset, a largely perceptual process valued in this increasingly globalized world. ■

LEARNING OBJECTIVES

After studying Chapter 3, you should be able to:

LO1 Describe the elements of self-concept and explain how they affect an individual's behavior and well-being.

LO2 Outline the perceptual process and discuss the effects of categorical thinking and mental models in that process.

LO3 Discuss how stereotyping, attribution, self-fulfilling prophecy, halo, false-consensus primacy, and recency influence the perceptual process.

LO4 Discuss three ways to improve perceptions, with specific application to organizational situations.

LO5 Outline the main features of a global mindset and justify its usefulness to employees and organizations.

Learning Objective

After reading this section, you should be able to

LO1 Describe the elements of self-concept and explain how they affect an individual's behavior and well-being.

SELF-CONCEPT: HOW WE PERCEIVE OURSELVES

We begin this chapter by looking at how people perceive themselves, that is, their self-concept. **Self-concept** refers to an individual's self-beliefs and self-evaluations. It is the "Who am I?" and "How do I feel about myself?" that people ask themselves and that guide their decisions and actions. Whether contemplating a career as an accountant or a chemical engineer, we compare our images of that job with our current (perceived self) and desired (ideal self) images of ourselves. We also evaluate our current and desired competencies to determine whether there is a good fit with that job. A growing number of organizational behavior experts are discovering that how people perceive themselves helps to explain their attitudes, motivation, decisions, and behavior in the workplace.

Self-Concept Complexity, Consistency, and Clarity

An individual's self-concept can be described by three characteristics: complexity, consistency, and clarity (see Exhibit 3.1).[2] First, self-concepts vary in their *complexity*, that is, the number of distinct and important roles or identities people perceive about themselves. Everyone has some degree of complexity because they see themselves in more than one role (accountant, friend, daughter, sports enthusiast, etc). Complexity is determined not only by the number of selves, but also by the separation of those selves.[3] A self-concept has low complexity when the individual's most important identities are highly interconnected, such as when they are all work related (manager, engineer, family income-earner).

A second characteristic of self-concept is its internal *consistency*. High internal consistency exists when most of the individual's self-perceived roles require similar personality traits, values, and other attributes. Low consistency occurs when some self-perceptions require personal characteristics that conflict with characteristics required for other aspects of self. Low self-concept consistency would exist if you see yourself as a very exacting engineer, yet also a cavalier and risk-oriented skier. *Clarity*, the third characteristic of self-concept, is the degree to which you have a clear, confidently defined, and stable self-concept. Clarity occurs when we are confident about "who we are," can describe our important identities to others, and provide

▼ **EXHIBIT 3.1** Self-Concept Characteristics and Processes

the same description of ourselves across time. Self-concept clarity increases with age as well as with the consistency of the person's multiple selves.[4]

Effects of Self-Concept Characteristics on Well-Being and Behavior Self-concept complexity, consistency, and clarity are important because they influence a person's well-being, behavior, and performance. People tend to have stronger psychological well-being when they have multiple selves (complexity) that are well established (clarity) and are similar to each other and compatible with personal traits (consistency). Complexity is important because it protects our self-evaluation when some roles are threatened or damaged.[5] A complex self-concept is rather like a ship with several compartments that can be sealed off from each

other. If one compartment is flooded, it can be sealed off so most of the ship remains afloat. People with low complexity, on the other hand, suffer severe loss when they experience failure because these events affect a large part of themselves.

A person's well-being also increases to some extent when his or her multiple selves are in harmony with each other (consistency).[6] Some self-concept diversity helps people to adapt, but too much variation causes internal tension and conflict. Finally, well-being tends to increase with self-concept clarity. When we lack confidence in ourselves, we are more easily influenced by others, experience more stress when making decisions, and feel more threatened by social forces that undermine our self-confidence and self-esteem.[7]

The effects of self-concept complexity, consistency, and clarity on behavior and performance are more varied.[8] On the one hand, people who define themselves mainly by their work (i.e., low complexity) tend to have lower absenteeism and turnover. They also potentially perform better due to more investment in skill development, longer hours, more concentration on work, and so forth. On the other hand, low complexity commonly results in higher stress and depression when the main self-aspect is damaged or threatened, which further undermines individual performance. Self-concept clarity tends to improve performance and is considered vital for leadership roles.[9] However, people with very high clarity may have role inflexibility and cannot adapt to changing job duties.

Complexity, consistency, and clarity describe characteristics of a person's self-concept. In addition to these characteristics are four processes that shape self-concept and influence a person's decisions and behavior. Let's look at each of these four "selves": self-enhancement, self-verification, self-evaluation, and social self (social identity).

Self-Enhancement

People across most (and likely all) cultures are inherently motivated to perceive themselves (and to be perceived by others) as competent, attractive, lucky, ethical, and important.[10] This **self-enhancement** is observed in many ways. Individuals tend to rate themselves above average, believe they have a better than average probability of success, and attribute their successes to personal motivation or ability while blaming the situation for their mistakes.

For instance, a recent U.S. government survey reported that 69 percent of government workers rated their performance above average compared to other coworkers in their unit; only 1 percent rated their performance below average. Even more extreme is that 94 percent of university professors in one study rated themselves above-average teachers compared with others at their university; two-thirds rated themselves in the top quartile![11] People don't see themselves as above average in all circumstances, but this bias is apparent for conditions that are common rather than rare and that are important to them.[12]

Self-enhancement has both positive and negative consequences in organizational settings.[13] On the positive side, individuals tend to experience better mental and physical health and adjustment when they view their self-concept in a positive light. On the negative side, self-enhancement can result in bad decisions. For example, some studies report that self-enhancement causes managers to overestimate the probability of success in investment decisions. Other research suggests that self-enhancement is a factor in high accident rates among novice drivers. Generally, though, successful companies strive to help employees feel valued and integral members of the organization.

> " People tend to have stronger psychological well-being when they have multiple selves (complexity) that are well established (clarity) and are similar to each other and compatible with personal traits (consistency). "

self-concept An individual's self-beliefs and self-evaluations.

self-enhancement A person's inherent motivation to have a positive self-concept (and to have others perceive him/her favorably), such as being competent, attractive, lucky, ethical, and important.

Many Recognition Programs, But Few Employees Feel Valued[14]

35% of employees say they received any recognition at all from their employer in the previous year.

Thank you

89% of human resources executives say they have employee recognition programs.

79% of employees say that lack of recognition is a key reason why they quit their jobs.

Self-Verification

Along with being motivated by self-enhancement, people try to confirm and maintain their existing self-concept.[15] This process, called **self-verification**, stabilizes an individual's self-concept, which, in turn, provides an important anchor that guides his or her thoughts and actions. Employees actively communicate their self-concept so coworkers can provide feedback that reinforces the self-concept. For example, you might let coworkers know you are a very organized person; later, they point out situations where you have indeed been very organized. Unlike self-enhancement, self-verification includes seeking out feedback that is not necessarily flattering (e.g., I'm a numbers person, not a people person). Social scientists continue to debate whether and under what conditions people prefer information that supports self-enhancement or self-verification.[16] In other words, do we prefer compliments rather than accurate criticism of our known limitations?

Self-verification has several implications for organizational behavior.[17] First, it affects the perceptual process because employees are more likely to remember information that is consistent with their self-concept and screen out information that seems inconsistent with it. Second, the clearer the individual's self-concept, the less he or she will accept feedback that contradicts that self-concept. Third, employees are motivated to interact with others who affirm their self-concept, and this affects how well they get along with their boss and team members.

Self-Evaluation

Almost everyone strives to have a positive self-concept, but some people have a more positive evaluation of themselves than do others. This *self-evaluation* is mostly defined by three elements: self-esteem, self-efficacy, and locus of control.[18]

Self-Esteem *Self-esteem*—the extent to which people like, respect, and are satisfied with themselves—represents a global self-evaluation. Some experts also believe self-esteem is a person's rating of his or her success at social inclusion. In other words, people have higher self-esteem when they believe they are connected to and accepted by others. People with high self-esteem are less influenced by others, tend to persist in spite of failure, and think more rationally. Self-esteem regarding specific aspects of self (e.g., a good student, a good driver, a good parent) predicts specific thoughts and behaviors, whereas a person's overall self-esteem predicts only large bundles of thoughts and behaviors.[19]

Self-Efficacy **Self-efficacy** refers to a person's belief that he or she can successfully complete a task.[20] Those with high self-efficacy have a "can do" attitude. They believe they possess the energy (motivation), resources (situational factors), understanding of the correct course of action (role perceptions), and competencies (ability) to perform the task. In other words, self-efficacy is an individual's perception regarding the MARS model in a specific situation. Although originally defined in terms of specific tasks, self-efficacy is also a general trait related to self-concept.[21] General self-efficacy is a perception of one's competence to perform across a variety of situations. The higher the person's general self-efficacy, the higher is his or her overall self-evaluation.

Locus of Control **Locus of control** is defined as a person's general beliefs about the amount of control he or she has over personal life events.[22] Individuals with more of an

Camp Fully Involved Builds Self-Esteem and Develops Self-Concept[23]

Women represent only 3.4 percent of firefighters in the United States. Camp Fully Involved aims to increase this number by helping young women to view firefighting as an exciting occupation compatible with their self-concept. During the six-day intensive course in Nashua, New Hampshire, teenage girls learn various firefighting skills, such as how to climb 100-foot ladders, fight fires in the woods, and repel off a building. Camp Fully Involved also helps to build their self-confidence for any career. "You see all these girls walk a little taller when they leave," says Nashua Fire Department lieutenant Jess Wyman, who organized the camp.

internal locus of control believe their personal characteristics (i.e., motivation and competencies) mainly influence life's outcomes. Those with more of an external locus of control believe events in their life are due mainly to fate, luck, or conditions in the external environment. Locus of control is a generalized belief, so people with an external locus can feel in control in familiar situations (such as performing common tasks). However, their underlying locus of control would be apparent in new situations in which control over events is uncertain.

People with a more internal locus of control have a more positive self-evaluation. They also tend to perform better in most employment situations, are more successful in their careers, earn more money, and are better suited for leadership positions. Internals are also more satisfied with their jobs, cope better in stressful situations, and are more motivated by performance-based reward systems.[24] One worrisome observation is that young people have significantly shifted from an internal to more of an external locus of control over the four decades since the early 1960s.[25]

The Social Self

Everyone has a self-concept that includes at least a few identities (manager, parent, golfer, etc), and each identity is defined by a set of attributes. These attributes highlight both the person's uniqueness (personal identity) or association with others (social identity).[26] *Personal identity* (also known as internal self-concept) consists of attributes that make us unique and distinct from people in the social groups to which we have a connection. For instance, an unusual achievement that distinguishes you from other people typically becomes a personal identity characteristic. Personal identity refers to something about you as an individual without reference to a larger group.

At the same time, human beings are social animals; they have an inherent drive to be associated with others and to be recognized as part of social communities. This drive to belong is reflected in self-concept by the fact

that all individuals define themselves to some degree by their relationships.[27] This *social identity* (also called external self-concept) is the central theme of **social identity theory**, which says people define themselves by the groups to which they belong or have an emotional attachment. For instance, someone might have a social identity as an American, a graduate of Indiana University, and an employee at Edward Jones (see Exhibit 3.2). Social identity is a complex combination of many memberships arranged in a hierarchy of importance. One factor determining importance is how easily we are identified as a member of the reference group, such as by our gender, age, and ethnicity. A second factor is your minority status in a group. It is difficult to ignore your gender in a class where most other students are the opposite gender, for example. In that context, gender tends to become a stronger defining feature of your social identity than it is in social settings where there are many people of your gender.

Along with demographic characteristics, the group's status is an important factor in determining whether we include it in our social identity because this association makes us feel better about ourselves (i.e., self-enhancement). Medical doctors usually define themselves by their profession because of its high status. Some people describe themselves by where they work ("I work at Mayo Clinic") because their employer has a good reputation. Others never mention where they work because their employer is noted for poor relations with employees or has a poor reputation in the community.[28]

▼ **EXHIBIT 3.2** Social Identity Theory Example

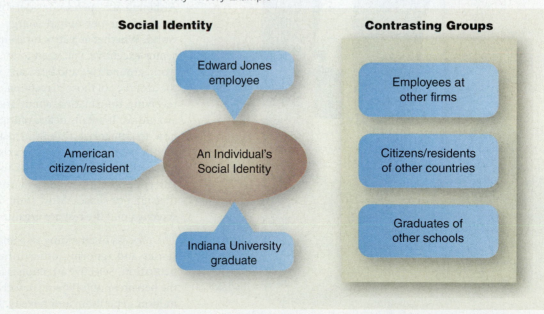

perception The process of receiving information about and making sense of the world around us.

selective attention The process of attending to some information received by our senses and ignoring other information.

confirmation bias The process of screening out information that is contrary to our values and assumptions and more readily accepting confirming information.

to recent studies, self-concept helps to explain leadership, team dynamics, employee motivation, decision making, influence, organizational commitment, and other organizational behavior topics.[30] Consequently, self-concept and its specific elements will be mentioned throughout this book, including later parts of this chapter.

Everyone tries to balance their personal and social identities, but the priority for uniqueness (personal identities) versus relatedness (social identities) differs from one person to the next. People whose self-concepts are heavily defined by social rather than personal identities are more motivated to abide by team norms and more easily influenced by peer pressure. Those who place more emphasis on personal identities, on the other hand, speak out more frequently against the majority and are less motivated to follow the team's wishes. Furthermore, expressing disagreement with others is a sign of distinctiveness and can help employees form a clearer self-concept, particularly when that disagreement is based on differences in personal values.[29]

Self-Concept and Organizational Behavior

Self-concept has become a hot topic in several disciplines and is now gaining attention in organizational behavior as a cluster of theories to explain employee attitudes and behavior. According

Many organizational leaders are well aware that performance and well-being are affected by how employees perceive themselves. For more than 50 years, Johnson & Johnson managers have lived by the health product company's credo that every employee "must be considered as an individual" and that the company "must respect their dignity and recognize their merit." Executives at Intercontinental Hotels Group (IHG) point out that the quality of service employees give their guests depends on how well those employees feel valued by management. As one IHG executive recently explained: "Everything you do in the business must make [employees] feel like heroes and heroines and you must acknowledge the huge contribution they make. Everyone says they do this, but very few companies do. That's how you galvanize an organization—by making people feel that they belong to something special."[31]

Learning Objective

After reading this section, you should be able to

LO2 Outline the perceptual process and discuss the effects of categorical thinking and mental models in that process.

PERCEIVING THE WORLD AROUND US

Although we spend considerable time perceiving ourselves, most of our perceptual energy is directed toward the outer world. Whether as a structural engineer, forensic accountant, or senior executive, you need to form accurate perceptions of the world around you, and be aware of the conditions that challenge the accuracy of those perceptions. **Perception** is the process of receiving information about and making sense of the world around us. It entails determining which information to notice, how to categorize this information, and how to interpret it within the framework of our existing knowledge. This perceptual process generally follows the steps shown in Exhibit 3.3. Perception begins when environmental stimuli are received through our senses. Most stimuli that bombard our senses are screened out; the rest are organized and interpreted.

The process of attending to some information received by our senses and ignoring other information is called **selective attention**. Selective attention is influenced by characteristics of the person or object being perceived, particularly size, intensity, motion, repetition, and novelty. For example, a small, flashing

red light on a nurse station console is immediately noticed because it is bright (intensity), flashing (motion), a rare event (novelty), and has symbolic meaning that a patient's vital signs are failing. Notice that selective attention is also influenced by the context in which the target is perceived. The selective attention process is triggered by things or people who might be out of context, such as someone with a foreign accent in a setting where most people have American accents.

Characteristics of the perceiver also influence selection attention, usually without the perceiver's awareness.[32] When information is received through the senses, our brain quickly and nonconsciously assesses whether it is relevant or irrelevant to us

> # We don't see things as they are. We see them as we are.
> —Anais Nin

and then attaches emotional markers (worry, happiness, boredom) to that information. These emotional markers help us to store information in memory; they also reproduce the same emotions when we are subsequently thinking about this information.[33] The selective attention process is far from perfect, however. The Greek philosopher Plato acknowledged this imperfection long ago when he wrote that we see reality only as shadows reflecting against the rough wall of a cave.[34]

One perceptual bias in selective attention is the effect of our assumptions and conscious anticipation of future events. You are more likely to notice a coworker's email among the daily bombardment of messages when you expect to receive that email (particularly when it is important to you). At the same time, expectations and assumptions also cause us to screen out potentially important information. In one study, students were asked to watch a 30-second video clip in which several people passed around two basketballs. Students who were instructed just to watch the video clip easily noticed someone dressed in a gorilla suit walking among the players for nine seconds and stopping to thump his or her chest. But only half of the students who were asked to count the number of times one basketball was passed around noticed the intruding gorilla.[35]

Another selective attention problem, called **confirmation bias**, is the tendency for people to screen out information that is contrary to their decisions, beliefs, values, and assumptions, whereas confirming information is more readily accepted through the perceptual process.[36] This bias occurs, for instance, when we form an opinion or theory about something, such as a consumer trend or an employee's potential. The preconception

▼ **EXHIBIT 3.3** Model of the Perceptual Process

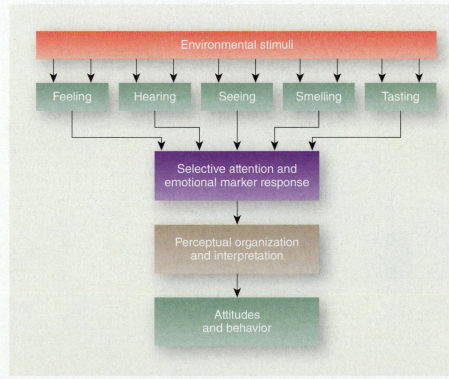

categorical thinking
Organizing people and objects into preconceived categories stored in our long-term memory.

mental models
Visual or relational images in our mind representing the external world.

stereotyping
The process of assigning traits to people based on their membership in a social category.

causes us to select information that is consistent with the theory and to ignore contrary or seemingly irrelevant information. Studies have reported this faulty selective attention occurs when police detectives and other forensic experts quickly form theories about what happened.[37]

There are many examples of confirmation bias in scientific research, where scientists have ignored or removed evidence that contradicts their prized theories. One classic case occurred in the 1970s when nuclear particle researchers at CERN (European Organization for Nuclear Research) found an unusual dip in the pattern formed by a colliding particle. This was an exciting discovery, until a growing chorus of nuclear researchers elsewhere reported they could not replicate that dip in their data. CERN vigorously defended the existence of the dip until the contrary evidence was overwhelming. What happened? CERN's researchers looked closely at batches of data that did not show any dip. They were convinced the missing dip was due to bad data, so they invariably found enough justification to discard batches that didn't have any dip. Meanwhile, batches of confirming data were accepted without scrutiny. In effect, CERN discarded the evidence that opposed their exciting, but short-lived, discovery![40]

Perceptual Organization and Interpretation

People make sense of information even before they become aware of it. This sense making partly includes **categorical thinking**—the mostly nonconscious process of organizing

> It is a capital mistake to theorize before you have all the evidence. It biases the judgment.[38]
> —Sir Arthur Conan Doyle in Sherlock Holmes's *A Study in Scarlet*

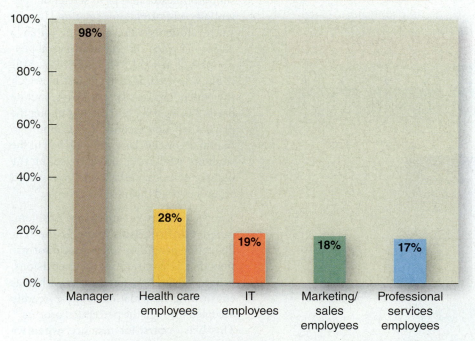

Manager-Employee Perceptual Misalignments[39]

Percentage of British managers who believe they "know their people well," compared with percentage of employees (by occupation) who believe their bosses know them well.

people and objects into preconceived categories stored in our long-term memory.[41] Categorical thinking relies on a variety of automatic perceptual grouping principles. Things are often grouped together based on their similarity or proximity to others. If you notice that a group of similar-looking people includes several professors, for instance, you will likely assume the others in that group are also professors. Another form of perceptual grouping is based on the need for cognitive closure, such as filling in missing information about what happened at a meeting you didn't attend (e.g., who was there, where it was held). A third form of grouping occurs when we think we see trends in otherwise ambiguous information. Several studies have found people have a natural tendency to see patterns that really are random events, such as presumed winning streaks among sports stars or in gambling.[42]

The process of "making sense" of the world around us also involves interpreting incoming information. This happens as quickly as selecting and organizing because the previously mentioned emotional markers are tagged to incoming stimuli, which are essentially quick judgments about whether that information is good or bad for us. How much time does it take to make these quick judgments? Recent studies estimate we make reliable judgments about another individual's trustworthiness based on viewing a facial image for as little as 50 milliseconds (1/20th of a second). In other words, we form similar opinions of another person whether we see that person's face for a minute or for only a fraction of one second.[43] Collectively, these studies reveal that selective attention, perceptual organization, and interpretation operate very quickly and to a large extent without our awareness.

Mental Models To achieve our goals with some degree of predictability and sanity, we need road maps of the environments in which we live. These road maps, called **mental models**, are internal representations of the external world.[44] They consist of visual or relational images in our mind, such as what the classroom looks like or what happens when we submit an assignment late. Mental models partly rely on the process of perceptual grouping to make sense of things; they fill in the missing pieces, including the causal connection among events. For example, you have a mental model about attending a class lecture or seminar, including assumptions or expectations about where the instructor and students arrange themselves in the room, how they ask and answer questions, and so forth. We can create a mental image of a class in progress.

The paradox of mental models is that although they help us to make sense of our environment, they also make it difficult to see that environment in new ways. For example, accounting professionals tend to see corporate problems from an accounting perspective, whereas marketing professionals see the same problems from a marketing perspective. Mental models also block our recognition of new opportunities. How do we change mental models? That's a tough challenge. After all, we developed models from several years of experience and reinforcement. The most important way to minimize the perceptual problems with mental models is to constantly question them. We need to ask ourselves about the assumptions we make. Working with people from diverse backgrounds is another way to break out of existing mental models. Colleagues from different cultures and areas of expertise tend to have different mental models, so working with them makes our own assumptions more obvious.

> " The paradox of mental models is that although they help us to make sense of our environment, they also make it difficult to see that environment in new ways. "

Learning Objective

After reading this section, you should be able to

LO3 Discuss how stereotyping, attribution, self-fulfilling prophecy, halo, false-consensus primacy, and recency influence the perceptual process.

SPECIFIC PERCEPTUAL PROCESSES AND PROBLEMS

Embedded within the general perceptual process are specific sub-processes and associated errors that have received considerable attention by social scientists. Over the next several pages, we will examine several of these perceptual processes and biases as well as their implications for organizational behavior. We begin with the most widely known perceptual process and bias: stereotyping.

Stereotyping in Organizations

Stereotyping is the perceptual process in which we assign characteristics to an identifiable group and then automatically transfer those features to anyone we believe is a member of that group.[45] The assigned characteristics tend to be difficult to observe, such as personality traits and abilities, but they can also include physical characteristics and a host of other qualities. For instance, most people hold the stereotype that professors are intelligent and absent-minded. Stereotypes are formed to some extent from personal experience, but they are mainly provided to us through media images (e.g., movie characters) and other cultural prototypes. They are beliefs held across an entire society and sometimes across several cultures, rather than beliefs that differ from one person to the next.

Stereotyping involves assigning a group's perceived attributes to individuals known or believed to be members of that group. Consequently, everyone identified with the stereotyped group is assumed to possess these characteristics. If we learn that someone is a professor, for example, we implicitly assume the person is also intelligent and absentminded. Historically, researchers also defined stereotypes as exaggerations or falsehoods. This is often true, but stereotypes often have some degree of accuracy.

Why People Stereotype One reason people engage in stereotyping is that, as a form of categorical thinking, it is a natural and mostly nonconscious "energy-saving" process that simplifies our understanding of the world. It is easier to remember features of a stereotype than the constellation of characteristics unique to everyone we meet.[46] A second reason is that we have an innate need to understand and anticipate how others will behave. We don't have much information when first meeting someone, so we rely heavily on stereotypes to fill in the missing pieces. The higher the perceiver's need for cognitive closure, the higher the reliance on stereotypes.

A third reason stereotyping occurs is because it enhances our self-concept. Earlier in this chapter we explained that people define themselves by the groups to which they belong or have an emotional attachment. They are also motivated to maintain a positive self-concept. This combination of social identity and self-enhancement leads to the process of categorization, homogenization, and differentiation:[47]

- *Categorization*. Social identity is a comparative process, and the comparison begins by categorizing people into distinct groups. By viewing someone (including yourself) as a Texan, for example, you remove that person's individuality and, instead, see him or her as a prototypical representative of the group called Texans. This categorization then allows you to distinguish Texans from people who live in, say, California or New Hampshire.

- *Homogenization*. To simplify the comparison process, we tend to think people within each group are very similar to each other. For instance, we think Texans collectively have similar attitudes and characteristics, whereas Californians collectively have their own set of characteristics. Of course, every individual is unique, but we tend to lose sight of this fact when thinking about our social identity and how we compare to people in other social groups.

- *Differentiation*. Self-enhancement motivates us to have a positive self-concept. Thus, in addition to categorizing and homogenizing people, we also differentiate them by assigning more favorable characteristics to people in our groups than to people in other groups. This differentiation is often subtle, but it can escalate into a "good guy–bad guy" contrast when groups are in conflict with each other.[48] In other words, when out-group members threaten our self-concept, we are particularly motivated (often without our awareness) to assign negative stereotypes to them.

Problems with Stereotyping Everyone engages in stereotyping, but this process distorts perceptions in various ways. First, although stereotypes are not completely fictional, neither do they accurately describe every person in a social category. Consider how accountants are typically stereotyped in films and literature. According to various studies, they are usually depicted as boring, monotonous, cautious, unromantic, obtuse, antisocial, shy, dysfunctional, devious, calculating, and malicious.[49] Fortunately, recent studies also note a more positive trend; some accountant characters are loyal, conscientious, and everyday heroes. The traditional accountant stereotype may fit the description of a few accountants, but it is certainly not characteristic of all—or even most—people in this profession. Even so, once we categorize someone as an accountant, the stereotypic features of accountants (boring, antisocial, etc.) are transferred to that person, even though we have not attempted to verify those characteristics in that person.

Another problem with stereotyping is that it lays the foundation for discriminatory attitudes and behavior. Most of this perceptual bias occurs as *unintentional (systemic) discrimination*, whereby decision makers rely on stereotypes to establish notions of the "ideal" person in specific roles. A person who doesn't fit the ideal tends to receive a less favorable evaluation. This subtle discrimination often shows up in age discrimination claims, such as the case in which Ryanair's recruitment advertising said it was looking for "young dynamic" employees. Recruiters at the Irish discount airline probably didn't intentionally discriminate against older people, but the tribunal concluded that systemic discrimination did occur because none of the job applicants was over 40 years old.[50]

The more serious form of stereotype bias is *intentional discrimination* or *prejudice*, in which people hold unfounded negative attitudes toward those belonging to a particular stereotyped group.[51] Is overt prejudice less common today? Perhaps, but there are plenty of examples to remind us it still exists. For example, a French study of 2,300 help-wanted ads found job applicants with French-sounding names were much more likely to get job interviews than were applicants with North African or sub-Saharan African names, even though employers received identical résumés for both names! Furthermore, when applicants personally visited human resource staff, those with foreign names were often told the job had been filled, whereas few of the applicants with French names received this message (even when visiting afterward). Similar studies also found degrees of job applicant discrimination involving Turkish applicants in Germany, Albanians in Greece, and Arabs in Sweden.[52]

If stereotyping is such a problem, shouldn't we try to avoid this process altogether? Unfortunately, it's not that simple. Most experts agree that categorical thinking (including stereotyping) is an automatic and nonconscious process. Specialized training programs can minimize stereotype activation to some extent, but for the most part the process is hardwired in our brain cells.[53] Also remember that stereotyping helps us in several valuable (although fallible) ways described earlier: minimizing mental effort, filling in missing information, and supporting our social identity. The good news is that while it is very difficult to prevent the *activation* of stereotypes, we can minimize the *application* of stereotypic information. In other words, although we automatically categorize people and assign stereotypic traits to them, we can consciously minimize the extent we rely on that stereotypic information. Later in this chapter, we identify ways to minimize stereotyping and other perceptual biases.

Attribution Theory

Another widely-discussed perceptual phenomenon in organizational settings is the **attribution process**. Attribution involves deciding whether an observed behavior or event is caused mainly by the person (internal factors) or by the environment (external factors).[54] Internal factors include the person's ability or motivation, whereas external factors include lack of resources, other people, or just luck. If a coworker doesn't show up for an important meeting, for instance, we infer either internal attributions (the coworker is forgetful, lacks motivation, etc.) or external attributions (traffic, a family emergency, or other circumstances prevented the coworker from attending).

People rely on the three attribution rules shown in Exhibit 3.4 to determine whether someone's behavior mainly has an internal or external attribution. Internal attributions are made when the observed individual behaved this way in the past (high consistency), he or she behaves like this toward other people or in different situations (low distinctiveness), and other people do not behave this way in similar situations (low consensus). On the other hand, an external attribution is made when there is low consistency, high distinctiveness, and high consensus.

To illustrate how these three attribution rules operate, suppose an employee is making poor-quality products one day on a particular machine. We would probably conclude there is something wrong with the machine (an external attribution) if the employee has made good-quality products on this machine in the past (low consistency), the employee makes good-quality products on other machines (high distinctiveness), and other employees have recently had quality problems on this machine (high consensus). We would make an internal attribution, on the other hand, if the employee usually makes poor-quality products on this machine (high consistency), other employees produce good-quality products on this machine (low consensus), and the employee also makes poor-quality products on other machines (low distinctiveness).[56]

Attribution is a necessary process; we need to form cause-effect relationships to survive in our environment. How we react to a coworker's poor performance depends on our internal or external attribution of that performance. Students who make internal attributions about their poor performance are more likely to drop out of their programs.[57] As we see next, however, people distort their perceptions through various attribution errors.

Attribution Errors Attribution is the source of a few perceptual errors, the two most common of which are fundamental attribution error and self-serving bias. **Fundamental attribution error** refers to our tendency to perceive that another person's actions are caused mainly by internal attributions, whereas we recognize both internal and external causes of our own actions.[58]

Women on Corporate Boards: Room to Grow[55]

Whether due to systemic or intentional discrimination, women remain significantly underrepresented on corporate boards in most countries. More than one-third of the workforce and upward of 20 percent of middle managers in many countries are women, yet they comprise less than 10 percent of corporate board members. The highest percentage of female corporate board members are in Norway (40.1%), Sweden (27.3%), Finland (24.5%), and the United States (16.1%). Further down the list are Germany (11.2%), Canada (10.3%), Hong Kong (9.0%), Austria (7.5%), and Mexico (6.8%). Women have the lowest representation on corporate boards (1% or less) in four Middle Eastern countries and Japan. Female board representation in France has nearly doubled over the past six years to 16.6%. This increase is likely due to recent government legislation mandating 40% female board membership by 2016.

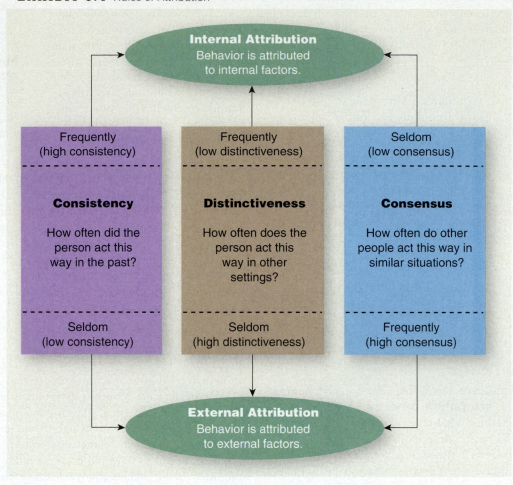

We tend to identify a coworker's motivation as the main reason why he or she is late for work (e.g., doesn't like the job), whereas we attribute our own lateness partly or mostly to external factors such as traffic jams, failed alarm clocks, or unexpected emergencies such as getting the kids ready for school. Fundamental attribution error occurs because observers can't easily see the external factors that constrain the person's behavior. We didn't see the traffic jam that caused the coworker to be late, for instance. Research suggests fundamental attribution error is more common in Western countries than in Asian cultures, where people are taught from an early age to pay attention to the context in interpersonal relations and to see everything as being connected in a holistic way.[59]

Nearly a century ago, fictional New York crime investigator Philo Vance quipped, "Bad luck is merely a defensive and self-consoling synonym for inefficiency." Vance was referring to an attribution error known as **self-serving bias**, which is the tendency to attribute our failures to external causes (such as bad luck) more than internal causes (e.g., inefficiency), while successes are due more to internal than external factors.[60] Simply put, we take credit for our successes and blame others or the situation for our mistakes. In annual reports, for example, executives mainly refer to their personal qualities as reasons for the company's successes and to external factors as reasons for the company's failures. Similarly, entrepreneurs in one recent study overwhelmingly cited situational causes for their business failure (funding, economy), whereas even in interviews they noticeably understated lack of vision, social skills, and other personal causes.[61] Philo Vance's comment about bad luck points out that self-serving bias is associated with self-enhancement. By relying on external causes of failure and internal causes of success, people generate a more positive (and self-consoling) self-concept.

Self-Fulfilling Prophecy

Self-fulfilling prophecy occurs when our expectations about another person cause that person to act in a way that is consistent with those expectations. In other words, our perceptions can influence reality. Exhibit 3.5 illustrates the four steps in the self-fulfilling prophecy process using the example of a supervisor and a subordinate.[62] The process begins when the supervisor forms expectations about the employee's future behavior and performance. These expectations are sometimes inaccurate because first impressions are usually formed from limited information. The supervisor's expectations influence his or her treatment of

Coaching Out the External Attribution

Coaching employees involves active listening and supportive goal setting, but it also involves reframing employee perceptions so they have a stronger internal attribution. Too often, employees blame the situation for past mistakes and, over time, believe good performance is beyond their control (an external attribution). Coaching reframes that perception to a stronger internal attribution. Through dialogue, employees can realize "that they have the ability and capacity to take responsibility for their situation and do something about it," says CJ Scarlet, who coaches employees through Roving Coach.[63]

employees. Specifically, high-expectancy employees (those expected to do well) receive more emotional support through nonverbal cues (e.g., more smiling and eye contact), more frequent and valuable feedback and reinforcement, more challenging goals, better training, and more opportunities to demonstrate good performance.

The third step in self-fulfilling prophecy includes two effects of the supervisor's behavior on the employee. First, through better training and more practice opportunities, a high-expectancy employee learns more skills and knowledge than a low-expectancy employee. Second, the employee becomes more self-confident, which results in higher motivation and willingness to set more challenging goals.[64] In the final step, high-expectancy employees have higher motivation and better skills, resulting in better performance, while the opposite is true of low-expectancy employees.

There are many examples of self-fulfilling prophecies in work and school settings.[65] Research has found women do not perform as well on math tests after being informed that men tend to perform better on them. Women perform better on these tests when they are not exposed to this negative self-fulfilling prophecy. Similarly, people over 65 years of age receive lower results on memory tests after hearing that mental ability declines with

self-serving bias The tendency to attribute our favorable outcomes to internal factors and our failures to external factors.

self-fulfilling prophecy The perceptual process in which our expectations about another person cause that person to act more consistently with those expectations.

▼ **EXHIBIT 3.5** The Self-Fulfilling Prophecy Cycle

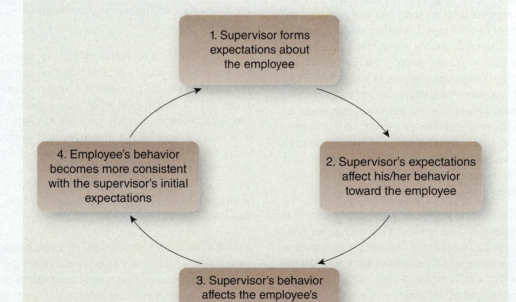

1. Supervisor forms expectations about the employee

2. Supervisor's expectations affect his/her behavior toward the employee

3. Supervisor's behavior affects the employee's ability and motivation (self-confidence)

4. Employee's behavior becomes more consistent with the supervisor's initial expectations

age. Another study reported that the performance of Israeli Defense Force trainees was influenced by their instructor's expectations regarding the trainee's potential in the program. Self-fulfilling prophecy was at work here because the instructor's expectations were based on a list researchers provided that showed which recruits had high and low potential, even though the researchers had actually listed these trainees randomly.

Contingencies of Self-Fulfilling Prophecy

Self-fulfilling prophecies are more likely to occur at the beginning of a relationship, such as when employees are first hired. It is also stronger when several people (rather than just one person) hold the same expectations of the individual. In other words, we might be able to ignore one person's doubts about our potential but not the collective doubts of several people. The self-fulfilling-prophecy effect is also stronger among people with a history of low achievement. High achievers can draw on their past successes to offset low expectations, whereas low achievers do not have past successes to support their self-confidence. Fortunately, the opposite is also true: Low achievers respond more favorably than high achievers to positive self-fulfilling prophecy. Low achievers don't receive this positive encouragement very often, so it probably has a stronger effect on their motivation to excel.[66]

The main lesson from the self-fulfilling-prophecy literature is that leaders need to develop and maintain a positive, yet realistic, expectation toward all employees. This recommendation is consistent with the emerging philosophy of **positive organizational behavior**, which suggests that focusing on the positive rather than negative aspects of life will improve organizational success and individual well-being. Communicating hope and optimism is so important it is identified as one of the critical success factors for physicians and surgeons.

Training programs that make leaders aware of the power of positive expectations seem to have minimal effect, however. Instead, generating positive expectations and hope depends on a corporate culture of support and learning. Hiring supervisors who are inherently optimistic toward their staff is another way of increasing the incidence of positive self-fulfilling prophecies.

Other Perceptual Effects

Self-fulfilling prophecy, attribution, and stereotyping are among the most common perceptual processes and biases in organizational settings, but there are many others. Four of them that have received attention in organizational settings are briefly described below.

Halo Effect The **halo effect** occurs when our general impression of a person, usually based on one prominent characteristic, distorts our perception of that person's other characteristics.[67] If a supervisor who values punctuality notices an employee is sometimes late for work, the supervisor might form a negative image of the employee and evaluate that person's other traits unfavorably as well. The halo effect is most likely to occur when concrete information about the perceived target is missing or we are not sufficiently motivated to search for it. Instead, we use our general impression of the person to fill in the missing information.

False-Consensus Effect The **false-consensus effect** (also called *similar-to-me effect*) occurs when people overestimate the extent to which others have similar beliefs or behaviors to our own.[68] Employees who are thinking of quitting their jobs overestimate the percentage of coworkers who are also thinking about quitting, for example. There are several explanations for false-consensus effect. One is that we are comforted by the belief that others are similar to us, particularly regarding less acceptable or divisive behavior. Put differently, we perceive "everyone does it" to reinforce our self-concept regarding behaviors that do not have a positive image (quitting, parking illegally, etc.). A second explanation is that we interact more with people who have similar views and behaviors, which causes us to overestimate how common those views/behaviors are in the entire organization or society. Third, as noted earlier in this chapter, we are more likely to remember information that is consistent with our own views and selectively screen out communication that is contrary to our beliefs. Finally, our social identity process homogenizes people within groups, so we tend to think everyone in that group has similar opinions and behavior, including the false-consensus topic.

Primacy Effect The **primacy effect** is our tendency to quickly form an opinion of people on the basis of the first information we receive about them.[69] It is the notion that first impressions are lasting impressions. This rapid perceptual organization and interpretation occur because we need to make sense of the world around us. The problem is that first impressions—particularly negative first impressions—are difficult to change. After categorizing someone, we tend to select subsequent information that supports our first impression and screen out information that opposes that impression.

Recency Effect The **recency effect** occurs when the most recent information dominates our perceptions.[71] This perceptual bias is most common when people (especially those with limited experience) are making an evaluation involving complex information. For instance, auditors must digest large volumes of information in their judgments about financial documents, and the most recent information received prior to the decision tends to get weighted more heavily than information received at the beginning of the audit. Similarly, when supervisors evaluate the performance of employees over the previous year, the most recent performance information dominates the evaluation because it is the most easily recalled.

First Impressions
Count in Job Applications[70]

72%
of executives say it is somewhat or very common for applicants with promising résumés not to live up to expectations during the interview.

Résumé Bloopers
"Hope to hear from you, **shorty**"
"Have a keen eye for **derail**"
"I'm **attacking** my resume for you to review"
"INTERESTS: **Exorcising** my sense of humor every day."
"Fluent in both English and **Spinach**."
"Dear Sir or **Madman**."

40%
of executives say that applicants with just one typo in their résumé are removed from further consideration.

76%
of executives say that applicants with just one or two typos in their résumé are removed from further consideration.

Survey consisted of telephone interviews with 150 senior executives at America's top 1,000 companies. Résumé gaffes were identified in documents received by Accountemps or parent company Robert Half.

Learning Objective
After reading this section, you should be able to

LO4 Discuss three ways to improve perceptions, with specific application to organizational situations.

IMPROVING PERCEPTIONS

We can't bypass the perceptual process, but we should try to minimize perceptual biases and distortions. Three potentially effective ways to improve perceptions include awareness of perceptual biases, self-awareness, and meaningful interaction.

Awareness of Perceptual Biases

One of the most obvious and widely practiced ways to reduce perceptual biases is to know they exist. For

Johari Window
A model of mutual understanding that encourages disclosure and feedback to increase our own open area and reduce the blind, hidden, and unknown areas.

contact hypothesis
A theory stating that the more we interact with someone, the less prejudiced or perceptually biased we will be against that person.

empathy A person's understanding of and sensitivity to the feelings, thoughts, and situations of others.

global mindset
An individual's ability to perceive, appreciate, and empathize with people from other cultures, and to process complex cross-cultural information.

example, diversity awareness training tries to minimize discrimination by making people aware of systemic discrimination as well as prejudices that occur through stereotyping. This training also attempts to dispel myths about people from various cultural and demographic groups. Awareness of perceptual biases can reduce them to some extent by making people more mindful of their thoughts and actions. However, awareness training has only a limited effect.[72] One problem is that teaching people to reject incorrect stereotypes has the unintended effect of reinforcing rather than reducing reliance on those stereotypes. Another problem is that diversity training is ineffective for people with deeply held prejudices against those groups.

Self-fulfilling prophecy awareness training has also failed to live up to expectations.[73] This training approach informs managers about the existence of the self-fulfilling prophecy effect and encourages them to engage in more positive rather than negative self-fulfilling prophecies. Unfortunately, research has found that managers continue to engage in negative self-fulfilling prophecies after they complete the training program.

Improving Self-Awareness

A more successful way to minimize perceptual biases is to increase self-awareness.[74] We need to become more aware of our beliefs, values, and attitudes and, from that insight, gain a better understanding of biases in our own decisions and behavior. This self-awareness tends to reduce perceptual biases by making people more open-minded and nonjudgmental toward others. Self-awareness is equally important in other ways. The emerging concept of authentic leadership emphasizes self-awareness as the first step in a person's ability to effectively lead others (see Chapter 11). Essentially, we need to understand our own values, strengths, and biases as a foundation for building a vision and leading others toward that vision.[75]

But how do we become more self-aware? One approach is to complete formal tests that indicate any implicit biases you might have toward others. One such procedure is the Implicit Association Test (IAT). Although scholars are hotly debating the

> ❝ Self-awareness tends to reduce perceptual biases by making people more open-minded and nonjudgmental toward others. ❞

accuracy of the IAT, it attempts to detect subtle racial, age, and gender bias by associating positive and negative words with specific demographic groups.[76] People are much more cautious about their stereotypes and prejudices after discovering they may have a personal bias against older people or individuals from different ethnic backgrounds.[77]

Another way to increase self-awareness and thereby reduce perceptual biases is to apply the **Johari Window**.[78] Developed by Joseph Luft and Harry Ingram (hence the name "Johari"), this model of self-awareness and mutual understanding divides information about you into four "windows"—open, blind, hidden, and unknown—based on whether your own values, beliefs, and experiences are known to you and to others (see Exhibit 3.6). The *open area* includes information about you that is known both to you and to others. The *blind area* refers to information that is known to others but not to

▼ **EXHIBIT 3.6** Johari Window Model of Self-Awareness and Mutual Understanding

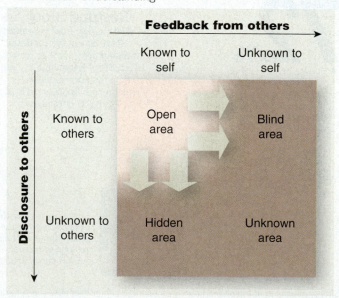

Source: Based on J. Luft, *Of Human Interaction* (Palo Alto, CA: National Press Books, 1969).

you. For example, your colleagues might notice you are self-conscious and awkward when meeting the company chief executive, but you are unaware of this fact. Information known to you but unknown to others is found in the *hidden area*. Finally, the *unknown area* includes your values, beliefs, and experiences that aren't known to you or others.

The main objective of the Johari Window is to increase the size of the open area so both you and your colleagues are aware of your perceptual limitations. This is partly accomplished by reducing the hidden area through *disclosure*—informing others of your beliefs, feelings, and experiences that may influence the work relationship. The open area also increases through *feedback* from others about your behavior. This information helps you to reduce your blind area because, according to recent studies, people near you are good sources of information about many (but not all) of your traits and behaviors.[79] Finally, the combination of disclosure and feedback occasionally produces revelations about information in the unknown area.

Meaningful Interaction

While the Johari Window relies on dialogue, self-awareness and mutual understanding can also improve through *meaningful interaction*.[80] Meaningful interaction is founded on the **contact hypothesis**, which states that, under certain conditions, people who interact with each other will be less prejudiced or perceptually biased against each other.[81] Simply spending time with members of other groups can improve your understanding and opinion of that person to some extent. However, meaningful interaction is strongest when people work together closely and frequently on a shared goal that requires cooperation and reliance on each other. Furthermore, everyone should have equal status in that context and should be engaged in a meaningful task.

Meaningful interaction reduces dependence on stereotypes to understand others because we gain better knowledge about individuals and experience the unique attributes of those people in action. Meaningful interaction also potentially improves empathy toward others. **Empathy** refers to understanding and being sensitive to the feelings, thoughts, and situations of others.[82] People empathize when they cognitively transpose themselves into the other person's place as if they are the other person. This perceptual experience is both cognitive and emotional, meaning that empathy is about understanding as well as feeling what the other person feels in that context. Empathizing with others improves our sensitivity to the external causes of another person's performance and behavior, thereby reducing fundamental attribution error. A supervisor who imagines what it's like to be a single mother, for example, would become more sensitive to the external causes of lateness and other events among such employees.

Learning Objective

After reading this section, you should be able to

LO5 Outline the main features of a global mindset and justify its usefulness to employees and organizations.

GLOBAL MINDSET: DEVELOPING PERCEPTIONS ACROSS BORDERS

Anne Connelly had previously worked outside North America, but her current job at Médecins Sans Frontières (Doctors Without Borders) pushed her even further onto the global stage. Connelly was sent to the Central African Republic to help the government with some of its financial programs. The setting wasn't for the fainthearted. "There has been civil unrest in the country for a while, mainly caused by poor government and warring rebel tribes coming in from neighboring countries," Connelly explains. But the experience of working in other lands with people who have different perceptions and experiences is exactly what Connelly had been seeking. "DeGroote [her MBA program] taught me to develop a global mindset of how businesses operate at the international level," she says. "By learning the culture, the languages, the people, the climate, everything, you can develop more holistic solutions to any given problem."[83]

Organizational leaders are paying much more attention these days to employees such as Anne Connelly who are developing a global mindset. A **global mindset** refers to an individual's ability to perceive, know about, and process information across cultures. It includes (a) an awareness of, openness to, and respect

for other views and practices in the world, (b) the capacity to empathize and act effectively across cultures, (c) ability to process complex information about novel environments, and (d) the ability to comprehend and reconcile intercultural matters with multiple levels of thinking.[84]

Let's look at each of these features. First, global mindset occurs as people develop more global than local/restricted perceptions of their business and its environment. They also have more knowledge and appreciation of many cultures and do not judge the competence of others by their national or ethnic origins. Second, global mindset includes understanding the mental models held by colleagues from other cultures as well as their emotional experiences in a given situation. Furthermore, this empathy translates into effective use of words and behaviors that are compatible with the local culture. Third, people with a strong global mindset are able to process and analyze large volumes of information in new and diverse situations. Finally, global mindset involves the capacity to quickly develop useful mental models of situations, particularly at both a local and global level of analysis.

As you can imagine, employees offer tremendous value to organizations as they develop a global mindset.[85] They develop better relationships across cultures by understanding and showing respect to distant colleagues and partners. They can sift through huge volumes of ambiguous and novel information transmitted in multinational relationships. They have a capacity to form networks and exchange resources more rapidly across borders. They also develop greater sensitivity and respond more quickly to emerging global opportunities.

Developing a Global Mindset

Developing a global mindset involves improving one's perceptions, so the practices described earlier on awareness, self-awareness, and meaningful interaction are relevant. As with most perceptual capabilities, a global mindset begins with self-awareness—understanding one's own beliefs, values, and attitudes. Through self-awareness, people are more open-minded and nonjudgmental when receiving and processing complex information for decision making. In addition, companies develop a global mindset by giving employees opportunities to compare their own mental models with those of coworkers or partners from other regions of the world. For example, employees might engage in virtual dialogues about how well the product's design or marketing strategy is received in the United States versus India or Chile. When companies encourage frequent discussion about global competitors, suppliers, and other stakeholders, they help employees to eventually shift their frame of thinking to a global level.

How do you develop a global mindset? Generally, our global mindset improves as we gain better knowledge of and more direct experience with people across cultures. Some of that knowledge is acquired through formal programs, such as diversity training, but deeper absorption results from immersion in those cultures. This immersion is a form of meaningful interaction, which we discussed earlier in the chapter as a way to improve perceptions. The more people embed themselves in the local environment (such as following local practices, eating local food, and using the local language), the more they tend to understand the perspectives and attitudes of their colleagues and others in those cultures.

Ernst & Young, IBM, Procter & Gamble, and a few other organizations have introduced special programs to accelerate global mindset development by sending teams of employees on social responsibility missions in developing countries for one or two months. IBM's Corporate Service Corps program is one of the leading examples. Each year about 500 IBMers from dozens of countries are organized into small teams and dispatched to developing countries. For one month, these diverse teams assist

local people on an economic or social development project. "These people actually go out and work in emerging markets, to work in NGOs [nongovernment organizations], to work in these other kinds of environments, so they can get a perspective and learn . . . how to think about problems from another perspective, from another point of view," explains an IBM executive.[87] ■

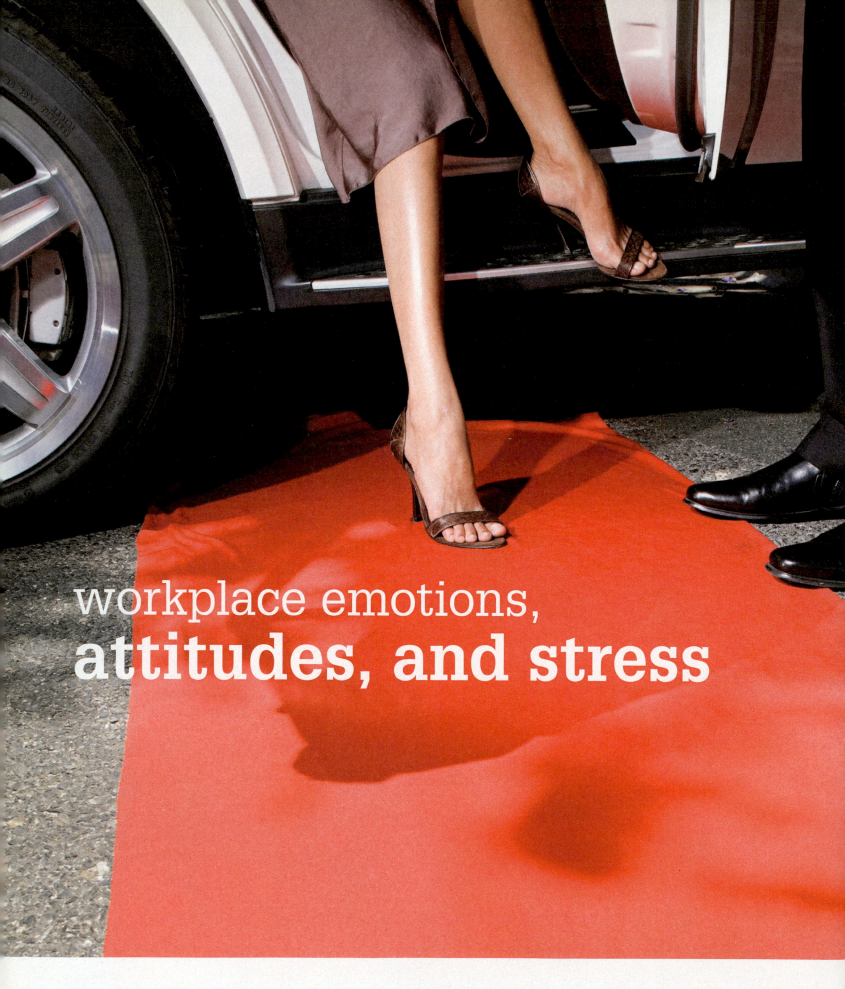

workplace emotions, **attitudes, and stress**

chapter four

OhioHealth literally gives employees the red carpet treatment when they reach 20 years of employment and every 5 years afterward. These long-service staff members at Ohio's largest health care provider are chauffeured to a local shopping mall for a shopping spree and cheered on by coworkers as they walk along a red carpet at a conference center. OhioHealth rewards these dedicated staff members with a day off, a free meal, and hundreds of dollars for shopping. Why does OhioHealth go to such lengths to create these upbeat, memorable events? "We want engaged, happy, well-compensated workers," says Ohio-Health CEO David Blom. "This reward and recognition (long-service shopping spree) stirs the emotions and passions of people."[1]

OhioHealth's leaders discovered long ago that emotions and attitudes are important, both for employee well-being and for the organization's success. This chapter looks closely at workplace emotions and attitudes. It begins by defining and describing emotions and explaining why researchers are so eager to discover how emotions influence attitudes and behavior. Next, we consider the dynamics of emotional labor, followed by the popular topic of emotional intelligence. The specific work attitudes of job satisfaction and organizational commitment are then discussed, including their association with various employee behaviors and work performance. The final section looks at work-related stress, including the stress experience, three prominent stressors, individual differences in stress, and ways to combat excessive stress. ■

LEARNING OBJECTIVES

After studying Chapter 4, you should be able to

LO1 Explain how emotions and cognition (logical thinking) influence attitudes and behavior.

LO2 Discuss the dynamics of emotional labor and the role of emotional intelligence in the workplace.

LO3 Summarize the consequences of job dissatisfaction as well as strategies to increase organizational (affective) commitment.

LO4 Describe the stress experience and review three major stressors.

LO5 Identify five ways to manage workplace stress.

emotions
Physiological, behavioral, and psychological episodes experienced toward an object, person, or event that create a state of readiness.

attitudes The cluster of beliefs, assessed feelings, and behavioral intentions toward a person, object, or event (called an attitude object).

Learning Objective

After reading this section, you should be able to

LO1 Explain how emotions and cognition (logical thinking) influence attitudes and behavior.

EMOTIONS IN THE WORKPLACE

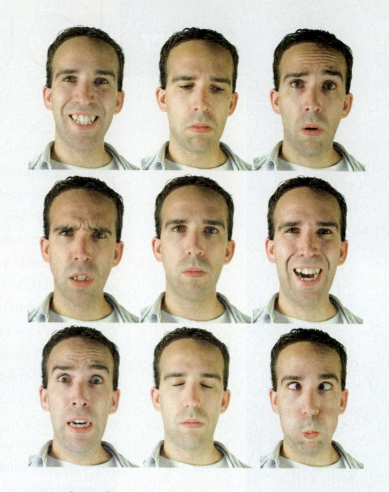

Emotions influence almost everything we do in the workplace. This is a strong statement, and one you would rarely find stated a dozen years ago among organizational behavior experts. Most OB theories still assume a person's thoughts and actions are governed primarily or exclusively by logical thinking (called *cognition*).[2] Yet groundbreaking neuroscience discoveries have revealed that our perceptions, attitudes, decisions, and behavior are influenced by emotions as well as cognitions.[3] In fact, emotions may have a greater influence because they often occur before cognitive processes and, consequently, influence the latter. By ignoring emotionality, many theories have overlooked a large piece of the puzzle about human behavior in the workplace.

Emotions are physiological, behavioral, and psychological episodes experienced toward an object, person, or event that create a state of readiness.[4] These "episodes" are very brief events that typically subside or occur in waves lasting from milliseconds to a few minutes. Emotions are directed toward someone or something. For example, we experience joy, fear, anger, and other emotional episodes toward tasks, customers, or a software program we are using. This differs from *moods*, which are not directed toward anything in particular and tend to be longer-term emotional states.[5]

events that influence our behavior without conscious awareness. Finally, emotions put us in a state of readiness. When we get worried, for example, our heart rate and blood pressure increase to make our body better prepared to engage in fight or flight. Strong emotions also trigger our conscious awareness of a threat or opportunity in the external environment.[6]

Types of Emotions

People experience many emotions as well as various combinations of emotions, but all of them have two common features, illustrated

[**Let's not forget that the little emotions are the great captains of our lives and we obey them without realizing it.**

—Vincent Van Gogh]

Emotions are experiences. They represent changes in our physiological state (e.g., blood pressure, heart rate), psychological state (e.g., thought process), and behavior (e.g., facial expression). Most of these emotional reactions are subtle and occur without our awareness. This is an important point because the topic of emotions often conjures images of people "getting emotional." In reality, most emotions are fleeting, low-intensity

in Exhibit 4.1.[7] First, all emotions have an associated valence: good or bad, helpful or harmful, positive or negative. In other words, all emotions signal that the perceived object or event should be approached or avoided. Second, emotions vary in their degree of activation; that is, they generate different levels of energy or motivational force within us. For instance, fear is a negative emotion that generates a high level of activation, whereas calm is a pleasant

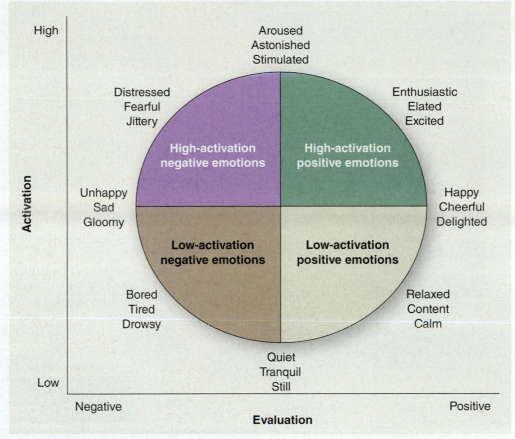

Source: Adapted from: J. Larson, E. Diener, and R. E. Lucas, "Emotion: Models, Measures, and Differences," in R. G. Lord, R. J. Klimoski, and R. Kanfer, eds., *Emotions in the Workplace* (San Francisco: Jossey-Bass, 2002), 64–113; J. A. Russell, "Core Affect and the Psychological Construction of Emotion," *Psychological Review* 110, no. 1 (2003): 145–72.

emotion that has fairly low activation. Some emotional experiences are strong enough that we are consciously aware of those emotions (joy, delight, etc), but most are far more subtle.

Positive and negative emotions are not equal. Instead, negative emotions tend to generate stronger levels of activation than positive emotions.[8] Fear and anger, for instance, are more intense experiences than joy and delight, so they have a stronger effect on our actions. This valence asymmetry likely occurs because negative emotions protect us from harm and are therefore more critical for our survival.

Emotions, Attitudes, and Behavior

To understand how emotions influence our thoughts and behavior in the workplace, we first need to know about attitudes. **Attitudes** represent the cluster of beliefs, assessed feelings, and behavioral intentions toward a person, object, or event (called an *attitude object*).[9] Attitudes are *judgments*, whereas emotions are *experiences*. In other words, attitudes involve conscious logical reasoning, whereas emotions operate as events, usually without our awareness. We also experience most emotions briefly, whereas our attitude toward someone or something is more stable over time.[10]

Until recently, experts believed that attitudes could be understood just by the three cognitive components illustrated on the left side of Exhibit 4.2: beliefs, feelings, and behavioral intentions. Now evidence suggests that a parallel emotional process is also at work, shown on the right side of the exhibit.[11] Using attitude toward mergers as an example, let's look more closely at this model, beginning with the traditional cognitive perspective of attitudes.

- *Beliefs.* These are your established perceptions about the attitude object—what you believe to be true. For example, you might believe that mergers reduce job security for employees in the merged firms, or that mergers increase the company's competitiveness in this era of globalization. These beliefs are perceived facts that you acquire from experience and other forms of learning.

- *Feelings.* Feelings represent your conscious positive or negative evaluations of the attitude object. Some people think mergers are good; others think they are bad. Your like or dislike of mergers represents your assessed feelings. According to the traditional cognitive perspective of attitudes (left side of the model), feelings are calculated from your beliefs about mergers. If you believe mergers typically have negative consequences such as layoffs and organizational politics, you will form negative feelings toward mergers in general or about a specific planned merger in your organization.

▼ **EXHIBIT 4.2** Model of Emotions, Attitudes, and Behavior

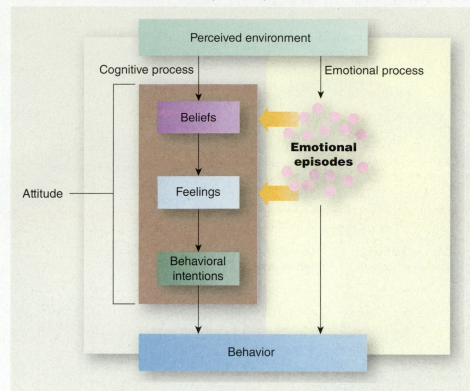

incoming sensory information with emotional markers based on a quick and imprecise evaluation of whether that information supports or threatens our innate drives. These markers are not calculated feelings; they are automatic and nonconscious emotional responses based on very thin slices of sensory information.[14]

Consider your attitude toward mergers. You might experience worry, nervousness, or relief upon learning your company intends to merge with a competitor. The fuzzy dots on the right side of Exhibit 4.2 illustrate the numerous emotional episodes you experience upon hearing the merger announcement, subsequently thinking about the merger, discussing the merger with co-workers, and so on. These emotions are transmitted to the reasoning process, where they are logically analyzed along with other information about the attitude object.[15] Thus, while you are consciously evaluating whether the merger is good or bad, your emotions are already sending normative (good-bad) signals, which then sways your conscious evaluation. In fact, we often deliberately "listen in" on our emotions to help us consciously decide whether to support or oppose something.[16]

• *Behavioral intentions.* Intentions represent your willingness to engage in a particular behavior regarding the attitude object.[12] Upon hearing the company will merge with another organization, you might increase your intention to look for a job elsewhere or possibly to complain to management about the merger decision. Your feelings toward mergers motivate your behavioral intentions, and which actions you choose depends on your past experience, personality, and social norms of appropriate behavior.

Exhibit 4.2 illustrates that behavioral intentions directly predict behavior. However, whether your intentions translate into behavior depends on the situation and possibly other elements of the MARS model. For example, you might intend to quit after hearing about the merger, but do not do so because of lack of better job opportunities (situation). Attitudes are also more likely to influence behavior when they are strong, meaning they are anchored by strong emotions.

How Emotions Influence Attitudes and Behavior

As we mentioned, emotions play a central role in forming and changing employee attitudes.[13] The right side of Exhibit 4.2 illustrates this process, which (like the cognitive process) also begins with perceptions of the world around us. Our brain tags

> " The influence of both cognitive reasoning and emotions on attitudes is most apparent when they disagree with each other. "

The influence of both cognitive reasoning and emotions on attitudes is most apparent when they disagree with each other. People occasionally experience this mental tug-of-war, sensing something isn't right even though they can't think of any logical reason to be concerned. This conflicting experience indicates the person's logical analysis of the situation (left side of Exhibit 4.2) can't identify reasons to support the automatic emotional reaction (right side of Exhibit 4.2).[17] Should we pay attention to our emotional response or our logical analysis? This question is not easy to answer, but some studies indicate that while executives tend to make quick decisions based on their gut feelings (emotional response), the best decisions tend to occur when executives spend time logically evaluating the situation.[18] Thus, we should pay attention to both the cognitive and emotional sides of the attitude model and hope they agree with each other most of the time!

cognitive dissonance Condition that occurs when we perceive an inconsistency between our beliefs, feelings, and behavior.

LeasePlan USA Injects Fun in the Workplace[19]

LeasePlan USA boasts one of the highest job satisfaction ratings in its category in North America. There are several reasons for the high morale, including the extracurricular activities planned by the Atlanta-based vehicle fleet leasing company's "Fun at Work" committee. This photo shows LeasePlan's human resource director handing out Atlanta Braves baseball tickets to winners of the Patty's Ping-Pong Tournament held on St. Patrick's Day.

Generating Positive Emotions at Work Some companies seem to be well aware of the dual cognitive–emotional attitude process because they try to inject more positive experiences in the workplace.[20] For instance, employees at Dixon Schwabl enjoy bocce tournaments, softball leagues, golf chipping contests, water balloon toss events, Halloween pumpkin-decorating contests, a padded primal scream room to release tension, and a spiral slide for those who want to descend more quickly to the main floor. "Fun is not just a word here, it is a way of life!" wrote one employee at the 75-person marketing and public relations firm in Rochester, New York.[21] Similarly, employees at Razer's Singapore offices zoom around on scooters and pit their gaming skills against each other on the state-of-the-art online gaming console. "Sometimes I can't believe that I have been here for seven months already," admits one employee at the gaming peripherals company. "I guess you don't feel the time passing when you are having so much fun."[22]

Some critics might argue that the organization's main focus should be to create positive emotions through the job itself as well as everyday natural occurrences such as supportive co-workers and polite customers. Still, most people perform work that produces some negative emotions, and research has found that humor and fun at work—whether natural or contrived—can potentially offset some of the negative experiences.[23] Overall, corporate leaders need to keep in mind that emotions shape employee attitudes and, as we will discuss later, attitudes influence various forms of work-related behavior.

One last comment about Exhibit 4.2: Notice the arrow from the emotional episodes to behavior. It indicates that emotions directly (without conscious thinking) influence a person's behavior. This occurs when we jump suddenly if someone sneaks up on us. It also occurs in everyday situations because even low-intensity emotions automatically change our facial expressions. These actions are not carefully thought out. They are automatic emotional responses that are learned or hardwired by heredity for particular situations.[24]

Cognitive Dissonance

Emotions and attitudes usually lead to behavior, but the opposite sometimes occurs through the process of **cognitive dissonance**.[25] Cognitive dissonance occurs when we perceive an inconsistency between our beliefs, feelings, and behavior. This inconsistency generates emotions (such as feeling hypocritical) that motivate us to create more consistency by

Best Employers to Work for in America, Europe, Latin America, and Japan[26]

Rank	Top 5 in America	Top 5 in Europe	Top 5 in Latin America	Top 5 in Japan
1	Google	Elica (Italy)	Kimberly Clark (several countries)	Google Japan Inc.
2	Boston Consulting Group	ATP (Denmark)	Telefónica (several countries)	Works Applications Co. Ltd.
3	SAS	EMC (Ireland & Poland)	Renault-Sofasa (Colombia)	Microsoft Co. Ltd.
4	Wegmans Food Markets	DIS AG (Germany)	Quala (Ecuador)	Asahi Breweries Ltd.
5	Edward Jones	domino-world TM (Germany)	Google (Brazil)	Plan.Do.See Inc.

None of the major "best employer" survey firms rank order companies across Asia. They rank order only for specific countries, so Japan is shown here as an illustration. The top 5 list in Europe represents only large companies. There is a separate list for small and mid-sized firms.

changing one or more of these elements. Suppose you think of yourself as someone who supports environmentalism. You also work at an oil company that seemed to be environmentally friendly until news reports accuse the company and others in the industry of creating environmental damage. This internal tension occurs because your "green" self-concept (beliefs) and positive regard for environmentalism (feelings) are inconsistent with your employment at a company with a poor environmental record (behavior). People experience an internal tension because they want to see themselves as rational creatures, which requires some alignment between their thoughts and actions.[27] Working for a company that has a poor environmental reputation seems inconsistent with your beliefs and attitudes about environmentalism, so you would be motivated to reduce that discrepancy.

How do people reduce cognitive dissonance? Changing behavior is one option, but it is more difficult and often more costly than changing beliefs and feelings. You might be very reluctant to quit your job with the oil company, for instance. Changing behavior is particularly difficult when others know about the behavior, you performed the behavior voluntarily, and the consequence of the behavior can't be undone. Although you could quit your job, you can't hide the fact that you had worked at that oil company or claim someone forced you to work there.

When it is difficult to change behavior or reverse its consequences, people instead reduce cognitive dissonance by changing their beliefs and feelings. As an employee at an oil company, you might convince yourself that problems with the company's environmental record have been exaggerated or that they fail to take into account the company's most recent environmental initiatives. Research suggests that people sometimes reduce cognitive dissonance by rebalancing their self-concept indirectly. So, rather than deny the company's environmental record, you might reduce the inconsistency by emphasizing your personal environmental behaviors (e.g., using public transport to work and composting food waste at home). Overall, these mental acrobatics maintain some degree of consistency between your behavior (working for the oil company) and your beliefs and attitudes toward environmentalism.

> " *When it is difficult to change behavior or reverse its consequences, people instead reduce cognitive dissonance by changing their beliefs and feelings.* "

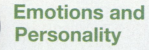

Emotions and Personality

Our coverage of the dynamics of workplace emotions wouldn't be complete unless we mention that emotions are also partly determined by a person's personality, not just workplace experiences.[28] Some people experience positive emotions as a natural trait. People with more positive emotions typically have higher emotional stability and are extraverted (see Chapter 2). Those who experience more negative emotions tend to have higher neuroticism (lower emotional stability) and are introverted. Positive and negative emotional traits affect a person's attendance, turnover, and long-term work attitudes.[29] While positive and negative personality traits have some effect, other research concludes the actual situation in which people work has a noticeably stronger influence on their attitudes and behavior.[30]

Learning Objective

After reading this section, you should be able to

LO2 Discuss the dynamics of emotional labor and the role of emotional intelligence in the workplace.

MANAGING EMOTIONS AT WORK

Whether as a customer service representative or chief executive officer, people are expected to manage their emotions in the workplace. They must conceal their frustration when serving an irritating customer, display compassion to an ill patient, and hide their boredom in a long meeting with other executives. These are all forms of **emotional labor**—the effort, planning, and control needed to express organizationally desired emotions during interpersonal transactions.[31] Almost everyone is expected to abide by *display rules*—norms requiring us to display specific emotions and to hide other emotions. Emotional labor demands are higher in jobs requiring a variety of emotions (e.g., anger as well as joy) and more intense emotions (e.g., showing delight rather than smiling weakly), as well as in jobs in which interaction with clients is frequent and longer. Emotional labor also increases when employees must precisely rather than casually abide by the display rules.[32] Precise emotional display rules are most common in the service industries, where employees have frequent face-to-face interaction with clients.

Emotional Display Norms across Cultures

Not long ago, the Paris-based magazine *L'Express* published a special series of articles about living in North America. Among other things, the magazine commented that American and Canadian restaurant servers provide "hyper-friendly, always smiling" service, which can seem a bit too insincere to many Europeans. "It's too much. It's too friendly," explains Laurence Pivot, who edited the special edition of *L'Express*.[33] The French magazine's comment highlights the fact that emotional display norms vary considerably across cultures.[34] In the United States and Canada, restaurant servers are expected to consistently show friendliness and other positive emotions toward customers. French customers appreciate friendly service, but they also expect servers to be more transparent than artificial in their duties. If a server is having a bad day, he or she should not completely hide the corresponding emotions.

One major study points to Ethiopia, Japan, and Austria (among others) as cultures that discourage emotional expression. Instead, people are expected to be subdued, have relatively monotonic voice intonation, and avoid physical movement and touching that display emotions. In contrast, cultures such as Kuwait, Egypt, Spain, and Russia allow or encourage more vivid display of emotions and expect people to act more consistently with their true emotions. In these cultures, people are expected to more honestly reveal their thoughts and feelings, be dramatic in their conversational tones, and be animated in their use of nonverbal behaviors. For example, 81 percent of Ethiopians and 74 percent of Japanese agreed it is considered unprofessional to express emotions overtly in their culture, whereas 43 percent of Americans, 33 percent of Italians, and only 19 percent of Spaniards, Cubans, and Egyptians agreed with this statement.[36]

Emotional Dissonance

Comedian George Burns once said, "The secret to being a good actor is honesty. If you can fake *that*, you've got it made." Burns's humor highlights an important reality in emotional labor, namely that it is very difficult to hide our true emotions in the workplace. Emotional labor can be challenging because it is difficult to conceal true emotions and to display the emotions required by the job. Joy, sadness, worry, and

> ## Emotional display norms vary considerably across cultures.

Malaysia Airlines Teaches Correct Emotions[35]

Managing emotions is an important part of flight attendant training at the Malaysia Airlines Academy in Petaling Jaya. Students learn how to smile, make eye contact, and keep their chin up at a level that displays confidence without arrogance. Students receive training in voice enrichment and public speaking. They also learn about personal grooming as well as different formalities of behavior in countries where the airline flies. The academy even has large mirrors on some walls so students constantly see how their facial expressions appear to others.

other emotions automatically activate a complex set of muscles (particularly facial)—an action that is difficult to prevent and equally difficult to fake. Pretending to be cheerful or concerned requires adjustment and coordination of several specific facial muscles and body positions. Meanwhile, our true emotions tend to reveal themselves as subtle gestures, usually without our awareness. More often than not, observers see when we are faking while we attempt to suppress our true emotions.[37]

Emotional labor also creates conflict between required and true emotions. The larger the gap, the more employees tend to experience stress, job burnout, and psychological separation from self.[38] This problem can be minimized through deep acting rather than surface acting.[39] *Surface acting* involves pretending to show the required emotions but continue to hold different internal feelings. *Deep acting* involves changing true emotions to match the required emotions. In other words, you train yourself to actually feel the emotion you are supposed to express. Deep acting also requires considerable emotional intelligence, which we discuss next.

EMOTIONAL INTELLIGENCE

Buckman Laboratories International Inc. pays close attention to the emotional intelligence (EI) of its job applicants and employees. The Memphis, Tennessee, chemical company has identified key emotional intelligence competencies of team players, which are then applied to job interviews. "By defining the concrete behaviors that demonstrate emotional intelligence, we can better focus our behavioral interviewing questions," explains Buckman's head of human resources. The company also evaluates its leaders on 19 leadership competencies, "many of which are based on the ability of the leader to perceive, influence, and manage the emotions of themselves and others."[40]

Buckman Labs is among the growing flock of companies that recognize **emotional intelligence (EI)** as a key factor in the organization's effectiveness. Emotional intelligence includes a set of *abilities* to perceive and express emotion, assimilate emotion in thought, understand and reason with emotion, and regulate emotion in oneself and others.[41] Although several emotional intelligence dimensions have been proposed over the past decade, the research findings seem to be converging around the four quadrant model shown in Exhibit 4.3.[42] This model organizes EI into four dimensions representing the recognition of emotions in ourselves and in others, as well as the regulation of emotions in ourselves and in others.

- *Awareness of own emotions.* This is the ability to perceive and understand the meaning of your own emotions. You are more sensitive to subtle emotional responses to events and understand their message. Self-aware people are better able

to eavesdrop on their emotional responses to specific situations and to use this awareness as conscious information.[43]

- *Management of own emotions.* Emotional intelligence includes the ability to manage your own emotions, something we all do to some extent. We keep disruptive impulses in check. We try not to feel angry or frustrated when events go against us. We try to feel and express joy and happiness toward others when the occasion calls for these emotional displays. We try to create a second wind of motivation later in the workday. Notice that management of your own emotions goes beyond displaying behaviors that represent desired emotions in a particular situation. It includes generating or suppressing emotions. In other words, the deep acting described earlier involves managing our own emotions.

- *Awareness of others' emotions.* This dimension refers to the ability to perceive and understand the emotions of other people. To a large extent, awareness of other people's emotions is represented by *empathy*—having an understanding of and sensitivity to the feelings, thoughts, and situations of others (see Chapter 3). This ability includes understanding the other person's situation, experiencing his or her emotions, and knowing his or her needs even though unstated. Awareness of others' emotions also includes being organizationally aware, such as sensing office politics and understanding social networks.

- *Management of others' emotions.* This dimension of EI involves managing other people's emotions. This includes consoling people who feel sad, emotionally inspiring your team members to complete a class project on time, getting strangers to feel comfortable working with you, and managing dysfunctional emotions among staff who experience conflict with customers or other employees.

These four dimensions of emotional intelligence form a hierarchy.[44] Awareness of your own emotions is lowest because you need awareness to engage in the higher levels of emotional intelligence. You can't manage your own emotions if you don't know what they are (i.e., low self-awareness). Managing other people's emotions is the highest level of EI because this ability requires awareness of our own and others' emotions. To diffuse an angry conflict between two employees, for example, you need to understand the emotions they are experiencing and manage your emotions (and display of emotions). To manage your own emotions, you also need to be aware of your current emotions.

Most jobs involve social interaction with coworkers or external stakeholders, so employees need emotional intelligence to work effectively. Emotional intelligence is particularly important for managers because their work requires management of their own emotions and the emotions of others. Research indicates that people with high EI are better at interpersonal relations, perform better in jobs requiring emotional labor, are superior leaders, make better decisions involving social exchanges, are more successful in many aspects of job interviews, and are better at organizational learning activities.

▼ **EXHIBIT 4.3** Dimensions of Emotional Intelligence

		Yourself	Others
Abilities	**Recognition of emotions**	Awareness of own emotions	Awareness of others' emotions
	Regulation of emotions	Management of own emotions	Management of others' emotions

Sources: D. Goleman, "An EI-Based Theory of Performance," in *The Emotionally Intelligent Workplace*, ed. C. Cherniss and D. Goleman (San Francisco: Jossey-Bass, 2001), 28; P. J. Jordan and S. A. Lawrence. "Emotional Intelligence in Teams: Development and Initial Validation of the Short Version of the Workgroup Emotional Intelligence Profile (WEIP-S)." *Journal of Management & Organization* 15 (2009): 452–69.

MOST JOBS INVOLVE SOCIAL INTERACTION, SO EMPLOYEES NEED EMOTIONAL INTELLIGENCE TO WORK EFFECTIVELY. "

Teams whose members have high emotional intelligence initially perform better than teams with low EI.[45] However, emotional intelligence does not improve some forms of performance, such as tasks that require minimal social interaction.[46]

Assessing and Developing Emotional Intelligence at Work

Emotional intelligence is associated with some personality traits, as well as with the emotional intelligence of one's parents. For this reason, many companies *try* to measure EI in job applicants. (We emphasize the word "try" because a high-quality test of emotional intelligence remains elusive.) The U.S. Air Force (USAF) offers one of the best-known examples of this practice. A decade or so ago, the USAF was hiring 400 recruiters each year, but approximately 100 of them failed to meet expectations. When the USAF discovered the top recruiters had significantly higher emotional intelligence scores, it began selecting recruiters partly on how well they score on this emotional intelligence test. The failure rate of new USAF recruiters has apparently fallen by as much as 90 percent.[47]

Within the past few years, the USAF has been investigating how emotional intelligence testing can improve trainee success in hard-to-fill, high-cost training programs with high attrition rates. One of those programs is pararescue jumper (PJ) training, which costs $250,000 per graduate and has an 80 percent failure rate. USAF research has found that trainees who score high on several emotional intelligence dimensions are two or more times as likely to successfully complete the PJ program.[48]

Emotional intelligence can also be learned. One recent study reported that a four-month training program resulted in a significant increase in emotional intelligence among staff members working in two Dutch residential operations for people with intellectual disabilities, compared with staff members who did not receive the training. In early stages of the program, trainees learned about the meaning and value of emotional intelligence, reviewed feedback on their initial EI test scores, applied EI dimensions to case studies, and developed two personal goals to improve their EI profile. Later stages of the program consisted of professional feedback to trainees based on videos showing trainees meeting with difficult clients.[49]

Sony Europe incorporates EI training in its executive development program, including an exercise in which leaders keep a journal of their emotional experiences throughout a week of work. At orthopedic device manufacturer Exactech Inc. two dozen leadership development participants learn how to improve their EI skills in self-awareness and interaction with other staff members.[50]

Medical Students Get an Emotional Intelligence Workout[51]

Based on a recent survey of its graduates, the University of South Florida (USF) College of Medicine concluded that emotional intelligence training would help its students to perform their job better. "We've created a lot of doctors that are like House," says USF medical college Dean Stephen Klasko, referring to the fictional TV physician with the caustic interpersonal style. Now, after two years at USF's medical school, a select group of students spend two years at Lehigh Valley Health Network in Pennsylvania, one of the country's top hospitals. Along with its advanced medical training, the Lehigh program includes special coaching and role modeling to help students develop their emotional intelligence. "You have to have an emotionally intelligent, collaborative, interdisciplinary team practicing if you want young trainees to adopt that as their model," explains Lehigh CEO, Ronald Swinfard.

Personal coaching, plenty of practice, and frequent feedback are particularly effective at developing EI. Emotional intelligence also increases with age; it is part of the process called maturity.[52]

Before leaving this topic, we should mention an ongoing debate about the usefulness of emotional intelligence as a concept.[53] The concept has not been as clear as some would hope. Even the label "intelligence" is inappropriate because EI is a skill, not a form of intelligence. Critics also suggest general intelligence and personality traits overlap with most of EI's contribution to knowledge. These criticisms are serious, yet the meaning of EI is becoming clearer and several studies (cited over the previous

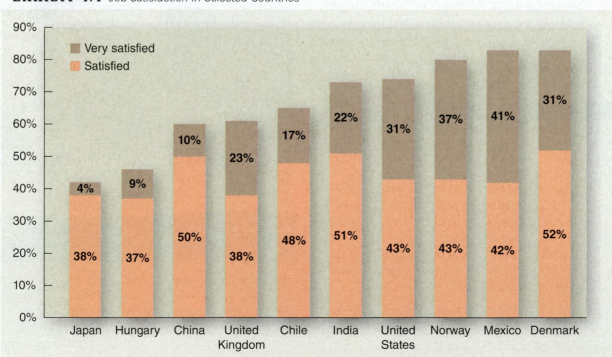

OB Theory to Practice

Improving Emotional Intelligence

1. Training programs—learning about emotional intelligence, then receiving ongoing feedback in realistic situations.

2. Self-reflection—After an event, employees write a journal report on their experience in which they reflect on what happened and how it could be improved in the future.

3. Coaching—A professional coach observes the individual in work situations and listens to his or her nonobserved experiences, then provides debriefing feedback about how to improve the person's emotions-based behavior in those situations.

4. Maturity—People tend to improve their emotional intelligence with age due to improved self-awareness, reinforcement of emotions management, and numerous opportunities to develop their emotional intelligence skills.

pages) suggest EI is relevant to workplace behavior. Overall, emotional intelligence offers considerable potential, but we also have a lot to learn about its measurement and effects on people in the workplace.

So far, this chapter has introduced the model of emotions and attitudes, as well as emotional intelligence as the means by which we manage emotions in the workplace. The next two sections look at two specific attitudes: job satisfaction and organizational commitment. These two attitudes are so important in our understanding of workplace behavior that some experts suggest the two combined should be called "overall job attitude."[54]

Learning Objective

After reading this section, you should be able to

LO3 Summarize the consequences of job dissatisfaction as well as strategies to increase organizational (affective) commitment.

JOB SATISFACTION

Probably the most studied attitude in organizational behavior is **job satisfaction**, a person's evaluation of his or her job and work context.[55] It is an *appraisal* of the perceived job characteristics, work environment, and emotional experiences at work. Satisfied employees have a favorable evaluation of their jobs, based on their observations and emotional experiences. Job satisfaction is best viewed as a collection of attitudes about different aspects of the job and work context. You might like your coworkers but be less satisfied with your workload, for instance.

How satisfied are employees at work? The answer depends on the person, the workplace, and the country. Global surveys, such as the one shown in Exhibit 4.4, indicate with some consistency that job satisfaction tends to be highest in Denmark,

▼ **EXHIBIT 4.4** Job Satisfaction in Selected Countries

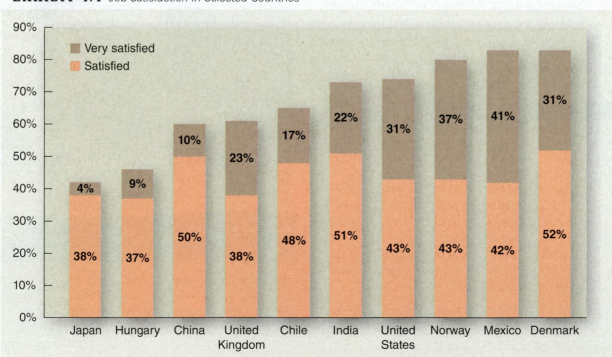

These survey results are from Randstad Workmonitor, June 2011. Data were collected from a minimum of 400 interviews per country of adults working 24 hours or more per week. Respondents were asked, "How satisfied are you in general working for your current employer?"

Norway, and other Nordic countries, as well as in Mexico, the United States, and India. The lowest levels of overall job satisfaction are usually recorded in Hungary and several Asian countries (e.g., Japan, Mainland China).[56] Other surveys report that more than four out of five working Americans are moderately or very satisfied with their jobs, a level that has been consistent for the past three decades.[57]

Can we conclude from these surveys that employees in Denmark, Mexico, Norway, and the United States are happy at work? Possibly, but not as much as these statistics suggest. One problem is that surveys often use a single direct question, such as, "How satisfied are you with your job?" Many dissatisfied employees are reluctant to reveal their feelings in a direct question because this is tantamount to admitting they made a poor job choice and are not enjoying life. There is some evidence that overall job satisfaction scores are inflated. Surveys that report high overall job satisfaction also found most employees are dissatisfied with several aspects of their job, including how much they are paid, promotion opportunities, and recognition for work accomplishments. Furthermore, studies report that a large percentage of employees plan to look for work within the next year or would leave their current employer if the right opportunity came along.[58] In summary, employees in the United States, Denmark, India, and other countries have fairly high job satisfaction, but probably not as much as they claim in the overall ratings.

A second problem is that cultural values make it difficult to compare job satisfaction across countries. People in China and Japan tend to subdue their emotions in public, and there is evidence they also avoid extreme survey ratings such as "very satisfied." A third problem is that job satisfaction changes with economic conditions. Employees with the highest job satisfaction in current surveys tend to be in countries where the economies are chugging along quite well.[59]

Job Satisfaction and Work Behavior

Brad Bird pays close attention to job satisfaction among his staff. "In my experience, the thing that has the most significant impact on a budget—but never shows up in a budget—is morale," advises Bird, who directed *Ratatouille* and other award-winning films at Pixar Animation Studios. "If you have low morale, for every dollar you spend, you get 25 cents of value. If you have high morale, for every dollar you spend, you get about $3 of value."[60]

Job satisfaction is important to many organizational leaders around the world. Many companies carefully monitor job satisfaction and related employee attitudes, and they actively compete to win best-workplace awards. In some firms, executive bonuses depend partly on employee satisfaction ratings. The reason for this attention is simple: Job satisfaction affects many of the individual behaviors introduced in Chapter 2 (task performance, organizational citizenship, quitting, absenteeism, etc.). A useful template for organizing and understanding the consequences of job dissatisfaction is the **exit–voice–loyalty–neglect**

(EVLN) model. As the name suggests, the EVLN model identifies four ways employees respond to job dissatisfaction:[61]

- *Exit.* Exit includes leaving the organization, transferring to another work unit, or at least trying to get away from the dissatisfying situation. The traditional theory is that job dissatisfaction builds over time and is eventually strong enough to motivate employees to search for better work opportunities elsewhere. This is likely true to some extent, but the most recent opinion is that specific "shock events" quickly energize employees to think about and engage in exit behavior. For example, the emotional reaction you experience to an unfair management decision or a conflict episode with a coworker motivates you to look at job ads and speak to friends about job opportunities where they work. This begins the process of realigning your self-concept more with another company than with your current employer.[62]

- *Voice.* Voice is any attempt to change, rather than escape from, the dissatisfying situation. Voice can be a constructive response, such as recommending ways for management to improve the situation, or it can be more confrontational, such as filing formal grievances or forming a coalition to oppose a decision.[63] In the extreme, some employees might engage in counterproductive behaviors to get attention and force changes in the organization.

- *Loyalty.* In the original version of this model, loyalty was not an outcome of dissatisfaction. Rather, it determined whether people chose exit or voice (i.e., high loyalty resulted in voice; low loyalty produced exit).[64] More recent writers describe loyalty as an outcome, but in various and somewhat unclear ways. Generally, they suggest "loyalists" are employees who respond to dissatisfaction by patiently waiting—some say they "suffer in silence"—for the problem to work itself out or be resolved by others.[65]

- *Neglect.* Neglect includes reducing work effort, paying less attention to quality, and increasing absenteeism and lateness. It is generally considered a passive activity that has negative consequences for the organization.

job satisfaction A person's evaluation of his or her job and work context.

exit–voice–loyalty–neglect (EVLN) model The four ways, as indicated in the name, that employees respond to job dissatisfaction.

service profit chain model A theory explaining how employees' job satisfaction influences company profitability indirectly through service quality, customer loyalty, and related factors.

organizational (affective) commitment The employee's emotional attachment to, identification with, and involvement in a particular organization. Also called *affective commitment*.

continuance commitment An employee's calculative attachment to the organization, whereby an employee is motivated to stay only because leaving would be costly.

Which of the four EVLN alternatives do employees use? It depends on the person and situation.[66] The individual's personality, values, and self-concept are important factors. For example, people with a high-conscientiousness personality are less likely to engage in neglect and more likely to engage in voice. Past experience also influences which EVLN action is applied. Employees who were unsuccessful with voice in the past are more likely to engage in exit or neglect when experiencing job dissatisfaction in the future. Another factor is loyalty, as it was originally intended in the EVLN model. Specifically, employees are more likely to quit when they have low loyalty to the company, and they are more likely to engage in voice when they have high loyalty. Finally, the response to dissatisfaction depends on the situation. Employees are less likely to use the exit option when there are few alternative job prospects, for example. Dissatisfied employees who hold central positions in the work process—that is, other employees are dependent on them—are more likely to use voice than the other options.[67]

Job Satisfaction and Performance

Is a happy worker a more productive worker? Most corporate leaders likely think so. Yet, for most of the past century, organizational behavior scholars have challenged this happy-productive employee belief, concluding that job satisfaction minimally affects job performance. Now OB experts are concluding that maybe the popular saying is correct after all; there is a *moderately* positive relationship between job satisfaction and performance. In other words, employees are more productive *to some extent* when they have more positive attitudes toward their job and workplace.[68]

their job. A third consideration is that job performance might cause job satisfaction, rather than vice versa.[69] Higher performers receive more rewards (including recognition) and, consequently, are more satisfied than low-performing employees who receive fewer rewards. The connection between job satisfaction and performance isn't stronger because many organizations do not reward good performance very well.

Job Satisfaction and Customer Satisfaction

Wegmans Food Markets in Rochester, New York, and HCL Technologies in Noida, India, are on the opposite sides of the planet and in quite different industries, yet they both have the same unusual motto: *Employees first, customers second*. Why don't these companies put customers at the top of the stakeholder list? Their rationale is that customer satisfaction is a natural outcome of employee satisfaction. Put differently, it is difficult to keep customers happy if employee morale is low.[70]

These companies are applying the **service profit chain model**, which proposes that job satisfaction has a positive effect on customer service, which flows on to shareholder financial returns. Exhibit 4.5 diagrams this process. Specifically, workplace practices affect job satisfaction, which influences employee retention, motivation, and behavior. These employee outcomes affect service quality, which then influence customer satisfaction and perceptions of value, customer referrals, and ultimately the company's profitability and growth.[71]

Behind the service profit chain model are two key explanations why satisfied employees tend to result in happier and more loyal customers.[72] First, employees are usually in a more positive mood when they feel satisfied with their jobs and working conditions. Employees in a good mood more naturally and frequently display friendliness and positive emotions. When

[**Employees are more productive *to some extent* when they have more positive attitudes toward their job and workplace.**]

Why isn't the job satisfaction-performance relationship even stronger? One reason is that general attitudes (such as job satisfaction) don't predict specific behaviors very well. As the EVLN model explained, dissatisfaction might lead to turnover, complaining, or patiently waiting rather than reducing one's performance (a form of neglect). A second reason is that dissatisfaction might affect performance only when employees have sufficient control over their job performance. People working on an assembly line, for example, would produce about the same quantity and quality output no matter what they think about

employees have good feelings, their behavior "rubs off" on customers (well, most of them), so customers feel happier and consequently form a positive evaluation of the service experience (i.e., higher service quality).

Second, satisfied employees are less likely to quit their jobs, so they have better knowledge and skills to serve clients. Lower turnover also enables customers to have the same employees serve them, so there is more consistent service. Some evidence indicates customers build their loyalty to specific employees,

▼**EXHIBIT 4.5** Service Profit Chain Model

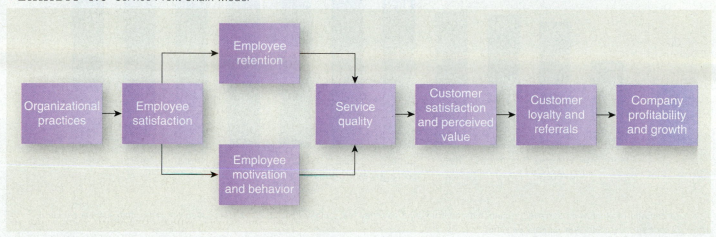

This model is based on J. I. Heskett, W. E. Sasser, and L. A. Schlesinger., *The Service Profit Chain* (New York: Free Press, 1997); A. J. Rucci, S. P. Kirn, and R. T. Quinn, "The Employee-Customer-Profit Chain at Sears," *Harvard Business Review* 76 (1998): 83–97; S. P. Brown and S. K. Lam, "A Meta-Analysis of Relationships Linking Employee Satisfaction to Customer Responses," *Journal of Retailing* 84, no. 3 (2008): 243–55.

not to the organization, so keeping employee turnover low tends to build customer loyalty.

Job Satisfaction and Business Ethics

Before leaving the topic of job satisfaction, we should mention it is also an ethical issue that influences the organization's reputation in the community. People spend a large portion of their time working in organizations, and many societies now expect companies to provide safe, enjoyable work environments. Indeed, employees in several countries closely monitor ratings of the best companies to work for, an indication that job satisfaction is a virtue worth considerable goodwill to employers. This virtue is apparent when an organization has low job satisfaction. The company tries to hide this fact, and when morale problems become public, corporate leaders are usually quick to improve the situation.

ORGANIZATIONAL COMMITMENT

Organizational commitment represents the other half (with job satisfaction) of what some experts call "overall job attitude." **Organizational commitment**—or more specifically **affective commitment**—is the employee's emotional attachment to, identification with, and involvement in a particular organization.[74] Affective commitment is a person's feeling of loyalty to the place where he or she works.

Affective commitment is often distinguished from **continuance commitment**, which is a calculative attachment to the organization. Employees have high continuance commitment when they feel bound to remain with the organization because it would be too costly to quit. In other words, they choose to stay because the calculated (typically financial) value of staying is higher than the value of working somewhere else. You can tell an employee has high calculative commitment when he or she says, "I hate this place but can't afford to quit!" This reluctance to quit may exist because the employee might lose a large bonus by leaving early or is well established in the community where he or she works.[75]

Consequences of Affective and Continuance Commitment

Affective commitment can be a significant competitive advantage.[76] Loyal employees are less likely to quit their jobs and be absent from work. They also have higher work motivation and organizational citizenship, as well as somewhat higher job performance. Organizational commitment also improves customer satisfaction because long-tenure employees have better knowledge of work practices and because clients like to do business with the same employees. One warning is that employees with very high loyalty tend to have high conformity, which

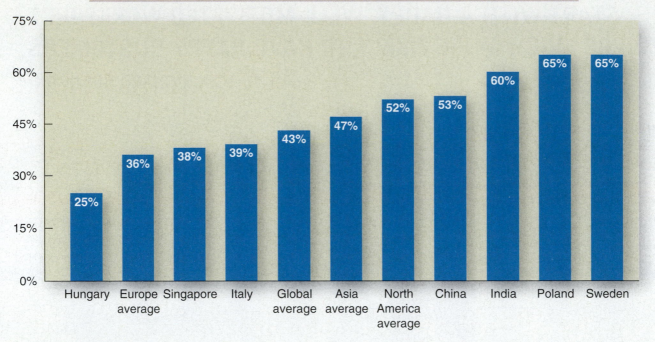

Totally Committed: Organizational Loyalty around the Planet[77]

Percentage of employees surveyed in selected countries who say they feel "totally committed" to their employer. More than 134,000 people in 29 countries were surveyed for Kelly Services.

> " Affective commitment includes a person's identification with the organization, and that identification is highest when employees believe their values are congruent with the organization's dominant values. "

results in lower creativity. There are also cases of dedicated employees who violated laws to defend the organization. However, most companies suffer from too little rather than too much employee loyalty.

In contrast to the benefits of affective commitment, employees with high levels of continuance commitment tend to have *lower* performance and are *less* likely to engage in organizational citizenship behaviors. Furthermore, unionized employees with high continuance commitment are more likely to use formal grievances, whereas employees with high affective commitment engage in more constructive problem solving when employee–employer relations sour.[78] Although some level of financial connection may be necessary, employers should not confuse continuance commitment with employee loyalty. Employers still need to win employees' hearts (affective commitment) beyond tying them financially to the organization (continuance commitment).

Building Organizational Commitment

There are almost as many ways to build organizational loyalty as there are topics in this textbook, but the following list is most prominent in the literature:

- *Justice and support.* Affective commitment is higher in organizations that fulfill their obligations to employees and abide by humanitarian values, such as fairness, courtesy, forgiveness, and moral integrity. These values relate to the concept of organizational justice, which we discuss in the next chapter. Similarly, organizations that support employee well-being tend to cultivate higher levels of loyalty in return.[79]

- *Shared values.* The definition of affective commitment includes a person's identification with the organization, and that identification is highest when employees believe their values are congruent with the organization's dominant values. Also, employees experience more comfort and predictability when they agree with the values underlying corporate decisions. This comfort increases their motivation to stay with the organization.[80]

- *Trust.* **Trust** refers to positive expectations one person has toward another person in situations involving risk.[81] Trust means putting faith in the other person or group. It is also a reciprocal activity: To receive trust, you must demonstrate trust. Employees identify with and feel obliged to work for an organization only when they trust its leaders. This explains why layoffs are one of the greatest blows to employee loyalty; by reducing job security, companies reduce the trust employees have in their employer and the employment relationship.[82]

- *Organizational comprehension.* Organizational comprehension refers to how well employees understand the organization, including its strategic direction, social dynamics, and physical layout.[83] This awareness is a necessary prerequisite to affective commitment because it is difficult to identify with or feel loyal to something you don't know very well. Furthermore, lack of information produces uncertainty, and the resulting stress can distance employees from that source of uncertainty (i.e., the organization). The practical implication here is to ensure employees develop a reasonably clear and complete mental model of the organization. This occurs by giving staff information and opportunities to keep up to date about organizational events, interact with coworkers, discover what goes on in different parts of the organization, and learn about the organization's history and future plans.[84]

- *Employee involvement.* Employee involvement increases affective commitment by strengthening the employee's psychological ownership and social identity with the organization.[85]

Employees feel they are part of the organization when they participate in decisions that guide the organization's future (see Chapter 6). Employee involvement also builds loyalty because giving this power is a demonstration of the company's trust in its employees.

Organizational commitment and job satisfaction represent two of the most often studied and discussed attitudes in the workplace. Each is linked to emotional episodes and cognitive judgments about the workplace and relationship with the company. Emotions also play an important role in another concept on everyone's mind these days: stress. The final section of this chapter provides an overview of work-related stress and how it can be managed.

Learning Objective

After reading this section, you should be able to

LO4 Describe the stress experience and review three major stressors.

WORK-RELATED STRESS AND ITS MANAGEMENT

When asked if they often feel stressed, most employees these days say, "Yes"! Not only do they understand the concept; they claim to have plenty of personal experience with it. **Stress** is described as an adaptive response to a situation perceived as challenging or threatening to the person's well-being.[86] It is a physiological and psychological condition that prepares us to adapt to hostile or noxious environmental conditions. Our heart rate increases, muscles tighten, breathing speeds up, and perspiration increases. Our body also moves more blood to the brain, releases adrenaline and other hormones, fuels the system by releasing more glucose and fatty acids, activates systems that sharpen our senses, and conserves resources by shutting down our immune system. One school of thought suggests stress is a negative evaluation of the external environment. However, critics of this "cognitive appraisal" perspective point out that stress is more accurately described as an emotional experience, which may occur before or after a conscious evaluation of the situation.[87]

Whether stress is a complex emotion or a cognitive evaluation of the environment, it has become a pervasive experience in most people's daily lives. Three out of four Americans (and a similar percentage of people in Germany, Canada, Australia, and the United Kingdom) say they frequently or sometimes feel stress in their daily lives. Another recent survey reported that 64 percent of American employees rate their stress as high.

good STRESS vs bad STRESS[88]

69% of 1,000 American employees surveyed are completely or somewhat satisfied with the amount of on-the-job stress.

69% of 42,000 American employees polled report they are neutral or energized by on-the-job stress.

27% of 1,000 American employees surveyed had an "excessive" score in a Rutgers University anxieties index.

13% of 115,000 employees polled globally say their work is so stressful it makes it hard for them to sleep at night.

More than one-third of adult Canadians report feeling stressed most of the time. And in a survey of 115,000 employees in 33 countries, respondents in Japan reported the most stress-related health complaints, followed by Canada, the Ukraine, Finland, Hong Kong, and Hungary.[89]

Stress is typically described as a negative experience. This is known as *distress*—the degree of physiological, psychological, and behavioral deviation from healthy functioning. However, some level of stress—called *eustress*—is a necessary part of life because it activates and motivates people to achieve goals, change their environments, and succeed in life's challenges. For example, more than two-thirds of 42,000 American employees polled report that on-the-job stress either energizes them or has no effect.[90] Our focus is on the causes and management of distress because it has become a chronic problem in many societies.

General Adaptation Syndrome

More than 500 years ago, people began using the word *stress* to describe the human response to harsh environmental conditions.

However, it wasn't until the 1930s that researcher Hans Selye (often described as the father of stress research) first documented the stress experience, called the **general adaptation syndrome**. Selye determined (initially by studying rats) that people have a fairly consistent and automatic physiological response to stressful situations, which helps them to cope with environmental demands.[91]

The general adaptation syndrome consists of the three stages shown in Exhibit 4.6. The *alarm reaction* stage occurs when a threat or challenge activates the physiological stress responses that were stated earlier. The individual's energy level and coping effectiveness decrease in response to the initial shock. The second stage, *resistance*, activates various biochemical, psychological, and behavioral mechanisms that give the individual more energy and engage coping mechanisms to overcome or remove the source of stress. To focus energy on the source of the stress, the body reduces resources to the immune system during this stage. This explains why people are more likely to catch a cold or some other illness when they experience prolonged stress. People have a limited resistance capacity, and if the source of stress persists, the individual will eventually move into the third stage, *exhaustion*. Most of us are able to remove the source of stress or remove ourselves from that source before becoming too exhausted. However, people who frequently reach exhaustion are more likely to suffer long-term physiological and psychological damage.[92]

Consequences of Distress

Stress takes its toll on the human body.[93] Many people experience tension headaches, muscle pain, and related problems mainly due to muscle contractions from the stress response. Studies have found that high stress levels also contribute to cardiovascular disease, including heart attacks and strokes, and may be associated with some forms of cancer. Stress also produces various psychological consequences, such as job dissatisfaction, moodiness, depression, and lower organizational commitment. Furthermore, various behavioral outcomes have been linked to high or persistent stress, including lower job performance, poor decision making, and increased workplace accidents and aggressive behavior.

▼ EXHIBIT 4.6 General Adaptation Syndrome

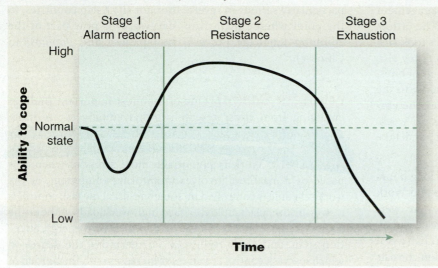

| Stage 1 Alarm reaction | Stage 2 Resistance | Stage 3 Exhaustion |

Y-axis: Ability to cope (High, Normal state, Low); X-axis: Time

Source: Adapted from H. Selye, *The Stress of Life* (New York: McGraw-Hill, 1956).

Most people react to stress through "fight or flight," so increased absenteeism is another outcome because it is a form of flight.[94]

Job Burnout

Job burnout is a particular stress consequence that refers to the process of emotional exhaustion, cynicism, and reduced feelings of personal accomplishment.[95] *Emotional exhaustion*, the first stage, is characterized by a lack of energy, tiredness, and a feeling that one's emotional resources are depleted. This is followed by *cynicism* (also called *depersonalization*), which is an indifferent attitude toward work, emotional detachment from clients, a cynical view of the organization, and a tendency to strictly follow rules and regulations rather than adapt to the needs of others. The final stage of burnout, called *reduced personal accomplishment*, entails feelings of diminished confidence in one's ability to perform the job well. In such situations, employees develop a sense of learned helplessness as they no longer believe their efforts make a difference.

Stressors: The Causes of Stress

Before identifying ways to manage work-related stress, we must first understand its causes, known as stressors. **Stressors** include any environmental conditions that place a physical or emotional demand on a person.[96] There are numerous stressors in the workplace and in life in general. In this section, we'll highlight three of the most common work-related stressors: harassment and incivility, workload, and lack of task control.

Harassment and Incivility

One of the fastest-growing sources of workplace stress is **psychological harassment**.

Psychological harassment includes repeated hostile or unwanted conduct, verbal comments, actions, and gestures that undermine an employee's dignity or psychological or physical integrity. This covers a broad landscape of behaviors, from threats and bullying to subtle yet persistent forms of incivility.[97]

Many people experience psychological harassment in the workplace. One recent global survey of 16,517 employees reported that 83 percent of Europeans, 65 percent of Americans, and 55 percent of people in Asia have been physically or emotionally bullied. More than two-thirds of teachers in the United Kingdom say they have experienced or witnessed workplace bullying within the past 12 months. The government of Quebec, Canada, which passed the first workplace anti-harassment legislation in North America, received more than 2,500 complaints in the first year alone! Labor bureaus in Japan received more than 32,000 complaints of harassments in a recent year, a fivefold increase from six years earlier.[98]

Sexual harassment is a type of harassment in which a person's employment or job performance is conditional and depends on unwanted sexual relations (called *quid pro quo* harassment) and/or the person experiences sexual conduct from others (such as posting pornographic material) that unreasonably interferes with work performance or creates an intimidating, hostile, or offensive working environment (called *hostile work environment* harassment).[99]

Work Overload

University of Michigan professor Dave Ulrich recalls visiting IBM's headquarters in Armonk,

New York, three decades ago to deliver executive programs. Almost everyone, including professional and management staff members, worked 35 to 45 hours per week. The offices were vacant by 5:30 p.m. Back then, IBM employees took sick leave whenever they experienced health problems. They also took real vacations of up to five weeks, with no cell phones, computers, or other electronics to keep them tethered to the job. Those days are long gone, says Ulrich. "Today the employees in that same building work 60 to 80 hours per week, keep on working through most health problems, and take almost no real vacation."[100]

IBM isn't the only company where employees work long hours and seldom take vacations. Surveys by the Families and Work Institute report that 44 percent of Americans say they are overworked, up from 28 percent who felt this way a few years earlier. In addition, 40 percent of Americans say they haven't had a real vacation within the previous two years (where vacation consists of leisure travel for a week or more to a destination at least 100 miles from home).[101]

Why do employees work such long hours? One explanation is the combined effects of technology and globalization. "Everyone in this industry is working harder now because of email, wireless access, and globalization," says marketing executive Christopher Lochhead. "You can't even get a rest on the weekend." A second factor is that many people are caught up in consumerism; they want to buy more goods and services, and doing so requires more income through longer work hours. A third reason, called the "ideal worker norm," is that professionals expect themselves and others to work longer work hours. For many, toiling away far beyond the normal workweek is a badge of honor, a symbol of their superhuman

capacity to perform above others.[103] This badge of honor is particularly serious in several (but not all) Asian countries, to the point where "death from overwork" is now part of the common language (*karoshi* in Japanese and *guolaosi* in Chinese).[104]

Low Task Control One of the most important findings emerging from stress research is that employees are more stressed when they lack control over how and when they perform their tasks as well as lack control over the pace of work activity. Work is potentially more stressful when it is paced by a machine, involves monitoring equipment, or the work schedule is controlled by someone else. Low task control is a stressor because employees face high workloads without the ability to adjust the pace of the load to their own energy, attention span, and other resources. Furthermore, the degree to which low task control is a stressor increases with the burden of responsibility the employee must carry.[105] Assembly-line workers have low task control, but their stress can be fairly low if their level of responsibility is also low. In contrast, sports coaches are under immense pressure to win games (high responsibility), yet they have little control over what happens on the playing field (low task control).

Individual Differences in Stress

People experience different stress levels when exposed to the same stressor. One factor is the employee's physical health. Regular exercise and a healthy lifestyle produce a larger store of energy to cope with stress. A second individual difference is the coping strategies employees use to ward off a particular stressor.[106] People sometimes figure out ways to remove the stressor or to minimize its presence. Seeking support from others, reframing the stressor in a more positive light, blaming others for the stressor, and denying the stressor's existence are some other coping mechanisms. Some coping strategies work better for some stressors, and some are better across all stressors.[107] Thus, someone who uses a less effective coping mechanism in a particular situation would experience more stress in response to that situation.

Six Jobs with High Stress Risk[102]

- Ambulance paramedics
- Teachers
- Social services caregivers
- Call center employees
- Prison officers
- Police officers

These jobs were identified based on job incumbent scores regarding physical health, psychological well-being, and job satisfaction.

People have a tendency to rely on one or two coping strategies, and those who rely on generally poor coping strategies (such as denying the stressor exists) are going to experience more stress.

Personality is the third and possibly the most important reason why people experience different levels of stress when faced with the same stressor.[108] Individuals with low neuroticism (high emotional stability) usually experience lower stress levels because, by definition, they are less prone to anxiety, depression, and other negative emotions. Extraverts also tend to experience lower stress than introverts, likely because extraversion includes a degree of positive thinking and extraverts interact with others, which helps buffer the effect of stressors. People with a positive self-concept—high self-esteem, self-efficacy, and internal locus of control (see Chapter 3)—feel more confident and in control when faced with a stressor. In other words, they tend to have a stronger sense of optimism.[109]

While positive self-concept protects us from stress, workaholism attracts more stressors and weakens the capacity to cope with them. The classic **workaholic** (also called *work addict*) is highly involved in work, feels compelled or driven to work because of inner pressures, and has a low enjoyment of work. Workaholics are compulsive and preoccupied with work, often to the exclusion and detriment of personal health, intimate relationships, and family.[110]

Learning Objective

After reading this section, you should be able to

LO5 Identify five ways to manage workplace stress.

MANAGING WORK-RELATED STRESS

Many people deny the existence of their stress until it has more serious outcomes. This avoidance strategy creates a vicious cycle because the failure to cope with stress becomes another stressor on top of the one that created the stress in the first place. To prevent this vicious cycle, employers and employees need to apply one or more of the stress management strategies described below: remove the stressor, withdraw from the stressor, change stress perceptions, control stress consequences, and receive social support.[111]

Remove the Stressor There are many ways to remove the stressor, but some of the more common actions involve assigning employees to jobs that match their skills and preferences, reducing excessive workplace noise, having a complaint system and taking corrective action against harassment, and giving employees more control over the work process. Another important way that companies can remove stressors is by facilitating better work/life balance. Work/life balance initiatives minimize conflict between the employee's work and nonwork demands. Five of the most common work/life balance initiatives are flexible and limited work time, job sharing, telecommuting, personal leave, and child care support.[112]

- *Flexible and limited work time.* An important way to improve work/life balance is limiting the number of hours that employees are expected to work and giving them flexibility in scheduling those hours. For example, electronics retailer Best Buy has also become a role model in work/life balance by giving employees very flexible work hours. The Minneapolis-based retailer's 3,000 head office employees are evaluated by their results, not their face time, through the results-only work environment (ROWE) initiative. San Jorge Children's Hospital offers a unique form of work flexibility that has dramatically reduced turnover and stress. The Puerto Rican medical center introduced a "ten month work program" in which employees can take summer months off to care for their children while out of school.[113]

- *Job sharing.* Job sharing splits a career position between two people so they experience less time-based stress between work and family. They typically work different parts of the week, with some overlapping work time in the weekly schedule to coordinate activities. This strategy gives employees the ability to work part-time in jobs naturally designed for full-time responsibilities.

- *Telecommuting.* Telecommuting (also called *teleworking*) involves working from home or a site close to home rather than commuting a longer distance to the office everyday (see Chapter 1). By reducing or eliminating commuting time, employees can more easily fulfill family obligations, such as temporarily leaving the home office to pick the kids up from school. Consequently, telecommuters tend to experience better work/life balance.[114] However, teleworking may increase stress for those who crave social interaction and who lack the space and privacy necessary to work at home.

- *Personal leave.* Employers with strong work/life values offer extended maternity, paternity, and personal leave for employees to care for a new family or take advantage of a personal experience. Most countries provide 12 to 16 weeks of paid leave, with some offering one year or more of fully or partially paid maternity leave.[115]

- *Child care support.* According to one estimate, almost one-quarter of large American companies provide on-site or subsidized child care facilities. Child care support reduces stress because employees are less rushed to drop off children and less worried during the day about how well their children are doing.[116]

Withdraw from the Stressor

Removing the stressor may be the ideal solution, but it is often not feasible. An alternative strategy is to permanently or temporarily remove employees from the stressor. Permanent withdrawal occurs when employees are transferred to jobs that better fit their competencies and values. Temporarily withdrawing from stressors is the most frequent way employees manage stress. Vacations and holidays are important opportunities for employees to recover from stress and reenergize for future challenges. A small number of companies offer paid or unpaid sabbaticals.[117] Many firms also provide innovative ways for employees to withdraw from stressful work throughout the day, such as games rooms, ice cream cart breaks, nap rooms, and cafeterias that include live piano recitals.

Change Stress Perceptions

Earlier, we learned that employees experience different stress levels because they have different levels of positive self-evaluation and optimism. Consequently, another way to manage stress is to help employees improve their self-concept so job challenges are not perceived as threatening. Personal goal setting and self-reinforcement can also reduce the stress people experience when they enter new work settings. Research also suggests that some (but not all) forms of humor can improve optimism and create positive emotions by taking some psychological weight off the situation.[118]

Control Stress Consequences

Regular exercise and maintaining a healthy lifestyle is an effective stress management strategy because it controls stress consequences. Research indicates that physical exercise reduces the physiological consequences of stress by helping employees moderate their breathing and heart rate, muscle tension, and stomach acidity.[119] Many companies offer Pilates, yoga, and other exercise and meditation classes during the workday. Research indicates that various forms of meditation reduce anxiety, reduce blood pressure and muscle tension, and moderate breathing and heart rate.[120] Wellness programs can also help control the consequences of stress. These programs inform employees about better nutrition and fitness, regular sleep, and other good health habits. Many large companies offer *employee assistance programs* (EAPs). EAPs are counseling services that help employees overcome work or nonwork-related challenges, such as marital conflict, financial distress, and bank robberies.

Receive Social Support

Social support occurs when coworkers, supervisors, family members, friends, and others provide emotional and/or informational support to buffer an individual's stress experience. For instance, one recent study reported that employees whose managers have good empathy skills experienced fewer stress symptoms than employees whose managers were less empathetic. Social support potentially (but not always) improves the person's optimism and self-confidence because support makes people feel valued and worthy. Social support also provides information to help the person interpret, comprehend, and possibly remove the stressor. For instance, to reduce a new employee's stress, coworkers could describe ways to handle difficult customers. Seeking social support is called a "tend and befriend" response to stress, and research suggests women often follow this route rather than the "fight-or-flight" response mentioned earlier.[121] ■

CHECK IT OUT!

www.mhhe.com/ McShaneM2e

for study materials

including quizzes

and other resources

employee motivation

Robert Meggy understands the importance of employee motivation and engagement for business success. "When I set out ... to turn around a box manufacturing company in receivership, the focus quickly became the employees," explains Meggy, who has turned Great Little Box Company Ltd. (GLBC) in Vancouver, Canada, into a strong competitor in the corrugated box and point-of-purchase display industry. "It is clear that happy and motivated employees are the key to success and longevity." Each year, Meggy establishes a "Big Outrageous eXtranvaganza (BOX) goal representing a stretch profit target for the coming year. If the BOX goal is achieved, all of GLBC's 180 employees receive an all-expense-paid vacation to a sunny location.

GLBC employees are also motivated through their involvement on one of several task forces to improve sales, reduce costs, or improve employee well-being. "We are always into improving what we do, and this motivates middle management and salespeople to put ideas on the table," Meggy explains. Employees are also motivated through a companywide profit-sharing plan. The same amount of bonus is distributed to everyone, which most staff members say is fair. "I certainly believe in fair pay," says Meggy. "You don't have to be the best paying but you do have to be fair."

Employee motivation has helped GLBC to withstand the challenges of increased competition and economic turbulence.

continued on p. 88

LEARNING OBJECTIVES

After studying Chapter 5, you should be able to:

LO1 Define employee engagement.

LO2 Explain how drives and emotions influence employee motivation, and summarize Maslow's needs hierarchy, McClelland's learned needs theory, and four-drive theory.

LO3 Apply the expectancy theory model to explain employee motivation.

LO4 Outline organizational behavior modification (OB Mod) and social cognitive theory and explain their relevance to employee motivation.

LO5 Summarize equity theory and describe ways to improve procedural justice.

LO6 Describe the characteristics of effective goal setting and feedback.

LO7 List the advantages and disadvantages of job specialization, and describe three ways to improve employee motivation through job design.

motivation Forces within a person that affect the direction, intensity, and persistence of voluntary behavior.

employee engagement Individual's emotional and cognitive motivation, particularly a focused, intense, persistent, and purposive effort toward work-related goals.

drives Hardwired characteristics of the brain that correct deficiencies or maintain an internal equilibrium by producing emotions to energize individuals.

needs Goal-directed forces that people experience.

continued from p. 87

Motivation refers to the forces within a person that affect the direction, intensity, and persistence of voluntary behavior.[1] Motivated employees are willing to exert a particular level of effort (intensity), for a certain amount of time (persistence), toward a particular goal (direction). Motivation is one of the four essential drivers of individual behavior and performance (see Chapter 2).

The theme of this chapter is employee motivation. We begin by discussing employee engagement, an increasingly popular concept associated with motivation. Next, we look briefly at employee drives and emotions, and introduce theories that focus on drives and needs. Next, two popular rational theories of employee motivation—expectancy theory and organizational justice (including equity theory)—are discussed. The latter part of this chapter describes goal setting, feedback, and job design. ■

Learning Objective

After reading this section, you should be able to

LO1 Define employee engagement.

EMPLOYEE ENGAGEMENT

When executives discuss employee motivation these days, they are just as likely to use the phrase **employee engagement**. Although its definition is still being debated,[2] employee engagement is best described as an individual's emotional and cognitive (logical) motivation, particularly a focused,

OB Theory to Practice

Company Evidence on the Value of Employee Engagement[3]

- Standard Chartered Bank: Bank branches with highly engaged employees produce 20 percent higher returns than branches with lower engagement scores.
- Marks & Spencer: A 1 percent improvement in employee engagement levels produces a 2.9 percent increase in sales per square foot.
- Best Buy: A 0.1 increase (on a 5.0 point scale) in a retail outlet's employee engagement score is associated with a $100,000 increase in that store's profitability for the year.
- JCPenney: Stores with the top-quartile engagement scores generate about 10 percent more in sales per square foot and 36 percent greater operating income than similar-size stores in the lowest quartile.

intense, persistent, and purposive effort toward work-related goals. It is an emotional involvement in, commitment to, and satisfaction with the work. Employee engagement also includes a high level of absorption in the work—the experience of focusing intensely on the task with limited awareness of events beyond that work. Finally, employee engagement is often described in terms of self-efficacy—the belief that you have the ability, role clarity, and resources to get the job done (see Chapter 3).

Employee engagement is on the minds of many business leaders these days because it seems to be a strong predictor of employee and work unit performance. A recent UK government report concluded employee engagement is so important to the country's international competitiveness that government should urgently raise awareness of and support for employee engagement practices throughout all sectors of the economy.[4] Although it is possible that company success makes employees more engaged, field studies suggest that employee engagement causes the company outcomes more than vice versa.

The challenge facing organizational leaders is that most employees aren't very engaged.[5] The numbers vary, but generally only about 30 percent of American employees are highly engaged, which is slightly above the global average. Approximately half of all employees are somewhat or not engaged, and approximately one-fifth have low engagement or are actively disengaged. Actively disengaged employees don't just lack motivation to

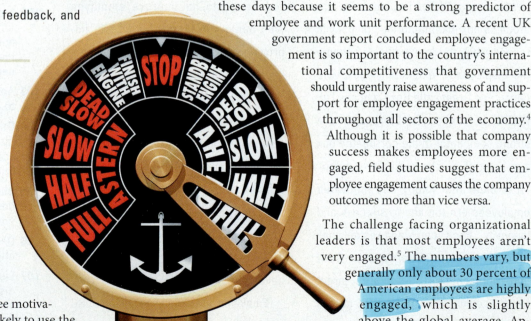

work; they are frustrated enough to actively disrupt the workplace and undermine other employees' motivation. Employees in several Asian countries (notably Japan, China, and South Korea) and a few European countries (notably Italy, the Netherlands, and France) have the lowest levels of employee engagement, whereas the highest scores are usually found in the United States, Brazil, and India.

This leads to the question: What are the drivers of employee engagement? Goal setting, employee involvement, organizational justice, organizational comprehension (knowing what's going on in the company), employee development opportunities, sufficient resources, and an appealing company vision are some of the more commonly-mentioned influences.[6] In other words, building an engaged workforce calls on most topics in this book, such as the MARS model (Chapter 2), building affective commitment (Chapter 4), motivation practices (Chapter 5), and leadership (Chapter 11).

Learning Objective

After reading this section, you should be able to

LO2   Explain how drives and emotions influence employee motivation, and summarize Maslow's needs hierarchy, McClelland's learned needs theory, and four-drive theory.

EMPLOYEE DRIVES AND NEEDS

To figure out how to nurture a more engaged and motivated workforce, we first need to understand the motivational "forces" or prime movers of employee behavior.[7] Our starting point is **drives** (also called *primary needs*), which we define as hardwired characteristics of the brain that attempt to keep us in balance by correcting deficiencies. Drives accomplish this task by producing emotions that energize us to act on our environment.[8] In Chapter 4, we learned that emotions put people in a state of readiness. In other words, emotions play a central role in motivation.[9] In fact, both words (*emotion* and *motivation*) originate from the same Latin word *movere*, which means "to move."

Drives and emotions are receiving increasing attention because recent neuroscience (brain) research has highlighted their central role in human decisions and behavior. There is no agreed-upon list of human drives, but several are consistently identified in research, such as the drive for social interaction, for competence or status, to know what's going on around us, and to defend ourselves against physiological and psychological harm.[10] These drives, and the emotions they produce, generate human needs. We define **needs** as goal-directed forces that people experience. They are the motivational forces of emotions channeled toward particular goals to correct deficiencies or imbalances. As one leading neuroscientist explained: "Drives express themselves directly in background emotions and we eventually become aware of their existence by means of background feelings."[11] These "feelings" are the needs that we consciously try to resolve through our decisions and actions.

Consider the following example: You arrive at work to discover a stranger sitting at your desk. Seeing this situation produces emotions (worry, curiosity) that motivate you to act. These emotions are generated from drives, such as the drive to defend and drive to know. When strong enough, they motivate you to do something about this situation, such as finding out who that person is and possibly seeking reassurance from coworkers that your job is still safe. In this case, you have a need to know what is going on, to feel secure, and possibly to correct a sense of personal violation. Notice that your emotional reactions to seeing the stranger sitting at your desk represent the forces that move you, but you channel those emotions toward specific goals.

Although everyone has the same drives, people develop different intensities of needs in a particular situation. We will revisit this notion of individual differences in needs later in this section, and later in this chapter we will explain why

[**The difference between a successful person and others is not a lack of strength, not a lack of knowledge, but rather in a lack of will.**]

—Vince Lombardi[12]

people who experience the same needs are motivated to take different actions to resolve those needs. Let's begin by looking at three motivation theories that try to explain why people have needs.

Maslow's Needs Hierarchy Theory

By far, the most widely known theory of human motivation is **Maslow's needs hierarchy theory** (see Exhibit 5.1). Developed by psychologist Abraham Maslow in the 1940s, the model condenses and integrates the long list of drives and needs that had been previously studied into a hierarchy of five basic categories (from lowest to highest):[13] *physiological* (need for food, air, water, shelter, etc.), *safety* (need for security and stability), *belongingness/love* (need for interaction with and affection from others), *esteem* (need for self-esteem and social esteem/status), and *self-actualization* (need for self-fulfillment, realization of one's potential). Along with developing these five categories, Maslow identified the desire to know and the desire for aesthetic beauty as two innate drives that do not fit within the hierarchy. Maslow suggested we are motivated simultaneously by several primary needs (drives), but the strongest source of motivation is the lowest unsatisfied need at the time. As the person satisfies a lower-level need, the next higher need in the hierarchy becomes the primary motivator and remains so even if never satisfied.

> Maslow deserves credit for bringing a more holistic, humanistic, and positive approach to the study of human motivation.

In spite of its popularity, most motivation experts dismiss Maslow's needs hierarchy theory.[14] Studies have concluded that people do not progress through the hierarchy as the theory predicts. Maslow's theory ultimately failed to explain human motivation because people don't fit into a one-size-fits-all needs hierarchy. Instead, there is growing evidence that people have different hierarchies. Some place social status at the top of their personal hierarchy; others view personal development and growth above social relations or status. Employee needs are strongly influenced by self-concept, personal values, and personality.[15] If your most important values lean toward stimulation and self-direction, you probably pay more attention to self-actualization needs. If power and achievement are at the top of your value system, status needs will likely be at the top of your needs hierarchy. This connection between values and needs suggests that a needs hierarchy is unique to each person and can possibly change over time, just as values change over a lifetime.[16]

Maslow's Contribution: Holistic, Humanistic, and Positive Human Motivation

Although needs hierarchy theory has failed the reality test, Maslow deserves credit for bringing a more holistic, humanistic, and positive approach to the study of human motivation.[17] First, Maslow explained that the various needs should be studied together (holistically) because human behavior is typically initiated by more than one need at the same time. Previously, motivation experts had splintered needs or drives into dozens of categories, each studied in isolation.[18] Second, Maslow introduced a more humanistic view of motivation by suggesting that higher-order needs are influenced by personal and social influences, not just instincts.[19] Previous motivation experts had focused almost entirely on human instincts without considering that human thought could shape motivation.

▼ **EXHIBIT 5.1** Maslow's Needs Hierarchy

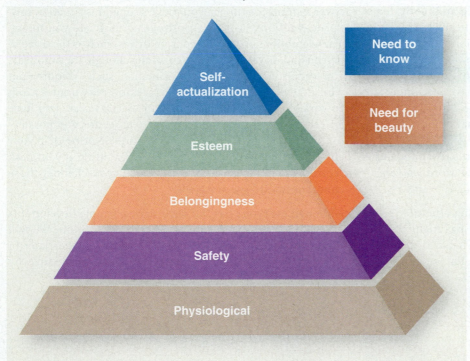

Source: Based on information in A. H. Maslow, "A Theory of Human Motivation," *Psychological Review* 50 (1943), 370–96.

Third, Maslow brought a positive approach to motivation theory by popularizing the concept of *self-actualization*. He emphasized that people are naturally motivated to reach their potential and that organizations and societies need to be structured to help people continue and develop this motivation.[20] This positive view of motivation contrasted with the dominant position that needs become activated by deficiencies such as hunger. Indeed, Maslow is considered a pioneer in *positive organizational behavior*. Positive OB says that focusing on the positive rather than negative aspects of life will improve organizational success and individual well-being (see Chapter 3). In other words, this approach advocates building positive qualities and perspectives within individuals or institutions as opposed to focusing on trying to fix what might be wrong with them.[21]

Learned Needs Theory

Although everyone has the same innate drives, there are considerable individual differences in the emotions those drives generate in a particular situation. Maslow noted this when he wrote that individual characteristics influence the strength of higher-order needs, such as the need to belong. Psychologist David McClelland further investigated the idea that need strength can be altered through social influences. In particular, he recognized that a person's needs can be strengthened through reinforcement, learning, and social conditions. McClelland examined three "learned" needs: achievement, power, and affiliation.[22]

Need for Achievement

People with a strong **need for achievement (nAch)** want to accomplish reasonably challenging goals through their own effort. They prefer working alone rather than in teams, and they choose tasks with a moderate degree of risk (i.e., neither too easy nor impossible to complete). High-nAch people also desire unambiguous feedback and recognition for their success. Money is a weak motivator, except when it provides feedback and recognition.[24] In contrast, employees with a low nAch perform their work better when money is used as an incentive. Successful entrepreneurs tend to have a high nAch, possibly because they establish challenging goals for themselves and thrive on competition.[25]

Need for Affiliation

Need for affiliation (nAff) refers to a desire to seek approval from others, conform to their wishes and expectations, and avoid conflict and confrontation. People with a strong nAff try to project a favorable image of themselves. They tend to actively support others and try to smooth out workplace conflicts. High nAff employees generally work well in coordinating roles to mediate conflicts and in sales positions where the main task is cultivating long-term relations. However, they tend to be less effective at allocating scarce resources and making other decisions that potentially generate conflict. People in decision-making positions must have a relatively low need for affiliation so their choices and actions are not biased by a personal need for approval.[26]

Need for Power

People with a high **need for power (nPow)** want to exercise control over others and are concerned about maintaining their leadership position. They tend to rely on persuasive communication, make more suggestions in meetings, and tend to publicly evaluate situations more frequently. McClelland pointed out that there are two types of nPow. Individuals who enjoy their power for its own sake, use it to advance personal interests, and

Aiming
for Self-Actualization[23]

74% of 160,000 employees polled globally identify the ability to grow/develop in their field as how they define or derive meaning from their work.

71% of 2,928 Australian employees (75% in management positions) agree or strongly agree that they are working to their full potential.

67% of older (age 50-69) middle-income American workers consider themselves ahead of the game at being intellectually stimulated, still learning, and working to their full potential.

57% of 9,441 petroleum engineers worldwide agree or strongly agree that their job uses their full potential.

wear their power as a status symbol have *personalized power*. Others mainly have a high need for *socialized power* because they desire power as a means to help others.[27] McClelland argues that effective leaders should have a high need for socialized rather than personalized power. They must have a high degree of altruism and social responsibility and be concerned about the consequences of their own actions on others.

Learning Needs McClelland believed needs can be learned (more accurately, strengthened or weakened), and the training programs he developed supported that proposition. In his achievement motivation program, trainees wrote achievement-oriented stories and practiced achievement-oriented behaviors in business games. They also completed a detailed achievement plan for the next two years and formed a reference group with other trainees to maintain their new-found achievement motivation.[28] Participants attending these achievement motivation programs subsequently started more new businesses, had greater community involvement, invested more in expanding their businesses, and employed twice as many people compared with a matched sample of nonparticipants. These training programs increased achievement motivation by helping participants to create a more achievement-focused self-concept and by rewarding them for engaging in achievement-oriented behavior. When writing an achievement plan, for example, participants were encouraged (and supported by other participants) to experience the anticipated thrill of succeeding.

Four-Drive Theory

One of the central messages of this chapter is that emotions play a key role in employee motivation. This view is supported by a groundswell of neuroscience research on emotions, decision making, and behavior. One of the few organizational behavior theories to apply this emerging knowledge is **four-drive theory**.[29] Developed by Harvard Business School professors Paul Lawrence and Nitin Nohria, four-drive theory states that everyone has the drive to acquire, bond, learn, and defend:

- *Drive to acquire.* This is the drive to seek, take, control, and retain objects and personal experiences. The drive to acquire extends beyond basic food and water; it includes gaining relative status and recognition in society.[30] Thus, it is the foundation of competition and the basis of our need for esteem. Four-drive theory states the drive to acquire is insatiable because the purpose of human motivation is to achieve a higher position than others, not just to fulfill one's physiological needs.

- *Drive to bond.* This is the drive to form social relationships and develop mutual caring commitments with others.[31] It explains why people form social identities by aligning their self-concept with various social groups (see Chapter 3). The drive to bond motivates people to cooperate and, consequently, is a fundamental ingredient in the success of organizations and the development of societies.

- *Drive to comprehend.* This is the drive to satisfy our curiosity, to know and understand ourselves and the environment around us.[32] This drive explains why we are motivated to seek out information when unfamiliar with our surroundings or where familiar surroundings have changed. In fact, people will even crave boring information (month-old stock exchange reports) when they lack an ongoing stream of knowledge.[33] The drive to comprehend is related to the higher-order needs of growth and self-actualization described earlier.

- *Drive to defend.* This is the drive to protect ourselves physically and socially. Probably the first drive to develop, it creates a "fight-or-flight" response in the face of personal danger. The drive to defend goes beyond protecting our physical self. It includes defending our relationships, our acquisitions, and our belief systems.

These four drives are innate and universal, which means they are hardwired in our brains and are found in all human beings. They are also independent of each other. There is no hierarchy of drives, so one drive is neither dependent on nor inherently inferior or superior to another drive. Four-drive theory also states these four drives are a complete set—there are no fundamental drives excluded from the model. Another key feature is that three of the four drives are proactive—we regularly try to fulfill them. Only the drive to defend is reactive—it is triggered by threat. Thus, any notion of fulfilling drives is temporary, at best.

B&Q Flash Mob: Fulfilling the Drive to Bond

B&Q, the world's third largest home improvement retailer, has one of the most engaged workforces on the planet. The British company trains, involves, and rewards employees; it also encourages fun activities where staff can fulfill their drive to bond. For example, employees at all 330 B&Q stores recently participated simultaneously in a five-minute dance routine during store hours. The charity event attempted to break a world record flash mob. "It puts a smile on the faces of our staff which hopefully transfers into great customer service," says one B&Q store manager about the flash mob event.[34]

quickly experience worry, curiosity, or both. These emotions are automatically created by one or more of the four drives. In this example, the emotions produced are likely strong enough to demand your attention and motivate you to act on this observation.

When these emotions become conscious experiences (i.e., needs), our mental skill set relies on social norms, past experience, and personal values to direct the motivational force of our emotions to actions that deal with that situation (see Exhibit 5.2). In other words, our mental skill set chooses courses of action that are acceptable to society, consistent with our own moral compass, and have a high probability of achieving the goal.[36]

Evaluating Four-Drive Theory
Although four-drive theory was introduced very recently, it is based on a deep foundation of research dating back more than three decades. The drives have been identified from psychological and anthropological studies. Furthermore, Shalom Schwartz recently reported that the four-drive theory maps well onto the ten dimensions in his circumplex model of personal values (see Chapter 2).[37] The translation of drives into goal-directed behavior originates from considerable research on emotions and neural processes. The theory explains why needs vary from one person to the next, but it avoids the assumption that everyone has the same needs hierarchy. Notice, too, that four-drive theory satisfies two of Maslow's criteria for any motivation theory: it is holistic (it relates to all drives, not just one or two) and humanistic (it acknowledges the role of human thought and social influences, not just instinct).

Even with its well-researched foundations, four-drive theory is far from complete. Most experts would argue one or two other

How Drives Influence Employee Motivation

According to recent neuroscience research, our perceptions of the world around us are quickly and nonconsciously tagged with emotional markers (as we described in Chapters 3 and 4).[35] Four-drive theory states the four drives determine which emotions are tagged to incoming stimuli. If you arrive at work one day to see a stranger sitting in your office chair, you might

▼ **EXHIBIT 5.2** Four-Drive Theory of Motivation

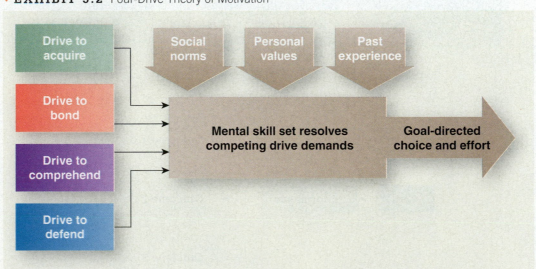

Source: Based on information in P. R. Lawrence and N. Nohria, *Driven: How Human Nature Shapes Our Choices* (San Francisco: Jossey-Bass, 2002).

drives exist that should be included. Furthermore, social norms, personal values, and past experience probably don't represent the full set of individual characteristics that translate emotions into goal-directed effort. For example, personality and self-concept likely also play a significant role in translating drives into needs and needs into decisions and behavior.

Practical Implications of Four-Drive Theory

Four-drive theory recommends organizations should ensure that jobs and workplaces provide a balanced opportunity to fulfill the four drives.[38] Employees continually seek fulfillment of their innate drives, so companies should provide sufficient rewards, learning opportunities, social interaction, and so forth, for all employees. At the same time, companies need to provide a balance of four drive fulfillment. Successful companies need to ensure employees do not experience too much or too little opportunity to fulfill each drive. The reason for this advice is that the four drives counterbalance each other. The drive to bond counterbalances the drive to acquire; the drive to defend counterbalances the drive to comprehend. An organization that fuels the drive to acquire without the drive to bond may eventually suffer from organizational politics and dysfunctional conflict. Change and novelty in the workplace will aid the drive to comprehend, but too much of it will trigger the drive to defend to such an extent that employees become territorial and resistant to change. Thus, the workplace should offer enough opportunity to keep all four drives in balance.

Learning Objective

After reading this section, you should be able to

LO3 Apply the expectancy theory model to explain employee motivation.

EXPECTANCY THEORY OF MOTIVATION

The theories described so far mainly explain what motivates employees as well as the mechanisms (drives and emotions) that motive us. But how do our needs translate into specific effort and behavior? Four-drive theory recognizes that social norms, personal values, and past experience direct our effort, but it doesn't offer any more detail. **Expectancy theory**, on the other hand, is an elegant rational logic model for predicting the employee's chosen direction, level, and persistence of motivation in a particular situation. Essentially, the theory states we are motivated to achieve the goals with the highest expected value, so work effort is directed toward behaviors people believe will lead to the best outcomes.[39] As Exhibit 5.3 illustrates, an individual's effort level depends on three factors: effort-to-performance (E-to-P) expectancy, performance-to-outcome (P-to-O) expectancy, and outcome valences. All three components of the expectancy theory model influence

▼ **EXHIBIT 5.3** Expectancy Theory of Motivation

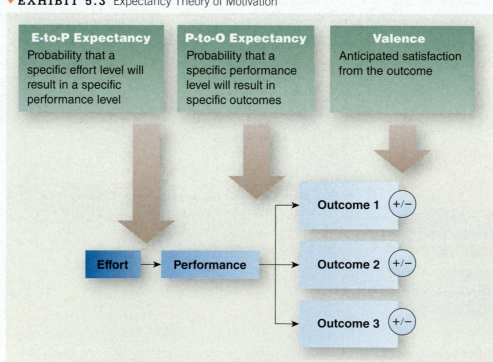

employee motivation. If any component weakens, motivation weakens.

- *E-to-P expectancy.* This is the individual's perception that his or her effort will result in a particular level of performance. In some situations, employees may believe they can unquestionably accomplish the task (a probability of 1.0). In other situations, they expect that even their highest level of effort will not result in the desired performance level (a probability of 0.0). In most cases, the E-to-P expectancy falls somewhere between these two extremes.

- *P-to-O expectancy.* This is the perceived probability that a specific behavior or performance level will lead to a particular outcome. In extreme cases, employees may believe accomplishing a particular task (performance) will definitely result in a particular outcome (a probability of 1.0), or they may believe successful performance will have no effect on this outcome (a probability of 0.0). More often, the P-to-O expectancy falls somewhere between these two extremes.

- *Outcome valences.* A *valence* is the anticipated satisfaction or dissatisfaction an individual feels toward an outcome. It ranges from negative to positive. (The actual range doesn't matter; it may be from -1 to $+1$ or from -100 to $+100$.)[40] Outcomes have a positive valence when they are consistent with our values and satisfy our needs; they have a negative valence when they oppose our values and inhibit need fulfillment.

Expectancy Theory in Practice

One of the appealing characteristics of expectancy theory is that it provides clear guidelines for increasing employee motivation.[41] Several practical applications of expectancy theory are listed in Exhibit 5.4 and described below.

Increasing E-to-P Expectancies
E-to-P expectancies are influenced by the individual's belief he or she can successfully complete the task. Some companies increase this can-do attitude by assuring employees they have the necessary competencies, clear role perceptions, and necessary resources to reach the desired levels of performance. An important part of this process involves matching employees' competencies to job requirements and clearly communicating the tasks required for the job. Similarly, E-to-P expectancies are learned, so behavioral modeling and supportive feedback (positive reinforcement) typically strengthen the individual's belief that he or she is able to perform the task.

Increasing P-to-O Expectancies
The most obvious ways to improve P-to-O expectancies are to measure employee performance accurately and distribute more valued rewards to those with higher job performance. P-to-O expectancies are perceptions, so employees also need to believe that higher

expectancy theory A motivation theory based on the idea that work effort is directed toward behaviors people believe will lead to desired outcomes.

▼ **EXHIBIT 5.4** Practical Applications of Expectancy Theory

Expectancy Theory Component	Objective	Applications
E → P expectancies	To increase the belief that employees are capable of performing the job successfully	• Select people with the required skills and knowledge. • Provide required training and clarify job requirements. • Provide sufficient time and resources. • Assign simpler or fewer tasks until employees can master them. • Provide examples of similar employees who have successfully performed the task. • Provide coaching to employees who lack self-confidence.
P → O expectancies	To increase the belief that good performance will result in certain (valued) outcomes	• Measure job performance accurately. • Clearly explain the outcomes that will result from successful performance. • Describe how the employee's rewards were based on past performance. • Provide examples of other employees whose good performance has resulted in higher rewards.
Outcome valences	To increase the expected value of outcomes resulting from desired performance	• Distribute rewards that employees value. • Individualize rewards. • Minimize the presence of countervalent outcomes.

Performance-to-Outcome Expectancy: the Missing Link [42]

56% of American managers polled say high performers in their company receive more money than do poor performers.

27% of 3,000 Canadian employees polled say there is a clear link between their job performance and pay.

41% of 10,000 American employees polled say high performers in their company receive more money than do poor performers.

44% of 97,000 employees in 30 countries say that their efforts at work are recognized and rewarded.

performance will result in higher rewards. Furthermore, they need to know how that connection occurs, so leaders should use examples, anecdotes, and public ceremonies to illustrate when behavior has been rewarded.

Increasing Outcome Valences One size does not fit all in the business of motivating and rewarding people. Organizational leaders need to find ways to individualize rewards or, where standard rewards are necessary, to identify rewards that do not have a negative valence for some staff. Consider the following story: Top-performing employees in one organization were rewarded with a one-week Caribbean cruise with the company's executive team. Many were likely delighted, but at least one top-performer was aghast at the thought of going on a cruise with senior management. "I don't like schmoozing, I don't like feeling trapped. Why couldn't they just give me the money?" she complained. The employee went on the cruise but spent most of her time working in her stateroom.[43]

One other observation about increasing outcome valences is to watch out for countervalent outcomes that offset outcomes with positive valences. For example, several employees in one work unit performed well when working alone because this achievement gave them a feeling of accomplishment and rewarded them with higher pay. But their performance was considerably lower when they worked together because peer pressure discouraged performance above a fairly low standard. In this situation, the positively valent outcomes (feeling of accomplishment, higher pay) were offset by the negatively valent outcome of peer pressure.

Overall, expectancy theory is a useful model that explains how people rationally figure out the best direction, intensity, and persistence of effort. It has been tested in a variety of situations and predicts employee motivation in different cultures.[44] However, critics have a number of concerns with how the theory has been tested. Another concern is that expectancy theory ignores the central role of emotion in employee effort and behavior. The valence element of expectancy theory captures some of this emotional process but only peripherally.[45] Finally, expectancy theory outlines how expectancies (probability of outcomes) affect motivation, but it doesn't explain how employees develop these expectancies. Two theories that provide this explanation are organizational behavior modification and social cognitive theory, which we describe next.

Learning Objective

After reading this section, you should be able to

LO4 Outline organizational behavior modification (OB Mod) and social cognitive theory and explain their relevance to employee motivation.

ORGANIZATIONAL BEHAVIOR MODIFICATION AND SOCIAL COGNITIVE THEORY

Expectancy theory states that employee beliefs about expected performance and outcomes determine motivation. But how do employees learn these expectancies? The answer to this question directs us to two theories: organizational behavior modification (OB Mod) and social cognitive theory. Although these theories explain how people *learn* what to expect from their actions, they are also theories of motivation because, as in expectancy theory, the learned expectancies affect the person's direction, intensity, and persistence of effort.

Organizational Behavior Modification

Organizational behavior modification or OB Mod adopts *behaviorism*—the view that good theory should rely exclusively on behavior and environmental events and ignore nonobservable cognitions and emotions.[46] Behaviorism has fallen out of favor, and most contemporary motivation models consider employee cognitions and emotions.[47] Even so, OB Mod offers useful ways to understand how workplace events can influence employee learning and motivation.

Organizational behavior modification is depicted in the A-B-C model, shown in Exhibit 5.5. Essentially, the model states that

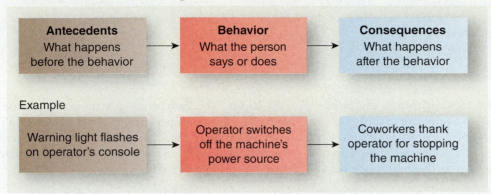

▼ **EXHIBIT 5.5** A-B-Cs of Organizational Behavior Modification

Antecedents What happens before the behavior	→	**Behavior** What the person says or does	→	**Consequences** What happens after the behavior

Example

Warning light flashes on operator's console	→	Operator switches off the machine's power source	→	Coworkers thank operator for stopping the machine

Sources: Adapted from T. K. Connellan, *How to Improve Human Performance* (New York: Harper & Row, 1978), 50; F. Luthans and R. Kreitner, *Organizational Behavior Modification and Beyond* (Glenview, IL: Scott, Foresman, 1985), 85–88.

organizational behavior modification A theory that explains employee behavior in terms of the antecedent conditions and consequences of that behavior.

social cognitive theory A theory that explains how learning and motivation occur by observing and modeling others as well as by anticipating the consequences of our behavior.

behavior (B) changes by managing its antecedents (A) and consequences (C).[48] *Consequences* are environmental events following a particular behavior that influence its future occurrence, such as the compliments or teasing received from coworkers when the employee wears safety goggles. Consequences also include no outcome at all, such as when no one says anything about how well you have been serving customers.

Antecedents are environmental events preceding the behavior, informing employees that a particular action will produce specific consequences. An antecedent may be a sound from your computer signaling an email has arrived or a request from your supervisor asking you to complete a specific task by tomorrow. Notice that antecedents do not cause behavior. The computer sound doesn't cause us to open our email. Rather, the sound (antecedent) is a cue telling us that if we check our email (behavior), we are certain to find a new message (consequence).

OB Mod identifies four types of consequences.[49] *Positive reinforcement* occurs when the introduction of a consequence increases or maintains the frequency or future probability of a specific behavior (e.g., receiving praise after completing a project). *Punishment* occurs when a consequence decreases the frequency or future probability of a behavior (e.g., being taunted or bullied by a coworker). *Negative reinforcement* increases or maintains the frequency of future probability of behavior. Essentially, it is the removal of punishment, such as when your boss stops complaining about your lateness when you show up for work on time. *Extinction* occurs when the target behavior decreases because no consequence follows it (e.g., you stop wearing your safety helmet when your boss stops thanking you for wearing it).[50]

> In most situations, positive reinforcement should follow desired behaviors and extinction (do nothing) should follow undesirable behaviors.

Which contingency of reinforcement works best? In most situations, positive reinforcement should follow desired behaviors and extinction (do nothing) should follow undesirable behaviors. This approach is preferred because punishment and negative reinforcement generate negative emotions and attitudes toward the punisher (e.g., supervisor) and organization. However, some form of punishment (dismissal, suspension, demotion, etc.) may be necessary for extreme behaviors, such as deliberately hurting a coworker or stealing inventory. Indeed, research suggests that, under certain conditions, punishment maintains a sense of fairness.[51]

The schedule (frequency and timing) of the reinforcers also motivates employees in different ways.[52] The most motivational schedule is a *variable ratio schedule* in which employee behavior is reinforced after a variable number of times. You tend to use this schedule to casually show appreciation to coworkers. You don't thank a coworker the same time each day or after a fixed number of successful tasks. Salespeople also experience variable ratio reinforcement because they make a successful sale (the reinforcer) after a varying number of client calls. The variable ratio schedule makes behavior highly resistant to extinction because the reinforcer is never expected at a particular time or after a fixed number of accomplishments.

Social Cognitive Theory

Social cognitive theory states that much learning and motivation occurs by observing and modeling others as well as by anticipating the consequences of our behavior.[53] Although observation and modeling (imitation) have been studied for many years as sources of motivation and learning, social scientist

Albert Bandura reframed these ideas within a cognitive (internal thoughts) perspective as an alternative to the behaviorist approach. There are several pieces to social cognitive theory, but the three most relevant to employee motivation are learning behavior consequences, behavioral modeling, and self-regulation.

Learning Behavior Outcomes
People learn the consequences of behavior by observing or hearing about what happened to other people, not just by directly experiencing the consequences.[54] Hearing that a coworker was fired for being rude to a client increases your perception that rude behavior will result in being fired. In the language of expectancy theory, learning behavior consequences changes a person's perceived P-to-O expectancy. Furthermore, people logically anticipate consequences in related situations. For instance, the story about the fired employee might also strengthen your P-to-O expectancy about getting fired if you are rude toward coworkers and suppliers.

Behavioral Modeling
People learn not only by observing others but also by imitating and practicing those behaviors.[55] Direct sensory experience helps to acquire tacit knowledge and skills, such as the subtle person-machine interaction while driving a vehicle. Behavioral modeling also increases self-efficacy

(see Chapter 3) because people gain more self-confidence after observing others and performing the task successfully themselves. Self-efficacy particularly improves when observers identify with the model, such as someone who is similar in age, experience, gender, and related features.

Self-Regulation
An important feature of social cognitive theory is that human beings set goals and engage in other forms of intentional, purposive action. They establish their own short- and long-term objectives, choose their own standards of achievement, work out a plan of action, consider back-up alternatives, and have the forethought to anticipate the consequences of their goal-directed behavior. Furthermore, people self-regulate by engaging in **self-reinforcement**; that is, they reward and punish themselves for exceeding or falling short of their self-set standards of excellence.[56] For example, you might have a goal of completing the rest of this chapter, after which you reward yourself by having a snack. Raiding the refrigerator is a form of self-induced positive reinforcement for completing this reading assignment.

Learning Objective
After reading this section, you should be able to

LO5 Summarize equity theory and describe ways to improve procedural justice.

ORGANIZATIONAL JUSTICE

Most organizational leaders know that treating employees fairly is both morally correct and good for employee motivation, loyalty, and well-being. Yet feelings of injustice and inequity are regular occurrences in the workplace. To minimize these incidents, we need to first understand that there are two forms of organizational justice: distributive justice and procedural justice.[57] **Distributive justice** refers to perceived fairness in the outcomes we receive compared to our contributions and the outcomes and contributions of others. **Procedural justice**, on the other hand, refers to fairness of the procedures used to decide the distribution of resources.

Equity Theory
At its most basic level, the employment relationship is about exchanging an employee's time and services for pay, skill development opportunities, fulfilling work, and so forth. What is

is the most common distributive justice rule in organizational settings, so let's look at it in more detail.

Feelings of equity are explained by **equity theory**, which says that employees determine feelings of equity by comparing their own outcome/input ratio to the outcome/input ratio of some other person.[58] As Exhibit 5.6 illustrates, the *outcome/input ratio* is the value of the outcomes you receive divided by the value of the inputs you provide in the exchange relationship. Inputs include such things as skill, effort, reputation, performance, experience, and hours worked. Outcomes are what employees receive from the organization, such as pay, promotions, recognition, interesting jobs, and opportunities to improve one's skills and knowledge.

We compare our outcome/input ratio with the ratio of a comparison other.[59] The comparison other might be another person or group of people in other jobs (e.g., comparing your pay with the CEO's pay) or another organization. For the most part, the comparison other varies from one person to the next and is not easily identifiable. The comparison of our own outcome/input ratio with the ratio of someone else results in perceptions of equity, underreward inequity, or overreward inequity. In the equity condition, people believe their outcome/input ratio is similar to the ratio of the comparison other. In the underreward inequity situation, people believe their outcome/input ratio is lower than the comparison other's ratio. In the overreward inequity condition, people believe their ratio of outcomes/inputs is higher than the comparison other's ratio.

Inequity and Employee Motivation How do equity or inequity perceptions affect employee motivation? The answer is illustrated in Exhibit 5.7. When people believe they are

considered "fair" in this exchange relationship varies with each person and situation. We apply an *equality principle* when we believe everyone in the group should receive the same outcomes, such as when everyone gets subsidized meals in the company cafeteria. The *need principle* is applied when we believe those with the greatest need should receive more outcomes than others with less need. The *equity principle* states that people should be paid in proportion to their contribution. The equity principle

▼ **EXHIBIT 5.6** Equity Theory Model

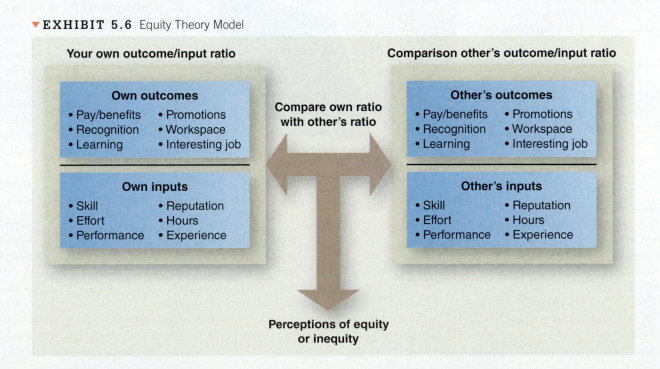

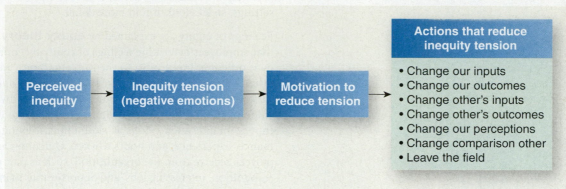

Perceived inequity → Inequity tension (negative emotions) → Motivation to reduce tension →

Actions that reduce inequity tension

- Change our inputs
- Change our outcomes
- Change other's inputs
- Change other's outcomes
- Change our perceptions
- Change comparison other
- Leave the field

under- or overrewarded, they experience negative emotions (called inequity tension). As we have pointed out throughout this chapter, emotions are the engines of motivation. In the case of inequity, people are motivated to reduce the emotional tension. Imagine the following: You discover a coworker earns slightly more than you do, even though he or she began the job at the same time you did, has the same background, and doesn't seem to perform any better. Most people have a strong emotional response to this information, and this emotion nags them until they take some sort of action to correct the perceived inequity. However, people do vary in their *equity sensitivity*, that is, how strongly they feel about outcome/input ratios with others.[60] Some are quite tolerant of situations where they are underrewarded, whereas others are more comfortable when they are overrewarded.

There are many ways people might try to reduce the inequity tension.[61] One action to reduce underreward inequity would be to reduce our inputs so the outcome/input ratio is similar to the higher-paid coworker. Some employees do this by working more slowly, offering fewer suggestions, and engaging in less organizational citizenship behavior. A second action might be to increase our outcomes. Some people who think they are underpaid ask for a pay raise. Others make unauthorized use of company resources. A third behavioral response is to increase the comparison other's inputs. You might subtly ask the better-paid coworker to do a larger share of the work, for instance. A fourth action would be to reduce the comparison other's outcomes. This might occur by ensuring the coworker gets less desirable jobs or working

Not Paid What They're Worth[62]

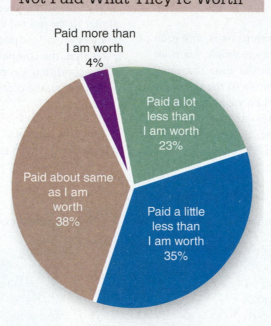

Fifty-eight percent of 1,000 American employees surveyed say they are paid a little or a lot less than they believe they are worth. Only 4 percent believe they are overpaid.

conditions. Another action, although uncommon, would be asking the company to reduce the coworker's pay so it is the same as yours.

A fifth action is perceptual rather than behavioral. It involves changing our beliefs about the situation. For example, you might believe the coworker really is doing more (e.g., working longer hours) for that higher pay. Alternatively, you might change your perceptions of the value of some outcomes. Although initially upset that a coworker gets more travel opportunities than you do, you eventually believe the travel is more a nuisance than desirable feature of the job. A sixth action to reduce the inequity tension would be to change the comparison other. You might compare yourself more with a friend or neighbor who works in a similar job rather than use the higher-paid coworker as the comparison. Finally, if the inequity tension is strong enough and can't be reduced through other actions, you might leave the field. This occurs by moving to another department, joining another company, or keeping away from the work site where the overpaid coworker is located.

The opposite of these seven responses to inequity would be applied by people who experience overreward inequity. Some overrewarded employees reduce their feelings of inequity by working harder. However, many overrewarded employees take an easier route. Some encourage the underrewarded employee to work at a more leisurely pace. A common reaction, however, is that the overrewarded employee changes his or her perceptions to justify the more favorable outcomes.

Evaluating Equity Theory Equity theory is widely studied and quite successful at predicting various situations involving feelings of workplace injustice.[63] However, equity theory isn't so easy to put into practice because it doesn't identify the comparison other and doesn't indicate which inputs or outcomes are most valuable to each employee. The best solution here is for leaders to know their employees well enough to minimize the risk of inequity feelings. Open communication is also a key, enabling employees to let decision makers know when they feel decisions are unfair. A second problem is that equity theory accounts for only some of our feelings of fairness or justice in the workplace. Experts now say procedural justice is at least as important as distributive justice.

Procedural Justice

Recall that *procedural justice* refers to fairness of the procedures used to decide the distribution of resources. How do companies improve procedural justice?[64] A good way to start is by giving employees "voice" in the process; encourage them to present their facts and perspectives on the issue. Voice also provides a "value-expressive" function; employees tend to feel better after having an opportunity to speak their mind. Procedural justice is also higher when the decision maker is perceived as unbiased, relies on complete and accurate information, applies existing policies consistently, and has

listened to all sides of the dispute. If employees still feel unfairness in the allocation of resources, their feelings tend to weaken if the company allows employees to appeal the decision to a higher authority.

Finally, people usually feel less injustice when they are given a full explanation of the decision and their concerns are treated with respect. If employees believe a decision is unfair, refusing to explain how the decision was made could fuel their feelings of inequity. For instance, one study found that nonwhite nurses who experienced racism tended to file grievances only after experiencing disrespectful treatment in their attempt to resolve the racist situation. Another study reported that employees with repetitive strain injuries were more likely to file workers' compensation claims after experiencing disrespectful behavior from management. A third study noted that employees have stronger feelings of injustice when the manager has a reputation of treating people unfairly most of the time.[66]

goal setting The process of motivating employees and clarifying their role perceptions by establishing performance objectives.

Learning Objective

After reading this section, you should be able to

LO6 Describe the characteristics of effective goal setting and feedback.

GOAL SETTING AND FEEDBACK

Walk into almost any customer contact center (i.e., call center)—whether it's Sitel's offices in Albuquerque, New Mexico, or Dell's contact center in Quezon City in the Philippines—and you will notice work activities are dominated by goal setting and plenty of feedback.[67] Contact-center performance is judged on several *key performance indicators (KPIs),* such as average time to answer the call, average handle time, and abandon rates (customers who hang up before the call is handled by a customer service representative). Some contact centers have large electronic boards showing how many customers are waiting, the average time they have been waiting, and the average time before

> ## I was underpaid for the first half of my life. I don't mind being overpaid for the second half.
>
> —Pierre Burton[65]

someone talks to them. A few even have "emotion detection" software, which translates words and voice intonation into a measure of the customer's level of happiness or anger during the telephone conversation.[68]

Goal setting is the process of motivating employees and clarifying their role perceptions by establishing performance objectives. It potentially improves employee performance in two ways: (1) by amplifying the intensity and persistence of effort and (2) by giving employees clearer role perceptions so their effort is channeled toward behaviors that will improve work performance. Goal setting is more complex than simply telling someone to "do your best." It requires several specific characteristics.[69] One popular acronym—SMARTER—captures these characteristics fairly well.[70] Effective goals are specific, measurable, achievable, relevant to the employee's job, set within a time-frame, exciting to create employee commitment, and reviewed both during and after the goal has been accomplished.

> ## SUCCESS IS ACHIEVED BY DEVELOPING OUR STRENGTHS, NOT BY ELIMINATING OUR WEAKNESSES.
>
> —MARILYN VOS SAVANT[74]

Characteristics of Effective Feedback

Feedback—information that lets us know whether we have achieved the goal or are properly directing our effort toward it—is a critical partner in goal setting. Along with clarifying role perceptions and improving employee skills and knowledge, feedback motivates when it is constructive and when employees have strong self-efficacy.[71] Effective feedback has many of the same characteristics as effective goal setting. It should be *specific* and *relevant*, that is, the information should refer to specific metrics (e.g., sales increased by 5 percent last month) and to the individual's behavior or outcomes within his or her control. Feedback should also be *timely*; the information should be available soon after the behavior or results occur so employees see a clear association between their actions and the consequences. Effective feedback is also *credible*. Employees are more likely to accept feedback from trustworthy and credible sources.

The final characteristic of effective feedback is that it should be *sufficiently frequent*. How frequent is "sufficiently"? The answer depends on at least two things. One consideration is the employee's knowledge and experience with the task. Feedback is a form of reinforcement, so employees working on new tasks should receive more frequent feedback because they require more behavior guidance and reinforcement. Employees who perform repetitive or familiar tasks can receive less frequent feedback. The second factor is how long it takes to complete the task. Feedback is necessarily less frequent in jobs with a long cycle time (e.g., executives and scientists) than in jobs with a short cycle time (e.g., grocery store cashiers).

Feedback through Strengths-Based Coaching

Forty years ago, Peter Drucker recognized leaders are more effective when they focus on strengths rather than weaknesses. "The effective executive builds on strengths—their own strengths, the strengths of superiors, colleagues, subordinates; and on the strength of the situation," wrote the late management guru.[72] This is the essence of **strengths-based coaching** (also known as *appreciative coaching*)—maximizing employees' potential by focusing on their strengths rather than weaknesses.[73] In strengths-based coaching, employees describe areas of work where they excel or demonstrate potential. The coach guides this discussion by asking exploratory questions that guide employees to discover ways of leveraging

OB Theory to Practice

The SMARTER Approach to Goal Setting

S—Specific: State what needs to be accomplished; how it should be accomplished; and where, when, and with whom it should be accomplished.

M—Measurable: Describe how much (quantity), how well (quality), and at what cost the goal should be achieved.

A—Achievable: Goals should be challenging without being so difficult that employees lose their motivation to achieve them.

R—Relevant: The goal needs to be relevant to the individual's job and within his or her control.

T—Time-framed: Specify when the goal should be completed or when it will be assessed.

E—Exciting: Support employee commitment (not just compliance) to the goal, such as by linking to the individual's growth needs and through involvement in the goal process.

R—Reviewed: Provide ongoing feedback about goal progress and attainment.

this strength. Situational barriers are identified as well as strategies to overcome those barriers to leveraging the employee's potential.

Strengths-based coaching can potentially motivate employees because they inherently seek feedback about their strengths, not their flaws. Thus, strengths-based feedback is consistent with the process of self-enhancement (see Chapter 3).

Strengths-based coaching also makes sense because personality becomes quite stable by around 30 years of age and this limits the flexibility of the person's interests, preferences, and competencies.[75] In spite of these research observations, most companies focus goal setting and feedback on tasks that employees are performing poorly. After the initial polite compliments, many coaching or performance feedback sessions analyze the employee's weaknesses, including determining what went wrong and what the employee needs to do to improve. These inquisitions sometimes produce so much negative feedback employees become defensive; they can also undermine self-efficacy, thereby making the employee's performance worse rather than better. By focusing on weaknesses, companies fail to realize the full potential of the employee's strengths.

Sources of Feedback

Feedback can originate from nonsocial or social sources. Nonsocial sources provide feedback without someone communicating that information. Employees at contact centers view electronic displays showing how many callers are waiting and the average time they have been waiting. Others receive feedback from a computer screen that monitors in real time the plant's operational capacity. Corporate intranets allow many executives to receive feedback instantaneously on their computer, usually in the form of graphic output on an executive dashboard. Almost half of Microsoft's employees use a dashboard to monitor project deadlines, sales, and other metrics. Microsoft CEO Steve Ballmer regularly reviews dashboard results in one-on-one meetings with his division leaders. "Every time I go to see Ballmer, it's an expectation that I bring my dashboard with me," says the head of the Microsoft Office division.[76]

Some companies set up *multisource (360-degree) feedback* which, as the name implies, is information about an employee's performance collected from a full circle of people, including subordinates, peers, supervisors, and customers. Multisource feedback tends to provide more complete and accurate information than feedback from a supervisor alone. It is particularly useful when the supervisor is unable to observe the employee's behavior or performance throughout the year.[77] However, multisource feedback can be expensive and time-consuming. It also tends to produce ambiguous and conflicting feedback. A third concern is that peers may provide inflated rather than accurate feedback to avoid conflicts during the forthcoming year. A final concern is that employees experience a stronger emotional reaction when they receive critical feedback from many people rather than from just one person (such as the boss).

> "Goal setting is rated by experts as one of the top OB theories in terms of validity and usefulness."

With so many sources of feedback—multisource feedback, executive dashboards, customer surveys, equipment gauges, nonverbal communication from your boss—which one works best under which conditions? The preferred feedback source depends on the purpose of the information. To learn about their progress toward goal accomplishment, employees usually prefer nonsocial feedback sources, such as computer printouts or feedback directly from the job. This is because information from nonsocial sources is considered more accurate than information from social sources. Corrective feedback from nonsocial sources is also less damaging to self-esteem. In contrast, social sources tend to delay negative information, leave some of it out, and distort the bad news in a positive way.[78] When employees want to improve their self-image, they seek out positive feedback from social sources. It feels better to have coworkers say you are performing the job well than to discover this from a computer screen.

Evaluating Goal Setting and Feedback

Goal setting represents one of the "tried-and-true" theories in organizational behavior, so much so it is rated by experts as one of the top OB theories in terms of validity and usefulness.[79] In partnership with goal setting, feedback also has an excellent reputation for improving employee motivation and performance. At the same time, putting goal setting into practice can create problems.[80] One concern is that goal setting tends to focus employees on a narrow subset of measurable performance indicators while ignoring aspects of job performance that are difficult to measure. The saying, "What gets measured, gets done" applies here. A second problem is that when goal achievement is tied to financial rewards, many employees are motivated to set easy goals (while making the boss think they are difficult) so they have a higher probability of the bonus or pay increase. As a former CEO at Ford once quipped: "At Ford, we hire very smart people. They quickly learn how to make relatively easy goals look difficult!"[81] A third problem is that setting performance goals is effective in established jobs but seems to interfere with the learning process in new, complex jobs. Thus, we need to be careful not to apply goal setting where an intense learning process is occurring.

strengths-based coaching A positive organizational behavior approach to coaching and feedback that focuses on building and leveraging the employee's strengths rather than trying to correct his or her weaknesses.

Learning Objective

After reading this section, you should be able to

LO7 List the advantages and disadvantages of job specialization, and describe three ways to improve employee motivation through job design.

JOB DESIGN PRACTICES

How do you build a better job? That question has challenged organizational behavior experts as well as psychologists, engineers, and economists for a few centuries. Some jobs have very few tasks and usually require very little skill. Other jobs are immensely complex and require years of experience and learning to master them. From one extreme to the other, jobs have different effects on work efficiency and employee motivation. The challenge for organizations is to design jobs in which the work is performed efficiently but employees are motivated and engaged.[82] This objective requires careful **job design**—the process of assigning tasks to a job, including the interdependency of those tasks with other jobs. A *job* is a set of tasks performed by one person. To understand this issue more fully, let's begin by describing early job design efforts aimed at increasing work efficiency through job specialization.

Job Design and Work Efficiency

Melody Zou earns close to $600 per month as an accountant for a media company in Shanghai, China, but the novelty of her work wore off after the first six months. "I do the same thing day by day, month by month, year by year," complains Zou.[83] Melody Zhou performs a job with a high degree of **job specialization**. Job specialization occurs when the work required to make a product or service is subdivided into separate jobs assigned to different people. Each resulting job includes a narrow subset of tasks, usually completed in a short cycle time. *Cycle time* is the time required to complete the task before starting over with a new work unit. Melody Zou clearly has a short cycle time, performing the same tasks several times every day, every week, and every month.

Why would companies divide work into tiny bits? The simple answer is that job specialization potentially improves work efficiency. One reason for this higher efficiency is that employees spend less time changing activities because they have fewer tasks to juggle. Even when people can change tasks quickly, their mental attention lingers on the previous task, which slows down performance on the new task.[84] A second reason for increased work efficiency is that specialized jobs require fewer physical and mental skills to accomplish the assigned work, so less time and fewer resources are needed for training. A third reason is that shorter work cycles give employees more frequent practice with the task, so jobs are mastered more quickly. A fourth reason why specialization tends to increase work efficiency is that employees with specific aptitudes or skills can be matched more precisely to the jobs for which they are best suited.[85]

The benefits of job specialization were noted more than 2,300 years ago by the Chinese philosopher Mencius and Greek philosopher Plato. Scottish economist Adam Smith wrote 250 years ago about the advantages of job specialization. Smith described a small factory where 10 pin makers collectively produced as many as 48,000 pins per day because they performed specialized tasks, such as straightening, cutting, sharpening, grinding, and whitening the pins. In contrast, Smith explained that if these 10 people worked alone producing complete pins, they would collectively manufacture no more than 200 pins per day.[86]

> " The challenge for organizations is to design jobs in which the work is performed efficiently but employees are motivated and engaged. "

Scientific Management One of the strongest advocates of job specialization was Frederick Winslow Taylor, an American industrial engineer who introduced the principles of **scientific management** in the early 1900s.[87] Scientific management consists of a toolkit of activities. Some of these interventions—employee selection, training, goal setting, and work incentives—are common today but

job characteristics model A job design model that relates the motivational properties of jobs to specific personal and organizational consequences of those properties.

efficiency of work (i.e., matching skills, faster learning, less switchover time). Yet they didn't seem to notice how extreme job specialization undermines employee motivation. Some jobs are so specialized they soon become tedious, trivial, and socially isolating. Employee turnover and absenteeism tend to be higher in specialized jobs with very short time cycles. Companies sometimes have to pay higher wages to attract job applicants to this dissatisfying, narrowly defined work.[88] Job specialization often reduces work quality because employees see only a small part of the process. As one observer of an automobile assembly line reports: "Often [employees] did not know how their jobs related to the total picture. Not knowing, there was no incentive to strive for quality—what did quality even mean as it related to a bracket whose function you did not understand?"[89]

Equally important, job specialization can undermine the motivational potential of jobs. As work becomes specialized, it tends to become easier to perform but less interesting. Complex jobs tend to be more motivating than are simple jobs, but complex jobs take longer to learn and fewer people are able to master them. Maximum job performance occurs somewhere between these two extremes, where most people can eventually perform the job tasks efficiently yet the work is interesting.

Job Design and Work Motivation

Industrial engineers may have overlooked the motivational effect of job characteristics, but it is now the central focus of many job design changes. Organizational behavior scholar Frederick Herzberg is credited with shifting the spotlight when he introduced **motivator-hygiene theory** in the 1950s.[90] Motivator-hygiene theory proposes that employees experience job satisfaction when they fulfill growth and esteem needs (called *motivators*), and they experience dissatisfaction when they have poor working conditions, job security, and other factors categorized as lower-order needs (called *hygienes*). Herzberg argued that only characteristics of the job itself motivate employees, whereas the hygiene factors merely prevent dissatisfaction. It might seem obvious to us today that the job itself is a source of motivation, but the concept was radical when Herzberg proposed the idea.

Motivator-hygiene theory has been soundly rejected by research studies, but Herzberg's ideas generated new thinking about the motivational potential of the job itself.[91] Out of subsequent research emerged the **job characteristics model**, shown in Exhibit 5.8. The job characteristics model identifies five core job dimensions that produce three psychological states. Employees who experience these psychological states tend to have higher levels of internal work motivation (motivation from the work itself), job satisfaction

were rare until Taylor popularized them. However, scientific management is mainly associated with high levels of job specialization and standardization of tasks to achieve maximum efficiency.

According to Taylor, the most effective companies have detailed procedures and work practices developed by engineers, enforced by supervisors, and executed by employees. Even the supervisor's tasks should be divided: One person manages operational efficiency, another manages inspection, and another is the disciplinarian. Taylor and other industrial engineers demonstrated that scientific management significantly improves work efficiency. No doubt, some of the increased productivity can be credited to the training, goal setting, and work incentives, but job specialization quickly became popular in its own right.

Problems with Job Specialization Frederick Taylor and his contemporaries focused on how job specialization reduces labor "waste" by improving the mechanical

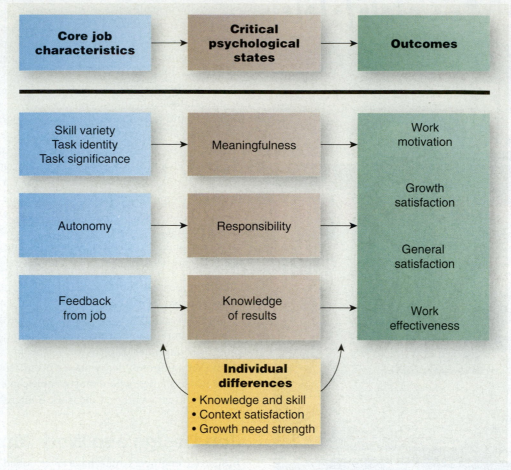

Source: J. R. Hackman and G. Oldham, *Work Redesign* (Reading, MA: Addison-Wesley, 1980), 90. Used with permission.

(particularly satisfaction with the work itself), and work effectiveness.[92]

Core Job Characteristics

The job characteristics model identifies five core job characteristics. Under the right conditions, employees are more motivated and satisfied when jobs have higher levels of these characteristics:

- *Skill variety.* **Skill variety** refers to the use of different skills and talents to complete a variety of work activities. For example, sales clerks who normally only serve customers might be assigned the additional duties of stocking inventory and changing storefront displays.

- *Task identity.* **Task identity** is the degree to which a job requires completion of a whole or identifiable piece of work, such as assembling an entire broadband modem rather than just soldering in the circuitry.

- *Task significance.* **Task significance** is the degree to which the job affects the organization and/or larger society. It is an observable characteristic of the job (you can see how it benefits others) as well as a perceptual awareness.

- *Autonomy.* Jobs with high levels of **autonomy** provide freedom, independence, and discretion in scheduling the work and

Customer Talks Raise Task Significance and Identity

Rolls Royce Engine Services facility in Oakland, California, invited customers to talk to production staff about the importance of their work. These sessions improve task significance because, as one Rolls Royce executive noted, they give "employees with relatively repetitive jobs the sense that they're not just working on a part but rather are key in keeping people safe.[93]

determining the procedures to be used to complete the work. In autonomous jobs, employees make their own decisions rather than relying on detailed instructions from supervisors or procedure manuals.

- *Job feedback.* Job feedback is the degree to which employees can tell how well they are doing on the basis of direct sensory information from the job itself. Airline pilots can tell how well they land their aircraft, and road crews can see how well they have prepared the roadbed and laid the asphalt.

Critical Psychological States

The five core job characteristics affect employee motivation and satisfaction through three critical psychological states, shown in Exhibit 5.8. One of these psychological states is *meaningfulness*—the belief that one's work is worthwhile or important. Skill variety, task identity, and task significance directly contribute to the job's meaningfulness. If the job has high levels of all three characteristics, employees are likely to feel their jobs are highly meaningful. The meaningfulness of a job drops as one or more of these characteristics declines.

Work motivation and performance increase when employees feel personally accountable for the outcomes of their efforts. Autonomy directly contributes to this feeling of *responsibility*. Employees must be assigned control of their work environment to feel responsible for their successes and failures. The third critical psychological state is *knowledge of results*. Employees want information about the consequences of their work effort. Knowledge of results can originate from coworkers, supervisors, or clients. However, job design focuses on knowledge of results from the work itself.

Individual Differences

Job design doesn't increase work motivation for everyone in every situation. Employees must have the required skills and knowledge to master the more challenging work. Otherwise, job design tends to increase stress and reduce job performance. The original model also suggests that increasing the motivational potential of jobs will not motivate employees who are dissatisfied with their work context (e.g., working conditions, job security) or who have a low growth-need strength. However, research findings have been mixed, suggesting employees might be motivated by job design no matter how they feel about their job context or how high or low they score on growth needs.[94]

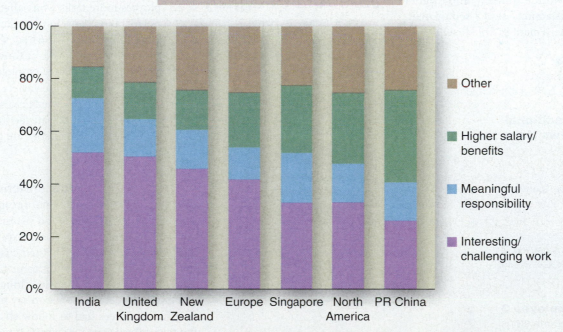

Preference for Enriched Jobs[95]

Percentage of employees in selected countries who identify job enrichment characteristics (meaningful responsibility and interesting/challenging work), higher salary/benefits, or other job features as the job condition that would make them most committed and engaged at work. Based on a sample of 134,000 people in 29 countries. United Kingdom sample is included in the European results as well as separately in this exhibit.

job rotation The practice of moving employees from one job to another.

job enlargement The practice of adding more tasks to an existing job.

job enrichment The practice of giving employees more responsibility for scheduling, coordinating, and planning their own work.

Job Design Practices That Motivate

Three main strategies can increase the motivational potential of jobs: job rotation, job enlargement, and job enrichment. This section also identifies several ways to implement job enrichment.

Job Rotation Most Chrysler assembly-line employees in the United States have a high degree of specialization. According to one estimate, these production workers have an average cycle time of about 65 seconds. Chrysler executives are aware of the motivational and physiological problems this repetitive work can create, so they have introduced **job rotation**, whereby employees work in teams and rotate to a different workstation within that team every few hours. "The whole idea of job rotation makes a big difference," says one Chrysler executive. "The job naturally gets better, quality improves, throughput improves." Chrysler reported significant improvements in productivity and morale within the first year of its job rotation program. Job rotation offers "important ergonomic benefits to workers, improvements in product quality, and higher employee satisfaction," says a senior manager at Chrysler's plant in Toledo, Ohio.[96]

> " *Job rotation minimizes health risks, supports multiskilling, and potentially reduces the boredom of highly repetitive jobs.* "

From the experience at Chrysler and many other companies, we can identify three potential benefits of job rotation. First, it minimizes health risks from repetitive strain and heavy lifting because employees use different muscles and physical positions in the various jobs. Second, it supports multi-skilling (employees learn several jobs), which increases workforce flexibility in staffing the production process and in finding replacements for employees on vacation. Third, it potentially reduces the boredom of highly repetitive jobs. However, organizational behavior experts continue to debate whether job rotation really is a form of job redesign because the jobs remain the same; they are still highly specialized. Critics argue that job redesign requires changes within the job, such as job enlargement.

Job Enlargement **Job enlargement** adds tasks to an existing job. This might involve combining two or more complete jobs into one or just adding one or two more tasks to an existing job. Either way, skill variety increases because there are more tasks to perform. Video journalist is an example of an enlarged job. As Exhibit 5.9 illustrates, a traditional news team consists of a camera operator, a sound and lighting specialist, and the journalist who writes and presents or narrates the story. One video journalist performs all of these tasks.

Job enlargement significantly improves work efficiency and flexibility. However, research suggests that simply giving employees more tasks won't affect motivation, performance, or job satisfaction. These benefits result only when skill variety is combined with more autonomy and job knowledge.[97] In other words, employees are motivated when they perform a variety of tasks *and* have the freedom and knowledge to structure their work to achieve the highest satisfaction and performance. These job characteristics are at the heart of job enrichment.

Job Enrichment **Job enrichment** occurs when employees are given more responsibility for scheduling, coordinating, and planning their own work.[98] For example, American Express and other companies are now allowing their customer service employees to go "off-script," meaning they use their own discretion regarding how long they should spend with a client and what to say to them.[99] Previously, employees had to follow strict statements and take a fixed time for specific types of customer issues. Generally, people in enriched jobs experience higher job satisfaction and work motivation, along with lower absenteeism and turnover.

▼ **EXHIBIT 5.9** Job Enlargement of Video Journalists

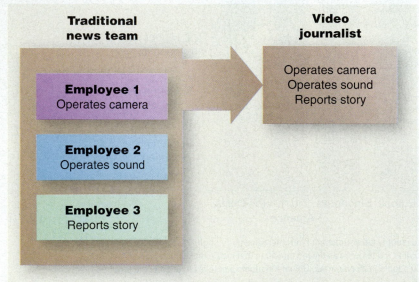

Traditional news team

Employee 1 Operates camera

Employee 2 Operates sound

Employee 3 Reports story

Video journalist

Operates camera Operates sound Reports story

Productivity is also higher when task identity and job feedback are improved. Product and service quality tend to improve because job enrichment increases the jobholder's felt responsibility and sense of ownership over the product or service.[100]

One way to increase job enrichment is to combine highly interdependent tasks into one job. This *natural grouping* approach is reflected in the video journalist job. Video journalist was earlier described as an enlarged job, but it is also an example of job enrichment because it naturally groups tasks together to complete an entire product (i.e., a news story). By forming natural work units, jobholders have stronger feelings of responsibility for an identifiable body of work. They feel a sense of ownership and, therefore, tend to increase job quality. Forming natural work units increases task identity and task significance because employees perform a complete product or service and can more readily see how their work affects others.

A second job enrichment strategy, called *establishing client relationships,* involves putting employees in direct contact with their clients rather than using the supervisor as a go-between. By being directly responsible for specific clients, employees have more information and can make decisions affecting those clients.[101] Establishing client relationships also increases task significance because employees see a line-of-sight connection between their work and consequences for customers. City Telecom in Hong Kong redesigned customer service jobs around customers for this reason. "We introduced a one-stop service for our customers," explains Ellis Ng, City Telecom's head of learning and development. "Each of our staff in the special duty unit (SDU) can handle all inquiries including sales, customer service and simple troubleshooting. They are divided into small working units and serve a set number of customers so they have the chance to build a rapport and create a personalized service."[102] ■

LEARNING OBJECTIVES

After studying Chapter 6, you should be able to:

LO1 Describe the rational choice paradigm of decision making.

LO2 Explain why people differ from the rational choice paradigm when identifying problems/opportunities, evaluating/choosing alternatives, and evaluating decision outcomes.

LO3 Discuss the roles of emotions and intuition in decision making.

LO4 Describe employee characteristics, workplace conditions, and specific activities that support creativity.

LO5 Describe the benefits of employee involvement and identify four contingencies that affect the optimal level of employee involvement.

decision making
and creativity

"My job as CEO is not to make business decisions—it's to push managers to be leaders," says Sergio Marchionne. In reality, the CEO of Fiat S.p.A. and Chrysler Group LLC makes more critical decisions in a week than most of us would make in a year. In "pushing managers to be leaders," Marchionne refers to developing their capacity to become better decision makers. At multiday weekend meetings, junior managers present their business plans to Marchionne and his 23 direct reports, who then vote on them using majority rule. Furthermore, he pushes decision making down the hierarchy, such as having Fiat and Chrysler teams work together to develop and launch new vehicles in record time. Marchionne has also brought in several people to instill more creative decision making, including Chrysler's "Imported

From Detroit" brand revival. "The creativity at Chrysler had been pushed very far underground [by its previous owners]," one auto industry expert observes. "Now Marchionne is bringing it out and he will put his mark on it."[1]

Sergio Marchionne views decision making as a critical management skill. He also recognizes that decision making occurs throughout the organization, which he supports through employee involvement. Furthermore, Chrysler and other organizations depend on creativity in the decision-making process. This chapter examines each of these themes. We begin by outlining the rational choice paradigm of decision making. Next, the limitations of this paradigm are discussed, including the human limitations of rational choice. We also examine the emerging paradigm that decisions

continued on p. 112

decision making
The conscious process of making choices among alternatives with the intention of moving toward some desired state of affairs.

rational choice paradigm The view in decision making that people should—and typically do—use logic and all available information to choose the alternative with the highest value.

subjective expected utility The probability (expectation) of satisfaction (utility) resulting from choosing a specific alternative in a decision.

continued from p. 111

consist of a complex interaction of logic and emotion. The latter part of this chapter focuses on creativity and employee involvement. We present these topics separately rather than within any stage of decision making because they deserve more detailed inspection and, in the case of creativity, because it occurs throughout the decision making process. ■

Learning Objective

After reading this section, you should be able to

LO1 Describe the rational choice paradigm of decision making.

RATIONAL CHOICE PARADIGM OF DECISION MAKING

Decision making is the process of making choices among alternatives with the intention of moving toward some desired state of affairs.[2] This is vital to an organization's health, rather like breathing is to a human being. Indeed, turnaround experts such as Sergio Marchionne sometimes see themselves as physicians who resuscitate organizations by encouraging and teaching employees at all levels to make decisions more quickly, effectively, and with more creative foundation. All businesses, governments, and not-for-profit agencies depend on employees to foresee and correctly identify problems, to survey alternatives and pick the best one based on a variety of stakeholder interests, and to execute those decisions effectively.

How should people make decisions in organizations? Most business leaders would likely answer this question by saying that effective decision making involves identifying, selecting, and applying the best possible alternative. In other words, the best decisions use pure logic and all available information to choose the alternative with the highest value—such as highest expected profitability, customer satisfaction, employee well-being, or some combination of these outcomes. These decisions sometimes involve complex calculations of data to produce a formula that points to the best choice.

In its extreme form, this calculative view of decision making represents the **rational choice paradigm**, which has dominated decision making philosophy in Western societies for most of written history.[3] It was established 2,500 years ago when Plato and his contemporaries in ancient Greece raised logical debate and reasoning to a fine art. About 400 years ago, Descartes and other European philosophers emphasized that the ability to make logical decisions is one of the most important accomplishments of human beings. In the 1700s, Scottish philosophers refined the notion that the best choice is the one that offers the greatest satisfaction or "utility."

The rational choice paradigm selects the choice with the highest utility through the calculation of **subjective expected utility**.[4] Subjective expected utility is the probability (expectancy) of satisfaction (utility) for each alternative. Suppose you want to select the best supplier of raw materials from among several vendors. Rationally, you would choose the supplier that will produce the highest overall satisfaction ("utility") for your company. That expected satisfaction depends on the expected satisfaction (utility) of each outcome as well as the probability ("expected" in subjective expected utility) that each supplier will provide that outcome. One outcome might be the timely delivery of raw materials. You might estimate that one supplier will consistently deliver the product on time whereas other

suppliers have lower probabilities of timely delivery. Another outcome might be the quality of raw materials. Again, you might estimate that the suppliers differ in their likelihood of maintaining high quality materials. Put these probabilities together across several outcomes and you can figure out which supplier has the highest overall subjective expected utility. The key point from this example is that all decisions rely to some degree on (a) the expected value of the outcomes (utility) and (b) the probability of those good or bad outcomes occurring (expectancy).

Rational Choice Decision-Making Process

Along with the principle of making decisions based on subjective expected utility, the rational choice paradigm assumes that decision makers follow the systematic process illustrated in Exhibit 6.1.[5] The first step is to identify the problem or recognize an opportunity. A *problem* is a deviation between the current and the desired situation—the gap between "what is" and "what ought to be." This deviation is a symptom of more fundamental causes that need to be corrected.[6] The "ought to be" refers to goals, and these goals later help to evaluate the selected choice. For instance, if the goal is to answer incoming client calls within 30 seconds, the problem is the gap between that goal and the actual time the call center takes to answer most client calls. An *opportunity* is a deviation between current expectations and a potentially better situation that was not previously expected. In other words,

> The rational choice paradigm assumes (incorrectly) that people are efficient and logical information-processing machines.

decision makers realize that some decisions may produce results beyond current goals or expectations.

The second step involves choosing the best decision process. This step is really a meta-decision—deciding how to decide—because it refers to choosing among the different approaches and processes to make the decision.[7] One meta-decision is whether to solve the problem alone or involve others in the process. Later in this chapter, we'll examine the contingencies of employee involvement in the decision. Another meta-decision is whether to assume the decision is programmed or nonprogrammed. *Programmed decisions* follow standard operating procedures; they have been resolved in the past, so the optimal solution has already been identified and documented. In contrast, *nonprogrammed decisions* require all steps in the decision process because the problems are new, complex, or ill-defined.

The third step in the rational choice decision process is to identify and/or develop a list of possible choices. This usually begins by searching for ready-made solutions, such as practices that have worked well on similar problems. If an acceptable solution cannot be found, then decision makers need to design a custom-made solution or modify an existing one. The fourth step is to select the choice with the highest subjective expected utility. This calls for all possible information about all possible alternatives and their outcomes, but the rational choice paradigm assumes this can be accomplished with ease.

The fifth step in the rational choice decision process is to implement the selected alternative. Rational choice experts have little to say about this step because they assume implementation occurs without any problems. This is followed by the sixth step, evaluating whether the gap has narrowed between "what is" and "what ought to be." Ideally, this information should come from systematic benchmarks so that relevant feedback is objective and easily observed.

Problems with the Rational Choice Paradigm

The rational choice paradigm seems so logical, yet it is impossible to apply in reality. One reason is that the model assumes people are efficient and logical information-processing machines. In reality, people have difficulty recognizing problems; they cannot (or will not) simultaneously process the huge volume of information needed to identify the best solution; and they have difficulty recognizing when their choices have failed. The second reason why the rational model doesn't fit reality is that it focuses on logical thinking and completely ignores the fact that emotions also influence—perhaps even dominate—the decision-making process. As we shall discover

▼ **EXHIBIT 6.1** Rational Choice Decision-Making Process

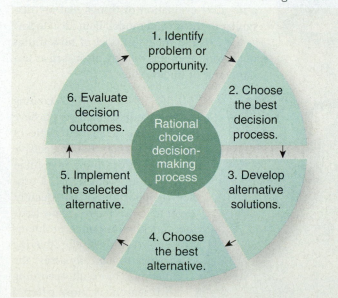

Rational choice decision-making process

1. Identify problem or opportunity.
2. Choose the best decision process.
3. Develop alternative solutions.
4. Choose the best alternative.
5. Implement the selected alternative.
6. Evaluate decision outcomes.

in this chapter, emotions both support and interfere with our quest to make better decisions.[8] With these points in mind, let's look again at each step in the rational choice decision-making process, but with more detail about what really happens.

Learning Objectives

After reading this section, you should be able to

LO2 Explain why people differ from the rational choice paradigm when identifying problems/opportunities, evaluating/choosing alternatives, and evaluating decision outcomes.

IDENTIFYING PROBLEMS AND OPPORTUNITIES

When Albert Einstein was asked how he would save the world in one hour, he replied that the first 55 minutes should be spent defining the problem and the last 5 minutes solving it.[9] Einstein's point is that problem identification is not just the first step in decision making; it is arguably the most important step. But problems and opportunities are not clearly labeled objects that appear on our desks. Instead, they are conclusions we form from ambiguous and conflicting information.[10]

Problems with Problem Identification

The problem identification stage is, itself, filled with problems. Here are five of the most widely recognized concerns.[11]

Mental Model Myopia of Hogwarts

Even though Harry Potter books were becoming the world's best-sellers, Hollywood filmmakers were reluctant to produce film versions unless the Hogwarts School of Witchcraft was set in the United States or, at least, that Harry was an American at the British academy. Some Hollywood decision makers insisted that all the main characters had to be Americans for the films to become blockbusters. Fortunately, after considerable persuasion by the British author's representatives, Hollywood reluctantly agreed to keep the location and characters all British. The result was the most successful film series in history![12]

Stakeholder Framing Employees, suppliers, customers, and other stakeholders have vested interests when bringing good or bad news to corporate decision makers. Whether deliberately or unwittingly, stakeholders filter information to amplify or suppress the seriousness of the situation, which highlights or hides specific problems and opportunities. Employees point to external factors rather than their own faults as the cause of production delays. Suppliers warn that problems will occur (or opportunities lost) if the decision maker does not buy their product or service. Stakeholder framing sometimes occurs by emphasizing or withholding information. Occasionally, stakeholders offer a concise statement of the problem in the hope the decision maker will accept their verdict without further analysis.

Decision makers easily fall prey to these constructed realities because they have a need to simplify the overwhelming volume of complex and often ambiguous information in the external environment. Consequently, as one popular management theory emphasizes, organizational decisions and actions are influenced mainly by what attracts management's attention, rather than by what is truly important.[13] This attention process is subject to a variety of cognitive biases, such as the decision maker's perceptual process, specific circumstances, and (as mentioned) the ways that stakeholders shape or filter incoming information.

Mental Models Even if stakeholders don't frame information, our mind creates its own framing through preconceived mental models. Mental models are visual or relational images in our mind of the external world; they fill in information that we don't immediately see, which helps us understand and navigate our surrounding environment (see Chapter 3). Many mental images are also prototypes—they represent models of how things should be. Unfortunately, these mental models also blind us from seeing unique problems or opportunities because they produce a negative evaluation of things that are dissimilar to the mental model. If an idea doesn't fit the existing mental model of how things should work, then it is quickly dismissed as unworkable or undesirable.

Decisive Leadership According to various studies, employees believe decisiveness is a characteristic of effective leaders.[14] Being decisive includes quickly forming an opinion of whether an event signals a problem or opportunity. Consequently, eager to look effective, many leaders quickly announce problems or opportunities before having a chance to logically assess the situation. The result, according to research, is more often a

> # WHEN THE ONLY TOOL YOU HAVE IS A HAMMER, ALL PROBLEMS BEGIN TO RESEMBLE NAILS.[15]
>
> —ABRAHAM MASLOW

poorer decision than would result if more time had been devoted to identifying the problem and evaluating the alternatives.

Solution-Focused Problems Decision makers tend to define problems as veiled solutions.[16] For instance, someone might say, "The problem is that we need more control over our suppliers." This statement doesn't describe the problem; it is really a slightly rephrased presentation of a solution to an ill-defined problem. Decision makers engage in solution-focused problem identification because it provides comforting closure to the otherwise ambiguous and uncertain nature of problems. People with a strong need for cognitive closure (those who feel uncomfortable with ambiguity) are particularly prone to solution-focused problems.

Perceptual Defense People sometimes block out bad news as a coping mechanism. Their brain refuses to see information that threatens their self-concept. This phenomenon is not true for everyone. Some people inherently avoid negative information, whereas others are more sensitive to it. Recent studies also report that people are more likely to disregard danger signals when they have limited control over the situation.[17]

Identifying Problems and Opportunities More Effectively

Recognizing problems and opportunities will always be a challenge, but one way to improve the process is to become aware of the five problem identification biases described above. For example, by recognizing that mental models restrict a person's perspective of the world, decision makers are more motivated to consider other perspectives of reality. Along with increasing their awareness of problem identification flaws, leaders require considerable willpower to resist the temptation of looking decisive when a more thoughtful examination of the situation should occur.

A third way to improve problem identification is for leaders to create a norm of "divine discontent." They are never satisfied with the status quo, and this aversion to complacency creates a mindset that more actively searches for problems and opportunities.[18] Finally, employees can minimize problem identification errors by discussing the situation with colleagues. It is much easier to discover blind spots in problem identification when listening to how others perceive the situation. Opportunities also become apparent when outsiders explore this information from their different mental models.

SEARCHING FOR, EVALUATING, AND CHOOSING ALTERNATIVES

According to the rational choice paradigm of decision making, people rely on logic to evaluate and choose alternatives. This paradigm assumes that decision makers have well-articulated and agreed-on organizational goals, that they efficiently and simultaneously process facts about all alternatives and the consequences of those alternatives, and that they choose the alternative with the highest payoff.

Nobel Prize–winning organizational scholar Herbert Simon questioned these assumptions a half century ago. He argued that people engage in **bounded rationality** because they process limited and imperfect information and rarely select the best choice.[19] Simon and other OB experts demonstrated that how people evaluate and choose alternatives differs from the rational choice paradigm in several ways, as illustrated in Exhibit 6.2. These differences are so significant that many economists are now shifting from rational choice to bounded rationality assumptions in their theories. Let's look at these differences in terms of goals, information processing, and maximization.

OB Theory to Practice

Identifying Problems and Opportunities More Effectively

- Be aware of the problem identification biases.
- Resist the temptation to look decisive.
- Have an aversion to complacency (practice divine discontent).
- Discuss the situation with others.

▼ EXHIBIT 6.2 Rational Choice Assumptions versus Organizational Behavior Findings about Choosing Alternatives

Rational choice paradigm assumptions	Observations from organizational behavior
Goals are clear, compatible, and agreed upon.	Goals are ambiguous, are in conflict, and lack full support.
Decision makers can calculate all alternatives and their outcomes.	Decision makers have limited information-processing abilities.
Decision makers evaluate all alternatives simultaneously.	Decision makers evaluate alternatives sequentially.
Decision makers use absolute standards to evaluate alternatives.	Decision makers evaluate alternatives against an implicit favorite.
Decision makers use factual information to choose alternatives.	Decision makers process perceptually distorted information.
Decision makers choose the alternative with the highest payoff.	Decision makers choose the alternative that is good enough (satisficing).

Problems with Goals

The rational choice paradigm assumes that organizational goals are clear and agreed-on. In fact, these conditions are necessary to identify "what ought to be" and, therefore, provide a standard against which each alternative is evaluated. Unfortunately, organizational goals are often ambiguous or in conflict with each other.

Problems with Information Processing

The rational choice paradigm also makes several assumptions about the human capacity to process information. It assumes that decision makers can process information about all alternatives and their consequences, whereas this is not possible in reality. Instead, people evaluate only a few alternatives and only

some of the main outcomes of those alternatives.[20] For example, there may be dozens of computer brands to choose from and dozens of features to consider, yet people typically evaluate only a few brands and a few features.

A related problem is that decision makers typically evaluate alternatives sequentially rather than all at the same time. This sequential evaluation occurs partly because all alternatives are

> **Problems are so complex that you have to be highly intelligent and well-informed just to be undecided about them.**
>
> —Laurence J. Peter

not usually available to the decision maker at the same time.[21] Consequently, as a new alternative comes along, it is immediately compared to an **implicit favorite**—an alternative that the decision maker prefers and that is used as a comparison with other choices. When choosing a new computer system, for example, people typically have an implicit favorite brand or model in their heads that they use to compare with the others. This sequential process of comparing alternatives with an implicit

implicit favorite A preferred alternative that the decision maker uses repeatedly as a comparison with other choices.

anchoring and adjustment heuristic A natural tendency for people to be influenced by an initial anchor point such that they do not sufficiently move away from that point as new information is provided.

availability heuristic A natural tendency to assign higher probabilities to objects or events that are easier to recall from memory, even though ease of recall is also affected by nonprobability factors (e.g., emotional response, recent events).

representativeness heuristic A natural tendency to evaluate probabilities of events or objects by the degree to which they resemble (are representative of) other events or objects rather than on objective probability information.

satisficing Selecting an alternative that is satisfactory or "good enough," rather than the alternative with the highest value (maximization).

favorite occurs even when decision makers aren't consciously aware they are doing this.[22]

Although the implicit favorite comparison process seems to be hardwired in human decision making (i.e., we naturally compare things), it often undermines effective decision making because people distort information to favor their implicit favorite over the alternative choices. They tend to ignore limitations of the implicit favorite and advantages of the alternative. Decision makers also overweight factors on which the implicit favorite is better and underweight areas in which the alternative is superior.[23]

Biased Decision Heuristics Subjective expected utility is the cornerstone of rational choice decision making, yet psychologists Amos Tversky and Daniel Kahneman discovered that human beings have built-in *decision heuristics* that automatically distort either the probability of outcomes or the value of those outcomes. Three of the most widely studied heuristic biases are anchoring and adjustment, availability, and representativeness:[24]

- **Anchoring and adjustment heuristic**. This heuristic states that we are influenced by an initial anchor point and do not sufficiently move away from that point as new information is provided.[25] The anchor point might be an initial offer price, someone's initial opinion, or initial estimated probability that something will occur. This bias affects the value we assign to choices and their outcomes. For example, suppose you ask

someone whether the population of Chile is above or below 50 million, then you ask that person to estimate Chile's population. Next, you ask a second person whether the population of Chile is above or below 10 million, then you ask him or her to estimate that country's actual population. If these two people don't actually know Chile's population, chances are that the first person will give a much higher population estimate than will the second person. The initial anchor point (50 million versus 10 million) biases their estimate.

- **Availability heuristic**. The availability heuristic is the tendency to estimate the probability of something occurring by how easily we can recall that event. Unfortunately, how easily we recall something is due to more than just its frequency (probability).[26] For instance, we easily remember emotional events (such as earthquakes and shark attacks), so we overestimate how often these traumatic events occur. We also have an easier time recalling recent events. If the media report several incidents of air pollution, we likely give more pessimistic estimates of air quality generally than if there have been no recent reports.

- **Representativeness heuristic**. This heuristic states that we pay more attention to whether something resembles (is representative of) something else than on more precise statistics about its probability.[27] Suppose that one-fifth of the students in your class are in engineering and the others are business majors. Statistically, there is a 20 percent chance that any individual in that class is an engineering student. Yet, if one student looks and acts like a stereotype of an engineer, we tend to believe the person is an engineer even though there is much stronger and more reliable statistical evidence that he or she is a business major. Another form of the representativeness heuristic, known as the *clustering illusion,* is the tendency to see patterns from a small sample of events when those events are, in fact, random. For example, most players and coaches believe that players are more likely to have a successful shot on the net when their previous two or three shots have been successful. The representativeness heuristic is at work here because players and coaches believe these sequences are causally connected (representative) when, in reality, they are more likely random events.

Problems with Maximization

One of the main assumptions of the rational choice paradigm is that people want to—and are able to—choose the alternative with the highest payoff (i.e., the highest "utility" in subjective expected utility). Yet rather than aiming for maximization, people engage in **satisficing**—they choose an alternative that

intuition The ability to know when a problem or opportunity exists and to select the best course of action without conscious reasoning.

is satisfactory or "good enough."[28] People satisfice when they select the first alternative that exceeds a standard of acceptance for their needs and preferences. Satisficing partly occurs because alternatives present themselves over time, not all at once. Consider the process of hiring new employees. It is impossible to choose the best possible job candidate because people apply over a period of time and the best candidate might not apply until next month, after earlier candidates have found other jobs. Consequently, as we mentioned earlier, decision makers rely on sequential evaluation of new alternatives against an implicit favorite. This necessarily calls for a satisficing decision rule—choose the first alternative that is "good enough."

A second reason why people engage in satisficing rather than maximization is that they lack the capacity and motivation to process the huge volume of information required to identify the best choice. Studies report that people like to have choices, but making decisions when there are many

> When presented with a large number of choices, people often choose the least cognitively challenging alternative—they don't make any decision at all!

alternatives can be cognitively and emotionally draining. Consequently, when exposed to many alternatives, decision makers become cognitive misers by engaging in satisficing.[30] They also discard many of those alternatives by using easily identifiable factors (i.e., color, size) and by evaluating alternatives using only a handful of criteria.

When presented with a large number of choices, people often choose a decision strategy that is even less cognitively challenging than satisficing; they don't make any decision at all! One study reported that many employees put off registering for the company's pension plan when they face dozens of investment options, even though signing up would give them tax benefits, company contributions to that plan, and long-term financial security. The company pension plan registration rate increases dramatically when employees are given only two or three initial investment options, such as a growth fund, balanced fund, and capital stable investment. The dozens of other investment choices are then presented after the employee has signed up.[31]

Too Many Choices

People avoid making choices in decisions that have too many alternatives. In one study, grocery store customers saw one of two jam-tasting booths. Thirty percent of consumers who visited the booth displaying 6 types of jam purchased one of those products. In contrast, only 3 percent of customers who saw the booth displaying 24 types of jam made a purchase. The larger number of choices discouraged them from making any decision. Other studies of decisions about chocolates, term essays, and pension plan investment options revealed similar results.[29]

Evaluating Opportunities

Opportunities are just as important as problems, but what happens when an opportunity is "discovered" is quite different from the process of problem solving. Research suggests that decision makers do not evaluate several alternatives when they find an opportunity; after all, the opportunity *is* the solution, so why look for others! An opportunity is usually experienced as an exciting and rare revelation, so decision makers tend to have an emotional attachment to the opportunity. Unfortunately, this emotional preference motivates decision makers to apply the opportunity and short-circuit any detailed evaluation of it.[32]

Learning Objectives

After reading this section, you should be able to

LO3 Discuss the roles of emotions and intuition in decision making.

Emotions and Making Choices

Herbert Simon and many other experts have found that people do not evaluate alternatives nearly as well as is assumed by the rational choice paradigm. However, they neglected to mention another glaring weakness with rational choice: It completely ignores the effect of emotions in human decision making. Just as both the rational and emotional brain centers alert us to problems, they also influence our choice of alternatives.[33] Emotions affect the evaluation of alternatives in three ways.

Emotions Form Early Preferences The emotional marker process described in previous chapters (Chapters 3 through 5) shapes our preferences for each alternative before we consciously evaluate those alternatives. Our brain very quickly attaches specific emotions to information about each alternative, and our preferred alternative is strongly influenced by those initial emotional markers.[34] Of course, logical analysis also influences which alternative we choose, but it requires strong logical evidence to change our initial preferences (initial emotional markers). Yet even logical analysis depends on emotions to sway our decision. Specifically, neuroscientific evidence says that information produced from logical analysis is tagged with emotional markers that then motivate us to choose or avoid a particular alternative. Ultimately, emotions, not rational logic, energize us to make the preferred choice. In fact, people with damaged emotional brain centers have difficulty making choices.

Emotions Change the Decision Evaluation Process Moods and specific emotions influence the *process* of evaluating alternatives.[35] For instance, we pay more attention to details when in a negative mood, possibly because a negative mood signals there is something wrong that requires attention. When in a positive mood, on the other hand, we pay less attention to details and rely on a more programmed decision routine. This phenomenon explains why executive teams in successful companies are often less vigilant about competitors and other environmental threats.[36] Research also suggests that decision makers rely on stereotypes and other shortcuts to speed up the choice process when they experience anger. Anger also makes them more optimistic about the success of risky alternatives, whereas the emotion of fear tends to make them less optimistic. Overall, emotions shape *how* we evaluate information, not just which choice we select.

Emotions Serve as Information When We Evaluate Alternatives The third way that emotions influence the evaluation of alternatives is through a process called "emotions as information." Marketing experts have found that we listen in on our emotions to gain guidance when making choices.[37] This process is similar to having a temporary improvement in emotional intelligence. Most emotional experiences remain below the level of conscious awareness, but people actively try to be more sensitive to these subtle emotions when making a decision.

When buying a new car, for example, you not only logically evaluate each vehicle's features; you also try to gauge your emotions when visualizing what it would be like to own each of the cars on your list of choices. Even if you have solid information about the quality of each vehicle on key features (purchase price, fuel efficiency, maintenance costs, resale value, etc.), you are swayed by your emotional reaction and actively try to sense that emotional response when thinking about

> "All gut feelings are emotional signals, but not all emotional signals are intuition."

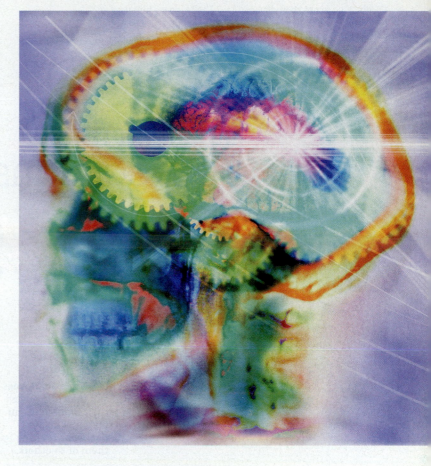

it. Some people pay more attention to these gut feelings, and personality tests such as the Myers-Briggs Type Indicator (see Chapter 2) identify individuals who listen in on their emotions more than others.[38] But everyone consciously pays attention to their emotions to some degree when choosing alternatives. This phenomenon ties directly into our next topic, intuition.

Intuition and Making Choices

Do you have a gut instinct—a feeling inside—when something isn't quite right? Or perhaps a different emotional experience occurs when you sense an opportunity in front of your eyes? These emotional experiences potentially (but not necessarily) indicate your **intuition**—the ability to know when a problem or opportunity exists and to select the best course of action without conscious reasoning.[39] Intuition is both an emotional experience and a rapid nonconscious analytic process. As mentioned in the previous section, the gut feelings we experience are emotional signals that have enough intensity to make us consciously aware of them. These signals warn us of impending danger or motivate us to take advantage of an opportunity. Some intuition also directs us to preferred choices relative to other alternatives in the situation.

Using Intuition to Make People Decisions[40]

39%
of British line managers surveyed say they rely on gut instinct as one of the most important factors when making any decisions about their people.

45%
of British employees say they don't trust their manager's gut instincts on staff decisions relating to them or to others.

All gut feelings are emotional signals, but not all emotional signals are intuition. The main distinction is that intuition involves rapidly comparing our observations with deeply held patterns learned through experience.[41] These "templates of the mind" represent tacit knowledge that has been implicitly acquired over time. They are mental models that help us to understand whether the current situation is good or bad, depending on how well that situation fits our mental model. When a template fits or doesn't fit the current situation, emotions are produced that motivate us to act. Studies have found that chess masters experience emotional signals when they see an opportunity through quick observation of a chessboard. They can't immediately analyze why this opportunity exists, but they can do so when given time to think about the situation. Their intuition signals the opportunity long before this rational analysis takes place.

As mentioned, some emotional signals are not intuition, so gut feelings shouldn't always guide our decisions. The problem is that emotional responses are not always based on well-grounded mental models. Instead, we sometimes compare the current situation to more remote templates, which may or may not be relevant. A new employee might feel confident about relations with a supplier, whereas an experienced employee senses potential problems. The difference is the new employee relies on templates from other experiences or industries that might not work well in this situation. Thus, the extent to which our gut feelings in a situation represent intuition depends on our level of experience in that situation.

So far, we have described intuition as an emotional experience (gut feeling) and a process in which we compare the current situation with well-established templates of the mind. Intuition also relies on *action scripts*—programmed decision routines that speed up our response to pattern matches or mismatches.[42] Action scripts effectively shorten the decision-making process by jumping from problem identification to selection of a solution. In other words, action scripting is a form of programmed decision making. Action scripts are generic, so we need to consciously adapt them to the specific situation.

Making Choices More Effectively

It is very difficult to get around the human limitations of making choices, but a few strategies help to minimize these concerns. One important discovery is that decisions tend to have a higher failure rate when leaders are decisive rather than contemplative about the available options. Of course, decisions can also be ineffective when leaders take too long to make a choice, but research indicates that a lack of logical evaluation of alternatives is a greater concern. By systematically assessing alternatives against relevant factors, decision makers minimize the implicit favorite and satisficing problems that occur when they rely on general subjective judgments. This recommendation does not suggest that we ignore intuition; rather, it suggests that we use it in combination with careful analysis of relevant information.[43]

A second piece of advice is to remember that decisions are influenced by both rational and emotional processes. With this point in mind, some decision makers deliberately revisit important issues later so they look at the information in different moods and have allowed their initial emotions to subside. For example, if you sense your team is feeling somewhat too self-confident when making an important competitive decision, you might decide to have the team members revisit the decision a few days later when they are thinking more critically. Another strategy is **scenario planning**, which is a disciplined method for imagining possible futures. It typically involves thinking about what would happen if a significant environmental

OB Theory to Practice

Making Choices More Effectively
- Be more contemplative than decisive for complex problems.
- Balance intuition with logical analysis.
- Practice scenario planning.

condition changed and what the organization should do to anticipate and react to such an outcome.[44] Scenario planning is a useful vehicle for choosing the best solutions under possible scenarios long before they occur because alternative courses of action are evaluated without the pressure and emotions that occur during real emergencies.

IMPLEMENTING DECISIONS

Implementing decisions is often skipped over in most writing about the decision-making process. Yet leading business writers emphasize that execution—translating decisions into action—is one of the most important and challenging tasks of leaders. "When assessing candidates, the first thing I looked for was energy and enthusiasm for execution," says Larry Bossidy, the former CEO of Honeywell and Allied Signal.[45]

EVALUATING DECISION OUTCOMES

Contrary to the rational choice paradigm, decision makers aren't completely honest with themselves when evaluating the effectiveness of their decisions. One problem is *confirmation bias* (also known as *post-decisional justification* in the context of decision evaluation), which is the "unwitting selectivity in the acquisition and use of evidence."[46] When evaluating decisions, people with confirmation bias ignore or downplay the negative features of the selected alternative and overemphasize its positive features. Confirmation bias gives people an excessively optimistic evaluation of their decisions, but only until they receive very clear and undeniable information to the contrary. Unfortunately, it also inflates the decision maker's initial evaluation of the decision, so reality often comes as a painful shock when objective feedback is finally received.

Escalation of Commitment

Another reason why decision makers don't evaluate their decisions very well is due to **escalation of commitment**— the tendency to repeat an apparently bad decision or allocate more resources to a failing course of action.[47] Why are decision makers led deeper and deeper into failing projects? Several explanations have been identified and discussed over the years, but the four main influences are self-justification, self-enhancement effect, prospect theory effect, and closing costs.

Self-Justification Decision makers typically want to appear rational and

effective. One such impression-management tactic is to demonstrate the importance of a decision by continuing to invest in it, whereas pulling the plug symbolizes the project's failure and the decision maker's incompetence. This self-justification effect is particularly evident when decision makers are personally identified with the project, have staked their reputations to some extent on the project's success, and have low self-esteem.[48]

Self-Enhancement Effect People have a natural tendency to feel good about themselves—to feel luckier, more competent, and more successful than average—regarding things that are important to them (see Chapter 3).[49] This self-enhancement

Classics in Escalation of Commitment[50]

- When proposed in 1997, Scotland's new parliament building had an estimated cost of £50 million. The project was completed in 2006, four years behind schedule and at a cost of more than £400 million.

- Planning for the Sydney Opera House began in the 1950s with a projected cost of AUD$7 million. The final scaled-down version of the building that everyone sees today cost ten times more than originally proposed, took 17 years to complete, and has never functioned well for its intended purpose. Fortunately, it has become a priceless iconic structure for Sydney and Australia.

- In the early 1980s, the London Stock Exchange formed a project team called Taurus to build an information technology system that would replace paper-based stock settlement. The original budget of £6 million blew out to more than £400 million before the project was abandoned in 1993.

- In the mid-1990s, executives at health boards across Ireland funded a common payroll system with an estimated cost of US$12 million. The project was officially axed in 2007 with losses somewhere between $250 and $350 million.

- Denver's International Airport was supposed to include a state-of-the-art automated baggage-handling system. Instead, the project was eventually abandoned in the mid-1990s, causing the airport to open 16 months late and $2 billion over budget.

maintains a positive self-concept, but it also increases the risk of escalation of commitment. When presented with evidence that a project is in trouble, the self-enhancement process biases our interpretation of the information as a deviation from an otherwise positive trend line. And when we eventually realize the project isn't going as well as planned, our better-than-average overly-optimistic self-view motivates us to invest more in rather than pull the plug on the project. Self-justification and self-enhancement often occur together, but they are different mechanisms. Self-justification is a deliberate attempt to act consistently and demonstrate support for a project, whereas self-enhancement operates mostly nonconsciously, biasing our probabilities of success and distorting information so we do not recognize the problem sooner.[51]

Prospect Theory Effect

Prospect theory effect is the tendency to experience stronger negative emotions when losing something of value than the positive emotions when gaining something of equal value. This prospect theory effect motivates us to avoid losses, which typically occurs by investing more in that losing project. Stopping a project is a certain loss, which is more painful to most people than the uncertainty of success associated with continuing to fund the project. Given the choice, decision makers choose escalation of commitment, which is the less painful option at the time.[52]

Closing Costs

Another disincentive to axing a failing project is the cost of doing so. Terminating a project may have financial penalties and loss of goodwill with partner organizations. Closing costs are particularly important in political situations because closing the project is acknowledgement that the decision makers made a grave mistake in their previous decisions.

Escalation of commitment is usually framed as poor decision making, but some experts argue that throwing more money into a failing project is sometimes a logical attempt to further understand an ambiguous situation. This strategy is essentially a variation of testing unknown waters. By adding more resources, the decision maker gains new information about the effectiveness of these funds, which provides more feedback about the project's future success. This strategy is particularly common where the project has high closing costs.[53]

Evaluating Decision Outcomes More Effectively

One of the most effective ways to minimize escalation of commitment and confirmation bias is to ensure that the people who made the original decision are not the same people who later evaluate that decision. This separation of roles minimizes the self-justification effect because the person responsible for evaluating the decision is not connected to the original decision. However, the second person might continue to escalate the

OB Theory to Practice

Evaluating Decision Outcomes More Effectively

- Those who evaluate the success of a decision should be different from those who made the decision.
- Publicly establish a preset level at which the decision is abandoned or reevaluated.
- Seek out sources of systematic and clear feedback for the decision's outcomes.
- Involve several people in the decision evaluation process.

project if he or she empathizes with the decision maker, has a similar mindset, or has similar attributes such as age. A second strategy is to publicly establish a preset level at which the decision is abandoned or reevaluated. This is similar to a stop-loss order in the stock market, whereby the stock is sold if it falls below a certain price. The problem with this solution is that conditions are often so complex it is difficult to identify an appropriate point to abandon a project.[54]

A third strategy is to find a source of systematic and clear feedback.[55] At some point, even the strongest escalation and confirmation bias effects deflate when the evidence highlights the project's failings. A fourth strategy to improve the decision evaluation process is to involve several people in the evaluation. Coworkers continuously monitor each other and might notice problems sooner than someone working alone on the project.

Learning Objective

After reading this section, you should be able to

LO4 Describe employee characteristics, workplace conditions, and specific activities that support creativity.

CREATIVITY

The entire decision-making process described over the preceding pages depends on **creativity**—the development of original ideas that make a socially recognized contribution.[56] Creativity is at work when imagining opportunities, such as how a company's expertise might be redirected to untapped markets. Creativity is present when developing alternatives, such as figuring out new places to look for existing solutions or working out the design of a custom-made solution. Creativity also helps us choose alternatives because we need to visualize the future in different ways and to figure out how each choice might be useful or a liability in those scenarios. In short, creativity is an essential component of decision making as well as a powerful resource for an organization's effectiveness and an individual's career development.

The value of creativity in decision making is evident at Google, the Internet search engine company. Google's creative culture includes a natural practice of experimenting with ideas and seeking out different uses of technology. Perhaps most famous is the company's policy of giving engineers 20 percent of their time to develop projects of their choosing. "Almost everything that is interesting which Google does started out as a 20 percent time idea," explains a Google executive. Google News and the photos linked to Google Maps were two projects developed from the 20 percent time rule.[57]

The Creative Process

How does creativity occur? That question has puzzled experts for hundreds of years and has been the fascination of Einstein, Poincaré, and many other scientists who have reflected on the creative experience that contributed to their own important discoveries. More than a century ago, German physicist Hermann von Helmholtz gave a public talk in which he described the process that led to his many innovations (energy physics, instruments for examining eyes, and many others). A few decades later, London School of Economics professor Graham Wallas built on Helmholtz's ideas to construct the four-stage model shown in Exhibit 6.3.[58] This remains the most reputable and influential model nearly a century later.

The first stage is *preparation*—the process of investigating the problem or opportunity in many ways. Preparation involves developing a clear understanding of what you are trying to achieve through a novel solution and then actively studying information seemingly related to the topic. It is a process of developing knowledge and possibly skills about the issue or object of attention. The second stage, called *incubation,* is the period of reflective thought. We put the problem aside, but our mind is still working on it in the background.[59] The important condition here is to maintain a

▼ **EXHIBIT 6.3** The Creative Process Model

Preparation	**Incubation**	**Illumination**	**Verification**
• Understand the problem or opportunity • Investigate information seemingly related to the issue	• Period of reflective thought • Nonconscious or low-level awareness, not direct attention to the issue • Active divergent thinking process	• Sudden awareness of a novel, although vague and incomplete, idea entering one's consciousness • May include an initial period of "fringe" awareness	• Detailed logical and experimental evaluation of the illuminated idea • Further creative thinking

Source: Based on G. Wallas, *The Art of Thought* (London: Jonathan Cape, 1926), Chap. 4.

divergent thinking
Reframing a problem in a unique way and generating different approaches to the issue.

low-level awareness by frequently revisiting the problem. Incubation does not mean that you forget about the problem or issue.

Incubation assists **divergent thinking**—reframing the problem in a unique way and generating different approaches to the issue. This contrasts with *convergent thinking*—calculating the conventionally accepted "right answer" to a logical problem. Divergent thinking breaks us away from existing mental models so we can apply concepts or processes from completely different areas of life. The discovery of Velcro is a case in point. In the 1940s, Swiss engineer Georges de Mestral had just returned home from a walk with his dog through the countryside when he noticed his clothing and the dog's fur were covered in burrs. While struggling to remove the barbed seeds, de Mestral engaged in divergent thinking by developing an idea that the adhesion used by burrs could be used to attach other things together. It took another dozen years of hard work, but de Mestral eventually perfected the hook-and-loop fastener, which he trademarked as Velcro.[60]

Illumination (also called insight), the third stage of creativity, refers to the experience of suddenly becoming aware of a unique idea.[61] Wallas and others also suggest this stage begins with a

> "The illumination stage of creativity likely begins with a "fringe" awareness before the idea fully enters our consciousness."

"fringe" awareness before the idea fully enters our consciousness. Illumination is often visually depicted as a light-bulb, but a better image would be a flash of light or perhaps a briefly flickering candle—these bits of inspiration are fleeting and can be quickly lost if not documented. For this reason, many creative people keep a journal or notebook nearby so they can jot down their ideas before they disappear. Also, flickering ideas don't keep a particular schedule; they might come to you at any time of day or night.

Illumination presents ideas that are usually vague, roughly drawn, and untested. Verification therefore provides the essential final stage of creativity, whereby we flesh out the illuminated ideas and subject them to detailed logical evaluation and experimentation. This stage often calls for further creativity as the ideas evolve into finished products or services. Thus, although *verification* is labeled the final stage of creativity, it is really the beginning of a long process of creative decision making toward development of an innovative product or service.

Characteristics of Creative People

Everyone is creative, but some people have a higher potential for creativity. Four of the main characteristics that give individuals more creative potential are intelligence, persistence, knowledge and experience, and a cluster of personality traits and values representing independent imagination (see Exhibit 6.4).

- *Cognitive and practical intelligence.* Creative people have above-average intelligence to synthesize information, analyze ideas, and apply their ideas.[62] Like the fictional sleuth Sherlock Holmes, creative people recognize the significance of small bits of information and are able to connect them in ways that few others can imagine. They also have *practical intelligence*—the capacity to evaluate the potential usefulness of their ideas.

- *Persistence.* Creative people have persistence, which includes a higher need for achievement, a strong motivation from the task itself, and a moderate or high degree of self-esteem. In support of this, one study reported that inventors have higher levels of confidence and optimism than do people in the general population, and these traits motivate inventors to continue working on and investing in a project after receiving diagnostic advice to quit.[63]

- *Knowledge and experience.* Creative people require a foundation of knowledge and experience to discover or acquire new knowledge (the idea of *absorptive capacity* that was discussed in Chapter 1).[64] However, this expertise is a double-edge sword. As people acquire knowledge and experience about a specific topic, their

▼ **EXHIBIT 6.4** Characteristics of Creative People

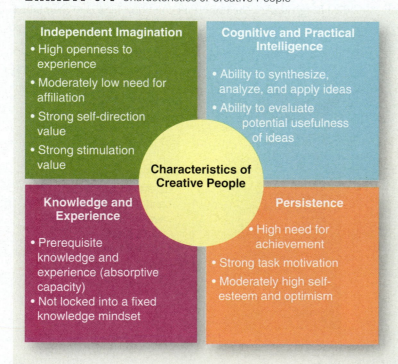

Independent Imagination
- High openness to experience
- Moderately low need for affiliation
- Strong self-direction value
- Strong stimulation value

Cognitive and Practical Intelligence
- Ability to synthesize, analyze, and apply ideas
- Ability to evaluate potential usefulness of ideas

Characteristics of Creative People

Knowledge and Experience
- Prerequisite knowledge and experience (absorptive capacity)
- Not locked into a fixed knowledge mindset

Persistence
- High need for achievement
- Strong task motivation
- Moderately high self-esteem and optimism

Generating a Creative Lightwave

When it comes to creative thinking, Alex Beim sees the light. The founder and chief creative technologist of Tangible Interaction Design in Vancouver, Canada, designed the digital graffiti walls at a Chanel outlet in New York City and Converse Shoes in Amsterdam, as well as the color-changing illuminated lightweight orbs (called zygotes) at the Vancouver Olympics. "I get ideas all the time for designs I want to create," says Beim, who now employs a team of people. "I love researching the idea, seeing it come to life and watching the happiness it brings to people."[65]

mental models tend to become more rigid. They are less adaptable to new information or rules about that knowledge domain. Some writers suggest that expertise also increases "mindless behavior" because expertise reduces the tendency to question why things happen.[66] To overcome the limitations of expertise, some corporate leaders like to hire people from other industries and areas of expertise. For instance, when Geoffrey Ballard, founder of Ballard Power Systems, hired a chemist to develop a better battery, the chemist protested that he didn't know anything about batteries. Ballard replied, "That's fine. I don't want someone who knows batteries. They know what won't work."[67]

- *Independent imagination.* Creative people possess a cluster of personality traits and values that support an independent imagination: high openness to experience, moderately low need for affiliation, and strong values around self-direction and stimulation.[68] Openness to experience is a Big Five personality dimension representing the extent to which a person is imaginative, curious, sensitive, open-minded, and original (see Chapter 2). Creative people have a moderately low need for affiliation, so they are less embarrassed when making mistakes. Self-direction includes the values of creativity and independent thought; stimulation includes the values of excitement and challenge. Together, these values form openness to change—representing the motivation to pursue innovative ways (see Chapter 2).

Organizational Conditions Supporting Creativity

Intelligence, persistence, expertise, and independent imagination represent a person's creative potential, but the extent to which these characteristics produce more creative output depends on how well the work environment supports the creative process.[69] Several job and workplace characteristics have been identified in the literature, and different combinations of situations can equally support creativity; there isn't one best work environment.[70]

One of the most important conditions that supports creative practice is that the organization has a *learning orientation;* that is, leaders recognize employees make reasonable mistakes as part of the creative process. "Creativity comes from failure," Samsung Electronics CEO and vice chairman Yun Jong-yong advises employees. "We should reform our corporate culture to forgive failure if workers did their best."[71] Motivation from the job itself is another important condition for creativity.[72] Employees tend to be more creative when they believe their work benefits the organization and/or larger society (i.e., task significance) and when they have the freedom to pursue novel ideas without bureaucratic delays (i.e., autonomy). Creativity is about changing things, and change is possible only when employees have the authority to experiment. More generally, jobs encourage creativity when they are challenging and aligned with the employee's competencies.

Along with supporting a learning orientation and intrinsically motivating jobs, companies foster creativity through open communication and sufficient resources. They also provide a comfortable degree of job security, which explains why creativity suffers during times of downsizing and corporate restructuring.[73] Some companies also support creativity by designing nontraditional workspaces, such as unique building design or unconventional office areas.[74] Google is one example. The Internet innovator has funky offices in several countries that include hammocks, gondola and hive-shaped privacy spaces, slides, and brightly painted walls.

OB Theory to Practice

Features of Creative Workplaces

- A learning orientation culture (reasonable mistakes are viewed as learning experiences).
- Jobs have high task significance and autonomy.
- Jobs are aligned with employee competencies.
- Open communication across the organization.
- Employees have sufficient resources to perform their work.
- Employees experience a comfortable degree of job security.
- Workspace is nontraditional.
- Leaders and coworkers provide mutual support.

To some degree, creativity also improves with support from leaders and coworkers. One study reported that effective product champions provide enthusiastic support for new ideas. Other studies suggest that coworker support can improve creativity in some situations whereas competition among coworkers improves creativity in other situations.[75] Similarly, it isn't clear how much pressure should be exerted on employees to produce creative ideas. Extreme time pressures are well-known creativity inhibitors, but lack of pressure doesn't seem to produce the highest creativity either.

Activities That Encourage Creativity

Hiring people with strong creative potential and providing a work environment that supports creativity are two cornerstones of a creative workplace. The third cornerstone consists of various activities that help employees think more creatively. One set of activities involves redefining the problem. Employees might be encouraged to revisit old projects that have been set aside. After a few months of neglect, these projects might be seen in new ways.[77] Another strategy involves asking people unfamiliar with the issue (preferably with different expertise) to explore the problem with you. You would state the objectives and give some facts and then let the other person ask questions to further understand the situation. By verbalizing the problem, listening to questions, and hearing what others think, you are more likely to form new perspectives on the issue.[78]

A second set of creativity activities, known as *associative play*, ranges from art classes to impromptu storytelling and acting. For example, British media giant OMD sends employees to two-day retreats in the countryside, where they play grapefruit croquet, chant like medieval monks, and pretend to be dog collars. "Being creative is a bit like an emotion; we need to be stimulated," explains Harriet Frost, one of OMD's specialists in building creativity. "The same is true for our imagination and its ability to come up with new ideas. You can't just sit in a room and devise hundreds of ideas."[79] Another associative play activity, called *morphological analysis*, involves listing different dimensions of a system and the elements of each dimension and then looking at each combination. This encourages people to carefully examine combinations that initially seem nonsensical.

A third set of activities that promote creative thinking falls under the category of *cross-pollination*.[80] Cross-pollination occurs when people from different areas of the organization exchange ideas or when new people are brought into an existing team. Mother, the London-based creative agency, has unusual policies and working conditions that apply this creative process. The company's 100 or so employees perform their daily work around one monster-size table—an 8-foot-wide reinforced-concrete slab that extends 300 feet like a skateboard ramp around the entire floor. Every three weeks, employees are asked to relocate their laptop, portable

Creativity
Advantage[76]

41% of 251,507 U.S. Federal Government employees surveyed agree or strongly agree that creativity and innovation are rewarded in their organization

85% of 1,461 American managers and consultants polled say that creativity has had a mild or strong positive effect on their career advancement

57% of 1,966 American employees say that innovation/creativity/out-of-the box thinking will prove to be the most useful skill over the next year

66% of 1,461 American managers and consultants polled believe their organization's management "to some degree" or "definitely" places a premium on people who are creative

60% of 600 senior global HR leaders polled identify creativity as one of the most important leadership qualities over the next five years (top choice, followed by integrity)

telephone, and trolley to another area around the table. Why the musical-chairs exercise? "It encourages cross-pollination of ideas," explains Stef Calcraft, one of Mother's founding partners. "You have people working on the same problem from different perspectives. It makes problem-solving much more organic."[81]

Cross-pollination highlights the fact that creativity rarely occurs alone. Some creative people may be individualistic, but most creative ideas are generated through teams and informal social interaction. "This whole thing about the solitary tortured artist is nonsense I think," says John Collee, the screenwriter who penned such films as *Happy Feet* and *Master and Commander*. "All the great creative people I know have become great precisely because they know how to get along with people and swim around in the communal unconscious."[82] This notion of improving creativity through social interaction leads us to the final section of this chapter: employee involvement in decision making.

Learning Objective

After reading this section, you should be able to

LO5 Describe the benefits of employee involvement and identify four contingencies that affect the optimal level of employee involvement.

EMPLOYEE INVOLVEMENT IN DECISION MAKING

Nishith Desai Associates (NDA) isn't your typical law firm. About 60 percent of decisions at the 100-member Mumbai, India-based organization occur through consensus. Another 25 percent are reached through majority vote of the partners, and the remainder are determined by the executive committee or the CEO. The law firm also has representative committees. The compensation committee, for example, consists of staff voted into the position and who have three or more years of professional experience. Overall, NDA strives to become a democratic organization by relying on various levels and forms of employee involvement in decision making.[83]

Employee involvement (also called *participative management*) refers to the degree to which employees influence how

their work is organized and carried out.[84] Employee involvement has become a natural process in every organization, but the level of involvement varies with the situation. In some organizations, such as NDA, almost everyone has a high degree of involvement in some corporate-wide decisions during a given year, whereas other organizations might give employees only low levels of involvement.

A low level of involvement occurs where employees are individually asked for specific information but the problem is not described to them. Somewhat higher involvement occurs where the problem is described and employees are asked individually or collectively for information relating to that problem. Moving further up the involvement scale, the problem is described to employees, who are collectively given responsibility for developing recommendations. However, the decision maker is not bound to accept those recommendations. At the highest level of involvement, the entire decision-making process is handed over to employees. They identify the problem, discover alternative solutions, choose the best alternative, and implement that choice. The original decision maker serves only as a facilitator to guide the team's decision process and keep everyone on track.[85]

Benefits of Employee Involvement

For the past half century, organizational behavior experts have advised that employee involvement potentially improves decision-making quality and commitment.[86] Involved employees can help improve decision quality by recognizing problems more quickly and defining them more accurately.

> ## "Tell me and I'll forget; show me and I may remember; involve me and I'll understand.
>
> —Chinese proverb"

Employees are, in many respects, the sensors of the organization's environment. When the organization's activities misalign with customer expectations, employees are usually the first to know. Employee involvement ensures that everyone in the organization is quickly alerted to such problems.[87] Employee involvement can also potentially improve the number and quality of solutions generated. In a well-managed meeting, team members create synergy by pooling their knowledge to form new alternatives. In other words, several people working together can potentially generate more and better solutions than the same people working alone.

Brasilata: The Ideas Company

Employee involvement has helped Brasilata to become one of the most innovative and productive manufacturing businesses in Brazil. Each year, the steel can manufacturer receives more than 200,000 ideas—an average of more than 220 ideas per employee—on a wide range of themes, from how to improve production efficiency to new product designs. Ideas are so important that Brasilata employees are called "inventors," and everyone signs an "innovation contract" that reinforces their commitment to continuous improvement. Brasilata holds a party every six months in which all employees are invited to celebrate teams and individuals with the best ideas[88]

A third benefit of employee involvement is that, under specific conditions, it improves the evaluation of alternatives. Numerous studies on participative decision making, constructive conflict, and team dynamics have found that involvement brings out more diverse perspectives, tests ideas, and provides more valuable knowledge, all of which help the decision maker to select the best alternative.[89] A mathematical theorem introduced in 1785 by the Marquis de Condorcet states that the alternative selected by the team's majority is more likely to be correct than is the alternative selected by any team member individually.[90]

Along with improving decision quality, involvement tends to strengthen employee commitment to the decision. Rather than viewing themselves as agents of someone else's decision, those who participate in a decision feel personally responsible for its success. Involvement also tends to improve employee motivation, satisfaction, and turnover. It also increases skill variety, feelings of autonomy, and task identity, all of which increase job enrichment and potentially employee motivation. Participation is also a critical practice in organizational change because employees are more motivated to implement the decision and less likely to resist changes resulting from the decision.[91]

Contingencies of Employee Involvement

If employee involvement is so wonderful, why don't leaders leave all decisions to employees? The answer is that the optimal level of employee involvement depends on the situation. The employee involvement model shown in Exhibit 6.5 lists four contingencies: decision structure, source of decision knowledge, decision commitment, and risk of conflict in the decision process.[92]

- *Decision structure.* At the beginning of this chapter, we learned that some decisions are programmed, whereas others are nonprogrammed. Programmed decisions are less likely to need employee involvement because the solutions are already worked out from past incidents. In other words, the benefits of employee involvement increase with the novelty and complexity of the problem or opportunity.

- *Source of decision knowledge.* Subordinates should be involved in some level of decision making when the leader lacks sufficient knowledge and subordinates have additional information to improve decision quality. In many cases, employees are closer to customers and production activities, so they often know where the company can save money, improve product or service quality, and realize opportunities. This is particularly

▼ **EXHIBIT 6.5** Model of Employee Involvement in Decision Making

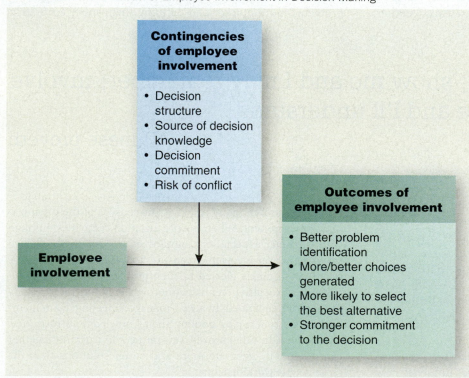

true for complex decisions where employees are more likely to possess relevant information.

- *Decision commitment.* Participation tends to improve employee commitment to the decision. If employees are unlikely to accept a decision made without their involvement, some level of participation is usually necessary.

- *Risk of conflict.* Two types of conflict undermine the benefits of employee involvement. First, if employee goals and norms conflict with the organization's goals, only a low level of employee involvement is advisable. Second, the degree of involvement depends on whether employees will agree on the preferred solution. If conflict is likely to occur, high involvement (i.e., employees make the decision alone) would be difficult to achieve.

Employee involvement is an important component of the decision-making process. To make the best decisions, we need to involve people who have the most valuable information and will increase commitment to implement the decision. Employee involvement is a formative stage of team dynamics, so it carries many of the benefits and challenges of working in teams. The next chapter provides a closer look at team dynamics, including processes for making decisions in teams. ■

CHECK IT OUT!

www.mhhe.com/ McShaneM2e

for study materials

including quizzes

and other resources

team **dynamics**

More than half of the organizations polled in a recent survey use teams to a high or very high extent to conduct day-to-day business. Furthermore, 77 percent of those firms rely on teams for one-time projects, and 67 percent rely on teams for ongoing projects. By comparison, a decade ago only 50 percent of executives said their work is done in teams. Two decades ago, only 20 percent of those executives said they worked in teams.[1] Team work has also become more important in scientific research. A recent study of almost 20 million research publications reported the percentage of journal articles written by teams rather than individuals has increased substantially over the past five decades. Team-based articles also had a much higher number of subsequent citations, suggesting that journal articles written by teams are superior to articles written by individuals.[2]

Why are teams becoming so important, and how can organizations strengthen

continued on p. 132

LEARNING OBJECTIVES

After studying Chapter 7, you should be able to:

LO1 Explain why employees join informal groups and discuss the benefits and limitations of teams.

LO2 Outline the team effectiveness model and discuss how task characteristics, team size, and team composition influence team effectiveness.

LO3 Discuss how the four team processes—team development, norms, cohesion, and trust—influence team effectiveness.

LO4 Discuss the characteristics and factors required for success of self-directed teams and virtual teams.

LO5 Identify four constraints on team decision making and discuss the advantages and disadvantages of four structures aimed at improving team decision making.

teams Groups of two or more people who interact with and influence each other, are mutually accountable for achieving common goals associated with organizational objectives, and perceive themselves as a social entity within an organization.

continued from p. 131

their potential for organizational effectiveness? We find the answers to these and other questions in this chapter on team dynamics. This chapter begins by defining *teams* and examining the reasons why organizations rely on teams and why people join informal groups in organizational settings. A large segment of this chapter examines a model of team effectiveness, which includes team and organizational environment, team design, and the team processes of development, norms, cohesion, and trust. We then turn our attention to two specific types of teams: self-directed teams and virtual teams. The final section of this chapter looks at the challenges and strategies for making better decisions in teams. ■

Learning Objective

After reading the next two sections, you should be able to

LO1 Explain why employees join informal groups and discuss the benefits and limitations of teams.

TEAMS AND INFORMAL GROUPS

Teams are groups of two or more people who interact with and influence each other, are mutually accountable for achieving common goals associated with organizational objectives, and perceive themselves as a social entity within an organization.[3] This definition has a few important components worth repeating. First, all teams exist to fulfill some purpose, such as repairing electric power lines, assembling a product, designing a new social welfare program, or making an important decision. Second, team members are held together by their interdependence and need for collaboration to achieve common goals. All teams require some form of communication so members can coordinate and share common objectives. Third, team members influence each other, although some members may be more influential than others regarding the team's goals and activities. Finally, a team exists when its members perceive themselves to be a team.

Exhibit 7.1 briefly describes various types of teams in organizations. Some teams are permanent, while others are temporary; some are responsible for making products or providing services, while others exist to make decisions or share knowledge. Each type of team has been created deliberately to serve an organizational purpose. Some teams, such as skunkworks teams, are not initially sanctioned by management, yet they are called "teams" because members' work toward an organization objective.

Informal Groups

For the most part, this chapter focuses on formal teams, but employees also belong to informal groups. All teams are groups, but many groups do not satisfy our definition of teams. Groups include people assembled together, whether or not they have any interdependence or organizationally focused objective. The friends you meet for lunch are an *informal group*, but they wouldn't be called a team because they have little or no interdependence (each person could just as easily eat lunch alone) and no organizationally mandated purpose. Instead, they exist primarily for the benefit of their members. Although the terms are used interchangeably, *teams* has largely replaced *groups* in the language of business when referring to employees who work together to complete organizational tasks.[4]

Why do informal groups exist? One reason is that human beings are social animals. Our drive to bond is hardwired through evolutionary development, creating a need to belong to informal groups.[5] This is evident by the fact that people invest considerable time and effort forming and maintaining social relationships without any special circumstances or ulterior motives. A second reason people join informal groups is provided by social identity theory, which states that individuals define themselves by their group affiliations (see Chapter 3). Thus, we join groups—particularly those that are viewed favorably by others and that have values similar to our own—because they shape and reinforce our self-concept.[6]

Third, informal groups exist because they accomplish goals that individuals working alone cannot achieve. For example, employees will sometimes congregate to oppose organizational changes because this collective effort has more power than individuals who try to bring about change alone. These informal groups, called coalitions, are discussed in Chapter 9. A fourth explanation for informal groups is that we are comforted by the mere presence of other people and are therefore motivated to be near them in stressful situations. When in danger, people congregate near each other even though doing so serves no protective purpose. Similarly, employees tend to mingle more often after hearing rumors the

Team Type	Description
Departmental teams	Teams that consist of employees who have similar or complementary skills and are located in the same unit of a functional structure; usually have minimal task interdependence because each person works with employees in other departments.
Production/service/ leadership teams	Typically multiskilled (employees have diverse competencies), team members collectively produce a common product/service or make ongoing decisions; production/service teams typically have an assembly-line type of interdependence, whereas leadership teams tend to have tight interactive (reciprocal) interdependence.
Self-directed teams	Similar to production/service teams except (1) they are organized around work processes that complete an entire piece of work requiring several interdependent tasks and (2) they have substantial autonomy over the execution of those tasks (i.e., they usually control inputs, flow, and outputs with little or no supervision).
Advisory teams	Teams that provide recommendations to decision makers; include committees, advisory councils, work councils, and review panels; may be temporary, but are often permanent, some with frequent rotation of members.
Task force (project) teams	Usually multiskilled, temporary teams whose assignment is to solve a problem, realize an opportunity, or design a product or service.
Skunkworks	Multiskilled teams that are usually located away from the organization and are relatively free of its hierarchy; often initiated by an entrepreneurial team leader who borrows people and resources (*bootlegging*) to design a product or service.
Virtual teams	Teams whose members operate across space, time, and organizational boundaries and are linked through information technologies to achieve organizational tasks; may be a temporary task force or permanent service team.
Communities of practice	Teams (but often informal groups) bound together by shared expertise and passion for a particular activity or interest; main purpose is to share information; often rely on information technologies as the main source of interaction.

company might be acquired by a competitor. As Chapter 4 explained, this social support minimizes stress by providing emotional and/or informational support to buffer the stress experience.[7]

Informal Groups and Organizational Outcomes

Informal groups are not created to serve organizational objectives. Nevertheless, they have a profound influence on organizations and employees. Informal groups potentially minimize employee stress because, as mentioned above, group members provide emotional and informational social support. This stress-reducing capability of informal groups improves employee well-being, thereby improving organizational effectiveness. Informal groups are also the backbone of *social networks*, which are important sources of trust building, information sharing, power, influence, and employee well-being in the workplace.[8] Chapter 8 describes the growing significance of social networking sites similar to Facebook and Linkedin to encourage the formation of informal groups and associated communication. Chapter 9 explains how social networks are a source of influence in organizational settings. Employees with strong informal networks tend to have more power and influence because they receive better information and preferential treatment from others and their talent is more visible to key decision makers.

ADVANTAGES AND DISADVANTAGES OF TEAMS

Employees don't work alone very often at Menlo Innovations. The software development company in Ann Arbor, Michigan, organizes employees into pairs each week. Two employees share one computer while discussing ideas on the same part of a large project. Each Monday, the company's two dozen employees not only switch partners, they often switch to a different part of the project or to another project altogether. "Just the act of one person bringing the other up to speed, saying things out loud, brings out things people hadn't noticed before," explains Richard Sheridan, one of Menlo Innovations' four cofounders. "That makes them smarter."[9]

The musical chairs arrangement at Menlo Innovations indicates teamwork is an important ingredient for the software company's business success. Why are teams so important? The answer to this question has a long history.[10] Early research on British coal mining in the 1940s, the Japanese economic miracle of the 1970s, and a huge number of investigations since then, have revealed that *under the right conditions,*

Ergon Energy's Team Culture

Teams are the foundation on which Ergon Energy does business. The electricity distribution company for regional Queensland, Australia, organizes its employees around teams and rewards them for team safety and performance. Teamwork is also one of Ergon's six core values. "Teamwork is a way of life, and it's something you can feel from your first day on the job," says Ergon's careers Web site. "Our employees really value teamwork," says an Ergon Energy executive. "It is a real key to our success and there's a real family culture, a sort of feeling that everyone is your mate."[11]

teams make better decisions, develop better products and services, and create a more engaged workforce than do employees working alone.[12] Similarly, team members can quickly share information and coordinate tasks, whereas these processes are slower and prone to more errors in traditional departments led by supervisors. Teams typically provide superior customer service because they provide more breadth of knowledge and expertise to customers than individual "stars" can offer.

In many situations, people are potentially more motivated when working in teams than when working alone.[13] One reason for this motivation is that, as we mentioned above, employees have a drive to bond and are motivated to fulfill the goals of groups to which they belong. This motivation is particularly strong when the team is part of the employee's social identity.

Second, people are more motivated in teams because they are accountable to fellow team members, who monitor performance more closely than a traditional supervisor. This is particularly true where the team's performance depends on the worst performer, such as on an assembly line, where how fast the product is assembled depends on the speed of the slowest employee. Third, under some circumstances, performance improves when employees work near others because coworkers become benchmarks of comparison. Employees are also motivated to work harder because of apprehension that their performance will be compared to others' performance.

OB Theory to Practice

What Organizations Say about Team Work[14]

Company	What They Say about Teamwork
A123 Systems (Waltham, MA)	A123 Systems is a team-oriented organization where open and honest communication is encouraged and bureaucracy is rejected.
Credit Suisse (Geneva)	Credit Suisse has a very team-oriented, cosmopolitan culture. . . . Applicants must demonstrate academic excellence as well as the ability to work in a team environment.
McKinsey & Company (New York/London)	We always work in teams, normally consisting of three to five consultants. The team is led by an engagement manager who is responsible for the day-to-day progress and for coaching the other team members.
Veolia Environnement (Paris)	Teamwork is a crucial element in the way Veolia Environnement works worldwide. Working together and pooling knowledge and experience ensures every success is a shared victory.
Whole Foods Market (Texas)	Working in our team environment means: (a) Communicating frequently, openly and compassionately; (b) Meeting regularly to discuss team operations and make consensus decisions; (c) Appreciating each other's contributions; (d) Working together to maximize rewards from team member incentive programs; (e) Celebrating our successes together; (f) Having fun!

The Challenges of Teams

In spite of their many benefits, teams are not always as effective as individuals working alone.[15] Teams are usually better suited to complex work, such as designing a building or auditing a company's financial records. Under these circumstances, one person rarely has all the necessary knowledge and skills. Instead, complex work is performed better by dividing its tasks into more specialized roles, with people in those specialized jobs coordinating with each other. In contrast, work is typically performed more effectively by individuals alone when they have all the necessary knowledge and skills and the work cannot be divided into specialized tasks or is not complex enough to benefit from specialization. Even where the work can and should be specialized, a team structure might not be necessary if the tasks performed by several people require minimal coordination.

The main problem with teams is that they have additional costs called **process losses**—resources (including time and energy) expended toward team development and maintenance rather than the task.[16] It is much more efficient for an individual to work out an issue alone than to resolve differences of opinion with other people. For a team to perform well, team members need to agree and have mutual understanding of their goals, the strategy for accomplishing those goals, their specific roles, and informal rules of conduct.[17] Team members need to divert time and energy away from performing the work so they can develop and maintain these team requirements.

The process-loss problem is particularly apparent when more people are added or replace others on the team. Team performance suffers when a team adds members because those employees need to learn how the team operates and how to coordinate efficiently with other team members. Process losses also occur because the workload often needs to be redistributed. The software industry even has a name for the problems of adding people to a team: **Brooks's law** (also called the "mythical man-month") says that adding more people to a late software project only makes it later!

Social Loafing
Perhaps the best-known limitation of teams is the risk of productivity loss due to **social loafing**. Social loafing occurs when people exert less effort (and usually perform at a lower level) when working in teams than when working alone.[18] Social loafing tends to be more serious when the individual's performance is less likely to be noticed, such as when people work together in very large teams. The individual's output is also less noticeable

where the team produces a single output (rather than each team member producing output), such as finding a single solution to a customer's problem. There is less social loafing when each team member's contribution is more noticeable; this can be achieved by reducing the size of the team, for example, or measuring each team member's performance. "When the group is smaller, there's nowhere to hide," explains Strategic Investments principal David Zebro. "You have to pull your weight."[19]

Social loafing also depends on the employee's motivation to perform the work. Social loafing is less prevalent when the task is interesting because individuals are more motivated by the work itself to perform their duties. For example, one recent study revealed that student apathy explains some of the social loafing that occurs in university student teams. Social loafing is also less common when the team's objective is important, possibly because individuals experience more pressure from co-workers to perform well. Finally, social loafing occurs less frequently among members who value team membership and believe in working toward the team's objectives.[20]

In summary, teams can be very powerful forces for competitive advantage, or they can be much more trouble than they are worth, so much so that job performance and morale decline when employees are placed in teams. To understand when teams are better than individuals working alone, we need to more closely examine the conditions that make teams effective or ineffective. The next few sections of this chapter discuss the model of team effectiveness.

OB Theory to Practice

Minimizing Social Loafing

- Make each team member's contribution more visible/identifiable.
- Redesign the work so it is more interesting (more job enrichment).
- Assign team objectives that are important or valued by team members.
- Increase the extent to which team members value their membership in the team.

process losses Resources (including time and energy) expended toward team development and maintenance rather than the task.

Brooks's law The principle that adding more people to a late software project only makes it later. Also called the mythical man-month.

social loafing The problem that occurs when people exert less effort (and usually perform at a lower level) when working in teams than when working alone.

Learning Objective

After reading the next two sections, you should be able to

LO2 Outline the team effectiveness model and discuss how task characteristics, team size, and team composition influence team effectiveness.

A MODEL OF TEAM EFFECTIVENESS

Why are some teams effective while others fail? To answer this question, we first need to clarify the meaning of team effectiveness. A team is effective when it benefits the organization, its members, and its own survival.[21] First, most teams exist to serve some organizational purpose, so effectiveness is partly measured by the achievement of those objectives. Second, a team's effectiveness relies on the satisfaction and well-being of its members. People join groups to fulfill their personal needs, so effectiveness is partly measured by this need fulfillment. Finally, team effectiveness includes the team's viability—its ability to survive. It must be able to maintain the commitment of its members, particularly during the turbulence of the team's development. Without this commitment, people leave and the team will fall apart. The team must also secure sufficient resources and find a benevolent environment in which to operate.

Researchers have developed several models over the years to identify the features or conditions that make some teams more effective than others.[22] Exhibit 7.2 integrates the main components of these team effectiveness models. We will closely examine each component over the next several pages. This model is best viewed as a template of several theories because each component (team development, team cohesion, etc.) includes its own set of theories and models to explain how that component operates.

Organizational and Team Environment

The organizational and team environment represents all conditions beyond the team's boundaries that influence its effectiveness. Team members tend to work together more effectively when they are at least partly rewarded for team performance.[23] Another environmental factor is the organizational structure. Teams flourish when organized around work processes because this structure increases interaction and interdependence among team members and reduces interaction with people outside the team. High-performance teams also depend on organizational leaders who provide support and strategic direction while team members focus on operational efficiency and flexibility.[24] The physical layout of the team's workspace can also make a difference. For example, Toyota Motor Company has relied on an "obeya room" to bring together project members with diverse backgrounds to more quickly resolve problems.

▼ **EXHIBIT 7.2** Team Effectiveness Model

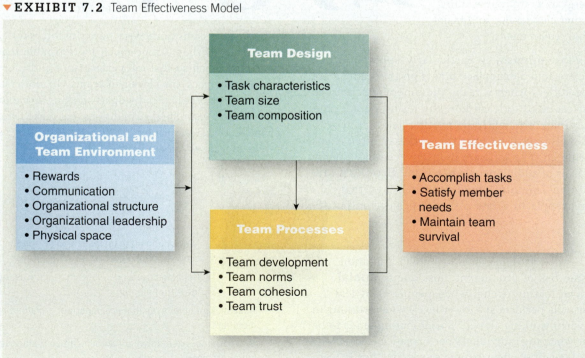

Teaming with Ideas in the Big Room

PSA Peugeot Citroën, Europe's second largest automaker, has set up an "obeya room" (Japanese for "big room") to speed up team decision making. The walls are plastered with graphs and notes so team members can visualize key issues. The obeya room creates a unique team environment that encourages face-to-face interaction to quickly solve important, well-defined problems. At one session, for example, managers figured out how to significantly reduce accidents among temporary workers. "The themes for projects in progress are displayed on the walls, with red when something is wrong," explains PSA Peugeot Citroën chief executive Philippe Varin. "Everyone takes the same problem and tries to fix it."[25]

TEAM DESIGN ELEMENTS

Along with setting up a team-friendly environment, leaders need to carefully design the team itself, including task characteristics, team size, team composition, and team roles.

Task Characteristics

Teams are more effective than individuals in specific types of tasks. They are better for work that is too complex for any individual to perform, such as launching the business in a new market, developing a computer operating system, or constructing a bridge. Complex work requires skills and knowledge beyond the competencies of one person. Teams are particularly well suited when the complex work can be divided into more specialized roles and the people in the specialized roles require frequent coordination with each other. Some evidence also suggests teams work best with well-structured tasks because it is easier to coordinate such work among several people.[26]

One task characteristic that is particularly important for teams is **task interdependence**—the extent to which team members must share materials, information, or expertise to perform their jobs.[27] Apart from complete independence, there are three levels of task interdependence, as illustrated in Exhibit 7.3. The lowest level of interdependence, called *pooled interdependence*, occurs when an employee or work unit shares a common resource, such as machinery, administrative support, or a budget, with other employees or work units. This would occur in a team setting where each member works alone but shares raw materials or machinery to perform her or his otherwise independent tasks. Interdependence is higher under *sequential interdependence,* in which the output of one person becomes the direct input for another person or unit. Sequential interdependence occurs where team members are organized in an assembly line.

Reciprocal interdependence, in which work output is exchanged back and forth among individuals, produces the highest degree of interdependence. People who design a new product or service would typically have reciprocal interdependence because their design decisions affect others involved in the design process. Any decision made by the design engineers would influence

▼ **EXHIBIT 7.3** Levels of Task Interdependence

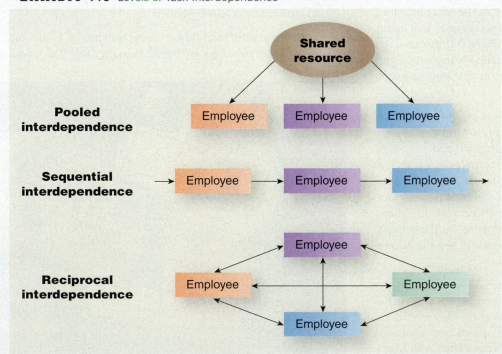

the work of the manufacturing engineer and purchasing specialist, and vice versa. Employees with reciprocal interdependence should be organized into teams to facilitate coordination in their interwoven relationship.

As a rule, the higher the level of task interdependence, the greater the need to organize people into teams rather than have them work alone. Team structure improves interpersonal communication and thus results in better coordination. High task interdependence also motivates most people to be part of the team. However, the rule that a team should be formed when employees have high interdependence applies when team members have the same task goals, such as serving the same clients or collectively assembling the same product. When team members have different goals (such as serving different clients) but must depend on other team members to achieve those unique goals, teamwork might create excessive conflict. Under these circumstances, the company should try to reduce the level of interdependence or rely on supervision as a buffer or mediator among employees.

Team Size

What is the ideal size for a team? Online retailer Amazon relies on the "two-pizza team" rule, namely that a team should be small enough to be fed comfortably with two large pizzas. This works out to between 5 and 7 employees. At the other extreme, a few experts suggest tasks are becoming so complex that many teams need to have more than 100 members.[28] Unfortunately, the former piece of advice (two-pizza teams) is too simplistic, and the latter seems to have lost sight of the meaning and dynamics of real teams.

Generally, teams should be large enough to provide the necessary competencies and perspectives to perform the work, yet small enough to maintain efficient coordination and meaningful involvement of each member.[29] Small teams (say, less than a dozen members) operate effectively because they have less process loss. Members of smaller teams also tend to feel more engaged because they get to know the other team members (which improves trust), have more influence on the group's norms and goals, and feel more responsible for the team's success and failure.

Should companies have 100-person teams if the task is highly complex? The answer is that a group this large probably isn't a team, even if management calls it one. A team exists when its members interact and influence each other, are mutually accountable for achieving common goals associated with organizational objectives, and perceive themselves as a social entity

within an organization. It is very difficult for everyone in a 100-person work unit to influence each other and experience enough cohesion to perceive themselves as team members.

Executives at Whole Foods Market were aware that real teams are much smaller than 100 people when the food retailer opened its huge store in New York City's Columbus Circle. The store had 140 cashiers—far too many people for one cashier team—so Whole Foods Market divided the group into teams with a dozen employees each. All cashiers meet as one massive group every month to discuss production issues, but the smaller groups work effectively as teams on a day-to-day basis.[31]

Team Composition

In most workplaces, employees must have more than technical skills; they must also be able and willing to work in a team environment. Team competencies are so important at Royal Dutch/Shell that the global energy giant hosts a special five-day "Gourami" exercise in Europe, North America, Asia, and the Middle East to observe how well university students (potential job applicants) work effectively under pressure in a team setting. "Dealing with the 'real-life' challenges of Gourami made us all aware of the value of other skills and aptitudes and the need to work as a team," says a mechanical engineering student who participated in one of these events.[32]

The most frequently mentioned characteristics or behaviors of effective team members are depicted in the "five C's" model

illustrated in Exhibit 7.4: cooperating, coordinating, communicating, comforting, and conflict resolving. The first three competencies are mainly (but not entirely) task related, while the last two primarily assist team maintenance:[33]

- *Cooperating.* Effective team members are willing and able to work together rather than alone. This includes sharing resources and being sufficiently adaptive or flexible to accommodate the needs and preferences of other team members, such as rescheduling use of machinery so another team member with a tighter deadline can use it.

- *Coordinating.* Effective team members actively manage the team's work so it is performed efficiently and harmoniously. For example, effective team members keep the team on track and help to integrate the work performed by different members. This typically requires that effective team members know the work of other team members, not just their own.

- *Communicating.* Effective team members transmit information freely (rather than hoarding), efficiently (using the best channel and language), and respectfully (minimizing arousal of negative emotions). They also listen actively to coworkers.

- *Comforting.* Effective team members help coworkers to maintain a positive and healthy psychological state. They show empathy, provide psychological comfort, and build coworker feelings of confidence and self-worth.

- *Conflict resolving.* Conflict is inevitable in social settings, so effective team members have the skills and motivation to resolve dysfunctional disagreements among team members. This requires effective use of various conflict-handling styles as well as diagnostic skills to identify and resolve the structural sources of conflict.

Which employees tend to have these team competencies? Top of the list are those with high conscientiousness and extroversion personality traits, as well as high emotional intelligence. Furthermore, the old saying "One bad apple spoils the barrel" seems to apply to teams; one team member who lacks these teamwork competencies may undermine the dynamics of the entire team.[34]

Team Diversity Another important dimension of team composition is diversity. Team diversity seems to have both positive and negative effects on team effectiveness.[35] Let's first look at the benefits of team diversity. Research suggests that, in specific situations, diverse teams are better than homogeneous teams at making decisions. One reason is that people from different backgrounds tend to see a problem or opportunity from different angles. Team members have different mental models, so they are more likely to identify viable solutions to difficult problems.

A second reason diverse teams tend to make better decisions is that they have a broader pool of technical competencies. For example, each team at Rackspace Hosting consists of more than a dozen people with diverse skills, such as account management, systems engineering, technical support, billing expertise, and data center support. The enterprise-level Web infrastructure company requires these diverse technical competencies within each team to serve the needs of customers assigned to the team. A third reason favoring teams with diverse members is that they provide better representation of the team's constituents, such as other departments or clients from similarly diverse backgrounds. A team responsible for designing and launching a new service, for instance, should have representation from the organization's various specializations so people in those work units will support the team's decisions.

Team diversity offers many advantages, but it also presents a number of opposing challenges.[36] Specifically, employees with diverse backgrounds take longer to become a high-performing team. This partly occurs because team members take longer to bond with people who are different from them, particularly when others hold different perspectives and values (i.e., deep-level diversity). Diverse teams are susceptible to "fault lines"—hypothetical dividing lines that may split a team into subgroups along gender, ethnic,

▼ **EXHIBIT 7.4** Five C's of Team Member Competency

Sources: Based on information in V. Rousseau, C. Aubé, and A. Savoie, "Teamwork Behaviors: A Review and an Integration of Frameworks," *Small Group Research* 37, no. 5 (2006), 540–70; M. L. Loughry, M. W. Ohland, and D. D. Moore, "Development of a Theory-Based Assessment of Team Member Effectiveness," *Educational and Psychological Measurement* 67, no. 3 (2007), 505–24.

Team Development

Team members must resolve several issues and pass through several stages of development before emerging as an effective work unit. They need to get to know and trust each other, understand and agree on their respective roles, discover appropriate and inappropriate behaviors, and learn how to coordinate with each other. The longer team members work together, the better they develop common or complementary mental models, mutual understanding, and effective performance routines to complete the work.

A popular model that captures many team development activities is shown in Exhibit 7.5.[37] The diagram shows teams moving systematically from one stage to the next, while the dashed lines illustrate that teams might fall back to an earlier stage of development as new members join or other conditions disrupt the team's maturity. *Forming*, the first stage of team development, is a period of testing and orientation in which members learn about each other and evaluate the benefits and costs of continued membership. People tend to be polite, will defer to authority, and try to find out what is expected of them and how they will fit into the team. The *storming* stage is marked by interpersonal conflict as members become more proactive and compete for various team roles. Members try to establish norms of appropriate behavior and performance standards.

professional, or other dimensions. These fault lines undermine team effectiveness by reducing the motivation to communicate and coordinate with teammates on the other side of the hypothetical divisions. In contrast, members of teams with minimal diversity experience higher satisfaction, less conflict, and better interpersonal relations. Consequently, homogeneous teams tend to be more effective on tasks requiring a high degree of cooperation and coordination, such as emergency response teams.

> " Team development is apparent when its members shift from viewing the team as something 'out there' to something that is part of themselves. "

During the *norming* stage, the team develops its first real sense of cohesion as roles are established and a consensus forms around group objectives and a common or complementary team-based mental model. By the *performing* stage, team members have learned to efficiently coordinate and resolve conflicts. In high-performance teams, members are highly cooperative, have a high level of trust in each other, are committed to group objectives, and identify with the team. Finally, the *adjourning* stage occurs when the team is about to disband. Team members shift their attention away from task orientation to a relationship focus.

The five-stage model represents the team development process fairly well, but it does not show that some teams remain in a particular stage longer than others. This model also masks two distinct processes during team development: developing team identity and developing team competence.[38]

- *Developing team identity.* Team development is apparent when its members shift from viewing the team as something "out there" to something that is part of themselves. In other words, team development occurs when employees take ownership of the team's success and make the team part of their self-concept.

Learning Objective

After reading this section, you should be able to

LO3 Discuss how the four team processes—team development, norms, cohesion, and trust—influence team effectiveness.

TEAM PROCESSES

The third set of elements in the team effectiveness model, collectively known as *team processes*, includes team development, norms, cohesion, and trust. These elements represent characteristics of the team that continuously evolve.

- *Developing team competence.* Team development includes developing habitual routines with teammates and forming shared or complementary mental models.[39] Team mental models are visual or relational mental images that are shared by team members, such as what good customer service looks like. One recent meta-analysis reported that teams are more effective when their members share common mental models of the work.[40]

Team Roles

An important part of the team development process is forming and reinforcing team roles. A **role** is a set of behaviors that people are expected to perform because they hold certain positions in a team and organization.[41] In a team setting, some roles help the team achieve its goals; other roles maintain relationships within the team. Some team roles are formally assigned to specific people. For example, team leaders are usually expected to initiate discussion, ensure everyone has an opportunity to present his or her views, and help the team reach agreement on the issues discussed.

Team members are assigned specific roles within their formal job responsibilities. Yet, team members also assume informal roles that suit their personality and values as well as the wishes of other team members. These informal roles, which are negotiated throughout the team development process, range from supporting others to initiating new ideas. Informal team roles are shared, but many are eventually associated with one or two people on the team.[42]

Accelerating Team Development through Team Building

Team building consists of formal activities intended to improve the development and functioning of a work team.[43] To a large extent, team building attempts to speed up the team development process. This process may be applied to new teams, but it is more commonly introduced for existing teams that have regressed to earlier stages of team development due to membership turnover or loss of focus.

Some team-building interventions are task focused. They clarify the team's performance goals, increase the team's motivation to accomplish these goals, and establish a mechanism for systematic feedback on the team's goal performance. A second type of team building tries to improve the team's problem-solving skills. A third category clarifies and reconstructs each member's

▼**EXHIBIT 7.5** Stages of Team Development

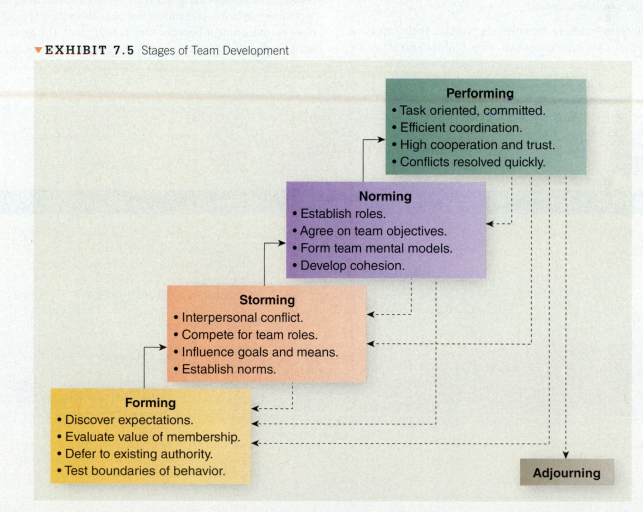

Performing
- Task oriented, committed.
- Efficient coordination.
- High cooperation and trust.
- Conflicts resolved quickly.

Norming
- Establish roles.
- Agree on team objectives.
- Form team mental models.
- Develop cohesion.

Storming
- Interpersonal conflict.
- Compete for team roles.
- Influence goals and means.
- Establish norms.

Forming
- Discover expectations.
- Evaluate value of membership.
- Defer to existing authority.
- Test boundaries of behavior.

Adjourning

perceptions of her or his role as well as the role expectations that member has of other team members. Role definition team building also helps the team to develop shared mental models—common internal representations of the external world, such as how to interact with clients, maintain machinery, and engage in meetings. As we mentioned earlier, team processes and performance depend on how well team members share common mental models about how they should work together.[44]

A fourth—and likely the most common—type of team building is aimed at improving relations among team members. Its objective is to help team members learn more about each other, build trust in each other, and develop ways to manage conflict within the team. Popular interventions such as wilderness team activities, paintball wars, and obstacle-course challenges are typically offered to build trust. "If two colleagues hold the rope for you while you're climbing 10 meters up, that is truly team building," suggests a partner in a German communications consulting firm who participated in that team-building event.[45]

Although team-building activities are popular, their success is less certain.[46] One problem is that team-building activities are used as general solutions to general team problems. A better approach is to begin with a sound diagnosis of the team's health and then select team-building interventions that address weaknesses.[48] Another problem is that team building is applied as a one-shot medical inoculation every team should receive when it is formed. In truth, team building is an ongoing process, not a three-day jump start.[49] Finally, we must remember that team building occurs on the job, not just on an obstacle course or in a national park. Organizations should encourage team members to reflect on their work experiences and to experiment with just-in-time learning for team development.

Team Norms

Norms are the informal rules and shared expectations that groups establish to regulate the behavior of their members. Norms apply only to behavior, not to private thoughts or feelings. Furthermore, norms exist only for behaviors that are important to the team.[50] Norms are enforced in various ways. Coworkers grimace if we are late for a meeting, or they make sarcastic comments if we don't have our part of the project completed on time. Norms are also directly reinforced through praise from high-status members, more access to valued resources, or other rewards available to the team. But team members often conform to prevailing norms without direct reinforcement or punishment because they identify with the group and want to align their behavior with the team's expectations. The

OB Theory to Practice

Popular Team Building Activities[47]

Team-Building Activity	Description	Example
Team volunteering events	Teams of employees spend a day providing a public service to the community.	Timberland Co. employees work in teams to clean up the environment, plant trees, and work on community revitalization projects.
Team scavenger/treasure hunt competitions	Teams follow instructions to find clues or objects collected throughout the community.	With instructions and GPS devices, teams of Verizon Wireless employees track down 32 clues around Tampa within a three-hour time limit.
Team sports/exercise competitions	Wide variety of sports or health activities, ranging from volleyball tournaments across departments to teams competing globally in health activities.	More than 200 teams (7 employees per team) at Nestlé UK compete each year in the Global Corporate Challenge. Each team has the challenge of taking a virtual walk around the world in 125 days, which is about 10,000 steps per person.
Team cooking competitions	Employees work in teams to prepare a meal under the guidance of a master chef.	Employees at the Singapore operations of German engineering firm Siemens attend lessons at a bakery and then test their baking skills in teams.

more closely the person's self-concept is connected to the group, the more the individual is motivated to avoid negative sanctions from that group.[51]

How Team Norms Develop

Norms develop when teams form because people need to anticipate or predict how others will act. Even subtle events during the team's formation, such as how team members initially greet each other and where they sit in the first meetings, can initiate norms that are later difficult to change. Norms also form as team members discover behaviors that help them function more effectively (such as the need to respond quickly to email). In particular, a critical event in the team's history can trigger formation of a norm or sharpen a previously vague one. A third influence on team norms are the experiences and values that members bring to the team. If members of a new team value work/life balance, norms are likely to develop that discourage long hours and work overload.[52]

Preventing and Changing Dysfunctional Team Norms

Team norms often become deeply anchored, so the best way to avoid norms that undermine organizational success or employee well-being is to establish desirable norms when the team is first formed. One way to do this is to clearly state desirable norms when the team is created. Another approach is to select people with appropriate values. If organizational leaders want their teams to have strong safety norms, they should hire people who already value safety and who clearly identify the importance of safety when the team is formed.

The suggestions so far refer to new teams, but how can organizational leaders maintain desirable norms in older teams? One solution, according to a recent study, is that leaders often have the capacity to alter existing norms.[53] By speaking up or actively coaching the team, they can often subdue dysfunctional norms while developing useful norms. A second suggestion is to introduce team-based rewards that counter dysfunction norms. However, studies report that employees might continue to adhere to a dysfunctional team norm (such as limiting output) even though this behavior reduces their paycheck. Finally, if dysfunctional norms are deeply ingrained and the previous solutions don't work, it may be necessary to disband the group and replace it with people having more favorable norms.

Team Cohesion

Team cohesion refers to the degree of attraction people feel toward the team and their motivation to remain members. It is a characteristic of the team, including the extent to which its members are attracted to the team, are committed to the team's goals or tasks, and feel a collective sense of team pride.[54] Thus, team cohesion is an emotional experience, not just a calculation of whether to stay or leave the team. It exists when team members make the team part of their self-concept. Team cohesion is associated with team development because team members develop a team identity as part of the team development process.

Influences on Team Cohesion

Several factors influence team cohesion: member similarity, team size, member interaction, difficult entry, team success, and external competition or challenges. For the most part, these factors reflect the individual's social identity with the group and beliefs about how team membership will fulfill personal needs.

- *Member similarity.* Social scientists have long known that people are attracted to others who are similar to them.[55] This similarity-attraction effect occurs because we assume people who look like us and have similar backgrounds are more trustworthy and are more likely to accept us. We also expect to have fewer negative experiences, such as conflicts and violations of our expectations and beliefs. Thus, teams have higher cohesion or become cohesive more quickly when members are similar to each other. In contrast, it is more difficult and takes longer for teams with diverse members to become cohesive. This difficulty depends on the form of diversity, however. Teams consisting of people from different job groups seem to gel together just as well as teams of people from the same job.[56]

- *Team size.* Smaller teams tend to have more cohesion than larger teams because it is easier for a few people to agree on goals and coordinate work activities. However, small teams have less cohesion when they lack enough members to perform the required tasks.

- *Member interaction.* Teams tend to have more cohesion when team members interact with each other fairly regularly. This occurs when team members perform highly interdependent tasks and work in the same physical area.

- *Somewhat difficult entry.* Teams tend to have more cohesion when entry to the team is restricted. The more elite the team, the more prestige it confers on its members, and the more they tend to value their membership in the unit. At the same time, research suggests that severe initiations can weaken team cohesion because of the adverse effects of humiliation, even for those who successfully endure the initiation.[57]

- *Team success.* Team cohesion increases with the team's level of success because people are attracted to groups that fulfill their needs and goals.[58] Furthermore, individuals are more likely to attach their social identity to successful teams than to those with a string of failures.[59]

- *External competition and challenges.* Team cohesion tends to increase when members face external competition or a valued objective that is challenging. This might include a threat from an external competitor or friendly competition from other teams. Employees value their membership on the team because of its ability to overcome the threat or competition and as a form of social support. However, cohesion can dissipate when external threats are severe because these threats are stressful and cause teams to make less effective decisions.[60]

Consequences of Team Cohesion Every team must have some minimal level of cohesion to maintain its existence. People who belong to high-cohesion teams are motivated to maintain their membership and to help the team achieve its mutually-agreed objectives. Compared to low-cohesion teams, high-cohesion team members spend more time together, share information more frequently, and are more satisfied with each other. They provide each other with better social support in

stressful situations.[61] Members of high-cohesion teams are generally more sensitive to each other's needs and develop better interpersonal relationships, thereby reducing dysfunctional conflict. When conflict does arise, members tend to resolve their differences swiftly and effectively. With better cooperation and more conformity to norms, high-cohesion teams usually perform better than low-cohesion teams.[62]

The relationship between cohesion and performance is somewhat more complex, however. Earlier in this section we said that team performance (success) increases cohesion, whereas we are now saying that team cohesion predicts team performance. Both statements are correct, but there is some evidence that team performance has a stronger effect on cohesion than vice versa. In other words, a team's performance will likely affect its cohesion, whereas a team's cohesion has less of an effect on its performance.[63]

The weaker effect of team cohesion on team performance might be explained by a second issue. Specifically, as Exhibit 7.6 illustrates, team cohesion increases team performance only when the team's norms are compatible with organizational values and objectives. When team norms are counterproductive (such as when norms encourage absenteeism or discourage employees from working productively), a cohesive team will typically perform worse than if the team had low cohesion. This effect occurs because cohesion motivates employees to perform at a level more consistent with team norms. When team norms undermine the organization's performance, high cohesion will motivate employees to reduce team performance.[64]

Team Trust

Any relationship—including the relationship among team members—depends on a certain degree of trust.[65] **Trust** refers to positive expectations one person has toward another person in situations involving risk (see Chapter 4).[66] A high level of trust occurs when others affect you in situations where you are at risk but you believe they will not harm you. Trust includes both your beliefs and conscious feelings about the relationship with other team members. In other words, a person both logically evaluates the situation as trustworthy and feels that it is trustworthy.[67] Trust is built on three foundations: calculus, knowledge, and identification (see Exhibit 7.7).

Calculus-based trust represents a logical calculation that other team members will act appropriately because they face sanctions if their actions violate reasonable expectations.[68] It offers the lowest potential trust and is easily broken by a violation of expectations. Some scholars even suggest that calculus-based trust is not trust at all. Instead, it might be trust in the system rather than in the other person. In any event, calculus-based trust alone cannot sustain a team's relationship because it relies on deterrence. *Knowledge-based trust* is based on the predictability of another team member's behavior. This predictability refers only to "positive expectations,"

▼ **EXHIBIT 7.6** Effect of Team Cohesion on Task Performance

	Low — Team cohesion — High
Team norms support company goals	Moderately high task performance / High task performance
Team norms conflict with company goals	Moderately low task performance / Low task performance

▼ **EXHIBIT 7.7** Three Foundations of Trust in Teams

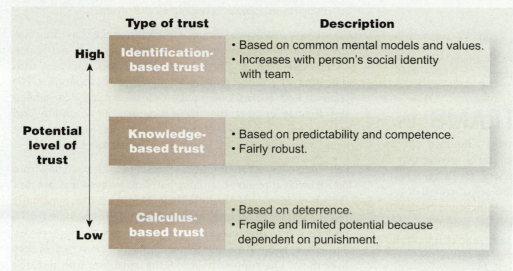

	Type of trust	Description
High ↑	**Identification-based trust**	• Based on common mental models and values. • Increases with person's social identity with team.
Potential level of trust	**Knowledge-based trust**	• Based on predictability and competence. • Fairly robust.
Low ↓	**Calculus-based trust**	• Based on deterrence. • Fragile and limited potential because dependent on punishment.

as the definition of trust states, because you would not trust someone who tends to engage in harmful or dysfunctional behavior. Knowledge-based trust includes our confidence in the other person's ability or competence, such as the confidence

a violation of this high-level trust because it strikes at the heart of their self-concept.

Dynamics of Team Trust

Employees typically join a team with a moderate or high level—not a low level—of trust in their new coworkers. The main explanation for the initially high trust (called *swift trust*) in organizational settings is that people usually believe fellow team members are reasonably competent (knowledge-based trust) and they tend to develop some degree of social identity with the team (identification-based trust). Even when working with strangers, most of us display some level of trust, if only because it supports our self-concept of being a good person.[70] However, trust is

> "One way to drive fear out of a relationship is to realize that your partner's values are the same as yours, that what you care about is exactly what they care about.
>
> —Steve Jobs[71]

that exists when we trust a physician.[69] Knowledge-based trust offers a higher potential level of trust and is more stable because it develops over time.

Identification-based trust is based on mutual understanding and an emotional bond among team members. It occurs when team members think, feel, and act like each other. High-performance teams exhibit this level of trust because they share the same values and mental models. Identification-based trust is potentially the strongest and most robust of all three types of trust. The individual's self-concept is based partly on membership in the team and he or she believes the members' values highly overlap, so any transgressions by other team members are quickly forgiven. People are more reluctant to acknowledge

fragile in new relationships because it is based on assumptions rather than well-established experience. Consequently, studies report that trust tends to decrease rather than increase over time. This is unfortunate because employees become less forgiving and less cooperative toward others as their level of trust decreases, and this undermines team and organizational effectiveness.[72]

The team effectiveness model is a useful template for understanding how teams work—and don't work—in organizations. With this knowledge in hand, let's briefly investigate two types of teams that have received considerable attention among OB experts and practitioners: self-directed teams and virtual teams.

Learning Objective

After reading the next two sections, you should be able to

LO4 Discuss the characteristics and factors required for success of self-directed teams and virtual teams.

SELF-DIRECTED TEAMS

Reckitt-Benckiser's plants in the United Kingdom operate with minimal management decision making or involvement in production line activities. The household goods company's manufacturing facilities rely instead on self-directed teams. **Self-directed teams (SDTs)** are cross-functional groups organized around work processes, that complete an entire piece of work requiring several interdependent tasks, and that have substantial autonomy over the execution of those tasks.[73]

This definition captures two distinct features of SDTs. First, these teams complete an entire piece of work requiring several interdependent tasks. This type of work arrangement clusters the team members together while minimizing interdependence and interaction with employees outside the team. The result is a close-knit group of employees who depend on each other to accomplish their individual tasks. For example, Reckitt-Benckiser employees responsible for manufacturing Lysol® disinfectant spray are responsible for that entire line of production—from receiving raw materials to packaging the product.

The second distinctive feature of SDTs is that they have substantial autonomy over the execution of their tasks. In particular, these teams plan, organize, and control work activities with little or no direct involvement of a higher-status supervisor. The teams at Reckitt-Benckiser's plants, for instance, are considered self-directed because they have considerable autonomy and responsibility for decisions in their work area, including managing inventory, production efficiency, and related matters.

Self-directed teams are found in several industries, ranging from petrochemical plants to aircraft parts manufacturing. Most of the top-rated manufacturing firms in North America apparently rely on SDTs.[75] Indeed, self-directed teams have become such a popular way to organize employees in manufacturing, services, and government work that many companies don't realize they have them. The popularity of SDTs is consistent with research indicating they potentially increase both productivity and job satisfaction. For instance, one study found car dealership service shops that organize employees into SDTs are significantly more profitable than shops where employees work without a team structure. Another study reported that both short- and long-term measures of customer satisfaction increased after street cleaners in a German city were organized into SDTs.[76]

Success Factors for Self-Directed Teams

The successful implementation of self-directed teams depends on several factors.[77] SDTs should be responsible for an entire work process, such as making an entire product or providing a service. This structure keeps each team sufficiently independent from other teams, yet it demands a relatively high degree of interdependence among employees within the team.[78] SDTs should also have sufficient autonomy to organize and coordinate their work. Autonomy allows them to respond more quickly and effectively to client and stakeholder demands. It also motivates team members through feelings of empowerment. Finally, SDTs are more successful when the work site and technology support coordination and communication among team members and increases job enrichment.[79] Too often, management calls a group of employees a "team," yet the work layout, assembly-line structure, and other technologies isolate the employees from each other.

VIRTUAL TEAMS

Virtual teams are teams whose members operate across space, time, and organizational boundaries and are linked through information technologies to achieve organizational tasks.[80] Virtual teams differ from traditional teams in two ways: (1) They are not usually colocated (do not work in the same physical area), and (2) due to their lack of colocation, members of virtual teams depend primarily on information technologies rather than face-to-face interaction to communicate and coordinate their work effort.

Self-Directed Teams at Whole Foods

Whole Foods Market operates with self-directed teams. Each store has about 10 teams, such as the prepared-foods team, the cashier/front-end team, and the seafood team. Teams are "self-directed" because team members make decisions about their work unit with minimal interference from management. "Each team is . . . responsible for managing its own business," explains Whole Foods Market cofounder John Mackey. "It gets a profit-and-loss statement, it's responsible for managing inventory, labor productivity, gross margins; and its members are responsible for many of the product-placement decisions."[74]

More Virtual Teams
More Virtual Challenges[81]

self-directed teams (SDTs) Cross-functional work groups that are organized around work processes, complete an entire piece of work requiring several interdependent tasks, and have substantial autonomy over the execution of those tasks.

virtual teams Teams whose members operate across space, time, and organizational boundaries and are linked through information technologies to achieve organizational tasks.

80% of managers polled in large American companies say their firm's reliance on virtual teams will grow in importance over the next three years.

58% of American managers polled say it is somewhat or very important that all members of their department work from the *same* location.

70% of American chief information officers polled indicate that managing virtual teams is a very important globalization challenge (highest rated issue on the list).

Virtual teams have spread throughout most organizations, and this trend will continue. Two-thirds of human resource managers estimate that reliance on virtual teams will grow rapidly over the next few years.[82] In global companies such as IBM, almost everyone in knowledge work is part of a virtual team. One reason why virtual teams have become so widespread is information technologies have made it easier than ever before to communicate and coordinate with people at a distance.[83] The shift from production-based to knowledge-based work is a second reason why virtual teamwork is feasible. It isn't yet possible to make a physical product when team members are located apart, but most of us are now in jobs that mainly process knowledge.

Information technologies and knowledge-based work make virtual teams *possible*, but organizational learning and globalization are two reasons why they are increasingly *necessary*. Virtual teams represent a natural part of the organizational learning process because they encourage employees to share and use knowledge where geography limits more direct forms of collaboration. Globalization also makes virtual teams increasingly necessary because employees are spread around the planet rather than around one building or city. Thus, global businesses depend on virtual teamwork to leverage their human capital.

Success Factors for Virtual Teams

Virtual teams have all the challenges of traditional teams, along with the complications of distance and time. Fortunately, OB researchers have been keenly interested in virtual teams, and their studies are now yielding ways to improve virtual team effectiveness.[84] First, along with having the team competencies described earlier in this chapter, members of successful virtual teams must have good communication technology skills, strong self-leadership skills to motivate and guide their behavior without peers or bosses nearby, and higher emotional intelligence so they can decipher the feelings of other team members from email and other limited communication media.

A second recommendation is that virtual teams should have a toolkit of communication channels (email, virtual whiteboards, video conferencing, etc.) as well as the freedom to choose the channels that work best for them. This may sound obvious, but unfortunately senior management tends to impose technology on virtual teams, often based on advice from external consultants, and expects team members to use the same communication technology throughout their work. In contrast, research suggests that communication channels gain and lose importance over time, depending on the task and level of trust.

Third, virtual teams need plenty of structure. In one recent review of effective virtual teams, many of the principles for successful virtual teams related mostly to creating these structures, such as clear operational objectives, documented work processes, and agreed-upon roles and responsibilities.[85] The final recommendation is that virtual team members should meet face-to-face fairly early in the team development process. This idea may seem contradictory to the entire notion of virtual teams, but so far, no technology has replaced face-to-face interaction for high-level bonding and mutual understanding.[86]

Learning Objective

After reading this section, you should be able to

LO5 Identify four constraints on team decision making and discuss the advantages and disadvantages of four structures aimed at improving team decision making.

TEAM DECISION MAKING

Self-directed teams, virtual teams, and practically all other groups are expected to make decisions. Under certain conditions, teams are more effective than individuals at identifying problems, choosing alternatives, and evaluating their decisions. To leverage these benefits, however, we first need to understand the constraints on effective team decision making. Then, we look at specific team structures that try to overcome these constraints.

Constraints on Team Decision Making

Anyone who has spent enough time in the workplace can recite several ways in which teams stumble in decision making. The four most common problems are time constraints, evaluation apprehension, pressure to conform, and some elements of groupthink.

Time Constraints There's a saying that committees keep minutes and waste hours. This reflects the fact that teams take longer than individuals to make decisions.[87] Unlike individuals, teams require extra time to organize, coordinate, and maintain relationships. The larger the group, the more time is required to make a decision. Team members need time to learn about each other and build rapport. They need to manage an imperfect communication process so there is sufficient understanding of each other's ideas. They also need to coordinate roles and rules of order within the decision process.

Another time-related constraint found in most team structures is that only one person can speak at a time.[88] This problem, known as **production blocking**, undermines idea generation in several ways. First, team members need to listen in on the conversation to find an opportune time to speak up, and this monitoring makes it difficult for them to concentrate on their own ideas. Second, ideas are fleeting, so the longer they wait to speak up, the more likely these flickering ideas will die out. Third, team members might remember their fleeting thoughts by concentrating on them, but this causes them to pay less attention to the conversation. By ignoring what others are saying, team members miss other potentially good ideas as well as the opportunity to convey their ideas to others in the group.

Evaluation Apprehension Team members are often reluctant to mention ideas that seem silly because they believe (often correctly) that other team members are silently evaluating them.[89] This **evaluation apprehension** is based on the individual's desire to create a favorable self-presentation and need to protect self-esteem. It is most common when meetings are attended by people with different levels of status or expertise or when members formally evaluate each other's performance throughout the year (as in 360-degree feedback). Creative ideas often sound bizarre or illogical when first presented, so evaluation apprehension tends to discourage employees from mentioning them in front of coworkers.

Pressure to Conform Team cohesion leads employees to conform to the team's norms. This control keeps the group organized around common goals, but it may also cause team members to suppress their dissenting opinions, particularly when a strong team norm is related to the issue. When someone does state a point of view that violates the majority opinion, other members might punish the violator or try to persuade him or her the opinion is incorrect. Conformity can also be subtle. To some extent, we depend on the opinions others hold to validate our own views. If coworkers don't agree with us, we begin to question our own opinions even without overt peer pressure.

Groupthink **Groupthink** refers to the tendency of highly cohesive groups to value consensus at the price of decision quality.[90] The concept includes the dysfunctional effects of conformity on team decision making, which we just described. It also includes the dysfunctional consequences of trying to maintain harmony within the team. This desire for harmony exists as a group norm and is most apparent when team members have a strong social identity with the group. Groupthink supposedly occurs most often when the team is isolated from outsiders, the team leader is opinionated (rather than impartial), the team is under stress due to an external threat, the team has experienced recent failures or other decision-making problems, and the team lacks clear guidance from corporate policies or procedures.

The term *groupthink* is now part of everyday language, but most experts have dismissed the concept. The main problem with the groupthink concept is it consists of several elements that don't cluster together very well, and some of those elements actually improve rather than undermine decision making in some situations. Also, almost all support for the groupthink effect comes from case studies, most of which are flawed.[91]

Although the groupthink concept is in doubt, there are specific elements that remain relevant as team decision-making problems. One of these elements, conformity, was identified earlier

OB Theory to Practice

Improving Team Decision Making

- Encourage critical thinking and vigorous debate.
- Provide opportunities for everyone to present their ideas (be sure discussion is not dominated by one or two people).
- The meeting should have enough people to provide necessary knowledge, yet few enough people that everyone has opportunities to participate in the discussion.
- Get everyone's preferences out in the open quickly.
- Narrow discussion to a few plausible options.
- Recognize the most senior person may have to make the final decision after everyone has debated the issue, particularly when the issue is messy or filled with conflict.

as a problem with team decision making. Overconfidence is another groupthink element that also deserves continued attention as a problem. Studies consistently report that highly confident teams have a false sense of invulnerability, which makes them less attentive in decision making than are moderately confident teams.[92] This overconfidence effect is related to problems with self-enhancement described in Chapter 3 and with the adverse effects of positive moods and emotions on the quality of decision making (see Chapter 6).

Team Structures to Improve Decision Making

Team decision making is fraught with problems, but several solutions also emerge from these bad news studies. Team members need to be confident in their decision making but not so confident they collectively feel invulnerable. This calls for team norms that encourage critical thinking as well as team membership with sufficient diversity. Checks and balances need to be in place to prevent one or two people from dominating the discussion. The team should also be large enough to possess the collective knowledge to resolve the problem yet small enough that the team doesn't consume too much time or restrict individual input.

Team structures also help to minimize the problems described over the previous few pages. Four structures potentially improve team decision making in team settings: constructive conflict, brainstorming, electronic brainstorming, and nominal group technique.

Constructive Conflict **Constructive conflict** occurs when people focus on the issue and maintain respect for people having other points of view. This conflict is called "constructive"

> [When two [people] in business always agree, one of them is unnecessary.[93]
>
> —William Wrigley Jr.]

because it encourages people to present their divergent viewpoints so ideas and recommendations can be clarified, redesigned, and tested for logical soundness. This critical thinking and analysis helps participants to reexamine their assumptions and logic. The main challenge with constructive conflict is that people get defensive when their ideas are questioned, even when those critiques are polite and logical. Consequently, constructive conflict often degenerates into defensive behavior and personal attacks. This tendency may explain why constructive conflict has not been consistently beneficial for team decision making across studies.[94] We explore this issue further in Chapter 11, along with specific strategies for minimizing the emotional effects of conflict while maintaining constructive debate.

Brainstorming

Brainstorming is a team event where participants try to think up as many ideas as possible. The process was introduced by advertising executive Alex Osborn in 1939 and has four simple rules to maximize the number and quality of ideas presented: (1) Speak freely—describe even the craziest ideas; (2) don't criticize others or their ideas; (3) provide as many ideas as possible—the quality of ideas increases with the quantity of ideas; and (4) build on the ideas that others have presented. These rules are supposed to encourage divergent thinking while minimizing evaluation apprehension and other team dynamics problems.[95]

Although brainstorming became immensely popular when first introduced, it lost credibility over the years—mostly for the wrong reasons. First, a business magazine article in the 1950s misrepresented and lampooned the process.[96] Second, numerous lab studies using college students concluded that brainstorming isn't very effective, mainly because production blocking and evaluation apprehension still interfere with team dynamics.[97]

These studies and the magazine article were unfortunate because subsequent work has found that brainstorming is potentially useful in real-world work settings.[98] Companies that use brainstorming emphasize that it takes considerable skill and experience to effectively lead brainstorm sessions, yet most lab studies involve

teams of college students who receive minimal training and have no previous experience with these activities. Executives say brainstorming requires a collaborative learning orientation culture where employees are not inhibited by evaluation apprehension, whereas the lab experiments involve students who often don't know each other and are sensitive about their image to others. Most studies also make the mistake of measuring brainstorming effectiveness by the number of ideas generated, whereas recent investigations indicate brainstorming tends to generate more *creative* ideas (not necessarily a greater number of ideas).[99]

Lab studies also ignore other benefits of brainstorming reported by companies that claim they are effective. The positive focus of brainstorming (no criticizing) tends to increase team cohesion and participant commitment to the eventual decision. Brainstorming sessions also tend to spread enthusiasm—a condition that often generates creativity beyond these events. Overall, while brainstorming might not always be the best team structure, it seems to be more valuable than many lab studies have concluded.

Electronic Brainstorming Electronic brainstorming

is a variation of brainstorming that relies on networked computers to submit and share creative ideas. After receiving the question or issue, participants enter their ideas using special computer software. The ideas are distributed anonymously to other participants, who are encouraged to piggyback on those ideas. Team members eventually vote electronically on the ideas presented. Face-to-face discussion usually follows. Electronic brainstorming can be quite effective at generating creative ideas with minimal production blocking, evaluation apprehension, or conformity problems.[100] Despite these numerous advantages, electronic brainstorming seems to be too structured and technology bound for some executives. Some leaders may also feel threatened by the honesty of statements generated through this process and by their limited ability to control the discussion.

Nominal Group Technique Nominal group technique

is another variation of traditional brainstorming that tries to combine the benefits of team decision making without the problems mentioned earlier.[101] The method is called "nominal" because participants form a group in name only during two of its three stages. After the problem is described, team members silently and independently write down as many solutions as they can. In the second stage, participants describe their solutions to the other team members, usually in a round-robin format. As with brainstorming, there is no criticism or debate, although members are encouraged to ask for clarification of the ideas presented. In the third stage, participants silently and independently rank-order or vote on each proposed solution.

Nominal group technique has been applied in numerous laboratory and real-world settings, such as identifying ways to improve tourism in various countries.[102] For the most part, these studies endorse the use of this structured form of team decision making. It tends to generate a higher number of ideas and better-quality ideas than do traditional interacting and possibly brainstorming groups.[103] Due to its high degree of structure, nominal group technique usually maintains a high task orientation and relatively low potential for conflict within the team. However, production blocking and evaluation apprehension still occur to some extent. At least one study also reports that participants require training to apply this structured approach to team decision making.[104] ◼

nominal group technique A variation of brainstorming consisting of three stages: Participants (1) silently and independently document their ideas, (2) collectively describe these ideas to the other team members without critique, and then (3) silently and independently evaluate the ideas presented.

CHECK IT OUT!

www.mhhe.com/ McShaneM2e

for study materials
including quizzes
and other resources

chapter eight

communicating in
teams and organizations

Atos Origin is at war with email. Executives at the Paris-based global information technology consulting firm believe the volume of email transmitted around the company has created "information pollution" that stifles productivity and undermines employee well-being. "We are producing data on a massive scale that is fast polluting our working environments and also encroaching into our personal lives," says Atos Origin chief executive Thierry Breton. The company estimates that reading and writing emails consume up to half of its managers' workweek.

Atos Origin's solution is to ban all email among the company's 50,000 staff within the next couple of years. The company will encourage staff to share ideas, engage in communities, and have virtual team meetings through instant messaging, web conferences, and an enterprise-strength social media site. "It is clearly going to be a big challenge for us because email is everywhere," admits Atos Origin vice-president for global innovation Marc-Henri Desportes. Desportes notes, however, that this transformation is less difficult for the company's Generation Y employees. "These people do not use email any more. They use social media tools."[1]

Communication is the lifeblood of all organizations. Yet, as Atos Origin executives have discovered, email and other channels can also overwhelm staff and reduce productivity. Technological developments have had a revolutionary effect on communication in organizations. In particular, social media technologies such as Facebook, Twitter, and LinkedIn have transformed how we communicate in society, yet we may still be at the beginning of this revolution. Wire cablegrams and telephones introduced a century ago are giving way to email, instant messaging, Weblogs, and now social media sites. Each of these inventions creates fascinating changes in how people communicate with each other in the workplace, as well as new opportunities to improve organizational effectiveness and employee well-being.

continued on p. 154

LEARNING OBJECTIVES

After studying Chapter 8, you should be able to:

LO1 Explain why communication is important in organizations and discuss four influences on effective communication encoding and decoding.

LO2 Compare and contrast the advantages of and problems with electronic mail, other verbal communication media, and nonverbal communication.

LO3 Explain how social acceptance and media richness influence the preferred communication channel.

LO4 Discuss various barriers (noise) to effective communication, including cross-cultural and gender-based differences in communication.

LO5 Explain how to get your message across more effectively, and summarize the elements of active listening.

LO6 Summarize effective communication strategies in organizational hierarchies, and review the role and relevance of the organizational grapevine.

153

continued from p. 153

communication
The process by which information is transmitted and understood between two or more people.

Communication refers to the process by which information is transmitted and *understood* between two or more people. We emphasize the word *understood* because transmitting the sender's intended meaning is the essence of good communication. This chapter begins by discussing the importance of effective communication, outlining the communication process model, and discussing factors that improve communication coding and decoding. Next, we identify types of communication channels, including email and social media sites, followed by factors to consider when choosing a communication medium. This chapter then identifies barriers to effective communication. The latter part of this chapter offers an overview of ways to communicate in organizational hierarchies and offers insight about the pervasive organizational grapevine. ■

Learning Objective

After reading the next two sections, you should be able to

LO1 Explain why communication is important in organizations and discuss four influences on effective communication encoding and decoding.

> "Communication effectiveness depends on the ability of sender and receiver to efficiently and accurately encode and decode information."

THE IMPORTANCE OF COMMUNICATION

Effective communication is vital to all organizations, so much so that no company could exist without it. The reason? Recall from Chapter 1 that organizations are defined as groups of people who work interdependently toward some purpose. People work interdependently only when they can communicate with each other. Although organizations rely on a variety of coordinating mechanisms (which we discuss in Chapter 12), frequent, timely, and accurate communication remains the primary means through which employees and work units effectively synchronize their work.[2] Chester Barnard, a telecommunications CEO and a respected pioneer in organizational behavior theory, made this observation back in 1938: "An organization comes into being when there are persons able to communicate with each other."[3]

In addition to coordination, communication plays a central role in organizational learning. It is the means through which knowledge enters the organization and is distributed to employees.[4] A third function of communication is decision making. Imagine the challenge of making a decision without any information about the decision context, the alternatives available, the likely outcomes of those options, or the extent to which the decision is achieving its objectives. All of these ingredients require communication from coworkers as well as from stakeholders in the external environment. For example, airline cockpit crews make much better decisions—and thereby cause far fewer accidents—when the captain encourages the crew to openly share information.[5]

A fourth function is to change behavior. When communicating to others, we are often trying to alter their beliefs and feelings and ultimately their behavior. This influence process might be passive, such as merely describing the situation more clearly and fully. Sometimes, the communication event is a deliberate attempt to change someone's thoughts and actions. We will discuss this under the topic of persuasion later in this chapter.

Finally, communication supports employee well-being.[6] Informationally, communication conveys knowledge that helps employees to better manage their work environment. For instance, research shows that new employees adjust much better to the organization when coworkers communicate subtle nuggets of wisdom, such as how to avoid office politics, complete work procedures correctly, find useful resources, handle difficult customers, and so on.[7]

Emotionally, the communication experience itself is a soothing balm. Indeed, people are less susceptible to colds, cardiovascular disease, and other physical and mental illnesses when they have regular social interaction (although research also finds that working in the same close office space with two or more coworkers increases the risk of getting colds!).[8] In essence, people have an inherent drive to bond, to validate their self-worth, and to maintain their social identity. Communication is the means through which these drives and needs are fulfilled.

A MODEL OF COMMUNICATION

To understand the key interpersonal features of effective communication, let's examine the model presented in Exhibit 8.1, which provides a useful "conduit" metaphor for thinking about the communication process.[9] According to this model, communication flows through channels between the sender and receiver. The sender forms a message and encodes it into words, gestures, voice intonations, and other symbols or signs. Next, the encoded message is transmitted to the intended receiver through one or more communication channels (media). The receiver senses the incoming message and decodes it into something meaningful. Ideally, the decoded meaning is what the sender had intended.

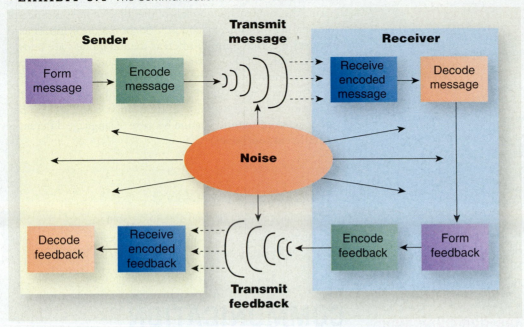

In most situations, the sender looks for evidence that the other person received and understood the transmitted message. This feedback may be a formal acknowledgment, such as "Yes, I know what you mean," or indirect evidence from the receiver's subsequent actions. Notice that feedback repeats the communication process. Intended feedback is encoded, transmitted, received, and decoded from the receiver to the sender of the original message. This model recognizes that communication is not a free-flowing conduit. Rather, the transmission of meaning from one person to another is hampered by *noise*—the psychological, social, and structural barriers that distort and obscure the sender's intended message. If any part of the communication process is distorted or broken, the sender and receiver will not have a common understanding of the message.

Influences on Effective Encoding and Decoding

The communication process model suggests that communication effectiveness depends on the ability of sender and receiver to efficiently and accurately encode and decode information. There are four main factors that influence the effectiveness of the encoding-decoding process: similar codebooks, experience at encoding that message, communication channel motivation and ability, and common mental models of the communication context.[10]

Similar Codebooks
The sender and receiver rely on "codebooks," which are dictionaries of symbols, language, gestures, idioms, and other tools used to convey information. With similar codebooks, the communication participants are able to encode and decode more accurately because they both have the same or similar meaning. Communication efficiency also improves because there is less need for redundancy (repeating the message in

different ways) and less need for confirmation feedback ("So, you are saying that . . . ?").

Message Encoding Experience
Even with the same codebooks, some people are better than others at communicating the message because, through experience, they have learned which words and gestures transmit the message best to that audience. For example, after speaking to several employee groups about the company's new product development plans, you have fine-tuned the presentation so the audience receives your message more efficiently and effectively. This is similar to the effect of job training or sports practice. The more experience and practice gained at communicating a subject, the more people learn how to effectively transmit that information to others.

Communication Channel Motivation and Ability
The encoding-decoding process also depends on the sender's and receiver's motivation and ability to use the selected communication channel. Some people prefer face-to-face conversations, whereas others would rather prepare or receive written documentation. Some people are skilled at communicating through Twitter tweets, whereas others are more effective at

writing detailed reports. So, even if both parties have the same codebooks and are skilled at using those codebooks for a particular message, message encoding and decoding can be hampered by a communication channel that the sender, receiver, or both dislike or lack proficiency.[11]

Shared Mental Models of the Communication Context The encoding and decoding process also depends on how similar and well developed are the sender's and receiver's mental models of the communication context. Mental models are internal representations of the external world that allow us to visualize elements of a setting and relationships among those elements (see Chapter 3). When sender and receiver have shared mental models, they have a common understanding of the location, time, and other contextual features of the information. Sharing the same mental models of the topic context is different from sharing the same codebook. Codebooks are symbols used to convey message content, whereas mental models are knowledge structures of the communication setting. For example, a Russian cosmonaut and American astronaut might have shared mental models about the design and technology onboard the international space station (communication context), yet they experience poor communication because of language differences (i.e., different codebooks).

Learning Objective

After reading this section, you should be able to

LO2 Compare and contrast the advantages of and problems with electronic mail, other verbal communication media, and nonverbal communication.

COMMUNICATION CHANNELS

A key component of the communication model is the channel or medium through which information is transmitted. There are two main types of channels: verbal and nonverbal. Verbal communication uses words and occurs through either spoken or written channels. Nonverbal communication is any part of

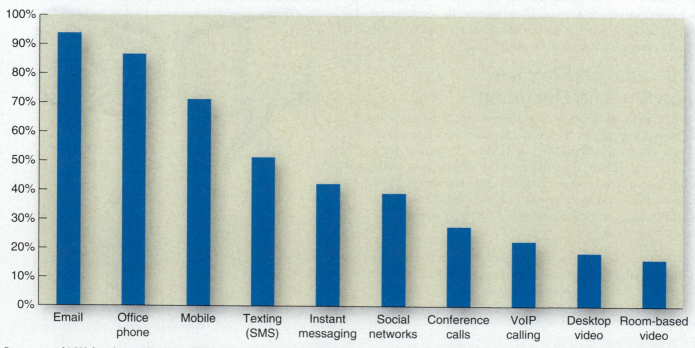

The Changing World of Workplace Communication Technology[12]

Percentage of 1,000 American technology-empowered workers who use various communications technologies in the workplace at least once per week.

communication that does not use words. Spoken and written communication are both verbal (i.e., they both use words), but they are quite different from each other and have different strengths and weaknesses in communication effectiveness, which we discuss later in this section. Also, written communication has traditionally been slower than spoken communication at transmitting messages, although electronic mail, Twitter "tweets," and other Internet-based communication channels have significantly improved written communication efficiency.

Internet-Based Communication

In the early 1960s, with funding from the U.S. Department of Defense, university researchers began discussing how to collaborate better by connecting their computers through a network. Their rough vision of connected computers became a reality in 1969 as the Advanced Research Projects Agency Network (ARPANET). ARPANET initially had only a dozen or so connections and was very slow and expensive by today's standards, but it marked the birth of the Internet. Two years later, a computer engineer developing ARPANET sent the first electronic mail (email) message between different computers on a network. By 1973, most communication on ARPANET was through email. ARPANET was mostly restricted to U.S. Defense-funded research centers, so in 1979 two graduate students at Duke University developed a public network system, called Usenet. Usenet allowed people to post information that could be retrieved by anyone else on the network, making it the first public computer-mediated social network.[13]

We have come a long way since the early days of ARPANET and Usenet. The medium of choice in most workplaces today is email because messages can be quickly written, edited, and transmitted. Information can be appended and conveyed to many people with a simple click of a mouse. Email is also asynchronous (messages are sent and received at different times), so there is no need to coordinate a communication session. With advances in computer search technology, email software has also become an efficient filing cabinet.[14]

Email tends to be the preferred medium for sending well-defined information for decision making. It is also central for coordinating work, although text messaging and Twitter tweets might overtake email for this objective. When email was introduced in the workplace over the past two decades, it tended to increase the volume of communication and significantly altered the flow of that information within groups and throughout the organization.[15] Specifically, it reduced some face-to-face and telephone communication but increased communication with people further up the hierarchy. Some social and organizational status differences still exist with email,[16] but they are somewhat less apparent than in face-to-face communication. By hiding age, race, and other features, email reduces stereotype biases. However, it also tends to increase reliance on stereotypes when we are already aware of the other person's personal characteristics.[17]

Problems with Email

In spite of the wonders of email, anyone who has used this communication medium knows that it has its limitations. Here are the top four complaints.

Poor Medium for Communicating Emotions People rely on facial expressions and other nonverbal cues to interpret the emotional meaning of words; email lacks this parallel communication channel. Indeed, people consistently and significantly underestimate the degree to which they understand the emotional tone of email messages.[18] Senders try to clarify the emotional tone of their messages by using expressive language ("Wonderful to hear from you!"), highlighting phrases in boldface or quotation marks, and inserting graphic faces (called emoticons or "smileys") representing the desired emotion. Recent studies suggest that writers are getting better at using these emotion symbols. Still, they do not replace the full complexity of real facial expressions, voice intonation, and hand movements.[19]

Reduces Politeness and Respect Email messages are often less diplomatic than written letters. Indeed, the term *flaming* has entered our language to describe email and other electronic messages that convey strong negative emotions to the receiver. People who receive email are partly to blame because they tend to infer a more negative or neutral interpretation of the email than was intended by the sender.[20] Even so, email flame wars occur mostly because senders are more likely to send disparaging messages by email than other communication channels. One reason is that individuals can post email messages before their emotions subside, whereas the sender of a traditional memo or letter would have time for sober second thoughts. A second reason is the low social presence (impersonal nature) of email; people are more likely to write things they would never say in face-to-face conversation. Fortunately, research has found that flaming decreases as teams move to later stages of development and when explicit norms and rules of communication are established.[21]

Poor Medium for Ambiguous, Complex, and Novel Situations
Email is usually fine for well-defined situations, such as giving basic instructions or presenting a meeting agenda, but it can be cumbersome and dysfunctional in ambiguous, complex, and novel situations. As we will describe later in this section, these circumstances require communication channels that transmit a larger volume of information with more rapid feedback. In other words, when the issue gets messy, stop emailing and start talking, preferably face-to-face.

Contributes to Information Overload
Email contributes to information overload.[22] Approximately 20 trillion emails (excluding 70 trillion spam emails) are now transmitted annually around the world, up from just 1.1 trillion in 1998. The email glut occurs because messages are created and copied to many people without much effort. The number of email messages will probably decrease as people become more familiar with it; until then, email volume continues to rise.

Workplace Communication through Social Media

Social media include Internet-based tools (Web sites, applications, etc.) that allow users to generate and exchange information. This "user-generated content" is creative content (developed by the user), published on the Internet (but may have restricted access), and produced outside of professional routines and practices.[23] Social media take many forms—blogs, wikis, instant messages, Twitter tweets, personal presentation sites (e.g., Facebook), viewer feedback forums, and the like. While earlier Internet activity involved passively reading or watching content, these emerging Internet activities are more interactive and dynamic.

One recent model suggests that social media serve several functions: presenting the individual's identity, enabling conversations, sharing information, sensing the presence of others in the virtual space, maintaining relationships, revealing reputation or status, and supporting communities (see Exhibit 8.2).[24] For instance, Facebook has a strong emphasis

▼**EXHIBIT 8.2** Functions of Communicating through Social Media

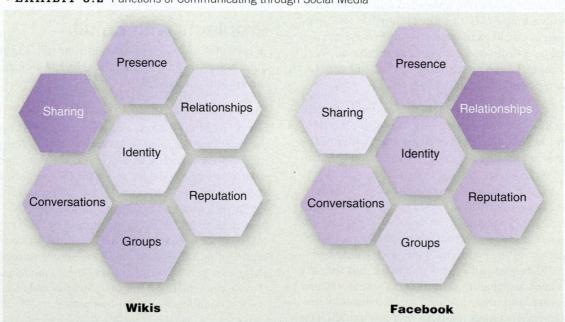

Source: Based on J. H. Kietzmann, K. Hermkens, I. P. McCarthy, and B. S. Silvestre, (2011). Social Media? Get Serious! Understanding the Functional Building Blocks of Social Media. *Business Horizons* 54, (no. 3): 241–51.

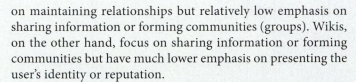

"THE MOST IMPORTANT THING IN COMMUNICATION IS HEARING WHAT ISN'T SAID.[25]

—PETER DRUCKER"

on maintaining relationships but relatively low emphasis on sharing information or forming communities (groups). Wikis, on the other hand, focus on sharing information or forming communities but have much lower emphasis on presenting the user's identity or reputation.

A few studies conclude (with caution) that social media offer considerable versatility and potential in the workplace.[26] Even so, companies have been reluctant to introduce these communication tools, mainly because they lack knowledge, staff/resources, and technical support to put them into practice.[27] Indeed, a common practice is to simply ban employee access to social media (usually after discovering excess employee activity on Facebook) without thinking through its potential.

Nonverbal Communication

Nonverbal communication includes facial gestures, voice intonation, physical distance, and even silence. This communication channel is necessary where noise or physical distance prevent effective verbal exchanges and the need for immediate feedback precludes written communication. But even in quiet face-to-face meetings, most information is communicated nonverbally. Rather like a parallel conversation, nonverbal cues signal subtle information to both parties, such as reinforcing their interest in the verbal conversation or demonstrating their relative status in the relationship.[28]

Nonverbal communication differs from verbal (i.e., written and spoken) communication in a couple of ways. First, it is less rule bound than verbal communication. We receive considerable formal training on how to understand spoken words but very little on how to understand the nonverbal signals that accompany those words. Consequently, nonverbal cues are generally more ambiguous and susceptible to misinterpretation. At the same time, many facial expressions (such as smiling) are hardwired and universal, thereby providing the only reliable means of communicating across cultures.

The other difference between verbal and nonverbal communication is that the former is typically conscious, whereas most nonverbal communication is automatic and nonconscious. We normally plan the words we say or write, but we rarely plan every blink, smile, or other gesture during a conversation. Indeed, as we just mentioned, many of these facial expressions communicate the same meaning across cultures because they are hardwired nonconscious responses to human emotions.[29] For example, pleasant emotions cause the brain centre to widen

the mouth, whereas negative emotions produce constricted facial expressions (squinting eyes, pursed lips, etc.).

Emotional Contagion
One of the most fascinating effects of emotions on nonverbal communication is the phenomenon called **emotional contagion**, which is the automatic process of "catching" or sharing another person's emotions by mimicking that person's facial expressions and other nonverbal behavior. Technically, human beings have brain receptors that cause them to mirror what they observe. In other words, to some degree our brain causes us to act as though we are the person we are watching.[30]

Consider what happens when you see a coworker accidentally bang his or her head against a filing cabinet. Chances are, you

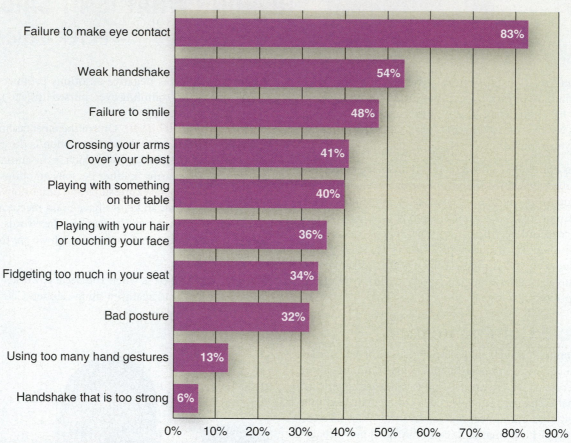

Top Ten Body Language Mistakes in Job Interviews[31]

Failure to make eye contact	83%
Weak handshake	54%
Failure to smile	48%
Crossing your arms over your chest	41%
Playing with something on the table	40%
Playing with your hair or touching your face	36%
Fidgeting too much in your seat	34%
Bad posture	32%
Using too many hand gestures	13%
Handshake that is too strong	6%

Percentage of U.K. employers surveyed who reported the biggest body language turnoffs in job interviews. Similar results were found in a U.S. survey one year earlier.

wince and put your hand on your own head as if you had hit the cabinet. Similarly, while listening to someone describe a positive event, you tend to smile and exhibit other emotional displays of happiness. While some of our nonverbal communication is planned, emotional contagion represents nonconscious behavior—we automatically mimic and synchronize our nonverbal behaviors with other people.[32]

Emotional contagion serves three purposes. First, mimicry provides continuous feedback, communicating that we understand and empathize with the sender. To consider the significance of this, imagine employees remaining expressionless after watching a coworker bang his or her head! The lack of parallel behavior conveys a lack of understanding or caring. Second, mimicking the nonverbal behaviors of other people seems to be a way of receiving emotional meaning from those people. If a coworker is angry with a client, your tendency to frown and show anger while listening helps you to experience that emotion more fully. In other words, we receive meaning by expressing the sender's emotions as well as by listening to the sender's words.

The third function of emotional contagion is to fulfill the drive to bond that was described in Chapter 5. Social solidarity is built out of each member's awareness of a collective sentiment. Through nonverbal expressions of emotional contagion, people see others share the same emotions that they feel. This strengthens relations among team members as well as between leaders and followers by providing evidence of their similarity.[33]

Learning Objective

After reading this section, you should be able to

LO3 Explain how social acceptance and media richness influence the preferred communication channel.

CHOOSING THE BEST COMMUNICATION CHANNEL

Which communication channel is most appropriate in a particular situation? Two important sets of factors to consider are (a) social acceptance and (b) media richness.

Social Acceptance

Social acceptance refers to how well the communication medium is approved and supported by the organization, teams, and individuals.[34] One factor in social acceptance is organizational and team norms regarding the use of specific communication channels. Norms partly explain why face-to-face meetings are daily events among staff in some firms, whereas computer-based video conferencing (such as Skype) and Twitter tweets are the media of choice in other organizations. Communication channel norms also vary across cultures. One recent study reported that when communicating with people further up the hierarchy, Koreans are much less likely than Americans to use email because this medium is less respectful of the superior's status.[35]

A second social acceptance factor is individual preferences for specific communication channels.[36] You may have noticed that some coworkers ignore (or rarely check) voice mail, yet they quickly respond to text messages or Twitter tweets. These preferences are due to personality traits as well as previous experience and reinforcement with particular channels.

A third social acceptance factor is the symbolic meaning of a channel. Some communication channels are viewed as impersonal, whereas others are more personal; some are considered professional, whereas others are casual; some are "cool," whereas others are old-fashioned. In one recent survey, 60 percent of employees say they use email to arrange meetings, whereas less than 10 percent use this channel to communicate with their boss about problems.[37] The importance of a channel's symbolic meaning is perhaps most apparent in stories about managers who use emails or text messages to inform employees that they are fired or laid off. These communication events make headlines because email and text messages are considered inappropriate (too impersonal) for transmission of that particular information.[38]

Media Richness

Along with social acceptance, people need to determine the best level of **media richness** for their message. Media richness refers to the medium's data-carrying capacity—the volume and variety of information that can be transmitted during a specific time.[39] Exhibit 8.3 illustrates various communication channels arranged in a hierarchy of richness, with face-to-face interaction at the top and lean data-only reports at the bottom. A communication channel has high richness when it is able to convey multiple cues (such as both verbal and nonverbal information),

> **media richness**
> A medium's data-carrying capacity, that is, the volume and variety of information that can be transmitted during a specific time.

▼**EXHIBIT 8.3** Media Richness Hierarchy

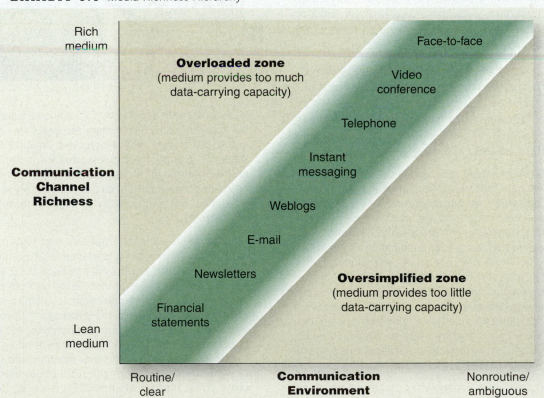

Source: Based on R. Lengel and R. Daft, "The Selection of Communication Media as an Executive Skill," *Academy of Management Executive* 2, no. 3 (August 1988), 226; R. L. Daft and R. H. Lengel, "Information Richness: A New Approach to Managerial Behavior and Organization Design," *Research in Organizational Behavior* (1984): 199.

allows timely feedback from receiver to sender, allows the sender to customize the message to the receiver, and makes use of complex symbols (such as words and phrases with multiple meanings).

Face-to-face communication is at the top of media richness because it allows us to communicate both verbally and nonverbally at the same time, to receive feedback almost immediately from the receiver, to quickly adjust our message and style, and to use complex language such as metaphors and idioms (e.g., "spilling the beans").

According to media richness theory, rich media are better than lean media when the communication situation is nonroutine and ambiguous. In nonroutine situations (such as an unexpected and unusual emergency), the sender and receiver have little common experience, so they need to transmit a large volume of information with immediate feedback. Lean media work well in routine situations because the sender and receiver have common expectations through shared mental models. Ambiguous situations also require rich media because the parties must share large amounts of information with immediate feedback to resolve multiple and conflicting interpretations of their observations and experiences.[40] Choosing the wrong medium reduces communication effectiveness. When the situation is routine or clear, using a rich medium—such as holding a special meeting—would seem like a waste of time. On the other hand, if a unique and ambiguous issue is handled through email or another lean medium, then issues take longer to resolve and misunderstandings are more likely to occur.

Exceptions to Media Richness Theory

Research generally supports the relevance of media richness for traditional channels (face-to-face, written memos, etc.). However, the model doesn't fit reality nearly as well when electronic communication channels are studied. Three factors seem to override or blur the medium's richness:

1. *Ability to multi-communicate:* It is usually difficult (as well as rude) to communicate face-to-face with someone while simultaneously transmitting messages to someone else using another medium. Most information technologies, on the other hand, require less social etiquette and attention, so employees can easily engage in two or more communication events at the same time. In other words, they can multi-communicate.[41] For example, people routinely scan webpages while carrying on telephone conversations. Some write text messages to a client while simultaneously listening to a discussion at a large meeting. People don't multitask as efficiently as they believe, but some are good enough that they likely exchange as much information through two or more lean media as through one high media richness channel.

2. *Communication proficiency:* Earlier in this chapter we explained that communication effectiveness is partially determined by the sender's competency and motivation with the communication channel. People with higher proficiency can "push" more information through the channel, thereby increasing the channel's information flow. Experienced smartphone users, for instance, can whip through messages in a flash, whereas new users struggle to type notes and organize incoming messages. In contrast, there is less variation in the ability to communicate through casual conversation and other natural channels because most of us develop good levels of proficiency throughout life and possibly through hardwired evolutionary development.[42]

3. *Social presence effects:* Channels with high media richness tend to have more social presence, that is, the participants experience a stronger physical presence of each other.[43] However, high social presence also sensitizes both parties to their relative status and self-presentation, which can distort or divert attention away from the message.[44] Face-to-face communication has very high media richness, yet its high social presence can disrupt the efficient flow of information through that medium. During a personal meeting with the company's CEO, for example, you might concentrate more on how you come across than on what the CEO is saying to you. In other words, the benefits of media richness channels may be offset by social presence distractions, whereas lean media have much less social presence to distract or distort the transmitted information.

Communication Channels and Persuasion

Media richness and social acceptance lay the foundation for understanding which communication channels are more effective for **persuasion**, that is, changing another person's beliefs and attitudes. Studies support the long-held view that spoken communication, particularly face-to-face interaction, is more persuasive than emails, Web sites, and other forms of written communication. There are three main reasons for this persuasive effect.[45] First, spoken communication is typically accompanied by nonverbal communication. People are persuaded more when they receive both emotional and logical messages, and the combination of spoken with nonverbal communication provides this dual punch. A lengthy pause, raised voice tone, and (in face-to-face interaction) animated hand gestures can amplify the emotional tone of the message, thereby signaling the vitality of the issue.

Second, spoken communication offers the sender high-quality immediate feedback whether the receiver understands and accepts the message (i.e., is being persuaded). This feedback allows the sender to adjust the content and emotional tone of the message more quickly than with written communication. Third, people are persuaded more under conditions of high social presence than low social presence. The sender can more easily monitor the receiver's listening in face-to-face

Learning Objective

After reading the next two sections, you should be able to

LO4 Discuss various barriers (noise) to effective communication, including cross-cultural and gender-based differences in communication.

COMMUNICATION BARRIERS (NOISE)

In spite of the best intentions of sender and receiver to communicate, several barriers (called "noise" earlier in Exhibit 8.1) inhibit the effective exchange of information. One barrier is the imperfect perceptual process of both sender and receiver. As receivers, we don't listen as well as senders assume, and our needs and expectations influence what signals get noticed and ignored. We aren't any better as senders, either. Some studies suggest that we have difficulty stepping out of our own perspectives and stepping into the perspectives of others, so we overestimate how well other people understand the message we are communicating.[46]

Language issues can be huge sources of communication noise because sender and receiver might not have the same "codebook." They might not speak the same language, or might have different meanings for particular words and phrases. The

> "The greatest problem with communication is the illusion that it has been accomplished.
> —George Bernard Shaw

conversations (high social presence), so listeners are more motivated to pay attention and consider the sender's ideas. When people receive persuasion attempts through a Web site, email, or other source of written communication, on the other hand, they experience a higher degree of anonymity and psychological distance from the persuader. These conditions reduce the motivation to think about and accept the persuasive message.

Although spoken communication tends to be more persuasive, written communication can also persuade others to some extent. Written messages have the advantage of presenting more technical detail than can occur through conversation. This factual information is valuable when the issue is important to the receiver. Also, people experience a moderate degree of social presence in written communication when they are exchanging messages with close associates, so messages from friends and coworkers can be persuasive.

English language (among others) also has built-in ambiguities that cause misunderstandings. Consider the question, "Can you close the door?" You might assume the sender is asking whether shutting the door is permitted. However, the question might be asking whether you are physically able to shut the door or whether the door is designed so it can be shut. In fact, this question might not be a question at all; the person could be politely *telling* you to shut the door.[47]

The ambiguity of language isn't always dysfunctional noise.[48] Corporate leaders are sometimes purposively vague to reflect the ambiguity of the topic or to avoid using precise language that carries unwanted emotional responses. They might use metaphors to represent an abstract vision of the company's future, or use obtuse phrases such as "rightsizing" and "restructuring" to obscure the underlying message that people would be fired or laid off. One study reported that people rely on more ambiguous language when communicating with people who have different values and beliefs. In these situations, ambiguity minimizes the risk of conflict.[49]

Jargon—specialized words and phrases for specific occupations or groups—is usually designed to improve communication efficiency. However, it is a source of communication noise when transmitted to people who do not possess the jargon codebook. Furthermore, people who use jargon excessively put themselves in an unflattering light. For example, former Home Depot and Chrysler CEO Robert Nardelli announced: "I'm blessed to have individuals with me who can take areas of responsibility and do vertical dives to really get the granularity and make sure that we're coupling horizontally across those functions so that we have a pure line of sight toward the customer." Business journalists weren't impressed, even if they did figure out what Nardelli meant.[50]

Another source of noise in the communication process is the tendency to filter messages. Filtering may involve deleting or delaying negative information or using less harsh words so the message sounds more favorable.[51] Filtering is less likely to occur when corporate leaders create a "culture of candor." This culture develops when leaders themselves communicate truthfully, seek out diverse sources for information, and protect and reward those who speak openly and truthfully.[52]

Information Overload

Start with a daily avalanche of email, then add in cell phone calls, text messages, PDF file downloads, webpages, hard copy documents, some Twitter tweets, blogs, wikis, and other sources of incoming information. Combined, these items are a perfect recipe for **information overload**.[53] As Exhibit 8.4 illustrates, information overload occurs whenever the job's information load exceeds the individual's capacity to get through it. Employees have a certain *information processing capacity*—the amount of information they are able to process in a fixed unit of time. At the same time, jobs have a varying *information load*—the amount of information to be processed per unit of time. Information overload creates noise in the communication system because information gets overlooked or misinterpreted when people can't process it fast enough. The result is poorer quality decisions as well as higher stress.[54]

▼ **EXHIBIT 8.4** Dynamics of Information Overload

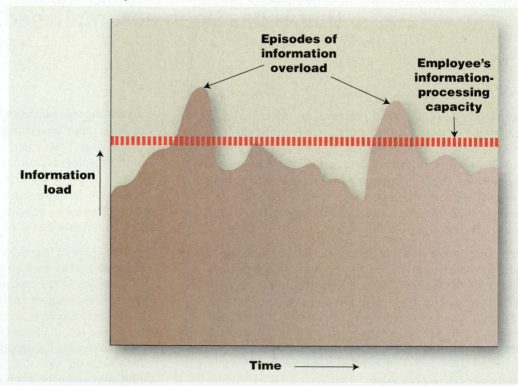

Episodes of information overload

Employee's information-processing capacity

Information load

Time

Information overload problems can be minimized by increasing our information processing capacity, reducing the job's information load, or through a combination of both. Studies suggest that employees often increase their information-processing capacity by temporarily reading faster, scanning through documents more efficiently, and removing distractions that slow information-processing speed. Time management also increases information-processing capacity. When information overload is temporary, information processing capacity can increase by working longer hours. We can reduce information load by buffering, omitting, and summarizing. Buffering involves having incoming communication filtered, usually by an assistant. Omitting occurs when we decide to overlook messages, such as using software rules to redirect emails from distribution lists to folders that we never look at. An example of summarizing would be where we read executive summaries rather than the full report.

> "Communication includes silence, but its use and meaning vary from one culture to another."

CROSS-CULTURAL AND GENDER COMMUNICATION

Increasing globalization and cultural diversity have brought more cross-cultural communication issues.[55] Voice intonation is one form of cross-cultural communication barrier. How loudly, deeply, and quickly people speak vary across cultures, and these voice intonations send secondary messages that have a different meaning in different cultures.

As mentioned earlier, language is an obvious cross-cultural communications challenge. Words are easily misunderstood in verbal communication, either because the receiver has a limited vocabulary or the sender's accent distorts the usual sound of some words. In one cross-cultural seminar, for example, participants at German electronics company Siemens were reminded that a French coworker might call an event a "catastrophe" as a casual exaggeration, whereas someone in Germany usually interprets this word literally as an earth-shaking event. Similarly, KPMG staff from the United Kingdom sometimes referred to another person's suggestions as "interesting." They had to clarify to their German colleagues that "interesting" isn't always a compliment to the idea.[56]

Communication includes silence, but its use and meaning vary from one culture to another.[57] One study estimated that silence and pauses represented 30 percent of conversation time between Japanese doctors and patients, compared to only 8 percent of the time between American doctors and patients. Why is there more silence in Japanese conversations? One reason is that interpersonal harmony and saving face are more important in Japanese culture, and silence is a way of disagreeing and upsetting that harmony or offending the other person.[58] In addition, silence symbolizes respect and indicates that the listener is thoughtfully contemplating what has just been said.[59] Empathy is very important in Japan, and this shared understanding is demonstrated without using words. In contrast, most people in the United States and many other cultures view silence as a *lack* of communication and often interpret long breaks as a sign of disagreement.

Conversational overlaps also send different messages in different cultures. Japanese people usually stop talking when they are interrupted, whereas talking over the other person's speech is more common in Brazil, France, and some other countries. The difference in communication behavior is, again, due to interpretations. Talking while someone is speaking to you is considered quite rude in Japan, whereas Brazilians and French are more likely to interpret this as the person's interest and involvement in the conversation.

Nonverbal Differences across Cultures

Nonverbal communication represents another potential area for misunderstanding across cultures. Many nonconscious or involuntary nonverbal cues (such as smiling) have the same meaning around the world, but deliberate gestures often have different interpretations. For example, most of us shake our head from side to side to say "No," but a variation of head shaking means "I understand" to many people in India. Filipinos raise their eyebrows to give an affirmative answer, yet Arabs interpret this expression (along with clicking one's tongue) as a negative response. Most Americans are taught to maintain eye contact with the speaker to show interest and respect, whereas some North American native groups learn at an early age to show respect by looking down when an older or more senior person is talking to them.[60]

Gender Differences in Communication

Men and women have similar communication practices, but there are subtle differences that can occasionally lead to misunderstanding and conflict (see Exhibit 8.5).[61] One distinction is that men are more likely than women to view conversations as negotiations of relative status and power. They assert their power by directly giving advice to others (e.g., "You should do the following") and using combative language. There is also evidence that men dominate the talk time in conversations with women, as well as

When Men Communicate	When Women Communicate
• Report talk—give advice, assert power	• Rapport talk—relationship building
• Give advice directly	• Give advice indirectly
• Dominant conversation style	• Flexible conversation style
• Apologize less often	• Apologize more often
• Less sensitive to nonverbal cues	• More sensitive to nonverbal cues

interrupt more and adjust their speaking style less than do women.

Men engage in more "report talk" in which the primary function of the conversation is impersonal and efficient information exchange. Women also do report talk, particularly when conversing with men, but conversations among women have a higher incidence of relationship building through "rapport talk." Women make more use of indirect requests ("Do you think you should . . ."), apologize more often, and seek advice from others more quickly than do men. Finally, research fairly consistently indicates that women are more sensitive than men to nonverbal cues in face-to-face meetings.[62] Together, these conditions can create communication conflicts. Women who describe problems get frustrated that men offer advice rather than rapport, whereas men become frustrated because they can't understand why women don't appreciate their advice.

Gender differences are also emerging in the use of social media to communicate.[63] Specifically, women are more likely to visit social networking sites like Facebook and Twitter, spend more time online, and clicked on more webpages than their male counterparts. Women are also more active participants in photo-sharing Web sites. Globally, women are outpacing men in signing up for Twitter accounts and are more active Twitter users. Their reasons for using this communication channel also differ. Women tend to use Twitter as a conversational rather than functional medium. Overall women spend an average of 24.8 hours per month online, whereas men spend 22.9 hours per month online.

Learning Objective

After reading this section, you should be able to

LO5 Explain how to get your message across more effectively, and summarize the elements of active listening.

IMPROVING INTERPERSONAL COMMUNICATION

Effective interpersonal communication depends on the sender's ability to get the message across and the receiver's performance as an active listener. In this section, we outline these two essential features of effective interpersonal communication.

OB Theory to Practice

Getting Your Message Across

Communication encoding and decoding are more effective when you:

• Empathize with the person receiving the message.

• Repeat the key points of your message a couple of times.

• Actively determine the best time to speak to the other person.

• Are descriptive by directing any negative comments toward the issue, not the person.

Getting Your Message Across

This chapter began with the statement that effective communication occurs when the other person receives and understands the message. This is more difficult to accomplish than most people believe. To get your message across to the other person, you first need to empathize with the receiver, such as being sensitive to words that may be ambiguous or trigger the wrong emotional response. Second, be sure you repeat the message, such as by rephrasing the key points a couple of times. Third, your message competes with other messages and noise, so find a time when the receiver is less likely to be distracted by these other matters. Finally, if you are communicating bad news or criticism, focus on the problem, not the person.

Active Listening

Active listening is a process of actively sensing the sender's signals, evaluating them accurately, and responding appropriately. These three components of listening—sensing, evaluating, and responding—reflect the listener's side of the communication model described at the beginning of this chapter. Listeners receive the sender's signals, decode them as intended, and provide appropriate and timely feedback to the sender (see Exhibit 8.6). Active listeners constantly cycle through sensing, evaluating, and responding during the conversation and engage in various activities to improve these processes.[65]

Sensing Sensing is the process of receiving signals from the sender and paying attention to them. Active listeners improve sensing in three ways. First, they postpone evaluation by not forming an opinion until the speaker has finished. Second, they avoid interrupting the speaker's conversation. Third, they remain motivated to listen to the speaker.

Evaluating This component of listening includes understanding the message meaning, evaluating

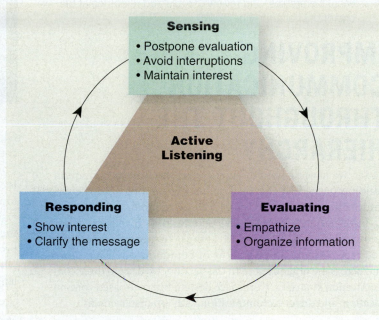

▼ **EXHIBIT 8.6** Active Listening Process and Strategies

Sensing
- Postpone evaluation
- Avoid interruptions
- Maintain interest

Active Listening

Responding
- Show interest
- Clarify the message

Evaluating
- Empathize
- Organize information

the message, and remembering the message. To improve their evaluation of the conversation, active listeners empathize with the speaker—they try to understand and be sensitive to the speaker's feelings, thoughts, and situation. Evaluation also improves by organizing the speaker's ideas during the communication episode.

Responding Responding, the third component of listening, is feedback to the sender, which motivates and directs the speaker's communication. Active listeners accomplish this by maintaining sufficient eye contact and sending back channel signals (e.g., "I see"), both of which show interest. They also respond by clarifying the message—rephrasing the speaker's ideas at appropriate breaks ("So you're saying that . . . ?").

Learning Objective

After reading the next two sections, you should be able to

LO6 Summarize effective communication strategies in organizational hierarchies, and review the role and relevance of the organizational grapevine.

IMPROVING COMMUNICATION THROUGHOUT THE HIERARCHY

So far, we have focused on micro-level issues in the communication process, namely, the dynamics of sending and receiving information between two employees or the informal exchanges of information across several people. But in this era where knowledge is competitive advantage, corporate leaders also need to maintain an open flow of communication up, down, and across the organization. In this section, we discuss three communication strategies: workspace design, Internet-based communication, and direct communication with top management.

Workspace Design

To improve information sharing and create a more sociable work environment, Intel is tearing down the cubicle walls at its microchip design center near Portland, Oregon. "We realized that we were inefficient and not as collaborative as we would have liked," acknowledges Neil Tunmore, Intel's director of corporate services. The refurbished building includes more shared space where employees set up temporary work areas. There are also more meeting rooms where employees can collaborate in private.[66]

Intel and many other companies are improving communication by tearing down walls.[67] The location and design of hallways, offices, cubicles, and communal areas (cafeterias, elevators) all shape whom we speak to as well as the frequency of that communication. For instance, face-to-face communication increased when GlaxoSmithKline employees moved to its new open-office environment in Raleigh, North Carolina, whereas the volume of email dropped significantly.

Although these open space arrangements increase the amount of face-to-face communication, they also potentially produce more noise, distractions, and loss of privacy.[68] For instance, one

GlaxoSmithKline employee described the pharmaceutical company's recent transition to open offices as "a big adjustment. There were a lot of distractions, and it was hard to stay focused."[69] Employees at one eBay call center also experienced too much distraction, so they agreed to hush up when coworkers draped a colorful bandana on their desk lamps or around their heads.[70] Others claim that open offices have minimal noise problems because employees tend to speak more softly and white noise technology blocks out most voices. Still, the challenge is to increase social interaction without these stressors.

Another workspace strategy is to cloister employees into team spaces, but also encourage sufficient interaction with people from other teams. Pixar Animation Studios constructed its campus in Emeryville, California with these principles in mind. The buildings encourage communication among team members. At the same time, the campus encourages happenstance interactions with people on other teams. Pixar executives call this the "bathroom effect" because team members must leave their isolated pods to fetch their mail, have lunch, or visit the restroom.[71]

Internet-Based Organizational Communication

For decades, employees received official company news through hard copy newsletters and magazines. Some firms still use these communication devices, but most have supplemented or replaced them completely with web-based sources of information. The traditional company magazine is now typically published on webpages or distributed in PDF format. The advantage of these *e-zines* is that company news can be prepared and distributed quickly.

Employees are increasingly skeptical of information that has been screened and packaged by management, so a few companies such as IBM are encouraging employees to post their own news on internal blogs and wikis. Wikis are collaborative web spaces in which anyone in a group can write, edit, or remove material from the Web site. *Wikipedia*, the popular online encyclopedia, is a massive public example of a wiki. IBM's WikiCentral now hosts more than 20,000 wiki projects involving 100,000 employees. The accuracy of wikis depends on the quality of participants, but IBM experts say errors are quickly identified by IBM's online community. Also, some wikis have failed to gain employee support, likely because wiki involvement takes time and the company does not reward or recognize those who provide this time to wiki development.[73]

Direct Communication with Top Management

During the great financial crisis, employee satisfaction scores at the U.S. Department of Transportation were among the lowest levels in the federal government. U.S. Secretary of Transportation Ray LaHood has improved that situation through more open communication and other management practices. Morale is already improving. "This boost in employee satisfaction is no accident," says LaHood. "Since joining DOT, I initiated town hall meetings with employees around the country, and I have also held regular open-door office hours where employees are free to let me know what's on their minds."[74]

The lesson from Ray LaHood's actions is that senior executives need to meet directly with employees and other stakeholders to improve morale as well as transmit and receive information more fully and meaningfully. Four decades ago, people at Hewlett-Packard coined a phrase for this communication strategy: **management by walking around (MBWA)**. Brian Scudamore, founder and CEO of 1-800-Got-Junk?, takes this practice further. "I don't have my own office, and I very often move around to different departments for a day at a time," says Scudamore.[75]

Along with MBWA, executives communicate more directly with employees through town hall meetings. Some executives also conduct employee roundtable forums to hear opinions from a small representation of staff about various issues. At the departmental level, some companies hold daily or weekly "huddles"—brief stand-up meetings in which staff and their manager discuss goals and hear good news stories. These direct communication strategies potentially minimize filtering because executives listen directly to employees. They also help executives acquire a deeper meaning and quicker understanding of internal organizational problems. A third benefit of direct communication is that employees might have more empathy for decisions made further up the corporate hierarchy.

COMMUNICATING THROUGH THE GRAPEVINE

Organizational leaders may try their best to communicate news to employees quickly through formal channels (e-zines, emails, and Twitter tweets), but employees will still rely to some extent on the corporate **grapevine**. The grapevine is an unstructured and informal network founded on social relationships rather than organizational charts or job descriptions. What do employees think about the grapevine? Surveys of employees in two firms—one in Florida, the other in California—found that almost all employees use the grapevine, but very few of them prefer this source of information. The Californian survey also

Zappos Communication

Tony Hsieh likes to tweet. Even as CEO of Zappos, one of the world's largest online retailers, Hsieh discovered that tweeting is a powerful way to connect with his staff and the wider community. "What I found was that people really appreciated the openness and honesty (of tweets), and that led people to feel more of a personal connection with Zappos and me," Hsieh wrote in one of his Weblogs. And for employees who want to communicate more directly with Zappos' top boss, Hsieh has the ultimate open-door policy. His desk is located in an open office setting in an area where anyone can speak with him. "The best way to have an open-door policy is not to have a door in the first place," Hsieh explains.[72]

When the Organizational Grapevine
Takes Top Priority[76]

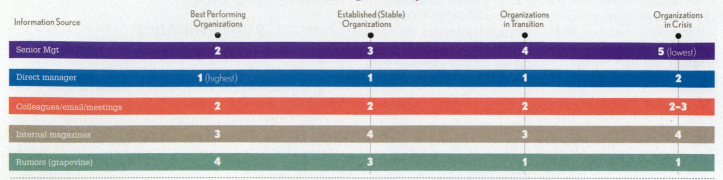

Information Source	Best Performing Organizations	Established (Stable) Organizations	Organizations in Transition	Organizations in Crisis
Senior Mgt	2	3	4	5 (lowest)
Direct manager	1 (highest)	1	1	2
Colleagues/email/meetings	2	2	2	2–3
Internal magazines	3	4	3	4
Rumors (grapevine)	4	3	1	1

Rank order (1=highest; 5=lowest) of preferred channels for receiving information identified by several thousand North American employees. The results show that the employee's direct manager and senior management are the most credible sources in the best performing firms, whereas rumors take top rank in organizations in transition and in crisis.

reported that only one-third of employees believe grapevine information is credible. In other words, employees turn to the grapevine when they have few other options.[77]

Grapevine Characteristics

Research conducted several decades ago reported that the grapevine transmits information very rapidly in all directions throughout the organization. The typical pattern is a cluster chain, whereby a few people actively transmit rumors to many others. The grapevine works through informal social networks, so it is more active where employees have similar backgrounds and are able to communicate easily. Many rumors seem to have at least a kernel of truth, possibly because they are transmitted through media-rich communication channels (e.g., face to face) and employees are motivated to communicate effectively. Nevertheless, the grapevine distorts information by deleting fine details and exaggerating key points of the story.[78]

Some of these characteristics might still be true, but the grapevine almost certainly has changed as email, social networking sites, and Twitter tweets have replaced the traditional water cooler as sources of gossip. For example, several Facebook sites are themed around specific companies, allowing employees and customers to vent their complaints about the organization. Along with altering the speed and network of corporate grapevines, the Internet has expanded these networks around the globe, not just around the next cubicle.

Grapevine Benefits and Limitations

Should the grapevine be encouraged, tolerated, or quashed? The difficulty in answering this question is that the grapevine has both benefits and limitations.[79] One benefit, as was mentioned earlier, is that employees rely on the grapevine when information is not available through formal channels. It is also the main conduit through which organizational stories and other symbols of the organization's culture are communicated. A third benefit of the grapevine is that this social interaction relieves anxiety. This explains why rumor mills are most active during times of uncertainty.[80] Finally, the grapevine is associated with the drive to bond. Being a recipient of gossip is a sign of inclusion, according to evolutionary psychologists. Trying to quash the grapevine is, in some respects, an attempt to undermine the natural human drive for social interaction.[81]

While the grapevine offers these benefits, it is not a preferred communication medium. Grapevine information is sometimes so distorted that it escalates rather than reduces employee anxiety. Furthermore, employees develop more negative attitudes toward the organization when management is slower than the grapevine in communicating information. What should corporate leaders do with the grapevine? The best advice seems to be to listen to the grapevine as a signal of employee anxiety, then correct the cause of this anxiety. Some companies also listen to the grapevine and step in to correct blatant errors and fabrications. Most important, corporate leaders need to view the grapevine as a competitor and meet this challenge by directly informing employees of news before it spreads throughout the grapevine. ■

power and influence
in the workplace

The Royal Canadian Mounted Police (RCMP) had become a hotbed of wayward power and organizational politics over the past decade. Up to a half-dozen years ago, Canada's largest law enforcement agency was led by a commissioner who "enjoyed the status and privileges of his office" and often reminded people that "I am the Commissioner." Following complaints, the Canadian government's independent investigation concluded that the RCMP suffered from this "absolute power exercised by the Commissioner," and that the solution is restructuring "aimed at whittling down the power of the Commissioner."

That commissioner's successor was the RCMP's first-ever civilian (i.e., not a police officer), a career civil servant who was supposed to clean out abuse of power. Instead, the new commissioner quickly developed a reputation for getting his way through bullying and intimidation, including screaming at senior officers and belittling their ideas in public. The deputy commissioner and a dozen other top RCMP leaders eventually complained directly to the federal government. An outside assessor heard these complaints, but the commissioner demoted some of the whistleblowers and forced others to take early retirement. Still facing media scrutiny, the civilian commissioner also retired soon after.[1]

Power and influence are never far from the actions of leaders and followers. Some senior RCMP officers concluded that the Commissioner abused his power by sidelining people and being assertive. Meanwhile, the Commissioner may have quietly thought these officers were using dysfunctional influence tactics to undermine organizational change. Although this story illustrates the dark

continued on p. 174

LEARNING OBJECTIVES

After studying Chapter 9, you should be able to:

LO1 Describe the dependence model of power and describe the five sources of power in organizations.

LO2 Discuss the four contingencies of power.

LO3 Explain how people and work units gain power through social networks.

LO4 Describe eight types of influence tactics, three consequences of influencing others, and three contingencies to consider when choosing an influence tactic.

LO5 Identify the organizational conditions and personal characteristics that support organizational politics, as well as ways to minimize organizational politics.

continued from p. 173

side of power and influence, power and influence are equally relevant to ethical conduct and organizational performance. In fact, some OB experts point out that power and influence are inherent in all organizations. They exist in every business and in every decision and action.

This chapter unfolds as follows: First, we define power and present a basic model depicting the dynamics of power in organizational settings. We then discuss the five bases of power. Next, we look at the contingencies necessary to translate those sources into meaningful power. Our attention then turns to social networks and how they provide power to members through social capital. The latter part of this chapter examines the various types of influence in organizational settings as well as the contingencies of effective influence strategies. The final section looks at organizational politics, including ways of minimizing political tactics in organizations. ■

Learning Objective

After reading the next two sections, you should be able to

LO1 Describe the dependence model of power and describe the five sources of power in organizations.

THE MEANING OF POWER

Power is the capacity of a person, team, or organization to influence others.[2] There are a few important features of this definition. First, power is not the act of changing someone's attitudes or behavior; it is only the *potential* to do so. People frequently have power they do not use; they might not even know they have power. Second, power is based on the target's *perception* that the power holder controls (i.e., possesses, has access to, or regulates), a valuable resource that can help them achieve their goals.[3] People might generate power by convincing others they control something of value, whether or not they actually control that resource. This perception is also formed from the power holder's behavior as someone who is not swayed by authority or norms. For instance, one recent study found that people are perceived as more powerful just by their behavior—such as putting their feet on a table, taking coffee from

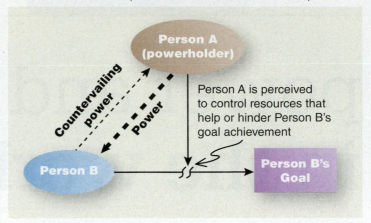

▼ EXHIBIT 9.1 Dependence in the Power Relationship

Person A (powerholder)

Countervailing power

Power

Person B

Person A is perceived to control resources that help or hinder Person B's goal achievement

Person B's Goal

someone else's container, and being less vigilant of bookkeeping rules.[4] Notice, too, that power is not a personal feeling of power. You might feel powerful or think you have power over others, but this is not power unless others believe you have that capacity.

Third, power involves asymmetric (unequal) *dependence* of one party on another party.[5] This dependent relationship is illustrated in Exhibit 9.1. The broken line from Person B to the goal shows that he or she believes Person A controls a resource that can help or hinder Person A in achieving that goal. Person A—the power holder in this illustration—might have power over Person B by controlling a desired job assignment, useful information, rewards, or even the privilege of being associated with him or her! For example, if you believe a coworker has expertise (the resource) that would substantially help you to write a better report (your goal), then that coworker has some power over you because you value that expertise to achieve your goal. Whatever the resources is, Person B is *dependent* on Person A (the power holder) to provide the resource so Person B can reach his/her goal.

Although dependence is a key element of power relationships, we use the phrase "asymmetric dependence" because the less powerful party still has some degree of power—called **countervailing power**—over the powerholder. In Exhibit 9.1, Person A dominates the power relationship, but Person B has enough countervailing power to keep Person A in the exchange relationship and ensure that person or department uses its dominant power judiciously. For example, although managers have power over subordinates in many ways (e.g., controlling job security, preferred work assignments), employees have countervailing power by possessing skills and knowledge to keep production humming and customers happy, something that management can't accomplish alone.

Finally, the power relationship depends on some minimum level of trust. Trust indicates a level of expectation that the more powerful party will deliver the resource. For example, you trust your employer to give you a paycheck at the end of each pay period. Even those in extremely dependent situations will usually walk away from the relationship if they lack a minimum level of trust in the more powerful party.

Let's look at this power dependence model in the employee–manager relationship. You depend on your boss for supporting your continued employment, satisfactory work arrangements, and other valued resources. At the same time, your manager depends on you to complete required tasks and to work effectively with others in the completion of their work. Managers (and the companies they represent) typically have more power, whereas employees have weaker countervailing power. But sometimes employees do have the stronger power base in the relationship. Notice that the strength of your power in the employee–manager relationship doesn't depend on your actual control over valued resources; it depends on the perceptions that your boss and others have about this resource control. Finally, trust is an essential ingredient in this relationship. Even with strong power, the employee–manager relationship comes apart when one party no longer sufficiently trusts the other.

The dependence model reveals only the core features of power dynamics between people and work units in organizations. We also need to learn about the specific sources of power and contingencies that allow that power to be effectively applied as influence. As Exhibit 9.2 illustrates, power is derived from five sources: legitimate, reward, coercive, expert, and referent. The model also identifies four contingencies of power: the employee's or department's substitutability, centrality, discretion, and visibility. Over the next few pages, we will discuss each of these sources and contingencies of power in the context of organizations.

SOURCES OF POWER IN ORGANIZATIONS

A half-century ago, social scientists John French and Bertrand Raven identified five sources of power found in organizations. Although variations of this list have been proposed over the years, the original list remains surprisingly intact.[6] Three sources of power—legitimate, reward, and coercive—originate mostly (but not completely) from the power holder's formal position or informal role. In other words, the person is granted these sources of power formally by the organization or informally by coworkers. Two other sources of power—expert and referent—originate mainly from the power holder's own characteristics; in other words, people carry these power bases around with them. However, even personal sources of power are not completely within the person because they depend on how others perceive them.

Legitimate Power

Legitimate power is an agreement among organizational members that people in certain roles can request a set of behaviors from others. This perceived right or obligation originates from formal job descriptions as well as informal rules of conduct. The most obvious example of legitimate power is a manager's right to tell employees what tasks to perform, who to work with, what office resources they can use, and so forth. Employees follow the boss's requests because there is mutual agreement that employees will follow a range of directives from

power The capacity of a person, team, or organization to influence others.

countervailing power The capacity of a person, team, or organization to keep a more powerful person or group in the exchange relationship.

legitimate power An agreement among organizational members that people in certain roles can request certain behaviors of others.

▼**EXHIBIT 9.2** Sources and Contingencies of Power

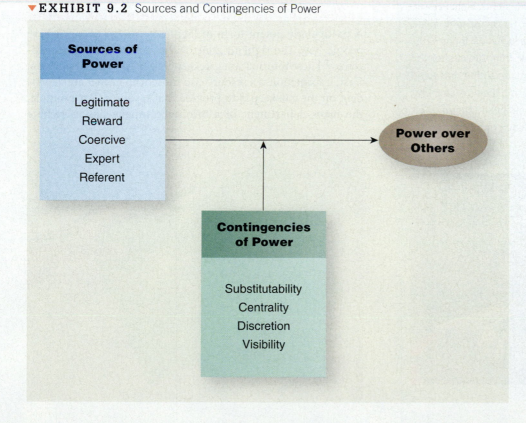

UNTHINKING RESPECT FOR AUTHORITY IS THE GREATEST ENEMY OF TRUTH.[7]

—ALBERT EINSTEIN ”

people in these positions of authority. Employees defer to this authority whether or not they will be rewarded or punished for complying with those requests.

Notice that legitimate power has restrictions; it only gives the power holder the *right* to ask for a *range* of behaviors from others. This range—known as the "zone of indifference"—is the set of behaviors that individuals are willing to engage in at the other person's request.[8] For example, although most employees accept the boss's right to deny them access to Facebook during company time, some might draw the line when the boss asks them to work several hours beyond the regular workday. There are also occasions where employees actively oppose the boss's actions.

The size of the zone of indifference (and, consequently, the magnitude of legitimate power) increases with the level of trust in the power holder. Some values and personality traits also make people more obedient to authority. Those who value conformity and tradition as well as have high power distance (i.e., they accept an unequal distribution of power) tend to have higher deference to authority. The organization's culture represents another influence on the willingness of employees to follow orders. A 3M scientist might continue to work on a project after being told by superiors to stop working on it because the 3M culture supports an entrepreneurial spirit, which includes ignoring your boss's authority from time to time.[10]

Managers are not the only people with legitimate power in organizations. Employees also have legitimate power over their bosses and coworkers through legal and administrative rights as well as informal norms.[11] For example, an organization might give employees the right to request information that is required for their job. Laws give employees the right to refuse work in unsafe conditions. More subtle forms of legitimate power also exist. Human beings have a **norm of reciprocity**—a feeling of obligation to help someone who has helped you.[12] If a coworker previously helped you handle a difficult client, that coworker has power because you feel an obligation to help him or her on something of similar value in the future. The norm of reciprocity is a form of legitimate power because it is an informal rule of conduct we are expected to follow.

Legitimate Power Takes People to the Extreme

A French television program recently revealed how far people are willing to follow orders. As a variation of the 1960s experiments conducted by Stanley Milgram, 80 contestants administered electric shocks whenever a volunteer (an actor who didn't receive the shocks at all) answered a question incorrectly. Shocks increased in 20-volt increments, from 20 volts for the first mistake through to 460 volts. Contestants often hesitated after hearing the volunteer screaming for them to stop, yet continued the shocks after the host reminded them of their duty. Only 16 of the 80 contestants refused to administer the strongest shocks.[9]

Legitimate Power through Information Control

A particularly potent form of legitimate power occurs where people have the right to control the information others receive.[13] These information gatekeepers gain power in two ways. First, information is a resource, so those who need it are dependent on the gatekeeper to provide that resource. For example, the maps department of a mining company has incredible

power when other departments are dependent on it to deliver maps required for exploration projects.

Second, information gatekeepers gain power by selectively distributing information so those receiving it perceive the situation differently.[14] Executives depend on middle managers and employees to provide an accurate picture of the company's operations. Yet, as we learned in the previous chapter on communication, information is often filtered as it flows up the hierarchy. Middle managers and employees filter information so it puts them in a more positive light and steers the executive team toward one decision rather than another. In other words, these information gatekeepers can potentially influence executive decisions by framing their reality through selective distribution of information.

Reward Power

Reward power is derived from the person's ability to control the allocation of rewards others value and to remove negative sanctions (i.e., negative reinforcement). Managers have formal authority that gives them power over the distribution of organizational rewards such as pay, promotions, time off, vacation schedules, and work assignments. Employees also have reward power over their bosses through their feedback and ratings in 360-degree feedback systems. These ratings affect supervisors' promotions and other rewards, so supervisors tend to behave differently toward employees after 360-degree feedback is introduced.

Coercive Power

Coercive power is the ability to apply punishment. For many of us, the first thought is managers threatening employees with dismissal. Yet, employees also have coercive power, such as being sarcastic toward coworkers or threatening to ostracize them if they fail to conform to team norms. Many firms rely on this coercive power to control coworker behavior in team settings. Nucor is one such example: "If you're not contributing with the team, they certainly will let you know about it," says an executive at the Charlotte, North Carolina, steelmaker. "The few poor players get weeded out by their peers." Similarly, when asked how AirAsia maintained attendance and productivity after the Malaysian discount airline removed the time clocks, chief executive Tony Fernandes replied, "Simple. Peer pressure sees to that. The fellow employees, who are putting their shoulders to the wheel, will see to that."[15]

Expert Power

For the most part, legitimate, reward, and coercive power originate from the position.[16] Expert power, on the other hand, originates mainly from within the powerholder. It is an individual's or work unit's capacity to influence others by possessing knowledge or skills others value. One important form of expert power is the (perceived) ability to manage uncertainties in the business environment. Organizations are more effective when they operate in predictable environments, so they value people who can cope with turbulence in the consumer trends, societal changes, unstable supply lines, and so forth.

Expertise can help companies cope with uncertainty in three ways. These coping strategies are arranged in a hierarchy of importance, with prevention being the most powerful:[17]

- *Prevention:* The most effective strategy is to prevent environmental changes from occurring. For example, financial experts acquire power by preventing the organization from experiencing a cash shortage or defaulting on loans.

- *Forecasting:* The next best strategy is to predict environmental changes or variations. In this respect, trendspotters and other marketing specialists gain power by predicting changes in consumer preferences.

- *Absorption:* People and work units also gain power by absorbing or neutralizing the impact of environmental shifts as they occur. An example is the maintenance crews' ability to come to the rescue when machines break down.

Many people respond to expertise just as they respond to authority—they mindlessly follow the guidance of these experts.[18] In one classic study, for example, a researcher posing as a hospital physician telephoned on-duty nurses to prescribe a specific dosage of medicine to a hospitalized patient. None of the nurses knew the person calling, and hospital policy forbade them from accepting treatment by telephone (i.e., they lacked legitimate power). Furthermore, the medication was unauthorized, and the prescription was twice the maximum daily dose. Yet, almost all 22 nurses who received the telephone call followed the "doctor's" orders until researchers stopped them.[19]

This doctor–nurse study is a few decades old, but the power of expertise remains just as strong today, sometimes with tragic consequences. The Canadian justice system recently discovered

norm of reciprocity
A felt obligation and social expectation of helping or otherwise giving something of value to someone who has already helped or given something of value to you.

referent power The capacity to influence others on the basis of an identification with and respect for the power holder.

charisma A personal characteristic or special "gift" that serves as a form of interpersonal attraction and referent power over others.

substitutability A contingency of power pertaining to the availability of alternatives.

centrality A contingency of power pertaining to the degree and nature of interdependence between the power holder and others.

that one of its "star" expert witnesses—a forensic child pathology expert—had provided inaccurate cause of death evaluations in at least 20 cases, a dozen of which resulted in wrongful or highly questionable criminal convictions. The pathologist's reputation as a renowned authority was the main reason why his often weak evidence was accepted without question. "Experts in a courtroom—we give great deference to experts," admits a Canadian defense lawyer familiar with this situation.[20]

Referent Power

People have **referent power** when others identify with them, like them, or otherwise respect them. As with expert power, referent power originates within the power holder. It is largely a function of the person's interpersonal skills and tends to develop slowly. Referent power is also associated with **charisma**. Experts have difficulty agreeing on the meaning of charisma, but it is most often described as a form of interpersonal attraction whereby followers ascribe almost magical powers to the charismatic individual.[21] Some writers describe charisma as a special "gift" or trait within the charismatic person, while others say it is mainly in the eyes of the beholder. However, all agree that charisma produces a high degree of trust, respect, and devotion toward the charismatic individual.

Learning Objective

After reading this section, you should be able to

LO2 Discuss the four contingencies of power.

CONTINGENCIES OF POWER

Let's say you have expert power because of your ability to forecast and possibly even prevent dramatic changes in the organization's environment. Does this expertise mean you are influential? Not necessarily. As was illustrated earlier in Exhibit 9.2, sources of power generate power only under certain conditions. Four important contingencies of power are substitutability, centrality, visibility, and discretion.[22]

Substitutability

Substitutability refers to the availability of alternatives. Power is strongest when someone has a monopoly over a valued resource. Conversely, power decreases as the number of alternative

sources of the critical resource increases. If you—and no one else—have expertise across the organization on an important issue, you would be more powerful than if several people in your company possess this valued knowledge. Conversely, power decreases as the number of alternative sources of the critical resource increases. Substitutability refers not only to other sources that offer the resource, but also to substitutions of the resource itself. For instance, labor unions are weakened when companies introduce technologies that replace the need for their union members. Technology is a substitute for employees and, consequently, reduces union power.

Nonsubstitutability is strengthened by controlling access to the resource. Professions and labor unions gain power by controlling knowledge, tasks, or labor to perform important activities. For instance, the medical profession is powerful because it controls who can perform specific medical procedures. Labor unions that dominate an industry effectively

Developing Your Personal Brand DNA

Developing your personal brand is one of the key drivers of career success. The first step is to identify your "DNA"—your distinct and notable attributes. This DNA is a talent or expertise that is both valuable *and* unique, which leverages the power of nonsubstitutability. "Be unique about something. Be a specialist in something. Be known for something. Drive something," advises Barry Salzberg, global chief executive of accounting and consulting firm Deloitte Touche Tohmatsu. "That's very, very important for success in leadership because there are so many highly talented people. What's different about you—that's your personal brand."[23]

control access to labor needed to perform key jobs. Employees become nonsubstitutable when they possess knowledge (such as operating equipment or serving clients) that is not documented or readily available to others. Nonsubstitutability also occurs when people differentiate their resource from the alternatives. Some people claim that consultants use this tactic. They take skills and knowledge that many other consulting firms can provide and wrap them into a package (with the latest buzz words, of course) so it looks like a service no one else can offer.

Centrality

Centrality refers to the power holder's importance based on the degree and nature of interdependence with others.[24] Your centrality—and therefore your power—increases with the number of people dependent on you as well as how quickly and strongly they are affected by that dependence. Think about your own centrality for a moment: If you decided not to show up for work or school tomorrow, how many people would have difficulty performing their jobs because of your absence? How soon after they arrive at work would these coworkers notice you are missing and would have to adjust their tasks and work schedule as a result? If you have high centrality, most people in the organization would be adversely affected by your absence, and they would be affected quickly.

The extent to which centrality leverages power is apparent in well-timed labor union strikes, such as the New York City transit strike during the busy Christmas shopping season a few years ago. The illegal three-day work stoppage clogged roads and prevented half of city workers to miss or arrive very late for work. "[The Metropolitan Transit Authority] told us we got no power, but we got power," said one striking transit worker. "We got the power to stop the city."[25]

Visibility

Lucy Shadbolt and her team members work from home and other remote locations for most of her workweek. While the manager of British Gas New Energy enjoys this freedom, she also knows that working remotely can be a career liability due to the lack of visibility. "When I go into the office, where we hot-desk, I have to make an effort to position myself near my boss," says Shadbolt. "You need to consciously build relationships when you don't have those water-cooler moments naturally occurring."[26]

Lucy Shadbolt recognizes that power does not flow to unknown people in the organization. Instead, employees gain power when their talents remain in the forefront of the minds of their boss,

> " *Your centrality— and therefore your power—increases with the number of people dependent on you as well as how quickly and strongly they are affected by that dependence.* "

coworkers, and others. In other words, power increases with your visibility. One way to increase visibility is to take people-oriented jobs and work on projects that require frequent interaction with senior executives. "You can take visibility in steps," advises an executive at a pharmaceutical firm. "You can start by making yourself visible in a small group, such as a staff meeting. Then when you're comfortable with that, seek out larger arenas."[27]

Employees also gain visibility by being, quite literally, visible. Some people (such as Lucy Shadbolt) strategically locate themselves in more visible work areas, such as those closest to the boss or where other employees frequently pass by. People often use public symbols as subtle (and not-so-subtle) cues to make their power sources known to others. Many professionals display their educational diplomas and awards on office walls to remind visitors of their expertise. Medical professionals wear white coats with a stethoscope around their neck to symbolize their legitimate and expert power in hospital settings. Other people play the game of "face time"—spending more time at work and showing they are working productively.

Discretion

The freedom to exercise judgment—to make decisions without referring to a specific rule or receiving permission from someone else—is another important contingency of power in organizations. Consider the plight of first-line supervisors. It may seem they have legitimate, reward, and coercive power over employees, but this power is often curtailed by specific rules. The lack of discretion makes supervisors less powerful than their positions would indicate. "Middle managers are very much 'piggy-in-the-middle,'" complains a middle manager at Britain's National Health System. "They have little power, only what senior managers are allowed to give them."[28] More generally, research indicates that managerial discretion varies considerably across industries, and that managers with an internal locus of control are viewed as more powerful because they don't act like they lack discretion in their job.[29]

Learning Objective

After reading this section, you should be able to

LO3 Explain how people and work units gain power through social networks.

THE POWER OF SOCIAL NETWORKS

"It's not what you know, but who you know that counts!" This often-heard statement reflects the idea that employees get ahead not just by developing their competencies, but by locating themselves within **social networks**—social structures of individuals or social units (e.g., departments, organizations) that are connected to each other through one or more forms of

interdependence.[30] Some networks are held together due to common interests, such as when employees who love fancy cars spend more time together. Other networks form around common status, expertise, kinship, or physical proximity. For instance, employees are more likely to form networks with coworkers who have common educational backgrounds and occupational interests.[31]

Social networks exist everywhere because people have a drive to bond. However, there are cultural differences in the norms of active network involvement. Several writers suggest that social networking is more of a central life activity in Asian cultures that emphasize *Guanxi,* a Chinese term referring to an individual's network of social connections. Guanxi is an expressive activity because being part of a close-knit network of family and friends reinforces one's self-concept. Guanxi is also an instrumental activity because it is a strategy for receiving favors and opportunities from others. People across all cultures rely on social networks for both expressive and instrumental purposes, but these activities seem to be somewhat more explicit in Confucian cultures.[32]

Social Capital and Sources of Power

Social networks generate power through **social capital**—the goodwill and resulting resources shared among members in a social network.[33] Social networks produce trust, support, sympathy, forgiveness, and similar forms of goodwill among network members, and this goodwill motivates and enables network members to share resources with each other.[34]

Social networks offer a variety of resources, each of which potentially enhances the power of its members. Probably the best-known resource is information from other network members, which improves the individual's expert power.[35] The goodwill of social capital opens communication pipelines among those within the network. Network members receive valuable knowledge more easily and more quickly from fellow network members than do people outside that network.[36] With better information access and timeliness, members have more power because their expertise is a scarce resource; it is not widely available to people outside the network.

Increased visibility is a second contributor to a person's power through social networks. When asked to recommend someone for valued positions, other network members more readily think of you than people outside the network. Similarly, they are more likely to mention your name when asked to identify people with expertise in your areas of knowledge. Referent power is a third source of power from networks. People tend to gain referent power because network members identify more with or at least have greater trust in network members. Referent power is also apparent by the fact that reciprocity increases among network members as they become more embedded in the network.[37]

The Power of
Personal Networks for Job Hunting[38]

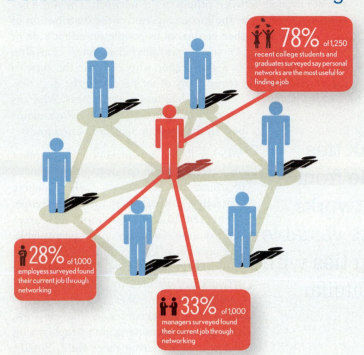

78% of 1,250 recent college students and graduates surveyed say personal networks are the most useful for finding a job

28% of 1,000 employees surveyed found their current job through networking

33% of 1,000 managers surveyed found their current job through networking

A common misperception is that social networks are free spirits that corporate leaders cannot orchestrate. In reality, company structures and practices can shape these networks to some extent.[39] But even if organizational leaders don't try to manage social networks, they need to be aware of them. Indeed, people gain power in organizations by knowing what the social networks around them look like.[40] "You look at an org chart within a company and you see the distribution of power that should be," says a senior marketing executive at Thomson Reuters. "You look at the dynamics in the social networks [to] see the distribution of power that is. It reflects where information is flowing—who is really driving things."[41]

Gaining Power from Social Networks

How do individuals (and teams and organizations) gain the most social capital from social networks? To answer this question, we need to consider the number, depth, variety, and centrality of connections that people have in their networks.

OB Theory to Practice

Introverts Can Be Effective Networkers, Too![42]

Networking requires communication and the confidence to introduce yourself to strangers. These practices come more naturally to extroverts, but networking experts say introverts can also be good at networking. Here's how.

Networking is about listening, not just talking. Networking is two-way communication, which means you need to listen to and develop empathy with others in your network. Introverts have a stronger preference than extroverts to listen, so it is an advantage they can use. Good listeners more quickly identify the needs of people they meet and therefore are more likely to convey information of value to others in the network.

Networking is personal, not mass production. People make the mistake that they need to "work the room" by introducing themselves to as many people as possible. But networking is about personal relationships, so it's fine to meet only a handful of people at a particular event. That deeper interaction could produce clearer understanding of the potential relationship and the means to strengthen that relationship.

Network rejection is about misalignment, not personal fault. Some people you meet don't want to form a network relationship. Introverts take these networking failures more personally than do extroverts, who just move on to the next social opportunity. While we always need to reflect and learn from life's events, introverts in particular need to recognize that social interaction rejections are usually misalignments of interests, not evidence of a personal fault.

Networking is a skill, not a personality trait. Introversion is a preference and behavioral tendency, not an innate lack of ability to interact with other people. Some very notable public speakers, politicians, and business leaders are introverts, yet are very good at the intense social interaction these jobs demand because they have developed appropriate skills and knowledge. While introverts might not enjoy social interaction as much as do extroverts, they can learn how to effectively meet strangers and form initial social bonds that lead to network relationships.

Networking is (partly) online, not just face-to-face. The Internet has created the best of both worlds for introverts. They can engage in effective networking without the stress or awkwardness of social interaction. At the same time, introverts can't always hide behind an Internet connection. Networking ultimately thrives on plenty of face-to-face interaction, not just emails, text messaging, and social media links.

Networking can be structured, to some extent. Some experts suggest that networking isn't a completely impromptu conversation. This is good news for introverts because they prefer structured social interaction. Before meeting people, introverts can think about specific questions to ask, practice ways to deliver those questions casually (not as a wooden interviewer), and practice answers to common questions that others will ask. When someone does ask an unexpected question, just give a polite short reply, then ask that question or another one back to the person who asked.

Strong Ties, Weak Ties, Many Ties The volume of information, favors, and other social capital that people receive from networks usually increases with the number of people connected to you. Some people have an amazing capacity to maintain their connectivity with many people, and emerging communication technologies (Facebook, LinkedIn, etc.) have further amplified this capacity to maintain these numerous connections.[43] At the same time, the more people you know, the less time and energy you have to form "strong ties." Strong ties are close-knit relationships, which are evident from how often we interact with people, how much we share resources with them, and whether we have multiple or single-purpose relationships with them (e.g., friend, coworker, sports partner). The main advantages of having strong ties are that they offer resources more quickly and sometimes more plentifully than are available in weak ties (i.e., acquaintances).

Some minimal connection strength is necessary to remain in any social network, but strong connections aren't necessarily the most valuable ties. Instead, weak ties (i.e., being merely acquaintances) with people from diverse networks can be more valuable than strong ties (i.e., having close friendships) with people in similar networks.[44] Why is this so? Close ties—our close-knit circle of friends—tend to be similar to us, and similar people tend to have the same information and connections we already have.[45] Weak ties, on the other hand, are acquaintances who are usually different from us and therefore offer resources we do not possess. Furthermore, by serving as a "bridge" across several unrelated networks, we receive unique resources from each network rather than more of the same resources.

The strength of weak ties is most apparent in job hunting and career development.[46] People with diverse networks tend to be more successful job seekers because they have a wider net to catch new job opportunities. In contrast, people who belong to similar overlapping networks tend to receive fewer leads, many of which they already knew about. As careers require more movement across many organizations and industries, you need to establish connections with people across a diverse range of industries, professions, and other spheres of life.

Social Network Centrality Earlier in this chapter, we explained that centrality is an important contingency of power. This contingency also applies to social networks.[47] The more central a person (or team or organization) is located in the network, the more social capital and therefore more power he or she acquires. Centrality is your

> ❝ Weak ties with people from diverse networks can be more valuable than strong ties with people in similar networks. ❞

importance in that network. What conditions give you more centrality than others in social networks? One important factor is your "betweenness," which literally refers to how much you are located between others in the network. The more betweenness you have, the more you control the distribution of information and other resources to people on either side of you. In Exhibit 9.3, Person A has high betweenness centrality because he or she is a gatekeeper who controls the flow of information to and from many other people in the network. Person G has less betweenness, whereas Person F and several other network members in the diagram have no betweenness.

Another factor in centrality is the number or percentage of connections you have to others in the network (called "degree centrality"). Recall that the more people connected to you, the more resources (information, favors, etc.) will be available. The number of connections also increases centrality because more members of the network are affected by your actions. Although being a member of a network gives you access to resources in that network, having a direct connection to people makes that resource-sharing more fluid. Finally, centrality is a function of the "closeness" of the relationship. High closeness occurs when a member has shorter, more direct, and efficient paths or connections with others in the network. For example, Person A has fairly high closeness centrality because he or she has direct paths to most of the network, and many of these paths are short (implying efficient and high quality communication links).

▼ **EXHIBIT 9.3** Centrality in Social Networks

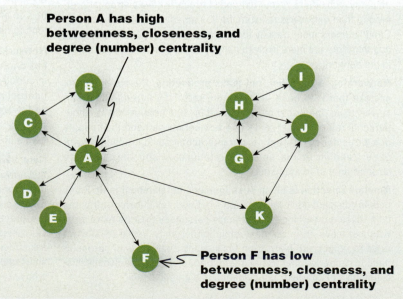

Person A has high betweenness, closeness, and degree (number) centrality

Person F has low betweenness, closeness, and degree (number) centrality

One last observation is that Exhibit 9.3 illustrates two clusters of people in the network. The gap between these two clusters is called a **structural hole**.[48] Notice that Person A provides the main bridge across this structural hole (connecting to H and K in the other cluster). This bridging role gives Person A additional power in the network. By bridging this gap, Person A becomes a broker—someone who connects two independent networks and controls information flow between them. Research shows that the more brokering relationships you have, the more likely you are to get early promotions and higher pay.

The Dark Side of Social Networks Social networks are natural elements of all organizations, yet they can create a formidable barrier to those who are not actively connected to them.[49] Women are often excluded from informal management networks because they do not participate in golf games and other male-dominated social events. Nina Smith, who leads Sage Software's Business Management Division, has had several conversations with female executives about these power dynamics. "I'm still trying to knock down the Boys Club and I still have women at Sage coming to me and saying, 'Nina, that's the boys' network and I can't get in.'"[50] Several years ago, executives at Deloitte Touche Tohmatsu discovered that inaccessibility to powerful social networks partly explained why many junior female employees left the accounting and consulting firm before reaching partnership level. The global accounting and consulting firm now relies on mentoring, formal women's network groups, and measurement of career progress to ensure that female staff members have the same career development opportunities as their male colleagues.[51]

CONSEQUENCES OF POWER

How does power affect the power holder? The answer depends to some extent on the type of power.[52] When people feel empowered (high self-determination, meaning, competence, and impact), they believe they have power over themselves and freedom from being influenced by others. Empowerment tends to increase motivation, job satisfaction, organizational commitment, and job performance. However, this feeling of being in control and free from others' authority also increases automatic rather than mindful thinking. In particular, people who feel powerful usually are more likely to rely on stereotypes, have difficulty empathizing, and generally have less accurate perceptions compared with people with less power.[53]

The other type of power is one in which an individual has power over others, such as the legitimate, reward, and coercive power that managers have over employees in the workplace. This type of power produces a sense of duty or responsibility for the people over whom you have power. Consequently, people who have power over others tend to be more mindful of their actions and engage in less stereotyping.

structural hole An area between two or more dense social network areas that lacks network ties.

influence Any behavior that attempts to alter someone's attitudes or behavior.

Learning Objective

After reading this section, you should be able to

LO4 Describe eight types of influence tactics, three consequences of influencing others, and three contingencies to consider when choosing an influence tactic.

INFLUENCING OTHERS

So far, this chapter has focused on the sources and contingencies of power as well as power derived from social networks. But power is only the *capacity* to influence others. It represents the potential to change someone's attitudes and behavior. **Influence**, on the other hand, refers to any behavior that attempts to alter someone's attitudes or behavior.[54] Influence is power in motion. It applies one or more sources of power to get people to alter their beliefs, feelings, and activities. Consequently, our interest in the remainder of this chapter is on how people use power to influence others.

Influence tactics are woven throughout the social fabric of all organizations. This is because influence is an essential process through which people coordinate their effort and act in concert to achieve organizational objectives. Indeed, influence is central to the definition of leadership. Influence operates down, across, and up the corporate hierarchy. Executives ensure that subordinates complete required tasks. Employees influence coworkers to help them with their job assignments. Subordinates engage in upward influence tactics so bosses make decisions compatible with subordinates' needs and expectations.

Types of Influence Tactics

Organizational behavior researchers have devoted considerable attention to the various types of influence tactics found in organizational settings. They do not agree on a definitive list, but the most commonly discussed influence tactics are identified in Exhibit 9.4 and described over the next few pages.[55] The first five are known as "hard" influence tactics because they force behavior change through position power (legitimate, reward, and coercion). The latter three—persuasion, ingratiation and impression management, and exchange—are called "soft" tactics because they rely more on personal sources of power (referent, expert) and appeal to the target person's attitudes and needs.

Silent Authority The silent application of authority occurs where someone complies with a request because of the requester's legitimate power as well as the target person's role expectations.[57] This deference occurs when you comply with your boss's request to complete a particular task. If the task is within your job scope and your boss has the right to make this request, then this influence strategy operates without negotiation, threats, persuasion, or other tactics. Silent authority is the most common form of influence in high power distance cultures.[58]

Assertiveness

The foreman at Otago Sheetmetal in New Zealand wasn't subtle about trying to improve staff performance. He often called the office administrator "useless" and, on one occasion, threatened to "plant her one." He also raised his voice and occasionally swore at other employees. One employee had his lawyer send a letter to Otago Sheetmetal urging the foreman to be less aggressive.[59] This incident of workplace bullying is an extreme form of assertiveness—influencing others through explicit reminders of one's obligations and sometimes explicit threats of punishment. Assertiveness might be called "vocal authority" because it involves actively applying legitimate and coercive power to influence others. This includes persistently reminding the

target of his or her obligations, frequently checking the target's work, confronting the target, and using threats of sanctions to force compliance.

Information Control

Earlier in this chapter we explained that people with centrality in social networks have the power to control information. This power translates into influence when the power holder selectively distributes information so that it reframes the situation and causes others to change their attitudes and/or behavior. Controlling information might include withholding information that is more critical or favorable, or distributing information to some people but not to others. According to one major survey, almost half of employees believe coworkers keep others in the dark about work issues if it helps their own cause. Another study found that CEOs influence their board of directors by selectively feeding and withholding information.[60]

Coalition Formation

When people lack sufficient power alone to influence others in the organization, they might form a

---

OB Theory to Practice

Managing Your Boss[61]

Managing your boss is the process of improving the relationship with your manager for the benefit of each other and the organization. It includes developing bases of power that enable you to influence the manager to achieve organizational objectives. Most executives say it is a key factor in everyone's career success. Here are the main strategies for managing your boss:

Build the relationship (i.e., build trust).

Clarify mutual expectations—work standards, work capacity.

Be reliable.

Build referent power through similarities.

Develop reciprocity (e.g., perform beyond expected duties, support your boss when he or she needs it).

Be an asset, not a liability.

Do your job well (aligned with your boss's expectations).

Be solution oriented, not problem oriented.

Find and apply complementary strengths/weaknesses (use your strengths to support your boss's weaknesses).

Adapt to your boss's style.

Be sensitive to your boss's preferences for communication, thinking, decision making, etc.

Be sensitive to your boss's values and expectations (formality, power distance, etc.).

---

coalition of people who support the proposed change. A coalition is influential in three ways.[62] First, it pools the power and resources of many people, so the coalition potentially has more influence than any number of people operating alone. Second, the coalition's mere existence can be a source of power by

coalition
A group that attempts to influence people outside the group by pooling the resources and power of its members.

upward appeal
A type of influence in which someone with higher authority or expertise is called on in reality or symbolically to support the influencer's position.

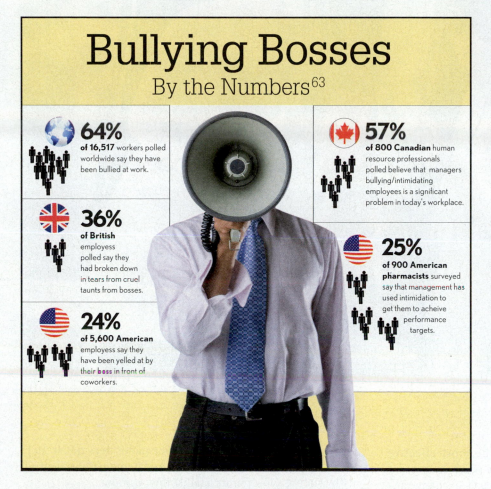

Bullying Bosses
By the Numbers[63]

64% of 16,517 workers polled worldwide say they have been bullied at work.

36% of British employees polled say they had broken down in tears from cruel taunts from bosses.

24% of 5,600 American employees say they have been yelled at by their boss in front of coworkers.

57% of 800 Canadian human resource professionals polled believe that managers bullying/intimidating employees is a significant problem in today's workplace.

25% of 900 American pharmacists surveyed say that management has used intimidation to get them to achieve performance targets.

symbolizing the legitimacy of the issue. In other words, a coalition creates a sense that the issue deserves attention because it has broad support. Third, coalitions tap into the power of the social identity process introduced in Chapter 3. A coalition is an informal group that advocates a new set of norms and behaviors. If the coalition has a broad-based membership (i.e., its members come from various parts of the organization), then other employees are more likely to identify with that group and, consequently, accept the ideas the coalition is proposing.

Upward Appeal Upward appeal involves calling upon higher authority or expertise, or symbolically relying on these sources to support the influencer's position. It occurs when someone says, "The boss likely agrees with me on this matter; let's find out!" Upward appeal also occurs when relying on the authority of the firm's policies or values. By reminding others that your request is consistent with the organization's overarching goals, you are implying support from senior executives without formally involving them.

▼**EXHIBIT 9.4** Types of Influence Tactics in Organizations

Influence Tactic	Description
Silent authority	Influencing behavior through legitimate power without explicitly referring to that power base.
Assertiveness	Actively applying legitimate and coercive power by applying pressure or threats.
Information control	Explicitly manipulating someone else's access to information for the purpose of changing their attitudes and/or behavior.
Coalition formation	Forming a group that attempts to influence others by pooling the resources and power of its members.
Upward appeal	Gaining support from one or more people with higher authority or expertise.
Persuasion	Using logical arguments, factual evidence, and emotional appeals to convince people of the value of a request.
Ingratiation/impression management	Attempting to increase liking by, or perceived similarity to, some targeted person.
Exchange	Promising benefits or resources in exchange for the target person's compliance.

Persuasion **Persuasion** is one of the most effective influence strategies for career success. The ability to present facts, logical arguments, and emotional appeals to change another person's attitudes and behavior is not just an acceptable way to influence others; in many societies, it is a noble art and a quality of effective leaders. The effectiveness of persuasion as an influence tactic depends on characteristics of the persuader, message content, communication medium, and the audience being persuaded (see Exhibit 9.5).[64] People are more persuasive when listeners believe they have expertise and credibility, such as when the persuader does not seem to profit from the persuasion attempt and demonstrates neutrality by stating a few points against the position.

The message is more important than the messenger when the issue is important to the audience. Persuasive message content acknowledges several points of view so the audience does not feel cornered by the speaker. The message should also be limited to a few strong arguments, which are repeated a few times, but not too frequently. The message should use emotional appeals

> " The effectiveness of persuasion as an influence tactic depends on characteristics of the persuader, message content, communication medium, and the audience being persuaded. "

(such as graphically showing the unfortunate consequences of a bad decision), but only in combination with logical arguments and specific recommendations to overcome the threat. Finally, message content is more persuasive when the audience is warned about opposing arguments. This **inoculation effect** causes listeners to generate counter-arguments to the anticipated persuasion attempts, which makes the opponent's subsequent persuasion attempts less effective.[65]

Two other considerations when persuading people are the medium of communication and characteristics of the audience. Generally, persuasion works best in face-to-face conversations and through other media-rich communication channels. The personal nature of face-to-face communication increases the persuader's credibility, and the richness of this channel provides faster feedback that the influence strategy is working. With respect to audience characteristics, it is more difficult to persuade people who have high self-esteem and intelligence, as well as a self-concept that is strongly tied to the opposing viewpoint.[66]

Ingratiation and Impression Management

Silent authority, assertiveness, information control, coalitions, and upward appeals are somewhat (or very!) forceful ways to influence other people. In contrast, a very "soft" influence tactic is **ingratiation**—any attempt to increase liking by, or perceived similarity to, some targeted person.[67] Ingratiation comes in several flavors. Employees might flatter their boss in front of others, demonstrate that they have similar attitudes as their boss (e.g., agreeing with the boss's proposal), and ask their boss for advice. Ingratiation is one of the more effective influence tactics at boosting a person's career success (i.e., with regard to performance appraisal feedback, salaries, and promotions).[68] However, people who engage in high levels of ingratiation are less (not more) influential and less likely to get promoted.[69] Why the opposite effect? Those who engage in too much ingratiation are viewed as insincere and self-serving. The terms "apple polishing" and "brown-nosing" are applied to those who ingratiate to excess or in ways that suggest selfish motives for the ingratiation.

Ingratiation is part of a larger influence tactic known as **impression management**, the practice of actively shaping our public images.[70] These public images might be crafted as being important, vulnerable, threatening, or pleasant. For the most part, employees routinely engage in pleasant impression management behaviors to satisfy the basic norms of social behavior, such as the way they dress and how they behave toward colleagues and customers.

Impression management is a common strategy for people trying to get ahead in the workplace. In fact, career professionals encourage people to develop a personal "brand"—that is, to demonstrate and symbolize a distinctive competitive advantage.[71] Furthermore, people who master the art of personal branding rely on impression management through distinctive personal characteristics such as black shirts, dyed hair, or unique signatures. "In today's economy, your personal brand is being judged every day," says Coca-Cola Company senior vice president Jerry Wilson. "Either position yourself, or others will position you."[72]

Unfortunately, a few individuals carry impression management beyond ethical boundaries by exaggerating their credentials and accomplishments. For instance, a Lucent Technologies

▼ **EXHIBIT 9.5** Elements of Persuasion

Persuasion Element	Characteristics of Effective Persuasion
Persuader characteristics	Expertise
	Credibility
	No apparent profit motive
	Appears somewhat neutral (acknowledges benefits of the opposing view)
Message content	Offers multiple viewpoints (does not exclusively support the desired option)
	Limited to a few strong arguments (not many arguments)
	Repeats arguments, but not excessively
	Uses emotional appeals in combination with logical arguments
	Offers specific solutions to overcome the stated problems
	Inoculation effect—audience warned of counterarguments that opposition will present
Communication medium	Media-rich channels are usually more persuasive
Audience characteristics	Lower self-esteem
	Lower intelligence
	Self-concept is not tied to the opposing view

OB Theory to Practice

Impression Management in Job Interviews[73]

Interviewer Question	Impression Management Principle	Do Say . . .	Don't Say . . .
What interests you about this job?	Demonstrate your interest in and respect for this company by seeking a specific job or career here.	"There are exciting things happening at this company, and this position would be a great way for me to grow my skills."	"Well, I just need a job, and this place looks as good as any to find one."
What are your greatest weaknesses?	Demonstrate honesty, self-awareness, and ability to develop yourself.	"Sometimes I take on more tasks than I should. I need to learn how to delegate more for better workload balance and to give others opportunities to develop their skills."	"Gee, I really don't have any weaknesses. I'm a model employee."
Why did you leave your last job?	Demonstrate that you are a positive forward-thinker who values this company's career opportunities. Avoid dwelling on negative past events.	"I have a goal to become head of marketing someday. The experience and new skills I would gain here look like an excellent fit with that aspiration."	"Working in my last job was like being on the *Titanic*. Also, I didn't like my boss. He always wanted me to work late, and it caused me to miss my favorite TV show a few times."
Describe a situation in which you had to deal with a professional disagreement or conflict.	Demonstrate that you are a good team player who is diplomatic at conflict handling and problem solving.	"My coworker and I once disagreed on (describe situation). We discussed our different methods and came up with a better way that combined the best of each of our methods."	"I've never had a disagreement. Everyone tends to know I'm right."
How many times do a clock's hands overlap in a day?	These unusual problem-solving questions test more than your technical skills; they also test your motivation and "can-do" attitude toward solving problems.	"Let's see, there are 24 hours in a day and every time on the clock happens twice, so. . . ."	"Gosh, I have no idea. I'm not that good at math."

executive lied about having a PhD from Stanford University and hid his criminal past involving forgery and embezzlement. Ironically, the executive was Lucent's director of recruiting![74] One of the most elaborate misrepresentations occurred a few years ago when a Singaporean entrepreneur sent out news releases claiming to be a renowned artificial intelligence researcher, the author of several books, and the recipient of numerous awards from MIT and Stanford University (one of the awards was illustrated on his Web site). These falsehoods were so convincing that the entrepreneur almost received a real award, the "Internet Visionary of the Year" at the Internet World Asia Industry Awards.[75]

Exchange Exchange activities involve the promise of benefits or resources in exchange for the target person's compliance with your request. Negotiation is an integral part of exchange influence activities. For instance, you might negotiate with your boss for a day off in return for working a less desirable shift at a future date. Exchange also includes applying the norm of reciprocity that we described earlier, such as reminding the target of past benefits or favors with the expectation that the target will now make up for that debt. Earlier in this chapter we explained how people gain power through social networks. They also use norms of reciprocity to influence others in the network. Active networkers build up "exchange credits" by helping colleagues in the short term for reciprocal benefits in the long term.

Consequences and Contingencies of Influence Tactics

Faced with a variety of influence strategies, you are probably asking, Which ones are best? The best way to answer this question is to describe how people react when others try to influence them: resistance, compliance, or commitment (see Exhibit 9.6).[76] *Resistance* occurs when people or work units oppose the behavior the influencer desires by refusing, arguing, or delaying engagement in the behavior. *Compliance* occurs when people are motivated to implement the influencer's request at a minimal level of effort and for purely instrumental reasons. Without external sources to prompt the desired behavior, compliance would not occur. *Commitment* is the strongest outcome of influence, whereby people identify with the influencer's request and are highly motivated to implement it even when extrinsic sources of motivation are no longer present.

Generally, people react more favorably to "soft" tactics than to "hard" tactics. Soft influence tactics rely on personal sources of power (expert and referent power), which tend to build commitment to the influencer's request. In contrast, hard tactics rely on position power (legitimate, reward, and coercion), so they tend to produce compliance or, worse, resistance. Hard tactics also tend to undermine trust, which can hurt future relationships.

Apart from the general preference for soft rather than hard tactics, the most appropriate influence strategy depends on a few contingencies. One obvious contingency is which sources of power are strongest. Those with expertise tend to have more influence

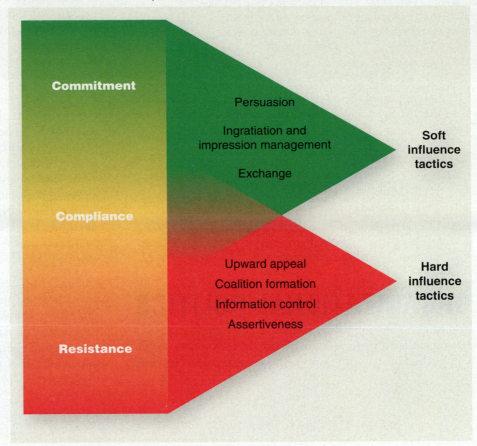

▼ **EXHIBIT 9.6**   Consequences of Hard and Soft Influence Tactics

Commitment

Persuasion

Ingratiation and impression management

Exchange

Soft influence tactics

Compliance

Upward appeal

Coalition formation

Information control

Assertiveness

Hard influence tactics

Resistance

using persuasion, whereas those with a strong legitimate power base are usually more successful applying silent authority.[77] A second contingency is whether the person being influenced is higher, lower, or at the same level in the organization. As an example, employees may face adverse career consequences by being too assertive with their boss. Meanwhile, supervisors who engage in ingratiation and impression management tend to lose the respect of their staff.

Finally, the most appropriate influence tactic depends on personal, organizational, and cultural values.[78] People with a strong power orientation might feel more comfortable using assertiveness, whereas those who value conformity might feel more comfortable with upward appeals. At an organizational level, firms with a competitive culture might foster more use of information control and coalition formation, whereas companies with a learning orientation would likely encourage more influence through persuasion. The preferred influence tactics also vary across societal cultures. Research indicates that ingratiation is much more common among managers in the United States than in

> " Soft influence tactics tend to build commitment to the influencer's request, whereas hard tactics tend to produce compliance or, worse, resistance. "

organizational politics Behaviors that others perceive as self-serving tactics at the expense of other people and possibly the organization.

Machiavellian values The beliefs that deceit is a natural and acceptable way to influence others and that getting more than one deserves is acceptable.

Hong Kong, possibly because this tactic disrupts the more distant roles that managers and employees expect in highpower distance cultures.

Learning Objective

After reading this section, you should be able to

LO5 Identify the organizational conditions and personal characteristics that support organizational politics, as well as ways to minimize organizational politics.

ORGANIZATIONAL POLITICS

You might have noticed that organizational politics has not been mentioned yet, even though some of the practices or examples described over the past few pages are usually considered political tactics. The phrase was carefully avoided because, for the most part, organizational politics is in the eye of the beholder. You might perceive a coworker's attempt to influence the boss as acceptable behavior for the good of the organization, whereas someone else might perceive the coworker's tactic as brazen organizational politics.

This perceptual issue explains why OB experts increasingly discuss influence tactics as behaviors and organizational politics as perceptions.[80] The influence tactics described earlier are perceived as **organizational politics** when they seem to be self-serving behaviors at the expense of others and possibly contrary to the interests of the entire organization. Of course, some tactics are so blatantly selfish and counterproductive that almost everyone correctly sees them as organizational politics. In other situations, however, a person's behavior might be viewed as political or in the organization's best interest, depending on your point of view.

Employees who experience organizational politics have lower job satisfaction, organizational commitment, organizational citizenship, and task performance, as well as higher levels of work-related stress and motivation to leave the organization.[81] And because political tactics serve individuals rather than organizations, they potentially divert resources away from the

> ## [Keep your friends close and your enemies closer.[82]]
> ### —Attributed to Sun-Tzu

Office Politics
by the Numbers[79]

53% of British managers polled feel that organizational politics is a major cause of stress at work (top-ranked cause of stress.)

47% of American employees polled say that office politics cuts into productive time (second highest cause, after fixing someone else's work).

36% of Canadian employees polled recently say that office politics is one of the biggest roadblocks to productivity.

19% of Canadian employees polled 10 years ago said that office politics is one of the biggest roadblocks to productivity.

29% of American employees polled say a coworker has taken credit for one of their ideas.

58% of Canadian employees polled say a coworker has taken credit for one of their ideas.

organization's effective functioning and potentially threaten its survival.

Minimizing Organizational Politics

Researchers have identified several conditions that support organizational politics, so we can identify corresponding strategies to keep political activities to a minimum.[83] First, organizational politics is triggered by scarce resources in the workplace. When budgets are slashed, people rely on political tactics to safeguard their resources and maintain the status quo. Although not easy to maintain or add resources, sometimes this action may be less costly than the consequences of organizational politics.

Second, organizational politics is suppressed when resource allocation decisions are clear and simplified. Political tactics are fueled by ambiguous, complex, or lack of formal rules because those tactics help people get what they want when decisions lack structural guidelines. Third, organizational change tends to bring out more

OB Theory to Practice

Minimizing Organizational Politics

- Clarify rules and procedures where ambiguity generates internal competition.
- Provide sufficient resources before scarcity starts generating political behavior.
- Manage organizational change effectively (i.e., communication, learning, and involvement).
- Alter reward systems and remove leaders who reinforce and role model self-serving behavior.
- Hire and promote people with low Machiavellian values.

organizational politics, mainly because change creates ambiguity and threatens the employee's power and other valued resources.[84] Consequently, leaders need to apply the organizational change strategies that we describe in Chapter 14, particularly through communication, learning, and involvement. Research has found that employees who are kept informed of what is going on in the organization and who are involved in organizational decisions are less likely to observe organizational politics.

Finally, political behavior is more common in work units and organizations where it is tolerated and reinforced. Some companies seem to nurture self-serving behavior through reward systems and by demonstrating it in the behaviors of organizational leaders. To minimize political norms, the organization needs to diagnose and alter systems and role modeling that support self-serving behavior. They should support organizational values that oppose political tactics, such as altruism and customer focus. One of the most important strategies is for leaders to become role models of organizational citizenship rather than symbols of successful organizational politicians.

Personal Characteristics Several personal characteristics affect a person's motivation to engage in self-serving behavior.[85] One such characteristic is a strong need for personal as opposed to socialized power. Those with a need for personal power seek power for its own sake and try to acquire more power. Some individuals have strong **Machiavellian values**. Machiavellianism is named after Niccolò Machiavelli, the sixteenth-century Italian philosopher who wrote *The Prince*, a famous treatise about political behavior. People with high Machiavellian values are comfortable with getting more than they deserve, and they believe that deceit is a natural and acceptable way to achieve this goal. They seldom trust coworkers and tend to use cruder influence tactics, such as bypassing one's boss or being assertive, to get their own way.[86] ■

managing workplace
conflict

Until a few years ago, Intel engineers were obsessed with designing computer processors that were faster and smaller, even though the processors were also becoming hotter and more power hungry. Key people at Intel's Israeli operations saw trouble brewing. Almost weekly, they would fly from Haifa to Intel's headquarters in California, pestering top executives with data and arguments that the company would soon hit the limits of chip speed. The Israeli crew also warned that Intel would lose out to competitors for cooler and more power-efficient "mobility" chips for laptops and other mobility devices.

The conflict may have rankled some Intel bosses, but the Israeli staff convinced Intel to change direction. Their persistent arguing also demonstrated the value of

continued on p. 194

LO1 Define conflict and debate its positive and negative consequences in the workplace.

LO2 Distinguish constructive from relationship conflict and describe three strategies to minimize relationship conflict during constructive conflict episodes.

LO3 Diagram the conflict process model and describe six structural sources of conflict in organizations.

LO4 Outline the five conflict handling styles and discuss the circumstances in which each would be most appropriate.

LO5 Apply the six structural approaches to conflict management and describe the three types of third-party dispute resolution.

LO6 Describe the bargaining zone model and outline strategies skilled negotiators use to claim value and create value in negotiations.

conflict A process in which one party perceives that his or her interests are being opposed or negatively affected by another party.

continued from p. 193

"constructive confrontation"—the art of argument and respectful debate. "The goal of a leader should be to maximize resistance—in the sense of encouraging disagreement and dissent," says Dov Frohman, founder of Intel Israel.[1]

Intel executives encourage constructive debate, believing that these interactions improve decision making and the company's overall effectiveness. At the same time, employees often shun conflict because disagreements can easily escalate into unpleasant experiences. This chapter investigates these dynamics of conflict in organizational settings. It begins by defining conflict and discussing the age-old question: Is conflict good or bad? Next, we look at the conflict process and examine in detail the main factors that cause or amplify conflict. The five styles of handling conflict are then described, including important contingencies of conflict handling as well as gender and cross-cultural differences. Next, we look at the role of managers and others in third-party conflict resolution. The final section of this chapter reviews key issues in negotiating conflict resolution. ■

conflict. **Conflict** is a process in which one party perceives that its interests are being opposed or negatively affected by another party.[2] It may occur when one party obstructs another's goals in some way, or just from one party's perception that the other party is going to do so. Conflict is ultimately based on perceptions; it exists whenever one party *believes* that another might obstruct its efforts, whether the other party actually intends to do so.

Is Conflict Good or Bad?

One of the oldest debates in organizational behavior is whether conflict is good or bad—or, more recently, what forms of conflict are good or bad—for organizations.[3] The dominant view over most of this time has been that conflict is dysfunctional.[4] At the turn of the previous century, European administrative theorists Henri Fayol and Max Weber independently recommended organizational structures that depended on harmonious relations and systematically discouraged conflict. Elton Mayo, who founded Harvard University's human relations school and is considered one of the founders of organizational behavior, was convinced that employee-management conflict undermines organizational effectiveness. These and other critics warn that even moderately low levels of disagreement tatter the fabric of workplace relations and sap energy from productive activities. Disagreement with one's supervisor, for example, wastes productive time, violates the hierarchy of command, and questions the efficient assignment of authority (where managers made the decisions and employees followed them).

Learning Objective

After reading this section, you should be able to

LO1 Define conflict and debate its positive and negative consequences in the workplace.

THE MEANING AND CONSEQUENCES OF CONFLICT

One of the facts of life is that organizations are continuously adapting to their external environment and introducing better ways to transform resources into outputs (see Chapter 1). There is no clear road map on how companies should change, and employees and other stakeholders rarely agree completely on the direction or form of these adjustments. Employees have divergent personal and work goals, which lead them to prefer different directions the organization should take.

These differences in goals and viewpoints, along with a few other key factors described in this chapter, lead to

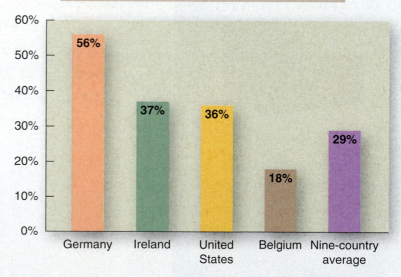

Frequently or Always Dealing with Workplace Conflict[5]

Percentage of 5,000 employees surveyed in nine countries (Belgium, Brazil, Denmark, France, Germany, Ireland, the Netherlands, the United Kingdom, and the United States) who say they always or frequently have to deal with workplace conflict. This chart shows selected countries and average results.

Conflict is the gadfly of thought. It stirs us to observation and memory. It instigates to invention. It shocks us out of sheeplike passivity, and sets us at noting and contriving.[6]

—John Dewey, educational philosopher/psychologist

Although the "conflict-is-bad" perspective is now considered too simplistic, conflict can indeed have negative consequences under some circumstances (see Exhibit 10.1).[7] Conflict has been criticized for consuming otherwise productive time. For instance, almost one-third of the 5,000 employees recently surveyed across nine countries reported that they are frequently or always dealing with workplace conflict. More than half of the employees in Germany complained that conflict was consuming their workday.[8]

Conflict can undermine job performance in other ways.[9] Conflict is often stressful, which consumes personal energy and distracts employees from their work. Conflict discourages people engaged in the dispute from sharing resources and coordinating with each other. It can reduce job satisfaction, resulting in higher turnover and lower customer service. Conflict fuels organizational politics, such as motivating employees to find ways to undermine the credibility of their opponents. Decision making suffers because people are less

Negative Consequences	Positive Consequences
Uses otherwise productive time	Fuller debate of decision choices
Less information sharing	Decision assumptions are questioned
Higher stress, dissatisfaction, and turnover	Potentially generates more creative decisions
Increases organizational politics	More responsive to changing environment
Wastes resources	Stronger team cohesion (when conflict occurs between the team and outside opponents)
Weakens team cohesion (when conflict occurs among team members)	

this view, organizations are most effective when employees experience some level of conflict, but they become less effective with high levels of conflict.[11] What are the benefits of conflict? Conflict energizes people to debate issues and evaluate alternatives more thoroughly. The debate tests the logic of arguments and encourages participants to reexamine their basic assumptions about the problem and its possible solution. It prevents individuals and groups from making inferior decisions. As individuals and teams strive to reach agreement, they learn more about each other and come to understand the underlying issues that need to be addressed. This helps them to develop more creative solutions that reflect the needs of multiple stakeholders. By generating active thinking, conflict also potentially improves creativity.[12]

A second potential benefit is that moderate levels of conflict prevent organizations from stagnating and becoming nonresponsive to their external environment. Through conflict, employees continuously question current practices and become more sensitive to dissatisfaction from stakeholders. In other words, conflict generates more vigilance.[13] Conflict offers a third positive consequence when team members have a dispute or competition with external sources. This form of conflict represents an external challenge which, as was noted in the team dynamics chapter (Chapter 7), potentially increases cohesion within the team. People are more motivated to work together when faced with an external threat, such as conflict with people outside the team.

motivated to communicate valuable information. Ironically, with less communication, the feuding parties are more likely to escalate their disagreement because each side relies increasingly on distorted perceptions and stereotypes of the other party. Finally, conflict among team members may undermine team cohesion.

Benefits of Conflict In the 1920s, when most organizational scholars viewed conflict as inherently dysfunctional, educational philosopher and psychologist John Dewey praised its benefits by calling it "the gadfly of thought." Three years later, political science and management theorist Mary Parker Follett similarly remarked that the "friction" of conflict should be put to use rather than treated as an unwanted consequence of differences.[10]

But it wasn't until the 1970s that conflict management experts began to embrace the "optimal conflict" perspective. According to

Learning Objective

After reading this section, you should be able to

LO2 Distinguish constructive from relationship conflict and describe three strategies to minimize relationship conflict during constructive conflict episodes.

The Emerging View: Constructive and Relationship Conflict

Although many writers still refer to the "optimal conflict" perspective, an emerging school of thought is that there are two types of conflict with opposing consequences: constructive conflict and relationship conflict.[14] **Constructive conflict** (also called *task-related conflict*) occurs when people focus their discussion around the issue while showing respect for people with other points of view. This conflict is called "constructive" because different positions are encouraged so ideas and recommendations can be clarified, redesigned, and tested for logical soundness. By keeping the debate focused on the issue, participants calmly reexamine their assumptions and beliefs without having hostile emotions triggered by their drive to defend their self-concept. Research indicates that teams and organizations with very low levels of constructive conflict are less effective.[15] At the same time, there is likely an upper limit to the intensity of any disagreement, above which it would be difficult to remain constructive.

In contrast to constructive conflict, **relationship conflict** (also known as *socioemotional conflict*) focuses on the adversary rather than the issue as the source of conflict. The parties refer to "personality clashes" and other interpersonal incompatibilities rather than legitimate differences of opinion regarding tasks or decisions. They try to undermine the other person's argument by questioning their competency. Attacking a person's credibility or displaying an aggressive response toward him or her triggers defense mechanisms and a competitive orientation. Relationship conflict also reduces trust because the strong negative emotions that typically accompany this conflict undermine any identification with the other person, leaving the relationship held together mainly by calculus-based trust.[16] The conflict more easily escalates because the adversaries become less motivated to communicate and share information, making it more

> " Most of us experience some degree of relationship conflict during and after any constructive debate. "

constructive conflict A type of conflict in which people focus their discussion around the issue while showing respect for people with other points of view.

relationship conflict A type of conflict in which people focus on characteristics of other individuals, rather than on the issues, as the source of conflict.

difficult for them to discover common ground and ultimately resolve the conflict. Instead, they rely more on distorted perceptions and stereotypes which, as we noted earlier, tend to further escalate the conflict.

Separating Constructive from Relationship Conflict

If there are two types of conflict, then the obvious advice is to encourage constructive conflict and minimize relationship conflict. This recommendation sounds good in theory, but separating these two types of conflict isn't easy. Research indicates that we experience some degree of relationship conflict whenever we are engaged in constructive debate.[17] No matter how diplomatically someone questions our ideas and actions, they potentially trigger our drive to defend our ideas, our sense of competence, and our public image. The stronger the level of debate and the more the issue is tied to our self-concept, the higher the chance that the constructive conflict will evolve into (or mix with) relationship conflict. Constructive debate has made Intel a more effective organization. However, some employees say they also experience relationship conflict.

Fortunately, three strategies or conditions potentially minimize the level of relationship conflict during constructive conflict episodes.[18]

- *Emotional Intelligence.* Relationship conflict is less likely to occur, or is less likely to escalate, when team members have high levels of emotional intelligence. Employees with higher emotional intelligence are better able to regulate their emotions during debate, which reduces the risk of escalating perceptions of interpersonal hostility. People with high emotional intelligence are also more likely to view a coworker's emotional reaction as valuable information about that person's needs and expectations rather than as a personal attack.

- *Cohesive Team.* Relationship conflict is suppressed when the conflict occurs within a highly cohesive team. The longer people work together, get to know each other, and develop mutual trust, the more latitude they give each other to show emotions without being personally offended. Strong cohesion also allows each person to know about and anticipate their teammates' behaviors and emotions. Another benefit is that cohesion produces a stronger social identity with the group, so team members are motivated to avoid escalating relationship conflict during otherwise emotionally turbulent discussions.

- *Supportive Team Norms.* Various team norms can hold relationship conflict at bay during constructive debate. When team norms encourage openness, for instance, team members learn to appreciate honest dialogue without personally reacting to any emotional display during the disagreements.[19] Other norms might discourage team members from displaying negative emotions toward coworkers. Team norms also encourage tactics that diffuse relationship conflict when it first appears. For instance, research has found that teams with low relationship conflict use humor to maintain positive group emotions, which offsets negative feelings team members might develop toward some coworkers during debate.

Learning Objective

After reading the next two sections, you should be able to

L03 Diagram the conflict process model and describe six structural sources of conflict in organizations.

CONFLICT PROCESS MODEL

Now that we have outlined the history and current knowledge about conflict and its outcomes, let's look at the model of the conflict process, shown in Exhibit 10.2.[20] This model begins with the sources of conflict, which we will describe in the next section. At some point, the sources of conflict lead one or both parties to perceive that conflict exists. They become aware that one party's statements and actions are incompatible with their own goals. These perceptions usually interact with emotions experienced about the conflict.[21]

Conflict perceptions and emotions produce manifest conflict—the decisions and behaviors of one party toward the other. These *conflict episodes* may range from subtle nonverbal behaviors to warlike aggression. Particularly when people experience high levels of conflict-generated emotions, they have difficulty finding the words and expressions that communicate effectively without further irritating the relationship.[22] Conflict is also manifested by the style each side uses to resolve the conflict. Some people tend to avoid the conflict, whereas others try to defeat those with opposing views.

Exhibit 10.2 shows arrows looping back from manifest conflict to conflict perceptions and emotions. These arrows illustrate that the conflict process is really a series of episodes that potentially cycle into conflict escalation.[23] It doesn't take much to start this conflict cycle—just an inappropriate comment, a misunderstanding, or action that lacks diplomacy. These behaviors cause the other party to perceive that conflict exists. Even if the first party did not intend to demonstrate conflict, the second party's response may create that perception.

STRUCTURAL SOURCES OF CONFLICT IN ORGANIZATIONS

The conflict model starts with the sources of conflict, so we need to understand these sources to effectively diagnose conflict episodes and subsequently resolve the conflict or occasionally generate conflict where it is lacking. The six main conditions that cause conflict in organizational settings are incompatible

▼**EXHIBIT 10.2** Model of the Conflict Process

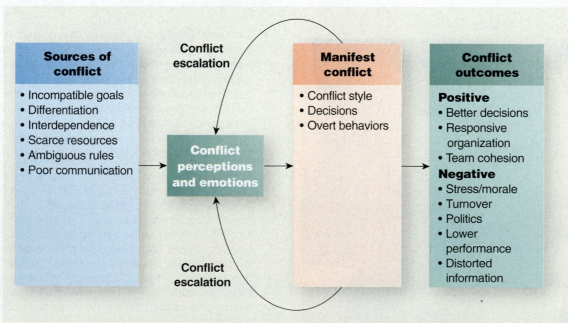

---

goals, differentiation, interdependence, scarce resources, ambiguous rules, and communication problems.

Incompatible Goals

Goal incompatibility occurs when the goals of one person or department seem to interfere with another person's or department's goals.[25] For example, the production department strives for cost efficiency by scheduling long production runs, whereas the sales team emphasizes customer service by delivering the client's product as quickly as possible. If inventory runs out of a particular product, the production team would prefer to have clients wait until the next production run. This infuriates sales representatives who would rather change production quickly to satisfy consumer demand.

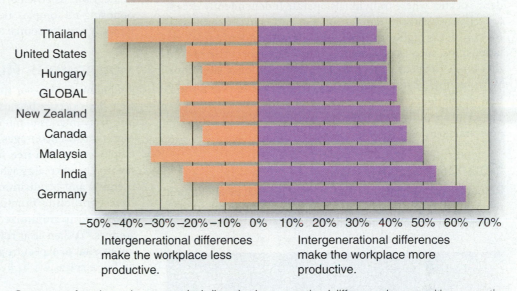

Do Intergenerational Differences Increase or Decrease Productivity?[27]

Intergenerational differences make the workplace less productive. / Intergenerational differences make the workplace more productive.

Percentage of employees by country who believe that intergenerational differences have a positive or negative effect on workplace productivity. Percentages do not add up to 100 percent because some respondents reported that generational differences have no effect on productivity. Based on a survey of 100,000 employees in 33 countries.

Differentiation

Another source of conflict is differentiation—differences among people and work units regarding their training, values, beliefs, and experiences. Differentiation can be distinguished from goal incompatibility; two people or departments may agree on a common goal (serving customers better) but have different beliefs about how to achieve that goal (e.g., standardize employee behavior versus give employees autonomy in customer interactions). Differentiation partly explains intergenerational conflicts. Younger and older employees have different needs, different expectations, and different workplace practices, which sometimes produces conflicting preferences and actions. Technological developments and pivotal social events help explain these unique characteristics of each generation.[26]

Differentiation also produces the classic tension between employees from two companies brought together through a merger. Even though everyone wants the merged company

to succeed, they fight over the "right way" to do things because of their unique experiences in the separate companies. A mid-sized retail clothing chain experienced another variation of differentiation-based conflict when the founder and CEO hired several senior managers from large organizations to strengthen the experience levels of its senior management group. The newly hired managers soon clashed with long-time executives at the clothing chain. "We ended up with an old team and a new team, and they weren't on the same wavelength," explains the company owner, who eventually fired most of the new managers.

Interdependence

Conflict tends to increase with the level of task interdependence. Task interdependence refers to the extent to which employees must share materials, information, or expertise to perform their jobs (see Chapter 7). This interdependence includes sharing common resources, exchanging work or clients back and forth, and receiving outcomes (such as rewards) that are partly determined by the performance of others.[28] Higher interdependence increases the risk of conflict because there is a greater chance that each side will disrupt or interfere with the other side's goals.[29]

Other than complete independence, employees tend to have the lowest risk of conflict when working with others in a pooled interdependence relationship. Pooled interdependence occurs where individuals operate independently except for reliance on a common resource or authority. The potential for conflict is higher in sequential interdependence work relationships, such as an assembly line. The highest risk of conflict tends to occur in reciprocal interdependence situations. With reciprocal interdependence, employees have high mutual dependence on each other and, consequently, have a higher probability of interfering with each other's work and personal goals.

Scarce Resources

Resource scarcity generates conflict because each person or unit requiring the same resource necessarily undermines others who also need that resource to fulfill their goals. Most labor strikes,

for instance, occur because there aren't enough financial and other resources for employees and company owners to each receive the outcomes they seek, such as higher pay (employees) and higher investment returns (shareholders). Budget deliberations within organizations also produce conflict because there aren't enough funds to satisfy the goals of each work unit. The more resources one group receives, the fewer resources stakeholders will receive. Fortunately, these interests aren't perfectly opposing in complex negotiations, but limited resources are typically a major source of friction.

Ambiguous Rules

Ambiguous rules—or the complete lack of rules—breed conflict. This occurs because uncertainty increases the risk that one party intends to interfere with the other party's goals. Ambiguity also encourages political tactics and, in some cases, employees enter a free-for-all battle to win decisions in their favor. This explains why conflict is more common during mergers and acquisitions. Employees from both companies have conflicting practices and values, and few rules have developed to minimize the maneuvering for power and resources.[30] When clear rules exist, on the other hand, employees know what to expect from each other and have agreed to abide by those rules.

Communication Problems

Conflict often occurs due to the lack of opportunity, ability, or motivation to communicate effectively. Let's look at each of these causes. First, when two parties lack the opportunity to communicate, they tend to rely more on stereotypes to understand the other party in the conflict. Unfortunately, stereotypes are sufficiently subjective that emotions can negatively distort the meaning of an opponent's actions, thereby escalating perceptions of conflict. Second, some people lack the necessary skills to communicate in a diplomatic, nonconfrontational manner. When one party communicates its disagreement arrogantly, the receivers of that message are more likely to heighten their perception that conflict exists. This may lead the other party to reciprocate with a similar response, which further escalates the conflict.[31]

A third problem is that relationship conflict is uncomfortable, so people are less motivated to communicate with others in a disagreement. Unfortunately, less communication can further escalate the conflict because each side has less accurate information about the other side's intentions. To fill in the missing pieces, they rely on distorted images and stereotypes of the other party. Perceptions are further distorted because people in conflict situations tend to accentuate differences between themselves and their opponents (see Chapter 3). This differentiation creates a more positive self-concept and a more negative image of the opponent. We begin to see competitors less favorably so our self-concept remains positive during these uncertain times.[32]

Learning Objective

After reading this section, you should be able to

LO4 Outline the five conflict handling styles and discuss the circumstances in which each would be most appropriate.

INTERPERSONAL CONFLICT HANDLING STYLES

The six structural conditions described in the previous section lead to conflict perceptions and emotions which, in turn, motivate people to take some sort of action to address the conflict. Along with her pioneering view that some conflict is beneficial, Mary Parker Follett suggested there are different conflict handling styles. Conflict management experts subsequently expanded and refined this taxonomy of conflict handling styles, with most of them adapting variations of the five-category model shown in Exhibit 10.3 and described below. This model recognizes that the use of a particular conflict handling style depends on the extent to which the person wants to maximize outcomes for themselves and

win–win orientation
The belief that conflicting parties will find a mutually beneficial solution to their disagreement.

win–lose orientation
The belief that conflicting parties are drawing from a fixed pie, so the more one party receives, the less the other party will receive.

> [**The more arguments you win, the fewer friends you will have.**[33]]
> —Mid-Twentieth-Century American Proverb

▼ **EXHIBIT 10.3** Interpersonal Conflict Handling Styles

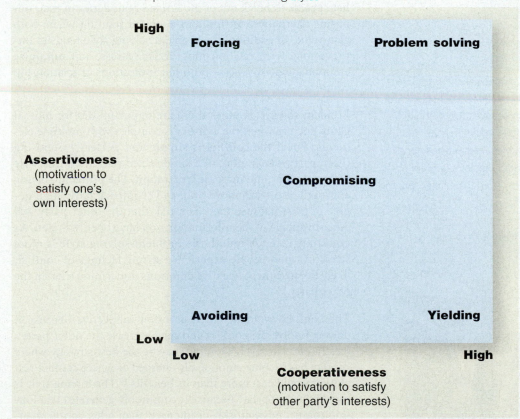

Source: C. K. W. de Dreu et al., "A Theory-Based Measure of Conflict Management Strategies in the Workplace," *Journal of Organizational Behavior,* 22 (2001), 645–68. For other variations of this model, see: T. L. Ruble and K. Thomas, "Support for a Two-Dimensional Model of Conflict Behavior," *Organizational Behavior and Human Performance,* 16 (1976), 145; R. R. Blake, H. A. Shepard, and J. S. Mouton, *Managing Intergroup Conflict in Industry* (Houston, TX: Gulf Publishing, 1964); M. A. Rahim, "Toward a Theory of Managing Organizational Conflict," *International Journal of Conflict Management 13,* no. 3 (2002): 206–35.

maximize outcomes for the other party.[34]

- *Problem solving:* Problem solving tries to find a solution that is beneficial for both parties. This is known as the **win–win orientation** because people using this style believe the resources at stake are expandable rather than fixed if the parties work together to find a creative solution. Information sharing is an important feature of this style because both parties collaborate to identify common ground and potential solutions that satisfy everyone involved.

- *Forcing:* Forcing tries to win the conflict at the other's expense. People who use this style typically have a **win–lose orientation**—they believe the parties are drawing from a fixed pie, so the more one party receives, the less the other party will receive. Consequently, this style relies on some of the "hard" influence tactics described in Chapter 9, particularly assertiveness, to get one's own way.

- *Avoiding:* Avoiding tries to smooth over or avoid conflict situations altogether. It represents a low concern for both self and the other party; in other words, avoiders try to find ways to avoid thinking about the conflict.[35] For instance, conflict avoiders might rearrange their work area or tasks to minimize interaction with certain coworkers.

- *Yielding:* Yielding involves giving in completely to the other side's wishes, or at least cooperating with little or no attention to your own interests. This style involves making unilateral concessions and unconditional promises, as well as offering help with no expectation of reciprocal help.

- *Compromising:* Compromising involves looking for a position in which your losses are offset by equally valued gains. It involves matching the other party's concessions, making conditional promises or threats, and actively searching for a middle ground between the interests of the two parties.

> " The best conflict-handling style depends on the situation, so we need to understand and develop the capacity to use each style for the appropriate occasions. "

Xerox: The Conflict Avoidance Company

"We are really, really, really nice," emphasizes Xerox CEO Ursula Burns (left in this photo) about social relationships in the technology company. But she also believes this "terminal niceness" encourages too much of an avoidance conflict handling style. For example, Burns notes that employees don't raise objections in meetings even when employees present ideas that aren't workable. "When we're in the family, you don't have to be as nice as when you're outside of the family," says Burns. "I want us to stay civil and kind, but we have to be frank—and the reason we can be frank is because we are all in the same family."[36]

Choosing the Best Conflict Handling Style

Chances are you have a preferred conflict handling style. You might typically engage in avoiding or yielding because disagreement makes you feel uncomfortable and is contrary to your self-view as someone who likes to get along with everyone. Or perhaps you prefer the compromising and forcing strategies because they reflect your strong need for achievement and to control your environment. People usually gravitate toward one or two conflict handling styles that match their personality, personal and cultural values, and past experience. However, the best style depends on the situation, so we need to understand and develop the capacity to use each style for the appropriate occasions.[37]

Exhibit 10.4 summarizes the main contingencies, as well as problems, with using each conflict handling style. Problem solving has long been identified as the preferred conflict handling style where possible because dialogue and clever thinking help people to break out of the limited boundaries of their opposing alternatives to find an integrated solution where both gain value. In addition, the problem solving style tends to improve long-term relationships, reduce stress, and minimize emotional defensiveness and other indications of relationship conflict.[38]

Problem solving assumes there are opportunities for mutual gains, such as when the conflict is complex with multiple elements. But if the conflict is simple and perfectly opposing (each party wants more of a single fixed pie), then this style will waste time and increase frustration. The problem-solving approach also takes more time and requires a fairly high degree of trust because there is a risk that the other party will take advantage of the information you have openly shared. As one study recently found, the problem-solving style is more stressful when people experience strong feelings of conflict, likely because these negative emotions undermine trust in the other party.[39]

The conflict avoidance style is often ineffective because it doesn't resolve the conflict and may increase the other party's frustration. However, avoiding may be the best strategy where conflict has become emotionally charged or where conflict resolution would cost more than its benefits.[40] The forcing style is usually inappropriate because it commonly generates relationship conflict more quickly or intensely than other conflict handling styles. However, forcing may be necessary where you know you are correct (e.g., the other party's position is unethical or based on obviously flawed logic), the dispute requires a quick solution, or the other party would take advantage of a more cooperative conflict handling style.

Conflict Handling Style	Preferred Style When...	Problems with This Style
Problem solving	• Interests are not perfectly opposing (i.e., not pure win–lose) • Parties have trust, openness, and time to share information • The issues are complex	• Sharing information the other party might use to their advantage
Avoiding	• Conflict has become too emotionally charged • Cost of trying to resolve the conflict outweighs the benefits	• Doesn't usually resolve the conflict • May increase other party's frustration
Forcing	• You have a deep conviction about your position (e.g., you believe other person's behavior is unethical) • Dispute requires a quick solution • The other party would take advantage of more cooperative strategies	• Highest risk of relationship conflict • May damage long-term relations, reducing future problem solving
Yielding	• Other party has substantially more power • Issue is much less important to you than to the other party • The value and logic of your position aren't as clear	• Increases other party's expectations in future conflict episodes
Compromising	• Parties have equal power • Time pressure to resolve the conflict • Parties lack trust/openness for problem solving	• Suboptimal solution where mutual gains are possible

The yielding style may be appropriate when the other party has substantially more power, the issue is not as important to you as to the other party, and you aren't confident that your position has the best value or logical consistency. On the other hand, yielding behaviors may give the other side unrealistically high expectations, thereby motivating them to seek more from you in the future. In the long run, yielding may produce more conflict rather than resolve it. "Raised voices, red faces and table thumping is a far less dysfunctional way of challenging each other than withdrawal, passivity and sullen acceptance," argues one conflict management consultant. "It doesn't mean that people agree with you: they just take their misgivings underground and spread them throughout the organization, which has a corrosive effect."[41]

The compromising style may be best when there is little hope for mutual gain through problem solving, both parties have equal power, and both are under time pressure to settle their differences. However, we rarely know whether the parties have perfectly opposing interests. Therefore, entering a conflict with the compromising style may cause the parties to overlook better solutions because they have not attempted to share enough information and creatively look for win–win alternatives.

Steering Clear of Workplace Conflict[42]

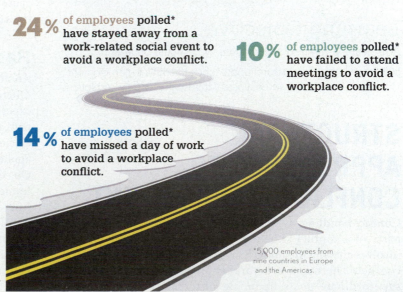

67% of employees polled* have gone out of their way to avoid a colleague because of a disagreement at work.

24% of employees polled* have stayed away from a work-related social event to avoid a workplace conflict.

10% of employees polled* have failed to attend meetings to avoid a workplace conflict.

14% of employees polled* have missed a day of work to avoid a workplace conflict.

*5,000 employees from nine countries in Europe and the Americas.

Cultural and Gender Differences in Conflict Handling Styles

Cultural differences are more than just a source of conflict. They also influence the preferred conflict handling style.[43] Some research suggests that people from collectivist cultures—where group goals are valued more than individual goals—are motivated to maintain harmonious relations and, consequently, are more likely than those from low collectivism cultures to manage disagreements through avoidance or problem solving. However, this view may be somewhat simplistic because people in some collectivist cultures are also more likely to publicly shame those whose actions oppose their own.[44] Cultural values and norms influence the conflict handling style used most often in a society, but they also represent an important contingency when outsiders choose the preferred conflict handling approach. For example, people who frequently use the conflict avoidance style might have more problems in cultures where the forcing style is common.

Conflict handling styles also seem to differ between men and women.[45] Some experts suggest that, compared to men, women pay more attention to the relationship between the parties. Consequently, women are more willing to adopt a problem-solving, compromise, or avoiding style to protect the relationship. Men tend to be more competitive and take a short-term orientation to the relationship. In low collectivism cultures, men are more likely than women to use the forcing approach to conflict handling. We must be cautious about these observations, however, because differences between men and women on preferred conflict handling styles are fairly small.

> "One of the oldest recommendations for resolving conflict is to focus attention on common superordinate goals."

Learning Objective

After reading the next two sections, you should be able to

LO5 Apply the six structural approaches to conflict management and describe the three types of third-party dispute resolution.

STRUCTURAL APPROACHES TO CONFLICT MANAGEMENT

Conflict handling styles describe how we approach the other party in a conflict situation. But conflict management also involves altering the underlying structural causes of potential conflict. The main structural approaches are emphasizing superordinate goals, reducing differentiation, improving communication and understanding, reducing task interdependence, increasing resources, and clarifying rules and procedures.

Emphasizing Superordinate Goals

One of the oldest recommendations for resolving conflict is to focus attention on common superordinate goals.[46] **Superordinate goals** are goals that the conflicting employees or departments value and whose attainment requires those parties' joint resources and effort.[47] These goals are called superordinate because they are higher-order aspirations such as the organization's strategic objectives rather than objectives specific to the individual or work unit. Research indicates the most effective executive teams frame their decisions as superordinate goals that rise above each executive's departmental or divisional goals. Similarly, one recent study reported that leaders reduce conflict through an inspirational vision that unifies employees and makes them less preoccupied with their subordinate goal differences.[48]

Suppose that marketing staff members want a new product released quickly, whereas engineers want more time to test and add new features. Leaders can potentially reduce this interdepartmental conflict by reminding both groups of the company's mission to serve customers, or by pointing out that competitors currently threaten the company's leadership in the industry. By increasing commitment to corporate-wide goals (customer focus, competitiveness), engineering and marketing employees pay less attention to their competing departmental-level goals, which reduces their perceived conflict with each other. Superordinate goals also potentially reduce the problem of differentiation because they establish feelings of a shared social identity (work for the same company).[49]

Reducing Differentiation

Another way to minimize dysfunctional conflict is to reduce the differences that generate conflict. As people develop common experiences and beliefs, they become more motivated to coordinate activities and resolve their disputes through constructive discussion.[50] SAP, the German enterprise software company, applied this approach when it recently acquired Business Objects, a French company with a strong American presence. Immediately after the merger, SAP began intermingling people from the two organizations. Several senior SAP executives transferred to Business Objects, and all of the acquired company's executives are on SAP's shared services team. "We also encourage cross-border, cross-functional teamwork on projects such as major product releases," says Business Objects CEO John Schwarz. "In this way team members come to depend on each other."[51] Essentially, SAP provided opportunities for managers and technical employees in the acquired firm to develop common experiences with their SAP counterparts by moving staff across the two companies or having them work together on joint projects.

Improving Communication and Mutual Understanding

A third way to resolve dysfunctional conflict is to give the conflicting parties more opportunities to communicate and understand each other. This recommendation applies two principles and practices introduced in Chapter 3: the Johari Window model and the contact hypothesis. Although both were previously described as ways to improve self-awareness, they are equally valuable to improve other-awareness. In the Johari Window process, you disclose more about yourself so others have a better understanding of the underlying causes of your behavior. The contact hypothesis is the proposition that we rely less on stereotypes to understand someone when we have more meaningful interaction with that person.[52] Through meaningful interaction, we develop a more person-specific and accurate understanding of others.

Several guidelines have developed over the years for resolving conflict through communication and mutual understanding.[53] The parties need to remain open-minded and avoid defensive emotional responses throughout this process. The process begins when each party describes their perceptions of the situation to the other party. Throughout this process, each party actively listens to the other party's views and shows understanding of those views. Also, each side needs to present their views as perceptions, not as though their perspective is "the truth." As viewpoints become understood, the parties suggest ways to resolve their differences. The solutions need to incorporate various perspectives to ensure buy-in.

Although communication and mutual understanding can work well, there are two important warnings. First, these interventions should be applied only where differentiation is sufficiently low or *after* differentiation has been reduced. If perceived differentiation remains high, attempts to manage conflict through dialogue might escalate rather than reduce relationship conflict. The reason is that when forced to interact with people who we believe are quite different and in conflict with us, we tend to select information that reinforces that view.[54] The second warning is that people in collectivist and high power distance cultures are less comfortable with the practice of resolving differences through direct and open communication.[55] As noted earlier, people in Confucian cultures prefer an avoidance conflict management style because it is the most consistent with harmony and face saving. Direct communication is a high-risk strategy because it easily threatens the need to save face and maintain harmony.

OB Theory to Practice

Resolving Conflict through Communication and Mutual Understanding

1. Begin with an open, curious, and emotionally stable frame of mind.
2. Ask the other people in the conflict to describe their perspectives of the situation.
3. Listen actively to the stories others tell, focusing on their perceptions, not on who is right or wrong.
4. Acknowledge and demonstrate that you understand the others' viewpoints as well as their feelings about the situation.
5. Present your perspective of the situation, describing it as your perception (not facts).
6. Refer to the others' viewpoints while you are describing your viewpoint.
7. Ask other people in the conflict for their ideas about how to overcome these differences.
8. Create solutions that incorporate ideas from everyone involved in the discussion.

Minimizing Generation Shock[56]

L'Oreal Canada executives anticipated their workplace would become more multigenerational, and this diversity might produce unwanted conflict. "We realized we could be faced with an interesting problem," says L'Oreal Canada executive Marjolaine Rompré (left in this photo). "We called it Generation Shock." To minimize generation shock, the company introduced seminars to improve mutual understanding. In one part of the session, employees sit together in their generational cohorts and are asked to answer questions; they then share their answers with the other cohorts. "Each group is interested and surprised to see what's important to the other group," says Rompré. These sessions have improved cross-generational relations and helped L'Oreal Canada to become one of the best places to work in Canada.

Reducing Task Interdependence

Conflict occurs where people are dependent on each other, so another way to reduce dysfunctional conflict is to minimize the level of interdependence between the parties. Three ways to reduce interdependence among employees and work units are to create buffers, use integrators, and combine jobs.

- *Create Buffers:* A buffer is any mechanism that loosens the coupling between two or more people or work units. This decoupling reduces the potential for conflict because the buffer reduces the effect of one party on the other. Building up inventories between people in an assembly line would be a buffer, for example, because each employee is less dependent in the short term on the previous person along that line.

- *Use Integrators:* Integrators are employees who coordinate the activities of work units toward the completion of a common task. For example, an individual might be responsible for coordinating the efforts of the research, production, advertising, and marketing departments in launching a new product line. In some respects, integrators are human buffers; they reduce the frequency of direct interaction among work units that have diverse goals and perspectives. Integrators rarely have direct authority over the departments they integrate, so they must rely on referent power and persuasion to manage conflict and accomplish the work.

- *Combine Jobs:* Combining jobs is both a form of job enrichment and a way to reduce task interdependence. Consider a toaster assembly system where one person inserts the heating element, another assembles the sides, and so on. By combining these tasks so that each person assembles an entire toaster, the employees now have a pooled rather than sequential form of task interdependence and the likelihood of dysfunctional conflict is reduced.

Increasing Resources

An obvious way to reduce conflict caused by resource scarcity is to increase the amount of resources available. Corporate decision makers might quickly dismiss this solution because of the costs involved. However, they need to carefully compare these costs with the costs of dysfunctional conflict arising out of resource scarcity.

Clarifying Rules and Procedures

Conflicts caused mainly by ambiguous rules can be minimized by establishing rules and procedures. If two departments are fighting over the use of a new laboratory, a schedule might be established that allocates the lab exclusively to each team at certain times of the day or week. Armstrong World Industries, Inc., applied the clarifying rules and procedures strategy when consultants and information systems employees clashed while working together on development of a client–server network. Information systems employees at the flooring and building materials company thought they should be in charge, whereas consultants believed they had the senior role. Also, the consultants wanted to work long hours and take Friday off to fly home,

whereas Armstrong employees wanted to work regular hours. The company reduced these conflicts by having both parties agree on specific responsibilities and roles. The agreement also assigned two senior executives at the companies to establish rules if future disagreements arose.[57]

THIRD-PARTY CONFLICT RESOLUTION

Most of this chapter has focused on people directly involved in a conflict, yet many disputes among employees and departments are resolved with the assistance of a manager. **Third-party conflict resolution** is any attempt by a relatively neutral person to help the parties resolve their differences. There are three main third-party dispute resolution activities: arbitration, inquisition, and mediation. These interventions can be classified by their level of control over the process and control over the decision (see Exhibit 10.5).[58]

- *Arbitration:* Arbitrators have high control over the final decision but low control over the process. Executives engage in this strategy by following previously agreed rules of due process, listening to arguments from the disputing employees, and making a binding decision. Arbitration is applied as the final stage of grievances by unionized employees in many countries, but it is also becoming more common in nonunion conflicts.

- *Inquisition:* Inquisitors control all discussion about the conflict. Like arbitrators, they have high decision control because they choose the form of conflict resolution. However, they also have high process control because they choose which information to examine and how to examine it, and they generally decide how the conflict resolution process will be handled.

▼**EXHIBIT 10.5** Types of Third-Party Intervention

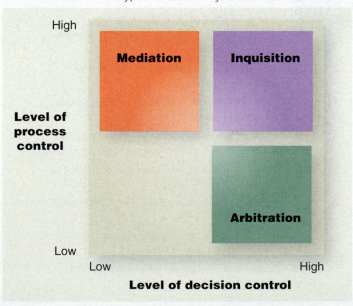

- *Mediation:* Mediators have high control over the intervention process. In fact, their main purpose is to manage the process and context of interaction between the disputing parties. However, the parties make the final decision about how to resolve their differences. Thus, mediators have little or no control over the conflict resolution decision.

Choosing the Best Third-Party Intervention Strategy

Team leaders, executives, and coworkers regularly intervene in workplace disputes. Sometimes they adopt a mediator role; other times they serve as arbitrators. Occasionally, they begin with one approach then switch to another. However, research suggests that people in positions of authority (e.g., managers) usually adopt an inquisitional approach whereby they dominate the intervention process as well as make a binding decision.[59]

Managers tend to rely on the inquisition approach because it is consistent with the decision-oriented nature of managerial jobs, gives them control over the conflict process and outcome, and tends to resolve disputes efficiently. However, inquisition is usually the least effective third-party conflict resolution method in organizational settings.[60] One problem is that leaders who take an inquisitional role tend to collect limited information about the problem, so their imposed decision may produce an ineffective solution to the conflict. Another problem is that employees often view inquisitional procedures and outcomes as unfair because they have little control over this approach. In particular, the inquisitional approach potentially violates several practices required to support procedural justice (see Chapter 5).

Which third-party intervention is most appropriate in organizations? The answer partly depends on the situation, such as the type of dispute, the relationship between the manager and employees, and cultural values such as power distance.[61] But generally speaking, for everyday disagreements between two employees, the mediation approach is usually best because this gives employees more responsibility for resolving their own disputes. The third-party representative merely establishes an appropriate context for conflict resolution. Although not as efficient as other strategies, mediation potentially offers the highest level of employee satisfaction with the conflict process and outcomes.[62] When employees cannot resolve their differences through mediation, arbitration seems to work best because the predetermined rules of evidence and other processes create a higher sense of procedural fairness.[63] Arbitration is also preferred where the organization's goals should take priority over individual goals.

third-party conflict resolution Any attempt by a relatively neutral person to help conflicting parties resolve their differences.

negotiation The process whereby two or more conflicting parties attempt to resolve their divergent goals by redefining the terms of their interdependence.

Learning Objective

After reading this section, you should be able to

LO6 Describe the bargaining zone model and outline strategies skilled negotiators use to claim value and create value in negotiations.

RESOLVING CONFLICT THROUGH NEGOTIATION

Think back through yesterday's events. Maybe you had to work out an agreement with other students about what tasks to complete for a team project. Chances are that you shared transportation with someone, so you had agreed on the timing of the ride. Then perhaps there was the question of who made dinner. Each of these daily events created potential conflict, and they were resolved through negotiation. **Negotiation** occurs whenever two or more conflicting parties attempt to resolve their divergent goals by redefining the terms of their interdependence. In other words, people negotiate when they think that discussion can produce a more satisfactory arrangement (at least for them) in their exchange of goods or services.

As you can see, negotiation is not an obscure practice reserved for labor and management bosses when hammering out a collective agreement. Everyone negotiates, every day. Most of the time, you don't even realize that you are in negotiations. Negotiation is particularly evident in the workplace because employees work interdependently with each other. They negotiate with their supervisors over next month's work assignments, with customers over the sale and delivery schedules of their product, and with coworkers over when to have lunch. And yes, they occasionally negotiate with each other in labor disputes and collective agreements.

Bargaining Zone Model of Negotiations

One way to view the negotiation process is that each party moves along a continuum in opposite directions with an area of

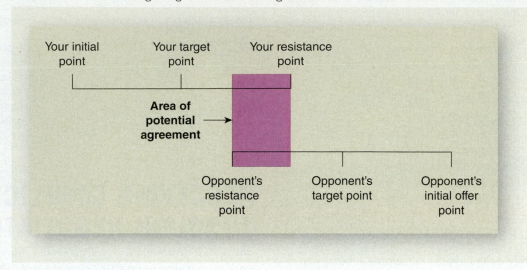

potential overlap called the *bargaining zone*.[64] Exhibit 10.6 displays one possible bargaining zone situation. This linear diagram illustrates a purely win–lose situation—one side's gain will be the other's loss. However, the bargaining zone model can also be applied to situations in which both sides potentially gain from the negotiations. As this model illustrates, the parties typically establish three main negotiating points. The *initial offer point* is the team's opening offer to the other party. This may be its best expectation or a pie-in-the-sky starting point. The *target point* is the team's realistic goal or expectation for a final agreement. The *resistance point* is the point beyond which the team will make no further concessions.

The parties begin negotiations by describing their initial offer point for each item on the agenda. In most cases, the participants know this is only a starting point that will change as both sides offer concessions. In win–lose situations, neither the target nor the resistance point is revealed to the other party. However, people try to discover the other side's resistance point because this knowledge helps them determine how much they can gain without breaking off negotiations.

The bargaining zone model implies that the parties compete against each other to reach their target point. Competition does exist to varying degrees because constituents expect the negotiator to *claim value*, that is, to get the best possible outcomes for themselves. Yet, the hallmark of successful negotiations is a combination of competition and cooperation. Negotiators need to cooperate with each other to *create value*, that is, to discover ways to achieve mutually satisfactory outcomes for both parties.[65] Cooperation maintains a degree of trust necessary to share information. To some degree, it may also improve concessions so the negotiations are resolved more quickly and with greater mutual gains.

Strategies for Claiming Value

Claiming value involves trying to obtain the best possible outcomes for yourself and your constituents. A purely competitive approach, in which you forcefully persuade the other party and assert your power (such as threatening to walk away from the negotiation), typically leads to failure because it generates negative emotions and undermines trust. Even so, some degree of value claiming is necessary to achieve a favorable outcome. Here are four skills to effectively claim value in negotiations: prepare and set goals, know your BATNA, manage time, and manage first offers and concessions.

Prepare and Set Goals
People negotiate more successfully when they carefully think through their three key positions in the bargaining zone model (initial, target, and resistance), consider alternative strategies to achieve those objectives, and test their underlying assumptions about the situation.[66] Equally important, they need to research what the other party wants from the negotiation. "You have to be prepared every which way about the people, the subject, and your fallback position," advises Paul Tellier, Chairman of Global Container Terminals and the former president of CN Railway and Bombardier, Inc. "Before walking into the room for the actual negotiation, I ask my colleagues to throw some curve balls at me."[67]

Know Your BATNA
To determine whether the opponent's offers are favorable, negotiators need to understand what outcome they might achieve through some other means (such as negotiating with someone else). This comparison is called the **best alternative to a negotiated agreement (BATNA)**. BATNA estimates your power in the negotiation because it represents the estimated cost of walking away from the

relationship. If others are willing to negotiate with you for the product or service you need, then you have a high BATNA and considerable power in the negotiation because it would not cost you much to walk away from the current negotiation. A common problem in negotiations, however, is that people tend to overestimate their BATNA; they wrongly believe there are plenty of other ways to achieve their objective rather than through this negotiation.

Manage Time
Negotiators make more concessions as the deadline gets closer.[68] This can be a liability if you are under time pressure, or it can be an advantage if the other party alone is under time pressure. Negotiators with more power in the relationship sometimes apply time pressure through an "exploding offer" whereby they give their opponent a very short time to accept their offer.[69] These time-limited offers are frequently found in consumer sales ("on sale today only!") and in some job offers. They produce time pressure, which can motivate the other party to accept the offer and forfeit the opportunity to explore their BATNA. Another time factor is that the more time someone has invested in the negotiation, the more committed they become to ensuring an agreement is reached. This commitment increases the tendency to make unwarranted concessions so the negotiations do not fail.

Manage First Offers and Concessions
Negotiators who make the first offer have the advantage of creating a position around which subsequent negotiations are anchored. As we explained in Chapter 6, people tend to adjust their expectations around the initial point, so if your initial request is high, opponents might move more quickly toward their resistance point along the bargaining zone.[70] It may even cause opponents to lower their resistance point.

After the first offer, negotiators need to make concessions, which serve at least three important purposes: (1) they enable the parties to move toward the area of potential agreement, (2) they symbolize each party's motivation to bargain in good faith, and (3) they tell the other party of the relative importance of the negotiating items.[71] However, concessions need to be clearly labeled as such and should be accompanied by an expectation that the other party will reciprocate. They should also be offered in installments because people experience more positive emotions from a few smaller concessions than from one large concession.[72] Generally, the best strategy is to be moderately tough and give just enough concessions to communicate sincerity and motivation to resolve the conflict.[73]

Strategies for Creating Value
Earlier in this section we pointed out that negotiations involve more than just claiming value; they also involve creating value—trying to obtain the best possible outcomes for both parties. In other words, negotiators need to apply the problem-solving approach to conflict handling. Information exchange is a critical feature of creating value, but it is also a potential pitfall. Information is power in negotiations, so information sharing gives the other party more power to leverage a better deal if the opportunity occurs.[74] Skilled negotiators address this dilemma by adopting a cautious problem-solving style at the outset. They begin by sharing information slowly and determining whether the other side will reciprocate. In this way, they try to establish trust with the other party. Here are three ways that skilled negotiators reap the benefits of problem-solving and value creation.

Gather Information
Information is the cornerstone of effective value creation.[75] Therefore, skilled negotiators heed the advice of management guru Stephen Covey: "Seek first to understand, then to be understood."[76] This means we should present our case only after spending more time listening closely to the other party and asking for details. It is particularly important to look beyond the opponent's stated justifications to the unstated motivation for their claims. Probing questions (such as asking "why") and listening intently can reveal better solutions for both parties. Nonverbal communication can also convey important information about the other party's priorities. Negotiating in teams can also aid the information-gathering process because some team members will hear information that others have ignored.

> ## TRUST IS CRITICAL FOR THE PROBLEM-SOLVING STYLE OF CONFLICT HANDLING AS WELL AS IN THE VALUE CREATION OBJECTIVE OF NEGOTIATIONS. "

Discover Priorities through Offers and Concessions

Some types of offers and concessions are better than others at creating value. The key objective is to discover and signal which issues are more and less important to each side. Suppose another division is "seconding" (temporarily transferring) some of your best staff to their projects, whereas you need these people on site for other assignments and to coach junior staff. Through problem-solving negotiation, you discover that the other division doesn't need those staff at their site; rather, the division head mainly needs some guarantee that these people will be available. The result is that your division keeps the staff (important to you), while the other division has some guarantee these people will be available at specific times for their projects (important to them).

One way to figure out the relative importance of the issues to each party is to make multi-issue offers rather than discussing one issue at a time.[77] You might offer a client a specific price, delivery date, and guarantee period, for example. The other party's counteroffer to multiple items signals which are more and which are less important to them. Your subsequent concessions similarly signal how important each issue is to your group.

Build the Relationship

Trust is critical for the problem-solving style of conflict handling as well as in the value creation objective of negotiations.[78] How do you build trust in negotiations? One approach is to discover common backgrounds and interests, such as places you have lived, favorite hobbies and sports teams, and so forth. If there are substantial differences between the parties (age, gender, etc), consider having team members that more closely match the backgrounds of the other party. First impressions are also important. Recall from earlier chapters in this book that people attach emotions to incoming stimuli in a fraction of a second. Therefore, you need to be sensitive to your nonverbal cues, appearance, and initial statements.

Signaling that we are trustworthy also helps strengthen the relationship. We can do this by demonstrating that we are reliable and will keep our promises as well as by identifying shared goals and values. Trustworthiness also increases by developing a shared understanding of the negotiation process, including its norms and expectations about speed and timing.[79] Finally, relationship building demands emotional intelligence.[80] This includes managing the emotions you display to the other party, particularly avoiding an image of superiority, aggressiveness, or insensitivity. Emotional intelligence also involves managing the other party's emotions. We can use well-placed flattery, humor, and other methods to keep everyone in a good mood and to break unnecessary tension.[81]

Situational Influences on Negotiations

The effectiveness of negotiating depends to some extent on the environment in which the negotiations occur. Three key situational factors are location, physical setting, and audience.

Location

It is easier to negotiate on your own turf because you are familiar with the negotiating environment and are able to maintain comfortable routines.[82] Also, there is no need to cope with travel-related stress or depend on others for resources during the negotiation. Of course, you can't walk out of negotiations as easily when on your own turf, but this is usually a minor issue. Considering these strategic benefits of home turf, many negotiators agree to neutral territory. Phone calls, video-conferences, and other forms of information technology potentially avoid territorial issues, but skilled negotiators usually prefer the media richness of face-to-face meetings. Frank Lowy, cofounder of retail property giant Westfield Group, says that telephones are "too cold" for negotiating: "From a voice I don't get all the cues I need. I go by touch and feel and I need to see the other person."[83]

Physical Setting

The physical distance between the parties and formality of the setting can influence their orientation toward each other and the disputed issues. So can the seating arrangements. People who sit face to face are more likely to develop a win–lose orientation toward the conflict situation. In contrast, some negotiation groups deliberately intersperse participants around the table to convey a win–win orientation. Others arrange the seating so both parties face a white board, reflecting the notion that both parties face the same problem or issue.

Audience Characteristics

Most negotiators have audiences—anyone with a vested interest in the negotiation outcomes, such as executives, other team members, or the general public. Negotiators tend to act differently when their audience observes the negotiation or has detailed information about the process, compared to situations in which the audience sees only the end results.[84] When the audience has direct surveillance over the proceedings, negotiators tend to be more competitive, less willing to make concessions, and more likely to engage in political tactics against the other party. This "hardline" behavior shows the audience that the negotiator is working for their interests. With their audience watching, negotiators also have more interest in saving face. ■

leadership in
organizational settings

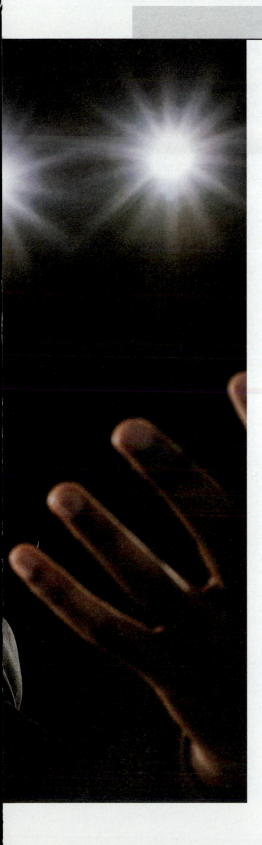

eadership is one of the most researched and discussed topics in the field of organizational behavior.[1] Google returns a whopping 499 million webpages where "leadership" is mentioned. Google Scholar lists 200,000 journal articles and books with one or both words in the title alone. Proquest identifies more than 565,000 scholarly and practitioner articles, dissertations, and other sources where one or both of these words appear in the title. Amazon lists more than 39,000 books in the English language with "leadership" in the title. From 2000 to 2009, the U.S. Library of Congress catalogue added 7,336 books or documents with the words "leader" or "leadership" in the citation, compared with 3,054 items added in the 1990s and only 146 items with these words (many of which were newspaper names) added during the first decade of the 1900s. ■

LEARNING OBJECTIVES

After studying Chapter 11, you should be able to:

LO1 Define *leadership* and *shared leadership*.

LO2 Identify eight competencies associated with effective leaders and describe authentic leadership.

LO3 Describe the key features of task-oriented, people-oriented, and servant leadership, and discuss their effects on followers.

LO4 Discuss the key elements of path–goal theory, Fiedler's contingency model, and leadership substitutes.

LO5 Describe the four elements of transformational leadership and distinguish this theory from transactional and charismatic leadership.

LO6 Describe the implicit leadership perspective.

LO7 Discuss cultural and gender similarities and differences in leadership.

Learning Objective

After reading this section, you should be able to

LO1   Define *leadership* and *shared leadership*.

The topic of leadership captivates us because we are awed by individuals who influence and motivate a group of people beyond expectations. This chapter explores leadership from five perspectives: competency, behavioral, contingency, transformational, and implicit.[2] Although some of these perspectives are currently more popular than others, each helps us to more fully understand the complex issue of leadership. In the final section, we also consider cross-cultural and gender issues in organizational leadership. But first, we learn about the meaning of leadership as well as shared leadership.

WHAT IS LEADERSHIP?

A few years ago, 54 leadership experts from 38 countries reached a consensus that **leadership** is about influencing, motivating, and enabling others to contribute toward the effectiveness and success of the organizations of which they are members.[3] This definition has two key components. First, leaders motivate others through persuasion and other influence tactics. They use their communication skills, rewards, and other resources to energize the collective to achieve challenging objectives. Second, leaders are enablers. They arrange the

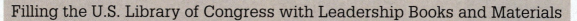

> My main job was developing talent. I was a gardener providing water and other nourishment to our top 750 people.[4]
>
> —Jack Welch, former GE CEO

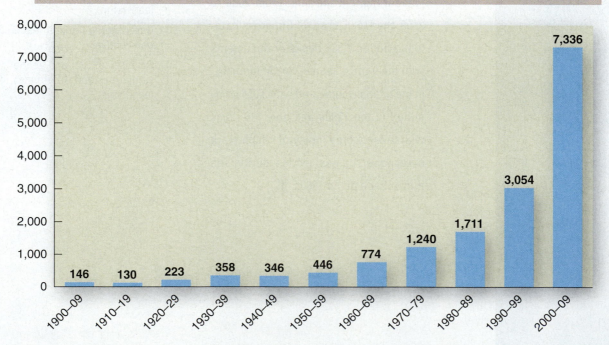

Filling the U.S. Library of Congress with Leadership Books and Materials

Number of books and other materials with "leader" or "leadership" in the title or citation catalogued by the U.S. Library of Congress and currently listed in its catalogue, by decade that the item was published or produced. The U.S. Library of Congress is the world's largest library.

work environment—such as allocating resources and altering communication patterns—so employees can achieve organizational objectives more easily.

Shared Leadership

As part of its employee engagement initiative, Rolls-Royce Engine Services in Oakland, California, involved employees directly with clients, encouraged weekly huddles for information sharing, and accepted employee requests for less micromanagement. Employees at the aircraft engine repair facility not only experienced higher levels of engagement and empowerment; they also accepted more leadership responsibilities. "I saw people around me, all front-line employees, who were leaders," say a machine programmer at the Rolls-Royce Oakland plant. "They weren't actually leading the company, but they were people you would listen to and follow. We didn't have titles, but people had respect for what we did."[6]

Rolls-Royce Engine Services has moved toward greater **shared leadership**, in which employees throughout the organization informally assume leadership responsibilities in various ways and at various times.[7] Shared leadership is based on the idea that leadership is plural, not singular. It doesn't operate out of one formally assigned position, role, or individual. Instead, employees lead each other as the occasion arises. Shared leadership typically supplements formal leadership. However, W. L. Gore & Associates and Semco SA rely almost completely on shared leadership because there is no formal hierarchy or organizational chart.[8] In fact, when Gore employees are asked in annual surveys, "Are you a leader?" more than 50 percent of them answer "Yes."

John Gardner, the White House cabinet member who introduced Medicare and public broadcasting, wrote more than two decades ago that the "vitality" of large organizations depends on shared leadership.[9] Employees across all levels of the organization need

to seek out opportunities and solutions to problems rather than rely on formal leaders to serve these roles. Gardner observed, for example, that successful teams consist of individuals other than the formal leader who take responsibility for healing rifts when conflicts arise, and for building confidence in others when events have turned for the worse. Various studies have also noted that employees who champion the introduction of new technologies and products are stepping unofficially into leadership positions.[10]

Shared leadership flourishes in organizations where the formal leaders are willing to delegate power and encourage employees to take initiative and risks without fear of failure (i.e., a learning orientation culture). Shared leadership also calls for a collaborative rather than internally competitive culture because employees take on shared leadership roles when coworkers support them for their initiative. Furthermore, shared leadership lacks formal authority, so it operates best when employees learn to influence others through their enthusiasm, logical analysis, and involvement of coworkers in their idea or vision.

Learning Objective

After reading this section, you should be able to

LO2 Identify eight competencies associated with effective leaders and describe authentic leadership.

COMPETENCY PERSPECTIVE OF LEADERSHIP

Since the beginning of recorded civilization, people have been interested in the personal characteristics that distinguish great leaders from the rest of us.[11] One ground-breaking review in the late 1940s concluded that no consistent list of traits could be distilled from previous research. This conclusion was revised a decade later, suggesting that a few traits are associated with effective leaders.[12] These nonsignificant findings caused many scholars to give up their search for personal characteristics that distinguish effective leaders.

Over the past two decades, leadership experts have returned to the notion that effective leaders possess specific personal characteristics.[13] The earlier research was apparently plagued by methodological problems, lack of theoretical foundation, and inconsistent definitions of leadership. The emerging work has identified several leadership *competencies,* that is, skills, knowledge, aptitudes, and other personal characteristics that lead to superior performance (see Chapter 2). The main categories of leadership competencies are listed in Exhibit 11.1 and described below.[14]

- *Personality.* Most of the Big Five personality dimensions (see Chapter 2) are associated with effective leadership to some extent, but the strongest predictors are high levels of extroversion (outgoing, talkative, sociable, and assertive) and conscientiousness (careful, dependable, and self-disciplined). With high extroversion, effective leaders are comfortable having an influential role in social settings.

With higher conscientiousness, effective leaders set higher goals for themselves (and others) and are more motivated to pursue those goals.

- *Self-concept.* Successful leaders have a complex, internally consistent, and clear self-concept as a leader (see Chapter 3). This "leader identity" also includes a positive self-evaluation, including high self-esteem, self-efficacy, and internal locus of control.[15] In short, effective leaders define themselves as leaders and are confident with this self-view.

- *Drive.* Related to their high conscientiousness and positive self-concept, successful leaders have a high need for achievement (see Chapter 5). This drive represents the inner motivation that leaders possess to pursue their goals and encourage others to move forward with theirs. Drive inspires inquisitiveness, an action orientation, and boldness to take the organization or team into uncharted waters.

- *Integrity.* Integrity involves truthfulness and consistency of words and actions, qualities that are related to honesty and ethical conduct. Leaders have a high moral capacity to judge dilemmas using sound values and to act accordingly. Notice that integrity is ultimately based on the leader's values, which provide an anchor for consistency. Several large-scale studies have reported that integrity and honesty are the most important characteristics of effective leaders.[16] Unfortunately, recent surveys also report that employees don't believe their leaders have integrity and, consequently, don't trust those leaders.

▼ **EXHIBIT 11.1** Competencies of Effective Leaders

Leadership Competency	Description
Personality	The leader's higher levels of extroversion (outgoing, talkative, sociable, and assertive) and conscientiousness (careful, dependable, and self-disciplined).
Self-concept	The leader's self-beliefs and positive self-evaluation about his or her own leadership skills and ability to achieve objectives.
Drive	The leader's inner motivation to pursue goals.
Integrity	The leader's truthfulness and tendency to translate words into deeds.
Leadership motivation	The leader's need for socialized power to accomplish team or organizational goals.
Knowledge of the business	The leader's tacit and explicit knowledge about the company's environment, enabling the leader to make more intuitive decisions.
Cognitive and practical intelligence	The leader's above-average cognitive ability to process information (cognitive intelligence) and ability to solve real-world problems by adapting to, shaping, or selecting appropriate environments (practical intelligence).
Emotional intelligence	The leader's ability to monitor his or her own and others' emotions, discriminate among them, and use the information to guide his or her thoughts and actions.

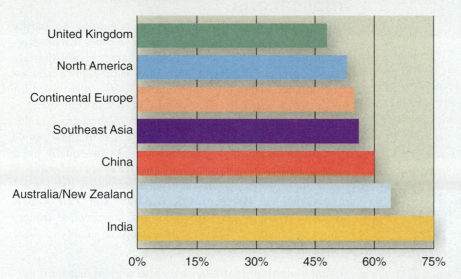

How Much Do Employees Trust Their Senior Leaders?[17]

- United Kingdom
- North America
- Continental Europe
- Southeast Asia
- China
- Australia/New Zealand
- India

0% 15% 30% 45% 60% 75%

Percent of 7,508 employees polled, by country/region, who agree or strongly agree that they trust senior leaders in their organization.

authentic leadership
The view that effective leaders need to be aware of, feel comfortable with, and act consistently with their values, personality, and self-concept.

Authentic Leadership

A few paragraphs ago, we said that successful leaders have a complex, internally consistent, and clear self-concept as a leader, and that they possess a strong positive self-evaluation. These characteristics lay the foundation for **authentic leadership**, which refers to how well leaders are aware of, feel comfortable with, and act consistently with their self-concept.[22] Authenticity is knowing yourself and being yourself (Exhibit 11.2). Leaders learn more about their personality, values, thoughts, and habits by reflecting on various situations and personal experiences. They also improve this self-awareness by receiving feedback from trusted people inside and outside the organization. Both self-reflection and receptivity to feedback require high levels of emotional intelligence.

As people learn more about themselves, they gain a greater understanding of their inner purpose which, in turn, generates a long-term passion for achieving something worthwhile for the organization or society. Some leadership experts suggest that this inner purpose emerges from a life story, typically a critical event or experience earlier in life that provides guidance for their later career and energy.

Authentic leadership is more than self-awareness; it also involves behaving in ways that are consistent with that self-concept rather than pretending to be someone else. To be themselves, great leaders regulate their decisions and behavior in several ways. First, they develop their own style and, where appropriate, place themselves in positions where that style is most effective. Although effective leaders adapt their behavior to the situation to some extent, they invariably understand and rely on decision methods and interpersonal styles that feel most comfortable to them.

- *Leadership motivation.* Effective leaders are motivated to lead others. They have a strong need for *socialized power,* meaning that they want power to lead others in accomplishing organizational objectives and similar good deeds. This contrasts with a need for *personalized power,* which is the desire to have power for personal gain or for the thrill one might experience from wielding power over others (see Chapter 5).[18] Leadership motivation is also necessary because, even in collegial firms, leaders are in contests for positions further up the hierarchy. Effective leaders thrive rather than wither in the face of this competition.[19]

- *Knowledge of the business.* Effective leaders possess tacit and explicit knowledge of the business environment in which they operate, including subtle indications of emerging trends. Knowledge of the business also includes a good understanding of how their organization works effectively.

- *Cognitive and practical intelligence.* Leaders have above-average cognitive ability to process enormous amounts of information. Leaders aren't necessarily geniuses; rather, they have a superior ability to analyze a variety of complex alternatives and opportunities. Furthermore, leaders have practical intelligence. Unlike cognitive intelligence, which is assessed by performance on clearly defined problems with sufficient information and usually one best answer, practical intelligence is assessed by performance in real-world settings, where problems are poorly defined, information is missing, and more than one solution may be plausible.[20]

- *Emotional intelligence.* Effective leaders have a high level of emotional intelligence.[21] They are able to recognize and regulate emotions in themselves and in other people (see Chapter 4).

▼ **EXHIBIT 11.2** Authentic Leadership

Know yourself:
- Engage in self-reflection.
- Receive feedback from trusted sources.
- Understand your life story.

Be yourself:
- Develop your own style.
- Apply your values.
- Maintain a positive core self-evaluation.

Second, effective leaders continually think about and consistently apply their stable hierarchy of personal values to those decisions and behaviors. Leaders face many pressures and temptations, such as achieving short-term stock price targets at the cost of long-term profitability. Experts note that authentic leaders demonstrate self-discipline by remaining anchored to their values. Third, leaders maintain consistency around their self-concept by having a strong, positive core self-evaluation. They have high self-esteem and self-efficacy as well as an internal locus of control (Chapter 3).

Competency Perspective Limitations and Practical Implications

Although the competency perspective is gaining popularity (again), it has a few limitations.[24] First, it assumes that all effective leaders have the same personal characteristics that are equally important in all situations. This is probably a false assumption; leadership is far too complex to have a universal list of traits that apply to every condition. Some competencies might not be important all the time. Second, alternative combinations of competencies may be equally successful; two people with different sets of competencies might be equally good leaders. Third, the competency perspective views leadership as something within a person, yet experts emphasize that leadership is relational. People are effective leaders because of their favorable relationships with followers, so effective leaders cannot be identified without considering the quality of these relationships.[25]

Several leadership researchers have also warned that some personal characteristics might influence only our perception that someone is a leader, not whether the individual really makes a difference to the organization's success. People who exhibit self-confidence, extroversion, and other traits are called leaders because they fit our stereotype of an effective leader. Or we might see a successful person, call that person a leader, and then attribute unobservable traits that we consider essential for great leaders. We will discuss this issue later in the implicit leadership perspective.

The competency perspective of leadership does not necessarily imply that leadership is a talent acquired at birth rather than developed throughout life. On the contrary, competencies indicate only leadership *potential*, not leadership performance. People with these characteristics become effective leaders only

The Leadership Report Card[26]

82% of U.K. board of directors surveyed rate senior leadership in their organization as either good or excellent.

52% of U.K. middle managers surveyed rate senior leadership in their organization as either good or excellent.

51% of U.K. public sector employees surveyed rate their leadership as poor or very poor.

53% of American employees surveyed rate management in their company as "so-so" or worse.

22% of Australia and New Zealand human resource professionals surveyed say their organization has high quality leadership.

after they have developed and mastered the necessary leadership behaviors. People with somewhat lower leadership competencies may become very effective leaders because they have leveraged their potential more fully.

Learning Objective

After reading this section, you should be able to

LO3 Describe the key features of task-oriented, people-oriented, and servant leadership, and discuss their effects on followers.

BEHAVIORAL PERSPECTIVE OF LEADERSHIP

In the 1940s and 1950s, leadership experts at several universities launched an intensive research investigation to answer the question "What behaviors make leaders effective?" Questionnaires were administered to subordinates, asking them to rate their supervisors on a large number of behaviors. These studies distilled two clusters of leadership behaviors from literally thousands of items (Exhibit 11.3).[27]

One cluster, called task-oriented leadership, includes behaviors that define and structure work roles. Task-oriented leaders assign employees to specific tasks, set goals and deadlines, clarify work duties and procedures, define work procedures, and plan work activities. The other cluster represents people-oriented behaviors. This cluster includes behaviors such as listening to employees for their opinions and ideas, creating a pleasant physical work environment, showing interest in staff, complimenting and recognizing employees for their effort, and showing consideration of employee needs.

Choosing Task- versus People-Oriented Leadership

Should leaders be task oriented or people oriented? This is a difficult question to answer because each style has its advantages and disadvantages. Recent evidence suggests that both styles are positively associated with leader effectiveness, but in different ways.[28] Not surprisingly, increasing people-oriented leadership reduces employee absenteeism, grievances, turnover,

> The task-oriented and people-oriented styles are both positively associated with leader effectiveness, but in different ways.

and job dissatisfaction, whereas increasing task-oriented leadership results in higher job performance. Research suggests that university students value task-oriented instructors because they want clear objectives and well-prepared lectures that abide by the unit's objectives.[29] Other research indicates that followers have few stress symptoms when leaders show empathy toward employees.[30]

One problem with the behavioral leadership perspective is that the two categories are broad generalizations that mask specific behaviors within each category. For instance, task-oriented leadership includes planning work activities, clarifying roles, and monitoring operations and performance. Each of these clusters of activities are fairly distinct and likely have different effects on employee well-being and performance. A second concern is that the behavioral approach assumes that high levels of both styles are best in all situations. In reality, the best leadership style depends on the situation.[31] On a positive note, the behavioral perspective lays the foundation for two of the main leadership styles—people-oriented and task-oriented—found in many contemporary leadership theories.

Servant Leadership

Servant leadership is an extension or variation of the people-oriented leadership style because it defines leadership as serving others toward their need fulfilment and personal development and growth.[32] Servant leaders ask, "How can I help you?" rather than expect employees to serve them. People who epitomize servant leadership have been described as selfless, egalitarian, humble, nurturing, empathetic, and ethical coaches.

▼**EXHIBIT 11.3** Task- and People-Oriented Leadership Styles

Leaders are task-oriented when they...	Leaders are people-oriented when they...
• Assign work and clarify responsibilities. • Set goals and deadlines. • Evaluate and provide feedback on work quality. • Establish well-defined best work procedures. • Plan future work activities.	• Show interest in others as people. • Listen to employees. • Make the workplace more pleasant. • Compliment employees for their work. • Are considerate of employee needs.

have described, many have included other characteristics that lack agreement and might confound the concept with its predictors and outcomes. Still, the notion of leader as servant has considerable currency and for many centuries has been embedded in the principles of most major religions.

Learning Objective

After reading this section, you should be able to

LO4 Discuss the key elements of path–goal theory, Fiedler's contingency model, and leadership substitutes.

The main objective of servant leadership is to help other stakeholders to fulfill their needs and potential, particularly "to become healthier, wiser, freer, more autonomous, more likely themselves to become servants."[33]

Servant leadership research suffers from ambiguous and conflicting definitions, but writers agree on a few features.[34] First, servant leaders have a natural desire or "calling" to serve others. This natural desire is a deep commitment to the growth of others for that purpose alone. It goes beyond the leader's role obligation to help others and is not merely an instrument to achieve company objectives. Second, servant leaders maintain a relationship with others that is humble, egalitarian, and accepting. Servant leaders do not view leadership as a position of power. Rather, they serve without drawing attention to themselves, without evoking superior status, and without being judgmental about others or defensive of criticisms received. Third, servant leaders anchor their decisions and actions in ethical principles and practices. They display sensitivity to and enactment of moral values and are not swayed by social pressures or expectations to deviate from those values. In this respect, servant leadership relies heavily on the idea of authentic leadership that we introduced a few pages ago.

Servant leadership was introduced four decades ago and has since had a steady following, particularly among practitioners and religious leaders. Scholarly interest in this topic has bloomed within the past few years, but the concept still faces a number of conceptual hurdles. Although servant leadership writers generally agree on the three features we

> " Servant leaders have a natural desire or "calling" to serve others—a deep commitment to the growth of others for that purpose alone. "

CONTINGENCY PERSPECTIVE OF LEADERSHIP

The contingency perspective of leadership is based on the idea that the most appropriate leadership style depends on the situation. Most (although not all) contingency leadership theories assume that effective leaders must be both insightful and flexible.[35] They must be able to adapt their behaviors and styles to the immediate situation. This isn't easy to do, however. Leaders typically have a preferred style. It takes considerable effort for leaders to choose and enact different styles to match the situation. As we noted earlier, leaders must have high emotional intelligence so they can diagnose the circumstances and match their behaviors accordingly.

Path–Goal Theory of Leadership

Several contingency theories have been proposed over the years, but **path–goal leadership theory** has withstood scientific critique better than the others. Indeed, one recent study found that the path–goal theory explained more about effective leadership than did another popular perspective of leadership (transformational, which we describe later in this chapter).[36] Path-goal leadership theory is founded on expectancy theory of motivation (see Chapter 5) because leaders create paths (expectancies) to effective performance (goals) for their employees.[37] Path–goal theory states that effective leaders ensure that good performers receive

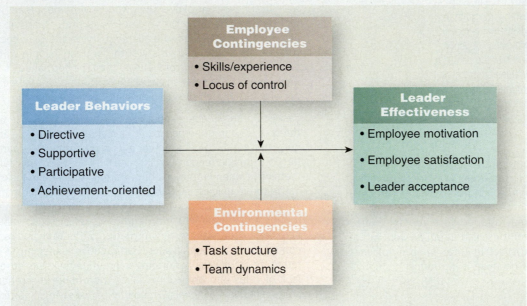

path–goal leadership theory
A contingency theory of leadership based on the expectancy theory of motivation that relates several leadership styles to specific employee and situational contingencies.

more valued rewards than poor performers. Effective leaders also provide the information, support, and other resources necessary to help employees complete their tasks.[38]

Path-Goal Leadership Styles

Exhibit 11.4 presents the path-goal theory of leadership. This model specifically highlights four leadership styles and several contingency factors leading to three indicators of leader effectiveness. The four leadership styles are directive, supportive, participative, and achievement-oriented.[39]

- *Directive.* This leadership style consists of clarifying behaviors that provide a psychological structure for subordinates. The leader clarifies performance goals, the means to reach those goals, and the standards against which performance will be judged. It also includes judicious use of rewards and disciplinary actions. Directive leadership is the same as task-oriented leadership, described earlier, and echoes our discussion in Chapter 2 on the importance of clear role perceptions in employee performance.

- *Supportive.* In this style, the leader's behaviors provide psychological support for subordinates. The leader is friendly and approachable; makes the work more pleasant; treats employees with equal respect; and shows concern for employees' status, needs, and well-being. Supportive leadership is the same as people-oriented leadership, described earlier, and reflects the benefits of social support to help employees cope with stressful situations.

- *Participative.* Participative leadership behaviors encourage and facilitate subordinate involvement in decisions beyond their normal work activities. The leader consults with employees, asks for their suggestions, and takes these ideas into serious consideration before making a decision. Participative leadership relates to involving employees in decisions (Chapter 6).

- *Achievement-oriented.* This leadership style emphasizes behaviors that encourage employees to reach their peak performance. The leader sets challenging goals, expects employees to perform at their highest level, continuously seeks improvement in employee performance, and shows a high degree of confidence that employees will assume responsibility and accomplish challenging goals. Achievement-oriented leadership applies goal-setting theory as well as positive expectations in self-fulfilling prophecy.

The path–goal model contends that effective leaders are capable of selecting the most appropriate behavioral style (or styles) for each situation. Also, leaders often use two or more styles at the same time, if these styles are appropriate for the circumstances.

Contingencies of Path–Goal Theory

As a contingency theory, path–goal theory states that each of the four leadership styles will be effective in some situations but not in others. The path–goal leadership model specifies two sets of situational variables that moderate the relationship between a leader's style and effectiveness: (1) employee characteristics and (2) characteristics of the employee's work environment. Several contingencies have already been studied within the path–goal framework, and the model is open for more variables in the future.[40] However, only four contingencies are reviewed here.

- *Skill and experience.* A combination of directive and supportive leadership is best for employees who are (or perceive themselves to be) inexperienced and unskilled.[41] Directive leadership gives subordinates information about how to accomplish the task, whereas supportive leadership helps them cope with the uncertainties of unfamiliar work situations. Directive leadership is detrimental when employees are skilled and experienced because it introduces too much supervisory control.

Leading with a Steel Fist in a Velvet Glove

The world's most respected leaders have the knack of keeping employees focused on the task while simultaneously being supportive. Anne Sweeney, cochair of Disney Media Networks and president of Disney/ABC Television Group, is a case in point. News Corporation founder Rupert Murdoch once said that Sweeney has "a steel fist in a velvet glove." Sweeney is renowned for her empathy and consideration. "She's very concerned about the people who work for her," says one executive. At the same time, she famously keeps her direct reports on their toes. "[Anne Sweeney] asks the tough questions. . . . It trains you to anticipate it," says one Disney executive.[42]

- *Locus of control.* People with an internal locus of control believe they have control over their work environment (see Chapter 3). Consequently, these employees prefer participative and achievement-oriented leadership styles and may become frustrated with a directive style. In contrast, people with an external locus of control believe their performance is due more to luck and fate, so they tend to be more satisfied and perform better with directive and supportive leadership.

- *Task structure.* Leaders should adopt the directive style when the task is nonroutine because this style minimizes role ambiguity that tends to occur in complex work situations (particularly for inexperienced employees).[43] The directive style is ineffective when employees have routine and simple tasks because the manager's guidance serves no purpose and may be viewed as unnecessarily close control. Employees in highly routine and simple jobs may require supportive leadership to help them cope with the tedious nature of the work and lack of control over the pace of work. Participative leadership is preferred for employees performing nonroutine tasks because the lack of rules and procedures gives them more discretion to achieve challenging goals. The participative style is ineffective for employees in routine tasks because they lack discretion over their work.

- *Team dynamics.* Cohesive teams with performance-oriented norms act as a substitute for most leader interventions. High team cohesion substitutes for supportive leadership, whereas performance-oriented team norms substitute for directive and possibly achievement-oriented leadership. Thus, when team cohesion is low, leaders should use the supportive style. Leaders should apply a directive style to counteract team norms that oppose the team's formal objectives. For example, the team leader may need to use legitimate power if team members have developed a norm to "take it easy" rather than get a project completed on time.

Path–goal theory has received more research support than other contingency leadership models, but the evidence is far from complete. A few contingencies (e.g., task structure) have limited research support. Other contingencies and leadership styles in the path–goal leadership model haven't been investigated at all.[44] Another concern is that as path–goal theory expands, the model may become too complex for practical use. Few people would be able to remember all the contingencies and the appropriate leadership styles for those contingencies. In spite of these limitations, path–goal theory remains a relatively robust contingency leadership theory.

Other Contingency Theories

Many leadership theories have developed over the years, several of which are found in the contingency perspective of leadership. Some overlap with the path–goal model's leadership styles, but most use simpler and more abstract contingencies. We will briefly mention only two here because of their popularity and historical significance to the field.

Situational Leadership Theory:
Widely Adopted in Spite of the Evidence[45]

1972
Year that Hersey and Blanchard introduced situational leadership theory (then known as "life-cycle leadership").

70
Percentage of Fortune 500 companies that currently use one or more situational leadership training products.

14 million
Estimated number of people who have received situational leadership training (as of 2010).

3 million
Estimated number of people who have received situational leadership training (as of 1997).

Situational Leadership Theory

One of the most popular contingency theories among practitioners is the **situational leadership theory (SLT)**, developed by Paul Hersey and Ken Blanchard.[46] SLT suggests that effective leaders vary their style with the ability and motivation (or commitment) of followers. The earliest versions of the model compressed the employee's ability and motivation into a single situational condition called maturity or readiness. The most recent version uses four labels, such as "enthusiastic beginner" (low ability, high motivation) and "disillusioned learner" (moderate ability and low motivation).

The situational leadership model also identifies four leadership styles—telling, selling, participating, and delegating—that Hersey and Blanchard distinguish by the amount of directive and supportive behavior provided. For example, "telling" has high task behavior and low supportive behavior. The situational leadership model has four quadrants, with each quadrant showing the leadership style that is most appropriate under different circumstances.

In spite of its popularity, several studies and at least three reviews have concluded that the situational leadership model lacks empirical support.[47] Only one part of the model apparently works, namely, that leaders should use "telling" (i.e., directive style) when employees lack motivation and ability. This relationship is also documented in path–goal theory. The model's elegant simplicity is attractive and entertaining, but most parts don't represent reality very well.

Fiedler's Contingency Model

Fiedler's contingency model, developed by Fred Fiedler and his associates, is the earliest contingency theory of leadership.[48] According to this model, leader effectiveness depends on whether the person's natural leadership style is appropriately matched to the situation. The theory examines two leadership styles that essentially correspond to the previously described people-oriented and task-oriented styles. Unfortunately, Fiedler's model relies on a questionnaire that does not measure either leadership style very well.

Fiedler's model suggests that the best leadership style depends on the level of *situational control*, that is, the degree of power and influence the leader possesses in a particular situation. Situational control is affected by three factors in the following order of importance: leader–member relations, task structure, and position power.[49] *Leader–member relations* refers to how much employees trust and respect the leader and are willing to follow his or her guidance. *Task structure* refers to the clarity or ambiguity of operating procedures. *Position power* is the extent to which the leader possesses legitimate, reward, and coercive power over subordinates. These three contingencies form the eight possible combinations of *situation favorableness* from the leader's viewpoint. Good leader–member relations, high task structure, and strong position power create the most favorable situation for the leader because he or she has the most power and influence under these conditions.

Fiedler has gained considerable respect for pioneering the first contingency theory of leadership, but his theory has fared less well. The leadership-style scale Fiedler used has been widely criticized, and there is no scientific justification for placing the three situational control factors in a hierarchy. Furthermore, the concept of leader–member relations is really an indicator of leader effectiveness (as in path–goal theory) rather than a situational factor. Finally, the theory considers only two leadership styles, whereas other models present a more complex and realistic array of behavior options. These concerns explain why the theory has limited empirical support.[50]

Changing the Situation to Match the Leader's Natural Style

Fiedler's contingency model may have become a historical footnote, but it does make an important and lasting contribution on one point. Fiedler argued that, contrary to most contingency theories, leaders might not be able to change their style easily to fit the situation. Instead, they tend to rely mainly on one style that is most consistent with their personality and values. Leaders with high agreeableness personality and benevolence values tend to prefer supportive leadership, for example, whereas leaders with high conscientiousness personality and achievement values feel more comfortable with the directive style of leadership.[51] More recent scholars have also proposed that leadership styles are "hardwired" more than most contingency leadership theories assume.[52] Leaders might be able to alter their style temporarily,

Leadership Substitutes

So far, we have looked at theories that recommend using different leadership styles in various situations. But one theory, called **leadership substitutes**, identifies conditions that either limit the leader's ability to influence subordinates or make a particular leadership style unnecessary. The literature identifies several conditions that possibly substitute for task-oriented or people-oriented leadership. Task-oriented leadership might be less important when performance-based reward systems keep employees directed toward organizational goals. Similarly, increasing employee skill and experience might reduce the need for task-oriented leadership. This proposition is consistent with path–goal leadership theory, which states that directive leadership is unnecessary—and may be detrimental—when employees are skilled or experienced.[53]

Some research suggests that effective leaders help team members learn to lead themselves through leadership substitutes; in other words, coworkers substitute for leadership in high-involvement team structures.[54] Coworkers instruct new employees, thereby providing directive leadership. They also provide social support, which reduces stress among fellow employees. Teams with norms that support organizational goals may substitute for achievement-oriented leadership because employees encourage (or pressure) coworkers to stretch their performance levels.[55]

The leadership substitutes model has intuitive appeal, but the evidence so far is mixed. Some studies show that a few substitutes do replace the need for task- or people-oriented leadership, but others do not. The difficulties of statistically testing for leadership substitutes may account for some problems, but a few writers contend that the limited support is evidence that leadership plays a critical role regardless of the situation.[56] At this point, we can conclude that leadership substitutes might reduce the need for leaders, but they do not completely replace leaders in these situations.

but they tend to rely mainly on one style that is most consistent with their personality and values.

If leadership style is influenced by an individual's personality and values, organizations should engineer the situation to fit the leader's dominant style, rather than expect leaders to change their style with the situation. A directive leader might be assigned inexperienced newcomers who need direction rather than skilled employees who work less effectively under a directive style. Alternatively, companies might transfer supervisors to workplaces where their dominant style fits best. For instance, directive leaders might be parachuted into work teams with counterproductive norms, whereas leaders who prefer a supportive style should be sent to departments in which employees face work pressures and other stressors.

> " Contrary to most contingency theories, leaders might not be able to change their style easily to fit the situation. "

After reading this section, you should be able to

LO5 Describe the four elements of transformational leadership and distinguish this theory from transactional and charismatic leadership.

TRANSFORMATIONAL PERSPECTIVE OF LEADERSHIP

By far the most popular leadership perspective today is **transformational leadership**, which views leaders as change agents. They create, communicate, and model a shared vision for the team or organization, and they inspire followers to strive for that vision.[57] Effective transformational leaders improve team and organizational effectiveness by changing what people do.

Transformational versus Transactional Leadership

Leadership experts often contrast transformational leadership with **transactional leadership**.[58] Transactional leaders influence others mainly by using rewards and penalties as well as by negotiating services from employees. James McGregor Burns, who coined the term four decades ago, describes transactional

For these reasons, we will avoid the "transactional leadership" concept. Instead, we believe a more appropriate comparison to transformational leadership is **managerial leadership** or managing. Managerial leadership refers to behaviors that make the current situation more effective. Managers "do things right" by helping employees to become more productive and satisfied within the existing corporate or work unit objectives.[61] The contingency and behavioral leadership theories described earlier refer to managerial leadership. In contrast, transformational leadership refers to behaviors that change the current situation. Transformational leaders "do the right things" by energizing and directing employees toward a better vision and set of objectives.

> ## Managers are people who do things right and leaders are people who do the right thing.[62]
>
> —Warren Bennis (also often attributed to Peter Drucker)

leadership with reference to political leaders who engage in vote buying or make transactional promises (e.g., I'll have a new hospital built if you vote for me).[59] Managers in organizations are rarely elected, yet transactional leadership has somehow been included in many organizational behavior leadership studies. The problem is compounded by a confusing and sometimes conflicting array of definitions and measures for transactional leadership. For example, Burns acknowledges that transactional leaders can appeal to follower wants and convictions about morality and justice, which is similar to transformational leadership.[60]

Organizations require both managerial and transformational leadership.[63] Managing improves organizational efficiency, whereas transformational leadership steers companies onto a better course of action. Transformational leadership is particularly important in organizations that require significant alignment with the external environment. Unfortunately, too many leaders get trapped in the daily activities that represent managerial leadership.[64] They lose touch with the transformational aspect of effective leadership. Without transformational leaders, organizations stagnate and eventually become seriously misaligned with their environments.

Transformational versus Charismatic Leadership

Another topic that has generated some confusion and controversy is charismatic leadership. Many researchers view charismatic leadership either as an essential ingredient of transformational leadership or as transformational leadership in its highest form of excellence.[65]

However, the emerging view, which this book adopts, comes from a third group of experts who contend that charisma is distinct from transformational leadership. These scholars point out that charisma is a personal trait or relational quality that provides referent power over followers, whereas transformational leadership is a set of behaviors that engage followers toward a better future.[66] This view is most consistent with the original and ongoing scholarly definition of charisma as an inherent characteristic of one's character, not something that can be easily learned or mimicked.[67] Transformational leadership motivates followers through behaviors that persuade and earn trust, whereas charismatic leadership motivates followers directly through existing referent power. For instance, communicating an inspiring vision is a transformational leadership behavior that motivates followers to strive for that vision. This motivational effect exists separate from the leader's degree of charisma. If the leader is highly charismatic, however, his or her charisma will amplify follower motivation.

Being charismatic is not inherently good or bad, but several writers have warned it can have negative consequences in leadership.[68] One concern is that leaders who possess the gift of charisma may become intoxicated by this power, which leads to a greater focus on self-interest than on the common good. "Charisma becomes the undoing of leaders," warns Peter Drucker. "It makes them inflexible, convinced of their own infallibility, unable to change."[69] The late management guru witnessed the destructive effects of charismatic political leaders in Europe a century ago and foresaw that this personal or relational characteristic would create similar problems for organizations.

Another concern with charismatic leadership is that it tends to produce dependent followers. Transformational leadership has the opposite effect—it builds follower empowerment, which tends to reduce dependence on the leader. One study also found that charismatic leadership has a negative effect on follower self-efficacy, which would further increase dependence on the leader. The main point here is that transformational leaders are not necessarily charismatic, and charismatic leaders are not necessarily transformational.

Elements of Transformational Leadership

There are several descriptions of transformational leadership, but most include the following four elements: Develop a strategic vision, communicate the vision, model the vision, and build commitment toward the vision (see Exhibit 11.5).

▼ **EXHIBIT 11.5** Elements of Transformational Leadership

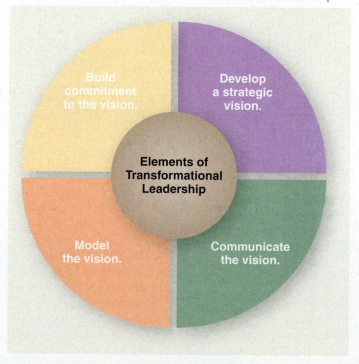

Develop a Strategic Vision A core element of transformational leadership is strategic vision—a realistic and attractive future that bonds employees together and focuses their energy toward a superordinate organizational goal.[71] Indeed, experts describe vision as the commodity or substance of transformational leadership. Strategic vision represents a "higher purpose" or superordinate goal that energizes and unifies employees and adds meaning to each person's self-concept.[72] It is typically described in a way that departs from the current situation and is both appealing and achievable. A strategic vision might originate with the leader, but it is just as likely to emerge from employees, clients, suppliers, or other stakeholders. When embraced by employees, a strategic vision plays an important role in organizational effectiveness.[73] It offers the same motivational benefits as goal setting (see Chapter 5), but also generates a common bond that builds employee commitment to this collective purpose.

Communicate the Vision If vision is the substance of transformational leadership, communicating that vision is

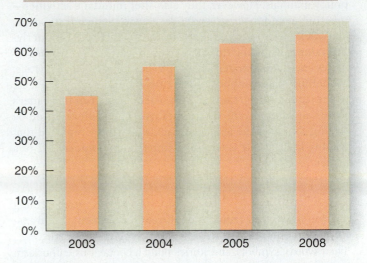

Does the Company's Senior Leadership Communicate a Clear Vision?[74]

Percentage of American employees, by year, who agree that senior management in their organization communicates a clear vision of the future.

the process. CEOs say that the most important leadership quality is being able to build and share their vision for the organization. "Part of a leader's role is to set the vision for the company and to communicate that vision to staff to get their buy-in," explains Dave Anderson, president of WorkSafeBC (the Workers' Compensation Board of British Columbia, Canada).[75]

Transformational leaders communicate meaning and elevate the importance of the visionary goal to employees. They frame messages around a grand purpose with emotional appeal that captivates employees and other corporate stakeholders. Framing generates positive emotions and motivation and establishes a common mental model so the group or organization will act collectively toward the desirable goal.[76] Transformational leaders bring their visions to life through symbols, metaphors, stories, and other vehicles that transcend plain language. Metaphors borrow images of other experiences, thereby creating richer meaning of the vision that has not yet been experienced.

Model the Vision Transformational leaders not only talk about a vision; they enact it. They "walk the talk" by stepping outside the executive suite and doing things that symbolize the vision.[77] "We hold our leaders to an even higher standard than our employees," says Nathan Bigler, human resource director at Eastern Idaho Regional Medical Center. "Leaders have to consistently walk the talk."[78]

Leaders walk the talk through significant events such as visiting customers, moving their offices closer to (or further from) employees, and holding ceremonies to destroy outdated policy manuals. However, they also alter mundane activities—meeting agendas, dress codes, executive schedules—so the activities are more consistent with the vision and its underlying values. Modeling the vision is important because it legitimizes and demonstrates what the vision looks like in practice. Modeling is also important because it builds employee trust in the leader. The greater the consistency between the leader's words and actions, the more employees will believe in and be willing to follow the leader. In fact, one survey reported that leading by example is the most important characteristic of a leader.[79]

Build Commitment toward the Vision Transforming a vision into reality requires employee commitment, and transformational leaders build this commitment in several ways. Their words, symbols, and stories build a contagious enthusiasm

Transformational leadership is currently the most popular leadership perspective, but it faces a number of challenges. One problem is that some writers engage in circular logic.[83] They define and measure transformational leadership by how well the leader inspires and engages employees rather than by whether they engage in specific transformational leadership behaviors (e.g., communicating a vision). This approach makes it impossible to evaluate transformational leadership because, by definition and measurement, all transformational leaders are effective!

Another concern is that transformational leadership is usually described as a universal rather than contingency-oriented model. Only very recently have writers begun to explore the idea that transformational leadership is more valuable in some situations than others.[84] For instance, transformational leadership is probably more appropriate when organizations need to adapt than when environmental conditions are stable. Preliminary evidence suggests that the transformational leadership perspective is relevant across

> "As an executive, you're always being watched by employees, and everything you say gets magnified. So you teach a lot by how you conduct yourself.[80]
>
> —Carl Bass, AutoDesk CEO

that energizes people to adopt the vision as their own. Leaders demonstrate a "can do" attitude by enacting their vision and staying on course. Their persistence and consistency reflect an image of honesty, trust, and integrity. Finally, leaders build commitment by involving employees in the process of shaping the organization's vision.

Evaluating the Transformational Leadership Perspective

Transformational leaders do make a difference.[81] Subordinates are more satisfied and have higher affective organizational commitment under transformational leaders. They also perform their jobs better, engage in more organizational citizenship behaviors, and make better or more creative decisions. One study of bank branches reported that organizational commitment and financial performance seem to increase where the branch manager completed a transformational leadership training program.[82]

cultures. However, there may be specific elements of transformational leadership, such as the way visions are formed and communicated, that are more appropriate in North America than other cultures.

Learning Objective

After reading this section, you should be able to

LO6 Describe the implicit leadership perspective.

IMPLICIT LEADERSHIP PERSPECTIVE

The competency, behavior, contingency, and transformational leadership perspectives make the basic assumption that leaders "make a difference." Certainly, there is evidence that senior executives do influence organizational performance. However, leadership also involves followers' perceptions about the characteristics and influence of people they call leaders. This perceptual perspective of leadership, called **implicit leadership theory**, has two components: leader prototypes and the romance or attribution of leadership.[85]

Charisma and Attribution of Leadership

As the CEO of a successful company (Semco SA) and the author of best-selling business books, Ricardo Semler is a giant among corporate leaders in South America. Yet he warns of the "romance of leadership" problems that can occur when employees are blinded by charismatic leadership. "People will naturally create and nurture a charismatic figure. The charismatic figure, on the other hand, feeds this," Semler explains. "The people at Semco don't look and act like me. They are not yes-men by any means. . . . [Yet] they credit me with successes that are not my own, and they don't debit me my mistakes."[86]

Prototypes of Effective Leaders

One aspect of implicit leadership theory states that everyone has *leadership prototypes*—preconceived beliefs about the features and behaviors of effective leaders.[87] These prototypes, which develop through socialization within the family and society, shape the follower's expectations and acceptance of others as leaders, and this in turn affects the willingness to remain as a follower. For example, one study reported that inherited personality characteristics significantly influence the perception that someone is a leader in a leaderless situation.[88]

Leadership prototypes not only support a person's role as leader; they also form or influence our perception of the leader's effectiveness. In other words, people are more likely to believe a leader is effective when he or she looks like and acts consistently with their prototype of a leader.[89] This prototype comparison process is a quick (although faulty) way of estimating the leader's capabilities. People want to trust their leader before they are willing to serve as followers, yet the leader's actual effectiveness usually isn't known for several months or possibly years.

The Romance of Leadership

Along with relying on implicit prototypes of effective leaders, followers tend to distort their perception of the influence that leaders have on the environment. This "romance of leadership" effect exists because in most cultures people want to believe that leaders make a difference. There are two basic reasons why people inflate their perceptions of the leader's influence over the environment.[90]

First, leadership is a useful way for us to simplify life events. It is easier to explain organizational successes and failures in terms of the leader's ability than by analyzing a complex array of other forces. Second, there is a strong tendency in the United States and other Western cultures to believe that life events are generated more from people than from uncontrollable natural forces.[91] This illusion of control is satisfied by believing that events result from the rational actions of leaders. In other words, employees feel better believing that leaders make a difference, so they actively look for evidence that this is so.

One way followers support their perceptions that leaders make a difference is through fundamental attribution error (see Chapter 3). Research has found (at least in Western cultures) that leaders are given credit or blame for the company's success or failure because employees do not readily see the external forces that also influence these events. Leaders reinforce this belief by taking credit for organizational successes.[92]

implicit leadership theory A theory stating that people evaluate a leader's effectiveness in terms of how well that person fits preconceived beliefs about the features and behaviors of effective leaders (leadership prototypes) and that people tend to inflate the influence of leaders on organizational events.

> ## LEADERSHIP IS A PERCEPTION OF FOLLOWERS AS MUCH AS THE ACTUAL BEHAVIORS AND FORMAL ROLES OF PEOPLE CALLING THEMSELVES LEADERS. ""

The implicit leadership perspective provides valuable advice to improve leadership acceptance. It highlights the fact that leadership is a perception of followers as much as the actual behaviors and formal roles of people calling themselves leaders. Potential leaders must be sensitive to this fact, understand what followers expect, and act accordingly. Individuals who do not make an effort to fit leadership prototypes will have more difficulty bringing about necessary organizational change.

Learning Objective

After reading this section, you should be able to

LO7 Discuss cultural and gender similarities and differences in leadership.

CROSS-CULTURAL AND GENDER ISSUES IN LEADERSHIP

Along with the five perspectives of leadership presented throughout this chapter, cultural values and practices affect what leaders do. Culture shapes the leader's values and norms, which influence his or her decisions and actions. Cultural values also shape the expectations that followers have of their

leaders. An executive who acts inconsistently with cultural expectations is more likely to be perceived as an ineffective leader. Furthermore, leaders who deviate from those values may experience various forms of influence to get them to conform to the leadership norms and expectations of the society. In other words, implicit leadership theory, described in the previous section of this chapter, explains differences in leadership practices across cultures.

Over the past decade, 150 researchers from dozens of countries have worked together on Project GLOBE (Global Leadership and Organizational Behavior Effectiveness) to identify the effects of cultural values on leadership.[93] The project organized countries into 10 regional clusters, of which the United States, Great Britain, and similar countries are grouped into the "Anglo" cluster. The results of this massive investigation suggest that some features of leadership are universal and some differ across cultures. Specifically, the GLOBE project reports that "charismatic visionary" is a universally recognized concept and that middle managers around the world believe it is characteristic of effective leaders. *Charismatic visionary* represents a cluster of concepts including visionary, inspirational, performance orientation, integrity, and decisiveness.[94]

In contrast, participative leadership is perceived as characteristic of effective leadership in low power distance cultures but less so in high power distance cultures. For instance, one study reported that Mexican employees expect managers to make decisions affecting their work. Mexico is a high power distance culture, so followers expect leaders to apply their authority rather than delegate their power most of the time.[95] In summary, there are similarities and differences in the concept and preferred practice of leadership across cultures.

Gender and Leadership

Studies in field settings have generally found that male and female leaders do not differ in their levels of task-oriented or people-oriented leadership. The main explanation is that real-world jobs require similar behavior from male and female job incumbents.[96] However, women do adopt a participative leadership style more readily than their male counterparts. One possible reason is that, compared to boys, girls are often raised to be more egalitarian and less status oriented, which is consistent with being participative. There is also some evidence that women have somewhat better interpersonal skills than men, and this translates into their relatively greater use of the participative leadership style. A third explanation is that subordinates, on the basis of their own gender stereotypes, expect female leaders to be more participative, so female leaders comply with follower expectations to some extent.

Surveys report that women are rated higher than men on the emerging leadership qualities of coaching, teamwork, and empowering employees.[97] Yet research also suggests that women are evaluated negatively when they try to apply the full range of leadership styles, particularly more directive and autocratic approaches. Thus, ironically, women may be well suited to contemporary leadership roles, yet they often continue to face limitations of leadership through the gender stereotypes and prototypes of leaders that are held by followers.[98] Overall, both male and female leaders must be sensitive to the fact that followers have expectations about how leaders should act, and negative evaluations may go to leaders who deviate from those expectations. ∎

designing organizational structures

LEARNING OBJECTIVES

After studying Chapter 12, you should be able to:

LO1 Describe three types of coordination in organizational structures.

LO2 Discuss the role and effects of span of control, centralization, and formalization, and relate these elements to organic and mechanistic organizational structures.

LO3 Identify and evaluate five types of departmentalization.

LO4 Explain how the external environment, organizational size, technology, and strategy are relevant when designing an organizational structure.

TAXI, Canada's creative agency of the decade, has grown to 350 employees in three countries (Canada, United States, and Netherlands), yet it continues to support flexibility and innovation through a unique organizational structure. "[Other advertising firms] operated on a nineteenth-century model of many secular departments trying to integrate everything ad hoc. Most cultures were so layered that a great idea was easily crushed," explains TAXI co-founder Paul Lavoie. "We needed a flexible infrastructure, able to move with the pace of change. TAXI started lean and nimble, and remains so today."

TAXI's structure assigns each client or project to "a nimble, autonomous team that is both empowered and responsible for results" says TAXI's Web site. The company claims the TAXI name reflects this small-team mandate: "We believe a small team of experts should drive every piece of the business—as many as can fit into a cab." And when a work center exceeds about 150 people, TAXI splits the unit into two centers. "Ancient nomadic tribes observed that a population exceeding 150 people had a tendency to form factions, erode group harmony, and render it dysfunctional," claims TAXI.[1]

continued on p. 234

organizational structure The division of labor as well as the patterns of coordination, communication, workflow, and formal power that direct organizational activities.

continued from p. 233

TAXI organizational structure has helped the creative agency to remain nimble and successful. **Organizational structure** refers to the division of labor as well as the patterns of coordination, communication, workflow, and formal power that direct organizational activities. It formally dictates what activities receive the most attention as well as financial, power, and information resources. For example, TAXI has an organizational structure that encourages employees to coordinate through information communication and to focus their attention around the client rather than their own job specializations. Organizational structure goes far beyond the organizational chart. Beyond these reporting relationships, the structure relates to job design, information flow, work standards and rules, team dynamics, and power relationships.

This chapter begins by introducing the two fundamental processes in organizational structure: division of labor and coordination. This is followed by a detailed investigation of the four main elements of organizational structure: span of control, centralization, formalization, and departmentalization. The latter part of this chapter examines the contingencies of organizational design, including external environment, organizational size, technology, and strategy. ■

Learning Objective

After reading this section, you should be able to

LO1 Describe three types of coordination in organizational structures.

DIVISION OF LABOR AND COORDINATION

All organizational structures include two fundamental requirements: the division of labor into distinct tasks and the coordination of that labor so employees are able to accomplish common goals.[2] Organizations are groups of people who work interdependently toward some purpose. To efficiently accomplish their goals, these groups typically divide the work into manageable chunks, particularly when there are many different tasks to perform. They also introduce various coordinating mechanisms to ensure that everyone is working effectively toward the same objectives.

Division of Labor

Division of labor refers to the subdivision of work into separate jobs assigned to different people. Subdivided work leads to job specialization because each job now includes a narrow subset of the tasks necessary to complete the product or service. TAXI organizes employees into a dozen or so specific jobs to effectively generate new advertisements, product designs, and other marketing resources. As companies get larger, this horizontal division of labor is accompanied by vertical division of labor: Some people are assigned the task of supervising employees, others are responsible for managing those supervisors, and so on.

Why do companies divide the work into several jobs? As we described in Chapter 5, job specialization increases work efficiency.[3] Job incumbents can master their tasks quickly because work cycles are shorter. Less time is wasted changing from one task to another. Training costs are reduced because employees require fewer physical and mental skills to accomplish the assigned work. Finally, job specialization makes it easier to match people with specific aptitudes or skills to the jobs for which they are best suited. Although one person working alone might be able to design a new ad campaign, for example, doing so would take much longer than having the work divided among several people with the required diversity of skills. Some employees are talented at thinking up innovative commercials, whereas others are better at preparing online drawings or working through financial costs.

Coordinating Work Activities

When people divide work among themselves, they require coordinating mechanisms to ensure that everyone works in concert. Coordination is so closely connected to division of labor that the optimal level of specialization is limited by the

feasibility of coordinating the work. In other words, an organization's ability to divide work among people depends on how well those people can coordinate with each other. Otherwise, individual effort is wasted due to misalignment, duplication, and mistiming of tasks. Coordination also tends to become more expensive and difficult as the division of labor increases, so companies specialize jobs only to the point where it isn't too costly or challenging to coordinate the people in those jobs.[4]

Every organization—from the two-person corner convenience store to the largest corporate entity—uses one or more of the following coordinating mechanisms:[5] informal communication, formal hierarchy, and standardization (see Exhibit 12.1). These forms of coordination align the work of staff within the same department as well as across work units. Coordinating mechanisms are also critical when several organizations work together, such as in joint ventures and humanitarian aid programs.[6]

Coordination through Informal Communication

All organizations rely on informal communication as a coordinating mechanism. This process includes sharing information on mutual tasks as well as forming common mental models so employees synchronize work activities using the same mental road map.[7] Informal communication is vital in nonroutine and ambiguous situations because employees can exchange a large volume of information through face-to-face communication and other media-rich channels.

Although coordination through informal communication is easiest in small firms, information technologies have further

> " Although coordination through informal communication is easiest in small firms, information technologies have further enabled this coordinating mechanism in large organizations. "

enabled this coordinating mechanism in large organizations.[8] Companies employing thousands of people also support informal communication by keeping each production site small. TAXI deliberately employs less than 150 people (most have 40 to 70 people) at its work units because it believes these smaller units support the informal coordination required for innovation.

Larger organizations also encourage coordination through informal communication by assigning *liaison roles* to employees, who are expected to communicate and share information with coworkers in other work units. Where coordination is required among several work units, companies create *integrator roles*. These people are responsible for coordinating a work process by encouraging employees in each work unit to share information and informally coordinate work activities. Integrators do not have authority over the people involved in that process, so they must rely on persuasion and commitment. Brand managers at Procter & Gamble have integrator roles because they coordinate work among marketing, production, and design groups.[9]

Another way larger organizations encourage coordination through informal communication is by organizing employees from several departments into temporary teams. Temporary cross-functional teams give employees more authority and opportunity to coordinate through informal communication. This process is now common in vehicle design. As the design engineer begins work on product specifications, team members from manufacturing, engineering, marketing, purchasing, and other departments are able to provide immediate feedback as

▼ **EXHIBIT 12.1** Coordinating Mechanisms in Organizations

Form of Coordination	Description	Subtypes/Strategies
Informal communication	Sharing information about mutual tasks; forming common mental models to synchronize work activities.	• Direct communication. • Liaison roles. • Integrator roles. • Temporary teams.
Formal hierarchy	Assigning legitimate power to individuals, who use this power to direct work processes and allocate resources.	• Direct supervision. • Formal communication channels.
Standardization	Creating routine patterns of behavior or output.	• Standardized skills. • Standardized processes. • Standardized output.

Sources: Based on information in J. Galbraith, *Designing Complex Organizations* (Reading, MA: Addison-Wesley, 1973), 8–19; H. Mintzberg, *The Structuring of Organizations* (Englewood Cliffs, NJ: Prentice Hall, 1979), Chap. 1; D. A. Nadler and M. L. Tushman, *Competing by Design: The Power of Organizational Architecture* (New York: Oxford University Press, 1997), Chap. 6.

Coordination Through
Micromanagement[10]

37%
of American employees surveyed say they occasionally or frequently feel micromanaged by their boss.

31%
of 97,000 employees surveyed in 30 countries describe their company's leadership as oppressive or authoritative.

25%
of 500 American employees surveyed say they work for a "micromanager."

17%
of 150 senior executives surveyed from the 1,000 largest American companies identify micromanaging as having the most negative impact on employee morale (third highest factor after lack of communication and recognition).

9%
of 11,045 American employees surveyed identify micromanagement as the most significant barrier to their productivity.

well as begin their contribution to the process. Without the informal coordination available through teams, the preliminary car design would pass from one department to the next—a much longer process.[11]

Coordination through Formal Hierarchy
Informal communication is the most flexible form of coordination, but it can become chaotic as the number of employees increases. Consequently, as organizations grow, they rely increasingly on a second coordinating mechanism: formal hierarchy.[12] Hierarchy assigns legitimate power to individuals, who then use this power to direct work processes and allocate resources. In other words, work is coordinated through direct supervision—the chain of command.

A century ago, management scholars applauded the formal hierarchy as the best coordinating mechanism for large organizations. They argued that organizations are most effective when managers exercise their authority and employees receive orders from only one supervisor. The chain of command—in which information flowed across work units only through supervisors and managers—was viewed as the backbone of organizational strength.

Although still important, formal hierarchy is much less popular today. One concern is that it is not as agile for coordination in complex and novel situations. Communicating through the chain of command is rarely as fast or accurate as direct communication between employees. For instance, product development—typically a complex and novel activity—tends to occur more quickly and produce higher-quality results when people coordinate

mainly through informal communication rather than formal hierarchy. Another concern with formal hierarchy is that managers are able to closely supervise only a limited number of employees. As the business grows, the number of supervisors and layers of management must increase, resulting in a costly bureaucracy. Finally, today's workforce demands more autonomy over work and more involvement in company decisions. Formal hierarchy coordination processes tend to conflict with employee autonomy and involvement.

Coordination through Standardization
Standardization, the third means of coordination, involves creating routine patterns of behavior or output. This coordinating mechanism takes three distinct forms: standardized processes, standardized outputs, and standardized skills.

- *Standardized processes.* Quality and consistency of a product or service can often be improved by standardizing work activities through job descriptions and procedures.[13] For example, flow charts represent a standardized process coordinating mechanism.

- *Standardized outputs.* This form of standardization involves ensuring that individuals and work units have clearly defined goals and output measures (e.g., customer satisfaction, production efficiency). For instance, to coordinate the work of salespeople, companies assign sales targets rather than specific behaviors.

- *Standardized skills.* When work activities are too complex to standardize through processes or goals, companies often coordinate work effort by extensively training employees or hiring people who have learned precise role behaviors from educational programs. Training is particularly critical as a coordinating mechanism in hospital operating rooms. Surgeons, nurses, and other operating room professionals coordinate their work more through training than through goals or company rules.

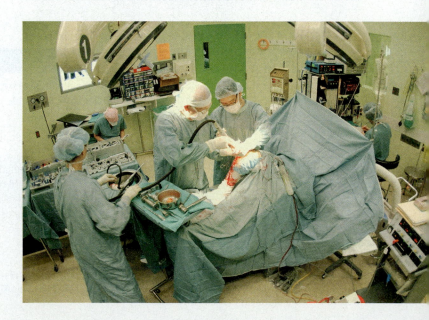

Division of labor and coordination of work represent the two fundamental ingredients of all organizations. But how work is divided, which coordinating mechanisms are emphasized, who makes decisions, and other issues are related to the four elements of organizational structure.

Learning Objective

After reading this section, you should be able to

LO2 Discuss the role and effects of span of control, centralization, and formalization, and relate these elements to organic and mechanistic organizational structures.

ELEMENTS OF ORGANIZATIONAL STRUCTURE

Organizational structure has four elements that apply to every organization. This section introduces three of them: span of control, centralization, and formalization. The fourth element—departmentalization—is presented in the next section.

Span of Control

Span of control (also called *span of management*) refers to the number of people directly reporting to the next level in the hierarchy. A narrow span of control exists when very few people report directly to a manager, whereas a wide span exists when a manager has many direct reports.[14] A century ago, French engineer and management scholar Henri Fayol strongly recommended a relatively narrow span of control, typically no more than 20 employees per supervisor and 6 supervisors per manager. Fayol championed formal hierarchy as the primary coordinating mechanism, so he believed supervisors should closely monitor and coach employees. His views were similar to those of Napoleon, who declared that 5 reporting officers is the maximum span of control for more senior leaders. These prescriptions were based on the belief that managers simply could not monitor and control any more subordinates closely enough.[15]

Today, we know better. The best-performing manufacturing plants currently have an average of 38 production employees per supervisor (see Exhibit 12.2).[16] What's the secret here? Did Fayol, Napoleon, and others miscalculate the optimal span of control? The answer is that those sympathetic to hierarchical control believed employees should perform the physical tasks, whereas supervisors and other management personnel should make the decisions and monitor employees to make sure they performed their tasks. In contrast, the best-performing manufacturing operations today rely on self-directed teams, so direct supervision (formal hierarchy) is supplemented with other coordinating mechanisms. Self-directed teams coordinate mainly through informal communication and various forms of standardization (i.e., training and processes), so formal hierarchy plays only a supporting role.

Many firms that employ doctors, lawyers, and other professionals also have a wider span of control because these staff members coordinate their work mainly through standardized skills. For example, more than two dozen people report directly to Cindy Zollinger, cofounder and president of Boston-based litigation-consulting firm Cornerstone Research. Zollinger explains that this large number of direct reports is possible because she leads professional staff members who don't require close supervision. "They largely run themselves," Zollinger explains. "I help them in dealing with obstacles they face, or in making the most of opportunities that they find."[17]

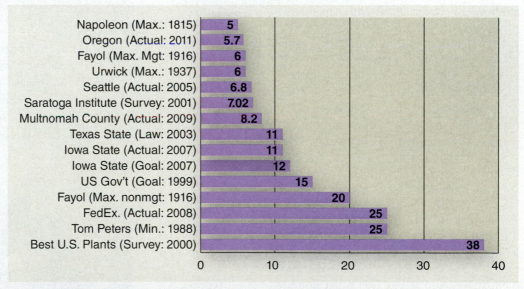

▼ **EXHIBIT 12.2** Recommended, Actual, and Enforced Spans of Control[18]

Napoleon (Max.: 1815)	5
Oregon (Actual: 2011)	5.7
Fayol (Max. Mgt: 1916)	6
Urwick (Max.: 1937)	6
Seattle (Actual: 2005)	6.8
Saratoga Institute (Survey: 2001)	7.02
Multnomah County (Actual: 2009)	8.2
Texas State (Law: 2003)	11
Iowa State (Actual: 2007)	11
Iowa State (Goal: 2007)	12
US Gov't (Goal: 1999)	15
Fayol (Max. nonmgt: 1916)	20
FedEx. (Actual: 2008)	25
Tom Peters (Min.: 1988)	25
Best U.S. Plants (Survey: 2000)	38

Figures represent the average number of direct reports per manager. "Max." figures represent the maximum spans of control recommended by Napoleon Bonaparte, Henri Fayol, and Lindall Urwick. "Min." figure represents the minimum span of control recommended by Tom Peters. "Goal" figures represent span of control targets that the U.S. Government and the State of Iowa have tried to achieve. The State of Texas figure represents the span of control mandated by law. The Saratoga Institute figure is the average span of control among U.S. companies surveyed. The Best U.S. Plants figure is the average span of control in American manufacturing facilities identified by *Industry Week* magazine as the most effective. "Actual" figures are spans of control in the city of Seattle, State of Oregon, Multnomah County (including Portland, Oregon), State of Iowa, and FedEx Corporation in the years indicated.

A second factor influencing the best span of control is whether employees perform routine tasks. A wider span of control is possible when employees perform routine jobs because there is less frequent need for direction or advice from supervisors. A narrow span of control is necessary when employees perform novel or complex tasks because these employees tend to require more supervisory decisions and coaching. This principle is illustrated in a survey of property and casualty insurers. The average span of control in commercial-policy processing departments is around 15 employees per supervisor, whereas the span of control is 6.1 in claims service and 5.5 in commercial underwriting. Staff members in the latter two departments perform more technical work, so they have more novel and complex tasks, which requires more supervisor involvement. Commercial-policy processing, on the other hand, is like production work. Tasks are routine and have few exceptions, so managers have less coordinating with each employee.[19]

A third influence on span of control is the degree of interdependence among employees within the department or team.[20] Generally, a narrow span of control is necessary where employees perform highly interdependent work with others. More supervision is required for highly interdependent jobs because employees tend to experience more conflict with each other, which requires more of a manager's time to resolve. Also, employees are less clear on their personal work performance in highly interdependent tasks, so supervisors spend more time providing coaching and feedback.

Tall versus Flat Structures

Span of control is interconnected with organizational size (number of employees) and the number of layers in the organizational hierarchy. Consider two companies with the same number of employees. If Company A has a wider span of control (more direct reports per manager) than Company B, then Company A necessarily has fewer layers of management (i.e., a flatter structure). The reason for this relationship is that a company with a wider span of control has more employees per supervisor, more supervisors for each middle manager, and so on. This larger number of direct reports, compared to a company with a narrower span of control, is possible only by removing layers of management.

The interconnection of span of control, organizational size (number of employees), and number of management layers has important implications for companies. As organizations employ more people, they must widen the span of control, build a taller hierarchy, or both. Most companies end up building taller structures because they rely on direct supervision to some extent as a coordinating mechanism and there are limits to how many people each manager can coordinate.

Unfortunately, building a taller hierarchy (more layers of management) creates problems. One concern is that taller structures have higher overhead costs because they have more managers per employee. This means there are more people administering the company and fewer actually making the product or supplying the service. A second problem is that senior managers in tall structures tend to receive lower-quality and less timely information. People tend to filter, distort, and simplify information before it is passed to higher levels in the hierarchy because they are motivated to frame the information in a positive light or to summarize it more efficiently. In contrast, information receives less manipulation in flat hierarchies and is often received much more quickly than in tall hierarchies. A third issue with tall hierarchies is that they tend to undermine employee empowerment and engagement. Hierarchies are power structures,

KenGen's Flatter Organizational Structure

KenGen, Kenya's leading electricity generation company, had more than 15 layers of hierarchy a few years ago. Today, the company's 1,500 employees are organized in a hierarchy with only 6 layers: the chief executive, executive directors, senior managers, chief officers, frontline management, and nonmanagement staff. "This flatter structure has reduced bureaucracy and it has also improved teamwork," explains KenGen executive Simon Ngure.[21]

so more levels of hierarchy tend to reduce the power distributed to people at the bottom of that hierarchy. Indeed, the size of the hierarchy itself tends to focus power around managers rather than employees.[22]

These problems have prompted leaders to "delayer"—remove one or more levels in the organizational hierarchy.[23] For instance, Chrysler Corp. CEO Sergio Marchionne recently warned that the automaker needs to have a flatter corporate structure to improve innovation, responsiveness, and customer service. "We need to be able to respond quickly, whether it's to customer complaints or consumer needs," he said. "Any new idea condemned to struggle upward through multiple levels of rigidly hierarchical, risk-averse management is an idea that won't see daylight until dusk—until it's too late." BASF's European Seal Sands plant came to the same conclusion several years ago; it was dramatically restructured around self-directed teams, cutting the hierarchy from seven to just two layers of management.[24]

> " Different degrees of decentralization can occur simultaneously in different parts of an organization. "

Centralization and Decentralization

Centralization means that formal decision-making authority is held by a small group of people, typically those at the top of the organizational hierarchy. Most organizations begin with centralized structures, as the founder makes most of the decisions and tries to direct the business toward his or her vision. As organizations grow, however, they diversify and their environments become more complex. Senior executives aren't able to process all the decisions that significantly influence the business. Consequently, larger organizations typically *decentralize;* that is, they disperse decision authority and power throughout the organization.

The optimal level of centralization or decentralization depends on several contingencies that we will examine later in this chapter. However, we also need to keep in mind that different degrees of decentralization can occur simultaneously in different parts of an organization. Nestlé, the Swiss-based food company, has decentralized marketing decisions to remain responsive to local markets, but it has centralized production, logistics, and supply chain management activities to improve cost efficiencies and avoid having too much complexity across the organization. "If you are too decentralized, you can become too complicated—you get too much complexity in your production system," explains a Nestlé executive.[25]

Likewise, 7-Eleven relies on both centralization and decentralization in different parts of the organization. The convenience store chain leverages buying power and efficiencies by centralizing decisions about information technology and supplier purchasing.

At the same time, it decentralizes local inventory decisions to store managers so they can adapt quickly to changing circumstances at the local level. Along with receiving ongoing product training and guidance from regional consultants, store managers have the best information about their customers and can respond quickly to local market needs. "We could never predict a busload of football players on a Friday night, but the store manager can," explains a 7-Eleven executive.[26]

Formalization

Formalization is the degree to which organizations standardize behavior through rules, procedures, formal training, and related mechanisms.[27] In other words, companies become more

Samsonite Drives Entrepreneurship through Decentralization

Samsonite, the Swiss-based luggage company, recently abandoned its centralized organizational structure by delegating more power to country managers. The reason? "We've learned that all of our customers are more different than similar," explains Samsonite chief financial officer Kyle Gendreau. Rather than follow global marketing and distribution practices dictated by the head office, country managers are now "empowered" to apply practices that best serve their local markets. "Letting people be entrepreneurial on the ground drives growth," says Gendreau. "It's really paying off for us."[28]

formalized as they increasingly rely on various forms of standardization to coordinate work. McDonald's and most other efficient fast-food chains typically have a high degree of formalization because they rely on standardization of work processes as a coordinating mechanism. Employees have precisely defined roles, right down to how much mustard should be dispensed, how many pickles should be applied, and how long each hamburger should be cooked.

Older companies tend to become more formalized because work activities become routinized, making them easier to document into standardized practices. Larger companies also tend to have more formalization because direct supervision and informal communication among employees are more costly or cumbersome when large numbers of people are involved. External influences, such as government safety legislation and strict accounting rules, also encourage formalization.

Formalization may increase efficiency and compliance, but it can also create problems.[29] Rules and procedures reduce organizational flexibility, so employees follow prescribed behaviors even when the situation clearly calls for a customized response. High levels of formalization tend to undermine organizational learning and creativity. Some work rules become so convoluted that organizational efficiency would decline if they were actually followed as prescribed. Formalization is also a source of job dissatisfaction and work stress. Finally, rules and procedures have been known to take on a life of their own in some organizations. They become the focus of attention rather than the organization's ultimate objectives of producing a product or service and serving its dominant stakeholders.

Mechanistic versus Organic Structures

We discussed span of control, centralization, and formalization together because they cluster around two broader organizational forms: mechanistic and organic structures (see Exhibit 12.3).[31] A

The Price of Formalization: More Red Tape[30]

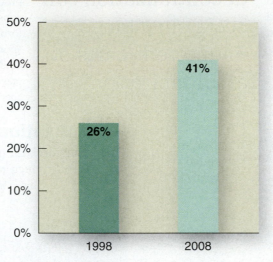

50%

41%

40%

30%

26%

20%

10%

0%

1998   2008

Percentage of 1,200 Canadian employees polled in 1998 and of 2,052 Canadian employees polled in 2008 who identified "red tape and bureaucracy" as one of the biggest barriers to their work productivity.

mechanistic structure is characterized by a narrow span of control and high degree of formalization and centralization. Mechanistic structures have many rules and procedures, limited decision making at lower levels, tall hierarchies of people in specialized roles, and vertical rather than horizontal communication flows. Tasks are rigidly defined and are altered only when sanctioned by higher authorities. Companies with an **organic structure** have the opposite characteristics. They operate with a wide span of control, decentralized decision making, and little formalization. Tasks are fluid, adjusting to new situations and organizational needs.

As a general rule, mechanistic structures operate better in stable environments because they rely on efficiency and routine behaviors, whereas organic structures work better in rapidly changing (i.e., dynamic) environments because they are more flexible and responsive to the changes. Organic structures are also more compatible with organizational learning, high-performance workplaces, and quality management because they emphasize information sharing and an empowered workforce rather than hierarchy and status.[32] However, organic structures tend to be better than mechanistic structures in dynamic environments only when employees have developed well-established roles and expertise.[33] Without these conditions, employees are unable to coordinate effectively with each other, resulting in errors and gross inefficiencies.

▼ **EXHIBIT 12.3** Contrasting Mechanistic and Organic Organizational Structures

Mechanistic Structure	Organic Structure
• Narrow span of control.	• Wide span of control.
• High centralization.	• High decentralization.
• High formalization.	• Low formalization.

Learning Objective

After reading this section, you should be able to

LO3   Identify and evaluate five types of departmentalization.

FORMS OF DEPARTMENTALIZATION

Span of control, centralization, and formalization are important elements of organizational structure, but most people think about organizational charts when the discussion of organizational structure arises. The organizational chart represents the fourth element in the structuring of organizations, called *departmentalization*. Departmentalization specifies how employees and their activities are grouped together. It is a fundamental strategy for coordinating organizational activities because it influences organizational behavior in the following ways:[34]

- Departmentalization establishes the chain of command—the system of common supervision among positions and units within the organization. It frames the membership of formal work teams and typically determines which positions and units must share resources. Thus, departmentalization establishes interdependencies among employees and subunits.

- Departmentalization focuses people around common mental models or ways of thinking, such as serving clients, developing products, or supporting a particular skill set. This focus is typically anchored around the common budgets and measures of performance assigned to employees within each departmental unit.

- Departmentalization encourages specific people and work units to coordinate through informal communication. With common supervision and resources, members within each configuration typically work near each other, so they can use frequent and informal interaction to get the work done.

There are almost as many organizational charts as there are businesses, but the five most common pure types of departmentalization are simple, functional, divisional, team-based, and matrix.

Simple Structure

Most companies begin with a *simple structure*.[35] They employ only a few people and typically offer only one distinct product or service. There is minimal hierarchy—usually just employees reporting to the owners. Employees perform broadly defined roles because there are insufficient economies of scale to assign them to more specialized jobs. The simple structure is highly flexible and minimizes the walls that form between employees in other structures. However, the simple structure usually depends on the owner's direct supervision to coordinate

work activities, so it is very difficult to operate as the company grows and becomes more complex.

Functional Structure

Growing organizations usually introduce a functional structure at some level of the hierarchy or at some time in their history. A **functional structure** organizes employees around specific knowledge or other resources (see Exhibit 12.4). Employees

▼ **EXHIBIT 12.4** A Functional Organizational Structure

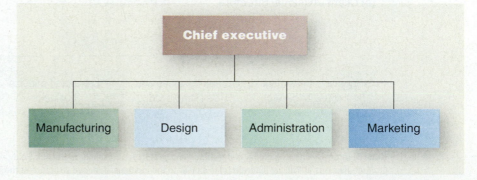

with marketing expertise are grouped into a marketing unit, those with production skills are located in manufacturing, engineers are found in product development, and so on. Organizations with functional structures are typically centralized to coordinate their activities effectively.

Evaluating the Functional Structure
The functional structure creates specialized pools of talent that typically serve everyone in the organization. This provides more economies of scale than are possible if functional specialists are spread over different parts of the organization. It increases employee identity with the specialization or profession. Direct supervision is easier in functional structures because managers oversee people with common issues and expertise.[36]

The functional structure also has limitations.[37] Grouping employees around their skills tends to focus attention on those skills and related professional needs rather than on the company's product, service, or client needs. Unless people are transferred from one function to the next, they might not develop a broader understanding of the business. Compared with other structures, the functional structure usually produces higher dysfunctional conflict and poorer coordination in serving clients or developing products. These problems occur because employees need to work with coworkers in other departments to complete organizational tasks, yet they have different subgoals and mental models of ideal work. Together, these problems require substantial formal controls and coordination when people are organized around functions.

Divisional Structure

The **divisional structure** (sometimes called the *multidivisional* or *M-form* structure) groups employees around geographic areas, outputs (products or services), or clients. Exhibit 12.5 illustrates these three variations of divisional structure. The *geographic divisional structure* organizes employees around distinct

▼**EXHIBIT 12.5** Three Types of Divisional Structure

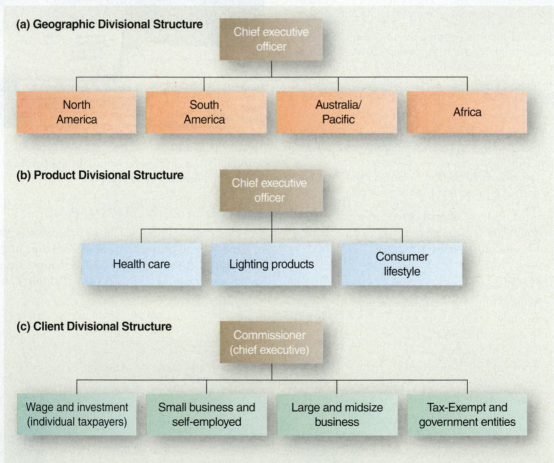

(a) Geographic Divisional Structure

Chief executive officer
- North America
- South America
- Australia/Pacific
- Africa

(b) Product Divisional Structure

Chief executive officer
- Health care
- Lighting products
- Consumer lifestyle

(c) Client Divisional Structure

Commissioner (chief executive)
- Wage and investment (individual taxpayers)
- Small business and self-employed
- Large and midsize business
- Tax-Exempt and government entities

Note: Diagram (a) shows a global geographic divisional structure similar to Barrick Gold Corporation; diagram (b) is similar to the product divisions at Philips; diagram (c) is similar to the customer-focused structure at the U.S. Internal Revenue Service.

regions of the country or world. Exhibit 12.5 (a) illustrates a geographic divisional structure adopted by Barrick Gold Corporation, the world's largest gold-mining company. The *product/service divisional structure* organizes employees around distinct outputs. Exhibit 12.5 (b) illustrates a simplified version of this type of structure at Philips. The Dutch electronics company divides its workforce mainly into three divisions: health care products, lighting products, and consumer products. (Philips also has a fourth organizational group consisting of the research and design functions.) The *client divisional structure* organizes employees around specific customer groups. Exhibit 12.5 (c) illustrates a customer-focused divisional structure similar to one adopted by the U.S. Internal Revenue Service.[38]

Which form of divisional structure should large organizations adopt? The answer depends mainly on the primary source of environmental diversity or uncertainty.[39] Suppose an organization has one type of product sold to people across the country. If customers have different needs across regions, or if state governments impose different regulations on the product, then a geographic structure would be best to be more vigilant of this diversity. On the other hand, if the company sells several types of products across the country and customer preferences and government regulations within each product are similar everywhere, then a product structure would likely work best.

Coca-Cola, Nestlé, and many other food and beverage companies are organized mainly around geographic regions because consumer tastes and preferred marketing strategies vary considerably around the world. Even though McDonald's makes the same Big Mac throughout the world, the company has more fish products in Hong Kong and more vegetarian products in India, in line with traditional diets in those countries. Philips, on the other hand, is organized around products because consumer preferences around the world are similar within each product group. Hospitals from Geneva, Switzerland, to Santiago, Chile, buy similar medical equipment from Philips, whereas the manufacturing and marketing of these products are quite different from Philips' consumer electronics business.

Many companies are moving away from structures that organize people around geographic clusters.[40] One reason is that clients can purchase products online and communicate with businesses from almost anywhere in the world, so local representation is less critical. Reduced geographic variation is another reason for the shift away from geographic structures; freer trade has reduced government intervention, and consumer preferences for many products and services are becoming more similar (converging) around the world. The third reason is that large companies increasingly have global business customers who demand one global point of purchase, not one in every country or region.

The Globally Integrated Enterprise

The shift away from geographic and toward product- or client-based divisional structures reflects the trend toward the **globally integrated enterprise.**[42] As the label implies, a globally integrated enterprise connects work processes around the world, rather than replicating them within each country or region. This type of organization typically organizes people around product or client divisions. Even functional units—production, marketing, design, human resources, and so on—serve the company worldwide rather than within specific geographic clusters. These functions are sensitive to cultural and market differences and have local representation to support that sensitivity, but local representatives are associates of a global function rather than a local subsidiary copied across several regions. Indeed, a globally integrated enterprise is marked by a dramatic increase in virtual teamwork because employees are assigned global projects and ongoing responsibilities for work units that transcend geographic boundaries.

The globally integrated enterprise no longer orchestrates its business from a single headquarters in one "home" country. Instead, its divisional and functional operations are led from where the work is concentrated, and this concentration depends on economics (cost of labor, infrastructure, etc.), expertise, and openness (trade, capital flow, knowledge sharing, etc.). For example, IBM has moved toward the globally integrated enterprise structure by locating its global data centers in Colorado, Web site management in Ireland, back-office finance in Brazil, software in India, and procurement in China.[43]

Evaluating the Divisional Structure

The divisional organizational structure is a building-block structure; it accommodates growth relatively easily and focuses employee attention on products or customers rather than tasks. Different products, services, or clients can be added on by sprouting new divisions. These advantages are offset by a number of limitations. First, the divisional structure tends to duplicate resources, such as production equipment and engineering or information technology expertise. Also, unless the division is quite large, resources are not used as efficiently as they are in functional structures where resources are pooled across the entire organization. The divisional structure also creates silos of knowledge. Expertise is spread across several autonomous business units, and this reduces the ability and perhaps motivation of the people in one division to share their knowledge with counterparts in other divisions. In contrast, a functional structure groups experts together, thereby supporting knowledge sharing.

Finally, the preferred divisional structure depends on the company's primary source of environmental diversity or uncertainty. This principle seems to be applied easily enough at Coca-Cola, McDonald's, and Philips, but many global organizations experience diversity and uncertainty in terms of geography, product, *and* clients. Consequently, some organizations revise their structures back and forth or create complex structures that attempt to give all three dimensions

> " Leaders of global organizations struggle to find the best divisional structure, often resulting in the departure of some executives and frustration among those who remain. "

equal status. This waffling generates further complications because organizational structure decisions shift power and status among executives. If the company switches from a geographic to product structure, people who lead the geographic fiefdoms suddenly get demoted under the product chiefs. In short, leaders of global organizations struggle to find the best divisional structure, often resulting in the departure of some executives and frustration among those who remain.

Team-Based Structure

A **team-based organizational structure** is built around self-directed teams that complete an entire piece of work, such as manufacturing a product or developing an electronic game. This type of structure is usually organic. There is a wide span of control because teams operate with minimal supervision. In extreme situations, there is no formal leader, just someone selected by other team members to help coordinate the work and liaise with top management. Team structures are highly decentralized because almost all day-to-day decisions are made by team members rather than someone further up the organizational hierarchy. Finally, many team-based structures have low formalization because teams are given relatively few rules about how to organize their work. Instead, executives assign quality and quantity output targets and often productivity improvement goals to each team. Teams are then encouraged to use available resources and their own initiative to achieve those objectives.

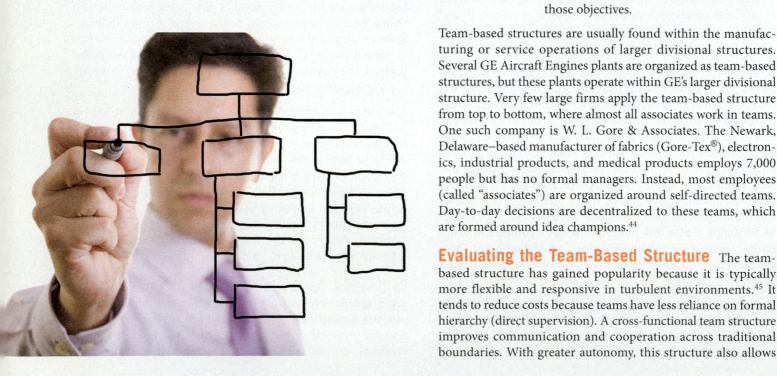

Team-based structures are usually found within the manufacturing or service operations of larger divisional structures. Several GE Aircraft Engines plants are organized as team-based structures, but these plants operate within GE's larger divisional structure. Very few large firms apply the team-based structure from top to bottom, where almost all associates work in teams. One such company is W. L. Gore & Associates. The Newark, Delaware–based manufacturer of fabrics (Gore-Tex®), electronics, industrial products, and medical products employs 7,000 people but has no formal managers. Instead, most employees (called "associates") are organized around self-directed teams. Day-to-day decisions are decentralized to these teams, which are formed around idea champions.[44]

Evaluating the Team-Based Structure The team-based structure has gained popularity because it is typically more flexible and responsive in turbulent environments.[45] It tends to reduce costs because teams have less reliance on formal hierarchy (direct supervision). A cross-functional team structure improves communication and cooperation across traditional boundaries. With greater autonomy, this structure also allows

quicker and more informed decision making.[46] For this reason, some hospitals have shifted from functional departments to cross-functional teams. Teams composed of nurses, radiologists, anesthetists, a pharmacology representative, possibly social workers, a rehabilitation therapist, and other specialists communicate and coordinate more efficiently, thereby reducing delays and errors.[47]

Against these benefits, the team-based structure can be costly to maintain due to the need for ongoing interpersonal skill training. Teamwork potentially takes more time to coordinate than formal hierarchy during the early stages of team development. Employees may experience more stress due to increased ambiguity in their roles. Team leaders also experience more stress due to increased conflict, loss of functional power, and unclear career progression ladders. In addition, team structures suffer from duplication of resources and potential competition (and lack of resource sharing) across teams.[48]

Matrix Structure

When physicians Ray Muzyka and Greg Zeschuk and a third partner (who later returned to medical practice) founded BioWare ULC, they initially organized employees at the electronic games company into a simple structure in which everyone worked together on the first game, *Shattered Steel*. Soon after, Muzyka and Zeschuk decided to create a second game

(*Baldur's Gate*), but they weren't sure what organizational structure would be best. Simply creating a second team might duplicate resources, undermine information sharing across teams, and weaken employee loyalty to the overall company. Alternatively, the game developer could adopt a functional structure by assigning employees to specialized departments such as art, programming, audio, quality assurance, and design. A functional structure would encourage employees within each specialization to share information, but it might undermine team dynamics on game projects and reduce employee commitment to the game they were developing.[49]

After carefully weighing the various organizational structure options, Muzyka and Zeschuk adopted a **matrix structure** to gain the benefits of both a functional structure and a project-based (team) structure. BioWare's matrix structure, which is similar to the diagram in Exhibit 12.6, is organized around both functions (art, audio, programming, etc.) and team-based game development projects. Employees are assigned to a cross-functional team responsible for a specific game project, yet they also belong to a permanent functional unit from which they are reassigned when their work is completed on a particular project.[50]

Muzyka and Zeschuk say the matrix structure focuses employees on the final product yet keeps them organized around their expertise to encourage knowledge sharing. "The matrix structure also supports our overall company culture where

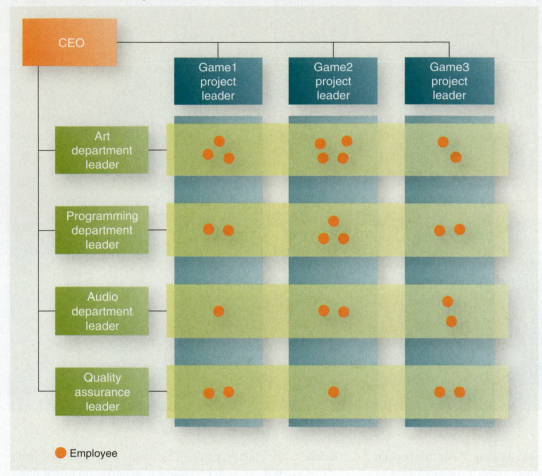

● Employee

companies with matrix structures, only employees at one level in the organization (typically country-specific brand managers) report to two bosses. For example, the manager responsible for Nestlé's bottled water brands in Mexico would have two bosses: Nestlé's Mexican country manager and the world headquarters executive responsible for Nestlé Waters. In contrast, sales and marketing employees further down the hierarchy report only to a Mexican manager.

Evaluating the Matrix Structure The matrix structure usually makes very good use of resources and expertise, making it ideal for project-based organizations with fluctuating workloads. When properly managed, it improves communication efficiency, project flexibility, and innovation, compared to purely functional or divisional designs. It focuses employees on serving clients or creating products yet keeps people organized around their specialization, so knowledge sharing improves and resources are used more efficiently. The matrix structure is also a logical choice when, as in the case of Nestlé, two different dimensions (regions and products) are equally important. Structures determine executive power and what is important; the matrix structure works when two different dimensions deserve equal attention.

BioWare is the team, and everyone is always willing to help each other whether they are on the same project or not," they add. BioWare's matrix structure was a good choice, particularly as the company (which is now an independent division of Electronic Arts) has grown to almost 800 employees working on numerous game projects at four centers around the United States and Canada.

BioWare's structure, in which project teams overlap with functional departments, is just one form of matrix structure. Another variation, found mainly in large global firms, has geographic divisions on one axis and products/services or client divisions on the other. Nestlé, Procter & Gamble, Shell, and many other global organizations have variations of a matrix structure that attempt to balance geography with products/services. Consider Nestlé Waters, which markets several brands of bottled water in more than three dozen countries. The manager responsible for Nestlé's Mexican bottled water brands would report to both the country manager and to the Nestlé Waters executive at the company's headquarters in Switzerland.[51]

A common error is the belief that everyone in a matrix organizational structure reports to two bosses. In multinational

In spite of these advantages, the matrix structure has several well-known problems.[52] One concern is that it increases conflict among managers who equally share power. Employees working at the matrix level have two bosses and, consequently, two sets of priorities that aren't always aligned with each other. Project leaders might squabble with functional leaders regarding the assignment of specific employees to projects as well as regarding the employee's technical competence. For example, Citigroup, Inc. recently adopted a geographic product matrix structure and apparently is already experiencing dysfunctional conflict between the regional and product group executives.[53]

Another challenge is ambiguous accountability. In a functional or divisional structure, one manager is responsible for everything, even the most unexpected issues. But in a matrix structure, the unusual problems don't get resolved because neither manager takes ownership of them.[54] Oracle president Mark Hurd warned of this problem a few years ago when he was CEO of Hewlett-Packard: "The more accountable I can make you, the easier it is for you to show you're a great performer," says Hurd. "The more I use a matrix, the easier I make it to blame someone else."[55] The combination of dysfunctional conflict and ambiguous accountability in matrix structures also explains why some employees experience more stress and some managers are less satisfied with their work arrangements.

Learning Objective

After reading this section, you should be able to

LO4 Explain how the external environment, organizational size, technology, and strategy are relevant when designing an organizational structure.

CONTINGENCIES OF ORGANIZATIONAL DESIGN

Most organizational behavior theories and concepts have contingencies: Ideas that work well in one situation might not work as well in another situation. This contingency approach is certainly relevant when choosing the most appropriate organizational structure.[56] In this section, we introduce four contingencies of organizational design: external environment, size, technology, and strategy.

External Environment

The best structure for an organization depends on its external environment. The external environment includes anything outside the organization, including most stakeholders (e.g., clients, suppliers, government), resources (e.g., raw materials, human resources, information, finances), and competitors. Four characteristics of external environments influence the type of organizational structure best suited to a particular situation: dynamism, complexity, diversity, and hostility.[57]

Dynamic versus Stable Environments

Dynamic environments have a high rate of change, leading to novel situations and a lack of identifiable patterns. Organic structures are better suited to this type of environment so that the organization can adapt more quickly to changes, but only if employees are experienced and coordinate well in teamwork.[58] In contrast, stable environments are characterized by regular cycles of activity and steady changes in supply and demand for inputs and outputs. Events are more predictable, enabling the firm to apply rules and procedures. Mechanistic structures are more efficient when the environment is predictable, so they tend to work better than organic structures.

Complex versus Simple Environments

Complex environments have many elements, whereas simple environments have few things to monitor. As an example, a major university library operates in a more complex environment than a small-town public library. The university library's clients require several types of services—book borrowing, online full-text databases, research centers, course reserve collections, and so on. A small-town public library has fewer of these demands placed on it. The more complex the environment, the more decentralized the organization should become. Decentralization is a logical choice for complex environments because decisions are pushed down to people and subunits with the necessary information to make informed choices.

Diverse versus Integrated Environments

Organizations located in diverse environments have a greater variety of products or services, clients, and regions. In contrast, an integrated environment has only one client, product,

organizational strategy The way the organization positions itself in its setting in relation to its stakeholders, given the organization's resources, capabilities, and mission.

and geographic area. The more diversified the environment, the more the firm needs to use a divisional structure aligned with that diversity. If it sells a single product around the world, a geographic divisional structure would align best with the firm's geographic diversity, for example.

Hostile versus Munificent Environments Firms located in a hostile environment face resource scarcity and more competition in the marketplace. Hostile environments are typically dynamic ones because they reduce the predictability of access to resources and demand for outputs. Organic structures tend to be best in hostile environments. However, when the environment is extremely hostile—such as a severe shortage of supplies or lower market share—organizations tend to temporarily centralize so decisions can be made more quickly and executives feel more comfortable being in control.[59] Ironically, centralization may result in lower-quality decisions during organizational crises because top management has less information, particularly when the environment is complex.

Organizational Size

Larger organizations should have different structures from smaller organizations.[60] As the number of employees increases, job specialization increases due to a greater division of labor. The greater division of labor requires more elaborate coordinating mechanisms. Thus, larger firms make greater use of standardization (particularly work processes and outcomes) to coordinate work activities. These coordinating mechanisms create an administrative hierarchy and greater formalization. Historically, larger organizations make less use of informal communication as a coordinating mechanism. However, emerging information technologies and increased emphasis on empowerment have caused informal communication to regain its importance in large firms.[61]

Larger organizations also tend to be more decentralized. Executives have neither sufficient time nor expertise to process all the decisions that significantly influence the business as it grows. Therefore, decision-making authority is pushed down to lower levels, where incumbents are able to cope with the narrower range of issues under their control.

Technology

Technology is another factor to consider when designing the best organizational structure for the situation.[62] *Technology* refers to the mechanisms or processes by which an organization turns out its product or service. One technological contingency

is *variability*—the number of exceptions to standard procedure that tend to occur. In work processes with low variability, jobs are routine and follow standard operating procedures. Another contingency is *analyzability*—the predictability or difficulty of the required work. The less analyzable the work, the more it requires experts with sufficient discretion to address the work challenges.

An organic, rather than a mechanistic, structure should be introduced where employees perform tasks with high variety and low analyzability, such as in a research setting. The reason is that employees face unique situations with little opportunity for repetition. In contrast, a mechanistic structure is preferred where the technology has low variability and high analyzability, such as an assembly line. The work is routine and highly predictable, an ideal situation for a mechanistic structure to operate efficiently.

Organizational Strategy

Organizational strategy refers to the way the organization positions itself in its setting in relation to its stakeholders, given the organization's resources, capabilities,

> " Organizational structures don't evolve as a natural response to environmental conditions; they result from conscious human decisions. "

and mission.[63] In other words, strategy represents the decisions and actions applied to achieve the organization's goals. Although size, technology, and environment influence the optimal organizational structure, these contingencies do not necessarily determine structure. Instead, corporate leaders formulate and implement strategies that shape both the characteristics of these contingencies as well as the organization's resulting structure.

This concept is summed up with the simple phrase "Structure follows strategy."[64] Organizational leaders decide how large to grow and which technologies to use. They take steps to define and manipulate their environments, rather than let the organization's fate be entirely determined by external influences. Furthermore, organizational structures don't evolve as a natural response to environmental conditions; they result from conscious human decisions. Thus, organizational strategy influences both the contingencies of structure and the structure itself.

If a company's strategy is to compete through innovation, a more organic structure would be preferred because it is easier for employees to share knowledge and be creative. If a company chooses a low-cost strategy, a mechanistic structure is preferred because it maximizes production and service efficiency.[65] Overall, it is now apparent that organizational structure is influenced by size, technology, and environment, but the organization's strategy may reshape these elements and loosen their connection to organizational structure. ■

CHECK IT OUT!

www.mhhe.com/ McShaneM2e

for study materials

including quizzes

and other resources

organizational **culture**

"**N**omura's Corporate Culture Still Flawed" (*The Daily Yomiuri*)[1]

"Volunteerism a Longtime By-product of Dannon's Corporate Culture" (*Westchester County Business Journal*)[2]

"Whistleblower: 'The Culture Ultimately Comes from the Top'" (*The Independent*)[3]

It seems that whenever a company is very successful or in deep trouble, its organizational culture is part of the explanation. These recent newspaper and magazine headlines illustrate this point. *The Daily Yomiuri* newspaper in Japan reports that a series of insider trading scandals at Nomura Securities Company over the past decade are due to an organizational culture that supports this wrongdoing. The *Westchester County Business Journal* explains how volunteerism and corporate social responsibility are ingrained in the organizational culture of New York–based food products company, The Dannon Company. And in *The Independent* newspaper article, a

continued on p. 252

LEARNING OBJECTIVES

After studying Chapter 13, you should be able to:

LO1 Describe the elements of organizational culture and discuss the importance of organizational subcultures.

LO2 List four categories of artifacts through which corporate culture is deciphered.

LO3 Discuss the importance of organizational culture and the conditions under which organizational culture strength improves organizational performance.

LO4 Compare and contrast four strategies for merging organizational cultures.

LO5 Identify four strategies for changing or strengthening an organization's culture, including the application of attraction–selection–attrition theory.

LO6 Describe the organizational socialization process and identify strategies to improve that process.

organizational culture The values and assumptions shared within an organization.

continued from p. 251

Barclays insider reveals that employees knew about the British financial institution's illegal interest rate fixing (Libor) but did not report this fraud to authorities because of "a culture of fear." ■

The phrase "organizational culture" was rarely uttered before 1982.[4] Today, it is the subject of popular press articles and the focus of most executives. **Organizational culture** consists of the values and assumptions shared within an organization.[5] It defines what is important and unimportant in the company and, consequently, directs everyone in the organization toward the "right way" of doing things. You might think of organizational culture as the company's DNA—invisible to the naked eye, yet a powerful template that shapes what happens in the workplace.

This chapter begins by identifying the elements of organizational culture and then describing how culture is deciphered through artifacts. This is followed by a discussion of the relationship between organizational culture and performance, including the effects of cultural strength, fit, and adaptability. Then we examine ways to change or strengthen organizational culture, including a closer look at the related topic of organizational socialization. The final section of this chapter turns our attention to the challenges of and solutions to merging organizational cultures.

Learning Objective

After reading this section, you should be able to

LO1 Describe the elements of organizational culture and discuss the importance of organizational subcultures.

ELEMENTS OF ORGANIZATIONAL CULTURE

As its definition states, organizational culture consists of shared values and assumptions. Exhibit 13.1 illustrates how these shared values and assumptions relate to each other and

▼**EXHIBIT 13.1** Organizational Culture Assumptions, Values, and Artifacts

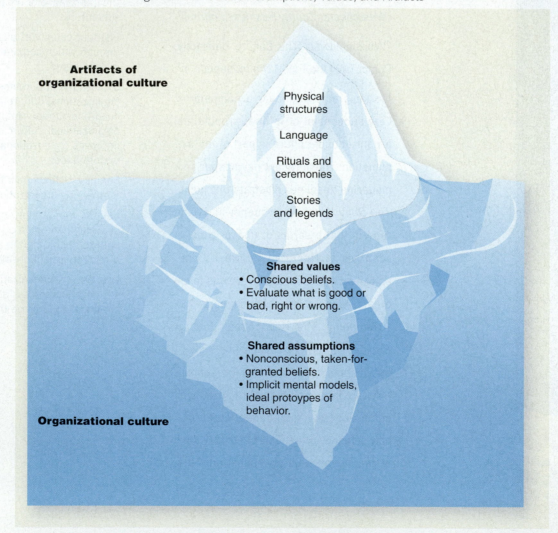

Artifacts of organizational culture

Physical structures

Language

Rituals and ceremonies

Stories and legends

Shared values
• Conscious beliefs.
• Evaluate what is good or bad, right or wrong.

Shared assumptions
• Nonconscious, taken-for-granted beliefs.
• Implicit mental models, ideal protoypes of behavior.

Organizational culture

Corporate Culture
Alignments and Misalignments[6]

93 % of American business leaders surveyed say that the organization's culture has an important influence on the effectiveness of performance management.

75 % of junior managers surveyed in the UK believe there is a mismatch between their company's "espoused values" and what actually goes on in the company.

69 % of American employees surveyed say that senior leadership acts in accordance with the company's core values and beliefs.

55 % of American employees surveyed say that senior leadership acts in accordance with the company's core values and beliefs.

27 % of American business leaders surveyed say their performance management strategy is aligned with the company's culture and values.

25 % of Board of Directors surveyed in the United Kingdom believe there is a mismatch between their company's "espoused values" and what actually goes on in the company.

are associated with artifacts, which are discussed later in this chapter. *Values* are stable, evaluative beliefs that guide our preferences for outcomes or courses of action in a variety of situations (see Chapters 1 and 2).[7] They are conscious perceptions about what is good or bad, right or wrong. In the context of organizational culture, values are discussed as *shared values*, which are values that people within the organization or work unit have in common and place near the top of their hierarchy of values.[8]

surveying employees. Only by observing employees, analyzing their decisions, and debriefing them on their actions would these assumptions rise to the surface.

Organizational culture has gained such reverence that leaders frequently identify and publicly state their organization's shared values. Online retailer Zappos lists ten core values, such as "Deliver WOW through Service," "Embrace and Drive Change," and "Create Fun and a Little Weirdness." Facebook's culture is described through three core values: focus on impact, be bold, and move fast (and break things). "We want people to take risks and be bold and really strive to make a huge impact, because that is what the company is trying to do" explains a Facebook employee in Austin, Texas.[10]

Do these values really represent the cultural content of Zappos and Facebook? Very probably in the case of these two organizations because their cultures are well known and deeply entrenched. However, the values statements of many organizations do not necessarily reflect the values that are widely shared and practiced in the organization. This difference occurs because corporate leaders typically describe *espoused values*—the values they want others to believe guide the organization's decisions and actions.[11] Espoused values are usually socially desirable, so they present a positive public image. Even if top management acts consistently with the espoused values, lower-level employees might not do so. Employees bring diverse personal values to the organization, some of which might conflict with the organization's espoused values.

Organizational culture is not represented by espoused values. Instead, it consists of shared *enacted values*—the values most leaders and employees truly rely on to guide their decisions and

> ## "The thing I have learned at IBM is that culture is everything.[9]
> ### —Louis V. Gerstner, Jr.

Organizational culture also consists of *shared assumptions*—a deeper element that some experts believe is the essence of corporate culture. Shared assumptions are nonconscious, taken-for-granted perceptions or ideal prototypes of behavior that are considered the correct way to think and act toward problems and opportunities. Shared assumptions are so deeply ingrained that you probably wouldn't discover them by

behavior. These "values-in-use" are apparent by watching executives and other employees in action, including their decisions, where they focus their attention and resources, and how they behave toward stakeholders. For example, BP's stated (espoused) value of responsibility seems to be wildly at odds with the decisions, priorities, and behavior of its leaders and many employees.

BP's Espoused Values Belie Its Enacted Values

BP describes one of its four core values as aiming "for no accidents, no harm to people and no damage to the environment," yet the British energy company's track record on safety and environmentalism indicates this value is espoused rather than enacted. BP and its partners were at the center of the Gulf of Mexico oil spill disaster. A few years earlier, a U.S. government agency concluded that a deadly explosion at BP's Texas City oil refinery was due to a lack of "safety culture leadership." The Norwegian government came to a similar conclusion in its investigation of a fatality on a BP oil platform.[12]

Content of Organizational Culture

Organizations differ in their cultural content, that is, the relative ordering of shared values. How many corporate cultures are there? Several models and measures classify organizational culture into a handful of easy-to-remember categories. One of these, shown in Exhibit 13.2, identifies seven corporate cultures. Another popular model identifies four organizational cultures organized in a two-by-two table representing internal versus external focus and flexibility versus control. Other models organize cultures around a circle with 8 or 12 categories. These circumplex models suggest that some cultures are opposite to others, such as an avoidance culture versus a self-actualization culture, or a power culture versus a collegial culture.[13]

Organizational culture models and surveys are popular with corporate leaders faced with the messy business of diagnosing their

> "Many organizational culture models and measures incorrectly assume that organizations have a fairly clear, unified culture that is easily decipherable."

▼ **EXHIBIT 13.2** Organizational Culture Profile Dimensions and Characteristics

Organizational Culture Dimension	Characteristics of the Dimension
Innovation	Experimenting, opportunity seeking, risk taking, few rules, low cautiousness.
Stability	Predictability, security, rule-oriented.
Respect for people	Fairness, tolerance.
Outcome orientation	Action-oriented, high expectations, results-oriented.
Attention to detail	Precise, analytic.
Team orientation	Collaboration, people-oriented.
Aggressiveness	Competitive, low emphasis on social responsibility.

Source: Based on information in C. A. O'Reilly III, J. Chatman, and D. F. Caldwell, "People and Organizational Culture: A Profile Comparison Approach to Assessing Person-Organization Fit," *Academy of Management Journal* 34, no. 3 (1991), 487–518.

company's culture and identifying what kind of culture they want to develop. Unfortunately, they oversimplify the diversity of cultural values in organizations. The fact is, there are dozens of individual values, and many more combinations of values, so the number of organizational cultures that these models describe likely falls considerably short of the full set. A second concern is that organizational culture includes shared assumptions, not just shared values. Most organizational culture measures ignore assumptions because they represent a more subterranean aspect of culture.

A third concern is that many organizational culture models and measures incorrectly assume that organizations have a fairly clear, unified, easily decipherable culture.[14] This "integration" perspective, as it is called, further assumes that when an organization's culture changes, it shifts from one unified condition to a new unified condition with only temporary ambiguity or weakness during the transition. These assumptions are probably incorrect or, at best, oversimplified. An organization's culture is usually quite blurry, so much so that it cannot be estimated through employee surveys alone. As we discuss next, organizations consist of diverse subcultures because employees across the organization have different clusters of experiences and backgrounds that have shaped their values and priorities.

Even these subcultural clusters can be ill-defined because values and assumptions

ultimately vary from one employee to the next. As long as employees differ, an organization's culture will have noticeable variability. Thus, many of the popular organizational culture models and measures oversimplify the variety of organizational cultures and falsely presume that organizations can easily be identified within these categories.

Organizational Subcultures

When discussing organizational culture, we are really referring to the *dominant culture*, that is, the values and assumptions the organization's members share most consistently and widely. The dominant culture is usually supported by senior management, but cultures can also persist in spite of senior management's desire for another culture. Furthermore, organizations are composed of *subcultures* located throughout their various divisions, geographic regions, and occupational groups.[15] Some subcultures enhance the dominant culture by espousing parallel assumptions and values. Others differ from, but do not conflict with, the dominant culture. Still others are called *countercultures* because they embrace values or assumptions that directly oppose the organization's dominant culture. It is also possible that some organizations (including some

> "Subcultures maintain the organization's standards of performance and ethical behavior and are the spawning grounds for emerging values that keep the firm aligned with its environment."

universities, according to one study) consist of subcultures with no decipherable dominant culture at all.[16]

Subcultures, particularly countercultures, potentially create conflict and dissension among employees, but they also serve two important functions.[17] First, they maintain the organization's standards of performance and ethical behavior. Employees who hold countercultural values are an important source of surveillance and critical review of the dominant order. They encourage constructive conflict and more creative thinking about how the organization should interact with its environment. Subcultures potentially support ethical conduct by preventing employees from blindly following one set of values. Subculture members continually question the majority's "obvious" decisions and actions, thereby making everyone more mindful of the consequences of their actions.

The second function of subcultures is that they are the spawning grounds for emerging values that keep the firm aligned with the evolving needs and expectations of customers, suppliers, communities, and other stakeholders. Companies eventually need to replace their dominant values with ones that are more appropriate for the changing environment. If subcultures are suppressed, the organization may take longer to discover and adopt values aligned with the emerging environment.

After reading this section, you should be able to

LO2 List four categories of artifacts through which corporate culture is deciphered.

DECIPHERING ORGANIZATIONAL CULTURE THROUGH ARTIFACTS

Shared values and assumptions are not easily measured through surveys and might not be accurately reflected in the organization's values statements. Instead, as Exhibit 13.1 illustrated earlier, an organization's culture needs to be deciphered through a thorough investigation of artifacts. **Artifacts** are the observable symbols and signs of an organization's culture, such as the way visitors are greeted, the organization's physical layout, and how employees are rewarded.[18] A few experts suggest that artifacts are the essence of organizational culture, whereas most others (including the authors of this book) view artifacts as symbols or indicators of culture. In other words, culture is cognitive (values and assumptions inside people's heads), whereas artifacts are observable manifestations of that culture. Either way, artifacts are important because they represent and reinforce an organization's culture.

Artifacts provide valuable evidence about a company's culture.[19] An organization's ambiguous (fragmented) culture is best understood by observing workplace behavior, listening to everyday conversations among staff and with customers, studying written documents and emails, viewing physical structures and settings, and interviewing staff about corporate stories. In other words, to truly understand an organization's culture, we need to sample information from a variety of organizational artifacts.

The Mayo Clinic conducted such an assessment a few years ago. An anthropologist was hired to decipher the medical organization's culture at its headquarters in Minnesota and to identify ways of transferring that culture to its two newer sites in Florida and Arizona. For six weeks, the anthropologist shadowed employees, posed as a patient in waiting rooms, did countless interviews, and accompanied physicians on patient visits. The final report outlined Mayo's dominant culture and how its satellite operations varied from that culture.[20]

> " The language of the workplace speaks volumes about the company's culture. "

In this section, we review the four broad categories of artifacts: organizational stories and legends, rituals and ceremonies, language, and physical structures and symbols.

Organizational Stories and Legends

Stories and legends about the company's founders and past events permeate strong organizational cultures. Some tales recount heroic deeds, whereas others ridicule past events that deviate from the firm's core values. Organizational stories and legends serve as powerful social prescriptions of the way things should (or should not) be done. They add human realism to corporate expectations, individual performance standards, and the criteria for getting fired.

Stories also produce emotions in listeners, and these emotions tend to improve listeners' memory of the lesson within the story.[21] Stories have the greatest effect on communicating corporate culture when they describe real people, are assumed to be true, and are known by employees throughout the organization. Stories are also prescriptive—they advise people what to do or not to do.[22]

Rituals and Ceremonies

Rituals are the programmed routines of daily organizational life that dramatize an organization's culture.[23] They include how visitors are greeted, how often senior executives visit subordinates, how people communicate with each other, how much time employees take for lunch, and so on. These rituals are repetitive, predictable, events that have

Cultural Artifact: Ogilvy's Giants

David Ogilvy is a legend in the advertising industry, but equally significant are the stories about him that have continued to reinforce the values he instilled. One story recounts how Ogilvy's board of directors arrived at a meeting to discover a Russian matryoshka doll at each of their seats. The directors opened each doll, one nested inside the other, until they discovered this message inside the tiniest doll: "If you hire people who are smaller than you are, we shall become a company of dwarfs. If you hire people who are bigger than you are, we shall become a company of giants." The Russian dolls became part of Ogilvy's culture, which demands hiring talent, not subservience.[24]

Zappos' Culture Revealed in Artifacts

Zappos is renowned for its "Wow" service. The online shoe and apparel company's customer-focused culture is equally apparent (along with a bit of weirdness) through artifacts at its headquarters in Nevada. Visitors are literally cheered by staff as they walk by. Employees seem to be perpetually upbeat when chatting with each other and customers. Probably the most unusual artifact at Zappos is a ceremony in which guests have their picture taken while seated on a royal throne wearing a regal crown.[25]

symbolic meaning of underlying cultural values and assumptions. For instance, BMW's fast-paced culture is quite literally apparent in the way employees walk around the German auto-maker's offices. "When you move through the corridors and hallways of other companies' buildings, people kind of crawl, they walk slowly," observes a BMW executive. "But BMW people tend to move faster."[26] **Ceremonies** are more formal artifacts than rituals. Ceremonies are planned activities conducted specifically for the benefit of an audience. This would include publicly rewarding (or punishing) employees or celebrating the launch of a new product or a newly won contract.

Organizational Language

The language of the workplace speaks volumes about the company's culture. How employees talk to each other, describe customers, express anger, and greet stakeholders are all verbal symbols of cultural values. The language of culture is apparent at The Container Store, where employees compliment each other about "being Gumby," meaning they are being as flexible as the once-popular green toy to help a customer or another employee.[27] Language also highlights values held by organizational subcultures. Consultants working at Whirlpool kept hearing employees talk about the appliance company's "Power-Point culture." This phrase, which names Microsoft's presentation software, implied that Whirlpool has a hierarchical culture in which communication is one-way (from executives to employees).[28]

Physical Structures and Symbols

Buildings both reflect and influence an organization's culture. The size, shape, location, and age of buildings might suggest a company's emphasis on teamwork, environmental friendliness, hierarchy, or any other set of values.[29] An extreme example is the "interplanetary headquarters" of Oakley, Inc. The ultra-hip eyewear and clothing company built a vault-like structure in Foothills Ranch, California, complete with towering metallic walls studded with oversize bolts, to represent its secretive and protective culture. "We've always had a fortress mentality," says an Oakley executive. "What we make is gold, and people will do anything to get it, so we protect it."[30]

Even if the building doesn't make much of a statement, there is a treasure trove of physical artifacts inside. Desks, chairs, office space, and wall hangings (or lack of them) are just a few of the

[**We shape our buildings; thereafter, they shape us.**[31]

—Winston Churchill]

> **CULTURE IS ONE OF THE MOST PRECIOUS THINGS A COMPANY HAS, SO YOU MUST WORK HARDER ON IT THAN ANYTHING ELSE.[37]**
>
> **HERB KELLEHER, COFOUNDER AND FORMER CEO OF SOUTHWEST AIRLINES**

items that might convey cultural meaning.[32] Each of these physical artifacts alone might not say much, but put enough of them together and you can see how they symbolize aspects of the company's culture.[33] For example, all of Facebook's offices have a similar open-space layout where employees work at wooden desks without any partitions. Many of these offices also have an unfinished look, reflecting the image of a start-up business with plenty of room to grow.

Learning Objective

After reading this section, you should be able to

LO3 Discuss the importance of organizational culture and the conditions under which organizational culture strength improves organizational performance.

IS ORGANIZATIONAL CULTURE IMPORTANT?

Does organizational culture improve organizational effectiveness? Leaders at Lee Kum Kee Health Products Company, Ltd., a subsidiary of Hong Kong-based food products company Lee Kum Kee, think so. "Two words explain why we are a Best Employer: corporate culture," says a Lee Kum Kee executive. "Our unique culture is our competitive edge. It plays a major role in the success of our organization."[34] Many writers of popular-press management books also assert that the most successful companies have strong cultures. In fact, one popular management book, *Built to Last*, suggests that successful companies are "cultlike" (although not actually cults, the authors are careful to point out.)[35]

So, are companies more effective when they have a strong culture? Possibly, but research evidence indicates that it depends on a few conditions.[36] Before discussing these contingencies, let's examine the meaning of a "strong" organizational culture and its potential benefits. The strength of an organization's culture refers to how widely and deeply employees hold the company's dominant values and assumptions. In a strong organizational culture, most employees across all subunits understand and embrace the dominant values. These values and assumptions are also institutionalized through well-established artifacts, which further entrench the culture. In addition, strong cultures tend to be long-lasting; some can be traced back to the values and assumptions established by the company's founder. In contrast, companies have weak cultures when the dominant values are held mainly by a few people at

the top of the organization, are barely discernible from artifacts, and are in flux.

As mentioned, companies with stronger cultures are potentially more effective, and this occurs through the three important functions listed in Exhibit 13.3 and described below:

1. *Control system.* Organizational culture is a deeply embedded form of social control that influences employee decisions and behavior.[38] Culture is pervasive and operates nonconsciously. You might think of it as an automatic pilot, directing employees in ways that are consistent with organizational expectations.

2. *Social glue.* Organizational culture is the "social glue" that bonds people together and makes them feel part of the organizational experience.[39] Employees are motivated to internalize the organization's dominant culture because it fulfills their need for social identity. This social glue is increasingly important as a way to attract new staff and retain top performers. It also becomes the common thread that holds together employees in global organizations. "The values of the company are really the bedrock—the glue which holds the firm together," says Nandan Nilekani, the head of the government of India's technology committee and former CEO of Infosys.[40]

3. *Sense making.* Organizational culture helps employees to make sense of what goes on and why things happen in the company.[41] Corporate culture also makes it easier for them to understand what is expected of them. For instance, research has found that sales staff in companies with stronger organizational cultures have clearer role perceptions and less role-related stress.[42]

Contingencies of Organizational Culture and Effectiveness

Studies have found only a modestly positive relationship between culture strength and organizational effectiveness. Why is there such a weak link? The answer is that strong cultures improve organizational effectiveness only under specific conditions (see Exhibit 13.3). Three important contingencies are: (1) whether the culture content is aligned with the environment, (2) whether the culture is moderately strong, not cultlike, and (3) whether the culture incorporates an adaptive culture.

Align Culture Content with Environment One contingency between cultural strength and organizational effectiveness is whether the organization's culture content—its dominant values and assumptions—is aligned with the external environment. Consider the challenges that Dell, Inc., faced a few years ago. The computer manufacturer's culture gave the highest priority to cost efficiency and competitiveness, yet these values and assumptions are no longer sufficient for the marketplace. Low-cost computers are still popular, but consumers increasingly demand computers that are innovative with elegant styling. Dell had a strong culture, but it was no longer the best culture for the external environment. "Dell's culture is not inspirational or aspirational," suggests one industry expert. "[Its] culture only wants to talk about execution."[43]

Avoid a Corporate Cult A second contingency is the degree of culture strength. Various experts suggest that

▼**EXHIBIT 13.3** Potential Benefits and Contingencies of Culture Strength

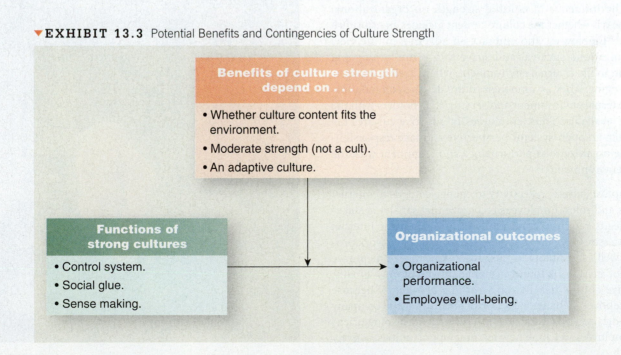

> ## "You have to create a culture that not only accepts change but seeks out how to change.[46]
>
> —Dan Akerson, General Motors CEO

companies with very strong cultures (i.e., corporate "cults") may be less effective than companies with moderately strong cultures.[44] Corporate cults may undermine organizational effectiveness because they tend to lock people into mental models, which can blind them to new opportunities and unique problems. The effect of these very strong cultures is that people overlook or incorrectly define subtle misalignments between the organization's activities and the changing environment.

Another problem with very strong cultures is that they suppress dissenting subcultural values. The challenge for organizational leaders is to maintain not only a strong culture but one that allows subcultural diversity. Subcultures encourage constructive conflict, which improves creative thinking and offers some level of ethical vigilance over the dominant culture. In the long run, a subculture's nascent values could become important dominant values as the environment changes. Corporate cults suppress subcultures, thereby undermining these benefits.

Create an Adaptive Culture A third contingency determining the influence of cultural strength on organizational effectiveness is whether the culture content includes an **adaptive culture**.[45] Employees who embrace an adaptive culture view the organization's survival and success in terms of ongoing adaptation to the external environment, which itself is continuously changing. They assume their future depends on monitoring the external environment and serving stakeholders with the resources available. Thus, employees in adaptive cultures see things from an open-systems perspective and take responsibility for the organization's performance and alignment with the external environment.

In an adaptive culture, receptivity to change extends to internal processes and roles. Employees recognize that satisfying stakeholder needs requires continuous improvement of internal work processes. They also support changing internal work processes as well as flexibility in their own work roles. The phrase "That's not my job" is found in nonadaptive cultures. Finally, an adaptive culture has a strong *learning orientation* because being receptive to change necessarily means that the company also supports action-oriented discovery. With a learning orientation, employees welcome new learning opportunities, actively experiment with new ideas and practices, view reasonable mistakes as a natural part of the learning process, and continuously question past practices.[47]

Organizational Culture and Business Ethics

An organization's culture influences its employees' ethical conduct. This makes sense because ethical values drive good behavior, and ethical values become embedded in an organization's dominant culture. Two apparent examples are

Nomura Securities in Japan and Barclays bank in the United Kingdom. As we briefly noted at the beginning of this chapter, sources suggest that Nomura's culture has reinforced insider trading over the past decade, and that a "culture of fear" discouraged Barclays employees from reporting the interest rate fixing that allegedly involved Barclays and other British banks over several years.

Another example may be Goldman Sachs, which one former executive recently described as having a corporate culture that rewards staff for deceiving clients and "making the most possible money off of them." Various artifacts depict this culture, such as the words to describe clients ("muppets") and to sell investments with the highest profit margin ("hunt elephants") rather than best value for their clients. Goldman Sachs' CEO replied that the former manager's statements "do not reflect our values, our culture." However, others point to numerous lawsuits against the investment firm in recent years, particularly charges that it engaged in conflicts of interest, failed to disclose vital information in the client's best interest, and actually bet against the investments it sold to clients.[48] The point here is that culture and ethics go hand-in-hand. To create a more ethical organization, leaders need to work on the embedded culture that steers employee behavior.

Mergers and acquisitions fail partly because corporate leaders are so focused on financial or marketing logistics of the merging organizations that they fail to conduct due-diligence audits on their respective corporate cultures.[50] Some forms of integration may allow successful mergers between companies with different cultures. However, research concludes that mergers typically suffer when organizations with significantly divergent corporate cultures merge into a single entity with a high degree of integration.[51]

For instance, a corporate culture clash occurred when Bank of America (BofA) hastily acquired Merrill Lynch during the great financial crisis. BofA's culture embraces cost efficiencies and penny pinching, whereas Merrill Lynch had more of an "entitlement" culture that encouraged big spending and bigger bonuses. BofA's culture is also more cautious and bureaucratic, requiring more signatures and higher-level authority, whereas Merrill Lynch's "thundering herd" culture was more aggressive, entrepreneurial and, some say, more likely to venture into ethically questionable territory.[52]

Bicultural Audit

Organizational leaders can minimize these cultural collisions and fulfill their duty of due diligence by conducting a bicultural

> **adaptive culture**
> An organizational culture in which employees are receptive to change, including the ongoing alignment of the organization to its environment and continuous improvement of internal processes.

Learning Objective

After reading this section, you should be able to

LO4 Compare and contrast four strategies for merging organizational cultures.

MERGING ORGANIZATIONAL CULTURES

4C Corporate Culture Clash and Chemistry is a company with an unusual name and mandate. The Dutch consulting firm helps clients to determine whether their culture is aligned ("chemistry") or incompatible with ("clash") a potential acquisition or merger partner. The firm also compares the company's culture with its strategy. There should be plenty of demand for 4C's expertise. One study estimated that only half of corporate acquisitions add value, whereas two other studies report that only 30 percent of acquisitions produce financial gains.[49] Meanwhile, mergers have a substantial disruptive effect on the organizations involved, often leading to neglected strategy, employee stress, and customer problems.

Losing Value and Talent with Mergers and Acquisitions[53]

85% of executives of failed mergers identify organizational culture differences as the major cause of the failure.

71% of acquisitions (on average across three major studies) destroyed rather than enhanced shareholder value.

75% of executives interviewed believed their acquisition was successful.

40% of executives in acquired firms left within two years after the acquisition (twice the usual executive turnover rate).

audit.[54] A **bicultural audit** diagnoses cultural relations between the companies and determines the extent to which cultural clashes will likely occur. The bicultural audit process begins by identifying cultural differences between the merging companies. Next, the bicultural audit data are analyzed to determine which differences between the two firms will result in conflict and which cultural values provide common ground on which to build a cultural foundation in the merged organization. The final stage involves identifying strategies and preparing action plans to bridge the two organizations' cultures.

Strategies for Merging Different Organizational Cultures

In some cases, the bicultural audit results in a decision to end merger talks because the two cultures are too different to merge effectively. However, even with substantially different cultures, two companies may form a workable union if they apply the appropriate merger strategy. The four main strategies for merging different corporate cultures are assimilation, deculturation, integration, and separation (see Exhibit 13.4).[55]

Assimilation Assimilation occurs when employees at the acquired company willingly embrace the cultural values of the acquiring organization. Typically, this strategy works best when the acquired company has a weak, dysfunctional culture and the acquiring company's culture is strong and aligned with the external environment. This assimilation strategy seems to be effective in Southwest Airlines' recent acquisition of AirTran. The two airlines have fairly similar cultures, but assimilation occurred mainly because the "Southwest Way" culture is widely respected. "It's helpful that Southwest has a great cultural reputation," says a Southwest executive about the AirTran acquisition.[56]

Deculturation Assimilation is rare. Employees usually resist organizational change, particularly when they are asked to throw away personal and cultural values. Under these conditions, some acquiring companies apply a *deculturation* strategy by imposing their culture and business practices on the acquired organization. The acquiring firm strips away artifacts and reward systems that support the old culture. People who cannot adopt the acquiring company's culture often lose their jobs. Deculturation may be necessary when the acquired firm's culture doesn't work, even when employees in the acquired company aren't convinced of this. However, this strategy is difficult to apply effectively because the acquired firm's employees resist the cultural intrusions from the buying firm, thereby delaying or undermining the merger process.

Integration A third strategy is to combine the two or more cultures into a new composite culture that preserves the best

▼ **EXHIBIT 13.4** Strategies for Merging Different Organizational Cultures

Merger Strategy	Description	Works Best When . . .
Assimilation	Acquired company embraces acquiring firm's culture.	Acquired firm has a weak culture.
Deculturation	Acquiring firm imposes its culture on unwilling acquired firm.	Rarely works—may be necessary only when acquired firm's culture doesn't work but employees don't realize it.
Integration	Merging companies combine the two or more cultures into a new composite culture.	Existing cultures can be improved.
Separation	Merging companies remain distinct entities with minimal exchange of culture or organizational practices.	Firms operate successfully in different businesses requiring different cultures.

Sources: Based on ideas in A. R. Malekzedeh and A. Nahavandi, "Making Mergers Work by Managing Cultures," *Journal of Business Strategy*, 11 (May/June 1990), 55–57; K. W. Smith, "A Brand-New Culture for the Merged Firm," *Mergers and Acquisitions*, 35 (June 2000), 45–50.

features of the previous cultures. Integration is slow and potentially risky because there are many forces preserving the existing cultures. Still, this strategy should be considered when the companies have relatively weak cultures or when their cultures include several overlapping values. Integration also works best when people realize their existing cultures are ineffective, which tends to increase their motivation to adopt a new set of dominant values.

Separation A separation strategy occurs when the merging companies agree to remain distinct entities with minimal exchange of culture or organizational practices. This strategy is most appropriate when the two merging companies are in unrelated industries or operate in different countries, because the most appropriate cultural values tend to differ by industry and corporate leaders. A few experts argue that an organization's culture "cannot be managed," so attempting to change the company's values and assumptions is a waste of time.[59] This may be an extreme view, but organizational culture experts generally agree that changing an organization's culture is a monumental challenge. At the same time, it is sometimes necessary to change one or more shared values and assumptions because the alignment of that culture with the external environment can influence the organization's survival and success. Over the next few pages, we will highlight four strategies that have had some success at altering corporate cultures. These strategies, illustrated in Exhibit 13.5, are not exhaustive, but each seems to work well under the right circumstances.

> # Unconsciously or consciously, senior people leave their marks on an organization's culture and legacy.[60]
> ## —Max de Pree, business author and former Herman Miller CEO

national culture. This strategy is also relevant advice for the corporate cultures of diversified conglomerates.

For example, Amazon has applied a separation strategy in its acquisition of Zappos. "The Amazon deal got us the best of all worlds," explains Zappos CEO Tony Hsieh. "We can continue to run independently and grow the Zappos brand and culture."[57] Amazon's cultural separation approach is rare, however. Executives in acquiring firms usually have difficulty keeping their hands off the acquired firm. According to one estimate, only 15 percent of mergers leave the acquired company as a stand-alone unit.[58]

Learning Objective

After reading this section, you should be able to

LO5 Identify four strategies for changing or strengthening an organization's culture, including the application of attraction-selection-attrition theory.

CHANGING AND STRENGTHENING ORGANIZATIONAL CULTURE

Is it possible to change an organization's culture? Yes, but doing so isn't easy, the change rarely occurs quickly, and often the culture ends up changing (or replacing)

Actions of Founders and Leaders

Leaders form their organization's culture during its early stages and introduce ways to make that culture "stick."[61]

▼ **EXHIBIT 13.5** Strategies for Changing and Strengthening Organizational Culture

Leaders Communicate and
Enact the Organization's Culture[62]

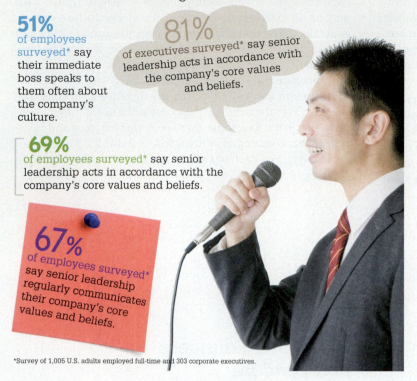

51%
of employees surveyed* say their immediate boss speaks to them often about the company's culture.

81%
of executives surveyed* say senior leadership acts in accordance with the company's core values and beliefs.

69%
of employees surveyed* say senior leadership acts in accordance with the company's core values and beliefs.

67%
of employees surveyed* say senior leadership regularly communicates their company's core values and beliefs.

*Survey of 1,005 U.S. adults employed full-time and 303 corporate executives.

Founders are often visionaries who provide a powerful role model for others to follow. The company's culture sometimes reflects the founder's personality, and this cultural imprint can remain with the organization for decades. The founder's activities are later retold as organizational stories to further reinforce the culture. In spite of the founder's cultural imprint, subsequent leaders are sometimes able to reshape that culture by applying transformational leadership and organizational change practices.[63]

Aligning Artifacts

Earlier in this chapter we pointed out that artifacts are the visible indicators of a company's culture. However, they are also mechanisms that keep the culture in place. By altering artifacts—or creating new ones—leaders can potentially adjust shared values and assumptions. Corporate cultures are also altered and strengthened through the artifacts of stories and behaviors. According to Max De Pree, former CEO of furniture manufacturer Herman Miller Inc., every organization needs "tribal storytellers" to keep the organization's history and culture alive.[64] Leaders play a role by creating memorable events that symbolize the cultural values they want to develop or maintain. Companies also strengthen culture in new operations by transferring current employees who abide by the culture.

Introducing Culturally Consistent Rewards

Reward systems are artifacts that often have a powerful effect on strengthening or reshaping an organization's culture.[65] Robert Nardelli used rewards to change Home Depot's freewheeling culture. Nardelli introduced precise measures of corporate performance and drilled managers with weekly performance objectives related to those metrics. A two-hour weekly conference call became a ritual in which Home Depot's top executives were held accountable for the previous week's goals. These actions reinforced a more disciplined (and centralized) performance-oriented culture.[66]

Attracting, Selecting, and Socializing Employees

Organizational culture is strengthened by attracting and hiring people who already embrace the cultural values. This process, along with weeding out people who don't fit the culture, is explained by **attraction–selection–attrition (ASA) theory**.[67] ASA theory states that organizations have a natural tendency to attract, select, and retain people with values and personality characteristics that are consistent with the organization's character, resulting in a more homogeneous organization and a stronger culture.

- *Attraction.* Job applicants engage in self-selection by avoiding employment in companies whose values seem incompatible with their own values.[68] They look for subtle artifacts during interviews and through public information that communicate the company's culture. Some organizations often encourage this self-selection by actively describing their cultures. At Reckitt Benckiser, for instance, applicants can complete an online simulation that estimates their fit with the British household products company's hard-driving culture. Participants indicate how they would respond to a series of business scenarios. The exercise then calculates their cultural fit score and asks them to decide whether to continue pursuing employment with the company.[69]

- *Selection.* Companies with strong cultures often put applicants through several interviews and other selection tests, in part to better gauge the applicant's values and their congruence with the company's values.[70] Consider Park Place Dealerships. As one of the top-rated luxury car dealerships in the United States, the Dallas–Fort Worth company relies on interviews and selection tests to carefully screen applicants for their culture fit. "Testing is one piece of our hiring process that enables us to find people who will not only be successful in our culture, but thrive and enjoy our culture," says Park Place chairman Ken Schnitzer. "It's not easy to get hired by Park Place."[71]

attraction–selection–attrition (ASA) theory A theory stating that organizations have a natural tendency to attract, select, and retain people with values and personality characteristics that are consistent with the organization's character, resulting in a more homogeneous organization and a stronger culture.

organizational socialization The process by which individuals learn the values, expected behaviors, and social knowledge necessary to assume their roles in the organization.

- *Attrition.* People are motivated to seek environments that are sufficiently congruent with their personal values and to leave environments that are a poor fit. This occurs because person-organization values congruence supports their social identity and minimizes internal role conflict. Even if employees aren't forced out, many quit when values incongruence is sufficiently high.[72]

Learning Objective

After reading this section, you should be able to

LO6 Describe the organizational socialization process and identify strategies to improve that process.

Organizational Culture
During the Hiring Process[73]

58% of 1,500 American job seekers want to know, during the hiring process, about the **company's culture.**

75% of 500 Canadian executives polled say **cultural fit** is more important than skills for selecting external candidates.

44% of Fortune 500 companies take steps to describe their **corporate culture** to job seekers.

51% of American managers surveyed say they use social media to see if a job candidate is a good fit for the company's culture.

23% of 91,000 employees surveyed across 30 countries identified corporate culture as the top consideration when deciding to apply for a job.

ORGANIZATIONAL SOCIALIZATION

Along with their use of attraction, selection, and attrition, organizations rely on organizational socialization to maintain a strong corporate culture. **Organizational socialization** is the process by which individuals learn the values, expected behaviors, and social knowledge necessary to assume their roles in the organization.[74] Organizations often try to use the socialization process to change employee values so they are more closely aligned with the company's culture. However, personal values change very little during adulthood. More likely, effective socialization gives newcomers clearer understanding about the company's values and how they are translated into specific on-the-job behaviors.[75]

Along with supporting the organization's culture, socialization helps newcomers adjust to coworkers, work procedures, and other corporate realities. Research indicates that when employees are effectively socialized into the organization, they tend to perform better, have higher job satisfaction, and remain longer with the organization.[76]

psychological contract The individual's beliefs about the terms and conditions of a reciprocal exchange agreement between that person and another party (the employer in most work situations).

reality shock The stress that results when employees perceive discrepancies between their preemployment expectations and on-the-job reality.

Organizational Socialization as a Learning and Adjustment Process

Organizational socialization is a process of both learning and adjustment. It is a learning process because newcomers try to make sense of the company's physical workplace, social dynamics, and strategic and cultural environment. They learn about the organization's performance expectations, power dynamics, corporate culture, company history, and jargon. They also need to form successful and satisfying relationships with other people from whom they can learn the ropes.[77] Thus, effective socialization enables new employees to form a cognitive map of the physical, social, and strategic and cultural dynamics of the organization without information overload.

Organizational socialization is also a process of adjustment because individuals need to adapt to their new work environment. They develop new work roles that reconfigure their social identity, adopt new team norms, and practice new behaviors.[78] Research reports that the adjustment process is fairly rapid for many people, usually occurring within a few months. However, newcomers with diverse work experience seem to adjust better than those with limited previous experience, possibly because they have a larger toolkit of knowledge and skills to make the adjustment possible.[79]

Organizational Socialization and Psychological Contracts

The learning process within organizational socialization is partly about developing a psychological contract. The **psychological contract** refers to the individual's beliefs about the terms and conditions of a reciprocal exchange agreement between that person and another party (the employer in most work situations). The psychological contract is a perception formed during recruitment and throughout the organizational socialization process about what the employee is entitled to receive and is obliged to offer the employer in return.[80]

Job applicants form perceptions of what the company will offer them by way of career and learning opportunities, job resources, pay and benefits, quality of management, job security, and so forth. They also form perceptions about what the company expects from them, such as hours of work, continuous

> "Organizational socialization is a process of both learning and adjustment."

skill development, and demonstrated loyalty. The psychological contract continues to develop and evolve after job applicants become employees, but they are also continuously testing the employer's fulfillment of that exchange relationship.

Types of Psychological Contracts Some psychological contracts are more transactional whereas others are more relational.[81] Transactional contracts are primarily short-term economic exchanges. Responsibilities are well defined around a fairly narrow set of obligations that do not change over the life of the contract. People hired in temporary positions and as consultants tend to have transactional contracts. To some extent, new employees also form transactional contracts until they develop a sense of continuity with the organization.

Relational contracts, on the other hand, are rather like marriages; they are long-term attachments that encompass a broad array of subjective mutual obligations. Employees with a relational psychological contract are more willing to contribute their time and effort without expecting the organization to pay back this debt in the short term. Relational contracts are also dynamic, meaning that the parties accept the idea that mutual obligations are not necessarily balanced in the short run. Not surprisingly, organizational citizenship behaviors are more likely to prevail under relational than transactional contracts. Permanent employees are more likely to believe they have a relational contract.

Stages of Organizational Socialization

Organizational socialization is a continuous process, beginning long before the first day of employment and continuing throughout one's career within the company. However, it is most intense when people move across organizational boundaries, such as when they first join a company or get transferred to an international assignment. Each of these transitions is a process that can be divided into three stages. Our focus here is on the socialization of new employees, so the three stages are called preemployment socialization, encounter, and role management (see Exhibit 13.6). These stages parallel the individual's transition from outsider to newcomer and then to insider.[82]

Stage 1: Preemployment Socialization Think back to the months and weeks before you began working in a new job (or attending a new school). You actively searched for information about the company, formed expectations about working there, and felt some anticipation about fitting into that environment. The preemployment socialization stage

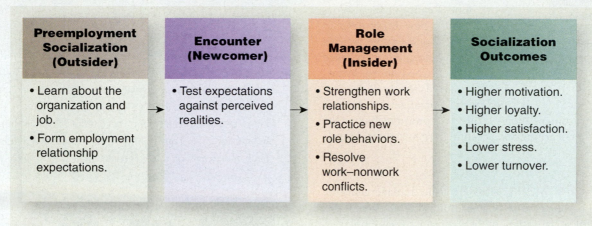

Preemployment Socialization (Outsider)	Encounter (Newcomer)	Role Management (Insider)	Socialization Outcomes
• Learn about the organization and job. • Form employment relationship expectations.	• Test expectations against perceived realities.	• Strengthen work relationships. • Practice new role behaviors. • Resolve work–nonwork conflicts.	• Higher motivation. • Higher loyalty. • Higher satisfaction. • Lower stress. • Lower turnover.

encompasses all the learning and adjustment that occurs before the first day of work. In fact, a large part of the socialization adjustment process occurs during this stage.[83]

The main problem with preemployment socialization is that outsiders rely on indirect information about what it is like to work in the organization. This information is often distorted by inherent conflicts during the mating dance between employer and applicant.[84] One conflict occurs between the employer's need to attract qualified applicants and the applicant's need for complete information to make accurate employment decisions. Many firms use a "flypaper" approach by describing only positive aspects of the job and company, causing applicants to accept job offers from incomplete or false expectations. Another

management when seeking employment, and this tends to motivate them to hide negative information, act out of character, and occasionally embellish information about their past accomplishments. At the same time, employers are sometimes reluctant to ask certain questions or use potentially valuable selection devices because they might scare off applicants. Unfortunately, exaggerated résumés from applicants and reluctance to ask for some information causes employers to form a less accurate opinion of the job candidate's potential as an employee.

Stage 2: Encounter The first day on the job typically marks the beginning of the encounter stage of organizational

> ## From the first day on the job, newcomers test how well their preemployment expectations fit reality. Many companies fail that test.

conflict that prevents accurate exchange of information occurs when applicants avoid asking important questions about the company because they want to convey a favorable image to their prospective employer. For instance, applicants usually don't like to ask about starting salaries and promotion opportunities because it makes them seem greedy or aggressive. Yet, unless the employer provides this information, applicants might fill in the missing information with false assumptions that produce an inaccurate psychological contract.

Two other types of conflict tend to distort preemployment information for employers. Applicants engage in impression

socialization. This is the stage in which newcomers test how well their preemployment expectations fit reality. Many companies fail that test, resulting in **reality shock**—the stress that results when employees perceive discrepancies between their preemployment expectations and on-the-job reality.[85] Reality shock doesn't necessarily occur on the first day; it might develop over several weeks or even months as newcomers form a better understanding of their new work environment.

Reality shock is common in many organizations.[86] Unmet expectations sometimes occur because the employer is unable to live up to its promises, such as failing to provide challenging

realistic job preview (RJP)
A method of improving organizational socialization in which job applicants are given a balance of positive and negative information about the job and work context.

projects or the resources to get the work done. Reality shock also occurs because new hires develop distorted work expectations through the information exchange conflicts described above. Whatever the cause, reality shock impedes the socialization process because the newcomer's energy is directed toward managing the stress rather than learning and accepting organizational knowledge and roles.[87]

Stage 3: Role Management

Role management, the third stage of organizational socialization, really begins during preemployment socialization, but it is most active as employees make the transition from newcomers to insiders. They strengthen relationships with coworkers and supervisors, practice new role behaviors, and adopt attitudes and values consistent with their new positions and the organization. Role management also involves resolving the conflicts between work and nonwork activities, including resolving discrepancies between their existing values and those emphasized by the organizational culture.

Improving the Socialization Process

One potentially effective way to improve the socialization process is through a **realistic job preview (RJP)**—a balance of positive and negative information about the job and work context.[88] Unfortunately, as mentioned earlier, many companies over-promise. They often exaggerate positive features of the job and neglect to mention the undesirable elements in the hope that the best applicants will get "stuck" on the organization.

In contrast, an RJP helps job applicants to decide for themselves whether their skills, needs, and values are compatible with the job and organization. RJPs scare away some applicants, but they also tend to reduce turnover and increase job performance.[89] This occurs because RJPs help applicants develop more accurate preemployment expectations, which, in turn, minimize reality shock. RJPs represent a type of vaccination by preparing employees for the more challenging and troublesome aspects of work life. There is also some evidence that RJPs increase organizational loyalty. A possible explanation for this is that companies providing candid information are easier to trust. They also show respect for the psychological contract and concern for employee welfare.[90]

Socialization Agents

Ask new employees what most helped them to adjust to their jobs and chances are they will mention helpful coworkers, bosses, or maybe even friends who

Landing Teams Embed Facebook's Corporate Culture

Facebook is rapidly expanding its operations around the world to keep up with its surging popularity. Yet as it opens offices in India (shown here) and elsewhere, the social network company is able to instill its unique corporate culture through "landing teams" of current employees. These teams carefully select applicants for their compatibility with Facebook's culture and coach newcomers on the Facebook way of life.[91]

work elsewhere in the organization. The fact is, socialization occurs mainly through these socialization agents.[92] Supervisors tend to provide technical information, performance feedback, and information about job duties. They also improve the socialization process by giving newcomers reasonably challenging first assignments, buffering them from excessive demands, and helping them form social ties with coworkers.

Coworkers are important socialization agents because they are easily accessible, can answer questions when problems arise, and serve as role models for appropriate behavior. New employees tend to receive this information and support when coworkers integrate them into the work team. Coworkers also aid the socialization process by being flexible and tolerant in their interactions with new hires.

Several companies organize a "buddy system," whereby newcomers are assigned to coworkers for sources of information and social support. Meridian Technology Center in Stillwater, Oklahoma, relies on a buddy system in the socialization of new staff members. Buddies introduce new hires to other employees, give them campus tours, and generally familiarize them with the physical layout of the workplace. They have lunch with employees on their first day and meet weekly with them for their first two months. Cxtec, the networking and voice technology company in Syracuse, New York, helps new staff meet other employees through food. On the first Friday of each month, new staff members take charge of the doughnut cart, introducing themselves as they distribute the morning snack to the company's 350 employees.[93] Collectively, these practices help newcomers to form social networks, which are powerful means of gaining information and influence in the organization. ■

organizational
change

ouis Gerstner Jr. led the legendary turnaround of IBM in the 1990s, but Sam Palmisano may have orchestrated an equally breathtaking transformation of the company over the past decade. Soon after taking over from Gerstner as CEO, Palmisano (who is now IBM's chairman) frankly warned staff that although IBM was good, it still wasn't an industry-leading business. He described four questions—about whether the business satisfied customers, employees, society, and stockholders—whose answers would transform IBM beyond expectations. "The hardest thing is answering those four questions," says Palmisano. "You've got to answer all four and work at answering all four to really execute with excellence."

The change process didn't come easily. In particular, the master stroke decision to sell IBM's PC business met with strong internal opposition and more

continued on p. 272

LEARNING OBJECTIVES

After studying Chapter 14, you should be able to:

L01 Describe the elements of Lewin's force field analysis model.

L02 Discuss the reasons why people resist organizational change and how change agents should view this resistance.

L03 Outline six strategies for minimizing resistance to change and debate ways to effectively create an urgency to change.

L04 Discuss how leadership, coalitions, social networks, and pilot projects influence organizational change.

L05 Describe and compare action research and appreciative inquiry as formal approaches to organizational change.

L06 Discuss two cross-cultural and three ethical issues in organizational change.

force field analysis Kurt Lewin's model of systemwide change that helps change agents diagnose the forces that drive and restrain proposed organizational change.

unfreezing The first part of the change process in which the change agent produces disequilibrium between the driving and restraining forces.

refreezing The latter part of the change process in which systems and conditions are introduced that reinforce and maintain the desired behaviors.

continued from p. 271

subtle forms of resistance. Palmisano eased these concerns by explaining how the PC business failed to deliver on the four questions. He also regularly cited the founding principle of Thomas J. Watson Jr. (IBM's second CEO) that IBM's ultimate purpose is to help solve society's challenges. "It's old-fashioned, but it's motivational," says Palmisano. This message and the four questions drove the change process, catapulting IBM to the top of the league once again.[1]

IBM's continuous transformation and reinvention illustrate many of the strategies and practices necessary to successfully change organizations. They reveal how leaders create an urgency for change, revise systems and structures to support the change, and continuously communicate the change process. Although IBM's ongoing change process sounds simple on paper, it has been complex in reality, requiring considerable leadership effort and vigilance. As we will describe throughout this chapter, the challenge of change is not just in deciding which way to go; the challenge is in the execution of this strategy. When leaders

discover the need for change and identify some ideas about the preferred route to a better future, the change process involves navigating around the numerous obstacles and gaining organization-wide support for that change.

This chapter unfolds as follows. We begin by introducing Lewin's model of change and its component parts. This discussion includes sources of resistance to change, ways to minimize this resistance, and ways to stabilize desired behaviors. Next, the chapter examines two approaches to organizational change—action research and appreciative inquiry. The last section of this chapter considers both cross-cultural and ethical issues in organizational change. ∎

Learning Objective

After reading this section, you should be able to

LO1 Describe the elements of Lewin's force field analysis model.

LEWIN'S FORCE FIELD ANALYSIS MODEL

"The velocity of change is so rapid, so quick, that if you don't accept the change and move with the change, you're going to be left behind."[2] This statement by BHP Billiton Chairman (and

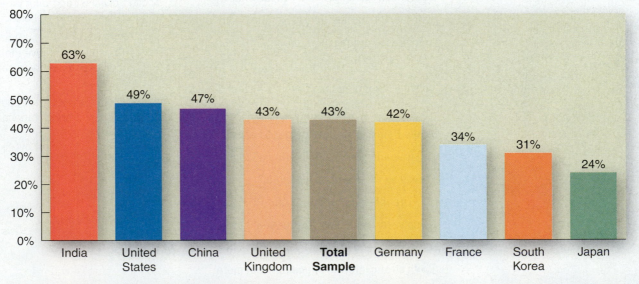

How Effectively Do Organizations around the World Handle Change?[3]

Country	Percentage
India	63%
United States	49%
China	47%
United Kingdom	43%
Total Sample	43%
Germany	42%
France	34%
South Korea	31%
Japan	24%

Percentage of employees, by selected countries, who agree or strongly agree that "change is handled effectively in my organization." Not all 28,810 employees across the 15 countries surveyed are shown here, but all are included in the "total sample" figure.

> ## I'VE ALWAYS BELIEVED THAT WHEN THE RATE OF CHANGE INSIDE AN INSTITUTION BECOMES SLOWER THAN THE RATE OF CHANGE OUTSIDE, THE END IS IN SIGHT.[4]
> —JACK WELCH, FORMER GENERAL ELECTRIC CEO

former Ford CEO) Jacques Nasser reflects the idea that organizations are open systems that survive and thrive by maintaining a good "fit" with their external environments. Successful organizations monitor consumer needs, global competition, technology, community expectations, and so forth, and they are continuously changing their internal structures, skills, and practices as these external conditions evolve. Rather than resist change, employees in successful companies embrace change as an integral part of organizational life.

It is easy to see that environmental forces push companies to change the way they operate. What is more difficult to see is the complex interplay of these forces on the internal dynamics of organizations. Social psychologist Kurt Lewin developed the force field analysis model to describe this process using the metaphor of a force field (see Exhibit 14.1).[5] Although it was developed more than 50 years ago, recent reviews affirm that Lewin's **force field analysis** model remains one of the most widely respected ways of viewing the change process.[6]

One side of the force field model represents the *driving forces* that push organizations toward a new state of affairs. These might include new competitors or technologies, evolving workforce expectations, or a host of other environmental changes. Corporate leaders also produce driving forces even when external forces for change aren't apparent. For instance, some experts call for "divine discontent" as a key feature of successful organizations, meaning that leaders continually urge employees to strive for higher standards or better practices even when the company outshines the competition. "We have a habit of divine discontent with our performance," says creative agency Ogilvy & Mather about its corporate culture. "It is an antidote to smugness."[7]

The other side of Lewin's model represents the *restraining forces* that maintain the status quo. These restraining forces are commonly called "resistance to change" because they appear to block the change process. Stability occurs when the driving and restraining forces are roughly in equilibrium—that is, they are of approximately equal strength in opposite directions.

Lewin's force field model emphasizes that effective change occurs by **unfreezing** the current situation, moving to a desired condition, and then **refreezing** the system so it remains in the desired state. Unfreezing involves producing disequilibrium between the driving and restraining forces. As we will describe later, this may occur by increasing the driving forces, reducing the restraining forces, or having a combination of both. Refreezing occurs when the organization's systems and structures are aligned with the desired behaviors. They must support and reinforce the new role patterns and prevent the organization from slipping back into the old way of doing things. Over the next few pages, we use Lewin's model to understand why change is blocked and how the process can evolve more smoothly.

▼ **EXHIBIT 14.1** Lewin's Force Field Analysis Model

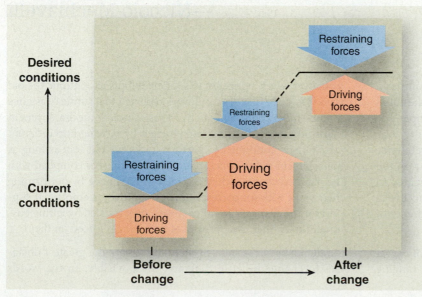

Learning Objective

After reading this section, you should be able to

LO2 Discuss the reasons why people resist organizational change and how change agents should view this resistance.

UNDERSTANDING RESISTANCE TO CHANGE

Robert Nardelli pushed hard to transform Home Depot from a loose configuration of fiefdoms to a more performance-oriented operation that delivered a consistent customer experience. Change did occur at the world's largest home improvement retailer, but at a price. A large

number of talented managers and employees left the company, and some of those who stayed continued to resent Nardelli's transformation. Disenchanted staff referred to the company as "Home Despot" because the changes took away their autonomy. Others named it "Home GEpot," a disparaging reference to the many former GE executives that Nardelli hired into top positions. After five years, the Home Depot board decided to replace Nardelli, partly because he made some unsuccessful strategic decisions and partly because of the aftereffects of Nardelli's changes.[8]

Robert Nardelli experienced considerable *resistance to change* at Home Depot. Resistance to change takes many forms, ranging from overt work stoppages to subtle attempts to continue the old ways.[10] A study of bank employees reported that subtle resistance is much more common than overt resistance. Some employees in that study avoided the desired changes by moving into different jobs. Others continued to perform tasks the old way as long as management didn't notice. Even when employees complied with the planned changes, they engaged in resistance by performing their work without corresponding cognitive or emotional support for the change.[11] In other words, they resisted by letting customers know they disapproved of the changes forced on them.

Subtle forms of resistance potentially create the greatest obstacles to change because they are not as visible. In the words of one manager, "[Change efforts] never die because of direct confrontation. Direct confrontation you can work with because it is known. Rather, they die a death of a thousand cuts. People and issues you never confront drain the life out of important [initiatives] and result in solutions that simply do not have the performance impact that they should have."[12]

Employee Resistance as a Resource for Change

Change agents are understandably frustrated by passive or active resistance to change, but they need to realize that resistance is a common and natural human response. Even when people support change, they typically assume that it is others—not themselves—who need to change. The problem, however, isn't so much that resistance to change exists. The main problem is that change agents typically view resistance as an unreasonable,

to change. Resistance aids change agents in three ways. First, it is a signal—a warning system—that the change agent has not sufficiently addressed the underlying conditions that support effective organizational change.[14] In some situations, employees may be worried about the *consequences* of change, such as how the new conditions will take away their power and status. In other situations, employees show resistance because of concerns about the *process* of change itself, such as the effort required to break old habits and learn new skills.

Second, resistance is a form of constructive conflict that can potentially improve decision making, including identifying ways to improve the organization's practices. However, constructive conflict is typically accompanied by dysfunctional relationship conflict. This appears to be the case when change agents see resistance to change as an impediment rather than a resource. They describe the people who resist as the problem, whereas

> Faced with the choice between changing one's mind and proving that there is no need to do so, almost everyone gets busy on the proof.[15]
> —John Kenneth Galbraith

dysfunctional, and irrational response to a desirable initiative. They often form an "us versus them" perspective without considering that the causes of resistance may, in fact, be traced back to their own actions or inaction.[13]

The emerging view among change management experts is that resistance to change is a useful indicator rather than an impediment

their focus should be on understanding the reasons why these people resist. Thus, by viewing resistance as a form of constructive conflict, change agents may be able to improve the change strategy or change process.

Finally, resistance should be viewed in the context of justice and motivation. Resistance is a form of voice, so it potentially improves procedural justice (see Chapter 5). By redirecting initial forms of resistance into constructive conversations, change agents can increase employee perceptions and feelings of fairness. Furthermore, resistance is motivational; it potentially engages people to think about the change strategy and process. Change agents can harness that motivational force to ultimately strengthen commitment to the change initiative.

Why Employees Resist Change

Some people resist change because of their personality and values.[16] Aside from these dispositional factors, however, employees lack a readiness for change when they believe the change will fail, is the wrong action for the situation, or will be costly to them personally.[17] This cost might be in the form of lost rewards and status, or it might represent negative consequences if they attempt to support the change. Another reason for resistance is the person's inability (or perceived inability) to change due to inadequate skills and knowledge. A third reason is that employees lack role clarity about the change. This lack of role clarity occurs when people misunderstand or magnify what is expected of them in the future. These three factors—motivation, ability, and role (mis)perceptions—are the foundations of the six most

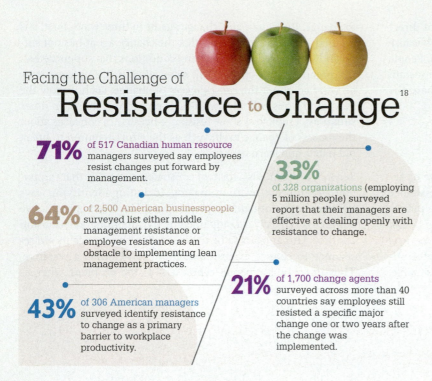

Facing the Challenge of
Resistance to Change[18]

71% of 517 Canadian human resource managers surveyed say employees resist changes put forward by management.

64% of 2,500 American businesspeople surveyed list either middle management resistance or employee resistance as an obstacle to implementing lean management practices.

43% of 306 American managers surveyed identify resistance to change as a primary barrier to workplace productivity.

33% of 328 organizations (employing 5 million people) surveyed report that their managers are effective at dealing openly with resistance to change.

21% of 1,700 change agents surveyed across more than 40 countries say employees still resisted a specific major change one or two years after the change was implemented.

commonly cited reasons why people resist change, which are summarized here:[19]

Direct Costs Employees lack commitment to (or even compliance with) a change initiative when their personal cost–benefit analysis calculation is negative rather than positive. They might believe the benefits for them (and possibly for the organization) are trivial (i.e., some pain for little gain). They might anticipate benefits from the change but also believe they will be worse off overall.

Saving Face Employees sometimes oppose changes that did not originate from them. Due to this "not-invented-here" syndrome, staff members sometimes deliberately inflate problems with changes they did not initiate, just to "prove" those ideas were not superior to their own. This form of resistance is widespread, according to change experts. Says one consultant, "Unless they're scared enough to listen, they'll never forgive you for being right and for knowing something they don't."[20]

Fear of the Unknown All change includes some degree of uncertainty. This uncertainty puts employees at risk. Their knowledge and skills might become obsolete; their valued work space, perquisites, or even social relationships might be disrupted and removed. Thus, people resist change out of worry that they cannot adjust to the new work requirements or that the change will produce unknown costs. Overall, this uncertainty is usually considered less desirable than the relative certainty of the status quo.

Breaking Routines People typically resist initiatives that force them out of their comfort zones and require them to invest

time and energy in learning new role patterns. Indeed, most employees in one survey admitted they don't follow through with organizational changes because they "like to keep things the way they are" or the changes seem to be too complicated or time wasting.[21]

Incongruent Team Dynamics Teams develop and enforce conformity to a set of norms that guide behavior. However, conformity to existing team norms may discourage employees from accepting organizational change. This form of resistance occurred at electronics retailer Best Buy when it introduced the results-only work environment (ROWE). ROWE evaluates employees by their results, not their face time, so employees can come to work and leave when they want. Yet coworkers often responded to deviations from the standard work schedule with half-humorous barbs such as, "Forgot to set your alarm clock again?" These jibes supported the old employment model but undermined the ROWE program. Best Buy's consultants eventually set up sessions that warned employees about these taunts, which they called "sludge."[22]

Incongruent Organizational Systems Rewards, information systems, patterns of authority, career paths, selection criteria, and other systems and structures are both

Rubber Band Resistance to Change

Ray Davis, CEO of Umpqua Bank, warns that employees tend to fall back into their old ways unless the change is reinforced through systems and structures. "When you are leading for growth, you know you are going to disrupt comfortable routines and ask for new behavior, new priorities, new skills," says Davis, whose Oregon-based bank is regarded as one of America's most innovative financial institutions. "Even when we want to change, and do change, we tend to relax and the rubber band snaps us back into our comfort zones."[23]

friends and foes of organizational change. When properly aligned, they reinforce desired behaviors. When misaligned, they pull people back into their old attitudes and behavior. Even enthusiastic employees lose momentum after failing to overcome the structural confines of the past.

Learning Objective

After reading this section, you should be able to

LO3 Outline six strategies for minimizing resistance to change and debate ways to effectively create an urgency to change.

UNFREEZING, CHANGING, AND REFREEZING

According to Lewin's force field analysis model, effective change occurs by unfreezing the current situation, moving to a desired condition, and then refreezing the system so it remains in this desired state. Unfreezing occurs when the driving forces are stronger than the restraining forces. This happens by making the driving forces stronger, weakening or removing the restraining forces, or combining both.

The first option is to increase the driving forces, motivating employees to change through fear or threats (real or contrived). This strategy rarely works, however, because the action of increasing the driving forces alone is usually met with an equal and opposing increase in the restraining forces. A useful metaphor is pushing against the coils of a mattress. The harder corporate leaders push for change, the stronger the restraining forces push back. This antagonism threatens the change effort by producing tension and conflict within the organization.

The second option is to weaken or remove the restraining forces. The problem with this change strategy is that it provides no motivation for change. To some extent, weakening the restraining forces is like clearing a pathway for change. An unobstructed road makes it easier to travel to the destination, but it does not produce the effort needed to go there. The preferred option, therefore, is to both increase the driving forces and reduce or remove the restraining forces. Increasing the driving forces creates an urgency for change, while reducing the restraining forces lessens motivation to oppose the change and removes obstacles such as lack of ability and situational constraints.

Creating an Urgency for Change

Organizational change requires employees to have an urgency for change.[24] This typically occurs by informing them about competitors, changing consumer trends, impending government

regulations, and other driving forces in the external environment. These pressures are the main driving forces in Lewin's model. They push people out of their comfort zones, energizing them to face the risks that change creates. In many organizations, however, leaders buffer employees from the external environment to such an extent that these driving forces are hardly felt by anyone below the top executive level. The result is that employees don't understand why they need to change, and leaders are surprised when their change initiatives do not have much effect.

Some companies fuel the urgency for change by putting employees in direct contact with customers. Dissatisfied customers represent a compelling driving force for change because the organization's survival typically depends on having customers who are satisfied with the product or service. Customers also provide a human element that further energizes employees to change current behavior patterns.[26]

Creating an Urgency for Change without External Forces Exposing employees to external forces can strengthen their commitment to the change process, but leaders often need to create an urgency for change long before problems come knocking at the company's door. The challenge is greatest when companies are successful in their markets.

Studies have found that success causes people to become less vigilant of external threats and to become more resistant to change.[27] "The biggest risk is that complacency can also come with that success," warns Richard Goyder, CEO of Australian conglomerate Wesfarmers. "That complacency may result in risk-aversion, or it may simply show up as a lack of urgency, as people take the foot off the accelerator and just assume that success will come as it always has."[28]

Creating an urgency for change when the organization is riding high requires a lot of persuasive influence. Employees need to visualize future competitive threats and environmental shifts. "You want to create a burning platform for change even when there isn't a need for one," says Steve Bennett, former CEO of financial software company Intuit.[29] Experts warn, however, that employees may see the burning-platform strategy as manipulative—a view that produces cynicism about change and undermines trust in the change agent.[30] Also, the urgency for change doesn't need to originate from problems or threats to the company; this motivation can also develop through a change champion's vision of a more appealing future. By creating a future vision of a better organization, leaders effectively make the current situation less appealing. When the vision connects to employee values and needs, it can be a motivating force for change even when external problems are not strong.

> "Leaders often need to create an urgency for change long before problems come knocking at the company's door."

Reducing the Restraining Forces

Employee resistance should be viewed as a resource, but its underlying causes—the restraining forces—still need to be addressed. As we explained earlier using the mattress coil metaphor, increasing the driving forces alone will not bring about change because employees often push back harder to offset the opposing forces. Instead, change agents need to address each of the sources of resistance. Six of the main strategies are outlined in Exhibit 14.2. If feasible, communication,

▼ **EXHIBIT 14.2** Strategies for Minimizing Resistance to Change

Strategy	Example	When Applied	Problems
Communication	Customer complaint letters are shown to employees.	When employees don't feel an urgency for change, don't know how the change will affect them, or resist change due to a fear of the unknown.	Time-consuming and potentially costly.
Learning	Employees learn how to work in teams as company adopts a team-based structure.	When employees need to break old routines and adopt new role patterns.	Time-consuming and potentially costly.
Employee involvement	Company forms task force to recommend new customer service practices.	When the change effort needs more employee commitment, some employees need to save face, and/or employee ideas would improve decisions about the change strategy.	Very time-consuming. Might lead to conflict and poor decisions if employees' interests are incompatible with organizational needs.
Stress management	Employees attend sessions to discuss their worries about the change.	When communication, training, and involvement do not sufficiently ease employee worries.	Time-consuming and potentially expensive. Some methods may not reduce stress for all employees.
Negotiation	Employees agree to replace strict job categories with multiskilling in return for increased job security.	When employees will clearly lose something of value from the change and would not otherwise support the new conditions. Also necessary when the company must change quickly.	May be expensive, particularly if other employees want to negotiate their support. Also tends to produce compliance but not commitment to the change.
Coercion	Company president tells managers to "get on board" the change or leave.	When other strategies are ineffective and the company needs to change quickly.	Can lead to more subtle forms of resistance, as well as long-term antagonism with the change agent.

Sources: Adapted from J. P. Kotter and L. A. Schlesinger, "Choosing Strategies for Change," *Harvard Business Review* 57 (1979), 106–14; P. R. Lawrence, "How to Deal with Resistance to Change," *Harvard Business Review*, May/June 1954, 49–57.

learning, employee involvement, and stress management should be attempted first.[31] However, negotiation and coercion are necessary for people who will clearly lose something from the change and in cases where the speed of change is critical.

Communication Communication is the highest priority and first strategy required for any organizational change. According to one recent survey, communication (together with involvement) is considered the top strategy for engaging employees in the change process.[32] Communication improves the change process in at least two ways.[33] One way, which we described earlier, is by generating an urgency to change. Leaders motivate employees to support the change by candidly telling them about the external threats and opportunities that make change so important. Whether through town hall meetings with senior management or by directly meeting with disgruntled customers, employees become energized to change when they understand and visualize those external forces.

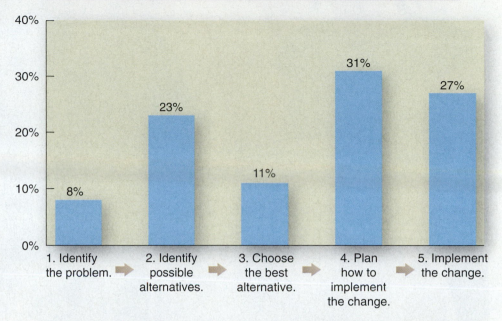

At What Stage in the Change Process Do Companies Activate the Internal Communication Function?[35]

Figures indicate percentage of 328 organizations (employing 5 million people) who activate the internal communication function at each stage of the change process. More than half (58 percent) of companies do not involve the internal communication function until after the change strategy has been selected.

The second way that communication minimizes resistance to change is by illuminating the future and thereby reducing fear of the unknown. The more corporate leaders communicate their vision of the future, particularly details about that future and milestones already achieved toward that future, the more easily employees can understand their own roles in that future. Similarly, as the leader communicates the future state more clearly, employees form a clearer picture about how the change relates to their jobs and responsibilities. "No. 1 is to always communicate, communicate, communicate," advises Randall Dearth, CEO of Calgon Carbon Corporation. "If you're bringing in change, you need to be able to make a very compelling case of what change looks like and why change is necessary."[34]

Learning Learning is an important process in most change initiatives because employees require new knowledge and skills to fit the organization's evolving requirements. For example, learning was an important strategy for change at CSC. The American business and technology consulting and services firm's executive team recognized that the company's culture required better alignment with its growth strategy.

> "Communication is the highest priority and first strategy required for any organizational change."

To achieve this, CSC launched a leadership development program, which would minimize resistance to the change by equipping managers with the skills to coach employees toward the emerging attitudes and values.[36]

Employee Involvement Unless the change must occur quickly or employee interests are highly incompatible with the organization's needs, employee involvement is almost an essential part of the change process. Chapter 6 (decision making) described several potential benefits of employee involvement, all of which are relevant to organizational change. Employees who participate in decisions about a change tend to feel more personal responsibility for its successful implementation, rather than being disinterested agents of someone else's decisions.[37] This sense of ownership also minimizes the problems of saving face and fear of the unknown. Furthermore, the complexity of today's work environment demands that more people provide ideas regarding the best direction of the change effort. Employee involvement is such an important component of organizational change that special initiatives have been developed to allow participation in large groups. These change interventions are described later in the chapter.

Stress Management

Organizational change is a stressful experience for many people because it threatens self-esteem and creates uncertainty about the future.[38] Communication, learning, and employee involvement can reduce some of the stressors. However, research indicates that companies also need to introduce stress management practices to help employees cope with changes.[39] In particular, stress management minimizes resistance by removing some of the direct costs and fear of the unknown of the change process. Stress also saps energy, so minimizing stress potentially increases employee motivation to support the change process.

Negotiation

As long as people resist change, organizational change strategies will require some influence tactics. Negotiation is a form of influence that involves the promise of benefits or resources in exchange for the target person's compliance with the influencer's request. This strategy potentially gains support from those who would otherwise lose out from the change. However, this support is mostly compliance with, rather than commitment to, the change effort, so it might not be effective in the long term.

Coercion

If all else fails, leaders rely on coercion to change organizations. Coercion can include persistently reminding people of their obligations, frequently monitoring behavior to ensure compliance, confronting people who do not change, and using threats of sanctions to force compliance. Replacing people who will not support the change is an extreme step, but it is fairly common. For instance, one year after Robert Nardelli was hired as CEO of Home Depot, most of the retailer's top management team had voluntarily or involuntarily left the company. Several years earlier, StandardAero CEO Bob Hamaberg threatened to fire senior managers who opposed his initiative to introduce lean management. "You must have senior management commitment," Hamaberg said bluntly at the time. "I had some obstacles. I removed the obstacles." Today, Standard-Aero is a world leader in the aircraft engine repair and overhaul business.[40]

Firing people is the least desirable way to change organizations. However, dismissals and other forms of coercion are sometimes necessary when speed is essential and other tactics are ineffective. For example, it may be necessary to remove several members of an executive team who are unwilling or unable to change their existing mental models of the ideal organization. This is also a radical form of organizational "unlearning" (see Chapter 1) because when executives leave, they remove knowledge of the organization's past routines that have become dysfunctional.[41] Even so, coercion is a risky strategy because survivors (employees who do not leave) may have less trust in corporate leaders and engage in more political tactics to protect their own job security.

Refreezing the Desired Conditions

Unfreezing and changing behavior won't produce lasting change. People are creatures of habit, so they easily slip back into past patterns. Therefore, leaders need to refreeze the new behaviors by realigning organizational systems and team dynamics with the desired changes.[42] The desired patterns of behavior can be "nailed down" by changing physical structures and situational conditions. Organizational rewards are also powerful systems that refreeze behaviors.[43] If the change process is supposed to encourage efficiency, then rewards should be realigned to motivate and reinforce efficient practices. Information systems play a complementary role in the change process, particularly as conduits for feedback.[44] Feedback mechanisms help employees learn how well they are moving toward the desired objectives. They are also a permanent architecture to support the new behavior patterns in the long term. The adage "What gets measured, gets done" applies here. Employees concentrate on the new priorities when they receive a continuous flow of feedback about how well they are achieving those goals.

Learning Objective

After reading this section, you should be able to

L04 Discuss how leadership, coalitions, social networks, and pilot projects influence organizational change.

LEADERSHIP, COALITIONS, AND PILOT PROJECTS

Kurt Lewin's force field analysis model is a useful template to explain the dynamics of organizational change. But it overlooks a few other ingredients in effective change processes: leadership, coalitions and social networks, and pilot projects.

Transformational Leadership and Change

Leadership is a key ingredient in most types of organizational change. Chapter 11 described how transformational leaders are agents of change.[45] They champion a vision of a better future, communicate that vision in ways that are meaningful to others, make decisions and act in ways that are consistent with that vision, and build commitment to that vision.

A key element of leading change is a strategic vision.[46] A leader's vision provides a sense of direction and establishes the critical success factors against which the real changes are evaluated. Furthermore, a vision provides an emotional foundation to the change because it links the individual's values and self-concept to the desired change.[47] A strategic vision also minimizes employee fear of the unknown and provides a better understanding of what behaviors employees must learn for the desired future.

Coalitions, Social Networks, and Change

One of the great truths of organizational change is that change agents cannot lead the initiative alone. They need the assistance of several people with a similar degree of commitment to the change.[48] Indeed, one recent study concluded that this group—often called a *guiding coalition*—appears to be the most important factor in the success of public sector organizational change programs.[49]

Membership in the guiding coalition extends beyond the executive team. Ideally, it includes a diagonal swath of employees representing different functions and most levels in the organization. In some cases, the guiding coalition is formed from a special task force that initially investigated the opportunities for change. Members of the guiding coalition should also be influence leaders; that is, they should be highly respected by peers in their area of the organization. At the same time, one recent report on organizational change warned that it takes more than a few dedicated disciples to generate widespread change.[50] Guiding coalitions may be very important, but they alone do not generate commitment to change in the rest of the workforce.

Social Networks and Viral Change

Social networks play a role in organizational change whether or not the change process includes a formal coalition. Social networks are social structures of individuals or social units (e.g., departments, organizations) that are connected to each other through one or more forms of interdependence (see Chapter 9). They have an important role in communication and influence, both of which are

> " Social networks have an important role in communication and influence, both of which are important drivers of organizational change. "

Sowing the Seeds of Viral Change

Viral change has become a hot topic among organizational change experts. Based on the power and influence of social networks, viral change begins by gaining support from key influencers. As these people change their behavior, others in the network eventually change their behavior. This mimicry occurs partly because of the influencer's referent power and partly because social networks make it easier for coworkers to observe and copy the influencer's changed behavior. Although the viral change process is difficult to manage, Pfizer, Novo Nordisk, and a few other firms have been reasonably successful at this approach to changing employee attitudes and behavior.[51]

found in word-of-mouth and viral marketing.[52] Viral and word-of-mouth marketing occur when information seeded to a few people is transmitted to others based on patterns of friendship. Within organizations, social networks represent the channels through which news and opinion about change initiatives are transmitted. Participants in that network have relatively high trust, so their information and views are more persuasive than many traditional ways that change is communicated. Social networks also provide opportunities for behavioral observation—employees observe each other's behavior and often adopt that behavior themselves. So, when a change initiative causes change in the behavior of some employees, the social network potentially spreads this behavior change to others in that network.[53]

Pilot Projects and Diffusion of Change

Earlier in this chapter we mentioned that American retailer Best Buy introduced a results-only work environment (ROWE) initiative to support work/life balance and employment expectations of a younger workforce. ROWE evaluates employees by their results, not their face time. This new arrangement gives employees at the electronics retailer the freedom to come to work when it suits them. ROWE is a significant departure from the traditional employment relationship, so Best Buy wisely introduced an early version of this initiative as a pilot project. Specifically, the program was first tested with a retail division of 320 employees who suffered from low morale and high turnover. The ROWE program expanded to other parts of the organization only after employee engagement scores increased and turnover fell over several months.[54]

Best Buy and many other companies often introduce change through a pilot project. This cautious approach tests the effectiveness of the change as well as the strategies to gain employee support for the change without the enormous costs and risk of companywide initiatives. Unlike centralized, systemwide changes, pilot projects are more flexible and less risky.[55] They also make it easier to select organizational groups that are most ready for change, thus increasing the pilot project's success.

But how do organizational leaders diffuse (spread out) change from the pilot project to other parts of the organization? The MARS model (see Chapter 2) provides a useful template for identifying strategies to diffuse pilot projects to other parts of the organization. First, employees are more likely to adopt the practices of a pilot project when they are motivated to do so.[56] This occurs when they see that the pilot project is successful and people in the pilot project receive recognition and rewards for changing their previous work practices. Diffusion also occurs more successfully when managers support and reinforce the desired behaviors. More generally, change agents need to minimize the sources of resistance to change that we discussed earlier in this chapter.

Second, employees must have the ability—the required skills and knowledge—to adopt the practices introduced in the pilot

important drivers of organizational change. In some cases, coalition members feed into these networks. Alternatively, change agents try to work directly with these social networks.

Social networks are not easily identified or influenced, but that has not stopped successful change agents from tapping into the power of these networks to build a groundswell of support for a change initiative. This *viral change* process adopts principles

OB Theory to Practice

Strategies for Diffusing Change from a Pilot Project

Motivation

Widely communicate and celebrate the pilot project's success.

Reward and recognize pilot project employees as well as those who work at transferring that change to other parts of the organization.

Ensure that managers support and reinforce the desired behaviors related to the pilot project's success.

Identify and address potential sources of resistance to change.

Ability

Give employees the opportunity to interact with and learn from those in the pilot project.

Reassign or temporarily transfer some pilot project employees to other work units, where they can coach and serve as role models.

Give employees technical training to implement practices identified in the pilot project.

Role Perceptions

Communicate and teach employees to discover how the pilot project practices are relevant for their own functional areas.

Ensure the pilot project is described in a way that is neither too specific nor too general.

Situational Factors

Give staff sufficient time and resources to learn and implement the pilot project practices in their work units.

---

project. According to innovation diffusion studies, people adopt ideas more readily when they have an opportunity to interact with and learn from others who have already applied the new practices.[57] Thus, pilot projects get diffused when employees in the original pilot are dispersed to other work units as role models and knowledge sources.

Third, pilot projects get diffused when employees have clear role perceptions—that is, when they understand how the practices in a pilot project apply to them even though they are in a completely different functional area. For instance, accounting department employees won't easily recognize how they can adopt quality improvement practices developed by employees in the production department. The challenge here is for change agents to provide guidance that is not too specific (not too narrowly defined around the pilot project environment) because it might not seem relevant to other areas of the organization. At the same time, the pilot project intervention should not be described too broadly or abstractly to other employees because this makes the information and role model too vague. Finally, employees require supportive situational factors, including the resources and time necessary to adopt the practices demonstrated in the pilot project.

Learning Objective

After reading this section, you should be able to

L05 Describe and compare action research and appreciative inquiry as formal approaches to organizational change.

> **action research**
> A problem-focused change process that combines action orientation (changing attitudes and behavior) and research orientation (testing theory through data collection and analysis).

TWO APPROACHES TO ORGANIZATIONAL CHANGE

So far, this chapter has examined the dynamics of change that occur every day in organizations. However, organizational change agents and consultants also apply various structured approaches to organizational change. This section introduces two of the most prominent approaches: action research and appreciative inquiry.

Action Research Approach

Along with introducing the force field model, Kurt Lewin recommended an **action research** approach to the change process. The philosophy of action research is that meaningful change is a combination of action orientation (changing attitudes and behavior) and research orientation (testing theory).[58] On the one hand, the change process needs to be action-oriented because the ultimate goal is to change the workplace. An action orientation involves diagnosing current problems and applying interventions that resolve those problems. On the other hand, the change process is a research study because change agents apply a conceptual framework (such as team dynamics

or organizational culture) to a real situation. As with any good research, the change process involves collecting data to diagnose problems more effectively and to systematically evaluate how well the theory works in practice.[59]

Within this dual framework of action and research, the action research approach adopts an open systems view. It recognizes that organizations have many interdependent parts, so change agents need to anticipate both the intended and the unintended consequences of their interventions. Action research is also a highly participative process because open systems change requires both the knowledge and the commitment of members within that system. Indeed, employees are essentially co-researchers as well as participants in the intervention. Overall, action research is a data-based, problem-oriented process that diagnoses the need for change, introduces the intervention, and then evaluates and stabilizes the desired changes. The main phases of action research are illustrated in Exhibit 14.3 and described here:[60]

1. *Form client–consultant relationship.* Action research usually assumes that the change agent originates outside the system (such as a consultant), so the process begins by forming the client–consultant relationship. Consultants need to determine the client's readiness for change, including whether people are motivated to participate in the process, are open to meaningful change, and possess the abilities to complete the process.

2. *Diagnose the need for change.* Action research is a problem-oriented activity that carefully diagnoses the problem through systematic analysis of the situation. Organizational diagnosis identifies the appropriate direction for the change effort by gathering and analyzing data about an ongoing system, such as through interviews and surveys of employees and other stakeholders. Organizational diagnosis also includes employee involvement in agreeing on the appropriate change method, the schedule for the actions involved, and the expected standards of successful change.

3. *Introduce intervention.* This stage in the action research model applies one or more actions to correct the problem. It may include any of the prescriptions mentioned in this book, such as building more effective teams, managing conflict, building a better organizational structure, or changing the

corporate culture. An important issue is how quickly the changes should occur.[61] Some experts recommend *incremental change* in which the organization fine-tunes the system and takes small steps toward a desired state. Others claim that *quantum change* is often required in which the system is overhauled decisively and quickly.

4. *Evaluate and stabilize change.* Action research recommends evaluating the effectiveness of the intervention against the standards established in the diagnostic stage. Unfortunately, even when these standards are clearly stated, the effectiveness of an intervention might not be apparent for several years or might be difficult to separate from other factors. If the activity has the desired effect, the change agent and participants need to stabilize the new conditions. This refers to the refreezing process that was described earlier. Rewards, information systems, team norms, and other conditions are redesigned so they support the new values and behaviors.

The action research approach has dominated organizational change thinking since it was introduced in the 1940s. However, some experts are concerned that the problem-oriented nature of action research—in which something is wrong that must be fixed—focuses on the negative dynamics of the group or system rather than its positive opportunities and potential. This concern with action research has led to the development of a more positive approach to organizational change, called *appreciative inquiry.*[62]

Appreciative Inquiry Approach

I Spy Marketing wanted to move to the next level of success. To accomplish this, the London-based digital marketing agency held workshops in which staff identified and reflected on the features of several famous teams—Apple's Macintosh team, an F1 race car team, a famous West Indies cricket team, and television's A-Team. This discussion created positive energy in the participants and subsequently guided them to award-winning accomplishments in a difficult economic climate. "Fueled by these pictures of success, happy in clearly defined roles, consciously thinking about choices and consequences and ensuring clear contracting on a daily basis, we became the A Team," says I Spy managing director Nick Jones.[63]

▼**EXHIBIT 14.3** The Action Research Process

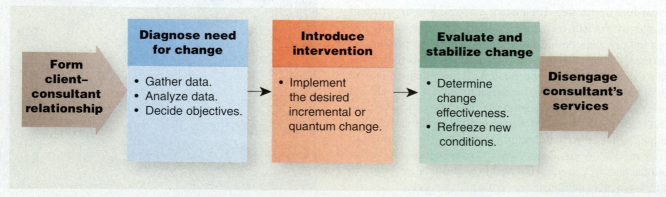

aware of their problems or already aware of their problems or already suffer from negativity in their relationships. The positive orientation of appreciative inquiry enables groups to overcome these negative tensions and build a more hopeful perspective of their future by focusing on what is possible.[65]

appreciative inquiry
An organizational change strategy that directs the group's attention away from its own problems and focuses participants on the group's potential and positive elements.

Appreciative Inquiry Principles Appreciative inquiry embraces five key principles (see Exhibit 14.4).[66] One of these is the positive principle, which we describe above. A second principle, called the *constructionist principle*, takes the position that conversations don't describe reality; they shape that reality. In other words, how we come to understand something depends on the questions we ask and the language we use. Thus appreciative inquiry requires sensitivity to and proactive management of the words and language used as well as the thoughts and feelings behind that communication. This relates to a third principle, called the *simultaneity principle*, which states that inquiry and change are simultaneous, not sequential. The moment we ask questions of others, we are changing those people. Furthermore, the questions we ask determine the information we receive, which in turn affects which change intervention we choose. The key learning point from this principle is to be mindful of effects that the inquiry has on the direction of the change process.

A fourth principle, called the *poetic principle*, states that organizations are open books, so we have choices in how they may be perceived, framed, and described. The poetic principle is reflected in the notion that a glass of water can be viewed as half full or half empty. Thus, appreciative inquiry actively frames reality in a way that provides constructive value for future development. *The anticipatory principle*, the fifth principle of appreciative inquiry, emphasizes the importance of a positive collective vision of the future state. People are motivated and guided by a vision they understand and can believe in. Images that are mundane or disempowering will affect current effort and behavior differently than will images that are inspiring and

I Spy Marketing applied a variation of **appreciative inquiry**, a change process that focuses attention on positive change rather than dwell on the problem-solving mentality of traditional change management practices. This approach to organizational change searches for strengths and capabilities—either within the organization or elsewhere—and then adapts or applies that knowledge for further success and well-being. Appreciative inquiry is therefore deeply grounded in the emerging philosophy of *positive organizational behavior*, which suggests that focusing on the positive rather than the negative aspects of life will improve organizational success and individual well-being.[64]

Appreciative inquiry is a form of behavioral modeling because it encourages participants to examine successful events, organizations, and work units. It is also a cognitive reframing process redirecting the group's attention away from its own problems. Appreciative inquiry is especially useful when participants are

▼ **EXHIBIT 14.4** Five Principles of Appreciative Inquiry

Appreciative Inquiry Principle	Description
Positive principle	Focusing on positive events and potential produces more positive, effective, and enduring change.
Constructionist principle	How we perceive and understand the change process depends on the questions we ask and language we use throughout that process.
Simultaneity principle	Inquiry and change are simultaneous, not sequential.
Poetic principle	Organizations are open books, so we have choices in how they may be perceived, framed, and described.
Anticipatory principle	People are motivated and guided by a vision they understand and can believe in.

Source: Based on D. L. Cooperrider and D. K. Whitney, *Appreciative Inquiry: A Positive Revolution in Change.* (San Francisco: Berrett-Koehler, 2005), Chap. 7; D. K. Whitney and A. Trosten-Bloom. *The Power of Appreciative Inquiry: A Practical Guide to Positive Change.* 2nd ed. (San Francisco: Berrett-Koehler Publishers, 2010), Chap. 3.

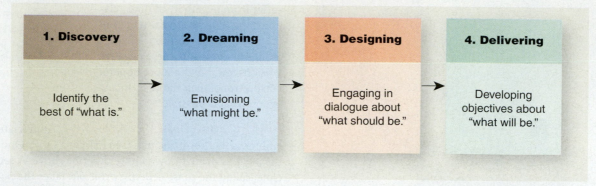

Sources: Based on F. J. Barrett and D. L. Cooperrider, "Generative Metaphor Intervention: A New Approach for Working with Systems Divided by Conflict and Caught in Defensive Perception," *Journal of Applied Behavioral Science* 26 (1990), 229; D. Whitney and C. Schau, "Appreciative Inquiry: An Innovative Process for Organization Change," *Employment Relations Today* 25 (Spring 1998), 11–21; D. L. Cooperrider and D. K. Whitney, *Appreciative Inquiry: A Positive Revolution in Change.* (San Francisco: Berrett-Koehler, 2005), Chap. 3.

engaging. We noted the importance of visions earlier in this chapter (change agents) and in our discussion of transformational leadership (Chapter 11).

The Four-D Model of Appreciative Inquiry

Building on these five principles, appreciative inquiry follows the "Four-D" process (named after its four stages) shown in Exhibit 14.5. Appreciative inquiry begins with *discovery*—identifying the positive elements of the observed events or organization.[67] This might involve documenting positive customer experiences elsewhere in the organization. Or it might include interviewing members of another organization to discover its fundamental strengths. As participants discuss their findings, they shift into the *dreaming* stage by envisioning what might be possible in an ideal organization. By pointing out a hypothetical ideal organization or situation, participants feel safer revealing their hopes and aspirations than they would if they were discussing their own organization or predicament.

As participants make their private thoughts public to the group, the process shifts into the third stage, called *designing*. Designing involves dialogue in which participants listen with selfless receptivity to each other's models and assumptions and eventually form a collective model for thinking within the team. In effect, they create a common image of what should be. As this model takes shape, group members shift the focus back to their own situation. In the final stage of appreciative inquiry, called *delivering* (also known as *destiny*), participants establish specific objectives and direction for their own organization on the basis of their model of what will be.

Appreciative inquiry was introduced more than two decades ago, but it really gained popularity only within the past few years. Appreciative inquiry has been a successful change process in a variety of organizational settings, including the British Broadcasting Corporation, Castrol Marine, Canadian Tire, AVON Mexico, American Express, Green Mountain Coffee Roasters, and Hunter Douglas.[68]

Although appreciative inquiry has much to offer, it is not always the best approach for changing teams or organizations, and, indeed, it has not always been successful. This approach depends on participants' ability to let go of the problem-oriented approach, including the "blame game" of determining who may have been responsible for past failures. It also requires leaders who are willing to accept appreciative inquiry's less structured process.[69] Another concern is that research has not yet examined the contingencies of this approach.[70] In other words, we don't yet know under what conditions appreciative inquiry is a useful approach to organizational change and under what conditions it is less effective. Overall, appreciative inquiry has much to offer the organizational change process, but there is much more to discover about its potential and limitations.

Learning Objective

After reading the next two sections, you should be able to

LO6 Discuss two cross-cultural and three ethical issues in organizational change.

CROSS-CULTURAL AND ETHICAL ISSUES IN ORGANIZATIONAL CHANGE

Cross-cultural and ethical issues must be considered in any change process. Many organizational change practices are built around Western cultural assumptions and values, which may differ from and sometimes conflict with assumptions and values in other cultures.[71] One possible cross-cultural limitation is that Western organizational change models, such as Lewin's force field analysis, often assume that change has a beginning and an ending in a logical linear sequence (that is, a straight line from point A to point B). Yet change is viewed more as a cyclical

ORGANIZATIONAL BEHAVIOR: THE JOURNEY CONTINUES

Nearly 100 years ago American industrialist Andrew Carnegie said, "Take away my people, but leave my factories, and soon grass will grow on the factory floors. Take away my factories, but leave my people, and soon we will have a new and better factory."[74] Carnegie's statement reflects the message woven throughout this textbook: Organizations are not buildings or machinery or financial assets; rather, they are the people in them. Organizations are human entities—full of life, sometimes fragile, and always exciting. ■

phenomenon in some cultures, such as the earth's revolution around the sun or a pendulum swinging back and forth. Other cultures have more of an interconnected view of change, whereby one change leads to another (often unplanned) change, which leads to another change, and so on until the change objective is ultimately achieved in a more circuitous way.

Another cross-cultural issue with some organizational change interventions is they assume that effective organizational change is necessarily punctuated by tension and overt conflict. Indeed, some change interventions encourage such conflict. But this direct confrontation approach is incompatible with cultures that emphasize harmony and equilibrium. These cross-cultural differences suggest that a more contingency-oriented perspective is required for organizational change to work effectively in a globalized world.

Some organizational change practices also face ethical issues.[72] One ethical concern is the risk of violating individual privacy rights. The action research model is built on the idea of collecting information from organizational members, yet this requires that employees provide personal information and emotions they may not want to divulge.[73] A second ethical concern is that some change activities potentially increase management's power by inducing compliance and conformity in organizational members. For instance, action research is a systemwide activity that requires employee participation rather than allowing individuals to get involved voluntarily. A third concern is that some organizational change interventions undermine the individual's self-esteem. The unfreezing process requires that participants disconfirm their existing beliefs, sometimes including their own competence at certain tasks or interpersonal relations.

Organizational change is usually more difficult than it initially seems. Yet the dilemma is that most organizations operate in hyperfast environments that demand continuous and rapid adaptation. Organizations survive and gain competitive advantage by mastering the complex dynamics of moving people through the continuous process of change as quickly as the external environment is changing.

CHECK IT OUT!

www.mhhe.com/ McShaneM2e

for study materials
including quizzes
and other resources

endnotes

CHAPTER 1

1. M. Warner, "Organizational Behavior Revisited," *Human Relations* 47 (October 1994): 1151–66; R. Westwood and S. Clegg, "The Discourse of Organization Studies: Dissensus, Politics, and Paradigms," in *Debating Organization: Point-Counterpoint in Organization Studies*, ed. R. Westwood and S. Clegg (Malden, MA: Blackwood, 2003), 1–42.

2. D. Katz and R. L. Kahn, *The Social Psychology of Organizations* (New York: Wiley, 1966), Chap. 2; R. N. Stern and S. R. Barley, "Organizations as Social Systems: Organization Theory's Neglected Mandate," *Administrative Science Quarterly* 41 (1996): 146–62.

3. L. E. Greiner, "A Recent History of Organizational Behavior," in *Organizational Behaviour*, ed. S. Kerr (Columbus, Ohio: Grid, 1979), 3–14; J. Micklethwait and A. Wooldridge, *The Company: A Short History of a Revolutionary Idea* (New York: Random House, 2003).

4. B. Schlender, "The Three Faces of Steve," *Fortune*, 9 November 1998, 96–101.

5. J. A. Conger, "Max Weber's Conceptualization of Charismatic Authority: Its Influence on Organizational Research," *The Leadership Quarterly* 4, no. 3–4 (1993): 277–88; R. Kanigel, *The One Best Way: Frederick Winslow Taylor and the Enigma of Efficiency* (New York: Viking, 1997); T. Takala, "Plato on Leadership," *Journal of Business Ethics* 17 (May 1998): 785–98; J. A. Fernandez, "The Gentleman's Code of Confucius: Leadership by Values," *Organizational Dynamics* 33, no. 1 (February 2004): 21–31.

6. C. D. Wrege, "Solving Mayo's Mystery: The First Complete Account of the Origin of the Hawthorne Studies-the Forgotten Contributions of C. E. Snow and H. Hibarger" in *Academy of Management Proceedings* 8, 12–16; J. A. Sonnenfeld, "Shedding Light on the Hawthorne Studies," *Journal of Occupational Behaviour* 6, no. 2 (1985): 111–30; O'Connor, "Minding the Workers: The Meaning of 'Human' and 'Human Relations' in Elton Mayo"; "A Field Is Born," *Harvard Business Review* 86, no. 7/8 (2008): 164–64.

7. W. L. M. King, *Industry and Humanity: A Study in the Principles Underlying Industrial Reconstruction* (Toronto: Thomas Allen, 1918); H. C. Metcalf and L. Urwick, *Dynamic Administration: The Collected Papers of Mary Parker Follett* (New York: Harper & Brothers, 1940); J. Smith, "The Enduring Legacy of Elton Mayo," *Human Relations* 51, no. 3 (1998): 221–49; E. O'Connor, "Minding the Workers: The Meaning of 'Human' and 'Human Relations' in Elton Mayo," *Organization* 6, no. 2 (May 1999): 223–46; K. Hallahan, "W. L. Mackenzie King: Rockefeller's 'Other' Public Relations Counselor in Colorado," *Public Relations Review* 29, no. 4 (2003): 401–14.

8. S. L. Rynes et al., "Behavioral Coursework in Business Education: Growing Evidence of a Legitimacy Crisis," *Academy of Management Learning & Education* 2, no. 3 (2003): 269–283; R. P. Singh and A. G. Schick, "Organizational Behavior: Where Does It Fit in Today's Management Curriculum?," *Journal of Education for Business* 82, no. 6 (July 2007): 349.

9. P. R. Lawrence and N. Nohria, *Driven: How Human Nature Shapes Our Choices* (San Francisco: Jossey-Bass, 2002), Chap. 6.

10. J. A. C. Baum, "Companion to Organizations: An Introduction," in *The Blackwell Companion to Organizations*, ed. J. A. C. Baum (Oxford, UK: Blackwell, 2002), 1–34.

11. OB scholars are currently in a heated debate regarding the field's relevance to practitioners. See, for example: P. R. Lawrence, "Historical Development of Organizational Behavior," in *Handbook of Organizational Behavior*, ed. L. W. Lorsch (Englewood Cliffs, NJ: Prentice Hall, 1987), 1–9; S. A. Mohrman, C. B. Gibson, and A. M. Mohrman Jr., "Doing Research That Is Useful to Practice: A Model and Empirical Exploration," *Academy of Management Journal* 44 (April 2001): 357–75; R. Gulati, "Tent Poles, Tribalism, and Boundary Spanning: The Rigor-Relevance Debate in Management Research," *Academy of Management Journal* 50, no. 4 (August 2007): 775–782; F. Vermeulen, "'I Shall Not Remain Insignificant': Adding a Second Loop to Matter More," *Academy of Management Journal* 50, no. 4 (2007): 754–61; J. P. Walsh et al., "On the Relationship between Research and Practice: Debate and Reflections," *Journal of Management Inquiry* 16, no. 2 (June 2007): 128–54; D. Palmer, B. Dick, and N. Freiburger, "Rigor and Relevance in Organization Studies," *Journal of Management Inquiry* 18, no. 4 (December 2009): 265–72; A. Nicolai and D. Seidl, "That's Relevant! Different Forms of Practical Relevance in Management Science," *Organization Studies* 31, no. 9–10 (September 2010): 1257–1285. At least one source argues that organizational scholarship does not need to be relevant to practitioners: M. W. Peng and G. G. Dess, "In the Spirit of Scholarship," *Academy of Management Learning & Education* 9, no. 2 (June 2010): 282–98.

12. M. S. Myers, *Every Employee a Manager* (New York: McGraw Hill, 1970).

13. B. N. Pfau and I. T. Kay, *The Human Capital Edge* (New York: McGraw-Hill, 2002); I. S. Fulmer, B. Gerhart, and K. S. Scott, "Are the 100 Best Better? An Empirical Investigation of the Relationship between Being a 'Great Place to Work' and Firm Performance," *Personnel Psychology* 56, no. 4 (Winter 2003): 965–93; Y. H. Ling and B.-S. Jaw, "The Influence of International Human Capital on Global Initiatives and Financial Performance," *The International Journal of Human Resource Management* 17, no. 3 (2006): 379–98; M. A. West et al., "Reducing Patient Mortality in Hospitals: The Role of Human Resource Management," *Journal of Organizational Behavior* 27, no. 7 (2006): 983–1002. However, one study warns that firm performance seems to predict the presence of OB practices as much as vice versa. See P. M. Wright et al., "The Relationship between HR Practices and Firm Performance: Examining Causal Order," *Personnel Psychology* 58, no. 2 (2005): 409–46.

14. Deloitte & Touche, *Human Capital Roi Study: Creating Shareholder Value through People*, (Toronto: Deloitte & Touche, 2002); D. Wheeler and J. Thomson, *Human Capital Based Investment Criteria for Total Shareholder Returns: A Canadian and International Perspective*, (Toronto: Schulich School of Business, York University, June 2004); P. Shokeen, T. M. Woodward, and D. Wheeler, "Refining the York Index Investment Criteria," *SSRN eLibrary* (December 13, 2006); L. Bassi and D. McMurrer, "Maximizing Your Return on People," *Harvard business Review* 85, no. 3 (March 2007): 115–23, 144. The AMP Capital example is cited in F. Smith, "Shareholders New Force in Employee Rights," *Australian Financial Review*, 29 (May 2007).

15. Mohrman, Gibson, and Mohrman Jr., "Doing Research That Is Useful to Practice: A Model and Empirical Exploration"; Walsh et al., "On the Relationship between Research and Practice: Debate and Reflections." Similarly, in 1961, Harvard business professor Fritz Roethlisberger proposed that the field of OB is concerned with human behavior "from the points of view of both (a) its determination . . . and (b) its improvement." See P. B. Vaill, "F. J. Roethlisberger and the Elusive Phenomena of Organizational Behavior," *Journal of Management Education* 31, no. 3 (June 2007): 321–38.

16. R. H. Hall, "Effectiveness Theory and Organizational Effectiveness," *Journal of Applied Behavioral Science* 16, no. 4 (October 1980): 536–45; K. Cameron, "Organizational Effectiveness: Its Demise and Re-Emergence through Positive Organizational Scholarship," in *Great Minds in Management*, ed. K. G. Smith and M. A. Hitt (New York: Oxford University Press, 2005), 304–30.

17. J. L. Price, "The Study of Organizational Effectiveness," *The Sociological Quarterly* 13 (1972): 3–15.

18. S. C. Selden and J. E. Sowa, "Testing a Multi-Dimensional Model of Organizational Performance: Prospects and Problems," *Journal of Public Administration Research and Theory* 14, no. 3 (July 2004): 395–416.

19. Chester Barnard gives one of the earliest descriptions of organizations as systems interacting with external environments and that are composed of subsystems. See: C. Barnard, *The Functions of the Executive* (Cambridge, MA: Harvard University Press, 1938), esp. Chap. 6. Also see: F. E. Kast and J. E. Rosenzweig, "General Systems Theory: Applications for Organization and Management," *Academy of Management Journal* 15, no. 4 (1972): 447–65; P. M. Senge, *The Fifth Discipline: The Art and Practice of the Learning Organization* (New York: Doubleday Currency, 1990); G. Morgan, *Images of Organization*, 2nd ed. (Newbury Park: Sage, 1996); A. De Geus, *The Living Company* (Boston: Harvard Business School Press, 1997).

20. D. P. Ashmos and G. P. Huber, "The Systems Paradigm in Organization Theory: Correcting the Record and Suggesting the Future," *The Academy of Management Review* 12, no. 4 (1987): 607–621.

21. Katz and Kahn, *The Social Psychology of Organizations*; V. P. Rindova and S. Kotha, "Continuous 'Morphing': Competing through Dynamic Capabilities, Form, and Function," *Academy of Management Journal* 44 (2001): 1263–80; J. McCann, "Organizational Effectiveness: Changing Concepts for Changing Environments," *Human Resource Planning* 27, no. 1 (2004): 42–50.

22. D. Steinbok, *The Nokia Revolution: The Story of an Extraordinary Company That Transformed an Industry* (New York: AMACOM, 2001).

23. C. Ostroff and N. Schmitt, "Configurations of Organizational Effectiveness and Efficiency," *Academy of Management Journal* 36, no. 6 (1993): 1345.

24. P. S. Adler et al., "Performance Improvement Capability: Keys to Accelerating Performance Improvement in Hospitals," *California Management Review* 45, no. 2 (2003): 12–33; J. Jamrog, M. Vickers, and D. Bear, "Building and Sustaining a Culture That Supports Innovation," *Human Resource Planning* 29, no. 3 (2006): 9–19.

25. K. E. Weick, *The Social Psychology of Organizing* (Reading, MA: Addison-Wesley, 1979); S. Brusoni and A. Prencipe, "Managing Knowledge in Loosely Coupled Networks: Exploring the Links between Product and Knowledge Dynamics," *Journal of Management Studies* 38, no. 7 (November 2001): 1019–35.

26. J. C. Barbieri and A. C. T. Ýlvares, "Innovation in Mature Industries: The Case of Brasilata S. A Metallic Packaging" (paper presented at International Conference on Technology Policy and Innovation, Curitiba, Brazil, 31 August 2000); "Participacāo É Desafio Nas Empresas (Participation Is a Challenge in Business)," *Gazeta do Povo*, November 16, 2008; "Brasilata Internal Suggestion System Is a Benchmark in Innovation in the Brazilian Market," 2010, accessed June 10, 2011, http://brasilata.jp/en/noticias_detalhada.php?cd_noticia=219; C. Heath and D. Heath, *Switch: How to Change Things When Change Is Hard* (New York: Broadway Books, 2010); "Brasilata Inventors Turned in 205,536 Innovative Suggestions in 2010," 2011, accessed June 10, 2011, http://brasilata.jp/en/noticias_detalhada.php?cd_noticia=264; "Simplification Project," 2011, accessed June 10, 2011, http://brasilata.jp/en/projeto_cronologia.php; "Business Management," 2011, accessed June 14, 2011, http://brasilata.jp/en/pessoal_negocios.php.

27. T. A. Stewart, *Intellectual Capital: The New Wealth of Organizations* (New York: Currency/ Doubleday, 1997); H. Saint-Onge and D. Wallace, *Leveraging Communities of Practice for Strategic Advantage* (Boston: Butterworth-Heinemann, 2003), 9–10; J.-A. Johannessen, B. Olsen, and J. Olaisen, "Intellectual Capital as a Holistic Management Philosophy: A Theoretical Perspective," *International Journal of Information Management* 25, no. 2 (2005): 151–71; L. Striukova, J. Unerman, and J. Guthrie, "Corporate Reporting of Intellectual Capital: Evidence from UK Companies," *British Accounting Review* 40, no. 4 (2008): 297–313.

28. J. Barney, "Firm Resources and Sustained Competitive Advantage," *Journal of Management* 17, no. 1 (1991): 99–120.

29. "Jim Goodnight, Chief Executive Officer, SAS," 2011, accessed June 13, 2011, http://www.sas.com/company/about/bios/jgoodnight.html.

30. S. C. Kang and S. A. Snell, "Intellectual Capital Architectures and Ambidextrous Learning: A Framework for Human Resource Management," *Journal of Management Studies* 46, no. 1 (2009): 65–92; L.-C. Hsu and C.-H. Wang, "Clarifying the Effect of Intellectual Capital on Performance: The Mediating Role of Dynamic Capability," *British Journal of Management* (2011): in press.

31. Some organizational learning researchers use the label "social capital" instead of relationship capital. Social capital is discussed later in this book as the goodwill and resulting resources shared among members in a social network. The two concepts may be identical (as those writers suggest). However, we continue to use "relationship capital" for intellectual capital because social capital typically refers to individual relationships whereas relationship capital also includes value not explicit in social capital, such as the organization's goodwill and brand value.

32. G. Huber, "Organizational Learning: The Contributing Processes and Literature," *Organizational Science* 2 (1991): 88–115; D. A. Garvin, *Learning in Action: A Guide to Putting the Learning Organization to Work* (Boston: Harvard Business School Press, 2000); H. Shipton, "Cohesion or Confusion? Towards a Typology for Organizational Learning Research," *International Journal of Management Reviews* 8, no. 4 (2006): 233–52; W. C. Bogner and P. Bansal, "Knowledge Management as the Basis of Sustained High Performance," *Journal of Management Studies* 44, no. 1 (2007): 165–88; D. Jiménez-Jiménez and J. G. Cegarra-Navarro, "The Performance Effect of Organizational Learning and Market Orientation," *Industrial Marketing Management* 36, no. 6 (2007): 694–708.

33 . R. Garud and A. Kumaraswamy, "Vicious and Virtuous Circles in the Management of Knowledge: The Case of Infosys Technologies," *MIS Quarterly* 29, no. 1 (March 2005): 9–33; S. L. Hoe and S. L. McShane, "Structural and Informal Knowledge Acquisition and Dissemination in Organizational Learning: An Exploratory Analysis," *The Learning Organization* 17, no. 4 (2010): 364–86.

34. M. N. Wexler, "Organizational Memory and Intellectual Capital," *Journal of Intellectual Capital* 3, no. 4 (2002): 393–414.

35. "A Cornerstone for Learning," *T&D*, October 2008, 66–89.

36. M. E. McGill and J. W. Slocum Jr., "Unlearn the Organization," *Organizational Dynamics* 22, no. 2 (1993): 67–79; A. E. Akgün, G. S. Lynn, and J. C. Byrne, "Antecedents and Consequences of Unlearning in New Product Development Teams," *Journal of Product Innovation Management* 23 (2006): 73–88.

37. E. Appelbaum et al., *Manufacturing Advantage: Why High-Performance Work Systems Pay Off* (Ithaca, N Y: Cornell University Press, 2000); A. Zacharatos, J. Barling, and R. D. Iverson, "High-Performance Work Systems and Occupational Safety," *Journal of Applied Psychology* 90, no. 1 (2005): 77–93; G. S. Benson, S. M. Young, and E. E. Lawler III, "High-Involvement Work Practices and Analysts' Forecasts of Corporate Earnings," *Human Resource Management* 45, no. 4 (2006): 519–537; L. Sels et al., "Unravelling the HRM-Performance Link: Value-Creating and Cost-Increasing Effects of Small Business HRM," *Journal of Management Studies* 43, no. 2 (2006): 319–42.

38. M. A. Huselid, "The Impact of Human Resource Management Practices on Turnover, Productivity, and Corporate," *Academy of Management Journal* 38, no. 3 (1995): 635; B. E. Becker and M. A. Huselid, "Strategic Human Resources Management: Where Do We Go from Here?," *Journal of Management* 32, no. 6 (December 2006): 898–925; J. Combs et al., "How Much Do High-Performance Work Practices Matter? A Meta-Analysis of Their Effects on Organizational Performance," *Personnel Psychology* 59, no. 3 (2006): 501–28.

39. E. E. Lawler III, S. A. Mohrman, and G. E. Ledford Jr., *Strategies for High Performance Organizations* (San Francisco: Jossey-Bass, 1998); S. H. Wagner, C. P. Parker, and D. Neil, "Employees That Think and Act Like Owners: Effects of Ownership Beliefs and Behaviors on Organizational Effectiveness," *Personnel Psychology* 56, no. 4 (Winter 2003): 847–71; P. J. Gollan, "High Involvement Management and Human Resource Sustainability: The Challenges and Opportunities," *Asia Pacific Journal of Human Resources* 43, no. 1 (April 2005): 18–33; Y. Liu et al., "The Value of Human Resource Management for Organizational Performance," *Business Horizons* 50 (2007): 503–11; P. Tharenou, A. M. Saks, and C. Moore, "A Review and Critique of Research on Training and Organizational-Level Outcomes," *Human Resource Management Review* 17, no. 3 (2007): 251–73.

40. M. Subramony, "A Meta-Analytic Investigation of the Relationship between HRM Bundles and Firm Performance," *Human Resource Management* 48, no. 5 (2009): 745–68.

41. S. Fleetwood and A. Hesketh, "HRM-Performance Research: Under-Theorized and Lacking Explanatory Power," *International Journal of Human Resource Management* 17, no. 12 (December 2006): 1977–93.

42. R. Takeuchi et al., "An Empirical Examination of the Mechanisms Mediating between High-Performance Work Systems and the Performance of Japanese Organizations," *Journal of Applied Psychology* 92, no. 4 (2007): 1069–83; L. Q. Wei and C.-M. Lau, "High Performance Work Systems and Performance: The Role of Adaptive Capability," *Human Relations* 63, no. 10 (2010): 1487–1511; J. Camps and R. Luna-Arocas, "A Matter of Learning: How Human Resources Affect Organizational Performance," *British Journal of Management* (in press).

43. J. Godard, "High Performance and the Transformation of Work? The Implications of Alternative Work Practices for the Experience and Outcomes of Work," *Industrial and Labor Relations Review* 54, no. 4 (July 2001): 776–805; G. Murray et al., eds., *Work and Employment Relations in the High-Performance Workplace* (London: Continuum, 2002); B. Harley, "Hope or Hype? High Performance Work Systems," in *Participation and Democracy at Work: Essays in Honour of Harvie Ramsay*, ed. B. Harley, J. Hyman, and P. Thompson (Houndsmills, UK: Palgrave Macmillan, 2005), 38–54.

44. A. L. Friedman and S. Miles, *Stakeholders: Theory and Practice* (New York: Oxford University Press, 2006); M. L. Barnett, "Stakeholder Influence Capacity and the Variability of Financial Returns to Corporate Social Responsibility," *Academy of Management Review* 32, no. 3 (2007): 794–816; R. E. Freeman, J. S. Harrison, and A. C. Wicks, *Managing for Stakeholders: Survival, Reputation, and Success* (New Haven, CT: Yale University Press, 2007).

45. C. Eden and F. Ackerman, *Making Strategy: The Journey of Strategic Management* (London: Sage, 1998).

46. G. R. Salancik and J. Pfeffer, *The External Control of Organizations: A Resource Dependence Perspective* (New York: Harper & Row, 1978); T. Casciaro and M. J. Piskorski, "Power Imbalance, Mutual Dependence, and Constraint Absorption: A Closer Look at Dependence Theory," *Administrative Science Quarterly* 50 (2005): 167–99; N. Roome and F. Wijen, "Stakeholder Power and Organizational Learning in Corporate Environmental Management," *Organization Studies* 27, no. 2 (2005): 235–63.

47. R. E. Freeman, A. C. Wicks, and B. Parmar, "Stakeholder Theory and 'the Corporate Objective Revisited'," *Organization Science* 15, no. 3 (May-June 2004): 364–69; Friedman and Miles, *Stakeholders: Theory and Practice*, Chap. 3; B. L. Parmar et al., "Stakeholder Theory: The State of the Art," *Academy of Management Annals* 4, no. 1 (2010): 403–445.

48. B. M. Meglino and E. C. Ravlin, "Individual Values in Organizations: Concepts, Controversies, and Research," *Journal of Management* 24, no. 3 (1998): 351–89; B. R. Agle and C. B. Caldwell, "Understanding Research on Values in Business," *Business and Society* 38, no. 3 (September 1999): 326–87; A. Bardi and S. H. Schwartz, "Values and Behavior: Strength and Structure of Relations," *Personality and Social Psychology Bulletin* 29, no. 10 (October 2003): 1207–20; S. Hitlin and J. A. Pilavin, "Values: Reviving a Dormant Concept," *Annual Review of Sociology* 30 (2004): 359–93.

49. Some popular books that emphasise the importance of values include: J. C. Collins and J. I. Porras, *Built to Last: Successful Habits of Visionary Companies* (London: Century, 1995); C. A. O'Reilly III and J. Pfeffer, *Hidden Value* (Cambridge, MA: Harvard Business School Press, 2000); R. Barrett, *Building a Values-Driven Organization: A Whole System Approach to Cultural Transformation* (Burlington, MA: Butterworth-Heinemann, 2006); J. M. Kouzes and B. Z. Posner, *The Leadership Challenge*, 4th ed/ (San Francisco: Jossey-Bass, 2007)

50. T. Hsieh, *Delivering Happiness: A Path to Profits, Passion, and Purpose* (New York: Hachette Book Group, 2010), pp. 155–59.

51. Aspen Institute, *Where Will They Lead? MBA Student Attitudes about Business & Society* (Washington, DC: Aspen Institute, April 2008).

52. M. van Marrewijk, "Concepts and Definitions of CSR and Corporate Sustainability: Between Agency and Communion," *Journal of Business Ethics* 44 (May 2003): 95–105; Barnett, "Stakeholder Influence Capacity and the Variability of Financial Returns to Corporate Social Responsibility."

53. L. S. Paine, *Value Shift* (New York: McGraw-Hill, 2003); A. Mackey, T. B. Mackey, and J. B. Barney, "Corporate Social Responsibility and Firm Performance: Investor Preferences and Corporate Strategies," *Academy of Management Review* 32, no. 3 (2007): 817–35.

54. S. Zadek, *The Civil Corporation: The New Economy of Corporate Citizenship* (London: Earthscan, 2001); S. Hart and M. Milstein, "Creating Sustainable Value," *Academy of Management Executive* 17, no. 2 (2003): 56–69.

55. MTN Group Limited, *2009 Sustainability Report* (Fairlands, South Africa: MTN Group, 26 June 2010); "21daysuganada," June 2011, accessed June 11, 2011, http://21daysuganda. wordpress.com; "MTN Plants 5,800 Trees in 21 Days of Y'ello Care," *Spy Ghana*, June 10, 2011.

56. M. Friedman, *Capitalism and Freedom*, 40th Anniversary ed. (Chicago: University of Chicago Press, 2002), Chap. 8; N. Vorster, "An Ethical Critique of Milton Friedman's Doctrine on Economics and Freedom," *Journal for the Study of Religions and Ideologies* 9, no. 26 (Summer 2010): 163–88.

57. Zadek, *The Civil Corporation: The New Economy of Corporate Citizenship*; "Canadians Inclined to Punish Companies Deemed Socially Irresponsible, Study Suggests," *Canadian Press*, April 23, 2005; M. Johne, "Show Us the Green, Workers Say," *Globe & Mail*, October 10, 2007, C1.

58. D. Kiron et al., "Sustainability Nears a Tipping Point," *MIT Sloan Management Review* 53, no. 2 (Winter 2012): 69–74; Net Impact, *Talent Report: What Workers Want in 2012*, (San Francisco: Net Impact, 2012).

59. W. Immen, "On the Move for Work," *Globe & Mail*, May 15, 2010, B16.

60. S. Fischer, "Globalization and Its Challenges," *American Economic Review* (May 2003): 1–29. For discussion of the diverse meanings of *globalization,* see M. F. Guillén, "Is Globalization Civilizing, Destructive or Feeble? A Critique of Five Key Debates in the Social Science Literature," *Annual Review of Sociology* 27 (2001): 235–260.

61. The ongoing debate regarding the advantages and disadvantages of globalization are discussed in Guillén, "Is Globalization Civilizing, Destructive or Feeble?"; D. Doane, "Can Globalization Be Fixed?," *Business Strategy Review* 13, no. 2 (2002): 51–58; J. Bhagwati, *In Defense of Globalization* (New York: Oxford University Press, 2004); M. Wolf, *Why Globalization Works* (New Haven, CT: Yale University Press, 2004).

62. K. Ohmae, *The Next Global Stage* (Philadelphia: Wharton School Publishing, 2005).

63. "Verizon again Named to Black Enterprise Magazine's List of 40 Best Companies for Diversity," M2 Presswire news release for Verizon, June 29, 2010; "Working Mother Magazine Ranks Verizon among the Best Companies for Multicultural Women," *PR Newswire* news release for Verizon, May 26, 2011; "No. 22: Verizon Communications," 2011, accessed June 14, 2011, http://diversityinc.com/article/8294/No-22–Verizon-Communications/.

64. M. F. Riche, "America's Diversity and Growth: Signposts for the 21st Century," *Population Bulletin* (June 2000): 3–43; U.S. Census Bureau, *Statistical Abstract of the United States: 2004–2005* (Washington: U.S. Census Bureau, May 2005).

65. D. A. Harrison et al., "Time, Teams, and Task Performance: Changing Effects of Surface- and Deep-Level Diversity on Group Functioning," *Academy of Management Journal* 45, no. 5 (2002): 1029–46.

66. R. Zemke, C. Raines, and B. Filipczak, *Generations at Work: Managing the Clash of Veterans, Boomers, Xers, and Nexters in Your Workplace* (New York: Amacom, 2000); S. H. Applebaum, M. Serena, and B. T. Shapiro, "Generation X and the Boomers: Organizational Myths and Literary Realities," *Management Research News* 27, no. 11/12 (2004): 1–28; N. Howe and W. Strauss, "The Next 20 Years: How Customer and Workforce Attitudes Will Evolve," *Harvard Business Review* (July-August 2007): 41–52.

67. E. Parry and P. Urwin, "Generational Differences in Work Values: A Review of Theory and Evidence," *International Journal of Management Reviews* 13 (2011): 79–96.

68. E. Ng, L. Schweitzer, and S. Lyons, "New Generation, Great Expectations: A Field Study of the Millennial Generation," *Journal of Business and Psychology* 25, no. 2 (2010): 281–92.

69. U.S. Bureau of Labor Statistics, *Household Data, Annual Averages: Employment Status of the Civilian Noninstitutional Population by Age, Sex, and Race,* (Washington, D.C.: U.S. Bureau of Labor Statistics, 2010).

70. J. M. Twenge and S. M. Campbell, "Generational Differences in Psychological Traits and Their Impact on the Workplace," *Journal of Managerial Psychology* 23, no. 8 (2008): 862–77; M. Wong et al., "Generational Differences in Personality and Motivation," *Journal of Managerial Psychology* 23, no. 8 (2008): 878–90; J. Deal, D. Altman, and S. Rogelberg, "Millennials at Work: What We Know and What We Need to Do (If Anything)," *Journal of Business and Psychology* 25, no. 2 (2010): 191–99; B. Kowske, R. Rasch, and J. Wiley, "Millennials' (Lack of) Attitude Problem: An Empirical Examination of Generational Effects on Work Attitudes," *Journal of Business and Psychology* 25, no. 2 (2010): 265–79; J. Twenge, "A Review of the Empirical Evidence on Generational Differences in Work Attitudes," *Journal of Business and Psychology* 25, no. 2 (2010): 201–10.

71. J. M. Twenge et al., "Generational Differences in Work Values: Leisure and Extrinsic Values Increasing, Social and Intrinsic Values Decreasing," *Journal of Management* 36, no. 5 (September 2010): 1117–42. Another temporal cohort study also reported an increasing preference for leisure, but these differences were not significant. See: J. Meriac, D. Woehr, and C. Banister, "Generational Differences in Work Ethic: An Examination of Measurement Equivalence across Three Cohorts," *Journal of Business and Psychology* 25, no. 2 (2010): 315–24.

72. O. C. Richard, "Racial Diversity, Business Strategy, and Firm Performance: A Resource-Based View," *Academy of Management Journal* 43 (2000): 164–77; T. Kochan et al., "The Effects of Diversity on Business Performance: Report of the Diversity Research Network," *Human Resource Management* 42 (2003): 3–21; R. J. Burke and E. Ng, "The Changing Nature of Work and Organizations: Implications for Human Resource Management," *Human Resource Management Review* 16 (2006): 86–94; M.-E. Roberge and R. van Dick, "Recognizing the Benefits of Diversity: When and How Does Diversity Increase Group Performance?," *Human Resource Management Review* 20, no. 4 (2010): 295–308.

73. D. Porras, D. Psihountas, and M. Griswold, "The Long-Term Performance of Diverse Firms," *International Journal of Diversity* 6, no. 1 (2006): 25–34; R. A. Weigand, "Organizational Diversity, Profits and Returns in U.S. Firms," *Problems & Perspectives in Management*, no. 3 (2007): 69–83.

74. "Working Mother Magazine Ranks Verizon among the Best Companies for Multicultural Women."

75. R. J. Ely and D. A. Thomas, "Cultural Diversity at Work: The Effects of Diversity Perspectives on Work Group Processes and Outcomes," *Administrative Science Quarterly* 46 (June 2001): 229–73; Kochan et al., "The Effects of Diversity on Business Performance: Report of the Diversity Research Network,"; D. van Knippenberg and S. A. Haslam, "Realizing the Diversity Dividend: Exploring the Subtle Interplay between Identity, Ideology and Reality," in *Social Identity at Work: Developing Theory for Organizational Practice*, ed. S. A. Haslam et al. (New York: Taylor and Francis, 2003), 61–80; D. van Knippenberg, C. K. W. De Dreu, and A. C. Homan, "Work Group Diversity and Group Performance: An Integrative Model and Research Agenda," *Journal of Applied Psychology* 89, no. 6 (2004): 1008–22; E. Molleman, "Diversity in Demographic Characteristics, Abilities and Personality Traits: Do Faultlines Affect Team Functioning?," *Group Decision and Negotiation* 14, no. 3 (2005): 173–93.

76. Regus, *A Better Balance* (Luxembourg: Regus, May 2012).

77. W. G. Bennis and R. J. Thomas, *Geeks and Geezers* (Boston: Harvard Business School Press, 2002), 74–79; E. D. Y. Greenblatt, "Work/Life Balance: Wisdom or Whining," *Organizational Dynamics* 31, no. 2 (2002): 177–93.

78. *WorldatWork, Telework Trendlines 2009* (Scottsdale, AZ: WorldatWork, February 2009).

79. M. Conlin, "The Easiest Commute of All," *Businessweek*, December 12, 2005, 78; "Increased Productivity Due to Telecommuting Generates an Estimated $277 Million in Annual Savings for Company," Cisco systems news release, June 25, 2009; D. Meinert, "Make Telecommuting Pay Off," *HRMagazine*, June 2011, 33.

80. A. Bourhis and R. Mekkaoui, "Beyond Work-Family Balance: Are Family-Friendly Organizations More Attractive?," *Relations Industrielles/Industrial Relations* 65, no. 1 (Winter 2010): 98–117; E. J. Hill et al., "Workplace Flexibility, Work Hours, and Work-Life Conflict: Finding an Extra Day or Two," *Journal of Family Psychology* 24, no. 3 (June 2010): 349–58

81. "Increased Productivity Due to Telecommuting Generates an Estimated $277 Million in Annual Savings for Company" news release; "Rep. Sarbane's Telework Improvements Act Passes House," news release for US Fed News Service, July 15, 2010); Meinert, "Make Telecommuting Pay Off."

82. D. E. Bailey and N. B. Kurland, "A Review of Telework Research: Findings, New Directions, and Lessons for the Study of Modern Work," *Journal of Organizational Behavior* 23 (2002): 383–400; D. W. McCloskey and M. Igbaria, "Does 'out of Sight' Mean 'out of Mind'? An Empirical Investigation of the Career Advancement Prospects of Telecommuters," *Information Resources Management Journal* 16 (April-June 2003): 19–34.

83. Most of these anchors are mentioned in: J. D. Thompson, "On Building an Administrative Science," *Administrative Science Quarterly* 1, no. 1 (1956): 102–11.

84. This anchor has a colorful history dating back to critiques of business schools in the 1950s. Soon after, systematic research became a mantra by many respected scholars. See, for example: Thompson, "On Building an Administrative Science."

85. J. Pfeffer and R. I. Sutton, *Hard Facts, Dangerous Half-Truths, and Total Nonsense* (Boston: Harvard Business School Press, 2006); D. M. Rousseau and S. McCarthy, "Educating Managers from an Evidence-Based Perspective," *Academy of Management Learning & Education* 6, no. 1 (2007): 84–101; R. B. Briner and D. M. Rousseau, "Evidence-Based I–O Psychology: Not There Yet," *Industrial and Organizational Psychology* 4, no. 1 (2011): 3–22.

86. M. N. Zald, "More Fragmentation? Unfinished Business in Linking the Social Sciences and the Humanities," *Administrative Science Quarterly* 41 (1996): 251–61; C. Heath and S. B. Sitkin, "Big-B Versus Big-O: What Is Organizational About Organizational Behavior?," *Journal of Organizational Behavior* 22 (2001): 43–58; C. Oswick, P. Fleming, and G. Hanlon, "From Borrowing to Blending: Rethinking the Processes of Organizational Theory Building," *Academy of Management Review* 36, no. 2 (April 2011): 318–37.

87. D. M. Rousseau and Y. Fried, "Location, Location, Location: Contextualizing Organizational Research," *Journal of Organizational Behavior* 22, no. 1 (2001): 1–13; C. M. Christensen and M. E. Raynor, "Why Hard-Nosed Executives Should Care about Management Theory," *Harvard Business Review* (September 2003): 66–74. For excellent critique of the "one best way" approach in early management scholarship, see P. F. Drucker, "Management's New Paradigms," *Forbes* (October 5, 1998): 152–77.

88. H. L. Tosi and J. W. Slocum Jr., "Contingency Theory: Some Suggested Directions," *Journal of Management* 10 (1984): 9–26.

89. D. M. H. Rousseau, R. J. House, "Meso Organizational Behavior: Avoiding Three Fundamental Biases," in *Trends in Organizational Behavior*, ed. C. L. Cooper and D. M. Rousseau (Chichester, UK: John Wiley & Sons, 1994), 13–30.

CHAPTER 2

1. H. Oliviero, "Chicken Chain Attracts Relatives," *Atlanta Journal-Constitution,* May 15, 2011, D1.

2. L. L. Thurstone, "Ability, Motivation, and Speed," *Psychometrika* 2, no. 4 (1937): 249–54; N. R. F. Maier, *Psychology in Industry,* 2nd ed. (Boston: Houghton Mifflin Company, 1955); V. H. Vroom, *Work and Motivation* (New York: John Wiley & Sons, 1964); J. P. Campbell et al., *Managerial Behavior, Performance, and Effectiveness* (New York: McGraw-Hill, 1970).

3. U. C. Klehe and N. Anderson, "Working Hard and Working Smart: Motivation and Ability during Typical and Maximum Performance," *Journal of Applied Psychology* 92, no. 4 (2007): 978–92; J. S. Gould-Williams and M. Gatenby, "The Effects of Organizational Context and Teamworking Activities on Performance Outcomes—a Study Conducted in England Local Government," *Public Management Review* 12, no. 6 (2010): 759–87.

4. E. E. I. Lawler and L. W. Porter, "Antecedent Attitudes of Effective Managerial Performance," *Organizational Behavior and Human Performance* 2 (1967): 122–42; M. A. Griffin, A. Neal, and S. K. Parker, "A New Model of Work Role Performance: Positive Behavior in Uncertain and Interdependent Contexts," *Academy of Management Journal* 50, no. 2 (April 2007): 327–47.

5. Only a few literature reviews have included all four factors. These include J. P. Campbell and R. D. Pritchard, "Motivation Theory in Industrial and Organizational Psychology," in *Handbook of Industrial and Organizational Psychology*, ed. M. D. Dunnette (Chicago: Rand McNally, 1976), 62–130; T. R. Mitchell, "Motivation: New Directions for Theory, Research, and Practice," *Academy of Management review* 7, no. 1 (Jan. 1982): 80–88;

G. A. J. Churchill et al., "The Determinants of Salesperson Performance: A Meta-Analysis," *Journal of Marketing Research* 22, no. 2 (1985): 103–18; R. E. Plank and D. A. Reid, "The Mediating Role of Sales Behaviors: An Alternative Perspective of Sales Performance and Effectiveness," *Journal of Personal Selling & Sales Management* 14, no. 3 (Summer 1994): 43–56. The MARS acronym was coined by senior officers in the Singapore armed forces. Chris Perryer at the University of Western Australia suggests the full model should be called the "MARS BAR" because the outcomes might be labeled "behavior and results"!

6. Technically, the model proposes that situation factors moderate the effects of the three within-person factors. For instance, the effect of employee motivation on behavior and performance depends on (is moderated by) the situation.

7. C. C. Pinder, *Work Motivation in Organizational Behavior* (Upper Saddle River, NJ: Prentice-Hall, 1998); G. P. Latham and C. C. Pinder, "Work Motivation Theory and Research at the Dawn of the Twenty-First Century," *Annual Review of Psychology* 56 (2005): 485–516.

8. T. J. Watson Jr., *A Business and Its Beliefs* (New York: McGraw-Hill, 2003, 1963), 4.

9. L. M. Spencer and S. M. Spencer, *Competence at Work: Models for Superior Performance* (New York: Wiley, 1993); R. Kurz and D. Bartram, "Competency and Individual Performance: Modelling the World of Work," in *Organizational Effectiveness: The Role of Psychology,* ed. I. T. Robertson, M. Callinan, and D. Bartram (Chichester, UK: John Wiley & Sons, 2002), 227–58; D. Bartram, "The Great Eight Competencies: A Criterion-Centric Approach to Validation," *Journal of Applied Psychology* 90, no. 6 (2005): 1185–1203; H. Heinsman et al., "Competencies through the Eyes of Psychologists: A Closer Look at Assessing Competencies," *International Journal of Selection and Assessment* 15, no. 4 (December 2007): 412–27.

10. Bartram, "The Great Eight Competencies."

11. J. N. Roy, "The Great 2012 Talent Migration," *Talent Management,* May 4, 2012. Based on interviews with 1,143 employed American adults in September 2011.

12. P. Tharenou, A. M. Saks, and C. Moore, "A Review and Critique of Research on Training and Organizational-Level Outcomes," *Human Resource Management Review* 17, no. 3 (2007): 251–73; T. W. H. Ng and D. C. Feldman, "How Broadly Does Education Contribute to Job Performance?," *Personnel Psychology* 62, no. 1 (Spring 2009): 89–134.

13. "Canadian Organizations Must Work Harder to Productively Engage Employees," Watson Wyatt Canada news release for Watson Wyatt Canada, January 25, 2005; BlessingWhite, *Employee Engagement Report 2011* (Princeton, NJ: BlessingWhite, January 2011).

14. J. Becker and L. Layton, "Safety Warnings Often Ignored at Metro," *Washington Post,* June 6, 2005, A01.

15. W. H. Cooper and M. J. Withey, "The Strong Situation Hypothesis," *Personality and Social Psychology Review* 13, no. 1 (February 2009): 62–72; D. C. Funder, "Persons, Behaviors and Situations: An Agenda for Personality Psychology in the Postwar Era," *Journal of Research in Personality* 43, no. 2 (2009): 120–26; R. D. Meyer, R. S. Dalal, and R. Hermida, "A Review and Synthesis of Situational Strength in the Organizational Sciences," *Journal of Management* 36, no. 1 (January 2010): 121–40; R. A. Sherman, C. S. Nave, and D. C. Funder, "Situational Similarity and Personality Predict Behavioral Consistency," *Journal of Personality and Social Psychology* 99, no. 2 (2010): 330–43.

16. K. F. Kane, "Special Issue: Situational Constraints and Work Performance," *Human Resource Management Review* 3 (Summer 1993): 83–175; S. B. Bacharach and P. Bamberger, "Beyond Situational Constraints: Job Resources Inadequacy and Individual Performance at Work," *Human Resource Management Review* 5, no. 2 (1995): 79–102; G. Johns, "Commentary: In Praise of Context," *Journal of Organizational Behavior* 22 (2001): 31–42.

17. Meyer, Dalal, and Hermida, "A Review and Synthesis of Situational Strength in the Organizational Sciences."

18. J. P. Campbell, "The Definition and Measurement of Performance in the New Age," in *The Changing Nature of Performance: Implications for Staffing, Motivation, and Development,* ed. D. R. Ilgen and E. D. Pulakos (San Francisco: Jossey-Bass, 1999), 399–429; R. D. Hackett, "Understanding and Predicting Work Performance in the Canadian Military," *Canadian Journal of Behavioural Science* 34, no. 2 (2002): 131–40.

19. O. Varela and R. Landis, "A General Structure of Job Performance: Evidence from Two Studies," *Journal of Business and Psychology* 25, no. 4 (2010): 625–38.

20. D. W. Organ, "Organizational Citizenship Behavior: It's Construct Clean-up Time," *Human Performance* 10 (1997): 85–97; J. A. LePine, A. Erez, and D. E. Johnson, "The Nature and Dimensionality of Organizational Citizenship Behavior: A Critical Review and Meta-Analysis," *Journal of Applied Psychology* 87 (February 2002): 52–65; R. S. Dalal, "A Meta-Analysis of the Relationship between Organizational Citizenship Behavior and Counterproductive Work Behavior," *Journal of Applied Psychology* 90, no. 6 (2005): 1241–55.

21. S. Majumdar, "Meaningful Engagement," *Business Standard (India),* March 5, 2009, 8.

22. K. Lee and N. J. Allen, "Organizational Citizenship Behavior and Workplace Deviance: The Role of Affect and Cognitions," *Journal of Applied Psychology* 87, no. 1 (2002): 131–42.

23. M. Rotundo and P. Sackett, "The Relative Importance of Task, Citizenship, and Counterproductive Performance to Global Ratings of Job Performance: A Policy-Capturing Approach," *Journal of Applied Psychology* 87 (February 2002): 66–80; P. D. Dunlop and K. Lee, "Workplace Deviance, Organizational Citizenship Behaviour, and Business Unit Performance: The Bad Apples Do Spoil the Whole Barrel," *Journal of Organizational Behavior* 25 (2004): 67–80; Dalal, "A Meta-Analysis of the Relationship between Organizational Citizenship Behavior and Counterproductive Work Behavior"; N. A. Bowling and M. L. Gruys, "Overlooked Issues in the Conceptualization and Measurement of Counterproductive Work Behavior," *Human Resource Management Review* 20, no. 1 (2010): 54–61.

24. P. I. Buerhaus, D. I. Auerbach, and D. O. Staiger, "The Recent Surge in Nurse Employment: Causes and Implications," *Health Affairs* 28, no. 4 (July 1, 2009 2009): w657–68; W. Dunham, "U.S. Healthcare System Pinched by Nursing Shortage," *Reuters* (Washington, D.C.), March 8, 2009; J. Skerritt, "Nursing Shortages Plague Reserves," *Winnipeg Free Press,* November 13, 2009, A4; S. Goodchild, "Babies Turned Away in Hospital Bed Crisis," *Evening Standard* (London), November 2, 2010. The recent survey is reported in P. Kujawa, "Beer Here, Bucks Here; Come Here?," *Workforce Management,* April 2012, 17.

25. "Social Recruiting Survey 2011," (Burlingame, CA: Jobvite, 2012), www.jobvite.com, accessed 15 June 2012; P. Brotherton, "Social Media and Referrals Are Best Sources for Talent," *T&D,* January 2012, 24; A. D. Wright, "Your Social Media Is Showing," *HRMagazine,* March 2012, 16.

26. N. Chaudhury et al., "Missing in Action: Teacher and Health Worker Absence in Developing Countries," *The Journal of Economic Perspectives* 20, no. 1 (2006): 91–116.

27. A. Furnham and M. Bramwell, "Personality Factors Predict Absenteeism in the Workplace," *Individual Differences Research* 4, no. 2 (2006): 68–77.

28. D. A. Harrison and J. J. Martocchio, "Time for Absenteeism: A 20–Year Review of Origins, Offshoots, and Outcomes," *Journal of Management* 24 (Spring 1998): 305–50; C. M. Mason and M. A. Griffin, "Group Absenteeism and Positive Affective Tone: A Longitudinal Study," *Journal of Organizational Behavior* 24 (2003): 667–87; A. Vaananen et al., "Job Characteristics, Physical and Psychological Symptoms, and Social Support as Antecedents of Sickness Absence among Men and Women in the Private Industrial Sector," *Social Science & Medicine* 57, no. 5 (2003): 807–24.

29. R. Lombardi, "Walking Wounded," *Canadian Occupational Safety,* November/December 2009, 14–15; G. Johns, "Presenteeism in the Workplace: A Review and Research Agenda," *Journal of Organizational Behavior* 31, no. 4 (2010): 519–42.

30. C. Crawshaw, "Personality Testing Can Be a Sticky Subject," *Edmonton Journal,* 29 March 29, 2008, D14.

31. Personality researchers agree on one point about the definition of personality: It is difficult to pin down. A definition necessarily captures one perspective of the topic more than others, and the concept of personality is itself very broad. The definition presented here is based on C. S. Carver and M. F. Scheier, *Perspectives on Personality,* 6th ed. (Boston: Allyn & Bacon, 2007); D. C. Funder, *The Personality Puzzle,* 4th ed. (New York: W. W. Norton & Company, 2007).

32. D. P. McAdams and J. L. Pals, "A New Big Five: Fundamental Principles for an Integrative Science of Personality," *American Psychologist* 61, no. 3 (2006): 204–17.

33. B. Reynolds and K. Karraker, "A Big Five Model of Disposition and Situation Interaction: Why a 'Helpful' Person May Not Always Behave Helpfully," *New Ideas in Psychology* 21 (April 2003): 1–13; W. Mischel, "Toward an Integrative Science of the Person," *Annual Review of Psychology* 55 (2004): 1–22.

34. I. B. Singer and R. Burgin, *Conversations with Isaac Bashevis Singer* (New York: Doubleday, 1985), 53.

35. B. W. Roberts and A. Caspi, "Personality Development and the Person-Situation Debate: It's DéjÃ Vu All over Again," *Psychological Inquiry* 12, no. 2 (2001): 104–9.

36. K. L. Jang, W. J. Livesley, and P. A. Vernon, "Heritability of the Big Five Personality Dimensions and Their Facets: A Twin Study," *Journal of Personality* 64, no. 3 (1996): 577–91; N. L. Segal, *Entwined Lives: Twins and What They Tell Us about Human Behavior* (New York: Plume, 2000); T. Bouchard and J. Loehlin, "Genes, Evolution, and Personality," *Behavior Genetics* 31, no. 3 (May 2001): 243–273; G. Lensvelt-Mulders and J. Hettema, "Analysis of Genetic Influences on the Consistency and Variability of the Big Five across Different Stressful Situations," *European Journal of Personality* 15, no. 5 (2001): 355–371; P. Borkenau et al., "Genetic and Environmental Influences on Person X Situation Profiles," *Journal of Personality* 74, no. 5 (2006): 1451–80.

37. B. W. Roberts and W. F. DelVecchio, "The Rank-Order Consistency of Personality Traits from Childhood to Old Age: A Quantitative Review of Longitudinal Studies," *Psychological Bulletin* 126, no. 1 (2000): 3–25; A. Terracciano, P. T. Costa, and R. R. McCrae, "Personality Plasticity after Age 30," *Personality and Social Psychology Bulletin* 32, no. 8 (Aug. 2006): 999–1009.

38. M. Jurado and M. Rosselli, "The Elusive Nature of Executive Functions: A Review of Our Current Understanding," *Neuropsychology Review* 17, no. 3 (2007): 213–33.

39. B. W. Roberts and E. M. Pomerantz, "On Traits, Situations, and Their Integration: A Developmental Perspective," *Personality & Social Psychology Review* 8, no. 4 (2004): 402–16; W. Fleeson, "Situation-Based Contingencies Underlying Trait-Content Manifestation in Behavior," *Journal of Personality* 75, no. 4 (2007): 825–62.

40. J. M. Digman, "Personality Structure: Emergence of the Five-Factor Model," *Annual Review of Psychology* 41 (1990): 417–40; O. P. John and S. Srivastava, "The Big Five Trait Taxonomy: History, Measurement, and Theoretical Perspectives," in *Handbook of Personality: Theory and Research,* ed. L. A. Pervin and O. P. John (New York: Guildford Press, 1999), 102–38; A. Caspi, B. W. Roberts, and R. L. Shiner, "Personality Development: Stability and Change," *Annual Review of Psychology* 56, no. 1 (2005): 453–84; McAdams and Pals, "A New Big Five."

41. J. Hogan and B. Holland, "Using Theory to Evaluate Personality and Job-Performance Relations: A Socioanalytic Perspective," *Journal of Applied Psychology* 88, no. 1 (2003): 100–12; D. S. Ones, C. Viswesvaran, and S. Dilchert, "Personality at Work: Raising Awareness and Correcting Misconceptions," *Human Performance* 18, no. 4 (2005): 389–404; I.-S. Oh and C. M. Berry, "The Five-Factor Model of Personality and Managerial Performance: Validity Gains through the Use of 360 Degree Performance Ratings," *Journal of Applied Psychology* 94, no. 6 (2009): 1498–1513.

42. M. R. Barrick and M. K. Mount, "Yes, Personality Matters: Moving on to More Important Matters," *Human Performance* 18, no. 4 (2005): 359–372; D. S. Ones et al., "In Support of Personality Assessment in Organizational Settings," *Personnel Psychology* 60, no. 4 (2007): 995–1027; S. J. Perry et al., "*P = F* (Conscientiousness X Ability): Examining the Facets of Conscientiousness," *Human Performance* 23, no. 4 (2010): 343–60.

43. M. R. Barrick, M. K. Mount, and T. A. Judge, "Personality and Performance at the Beginning of the New Millennium: What Do We Know and Where Do We Go Next?," *International Journal of Selection and Assessment* 9, no. 1 & 2 (2001): 9–30; T. A. Judge and R. Ilies, "Relationship of Personality to Performance Motivation: A Meta-Analytic Review," *Journal of Applied Psychology* 87, no. 4 (2002): 797–807; A. Witt, L. A. Burke, and M. R. Barrick, "The Interactive Effects of Conscientiousness and Agreeableness on Job Performance," *Journal of Applied Psychology* 87 (February 2002): 164–169; J. Moutafi, A. Furnham, and J. Crump, "Is Managerial Level Related to Personality?," *British Journal of Management* 18, no. 3 (2007): 272–80.

44. R. Ilies, M. W. Gerhardt, and H. Le, "Individual Differences in Leadership Emergence: Integrating Meta-Analytic Findings and Behavioral Genetics Estimates," *International Journal of Selection and Assessment* 12, no. 3 (September 2004): 207–19; Oh and Berry, "The Five-Factor Model of Personality and Managerial Performance: Validity Gains through the Use of 360 Degree Performance Ratings."

45. K. M. DeNeve and H. Cooper, "The Happy Personality: A Meta-Analysis of 137 Personality Traits and Subjective Well-Being," *Psychological Bulletin* 124 (September 1998): 197–229; M. L. Kern and H. S. Friedman, "Do Conscientious Individuals Live Longer? A Quantitative Review," *Health Psychology* 27, no. 5 (2008): 505–12; P. S. Fry and D. L. Debats, "Perfectionism and the Five-Factor Personality Traits as Predictors of

Mortality in Older Adults," *Journal of Health Psychology* 14, no. 4 (May 1, 2009): 513–24; F. C. M. Geisler, M. Wiedig-Allison, and H. Weber, "What Coping Tells about Personality," *European Journal of Personality* 23, no. 4 (2009): 289–306; H. S. Friedman, M. L. Kern, and C. A. Reynolds, "Personality and Health, Subjective Well-Being, and Longevity," *Journal of Personality* 78, no. 1 (2010): 179–216.

46. C. G. Jung, *Psychological Types,* trans. H. G. Baynes (Princeton, NJ: Princeton University Press, 1971); I. B. Myers, *The Myers-Briggs Type Indicator* (Palo Alto, CA: Consulting Psychologists Press, 1987).

47. Adapted from an exhibit found at http://www.16–personality-types.com.

48. M. Gladwell, "Personality Plus," *New Yorker,* September 20, 2004, 42–48; R. B. Kennedy and D. A. Kennedy, "Using the Myers-Briggs Type Indicator in Career Counseling," *Journal of Employment Counseling* 41, no. 1 (March 2004): 38–44.

49. R. M. Capraro and M. M. Capraro, "Myers-Briggs Type Indicator Score Reliability across Studies: A Meta-Analytic Reliability Generalization Study," *Educational and Psychological Measurement* 62 (August 2002): 590–602; J. Michael, "Using the Myers -Briggs Type Indicator as a Tool for Leadership Development? Apply with Caution," *Journal of Leadership & Organizational Studies* 10 (Summer 2003): 68–81; Moutafi, Furnham, and Crump, "Is Managerial Level Related to Personality?"; F. W. Brown and M. D. Reilly, "The Myers-Briggs Type Indicator and Transformational Leadership," *Journal of Management Development* 28, no. 10 (2009): 916–32; B. S. Kuipers et al., "The Influence of Myers-Briggs Type Indicator Profiles on Team Development Processes," *Small Group Research* 40, no. 4 (August 2009): 436–64.

50. R. R. McCrae and P. T. Costa, "Reinterpreting the Myers-Briggs Type Indicator from the Perspective of the Five-Factor Model of Personality," *Journal of Personality* 57 (1989): 17–40; A. Furnham, "The Big Five versus the Big Four: The Relationship between the Myers-Briggs Type Indicator (MBTI) and NEO-PI Five Factor Model of Personality," *Personality and Individual Differences* 21, no. 2 (1996): 303–07.

51. S. Vazire and S. D. Gosling, "E-Perceptions: Personality Impressions Based on Personal Websites," *Journal of Personality and Social Psychology* 87, no. 1 (2004): 123–32; A. J. Gill, J. Oberlander, and E. Austin, "Rating E-Mail Personality at Zero Acquaintance," *Personality and Individual Differences* 40, no. 3 (2006): 497–507; R. E. Guadagno, B. M. Okdie, and C. A. Eno, "Who Blogs? Personality Predictors of Blogging," *Computers in Human Behavior* 24, no. 5 (2008): 1993–2004; D. H. Kluemper and P. A. Rosen, "Future Employment Selection Methods: Evaluating Social Networking Web Sites," *Journal of Managerial Psychology* 24, no. 6 (2009): 567–80; C. Ross et al., "Personality and Motivations Associated with Facebook Use," *Computers in Human Behavior* 25, no. 2 (2009): 578–586; M. D. Back et al., "Facebook Profiles Reflect Actual Personality, Not Self-Idealization," *Psychological Science* (January 2010); T. Yarkoni, "Personality in 100,000 Words: A Large-Scale Analysis of Personality and Word Use among Bloggers," *Journal of Research in Personality* 44, no. 3 (2010): 363–373.

52. K. M. Butler, "Using Positive Four-Letter Words," *Employee Benefit News,* April 2007; M. Weinstein, "Personality Assessment Soars at Southwest," *Training,* 3, January 2008.

53. "Metrolink Train Crews in Southern California Threaten Boycott over New Personality Tests," *Associated Press,* April 1, 2010, Lopez, 2010 #542.

54. K. C. Neel, "Abdoulah Sets Wow Apart," *Multichannel News,* January 29, 2007, 2; D. Graham, "She Walks the Talk," *Denver Woman,* April 2009; "Wow! Management Team," 2010, accessed December 6, 2010, http://www.wowway.com/internet-cable-phone-company/wow-management-executive-bios/.

55. B. M. Meglino and E. C. Ravlin, "Individual Values in Organizations: Concepts, Controversies, and Research," *Journal of Management* 24, no. 3 (1998): 351–89; B. R. Agle and C. B. Caldwell, "Understanding Research on Values in Business," *Business and Society* 38, no. 3 (September 1999): 326–87; S. Hitlin and J. A. Pilavin, "Values: Reviving a Dormant Concept," *Annual Review of Sociology* 30 (2004): 359–93.

56. D. Lubinski, D. B. Schmidt, and C. P. Benbow, "A 20–Year Stability Analysis of the Study of Values for Intellectually Gifted Individuals from Adolescence to Adulthood," *Journal of Applied Psychology* 81 (1996): 443–51.

57. L. Parks and R. P. Guay, "Personality, Values, and Motivation," *Personality and Individual Differences* 47, no. 7 (2009): 675–84.

58. Hitlin and Pilavin, "Values: Reviving a Dormant Concept," A. Pakizeh, J. E. Gebauer, and G. R. Maio, "Basic Human Values: Inter-Value Structure in Memory," *Journal of Experimental Social Psychology* 43, no. 3 (2007): 458–65.

59. S. H. Schwartz, "Universals in the Content and Structure of Values: Theoretical Advances and Empirical Tests in 20 Countries," *Advances in Experimental Social Psychology* 25 (1992): 1–65; S. H. Schwartz, "Are There Universal Aspects in the Structure and Contents of Human Values?," *Journal of Social Issues* 50 (1994): 19–45; D. Spini, "Measurement Equivalence of 10 Value Types from the Schwartz Value Survey across 21 Countries," *Journal of Cross-Cultural Psychology* 34, no. 1 (January 2003): 3–23; S. H. Schwartz and K. Boehnke, "Evaluating the Structure of Human Values with Confirmatory Factor Analysis," *Journal of Research in Personality* 38, no. 3 (2004): 230–55.

60. M. Schrage, *Serious Play: How the World's Best Companies Simulate to Innovate* (Cambridge, MA: Harvard Business School Press, 1999), 98.

61. G. R. Maio and J. M. Olson, "Values as Truisms: Evidence and Implications," *Journal of Personality and Social Psychology* 74, no. 2 (1998): 294–311; G. R. Maio et al., "Addressing Discrepancies between Values and Behavior: The Motivating Effect of Reasons," *Journal of Experimental Social Psychology* 37, no. 2 (2001): 104–17; B. Verplanken and R. W. Holland, "Motivated Decision Making: Effects of Activation and Self-Centrality of Values on Choices and Behavior," *Journal of Personality and Social Psychology* 82, no. 3 (2002): 434–47; A. Bardi and S. H. Schwartz, "Values and Behavior: Strength and Structure of Relations," *Personality and Social Psychology Bulletin* 29, no. 10 (October 2003): 1207–20; M. M. Bernard and G. R. Maio, "Effects of Introspection about Reasons for Values: Extending Research on Values-as-Truisms," *Social Cognition* 21, no. 1 (2003): 1–25.

62. N. Mazar, O. Amir, and D. Ariely, "The Dishonesty of Honest People: A Theory of Self-Concept Maintenance," *Journal of Marketing Research* 45 (December 2008): 633–44.

63. A. L. Kristof, "Person-Organization Fit: An Integrative Review of Its Conceptualizations, Measurement, and Implications," *Personnel Psychology* 49, no. 1 (Spring 1996): 1–49; M. L. Verquer, T. A. Beehr, and S. H. Wagner, "A Meta-Analysis of Relations between Person-Organization Fit and Work Attitudes," *Journal of Vocational Behavior* 63 (2003): 473–89; J. W. Westerman and L. A. Cyr, "An Integrative Analysis of

Person-Organization Fit Theories," *International Journal of Selection and Assessment* 12, no. 3 (September 2004): 252–61; D. Bouckenooghe et al., "The Prediction of Stress by Values and Value Conflict," *Journal of Psychology* 139, no. 4 (2005): 369–82.

64. Aspen Institute, *Where Will They Lead?* (New York: Aspen Institute, 17 April 2008).

65. K. Hornyak, "Upward Move: Cynthia Schwalm," *Medical Marketing & Media,* June 2008, 69. For research on the consequences on values congruence, see Kristof, "Person-Organization Fit: An Integrative Review of Its Conceptualizations, Measurement, and Implications"; Verquer, Beehr, and Wagner, "A Meta-Analysis of Relations between Person-Organization Fit and Work Attitudes"; Westerman and Cyr, "An Integrative Analysis of Person-Organization Fit Theories"; Bouckenooghe et al., "The Prediction of Stress by Values and Value Conflict."

66. T. Simons, "Behavioral Integrity: The Perceived Alignment be-tween Managers' Words and Deeds as a Research Focus," *Organization Science* 13, no. 1 (January-February 2002): 18–35; Watson Wyatt, "Employee Ratings of Senior Management Dip, Watson Wyatt Survey Finds," Watson Wyatt news release, January 4, 2007).

67. Z. Aycan, R. N. Kanungo, and J. B. P. Sinha, "Organizational Culture and Human Resource Management Practices: The Model of Culture Fit," *Journal of Cross-Cultural Psychology* 30 (July 1999): 501–26; M. Naor, K. Linderman, and R. Schroeder, "The Globalization of Operations in Eastern and Western Countries: Unpacking the Relationship between National and Organizational Culture and Its Impact on Manufacturing Performance," *Journal of Operations Management* 28, no. 3 (2010): 194–205. This type of values incongruence can occur even when the company is founded in that country, that is, when a local company tries to introduce a culture incompatible with the national culture. See for example: A. Danisman, "Good Intentions and Failed Implementations: Understanding Culture-Based Resistance to Organizational Change," *European Journal of Work and Organizational Psychology* 19, no. 2 (2010): 200–20.

68. C. Savoye, "Workers Say Honesty Is Best Company Policy," *Christian Science Monitor,* June 15 2000; J. M. Kouzes and B. Z. Posner, *The Leadership Challenge,* 3rd ed. (San Francisco: Jossey-Bass, 2002); J. Schettler, "Leadership in Corporate America," *Training & Development,* September 2002, 66–73; Ekos Politics, *Women See It Differently,* (Ottawa: Ekos Politics, 6 May 2010).

69. P. L. Schumann, "A Moral Principles Framework for Human Resource Management Ethics," *Human Resource Management Review* 11 (Spring-Summer 2001): 93–111; J. Boss, *Analyzing Moral Issues,* 3rd ed. (New York: McGraw-Hill, 2005), Chap. 1; M. G. Velasquez, *Business Ethics: Concepts and Cases,* 6th ed. (Upper Saddle River, NJ: Prentice-Hall, 2006), Chap. 2.

70. For a recent analysis of these predictors of ethical conduct, see: J. J. Kish-Gephart, D. A. Harrison, and L. K. Treviño, "Bad Apples, Bad Cases, and Bad Barrels: Meta-Analytic Evidence about Sources of Unethical Decisions at Work," *Journal of Applied Psychology* 95, no. 1 (2010): 1–31.

71. T. J. Jones, "Ethical Decision Making by Individuals in Organizations: An Issue Contingent Model," *Academy of Management Review* 16 (1991): 366–95; B. H. Frey, "The Impact of Moral Intensity on Decision Making in a Business Context," *Journal of Business Ethics* 26 (August 2000): 181–95; D. R. May and K. P. Pauli, "The Role of Moral Intensity in Ethical Decision Making," *Business and Society* 41 (March 2002): 84–117.

72. J. R. Sparks and S. D. Hunt, "Marketing Researcher Ethical Sensitivity: Conceptualization, Measurement, and Exploratory Investigation," *Journal of Marketing* 62 (April 1998): 92–109.

73. Ethics Resource Center, *2011 National Business Ethics Survey: Workplace Ethics in Transition* (Arlington, VA: Ethics Resource Center, 2012).

74. K. F. Alam, "Business Ethics in New Zealand Organizations: Views from the Middle and Lower Level Managers," *Journal of Business Ethics* 22 (November 1999): 145–53; Human Resource Institute, *The Ethical Enterprise: State-of-the-Art,* (St. Petersburg, Florida: Human Resource Institute, January 2006).

75. S. J. Reynolds, K. Leavitt, and K. A. DeCelles, "Automatic Ethics: The Effects of Implicit Assumptions and Contextual Cues on Moral Behavior," *Journal of Applied Psychology* 95, no. 4 (2010): 752–60.

76. D. R. Beresford, N. d. Katzenbach, and C. B. Rogers Jr, *Report of Investigation by the Special Investigative Committee of the Board of Directors of Worldcom, Inc.,* (March 31, 2003).

77. H. Donker, D. Poff, and S. Zahir, "Corporate Values, Codes of Ethics, and Firm Performance: A Look at the Canadian Context," *Journal of Business Ethics* 82, no. 3 (2008): 527–37; L. Preuss, "Codes of Conduct in Organisational Context: From Cascade to Lattice-Work of Codes," *Journal of Business Ethics* 94, no. 4 (2010): 471–87.

78. B. Farrell, D. M. Cobbin, and H. M. Farrell, "Codes of Ethics: Their Evolution, Development and Other Controversies," *Journal of Management Development* 21, no. 2 (2002): 152–63; G. Wood and M. Rimmer, "Codes of Ethics: What Are They Really and What Should They Be?," *International Journal of Value-Based Management* 16, no. 2 (2003): 181.

79. S. Greengard, "Golden Values," *Workforce Management,* March 2005, 52–53; K. Tyler, "Do the Right Thing," *HRMagazine,* February 2005, 99–102.

80. Texas Instruments, *The Values and Ethics of TI* (Dallas: 18 February 2011).

81. G. Svensson et al., "Ethical Structures and Processes of Corporations Operating in Australia, Canada, and Sweden: A Longitudinal and Cross-Cultural Study," *Journal of Business Ethics* 86, no. 4 (2009): 485–506.

82. E. Aronson, "Integrating Leadership Styles and Ethical Perspectives," *Canadian Journal of Administrative Sciences* 18 (December 2001): 266–76; D. R. May et al., "Developing the Moral Component of Authentic Leadership," *Organizational Dynamics* 32 (2003): 247–60. The Vodafone director quota-tion is from R. Van Lee, L. Fabish, and N. McGaw, "The Value of Corporate Values," *strategy+business,* no. 39 (Summer 2005): 1–13.

83. V. Galt, "A World of Opportunity for Those in Mid-Career," *Globe & Mail,* June 7, 2006, C1.

84. A. Fisher, "How to Be a Better Global Manager," *Fortune,* July 9, 2009.

85. Individual and collectivism information are from the meta-analysis by Oyserman, Coon, and Kemmelmeier, not the earlier findings by Hofstede. See: D. Oyserman, H. M. Coon, and M. Kemmelmeier, "Rethinking Individualism and Collectivism: Evaluation of Theoretical Assumptions and Meta-Analyses," *Psychological Bulletin* 128 (2002): 3–72. Consistent with Oyserman et al., a recent study found high rather than low indi-vidualism among Chileans. See: A. Kolstad and S. Horpestad, "Self-Construal in Chile and Norway," *Journal of Cross-Cultural Psychology* 40, no. 2 (March 2009): 275–81.

86. C. P. Earley and C. B. Gibson, "Taking Stock in Our Progress on Individualism-Collectivism: 100 Years of Solidarity and Community," *Journal of Management* 24 (May 1998): 265–304; F. S. Niles, "Individualism-Collectivism Revisited," *Cross-Cultural Research* 32 (November 1998): 315–41; C. L. Jackson et al., "Psychological Collectivism: A Measurement Validation and Linkage to Group Member Performance," *Journal of Applied Psychology* 91, no. 4 (2006): 884–99.

87. Oyserman, Coon, and Kemmelmeier, "Rethinking Individualism and Collectivism." Also see F. Li and L. Aksoy, "Dimensionality of Individualism–Collectivism and Measurement Equivalence of Triandis and Gelfand's Scale," *Journal of Business and Psychology* 21, no. 3 (2007): 313–29. The relationship between individualism and collectivism is still being debated, but most experts now agree that individualism and collectivism have serious problems with conceptualization and measurement.

88. M. Voronov and J. A. Singer, "The Myth of Individualism-Collectivism: A Critical Review," *Journal of Social Psychology* 142 (August 2002): 461–480; Y. Takano and S. Sogon, "Are Japanese More Collectivistic than Americans?," *Journal of Cross-Cultural Psychology* 39, no. 3 (May 1, 2008 2008): 237–50; D. Dalsky, "Individuality in Japan and the United States: A Cross-Cultural Priming Experiment," *International Journal of Intercultural Relations* 34, no. 5 (2010): 429–35.

89. G. Hofstede, *Culture's Consequences: Comparing Values, Behaviors, Institutions, and Organizations across Nations,* 2nd ed. (Thousand Oaks, CA: Sage, 2001).

90. S. Klie, "Program Breaks Cultural Barriers," *Canadian HR Reporter,* September 10, 2007.

91. Hofstede, *Culture's Consequences: Comparing Values, Behaviors, Institutions, and Organizations across Nations.* Hofstede used the terms *masculinity* and *femininity* for *achievement* and *nurturing orientation,* respectively. We (along with other writers) have adopted the latter two terms to minimize the sexist perspective of these concepts. Also, readers need to be aware that achievement orientation is assumed to be opposite of nurturing orientation, but this opposing relationship might be questioned.

92. V. Taras, J. Rowney, and P. Steel, "Half a Century of Measuring Culture: Review of Approaches, Challenges, and Limitations Based on the Analysis of 121 Instruments for Quantifying Culture," *Journal of International Management* 15, no. 4 (2009): 357–73.

93. R. L. Tung and A. Verbeke, "Beyond Hofstede and GLOBE: Improving the Quality of Cross–Cultural Research," *Journal of International Business Studies* 41, no. 8 (2010): 1259–74.

94. D. S. Berry, G. M. Jones, and S. A. Kuczaj, "Differing States of Mind: Regional Affiliation, Personality Judgment, and Self-View," *Basic and Applied Social Psychology* 22, no. 1 (2000): 43–56; K. H. Rogers and D. Wood, "Accuracy of United States Regional Personality Stereotypes," *Journal of Research in Personality* 44, no. 6 (2010): 704–13.

95. J. A. Vandello and D. Cohen, "Patterns of Individualism and Collectivism across the United States," *Journal of Personality and Social Psychology* 77, no. 2 (1999): 279–92.

96. W. K. W. Choy, A. B. E. Lee, and P. Ramburuth, "Multinationalism in the Workplace: A Myriad of Values in a Singaporean Firm," *Singapore Management Review* 31, no. 1 (January 2009).

97. N Jacob, "Cross-Cultural Investigations: Emerging Concepts," *Journal of Organizational Change Management* 18, no. 5 (2005): 514–28; V. Taras, B. L. Kirkman, and P. Steel, "Examining the Impact of Culture's Consequences: A Three-Decade, Multilevel, Meta-Analytic Review of Hofstede's Cultural Value Dimensions," *Journal of Applied Psychology* 95, no. 3 (2010): 405–39.

CHAPTER 3

1. I. M. O'Bannon, "The 'Certifiable' Public Accountant," *CPA Technology Advisor* 20, no. 7 (November 2010): 28–29. Blumer's comment can be found in a response to Joey Brannon's blog. See: J. Brannon, "10 Ways You Know You Were Born to Be an Accountant (or Not)," 2010, accessed 12 May 2011.

2. J. D. Campbell, S. Assanand, and A. Di Paula, "The Structure of the Self-Concept and Its Relation to Psychological Adjustment," *Journal of Personality* 71, no. 1 (2003): 115–40; M. J. Constantino et al., "The Direct and Stress-Buffering Effects of Self-Organization on Psychological Adjustment," *Journal of Social & Clinical Psychology* 25, no. 3 (2006): 333–60.

3. E. J. Koch and J. A. Shepperd, "Is Self-Complexity Linked to Better Coping? A Review of the Literature," *Journal of Personality* 72, no. 4 (2004): 727–60; A. R. McConnell, R. J. Rydell, and C. M. Brown, "On the Experience of Self-Relevant Feedback: How Self-Concept Organization Influences Affective Responses and Self-Evaluations," *Journal of Experimental Social Psychology* 45, no. 4 (2009): 695–707.

4. J. Lodi-Smith and B. W. Roberts, "Getting to Know Me: Social Role Experiences and Age Differences in Self-Concept Clarity during Adulthood," *Journal of Personality* 78, no. 5 (2010): 1383–1410.

5. Koch and Shepperd, "Is Self-Complexity Linked to Better Coping? A Review of the Literature"; A. R. McConnell et al., "The Simple Life: On the Benefits of Low Self-Complexity," *Personality and Social Psychology Bulletin* 35, no. 7 (July 2009): 823–35. On the process of self-concept repair, see: S. Chen and H. C. Boucher, "Relational Selves as Self-Affirmational Resources," *Journal of Research in Personality* 42, no. 3 (2008): 716–33.

6. A. T. Brook, J. Garcia, and M. A. Fleming, "The Effects of Multiple Identities on Psychological Well-Being," *Personality and Social Psychology Bulletin* 34, no. 12 (December 2008): 1588–1600.

7. J. D. Campbell, "Self-Esteem and Clarity of the Self-Concept," *Journal of Personality and Social Psychology* 59, no. 3 (1990).

8. T. W. H. Ng, K. L. Sorensen, and D. C. Feldman, "Dimensions, Antecedents, and Consequences of Workaholism: A Conceptual Integration and Extension," *Journal of Organizational Behavior* 28 (2007): 111–36; S. Pachulicz, N. Schmitt, and G. Kuljanin, "A Model of Career Success: A Longitudinal Study of Emergency Physicians," *Journal of Vocational Behavior* 73, no. 2 (2008): 242–53.

9. B. George, *Authentic Leadership* (San Francisco: Jossey-Bass, 2004); S. T. Hannah and B. J. Avolio, "Ready or Not: How Do We Accelerate the Developmental Readiness of Leaders?" *Journal of Organizational Behavior* 31, no. 8 (2010): 1181–87.

10. C. Sedikides and A. P. Gregg, "Portraits of the Self," in *The Sage Handbook of Social Psychology,* ed. M. A. Hogg and J. Cooper (London: Sage Publications, 2003), 110–38; M. D. Alicke and C. Sedikides, "Self-Enhancement and Self-Protection: What They Are and What They Do," *European Review of Social Psychology* 20 (2009): 1–48; C. L. Guenther and M. D. Alicke, "Deconstructing the Better-than-Average Effect," *Journal of Personality and Social Psychology* 99, no. 5 (2010): 755–70; S. Loughnan et al., "Universal Biases in Self-Perception: Better and More Human than Average," *British Journal of Social Psychology* 49 (2010): 627–36.

11. K. P. Cross, "Not Can, but *Will* College Teaching Be Improved?" *New Directions for Higher Education,* no. 17 (Spring 1977): 1–15; U.S. Merit Systems Protection Board, *Accomplishing Our*

Mission: Results of the 2005 Merit Principles Survey, (Washington, DC: U.S. Merit Systems Protection Board, December 6, 2007).

12. D. A. Moore, "Not So above Average after All: When People Believe They Are Worse than Average and Its Implications for Theories of Bias in Social Comparison," *Organizational Behavior and Human Decision Processes* 102, no. 1 (2007): 42–58.

13. M. S. Horswill, A. E. Waylen, and M. I. Tofield, "Drivers' Ratings of Different Components of Their Own Driving Skill: A Greater Illusion of Superiority for Skills That Relate to Accident Involvement," *Journal of Applied Social Psychology* 34, no. 1 (2004): 177–95; N. J. Hiller and D. C. Hambrick, "Conceptualizing Executive Hubris: The Role of (Hyper-) Core Self-Evaluations in Strategic Decision-Making," *Strategic Management Journal* 26, no. 4 (2005): 297–319; U. Malmendier and G. Tate, "CEO Overconfidence and Corporate Investment," *The Journal of Finance* 60, no. 6 (2005): 2661–2700; J. A. Doukas and D. Petmezas, "Acquisitions, Overconfident Managers and Self-Attribution Bias," *European Financial Management* 13, no. 3 (2007): 531–77; N. Harrè and C. G. Sibley, "Explicit and Implicit Self-Enhancement Biases in Drivers and Their Relationship to Driving Violations and Crash-Risk Optimism," *Accident Analysis & Prevention* 39, no. 6 (2007): 1155–61; D. A. Moore and P. J. Healy, "The Trouble with Overconfidence," *Psychological Review* 115, no. 2 (2008): 502–17.

14. "New Worldatwork Survey: Trends in Employee Recognition 2008," PRWeb news release for HRMarketer, April 23, 2008; A. Gostick and C. Elton, *The Carrot Principle,* reissued ed. (New York: Free Press, 2009); Kelly Services, *Acquisition and Retention in the War for Talent,* Kelly Global Workforce Index (Troy, MI: Kelly Services, April 2012). The WorldatWork survey provided the percentage of companies with recognition programs. Other survey statistics are from the remaining two sources. The global statistics consists of 168,000 respondents in 30 countries.

15. W. B. Swann Jr, "To Be Adored or to Be Known? The Interplay of Self-Enhancement and Self-Verification," in *Foundations of Social Behavior,* ed. R. M. Sorrentino and E. T. Higgins (New York: Guildford, 1990), 408–48; W. B. Swann Jr., P. J. Rentfrow, and J. S. Guinn, "Self-Verification: The Search for Coherence," in *Handbook of Self and Identity,* ed. M. R. Leary and J. Tagney (New York: Guildford, 2002), 367–83.

16. F. Anseel and F. Lievens, "Certainty as a Moderator of Feedback Reactions? A Test of the Strength of the Self-Verification Motive," *Journal of Occupational & Organizational Psychology* 79, no. 4 (2006): 533–51; T. Kwang and W. B. Swann, "Do People Embrace Praise Even When They Feel Unworthy? A Review of Critical Tests of Self-Enhancement versus Self-Verification," *Personality and Social Psychology Review* 14, no. 3 (August 2010): 263–80.

17. M. R. Leary, "Motivational and Emotional Aspects of the Self," *Annual Review of Psychology* 58, no. 1 (2007): 317–44.

18. T. A. Judge and J. E. Bono, "Relationship of Core Self-Evaluations Traits—Self-Esteem, Generalized Self-Efficacy, Locus of Control, and Emotional Stability—with Job Satisfaction and Job Performance: A Meta-Analysis," *Journal of Applied Psychology* 86, no. 1 (2001): 80–92; T. A. Judge and C. Hurst, "Capitalizing on One's Advantages: Role of Core Self-Evaluations," *Journal of Applied Psychology* 92, no. 5 (2007): 1212–27. We have described the three most commonly noted components of self-evaluation. The full model also includes emotional stability (low neuroticism). However, the core self-evaluation model has received limited research and its dimensions are being debated. For example, see T. W. Self, "Evaluating Core Self-Evaluations: Application of a Multidimensional, Latent-Construct, Evaluative Framework to Core Self-Evaluations Research" (Ph.D. thesis, University of Houston, 2007); R. E. Johnson, C. C. Rosen, and P. E. Levy, "Getting to the Core of Core Self-Evaluation: A Review and Recommendations," *Journal of Organizational Behavior* 29 (2008): 391–413.

19. R. F. Baumeister and J. M. Twenge, *The Social Self, Handbook of Psychology* (New York: John Wiley & Sons, Inc., 2003); W. B. Swann Jr., C. Chang-Schneider, and K. L. McClarty, "Do People's Self-Views Matter?: Self-Concept and Self-Esteem in Everyday Life," *American Psychologist* 62, no. 2 (2007): 84–94.

20. A. Bandura, *Self-Efficacy: The Exercise of Control* (New York: W. H. Freeman, 1997). However, one recent review found that self-efficacy's effect on task and job performance is much lower when also including the effects of personality traits on performance. See: T. A. Judge et al., "Self-Efficacy and Work-Related Performance: The Integral Role of Individual Differences," *Journal of Applied Psychology* 92, no. 1 (2007): 107–27.

21. G. Chen, S. M. Gully, and D. Eden, "Validation of a New General Self-Efficacy Scale," *Organizational Research Methods* 4, no. 1 (Jan. 2001): 62–83.

22. J. B. Rotter, "Generalized Expectancies for Internal Versus External Control of Reinforcement," *Psychological Monographs* 80, no. 1 (1966): 1–28.

23. C. Kittle, "Camp Teaches Girls Firefighting," *The Telegraph* (Nashua, New Hampshire), August 15, 2010. Firefighter statistics are reported in U.S. Census Bureau, *Table 615. Employed Civilians by Occupation, Sex, Race, and Hispanic Origin: 2009, Statistical Abstract of the United States: 2011* (Washington, DC: U.S. Census Bureau, 2011).

24. P. E. Spector, "Behavior in Organizations as a Function of Employee's Locus of Control," *Psychological Bulletin* 91 (1982): 482–97; K. Hattrup, M. S. O'Connell, and J. R. Labrador, "Incremental Validity of Locus of Control after Controlling for Cognitive Ability and Conscientiousness," *Journal of Business and Psychology* 19, no. 4 (2005): 461–81; T. W. H. Ng, K. L. Sorensen, and L. T. Eby, "Locus of Control at Work: A Meta-Analysis," *Journal of Organizational Behavior* 27 (2006): 1057–87; Kwang and Swann, "Do People Embrace Praise Even When They Feel Unworthy?"

25. J. M. Twenge, L. Zhang, and C. Im, "It's Beyond My Control: A Cross-Temporal Meta-Analysis of Increasing Externality in Locus of Control, 1960–2002," *Personality and Social Psychology Review* 8, no. 3 (August 2004): 308–19.

26. H. Tajfel, *Social Identity and Intergroup Relations* (Cambridge: Cambridge University Press, 1982); B. E. Ashforth and F. Mael, "Social Identity Theory and the Organization," *Academy of Management Review* 14 (1989): 20–39; M. A. Hogg and D. J. Terry, "Social Identity and Self-Categorization Processes in Organizational Contexts," *Academy of Management Review* 25 (January 2000): 121–40; L. L. Gaertner et al., "The 'I,' the 'We,' and the 'When': A Meta-Analysis of Motivational Primacy in Self-Definition," *Journal of Personality and Social Psychology* 83, no. 3 (2002): 574; S. A. Haslam, R. A. Eggins, and K. J. Reynolds, "The Aspire Model: Actualizing Social and Personal Identity Resources to Enhance Organizational Outcomes," *Journal of Occupational and Organizational Psychology* 76 (2003): 83–113.

27. Sedikides and Gregg, "Portraits of the Self," The history of the social self in human beings is described in M. R. Leary and N. R. Buttermore, "The Evolution of the Human Self: Tracing

the Natural History of Self-Awareness," *Journal for the Theory of Social Behaviour* 33, no. 4 (2003): 365–404.

28. M. R. Edwards, "Organizational Identification: A Conceptual and Operational Review," *International Journal of Management Reviews* 7, no. 4 (2005): 207–30; D. A. Whetten, "Albert and Whetten Revisited: Strengthening the Concept of Organizational Identity," *Journal of Management Inquiry* 15, no. 3 (Sept. 2006): 219–34.

29. M. B. Brewer, "The Social Self: On Being the Same and Different at the Same Time," *Personality and Social Psychology Bulletin* 17, no. 5 (October 1991): 475–82; R. Imhoff and H.-P. Erb, "What Motivates Nonconformity? Uniqueness Seeking Blocks Majority Influence," *Personality and Social Psychology Bulletin* 35, no. 3 (March 1, 2009): 309–20; M. G. Mayhew, J. Gardner, and N. M. Ashkanasy, "Measuring Individuals' Need for Identification: Scale Development and Validation," *Personality and Individual Differences* 49, no. 5 (2010): 356–61; K. R. Morrison and S. C. Wheeler, "Nonconformity Defines the Self: The Role of Minority Opinion Status in Self-Concept Clarity," *Personality and Social Psychology Bulletin* 36, no. 3 (March 2010): 297–308.

30. See, for example: W. B. Swann Jr., R. E. Johnson, and J. K. Bosson, "Identity Negotiation at Work," *Research in Organizational Behavior* 29 (2009): 81–109; M. N. Bechtoldt et al., "Self-Concept Clarity and the Management of Social Conflict," *Journal of Personality* 78, no. 2 (2010): 539–74; Hannah and Avolio, "Ready or Not: How Do We Accelerate the Developmental Readiness of Leaders?"; H. L. Yang and C. Y. Lai, "Motivations of Wikipedia Content Contributors," *Computers in Human Behavior* 26, no. 6 (2010): 1377–83.

31. G. Joseph, "Man of the People," *Business Times Singapore,* November 13, 2010.

32. The effect of the target in selective attention is known as "bottom-up selection"; the effect of the perceiver's psychodynamics on this process is known as "top-down selection." See C. E. Connor, H. E. Egeth, and S. Yantis, "Visual Attention: Bottom-up versus Top-down," *Current Biology* 14, no. 19 (2004): R850–52; E. I. Knudsen, "Fundamental Components of Attention," *Annual Review of Neuroscience* 30, no. 1 (2007): 57–78.

33. A. Mack et al., "Perceptual Organization and Attention," *Cognitive Psychology* 24, no. 4 (1992): 475–501; A. R. Damasio, *Descartes' Error: Emotion, Reason, and the Human Brain* (New York: Putnam Sons, 1994); C. Frith, "A Framework for Studying the Neural Basis of Attention," *Neuropsychologia* 39, no. 12 (2001): 1367–71; N. Lavie, "Distracted and Confused?: Selective Attention under Load," *Trends in Cognitive Sciences* 9, no. 2 (2005): 75–82; M. Shermer, "The Political Brain," *Scientific American* 295, no. 1 (July 2006): 36; D. Westen, *The Political Brain: The Role of Emotion in Deciding the Fate of the Nation* (Cambridge, MA: PublicAffairs, 2007).

34. Plato, *The Republic,* trans. D. Lee (Harmondsworth, England: Penguin, 1955).

35. D. J. Simons and C. F. Chabris, "Gorillas in Our Midst: Sustained Inattentional Blindness for Dynamic Events," *Perception* 28 (1999): 1059–74.

36. Confirmation bias is defined as "unwitting selectivity in the acquisition and use of evidence." R. S. Nickerson, "Confirmation Bias: A Ubiquitous Phenomenon in Many Guises," *Review of General Psychology* 2, no. 2 (1998): 175–220. This occurs in a variety of ways, including overweighting positive information, perceiving only positive information, and restricting cognitive attention to a favored hypothesis.

Research has found that confirmation bias is typically nonconscious and driven by emotions.

37. K. A. Lane, J. Kang, and M. R. Banaji, "Implicit Social Cognition and Law," *Annual Review of Law and Social Science* 3, no. 1 (2007).

38. S. A. Conan Doyle, "A Study in Scarlet," in *The Complete Sherlock Holmes* (New York: Fine Creative Media, 2003), 3–96. Sherlock Holmes offers similar advice in "A Scandal in Bohemia," 189.

39. D. Woods, "Managers Make Decisions about People Based on Gut Instinct Rather than Objective Data," *HR Magazine* (UK), February 16, 2010, http://www.hrmagazine.co.uk.

40. A. Cromer, "Pathological Science: An Update," *The Skeptical Inquirer* 17, no. 4 (Summer 1993): 400–7.

41. C. N. Macrae and G. V. Bodenhausen, "Social Cognition: Thinking Categorically about Others," *Annual Review of Psychology* 51 (2000): 93–120. For literature on the automaticity of the perceptual organization and interpretation process, see J. A. Bargh, "The Cognitive Monster: The Case against the Controllability of Automatic Stereotype Effects," in *Dual Process Theories in Social Psychology,* ed. S. Chaiken and Y. Trope (New York: Guilford, 1999), 361–82; J. A. Bargh and M. J. Ferguson, "Beyond Behaviorism: On the Automaticity of Higher Mental Processes," *Psychological Bulletin* 126, no. 6 (2000): 925–45; M. Gladwell, *Blink: The Power of Thinking without Thinking* (New York: Little, Brown, 2005).

42. E. M. Altmann and B. D. Burns, "Streak Biases in Decision Making: Data and a Memory Model," *Cognitive Systems Research* 6, no. 1 (2005): 5–16. For a discussion of cognitive closure and perception, see A. W. Kruglanski, *The Psychology of Closed Mindedness* (New York: Psychology Press, 2004).

43. J. Willis and A. Todorov, "First Impressions: Making up Your Mind after a 100–Ms Exposure to a Face," *Psychological Science* 17, no. 7 (Jul 2006): 592–98; A. Todorov, M. Pakrashi, and N. N. Oosterhof, "Evaluating Faces on Trustworthiness after Minimal Time Exposure," *Social Cognition* 27, no. 6 (December 2009): 813–33; C. Olivola and A. Todorov, "Elected in 100 Milliseconds: Appearance-Based Trait Inferences and Voting," *Journal of Nonverbal Behavior* 34, no. 2 (2010): 83–110. For related research on thin slices, see: N. Ambady et al., "Surgeons' Tone of Voice: A Clue to Malpractice History," *Surgery* 132, no. 1 (July 2002): 5–9; D. J. Benjamin and J. M. Shapiro, "Thin-Slice Forecasts of Gubernatorial Elections," *Review of Economics and Statistics* 91, no. 3 (2009): 523–36.

44. P. M. Senge, *The Fifth Discipline: The Art and Practice of the Learning Organization* (New York: Doubleday Currency, 1990), Chap. 10; P. N. Johnson-Laird, "Mental Models and Deduction," *Trends in Cognitive Sciences* 5, no. 10 (2001): 434–42; A. B. Markman and D. Gentner, "Thinking," *Annual Review of Psychology* 52 (2001): 223–47; T. J. Chermack, "Mental Models in Decision Making and Implications for Human Resource Development," *Advances in Developing Human Resources* 5, no. 4 (2003): 408–22.

45. G. W. Allport, *The Nature of Prejudice* (Reading, MA: Addison-Wesley, 1954); J. C. Brigham, "Ethnic Stereotypes," *Psychological Bulletin* 76, no. 1 (1971): 15–38; D. J. Schneider, *The Psychology of Stereotyping* (New York: Guilford, 2004); S. Kanahara, "A Review of the Definitions of Stereotype and a Proposal for a Progressional Model," *Individual Differences Research* 4, no. 5 (2006): 306–21.

46. C. N. Macrae, A. B. Milne, and G. V. Bodenhausen, "Stereotypes as Energy-Saving Devices: A Peek inside the Cognitive Toolbox," *Journal of Personality and Social Psychology* 66 (1994):

37–47; J. W. Sherman et al., "Stereotype Efficiency Reconsidered: Encoding Flexibility under Cognitive Load," *Journal of Personality and Social Psychology* 75 (1998): 589–606; Macrae and Bodenhausen, "Social Cognition: Thinking Categorically about Others."

47. J. C. Turner and S. A. Haslam, "Social Identity, Organizations, and Leadership," in *Groups at Work: Theory and Research,* ed. M. E. Turner (Mahwah, NJ: Lawrence Erlbaum Associates, 2001), 25–65; M. A. Hogg et al., "The Social Identity Perspective: Intergroup Relations, Self-Conception, and Small Groups," *Small Group Research* 35, no. 3 (June 2004): 246–76; J. Jetten, R. Spears, and T. Postmes, "Intergroup Distinctiveness and Differentiation: A Meta-Analytic Integration," *Journal of Personality and Social Psychology* 86, no. 6 (2004): 862–79; K. Hugenberg and D. F. Sacco, "Social Categorization and Stereotyping: How Social Categorization Biases Person Perception and Face Memory," *Social and Personality Psychology Compass* 2, no. 2 (2008): 1052–72.

48. J. W. Jackson and E. R. Smith, "Conceptualizing Social Identity: A New Framework and Evidence for the Impact of Different Dimensions," *Personality & Social Psychology Bulletin* 25 (January 1999): 120–35.

49. S. N. Cory, "Quality and Quantity of Accounting Students and the Stereotypical Accountant: Is There a Relationship?" *Journal of Accounting Education* 10, no. 1 (1992): 1–24; P. D. Bougen, "Joking Apart: The Serious Side to the Accountant Stereotype," *Accounting, Organizations and Society* 19, no. 3 (1994): 319–35; A. L. Friedman and S. R. Lyne, "The Beancounter Stereotype: Towards a General Model of Stereotype Generation," *Critical Perspectives on Accounting* 12, no. 4 (2001): 423–51; A. Hoffjan, "The Image of the Accountant in a German Context," *Accounting and the Public Interest* 4 (2004): 62–89; T. Dimnik and S. Felton, "Accountant Stereotypes in Movies Distributed in North America in the Twentieth Century," *Accounting, Organizations and Society* 31, no. 2 (2006): 129–55.

50. "Employers Face New Danger: Accidental Age Bias," *Omaha World-Herald,* October 10, 2005, D1; "Tiptoeing through the Employment Minefield of Race, Sex, and Religion? Here's Another One," *North West Business Insider* (Manchester, UK), February 2006.

51. S. O. Gaines and E. S. Reed, "Prejudice: From Allport to Dubois," *American Psychologist* 50 (February 1995): 96–103; S. T. Fiske, "Stereotyping, Prejudice, and Discrimination," in *Handbook of Social Psychology,* ed. D. T. Gilbert, S. T. Fiske, and G. Lindzey, 4th ed. (New York: McGraw-Hill, 1998), 357–411; M. Hewstone, M. Rubin, and H. Willis, "Intergroup Bias," *Annual Review of Psychology* 53 (2002): 575–604.

52. P. Gumbel, "The French Exodus," *Time International,* April 16, 2007, 18; E. Cediey and F. Foroni, *Discrimination in Access to Employment on Grounds of Foreign Origin in France,* (Geneva: International Labour Organization, 2008); "Study Finds Major Discrimination against Turkish Job Applicants," *The Local* (Berlin), February 9, 2010.

53. J. A. Bargh and T. L. Chartrand, "The Unbearable Automaticity of Being," *American Psychologist* 54, no. 7 (July 1999): 462–79; S. T. Fiske, "What We Know Now about Bias and Intergroup Conflict, the Problem of the Century," *Current Directions in Psychological Science* 11, no. 4 (August 2002): 123–28. For recent evidence that shows that intensive training can minimize stereotype activation, see K. Kawakami et al., "Just Say No (to Stereotyping): Effects of Training in the Negation of Stereotypic Associations on Stereotype Activation," *Journal of Personality and Social Psychology* 78, no. 5 (2000): 871–88; E. A. Plant,

B. M. Peruche, and D. A. Butz, "Eliminating Automatic Racial Bias: Making Race Non-Diagnostic for Responses to Criminal Suspects," *Journal of Experimental Social Psychology* 41, no. 2 (2005): 141. On the limitations of some stereotype training, see: B. Gawronski et al., "When 'Just Say No' Is Not Enough: Ayrmation versus Negation Training and the Reduction of Automatic Stereotype Activation," *Journal of Experimental Social Psychology* 44 (2008): 370–77.

54. H. H. Kelley, *Attribution in Social Interaction* (Morristown, NJ: General Learning Press, 1971).

55. Catalyst, *Quick Takes: Women on Boards,* (New York: Catalyst, April 9, 2012); K. Gladman and M. Lamb, *Gmi Ratings' 2012 Women on Boards Survey* (New York: GovernanceMetrics International, 2012).

56. J. M. Feldman, "Beyond Attribution Theory: Cognitive Processes in Performance Appraisal," *Journal of Applied Psychology* 66 (1981): 127–48.

57. J. M. Crant and T. S. Bateman, "Assignment of Credit and Blame for Performance Outcomes," *Academy of Management Journal* 36 (1993): 7–27; B. Weiner, "Intrapersonal and Interpersonal Theories of Motivation from an Attributional Perspective," *Educational Psychology Review* 12 (2000): 1–14; N. Bacon and P. Blyton, "Worker Responses to Teamworking: Exploring Employee Attributions of Managerial Motives," *International Journal of Human Resource Management* 16, no. 2 (February 2005): 238–55.

58. Fundamental attribution error is part of a larger phenomenon known as correspondence bias. See D. T. Gilbert and P. S. Malone, "The Correspondence Bias," *Psychological Bulletin* 117, no. 1 (1995): 21–38.

59. I. Choi, R. E. Nisbett, and A. Norenzayan, "Causal Attribution across Cultures: Variation and Universality," *Psychological Bulletin* 125, no. 1 (1999): 47–63; D. S. Krull et al., "The Fundamental Fundamental Attribution Error: Correspondence Bias in Individualist and Collectivist Cultures," *Personality and Social Psychology Bulletin* 25, no. 10 (October 1999): 1208–19; R. E. Nisbett, *The Geography of Thought: How Asians and Westerners Think Differently—and Why* (New York: Free Press, 2003), Chap. 5.

60. D. T. Miller and M. Ross, "Self-Serving Biases in the Attribution of Causality: Fact or Fiction?" *Psychological Bulletin* 82, no. 2 (1975): 213–25; J. Shepperd, W. Malone, and K. Sweeny, "Exploring Causes of the Self-Serving Bias," *Social and Personality Psychology Compass* 2, no. 2 (2008): 895–908. The Philo Vance quotation is from: S. S. Van Dine (Willard Huntington Wright), *The Benson Murder Mystery* (New York: Charles Scribner's Sons, 1926), Chap. 6.

61. E. W. K. Tsang, "Self-Serving Attributions in Corporate Annual Reports: A Replicated Study," *Journal of Management Studies* 39, no. 1 (January 2002): 51–65; N. J. Roese and J. M. Olson, "Better, Stronger, Faster: Self-Serving Judgment, Affect Regulation, and the Optimal Vigilance Hypothesis," *Perspectives on Psychological Science* 2, no. 2 (2007): 124–41; R. Hooghiemstra, "East–West Differences in Attributions for Company Performance: A Content Analysis of Japanese and U.S. Corporate Annual Reports," *Journal of Cross-Cultural Psychology* 39, no. 5 (September 1, 2008): 618–29; M. Franco and H. Haase, "Failure Factors in Small and Medium-Sized Enterprises: Qualitative Study from an Attributional Perspective," *International Entrepreneurship and Management Journal* 6, no. 4 (2010): 503–21.

62. Similar models are presented in D. Eden, "Self-Fulfilling Prophecy as a Management Tool: Harnessing Pygmalion,"

Academy of Management Review 9 (1984): 64–73; R. H. G. Field and D. A. Van Seters, "Management by Expectations (MBE): The Power of Positive Prophecy," *Journal of General Management* 14 (Winter 1988): 19–33; D. O. Trouilloud et al., "The Influence of Teacher Expectations on Student Achievement in Physical Education Classes: Pygmalion Revisited," *European Journal of Social Psychology* 32 (2002): 591–607.

63. A. Davis, "Moving to Greener Pastures," *Employee Benefit News,* December 2010, 18.

64. D. Eden, "Interpersonal Expectations in Organizations," in *Interpersonal Expectations: Theory, Research, and Applications* (Cambridge, UK: Cambridge University Press, 1993), 154–78.

65. D. Eden, "Pygmalion Goes to Boot Camp: Expectancy, Leadership, and Trainee Performance," *Journal of Applied Psychology* 67 (1982): 194–99; R. P. Brown and E. C. Pinel, "Stigma on My Mind: Individual Differences in the Experience of Stereotype Threat," *Journal of Experimental Social Psychology* 39, no. 6 (2003): 626–33.

66. S. Madon, L. Jussim, and J. Eccles, "In Search of the Powerful Self-Fulfilling Prophecy," *Journal of Personality and Social Psychology* 72, no. 4 (April 1997): 791–809; A. E. Smith, L. Jussim, and J. Eccles, "Do Self-Fulfilling Prophecies Accumulate, Dissipate, or Remain Stable over Time?" *Journal of Personality and Social Psychology* 77, no. 3 (1999): 548–65; S. Madon et al., "Self-Fulfilling Prophecies: The Synergistic Accumulative Effect of Parents' Beliefs on Children's Drinking Behavior," *Psychological Science* 15, no. 12 (2005): 837–45.

67. W. H. Cooper, "Ubiquitous Halo," *Psychological Bulletin* 90 (1981): 218–44; K. R. Murphy, R. A. Jako, and R. L. Anhalt, "Nature and Consequences of Halo Error: A Critical Analysis," *Journal of Applied Psychology* 78 (1993): 218–25; T. H. Feeley, "Comment on Halo Effects in Rating and Evaluation Research," *Human Communication Research* 28, no. 4 (October 2002): 578–86. For a variation of the classic halo effect in business settings, see P. Rosenzweig, *The Halo Effect . . . And the Eight Other Business Delusions That Deceive Managers* (New York: Free Press, 2007).

68. B. Mullen et al., "The False Consensus Effect: A Meta-Analysis of 115 Hypothesis Tests," *Journal of Experimental Social Psychology* 21, no. 3 (1985): 262–83; G. Marks and N. Miller, "Ten Years of Research on the False-Consensus Effect: An Empirical and Theoretical Review," *Psychological Bulletin* 102, no. 1 (1987): 72–90; R. L. Cross and S. E. Brodt, "How Assumptions of Consensus Undermine Decision Making," *MIT Sloan Management Review* 42, no. 2 (Winter 2001): 86–94; F. J. Flynn and S. S. Wiltermuth, "Who's with Me? False Consensus, Brokerage, and Ethical Decision Making in Organizations," *Academy of Management Journal* 53, no. 5 (October 2010): 1074–89; S. Goel, W. Mason, and D. J. Watts, "Real and Perceived Attitude Agreement in Social Networks," *Journal of Personality and Social Psychology* 99, no. 4 (2010): 611–21.

69. C. L. Kleinke, *First Impressions: The Psychology of Encountering Others* (Englewood Cliffs, NJ: Prentice Hall, 1975); E. A. Lind, L. Kray, and L. Thompson, "Primacy Effects in Justice Judgments: Testing Predictions from Fairness Heuristic Theory," *Organizational Behavior and Human Decision Processes* 85 (July 2001): 189–210; O. Ybarra, "When First Impressions Don't Last: The Role of Isolation and Adaptation Processes in the Revision of Evaluative Impressions," *Social Cognition* 19 (October 2001): 491–520; S. D. Bond et al., "Information Distortion in the Evaluation of a Single Option," *Organizational Behavior and Human Decision Processes* 102, no. 2 (2007): 240–54.

70. "Survey: Candidates with Strong Resumes Often Fail to Meet Expectations in Interview," PR news release, Menlo Park, CA, July 23, 2009; L. Smith, "How Typos on Resume Can Ruin Your Career Prospects," *ABC15* (Phoenix, Arizona), July 15, 2009.

71. D. D. Steiner and J. S. Rain, "Immediate and Delayed Primacy and Recency Effects in Performance Evaluation," *Journal of Applied Psychology* 74 (1989): 136–42; K. T. Trotman, "Order Effects and Recency: Where Do We Go from Here?" *Accounting & Finance* 40 (2000): 169–82; W. Green, "Impact of the Timing of an Inherited Explanation on Auditors' Analytical Procedures Judgements," *Accounting & Finance* 44 (2004): 369–92.

72. L. Roberson, C. T. Kulik, and M. B. Pepper, "Using Needs Assessment to Resolve Controversies in Diversity Training Design," *Group & Organization Management* 28, no. 1 (March 2003): 148–74; D. E. Hogan and M. Mallott, "Changing Racial Prejudice through Diversity Education," *Journal of College Student Development* 46, no. 2 (March/April 2005): 115–25; Gawronski et al., "When 'Just Say No' Is Not Enough: Ayrmation."

73. Eden, "Self-Fulfilling Prophecy as a Management Tool: Harnessing Pygmalion"; S. S. White and E. A. Locke, "Problems with the Pygmalion Effect and Some Proposed Solutions," *Leadership Quarterly* 11 (Autumn 2000): 389–415.

74. T. W. Costello and S. S. Zalkind, *Psychology in Administration: A Research Orientation* (Englewood Cliffs, NJ: Prentice Hall, 1963), 45–46; J. M. Kouzes and B. Z. Posner, *The Leadership Challenge*, 4th ed. (San Francisco: Jossey-Bass, 2007), Chap. 3.

75. George, *Authentic Leadership;* W. L. Gardner et al., "'Can You See the Real Me?' A Self-Based Model of Authentic Leader and Follower Development," *Leadership Quarterly* 16 (2005): 343–72; B. George, *True North* (San Francisco: Jossey-Bass, 2007).

76. For a discussion of the Implicit Association Test, including critique, see H. Blanton et al., "Decoding the Implicit Association Test: Implications for Criterion Prediction," *Journal of Experimental Social Psychology* 42, no. 2 (2006): 192–212; A. G. Greenwald, B. A. Nosek, and N. Sriram, "Consequential Validity of the Implicit Association Test: Comment on Blanton and Jaccard (2006)," *American Psychologist* 61, no. 1 (2006): 56–61; W. Hofmann et al., "Implicit and Explicit Attitudes and Interracial Interaction: The Moderating Role of Situationally Available Control Resources," *Group Processes Intergroup Relations* 11, no. 1 (Jan. 2008): 69–87.

77. Hofmann et al., "Implicit and Explicit Attitudes and Interracial Interaction"; J. T. Jost et al., "The Existence of Implicit Bias Is Beyond Reasonable Doubt: A Refutation of Ideological and Methodological Objections and Executive Summary of Ten Studies That No Manager Should Ignore," *Research in Organizational Behavior* 29 (2009): 39–69; Jost et al., "The Existence of Implicit Bias Is Beyond Reasonable Doubt."

78. J. Luft, *Of Human Interaction* (Palo Alto, CA: National Press, 1969). For a variation of this model, see J. Hall, "Communication Revisited," *California Management Review* 15 (Spring 1973): 56–67.

79. S. Vazire and M. R. Mehl, "Knowing Me, Knowing You: The Accuracy and Unique Predictive Validity of Self-Ratings and Other-Ratings of Daily Behavior," *Journal of Personality and Social Psychology* 95, no. 5 (2008): 1202–16; S. Vazire, "Who Knows What about a Person? The Self-Other Knowledge Asymmetry (Soka) Model," *Journal of Personality and Social Psychology* 98, no. 2 (2010): 281–300.

80. J. Dixon and K. Durrheim, "Contact and the Ecology of Racial Division: Some Varieties of Informal Segregation," *British Journal of Social Psychology* 42 (March 2003): 1–23; P. J. Henry and C. D. Hardin, "The Contact Hypothesis Revisited: Status Bias in the Reduction of Implicit Prejudice in the United States and Lebanon," *Psychological Science* 17, no. 10 (2006): 862–68; T. F. Pettigrew and L. R. Tropp, "A Meta-Analytic Test of Intergroup Contact Theory," *Journal of Personality and Social Psychology* 90, no. 5 (2006): 751–83; C. Tredoux and G. Finchilescu, "The Contact Hypothesis and Intergroup Relations 50 Years on: Introduction to the Special Issue," *South African Journal of Psychology* 37, no. 4 (2007): 667–78; T. F. Pettigrew, "Future Directions for Intergroup Contact Theory and Research," *International Journal of Intercultural Relations* 32, no. 3 (2008): 187–99.

81. The contact hypothesis was first introduced in: Allport, *The Nature of Prejudice,* Chap. 16.

82. C. Duan and C. E. Hill, "The Current State of Empathy Research," *Journal of Counseling Psychology* 43 (1996): 261–74; W. G. Stephen and K. A. Finlay, "The Role of Empathy in Improving Intergroup Relations," *Journal of Social Issues* 55 (Winter 1999): 729–43; S. K. Parker and C. M. Axtell, "Seeing Another Viewpoint: Antecedents and Outcomes of Employee Perspective Taking," *Academy of Management Journal* 44 (December 2001): 1085–1100; G. J. Vreeke and I. L. van der Mark, "Empathy, an Integrative Model," *New Ideas in Psychology* 21, no. 3 (2003): 177–207.

83. D. Calderwood-Smith, "Degroote Grad Uses MBA Training to Aid a Developing Economy," *McMaster Daily News* (Hamilton, Ontario.), June 15, 2010

84. S. J. Black, W. H. Mobley, and E. Weldon, "The Mindset of Global Leaders: Inquisitiveness and Duality," in *Advances in Global Leadership* (JAI, 2006), 181–200; O. Levy et al., "What We Talk about When We Talk about 'Global Mindset': Managerial Cognition in Multinational Corporations," *Journal of International Business Studies* 38, no. 2 (2007): 231–58; S. Beechler and D. Baltzley, "Creating a Global Mindset," *Chief Learning Officer* 7, no. 6 (2008): 40–45.

85. A. K. Gupta and V. Govindarajan, "Cultivating a Global Mindset," *Academy of Management Executive* 16, no. 1 (2002): 116–26.

86. U. Hedquist, "Kiwi Volunteer in Tanzania Project Receives Lessons in Life," *Computerworld* (NZ), January 22, 2009.

87. IBM, "Sam Palmisano Discusses IBM's New Corporate Service Corps," IBM news release, July, 25, 2007;"IBM's Corporate Service Corps Heading to Six Emerging Countries to Spark Socio-Economic Growth While Developing Global Leaders," IBM news release, March 26, 2008 C. Hymowitz, "IBM Combines Volunteer Service, Teamwork to Cultivate Emerging Markets," *Wall Street Journal,* August 4, 2008, B6.

CHAPTER 4

1. H. Poturalski, "Shopping Salute," *Columbus Dispatch* (Ohio), June 23, 2010.

2. Emotions are also cognitive processes. However, we use the narrow definition of cognition as a well-used label referring only to reasoning processes. Also, this and other chapters emphasize that emotional and cognitive processes are intertwined.

3. For discussion of emotions in marketing, economics, sociology, and political science, see G. Loewenstein, "Emotions in Economic Theory and Economic Behavior," *American Economic Review* 90, no. 2 (May 2000): 426–32; D. S. Massey, "A Brief History of Human Society: The Origin and Role of Emotion in Social Life," *American Sociological Review* 67 (February 2002): 1–29; J. O'Shaughnessy and N. J. O'Shaughnessy, *The Marketing Power of Emotion* (New York: Oxford University Press, 2003); J. Druckman and R. McDermott, "Emotion and the Framing of Risky Choice," *Political Behavior* 30, no. 3 (2008): 297–321; E. Petit, "The Role of Affects in Economics," *Revue d'économie politique* 119, no. 6 (2009): 859–97; M. Hubert, "Does Neuroeconomics Give New Impetus to Economic and Consumer Research?" *Journal of Economic Psychology* 31, no. 5 (2010): 812–17.

4. The definition presented here is constructed from the following sources: N. M. Ashkanasy, W. J. Zerbe, and C. E. J. Hartel, "Introduction: Managing Emotions in a Changing Workplace," in *Managing Emotions in the Workplace,* ed. N. M. Ashkanasy, W. J. Zerbe, and C. E. J. Hartel (Armonk, NY: M. E. Sharpe, 2002), 3–18; H. M. Weiss, "Conceptual and Empirical Foundations for the Study of Affect at Work," in *Emotions in the Workplace,* ed. R. G. Lord, R. J. Klimoski, and R. Kanfer (San Francisco: Jossey-Bass, 2002), 20–63. However, the meaning of emotions is still being debated. See, for example, M. Cabanac, "What Is Emotion?" *Behavioral Processes* 60 (2002): 69–83; J. Gooty, M. Gavin, and N. M. Ashkanasy, "Emotions Research in OB: The Challenges That Lie Ahead," *Journal of Organizational Behavior* 30, no. 6 (2009): 833–38.

5. R. Kanfer and R. J. Klimoski, "Affect and Work: Looking Back to the Future," in *Emotions in the Workplace,* ed. R. G. Lord, R. J. Klimoski, and R. Kanfer (San Francisco: Jossey-Bass, 2002), 473–90; J. A. Russell, "Core Affect and the Psychological Construction of Emotion," *Psychological Review* 110, no. 1 (2003): 145–72.

6. R. B. Zajonc, "Emotions," in *Handbook of Social Psychology,* ed. D. T. Gilbert, S. T. Fiske, and L. Gardner (New York: Oxford University press, 1998), 591–634.

7. N. A. Remington, L. R. Fabrigar, and P. S. Visser, "Reexamining the Circumplex Model of Affect," *Journal of Personality and Social Psychology* 79, no. 2 (2000): 286–300; R. J. Larson, E. Diener, and R. E. Lucas, "Emotion: Models, Measures, and Differences," in *Emotions in the Workplace,* ed. R. G. Lord, R. J. Klimoski, and R. Kanfer (San Francisco: Jossey- Bass, 2002), 64–113; L. F. Barrett et al., "The Experience of Emotion," *Annual Review of Psychology* 58, no. 1 (2007): 373–403.

8. R. F. Baumeister, E. Bratslavsky, and C. Finkenauer, "Bad Is Stronger than Good," *Review of General Psychology* 5, no. 4 (2001): 323–70; A. Vaish, T. Grossmann, and A. Woodward, "Not All Emotions Are Created Equal: The Negativity Bias in Social-Emotional Development," *Psychological Bulletin* 134, no. 3 (May 2008): 383–403; B. E. Hilbig, "Good Things Don't Come Easy (to Mind) Explaining Framing Effects in Judgments of Truth," *Experimental Psychology* 59, no. 1 (2012): 38–46.

9. A. H. Eagly and S. Chaiken, *The Psychology of Attitudes* (Orlando, FL: Harcourt Brace Jovanovich, 1993); A. P. Brief, *Attitudes in and around Organizations* (Thousand Oaks, CA: Sage, 1998). There is an amazing lack of consensus on the definition of attitudes. This book adopts the three-component model, whereas some experts define attitude as only the "feelings" component, with "beliefs" as a predictor and "intentions" as an outcome. Some writers specifically define attitudes as an "evaluation" of an attitude object, whereas others distinguish attitudes from evaluations of an attitude object. Some even define specific attitudes as "affects" (emotions), although there is also confusion whether affect is emotion as well as

cognitive feelings. For some of these definitional variations, see I. Ajzen, "Nature and Operation of Attitudes," *Annual Review of Psychology* 52 (2001): 27–58; D. Albarracín et al., "Attitudes: Introduction and Scope," in *The Handbook of Attitudes,* ed. D. Albarracín, B. T. Johnson, and M. P. Zanna (Mahwah, NJ: Lawrence Erlbaum Associates, 2005), 3–20; W. A. Cunningham and P. D. Zelazo, "Attitudes and Evaluations: A Social Cognitive Neuroscience Perspective," *TRENDS in Cognitive Sciences* 11, no. 3 (2007): 97–104.

10. Neuroscience has a slightly more complicated distinction in that conscious awareness is "feeling a feeling" whereas "feeling" is a nonconscious sensing of the body state created by emotion, which itself is a nonconscious neural reaction to a stimulus. However, this distinction is not significant for scholars focused more on human behavior than brain activity, and the labels collide with popular understanding of "feeling." See: A. R. Damasio, *The Feeling of What Happens: Body and Emotion in the Making of Consciousness* (New York: Harcourt Brace and Company, 1999); T. Bosse, C. M. Jonker, and J. Treur, "Formalisation of Damasio's Theory of Emotion, Feeling and Core Consciousness," *Consciousness and Cognition* 17, no. 1 (2008): 94–113.

11. C. D. Fisher, "Mood and Emotions while Working: Missing Pieces of Job Satisfaction?" *Journal of Organizational Behavior* 21 (2000): 185–202; Cunningham and Zelazo, "Attitudes and Evaluations"; M. D. Lieberman, "Social Cognitive Neuroscience: A Review of Core Processes," *Annual Review of Psychology* 58, no. 1 (2007): 259–89; M. Fenton-O'Creevy et al., "Thinking, Feeling and Deciding: The Influence of Emotions on the Decision Making and Performance of Traders," *Journal of Organizational Behavior* 32, no. 8 (2010): 1044–61. The dual emotion-cognition processes are likely the same as the implicit-explicit attitude processes reported by a few scholars. See: W. J. Becker and R. Cropanzano, "Organizational Neuroscience: The Promise and Prospects of an Emerging Discipline," *Journal of Organizational Behavior* 31, no. 7 (2010): 1055–59.

12. S. Orbell, "Intention-Behavior Relations: A Self-Regulation Perspective," in *Contemporary Perspectives on the Psychology of Attitudes,* ed. G. Haddock and G. R. Maio (East Sussex, UK: Psychology Press, 2004), 145–68.

13. H. M. Weiss and R. Cropanzano, "Affective Events Theory: A Theoretical Discussion of the Structure, Causes and Consequences of Affective Experiences at Work," *Research in Organizational Behavior* 18 (1996): 1–74; H. A. Elfenbein, "Chapter 7: Emotion in Organizations," *The Academy of Management Annals* 1 (2007): 315–86.

14. J. A. Bargh and M. J. Ferguson, "Beyond Behaviorism: On the Automaticity of Higher Mental Processes," *Psychological Bulletin* 126, no. 6 (2000): 925–45; P. Winkielman and K. C. Berridge, "Unconscious Emotion," *Current Directions in Psychological Science* 13, no. 3 (2004): 120–23; J. M. George, "The Illusion of Will in Organizational Behavior Research: Nonconscious Processes and Job Design," *Journal of Management* 35, no. 6 (December 1, 2009): 1318–39; K. I. Ruys and D. A. Stapel, "The Unconscious Unfolding of Emotions," *European Review of Social Psychology* 20 (2009): 232–71.

15. A. R. Damasio, *Descartes' Error: Emotion, Reason, and the Human Brain* (New York: Putnam, 1994); Damasio, *The Feeling of What Happens: Body and Emotion in the Making of Consciousness;* P. Ekman, "Basic Emotions," in *Handbook of Cognition and Emotion,* ed. T. Dalgleish and M. Power (San Francisco: Jossey-Bass, 1999), 45–60; J. E. LeDoux,

"Emotion Circuits in the Brain," *Annual Review of Neuroscience* 23 (2000): 155–84; R. J. Dolan, "Emotion, Cognition, and Behavior," *Science* 298, no. 5596 (November 8. 2002): 1191–94.

16. N. Schwarz, "Emotion, Cognition, and Decision Making," *Cognition and Emotion* 14, no. 4 (2000): 433–40; M. T. Pham, "The Logic of Feeling," *Journal of Consumer Psychology* 14, no. 4 (2004): 360–69. One recent proposition is that a person's confidence in their beliefs is also influenced by their emotional experiences regarding those beliefs. See: Z. Memon and J. Treur, "On the Reciprocal Interaction between Believing and Feeling: An Adaptive Agent Modelling Perspective," *Cognitive Neurodynamics* 4, no. 4 (2010): 377–94.

17. G. R. Maio, V. M. Esses, and D. W. Bell, "Examining Conflict between Components of Attitudes: Ambivalence and Inconsistency Are Distinct Constructs," *Canadian Journal of Behavioural Science* 32, no. 2 (2000): 71–83.

18. P. C. Nutt, *Why Decisions Fail* (San Francisco, CA: Berrett-Koehler, 2002); S. Finkelstein, *Why Smart Executives Fail* (New York: Viking, 2003); P. C. Nutt, "Search During Decision Making," *European Journal of Operational Research* 160 (2005): 851–76.

19. M. Tierney, "They're All in It Together," *Atlanta Journal-Constitution,* April 16, 2011, G7.

20. S. C. Bolton and M. Houlihan, "Are We Having Fun Yet? A Consideration of Workplace Fun and Engagement," *Employee Relations* 31, no. 6 (2009): 556–68.

21. E. Maltby, "Boring Meetings? Get out the Water Guns," *Wall Street Journal,* January 7, 2010; E. Shearing, "Dixon Schwabl Focuses on Having Fun at Its Office Playground," *Democrat & Chronicle* (Rochester, NY), September 5, 2010.

22. C. Foster, "Turning Ha-Ha into a-Ha!," *Employee Benefit News Canada,* December 2007; S. Davies, "Razer Employees Wear Shorts, T-Shirts and Flip-Flops to Work," *Straits Times* (Singapore), May 10, 2008.

23. C. Cooper, "Elucidating the Bonds of Workplace Humor: A Relational Process Model," *Human Relations* 61, no. 8 (August 1, 2008): 1087–1115; B. Plester and M. Orams, "Send in the Clowns: The Role of the Joker in Three New Zealand It Companies," *Humor: International Journal of Humor Research* 21, no. 3 (2008): 253–81.

24. Weiss and Cropanzano, "Affective Events Theory."

25. L. Festinger, *A Theory of Cognitive Dissonance* (Evanston, IL: Row, Peterson, 1957); G. R. Salancik, "Commitment and the Control of Organizational Behavior and Belief," in *New Directions in Organizational Behavior,* ed. B. M. Staw and G. R. Salancik (Chicago: St. Clair, 1977), 1–54; A. D. Galinsky, J. Stone, and J. Cooper, "The Reinstatement of Dissonance and Psychological Discomfort Following Failed Affirmation," *European Journal of Social Psychology* 30, no. 1 (2000): 123–47.

26. These lists are found at www.greatplacetowork.com. They present the top-listed companies for 2012 in the United States and 2011 elsewhere. Hewitt Associates produces a related list, particularly for Asia, Europe, and the Middle East. See https://ceplb03.hewitt.com/bestemployers/pages/index.htm.

27. J. Cooper, *Cognitive Dissonance: Fifth Years of a Classic Theory* (London: Sage, 2007); A. R. McConnell and C. M. Brown, "Dissonance Averted: Self-Concept Organization Moderates the Effect of Hypocrisy on Attitude Change,"

Journal of Experimental Social Psychology 46, no. 2 (2010): 361–66; J. M. Jarcho, E. T. Berkman, and M. D. Lieberman, "The Neural Basis of Rationalization: Cognitive Dissonance Reduction During Decision-Making," *Social Cognitive and Affective Neuroscience* (2011): in press.

28. T. A. Judge, E. A. Locke, and C. C. Durham, "The Dispositional Causes of Job Satisfaction: A Core Evaluations Approach," *Research in Organizational Behavior* 19 (1997): 151–88; T. W. H. Ng and K. L. Sorensen, "Dispositional Affectivity and Work-Related Outcomes: A Meta-Analysis," *Journal of Applied Social Psychology* 39, no. 6 (2009): 1255–87.

29. C. M. Brotheridge and A. A. Grandey, "Emotional Labor and Burnout: Comparing Two Perspectives of 'People Work,'" *Journal of Vocational Behavior* 60 (2002): 17–39; P. G. Irving, D. F. Coleman, and D. R. Bobocel, "The Moderating Effect of Negative Affectivity in the Procedural Justice-Job Satisfaction Relation," *Canadian Journal of Behavioural Science* 37, no. 1 (January 2005): 20–32.

30. J. Schaubroeck, D. C. Ganster, and B. Kemmerer, "Does Trait Affect Promote Job Attitude Stability?" *Journal of Organizational Behavior* 17 (1996): 191–96; C. Dormann and D. Zapf, "Job Satisfaction: A Meta-Analysis of Stabilities," *Journal of Organizational Behavior* 22 (2001): 483–504.

31. B. E. Ashforth and R. H. Humphrey, "Emotional Labor in Service Roles: The Influence of Identity," *Academy of Management Review* 18 (1993): 88–115. For a recent review of the emotional labor concept, see T. M. Glomb and M. J. Tews, "Emotional Labor: A Conceptualization and Scale Development," *Journal of Vocational Behavior* 64, no. 1 (2004): 1–23.

32. J. A. Morris and D. C. Feldman, "The Dimensions, Antecedents, and Consequences of Emotional Labor," *Academy of Management Review* 21 (1996): 986–1010; D. Zapf, "Emotion Work and Psychological Well-Being: A Review of the Literature and Some Conceptual Considerations," *Human Resource Management Review* 12 (2002): 237–68.

33. L. Pivot, "Objectif Canada: A Vos Marques, PrêTs . . . Partez !," *L'Express,* June 4, 2008; P. O'Neil, "Canada a Top Draw for French Seeking Jobs," *Montreal Gazette,* November 18, 2010, B2.

34. A. E. Raz and A. Rafaeli, "Emotion Management in Cross-Cultural Perspective: 'Smile Training' in Japanese and North American Service Organizations," *Research on Emotion in Organizations* 3 (2007): 199–220; D. Matsumoto, S. H. Yoo, and J. Fontaine, "Mapping Expressive Differences around the World," *Journal of Cross-Cultural Psychology* 39, no. 1 (January 1, 2008): 55–74; S. Ravid, A. Rafaeli, and A. Grandey, "Expressions of Anger in Israeli Workplaces: The Special Place of Customer Interactions," *Human Resource Management Review* 20, no. 3 (2010): 224–34. Emotional display norms might also explain differences in aggression across cultures. See: N. Bergeron and B. H. Schneider, "Explaining Cross-National Differences in Peer-Directed Aggression: A Quantitative Synthesis," *Aggressive Behavior* 31, no. 2 (2005): 116–37.

35. "Reach for the Sky," *New Sunday Times* (Kuala Lumpur), November 16, 2008, 4; C. Platt, "Inside Flight Attendant School," *WA Today* (Perth), February 24, 2009.

36. F. Trompenaars and C. Hampden-Turner, *Riding the Waves of Culture,* 2nd ed. (New York: McGraw-Hill, 1998), Chap. 6. One recent study reveals cultural differences in emotional display norms among American, Canadian, and Japanese students. See: S. Safdar et al., "Variations of Emotional Display Rules within and across Cultures: A Comparison between Canada, USA, and Japan," *Canadian Journal of Behavioural Science* 41, no. 1 (2009): 1–10.

37. This relates to the automaticity of emotion, which is summarized in Winkielman and Berridge, "Unconscious Emotion"; K. N. Ochsner and J. J. Gross, "The Cognitive Control of Emotions," *TRENDS in Cognitive Sciences* 9, no. 5 (May 2005): 242–49.

38. W. J. Zerbe, "Emotional Dissonance and Employee Well-Being," in *Managing Emotions in the Workplace,* ed. N. M. Ashkanasy, W. J. Zerbe, and C. E. J. Hartel (Armonk, NY: M. E. Sharpe, 2002), 189–214; R. Cropanzano, H. M. Weiss, and S. M. Elias, "The Impact of Display Rules and Emotional Labor on Psychological Well-Being at Work," *Research in Occupational Stress and Well Being* 3 (2003): 45–89.

39. Brotheridge and Grandey, "Emotional Labor and Burnout: Comparing Two Perspectives of 'People Work'"; Zapf, "Emotion Work and Psychological Well-Being"; J. M. Diefendorff, M. H. Croyle, and R. H. Gosserand, "The Dimensionality and Antecedents of Emotional Labor Strategies," *Journal of Vocational Behavior* 66, no. 2 (2005): 339–57.

40. M. Weinstein, "Emotional Evaluation," *Training,* July 29, 2009.

41. J. D. Mayer, P. Salovey, and D. R. Caruso, "Models of Emotional Intelligence," in *Handbook of Human Intelligence,* 2nd ed., ed. R. J. Sternberg (New York: Cambridge University Press, 2000), 396–420. This definition is also recognized in C. Cherniss, "Emotional Intelligence and Organizational Effectiveness," in *The Emotionally Intelligent Workplace,* ed. C. Cherniss and D. Goleman (San Francisco: Jossey-Bass, 2001), 3–12; M. Zeidner, G. Matthews, and R. D. Roberts, "Emotional Intelligence in the Workplace: A Critical Review," *Applied Psychology: An International Review* 53, no. 3 (2004): 371–99.

42. This model is very similar to Goleman's revised emotional intelligence model. See R. Boyatzis, D. Goleman, and K. S. Rhee, "Clustering Competence in Emotional Intelligence," in *The Handbook of Emotional Intelligence,* ed. R. Bar-On and J. D. A. Parker (San Francisco: Jossey-Bass, 2000), 343–62; D. Goleman, "An EI-Based Theory of Performance," in *The Emotionally Intelligent Workplace* ed. C. Cherniss and D. Goleman (San Francisco: Jossey-Bass, 2001), 27–44; D. Goleman, R. Boyatzis, and A. McKee, *Primal Leadership* (Boston: Harvard Business School Press, 2002), Chap. 3. Goleman's revised model received a cool reception by most scholars. Yet recent studies indicate that variations of this model (when properly framed as a set of abilities) provide a better fit than other models. See, in particular C.-S. Wong and K. S. Law, "The Effects of Leader and Follower Emotional Intelligence on Performance and Attitude: An Exploratory Study," *Leadership Quarterly* 13 (2002): 243–74; R. P. Tett and K. E. Fox, "Confirmatory Factor Structure of Trait Emotional Intelligence in Student and Worker Samples," *Personality and Individual Differences* 41 (2006): 1155–68; P. J. Jordan and S. A. Lawrence, "Emotional Intelligence in Teams: Development and Initial Validation of the Short Version of the Workgroup Emotional Intelligence Profile (WEIP-S)," *Journal of Management & Organization* 15 (2009): 452–69; D. L. Joseph and D. A. Newman, "Emotional Intelligence: An Integrative Meta-Analysis and Cascading Model," *Journal of Applied Psychology* 95, no. 1 (2010): 54–78.

43. H. A. Elfenbein and N. Ambady, "Predicting Workplace Outcomes from the Ability to Eavesdrop on Feelings," *Journal of Applied Psychology* 87, no. 5 (2002): 963–71.

44. The hierarchical nature of the four EI dimensions is discussed by Goleman, but it is more explicit in the Salovey and Mayer model. See D. R. Caruso and P. Salovey, *The Emotionally Intelligent Manager* (San Francisco: Jossey-Bass, 2004). This hierarchy is also identified (without the self-other distinction) as a sequence in Joseph and Newman, "Emotional Intelligence."

45. P. N. Lopes et al., "Emotional Intelligence and Social Interaction," *Personality and Social Psychology Bulletin* 30, no. 8 (August 2004): 1018–34; C. S. Daus and N. M. Ashkanasy, "The Case for the Ability-Based Model of Emotional Intelligence in Organizational Behavior," *Journal of Organizational Behavior* 26 (2005): 453–66; J. E. Barbuto Jr. and M. E. Burbach, "The Emotional Intelligence of Transformational Leaders: A Field Study of Elected Officials," *Journal of Social Psychology* 146, no. 1 (2006): 51–64; M. A. Brackett et al., "Relating Emotional Abilities to Social Functioning: A Comparison of Self-Report and Performance Measures of Emotional Intelligence," *Journal of Personality and Social Psychology* 91, no. 4 (2006): 780–95; D. L. Reis et al., "Emotional Intelligence Predicts Individual Differences in Social Exchange Reasoning," *NeuroImage* 35, no. 3 (2007): 1385–91; S. K. Singh, "Role of Emotional Intelligence in Organisational Learning: An Empirical Study," *Singapore Management Review* 29, no. 2 (2007): 55–74.

46. Some studies have reported situations where EI has a limited effect on individual performance. For example, see A. L. Day and S. A. Carroll, "Using an Ability-Based Measure of Emotional Intelligence to Predict Individual Performance, Group Performance, and Group Citizenship Behaviors," *Personality and Individual Differences* 36 (2004): 1443–58; Z. Ivcevic, M. A. Brackett, and J. D. Mayer, "Emotional Intelligence and Emotional Creativity," *Journal of Personality* 75, no. 2 (2007): 199–236; J. C. Rode et al., "Emotional Intelligence and Individual Performance: Evidence of Direct and Moderated Effects," *Journal of Organizational Behavior* 28, no. 4 (2007): 399–421.

47. R. Bar-On, R. Handley, and S. Fund, "The Impact of Emotional Intelligence on Performance," in *Linking Emotional Intelligence and Performance at Work,* ed. V. U. Druskat, F. Sala, and G. Mount (Mahwah, NJ: Lawrence Erlbaum, 2006), 3–19. However, the most important predictor of recruiter success was "assertiveness," which is a motivational disposition, so probably would not be considered emotional intelligence ability.

48. "Occupational Analysts Influence Air Force Decision Makers," *US Fed News,* November 3, 2010; R. Bar-On, *Preliminary Report: A New Us Air Force Study Explores the Cost-Effectiveness of Applying the Bar-on EQ-I,* (eiconsortium, August 2010); W. Gordon, "Climbing High for EI," *T + D* 64, no. 8 (August 2010): 72–73.

49. L. J. M. Zijlmans et al., "Training Emotional Intelligence Related to Treatment Skills of Staff Working with Clients with Intellectual Disabilities and Challenging Behaviour," *Journal of Intellectual Disability Research* 55, no. 2 (February 2011): 219–30.

50. R. Johnson, "Can You Feel It?" *People Management,* 23 August 2007, 34–37; K. K. Spors, "Top Small Workplaces 2007," *Wall Street Journal,* October 1, 2007, R1. Also see: S. C. Clark, R. Callister, and R. Wallace, "Undergraduate Management Skills Courses and Students' Emotional Intelligence," *Journal of Management Education* 27, no. 1 (February 2003): 3–23; D. Nelis et al., "Increasing Emotional Intelligence: (How) Is It Possible?" *Personality and Individual Differences* 47, no. 1 (2009): 36–41.

51. L. Peterson, "USF Seeking Medical Students Nicer Than 'House'," *Tampa Tribune,* June 20, 2011.

52. Goleman, Boyatzis, and McKee, *Primal Leadership;* Lopes et al., "Emotional Intelligence and Social Interaction"; H. A. Elfenbein, "Learning in Emotion Judgments: Training and the Cross-Cultural Understanding of Facial Expressions," *Journal of Nonverbal Behavior* 30, no. 1 (2006): 21–36; C.-S. Wong et al., "The Feasibility of Training and Development of EI: An Exploratory Study in Singapore, Hong Kong and Taiwan," *Intelligence* 35, no. 2 (2007): 141–50.

53. E. A. Locke, "Why Emotional Intelligence Is an Invalid Concept," *Journal of Organizational Behavior* 26 (2005): 425–31; J. Antonakis, "Emotional Intelligence: What Does It Measure and Does It Matter for Leadership?" in *Lmx Leadership—Game-Changing Designs: Research-Based Tools,* ed. G. B. Graen (Greenwich, CT: Information Age Publishing, 2009), 163–92; J. Antonakis, N. M. Ashkanasy, and M. T. Dasborough, "Does Leadership Need Emotional Intelligence?" *Leadership Quarterly* 20 (2009): 247–61; M. Fiori and J. Antonakis, "The Ability Model of Emotional Intelligence: Searching for Valid Measures," *Personality and Individual Differences* 50, no. 3 (2011): 329–34.

54. D. A. Harrison, D. A. Newman, and P. L. Roth, "How Important Are Job Attitudes? Meta-Analytic Comparisons of Integrative Behavioral Outcomes and Time Sequences," *Academy of Management Journal* 49, no. 2 (2006): 305–25. Another recent study concluded that job satisfaction and organizational commitment are so highly correlated that they represent the same construct. See: H. Le et al., "The Problem of Empirical Redundancy of Constructs in Organizational Research: An Empirical Investigation," *Organizational Behavior and Human Decision Processes* 112, no. 2 (2010): 112–25. They are also considered the two central work-related variables in the broader concept of happiness at work. See: C. D. Fisher, "Happiness at Work," *International Journal of Management Reviews* 12, no. 4 (2010): 384–412.

55. E. A. Locke, "The Nature and Causes of Job Satisfaction," in *Handbook of Industrial and Organizational Psychology,* ed. M. Dunnette (Chicago: Rand McNally, 1976), 1297–1350; H. M. Weiss, "Deconstructing Job Satisfaction: Separating Evaluations, Beliefs and Affective Experiences," *Human Resource Management Review,* no. 12 (2002): 173–94. Some definitions still include emotion as an element of job satisfaction, whereas the definition presented in this book views emotion as a cause of job satisfaction. Also, this definition views job satisfaction as a "collection of attitudes," not several "facets" of job satisfaction.

56. Ipsos-Reid, "Ipsos-Reid Global Poll Finds Major Differences in Employee Satisfaction around the World," news release, January 8, 2001); International Survey Research, *Employee Satisfaction in the World's 10 Largest Economies: Globalization or Diversity?* (Chicago: International Survey Research, 2002); Watson Wyatt Worldwide, "Malaysian Workers More Satisfied with Their Jobs Than Their Companies' Leadership and Supervision Practices," Watson Wyatt Worldwide news release, November 30, 2004; Kelly Global Workforce Index, *American Workers Are Happy with Their Jobs and Their Bosses,* (Troy, Michigan: Kelly Services, November 2006).

57. T. W. Smith, *Job Satisfaction in America: Trends and Socio-Demographic Correlates,* (Chicago: National Opinion Research Center/University of Chicago, August 2007); T. W. Smith, *Trends in Well-Being, 1972–2010,* General Social Survey

(Chicago: NORC/University of Chicago, March 2011). Similar consistently high levels of job satisfaction are reported by other major surveys. For a review of these results, see: K. Bowman and A. Rugg, *The State of the American Workers 2010: Attitudes about Work in America,* (Washington, DC: American Enterprise Institute for Public Policy Research, August 2010).

58. L. Saad, *Job Security Slips in U.S. Worker Satisfaction Rankings,* (Princeton, NJ: Gallup, Inc., August 27, 2009); *Employee Engagement Report 2011* (Princeton, NJ: BlessingWhite, 2011). A recent Kelly Services Workforce Index survey reported that 66 percent of the 170,000 respondents in 30 countries plan to look for a job with another organization within the next year. See: Kelly Services, *Acquisition and Retention in the War for Talent,* Kelly Global Workforce Index (Troy, MI: Kelly Services, April 2012).

59. The problems with measuring attitudes and values across cultures is discussed in G. Law, "If You're Happy & You Know It, Tick the Box," *Management-Auckland,* no. 45 (March 1998): 34–37; P. E. Spector et al., "Do National Levels of Individualism and Internal Locus of Control Relate to Well-Being: An Ecological Level International Study," *Journal of Organizational Behavior,* no. 22 (2001): 815–32; L. Saari and T. A. Judge, "Employee Attitudes and Job Satisfaction ," *Human Resource Management* 43, no. 4 (Winter 2004): 395–407.

60. H. Rao and R. I. Sutton, "Innovation Lessons from Pixar: An Interview with Oscar-Winning Director Brad Bird," *McKinsey Quarterly* (April 2008): 1–9.

61. M. J. Withey and W. H. Cooper, "Predicting Exit, Voice, Loyalty, and Neglect," *Administrative Science Quarterly,* no. 34 (1989): 521–39; W. H. Turnley and D. C. Feldman, "The Impact of Psychological Contract Violations on Exit, Voice, Loyalty, and Neglect," *Human Relations,* no. 52 (July 1999): 895–922. Subdimensions of silence and voice also exist. See L. van Dyne, S. Ang, and I. C. Botero, "Conceptualizing Employee Silence and Employee Voice as Multidimensional Constructs," *Journal of Management Studies* 40, no. 6 (Sept. 2003): 1359–92.

62. T. R. Mitchell, B. C. Holtom, and T. W. Lee, "How to Keep Your Best Employees: Developing an Effective Retention Policy," *Academy of Management Executive* 15 (November 2001): 96–108; C. P. Maertz and M. A. Campion, "Profiles of Quitting: Integrating Process and Content Turnover Theory," *Academy of Management Journal* 47, no. 4 (2004): 566–82; K. Morrell, J. Loan-Clarke, and A. Wilkinson, "The Role of Shocks in Employee Turnover," *British Journal of Management* 15 (2004): 335–49; B. C. Holtom, T. R. Mitchell, and T. W. Lee, "Increasing Human and Social Capital by Applying Job Embeddedness Theory," *Organizational Dynamics* 35, no. 4 (2006): 316–31.

63. A. A. Luchak, "What Kind of Voice Do Loyal Employees Use?" *British Journal of Industrial Relations* 41 (March 2003): 115–34. For a critique and explanation for historical errors in the EVLN model's development, see S. L. McShane, "Reconstructing the Meaning and Dimensionality of Voice in the Exit-Voice-Loyalty-Neglect Model (paper presented in the Voice and Loyalty Symposium)," paper presented at Annual Conference of the Administrative Sciences Association of Canada, Organizational Behaviour Division, Halifax, May 21, 2008.

64. A. O. Hirschman, *Exit, Voice, and Loyalty: Responses to Decline in Firms, Organizations, and States* (Cambridge, MA: Harvard University Press, 1970); E. A. Hoffmann, "Exit and Voice: Organizational Loyalty and Dispute Resolution Strategies," *Social Forces* 84, no. 4 (June 2006): 2313–30.

65. J. D. Hibbard, N. Kumar, and L. W. Stern, "Examining the Impact of Destructive Acts in Marketing Channel Relationships," *Journal of Marketing Research* 38 (February 2001): 45–61; J. Zhou and J. M. George, "When Job Dissatisfaction Leads to Creativity: Encouraging the Expression of Voice," *Academy of Management Journal* 44 (August 2001): 682–96.

66. M. J. Withey and I. R. Gellatly, "Situational and Dispositional Determinants of Exit, Voice, Loyalty and Neglect," *Proceedings of the Administrative Sciences Association of Canada, Organizational Behaviour Division* (June 1998); D. C. Thomas and K. Au, "The Effect of Cultural Differences on Behavioral Responses to Low Job Satisfaction," *Journal of International Business Studies* 33, no. 2 (2002): 309–26; S. F. Premeaux and A. G. Bedeian, "Breaking the Silence: The Moderating Effects of Self-Monitoring in Predicting Speaking up in the Workplace," *Journal of Management Studies* 40, no. 6 (2003): 1537–62.

67. V. Venkataramani and S. Tangirala, "When and Why Do Central Employees Speak Up? An Examination of Mediating and Moderating Variables," *Journal of Applied Psychology* 95, no. 3 (2010): 582–91.

68. T. A. Judge et al., "The Job Satisfaction-Job Performance Relationship: A Qualitative and Quantitative Review," *Psychological Bulletin* 127, no. 3 (2001): 376–407; C. D. Fisher, "Why Do Lay People Believe That Satisfaction and Performance Are Correlated? Possible Sources of a Commonsense Theory," *Journal of Organizational Behavior* 24, no. 6 (2003): 753–77; Saari and Judge, "Employee Attitudes and Job Satisfaction". Other studies report stronger correlations with job performance when both the belief and feeling components of job satisfaction are consistent with each other and when overall job attitude (satisfaction and commitment combined) is being measured. See D. J. Schleicher, J. D. Watt, and G. J. Greguras, "Reexamining the Job Satisfaction-Performance Relationship: The Complexity of Attitudes," *Journal of Applied Psychology* 89, no. 1 (2004): 165–77; Harrison, Newman, and Roth, "How Important Are Job Attitudes?". The positive relationship between job satisfaction and employee performance is also consistent with emerging research on the outcomes of positive organizational behavior. For example, see: J. R. Sunil, "Enhancing Employee Performance through Positive Organizational Behavior," *Journal of Applied Social Psychology* 38, no. 6 (2008): 1580–1600.

69. However, panel studies suggest that satisfaction has a stronger effect on performance than the other way around. For a summary, see: Fisher, "Happiness at Work."

70. J. Bonasia, "When Employees Occupy the Top Spot at Work," *Investor's Business Daily,* 5 November 2007; S. R. Ezzedeen, C. M. Hyde, and K. R. Laurin, "Is Strategic Human Resource Management Socially Responsible? The Case of Wegman's Food Markets, Inc.," *Employee Rights and Responsibilities Journal* 18 (2007): 295–307.

71. J. I. Heskett, W. E. Sasser, and L. A. Schlesinger, *The Service Profit Chain* (New York: Free Press, 1997); R. W. Y. Yee et al., "The Service-Profit Chain: A Review and Extension," *Total Quality Management & Business Excellence* 20, no. 6 (2009): 617–32. Several studies and meta-analyses have found substantial support for most parts of this model. See: G. A. Gelade and S. Young, "Test of a Service Profit Chain Model in the Retail Banking Sector," *Journal of Occupational &*

Organizational Psychology 78 (2005): 1–22; S. P. Brown and S. K. Lam, "A Meta-Analysis of Relationships Linking Employee Satisfaction to Customer Responses," *Journal of Retailing* 84, no. 3 (2008): 243–55; C. G. Chi and D. Gursoy, "Employee Satisfaction, Customer Satisfaction, and Financial Performance: An Empirical Examination," *International Journal of Hospitality Management* 28, no. 2 (2009): 245–53; R. G. Netemeyer, J. G. Maxham Iii, and D. R. Lichtenstein, "Store Manager Performance and Satisfaction: Effects on Store Employee Performance and Satisfaction, Store Customer Satisfaction, and Store Customer Spending Growth," *Journal of Applied Psychology* 95, no. 3 (2010): 530–45; T. J. Gerpott and M. Paukert, "The Relationship between Employee Satisfaction and Customer Satisfaction: A Meta-Analysis (Der Zusammenhang Zwischen Mitarbeiter- Und Kundenzufriedenheit: Eine Metaanalyse)," *Zeitschrift für Personalforschung* 25, no. 1 (2011): 28–54.

72. W.-C. Tsai and Y.-M. Huang, "Mechanisms Linking Employee Affective Delivery and Customer Behavioral Intentions," *Journal of Applied Psychology* 87, no. 5 (2002): 1001–8; P. Guenzi and O. Pelloni, "The Impact of Interpersonal Relationships on Customer Satisfaction and Loyalty to the Service Provider," *International Journal Of Service Industry Management* 15, no. 3–4 (2004): 365–84; S. J. Bell, S. Auh, and K. Smalley, "Customer Relationship Dynamics: Service Quality and Customer Loyalty in the Context of Varying Levels of Customer Expertise and Switching Costs," *Journal of the Academy of Marketing Science* 33, no. 2 (Spring 2005): 169–83; P. B. Barger and A. A. Grandey, "Service with a Smile and Encounter Satisfaction: Emotional Contagion and Appraisal Mechanisms," *Academy of Management Journal* 49, no. 6 (2006): 1229–38.

73. "The Greatest Briton in Management and Leadership," *Personnel Today* (February 18, 2003): 20.

74. R. T. Mowday, L. W. Porter, and R. M. Steers, *Employee Organization Linkages: The Psychology of Commitment, Absenteeism, and Turnover* (New York: Academic Press, 1982); J. P. Meyer, "Organizational Commitment," *International Review of Industrial and Organizational Psychology* 12 (1997): 175–228 Along with affective and continuance commitment, Meyer identifies "normative commitment," which refers to employee feelings of obligation to remain with the organization. This commitment has been excluded so students focus on the two most common perspectives of commitment. Also, there is some question whether continuance and normative commitment are comparable to affective commitment; they are attitudes toward quitting and repaying a debt, respectively, rather than toward the organization. See: O. N. Solinger, W. van Olffen, and R. A. Roe, "Beyond the Three-Component Model of Organizational Commitment," *Journal of Applied Psychology* 93, no. 1 (2008): 70–83.

75. R. D. Hackett, P. Bycio, and P. A. Hausdorf, "Further Assessments of Meyer and Allen's (1991) Three-Component Model of Organizational Commitment," *Journal of Applied Psychology* 79 (1994): 15–23.

76. J. P. Meyer et al., "Affective, Continuance, and Normative Commitment to the Organization: A Meta-Analysis of Antecedents, Correlates, and Consequences," *Journal of Vocational Behavior* 61 (2002): 20–52; M. Riketta, "Attitudinal Organizational Commitment and Job Performance: A Meta-Analysis," *Journal of Organizational Behavior* 23 (2002): 257–66; J. P. Meyer, T. E. Becker, and C. Vandenberghe, "Employee Commitment and Motivation: A Conceptual Analysis and Integrative Model," *Journal of Applied Psychology*

89, no. 6 (2004): 991–1007; J. P. Meyer and E. R. Maltin, "Employee Commitment and Well-Being: A Critical Review, Theoretical Framework and Research Agenda," *Journal of Vocational Behavior* 77, no. 2 (2010): 323–37.

77. Data provided in several country-specific news releases from Kelly Services. For a white paper summary of the survey, see Kelly Services, *Employee Loyalty Rises during Global Economic Recession, Kelly International Workforce Survey Finds* (Troy, MI: Kelly Services, March 8, 2010).

78. J. P. Meyer et al., "Organizational Commitment and Job Performance: It's the Nature of the Commitment That Counts," *Journal of Applied Psychology* 74 (1989): 152–56; A. A. Luchak and I. R. Gellatly, "What Kind of Commitment Does a Final-Earnings Pension Plan Elicit?" *Relations Industrielles* 56 (Spring 2001): 394–417; Z. X. Chen and A. M. Francesco, "The Relationship between the Three Components of Commitment and Employee Performance in China," *Journal of Vocational Behavior* 62, no. 3 (2003): 490–510; D. M. Powell and J. P. Meyer, "Side-Bet Theory and the Three-Component Model of Organizational Commitment," *Journal of Vocational Behavior* 65, no. 1 (2004): 157–77.

79. J. E. Finegan, "The Impact of Person and Organizational Values on Organizational Commitment," *Journal of Occupational and Organizational Psychology* 73 (June 2000): 149–69; A. Panaccio and C. Vandenberghe, "Perceived Organizational Support, Organizational Commitment and Psychological Well-Being: A Longitudinal Study," *Journal of Vocational Behavior* 75, no. 2 (2009): 224–36.

80. J. W. Westerman and L. A. Cyr, "An Integrative Analysis of Person-Organization Fit Theories," *International Journal of Selection and Assessment* 12, no. 3 (September 2004): 252–61; A. L. Kristof-Brown, R. D. Zimmerman, and E. C. Johnson, "Consequences of Individuals' Fit at Work: A Meta-Analysis of Person-Job, Person-Organization, Person-Group, and Person-Supervisor Fit," *Personnel Psychology* 58, no. 2 (2005): 281–342; J. R. Edwards, "Chapter 4: Person-Environment Fit in Organizations: An Assessment of Theoretical Progress," *The Academy of Management Annals* 2 (2008): 167–230.

81. D. M. Rousseau et al., "Not So Different after All: A Cross-Discipline View of Trust," *Academy of Management Review* 23 (1998): 393–404.

82. A. Travaglione and B. Cross, "Diminishing the Social Network in Organizations: Does There Need to Be Such a Phenomenon as 'Survivor Syndrome' after Downsizing?" *Strategic Change* 15 (January-February 2006): 1–13; D. K. Datta et al., "Causes and Effects of Employee Downsizing: A Review and Synthesis," *Journal of Management* 36, no. 1 (January 2010): 281–348.

83. Similar concepts on information acquisition are found in socialization and organizational change research. See, for example, P. Bordia et al., "Uncertainty during Organizational Change: Types, Consequences, and Management Strategies," *Journal of Business and Psychology* 18, no. 4 (2004): 507–32; H. D. Cooper-Thomas and N. Anderson, "Organizational Socialization: A Field Study into Socialization Success and Rate," *International Journal of Selection and Assessment* 13, no. 2 (2005): 116–28; T. N. Bauer, "Newcomer Adjustment during Organizational Socialization: A Meta-Analytic Review of Antecedents, Outcomes, and Methods," *Journal of Applied Psychology* 92, no. 3 (2007): 707–21.

84. T. S. Heffner and J. R. Rentsch, "Organizational Commitment and Social Interaction: A Multiple Constituencies Approach," *Journal of Vocational Behavior* 59 (2001): 471–90.

85. J. L. Pierce, T. Kostova, and K. T. Dirks, "Toward a Theory of Psychological Ownership in Organizations," *Academy of Management Review* 26, no. 2 (2001): 298–310; M. Mayhew et al., "A Study of the Antecedents and Consequences of Psychological Ownership in Organizational Settings," *The Journal of Social Psychology* 147, no. 5 (2007): 477–500; T.-S. Han, H.-H. Chiang, and A. Chang, "Employee Participation in Decision Making, Psychological Ownership and Knowledge Sharing: Mediating Role of Organizational Commitment in Taiwanese High-Tech Organizations," *The International Journal of Human Resource Management* 21, no. 12 (2010): 2218–33.

86. J. C. Quick et al., *Preventive Stress Management in Organizations* (Washington, D.C.: American Psychological Association, 1997), pp. 3–4; R. S. DeFrank and J. M. Ivancevich, "Stress on the Job: An Executive Update," *Academy of Management Executive* 12 (August 1998): 55–66; A. L. Dougall and A. Baum, "Stress, Coping, and Immune Function," in *Handbook of Psychology,* ed. M. Gallagher and R. J. Nelson (Hoboken, NJ: John Wiley & Sons, 2003), 441–55. There are at least three schools of thought regarding the meaning of stress, and some reviews of the stress literature describe these schools without pointing to any one as the preferred definition. One reviewer concluded the stress concept is so broad it should be considered an umbrella concept, capturing a broad array of phenomena and providing a simple term for the public to use. See T. A. Day, "Defining Stress as a Prelude to Mapping Its Neurocircuitry: No Help from Allostasis," *Progress in Neuro-Psychopharmacology and Biological Psychiatry* 29, no. 8 (2005): 1195–1200; R. Cropanzano and A. Li, "Organizational Politics and Workplace Stress," in *Handbook of Organizational Politics,* ed. E. Vigoda-Gadot and A. Drory (Cheltenham, UK: Edward Elgar, 2006), 139–60; R. L. Woolfolk, P. M. Lehrer, and L. A. Allen, "Conceptual Issues Underlying Stress Management," in *Principles and Practice of Stress Management,* ed. P. M. Lehrer, R. L. Woolfolk, and W. E. Sime (New York: Guilford Press, 2007), 3–15.

87. Finegan, "The Impact of Person and Organizational Values on Organizational Commitment"; Dougall and Baum, "Stress, Coping, and Immune Function"; R. S. Lazarus, *Stress and Emotion: A New Synthesis* (New York: Springer Publishing, 2006); L. W. Hunter and S. M. B. Thatcher, "Feeling the Heat: Effects of Stress, Commitment, and Job Experience on Job Performance," *Academy of Management Journal* 50, no. 4 (2007): 953–68.

88. "The Anxious American Worker: Jobs, the Economy, and a Call for Help," Rutgers University news release, August 28, 2008; M. Fahmy, "Survey Says Work Really Is Hazardous to Your Health," *Reuters* (Singapore), December 5, 2008; Towers Watson, "Debunking Workforce Myths," Towers Watson news release, March 2008; Saad, *Job Security Slips in U.S. Worker Satisfaction Rankings.*

89. W. Lester, "Poll: Stress Knows Few Boundaries for People in Industrial Democracies," *USA Today,* December 20, 2006; "Survey Reveals 77% of Americans Stressed about Something at Work," PR Newswire news release, March 30, 2011; Leger Marketing, *Cbc: The Health of Canadians* (Toronto: Leger Marketing, 2011); Right Management, "Most Employees Say Their Workplace Is Stressful," Right Management news release for R. Management, April 30, 2012.

90. Quick et al., *Preventive Stress Management in Organizations,* 5–6; B. L. Simmons and D. L. Nelson, "Eustress at Work: The Relationship between Hope and Health in Hospital Nurses," *Health Care Management Review* 26, no. 4 (October 2001): 7ff.

91. H. Selye, "A Syndrome Produced by Diverse Nocuous Agents," *Nature* 138, no. 1 (4 July 1936): 32; H. Selye, *Stress without Distress* (Philadelphia: J. B. Lippincott, 1974). The earliest use of the word stress is described in R. M. K. Keil, "Coping and Stress: A Conceptual Analysis," *Journal of Advanced Nursing* 45, no. 6 (2004): 659–65.

92. S. E. Taylor, R. L. Repetti, and T. Seeman, "Health Psychology: What Is an Unhealthy Environment and How Does It Get under the Skin?" *Annual Review of Psychology* 48 (1997): 411–47.

93. D. Ganster, M. Fox, and D. Dwyer, "Explaining Employees' Health Care Costs: A Prospective Examination of Stressful Job Demands, Personal Control, and Physiological Reactivity," *Journal of Applied Psychology* 86 (May 2001): 954–64; M. Kivimaki et al., "Work Stress and Risk of Cardiovascular Mortality: Prospective Cohort Study of Industrial Employees," *British Medical Journal* 325 (October 19, 2002): 857–60; S. Andrew and S. Ayers, "Stress, Health, and Illness," in *The Sage Handbook of Health Psychology,* ed. S. Sutton, A. Baum, and M. Johnston (London: Sage, 2004), 169–96; A. Rosengren et al., "Association of Psychosocial Risk Factors with Risk of Acute Myocardial Infarction in 11 119 Cases and 13 648 Controls from 52 Countries (the Interheart Study): Case-Control Study," *The Lancet* 364, no. 9438 (September 11, 2004): 953–62.

94. R. C. Kessler, "The Effects of Stressful Life Events on Depression," *Annual Review of Psychology* 48 (1997): 191–214; L. Greenburg and J. Barling, "Predicting Employee Aggression against Coworkers, Subordinates and Supervisors: The Roles of Person Behaviors and Perceived Workplace Factors," *Journal of Organizational Behavior* 20 (1999): 897–913; M. Jamal and V. V. Baba, "Job Stress and Burnout among Canadian Managers and Nurses: An Empirical Examination," *Canadian Journal of Public Health* 91, no. 6 (Nov-Dec 2000): 454–58; L. Tourigny, V. V. Baba, and T. R. Lituchy, "Job Burnout among Airline Employees in Japan: A Study of the Buffering Effects of Absence and Supervisory Support," *International Journal of Cross Cultural Management* 5, no. 1 (April 2005): 67–85; M. S. Hershcovis et al., "Predicting Workplace Aggression: A Meta-Analysis," *Journal of Applied Psychology* 92, no. 1 (2007): 228–38.

95. C. Maslach, W. B. Schaufeli, and M. P. Leiter, "Job Burnout," *Annual Review of Psychology* 52 (2001): 397–422; J. R. B. Halbesleben and M. R. Buckley, "Burnout in Organizational Life," *Journal of Management* 30, no. 6 (2004): 859–79.

96. K. Danna and R. W. Griffin, "Health and Well-Being in the Workplace: A Review and Synthesis of the Literature," *Journal of Management* (Spring 1999): 357–84.

97. This is a slight variation of the definition in the Quebec anti-harassment legislation. See http://www.cnt.gouv.qc.ca/en/in-case-of/psychological-harassment-at-work/index.html. For related definitions and discussion of workplace incivility, see H. Cowiea et al., "Measuring Workplace Bullying," *Aggression and Violent Behavior* 7 (2002): 33–51; C. M. Pearson and C. L. Porath, "On the Nature, Consequences and Remedies of Workplace Incivility: No Time for 'Nice'? Think Again," *Academy of Management Executive* 19, no. 1 (February 2005): 7–18. For recent discussion of workplace harassment legislation in the United States, see: D. C. Yamada, "Workplace Bully and American Employment Law: A Ten-Year Progress Report and Assessment," *Comparative Labor Law and Policy Journal* 32, no. 1 (2010): 251–84.

98. "Power Harassment Cases Rising," *Daily Yomiuri* (Tokyo), June 10, 2009, 2; "Monster Global Poll Reveals Workplace

Bullying Is Endemic" 2011, accessed June 26, 2012, http://www.onrec.com; H. Mulholland, "Bullied Teachers Fear Culture of 'Macho Managers'," *The Observer* (London), April 8, 2012, 4.

99. For a legal discussion of types of sexual harassment, see: B. Lindemann and D. D. Kadue, Sexual Harassment in Employment Law (Washington: BNA Books, 1999), 7–9.

100. D. Ulrich and W. Ulrich, *The Why of Work: How Great Leaders Build Abundant Organizations That Win* (New York: McGraw-Hill, 2010), v.

101. E. Galinsky et al., *Overwork in America: When the Way We Work Becomes Too Much* (New York: Families and Work Institute, March 2005); A. Fung, "Poll: 40% Haven't Vacationed in 2 Years," *Richmond Times-Dispatch,* July 1, 2010, B3.

102. S. Johnson et al., "The Experience of Work-Related Stress across Occupations," in *Stress and the Quality of Working Life,* ed. A. M. Rossi, J. C. Quick, and P. L. Perrewé (Charlotte, NC: Information Age Publishing, 2009), 67–77.

103. R. Drago, D. Black, and M. Wooden, *The Persistence of Long Work Hours,* Melbourne Institute Working Paper Series (Melbourne: Melbourne Institute of Applied Economic and Social Research, University of Melbourne, August 2005); L. Golden, "A Brief History of Long Work Time and the Contemporary Sources of Overwork," *Journal of Business Ethics* 84, no. S2 (2009): 217–27.

104. C. B. Meek, "The Dark Side of Japanese Management in the 1990s: Karoshi and Ijime in the Japanese Workplace," *Journal of Managerial Psychology* 19, no. 3 (2004): 312–31; "Nagoya Court Rules Toyota Employee Died from Overwork," *Japan Times,* December 1, 2007; Y. Kageyama, "Questions Rise about Temps, Overwork at Toyota," *Associated Press Newswires,* September 10, 2008; Y. Kawanishi, "On Karo-Jisatsu (Suicide by Overwork)," *International Journal of Mental Health* 37, no. 1 (Spring2008): 61–74; P. Novotny, "Overwork a Silent Killer in Japan," *Agence France Presse,* January 11, 2009.

105. R. Karasek and T. Theorell, *Healthy Work: Stress, Productivity, and the Reconstruction of Working Life* (New York: Basic Books, 1990); N. Turner, N. Chmiel, and M. Walls, "Railing for Safety: Job Demands, Job Control, and Safety Citizenship Role Definition," *Journal of Occupational Health Psychology* 10, no. 4 (2005): 504–12.

106. Lazarus, *Stress and Emotion: A New Synthesis,* Chap. 5.

107. M. Zuckerman and M. Gagne, "The Cope Revised: Proposing a 5–Factor Model of Coping Strategies," *Journal of Research in Personality* 37 (2003): 169–204; S. Folkman and J. T. Moskowitz, "Coping: Pitfalls and Promise," *Annual Review of Psychology* 55 (2004): 745–74; C. A. Thompson et al., "On the Importance of Coping: A Model and New Directions for Research on Work and Family," *Research in Occupational Stress and Well-Being* 6 (2007): 73–113.

108. S. E. Taylor et al., "Psychological Resources, Positive Illusions, and Health," *American Psychologist* 55, no. 1 (January 2000): 99–109; F. Luthans and C. M. Youssef, "Emerging Positive Organizational Behavior," *Journal of Management* 33, no. 3 (June 1, 2007 2007): 321–49; P. Steel, J. Schmidt, and J. Shultz, "Refining the Relationship between Personality and Subjective Well-Being," *Psychological Bulletin* 134, no. 1 (2008): 138–61; G. Alarcon, K. J. Eschleman, and N. A. Bowling, "Relationships between Personality Variables and Burnout: A Meta-Analysis,"

Work & Stress 23, no. 3 (2009): 244–63; R. Kotov et al., "Linking "Big" Personality Traits to Anxiety, Depressive, and Substance Use Disorders: A Meta-Analysis," *Psychological Bulletin* 136, no. 5 (2010): 768–821.

109. G. A. Bonanno, "Loss, Trauma, and Human Resilience: Have We Underestimated the Human Capacity to Thrive after Extremely Aversive Events?" *American Psychologist* 59, no. 1 (2004): 20–28; F. Luthans, C. M. Youssef, and B. J. Avolio, *Psychological Capital: Developing the Human Competitive Edge* (New York: Oxford University Press, 2007).

110. J. T. Spence and A. S. Robbins, "Workaholism: Definition, Measurement and Preliminary Results," *Journal of Personality Assessment* 58 (1992): 160–178; R. J. Burke, "Workaholism in Organizations: Psychological and Physical Well-Being Consequences," *Stress Medicine* 16, no. 1 (2000): 11–16; I. Harpaz and R. Snir, "Workaholism: Its Definition and Nature," *Human Relations* 56 (2003): 291–319; R. J. Burke, A. M. Richardson, and M. Martinussen, "Workaholism among Norwegian Senior Managers: New Research Directions," *International Journal of Management* 21, no. 4 (December 2004): 415–26; T. W. H. Ng, K. L. Sorensen, and D. C. Feldman, "Dimensions, Antecedents, and Consequences of Workaholism: A Conceptual Integration and Extension," *Journal of Organizational Behavior* 28 (2007): 111–36.

111. M. Siegall and L. L. Cummings, "Stress and Organizational Role Conflict," *Genetic, Social, and General Psychology Monographs* 12 (1995): 65–95.

112. L. T. Eby et al., "Work and Family Research in IO/OB: Content Analysis and Review of the Literature (1980–2002)," *Journal of Vocational Behavior* 66, no. 1 (2005): 124–97.

113. N. Davidson, "Vancouver Developer Looks to Make Video Games without Burning out Staff," *Canadian Press,* February 21, 2006; F. Jossi, "Clocking Out," *HRMagazine,* June 2007, 46–50; American Psychological Association, "San Jorge Children's Hospital: A Culture of Collaboration and Care," news release for A. P. Association, 2011.

114. S. R. Madsen, "The Effects of Home-Based Teleworking on Work-Family Conflict," *Human Resource Development Quarterly* 14, no. 1 (2003): 35–58; S. Raghuram and B. Wiesenfeld, "Work-Nonwork Conflict and Job Stress among Virtual Workers," *Human Resource Management* 43, no. 2/3 (Summer/Fall 2004): 259–77.

115. Organization for Economic Co-operation and Development, *Babies and Bosses: Reconciling Work and Family Life,* vol. 4 (Canada, Finland, Sweden and the United Kingdom) (Paris: OECD Publishing, 2005); J. Heymann et al., *The Work, Family, and Equity Index: How Does the United States Measure Up?,* Project on Global Working Families (Montreal: Institute for Health and Social Policy, June 2007).

116. M. Secret, "Parenting in the Workplace: Child Care Options for Consideration," *The Journal of Applied Behavioral Science* 41, no. 3 (September 2005): 326–47.

117. A. E. Carr and T. L.-P. Tang, "Sabbaticals and Employee Motivation: Benefits, Concerns, and Implications," *Journal of Education for Business* 80, no. 3 (Jan/Feb 2005): 160–64; S. Overman, "Sabbaticals Benefit Companies as Well as Employees," *Employee Benefit News,* April 15, 2006; O. B. Davidson et al., "Sabbatical Leave: Who Gains and How Much?" *Journal of Applied Psychology* 95, no. 5 (2010): 953–64. For discussion of psychological detachment and stress management, see C. Fritz et al., "Happy, Healthy, and Productive: The Role of Detachment from Work During

Nonwork Time," *Journal of Applied Psychology* 95, no. 5 (2010): 977–83.

118. M. H. Abel, "Humor, Stress, and Coping Strategies," *Humor: International Journal of Humor Research* 15, no. 4 (2002): 365–81; N. A. Kuiper et al., "Humor Is Not Always the Best Medicine: Specific Components of Sense of Humor and Psychological Well-Being," *Humor: International Journal of Humor Research* 17, no. 1/2 (2004): 135–68; E. J. Romero and K. W. Cruthirds, "The Use of Humor in the Workplace," *Academy of Management Perspectives* 20, no. 2 (2006): 58–69; M. McCreaddie and S. Wiggins, "The Purpose and Function of Humor in Health, Health Care and Nursing: A Narrative Review," *Journal of Advanced Nursing* 61, no. 6 (2008): 584–95.

119. W. M. Ensel and N. Lin, "Physical Fitness and the Stress Process," *Journal of Community Psychology* 32, no. 1 (January 2004): 81–101.

120. S. Armour, "Rising Job Stress Could Affect Bottom Line," *USA Today,* July 29, 2003; V. A. Barnes, F. A. Treiber, and M. H. Johnson, "Impact of Transcendental Meditation on Ambulatory Blood Pressure in African-American Adolescents," *American Journal of Hypertension* 17, no. 4 (2004): 366–69; P. Manikonda et al., "Influence of Non-Pharmacological Treatment (Contemplative Meditation and Breathing Technique) on Stress Induced Hypertension- a Randomized Controlled Study," *American Journal of Hypertension* 18, no. 5, Supplement 1 (2005): A89–A90.

121. C. Viswesvaran, J. I. Sanchez, and J. Fisher, "The Role of Social Support in the Process of Work Stress: A Meta-Analysis," *Journal of Vocational Behavior* 54, no. 2 (1999): 314–34; S. E. Taylor et al., "Biobehavioral Responses to Stress in Females: Tend-and-Befriend, Not Fight-or-Flight," *Psychological Review* 107, no. 3 (July 2000): 411–29; R. Eisler and D. S. Levine, "Nurture, Nature, and Caring: We Are Not Prisoners of Our Genes," *Brain and Mind* 3 (2002): 9–52; T. A. Beehr, N. A. Bowling, and M. M. Bennett, "Occupational Stress and Failures of Social Support: When Helping Hurts," *Journal of Occupational Health Psychology* 15, no. 1 (Jan 2010): 45–59; B. A. Scott et al., "A Daily Investigation of the Role of Manager Empathy on Employee Well-Being," *Organizational Behavior and Human Decision Processes* 113, no. 2 (2010): 127–40.

CHAPTER 5

1. C. C. Pinder, *Work Motivation in Organizational Behavior* (Upper Saddle River, NJ: Prentice-Hall, 1998); R. M. Steers, R. T. Mowday, and D. L. Shapiro, "The Future of Work Motivation Theory," *Academy of Management Review* 29 (2004): 379–87.

2. A. B. Bakker and W. B. Schaufeli, "Positive Organizational Behavior: Engaged Employees in Flourishing Organizations," *Journal of Organizational Behavior* 29, no. 2 (2008): 147–54; W. H. Macey and B. Schneider, "The Meaning of Employee Engagement," *Industrial and Organizational Psychology* 1 (2008): 3–30.

3. M. Millar, "Getting the Measure of Its People," *Personnel Today,* December 14, 2004, 6; K. Ockenden, "Inside Story," *Utility Week,* January 28, 2005, 26; J. Engen, "Are Your Employees Truly Engaged?" *Chief Executive,* March 2008, 42; P. Flade, "Employee Engagement Drives Shareholder Value," *Director of Finance Online,* February 13, 2008; S. Flander, "Terms of Engagement," *Human Resource Executive Online,* January 2008.

4. Engen, "Are Your Employees Truly Engaged?"; Flander, "Terms of Engagement"; D. Macleod and N. Clarke, *Engaging for Success: Enhancing Performance through Employee Engagement,* (London: July 2009).

5. Gallup Consulting, *The Gallup Q12–Employee Engagement-Poll 2008 Results* (Gallup Consulting, February 2009); A. Fox, "Raising Engagement," *HRMagazine,* May 2010, 34; BlessingWhite, *Employee Engagement Report 2011,* (Princeton, NJ: BlessingWhite, January 2011).

6. Several sources attempt to identify and organize the drivers of employee engagement. See, for example: D. Robinson, S. Perryman, and S. Hayday, *The Drivers of Employee Engagement* (Brighton, UK: Institute for Employment Studies., 2004); W. H. Macey et al., *Employee Engagement: Tools for Analysis, Practice, and Competitive Advantage* (Malden, MA: Wiley-Blackwell, 2009); Macleod and Clarke, *Engaging for Success;* M. Stairs and M. Galpin, "Positive Engagement: From Employee Engagement to Workplace Happiness," in *Oxford Handbook of Positive Psychology of Work,* ed. P. A. Linley, S. Harrington, and N. Garcea (New York: Oxford University Press, 2010), 155–72.

7. The confusing array of definitions about drives and needs has been the subject of criticism for a half century. See, for example, R. S. Peters, "Motives and Motivation," *Philosophy* 31 (1956): 117–30; H. Cantril, "Sentio, Ergo Sum: 'Motivation' Reconsidered," *Journal of Psychology* 65, no. 1 (January 1967): 91–107; G. R. Salancik and J. Pfeffer, "An Examination of Need-Satisfaction Models of Job Attitudes," *Administrative Science Quarterly* 22, no. 3 (Sep. 1977): 427–56.

8. A. Blasi, "Emotions and Moral Motivation," *Journal for the Theory of Social Behaviour* 29, no. 1 (1999): 1–19; D. W. Pfaff, *Drive: Neurobiological and Molecular Mechanisms of Sexual Motivation* (Cambridge, MA: MIT Press, 1999); T. V. Sewards and M. A. Sewards, "Fear and Power-Dominance Drive Motivation: Neural Representations and Pathways Mediating Sensory and Mnemonic Inputs, and Outputs to Premotor Structures," *Neuroscience and Biobehavioral Reviews* 26 (2002): 553–79; K. C. Berridge, "Motivation Concepts in Behavioral Neuroscience," *Physiology & Behavior* 81, no. 2 (2004): 179–209. We distinguish drives from emotions, but future research may find the two concepts are not so different as is stated here. Woodworth is credited with either coining or popularizing the term *drives* in the context of human motivation. His classic book is certainly the first source to discuss the concept in detail. See: R. S. Woodworth, *Dynamic Psychology* (New York: Columbia University Press, 1918).

9. K. Passyn and M. Sujan, "Self-Accountability Emotions and Fear Appeals: Motivating Behavior," *Journal of Consumer Research* 32, no. 4 (2006): 583–89; S. G. Barsade and D. E. Gibson, "Why Does Affect Matter in Organizations?" *Academy of Management Perspectives* 21, no. 2 (February 2007): 36–59.

10. G. Loewenstein, "The Psychology of Curiosity: A Review and Reinterpretation," *Psychological Bulletin* 116, no. 1 (1994): 75–98; R. E. Baumeister and M. R. Leary, "The Need to Belong: Desire for Interpersonal Attachments as a Fundamental Human Motivation," *Psychological Bulletin* 117 (1995): 497–529; A. E. Kelley, "Neurochemical Networks Encoding Emotion and Motivation: An Evolutionary Perspective," in *Who Needs Emotions? The Brain Meets the Robot,* ed. J.-M. Fellous and M. A. Arbib (New York: Oxford University Press, 2005), 29–78; L. A. Leotti, S. S. Iyengar, and K. N. Ochsner, "Born to Choose: The Origins and Value of the Need for Control," *Trends in Cognitive Sciences* 14, no. 10 (2010): 457–63.

11. A. R. Damasio, *The Feeling of What Happens: Body and Emotion in the Making of Consciousness* (New York: Harcourt Brace & Company, 1999), 286.

12. V. Lombardi Jr., *What It Takes to Be #1: Vince Lombardi on Leadership* (New York: McGraw-Hill, 2001), 39.

13. A. H. Maslow, "A Theory of Human Motivation," *Psychological Review* 50 (1943): 370–96; A. H. Maslow, *Motivation and Personality* (New York: Harper & Row, 1954).

14. D. T. Hall and K. E. Nougaim, "An Examination of Maslow's Need Hierarchy in an Organizational Setting," *Organizational Behavior and Human Performance* 3, no. 1 (1968): 12; M. A. Wahba and L. G. Bridwell, "Maslow Reconsidered: A Review of Research on the Need Hierarchy Theory," *Organizational Behavior and Human Performance* 15 (1976): 212–40; E. L. Betz, "Two Tests of Maslow's Theory of Need Fulfillment," *Journal of Vocational Behavior* 24, no. 2 (1984): 204–20; P. A. Corning, "Biological Adaptation in Human Societies: A 'Basic Needs' Approach," *Journal of Bioeconomics* 2, no. 1 (2000): 41–86. For a recent proposed revision of the model, see: D. T. Kenrick et al., "Renovating the Pyramid of Needs: Contemporary Extensions Built upon Ancient Foundations," *Perspectives on Psychological Science* 5, no. 3 (May 2010): 292–314.

15. L. Parks and R. P. Guay, "Personality, Values, and Motivation," *Personality and Individual Differences* 47, no. 7 (2009): 675–84.

16. B. A. Agle and C. B. Caldwell, "Understanding Research on Values in Business," *Business and Society* 38 (September 1999): 326–87; B. Verplanken and R. W. Holland, "Motivated Decision Making: Effects of Activation and Self-Centrality of Values on Choices and Behavior," *Journal of Personality and Social Psychology* 82, no. 3 (2002): 434–47; S. Hitlin and J. A. Pilavin, "Values: Reviving a Dormant Concept," *Annual Review of Sociology* 30 (2004): 359–93.

17. K. Dye, A. J. Mills, and T. G. Weatherbee, "Maslow: Man Interrupted—Reading Management Theory in Context," *Management Decision* 43, no. 10 (2005): 1375–95.

18. A. H. Maslow, "A Preface to Motivation Theory," *Psychsomatic Medicine* 5 (1943): 85–92.

19. S. Kesebir, J. Graham, and S. Oishi, "A Theory of Human Needs Should Be Human-Centered, Not Animal-Centered," *Perspectives on Psychological Science* 5, no. 3 (May 2010): 315–19.

20. A. H. Maslow, *Maslow on Management* (New York: John Wiley & Sons, 1998).

21. F. F. Luthans, "Positive Organizational Behavior: Developing and Managing Psychological Strengths," *The Academy of Management Executive* 16, no. 1 (2002): 57–72; S. L. Gable and J. Haidt, "What (and Why) Is Positive Psychology?" *Review of General Psychology* 9, no. 2 (2005): 103–10; M. E. P. Seligman et al., "Positive Psychology Progress: Empirical Validation of Interventions," *American Psychologist* 60, no. 5 (2005): 410–21.

22. D. C. McClelland, *The Achieving Society* (New York: Van Nostrand Reinhold, 1961); D. C. McClelland and D. H. Burnham, "Power Is the Great Motivator," *Harvard Business Review* 73 (January/February 1995): 126–39; D. Vredenburgh and Y. Brender, "The Hierarchical Abuse of Power in Work Organizations," *Journal of Business Ethics* 17 (September 1998): 1337–47; S. Shane, E. A. Locke, and C. J. Collins, "Entrepreneurial Motivation," *Human Resource Management Review* 13, no. 2 (2003): 257–79.

23. Australian Institute of Management, *There Are No Limits: What Keeps Employees Engaged with Their Workplace?* (St. Kilda, VIC: Australian Institute of Management, November 29, 2006); Society of Petroleum Engineers, "Spe Survey Rates Employee Satisfaction," *Talent & Technology* 2007; "Charles Schwab's Older Workers & Money Survey Reveals Surprising Findings about Job Sentiment among Americans in Their 50s and 60s," Business Wire news release for C. S. Co., April 24 2012; Kelly Services, *Acquisition and Retention in the War for Talent,* Kelly Global Workforce Index (Troy, MI: Kelly Services, April 2012).

24. McClelland, *The Achieving Society.*

25. Shane, Locke, and Collins, "Entrepreneurial Motivation."

26. McClelland and Burnham, "Power Is the Great Motivator"; J. L. Thomas, M. W. Dickson, and P. D. Bliese, "Values Predicting Leader Performance in the U.S. Army Reserve Officer Training Corps Assessment Center: Evidence for a Personality-Mediated Model," *The Leadership Quarterly* 12, no. 2 (2001): 181–96.

27. Vredenburgh and Brender, "The Hierarchical Abuse of Power in Work Organizations."

28. D. Miron and D. C. McClelland, "The Impact of Achievement Motivation Training on Small Business," *California Management Review* 21 (1979): 13–28.

29. P. R. Lawrence and N. Nohria, *Driven: How Human Nature Shapes Our Choices* (San Francisco: Jossey-Bass, 2002); N. Nohria, B. Groysberg, and L.-E. Lee, "Employee Motivation: A Powerful New Model," *Harvard Business Review* (July/August 2008): 78–84. On the application of four-drive theory to leadership, See: P. R. Lawrence, *Driven to Lead* (San Francisco: Jossey-Bass, 2010).

30. The drive to acquire is likely associated with research on getting ahead, desire for competence, the selfish gene, and desire for social distinction. See R. H. Frank, *Choosing the Right Pond: Human Behavior and the Quest for Status* (New York: Oxford University Press, 1985); L. Gaertner et al., "The 'I,' the 'We,' and the 'When': A Meta-Analysis of Motivational Primacy in Self-Definition," *Journal of Personality and Social Psychology* 83, no. 3 (2002): 574–91; J. Hogan and B. Holland, "Using Theory to Evaluate Personality and Job-Performance Relations: A Socioanalytic Perspective," *Journal of Applied Psychology* 88, no. 1 (2003): 100–12; R. Dawkins, *The Selfish Gene,* 30th Anniversary ed. (Oxford, UK: Oxford University Press, 2006); B. S. Frey, "Awards as Compensation," *European Management Journal* 4 (2007): 6–14; M. R. Leary, "Motivational and Emotional Aspects of the Self," *Annual Review of Psychology* 58, no. 1 (2007): 317–44.

31. Baumeister and Leary, "The Need to Belong."

32. J. Litman, "Curiosity and the Pleasures of Learning: Wanting and Liking New Information," *Cognition and Emotion* 19, no. 6 (2005): 793–814; T. G. Reio Jr. et al., "The Measurement and Conceptualization of Curiosity," *Journal of Genetic Psychology* 167, no. 2 (2006): 117–35.

33. W. H. Bexton, W. Heron, and T. H. Scott, "Effects of Decreased Variation in the Sensory Environment," *Canadian Journal of Psychology* 8 (1954): 70–76; Loewenstein, "The Psychology of Curiosity."

34. "Come and Join Our Mob!," *St. Helens Reporter* (UK), March 2, 2011; B. Gibson, "Huddersfield B&Q Customers Surprised by Staff Flash Mob," *Huddersfield Daily Examiner* (UK), March 7, 2011.

35. A. R. Damasio, *Descartes' Error: Emotion, Reason, and the Human Brain* (New York: Putnam, 1994); J. E. LeDoux,

"Emotion Circuits in the Brain," *Annual Review of Neuroscience* 23 (2000): 155–84; P. Winkielman and K. C. Berridge, "Unconscious Emotion," *Current Directions in Psychological Science* 13, no. 3 (2004): 120–23.

36. Lawrence and Nohria, *Driven,* 145–47.

37. S. H. Schwartz, B. A. Hammer, and M. Wach, "Les Valeurs De Base De La Personne: The Orie, Mesures Et Applications," *Revue Francaises de Sociologie* 47, no. 4 (October/December 2006): 929–68.

38. Lawrence and Nohria, *Driven,* Chap. 11.

39. Expectancy theory of motivation in work settings originated in V. H. Vroom, *Work and Motivation* (New York: Wiley, 1964). The version of expectancy theory presented here was developed by Edward Lawler. Lawler's model provides a clearer presentation of the model's three components. P-to-O expectancy is similar to "instrumentality" in Vroom's original expectancy theory model. The difference is that instrumentality is a correlation whereas P-to-O expectancy is a probability. See J. P. Campbell et al., *Managerial Behavior, Performance, and Effectiveness* (New York: McGraw-Hill, 1970); E. E. Lawler III, *Motivation in Work Organizations* (Monterey, CA: Brooks-Cole, 1973); D. A. Nadler and E. E. Lawler, "Motivation: A Diagnostic Approach," in *Perspectives on Behavior in Organizations,* 2d ed. J. R. Hackman, E. E. Lawler III, and L. W. Porter (New York: McGraw-Hill, 1983), 67–78.

40. M. Zeelenberg et al., "Emotional Reactions to the Outcomes of Decisions: The Role of Counterfactual Thought in the Experience of Regret and Disappointment," *Organizational Behavior and Human Decision Processes* 75, no. 2 (1998): 117–41; B. A. Mellers, "Choice and the Relative Pleasure of Consequences," *Psychological Bulletin* 126, no. 6 (November 2000): 910–24; R. P. Bagozzi, U. M. Dholakia, and S. Basuroy, "How Effortful Decisions Get Enacted: The Motivating Role of Decision Processes, Desires, and Anticipated Emotions," *Journal of Behavioral Decision Making* 16, no. 4 (October 2003): 273–95.

41. Nadler and Lawler, "Motivation: A Diagnostic Approach."

42. Watson Wyatt, *WorkCanada 2004/2005—Pursuing Productive Engagement* (Toronto: Watson Wyatt, January 2005); Hudson, *Rising above the Average: 2007 Compensation & Benefits Report* (New York: June 2007).

43. B. Moses, "Time to Get Serious about Rewarding Employees," *Globe & Mail,* April 28, 2010, B16.

44. T. Matsui and T. Terai, "A Cross-Cultural Study of the Validity of the Expectancy Theory of Motivation," *Journal of Applied Psychology* 60 (1975): 263–65; D. H. B. Welsh, F. Luthans, and S. M. Sommer, "Managing Russion Factory Workers: The Impact of U.S.-Based Behavioral and Participative Techniques," *Academy of Management Journal* 36 (1993): 58–79.

45. This limitation was recently acknowledged by Victor Vroom, who had introduced expectancy theory in his 1964 book. See G. P. Latham, *Work Motivation: History, Theory, Research, and Practice* (Thousand Oaks, CA: Sage, 2007), 47–48.

46. B. F. Skinner, *About Behaviorism* (New York: Alfred A. Knopf, 1974); J. Komaki, T. Coombs, and S. Schepman, "Motivational Implications of Reinforcement Theory," in *Motivation and Leadership at Work,* ed. R. M. Steers, L. W. Porter, and G. A. Bigley (New York: McGraw-Hill, 1996), 34–52; R. G. Miltenberger, *Behavior Modification: Principles and Procedures* (Pacific Grove, CA: Brooks/Cole, 1997). For early writing on behaviorism, see: J. B. Watson, *Behavior: An Introduction to Comparative Psychology* (New York: Henry Holt & Co., 1914).

47. J. A. Bargh and M. J. Ferguson, "Beyond Behaviorism: On the Automaticity of Higher Mental Processes," *Psychological Bulletin* 126, no. 6 (2000): 925–45. Some writers argue that behaviorists long ago accepted the relevance of cognitive processes in behavior modification. See I. Kirsch et al., "The Role of Cognition in Classical and Operant Conditioning," *Journal of Clinical Psychology* 60, no. 4 (April 2004): 369–92.

48. T. K. Connellan, *How to Improve Human Performance* (New York: Harper & Row, 1978), 48–57; F. Luthans and R. Kreitner, *Organizational Behavior Modification and Beyond* (Glenview, IL: Scott, Foresman, 1985), 85–88.

49. B. F. Skinner, *Science and Human Behavior* (New York: The Free Press, 1965); Miltenberger, *Behavior Modification: Principles and Procedures,* Chap. 4–6.

50. T. R. Hinkin and C. A. Schriesheim, "'If You Don't Hear from Me You Know You Are Doing Fine'," *Cornell Hotel & Restaurant Administration Quarterly* 45, no. 4 (November 2004): 362–72.

51. L. K. Trevino, "The Social Effects of Punishment in Organizations: A Justice Perspective," *Academy of Management Review* 17 (1992): 647–76; L. E. Atwater et al., "Recipient and Observer Reactions to Discipline: Are Managers Experiencing Wishful Thinking?" *Journal of Organizational Behavior* 22, no. 3 (May 2001): 249–70.

52. G. P. Latham and V. L. Huber, "Schedules of Reinforcement: Lessons from the Past and Issues for the Future," *Journal of Organizational Behavior Management* 13 (1992): 125–49; B. A. Williams, "Challenges to Timing-Based Theories of Operant Behavior," *Behavioural Processes* 62 (April 2003): 115–23.

53. A. Bandura, *Social Foundations of Thought and Action: A Social Cognitive Theory* (Englewood Cliffs, NJ: Prentice Hall, 1986); A. Bandura, "Social Cognitive Theory of Self-Regulation," *Organizational Behavior and Human Decision Processes* 50, no. 2 (1991): 248–87; A. Bandura, "Social Cognitive Theory: An Agentic Perspective," *Annual Review of Psychology* 52, no. 1 (2001): 1–26.

54. M. E. Schnake, "Vicarious Punishment in a Work Setting," *Journal of Applied Psychology,* 71 (1986): 343–45; Trevino, "The Social Effects of Punishment in Organizations"; J. Malouff et al., "Effects of Vicarious Punishment: A Meta-Analysis," *Journal of General Psychology* 136, no. 3 (2009): 271–86.

55. A. Pescuric and W. C. Byham, "The New Look of Behavior Modeling," *Training & Development* 50 (July 1996): 24–30.

56. A. Bandura, "Self-Reinforcement: Theoretical and Methodological Considerations," *Behaviorism* 4 (1976): 135–55; C. A. Frayne and J. M. Geringer, "Self-Management Training for Improving Job Performance: A Field Experiment Involving Salespeople," *Journal of Applied Psychology* 85, no. 3 (June 2000): 361–72; J. B. Vancouver and D. V. Day, "Industrial and Organisation Research on Self-Regulation: From Constructs to Applications," *Applied Psychology: an International Journal* 54, no. 2 (April 2005): 155–85.

57. J. Greenberg and E. A. Lind, "The Pursuit of Organizational Justice: From Conceptualization to Implication to Application," in *Industrial and Organizational Psychology: Linking Theory with Practice* ed. C. L. Cooper and E. A. Locke (London: Blackwell, 2000), 72–108; R. Cropanzano and M. Schminke, "Using Social Justice to Build Effective Work Groups," in *Groups at Work: Theory and Research,* ed. M. E. Turner (Mahwah, NJ: Lawrence Erlbaum Associates, 2001), 143–71;

D. T. Miller, "Disrespect and the Experience of Injustice," *Annual Review of Psychology* 52 (2001): 527–53.

58. J. S. Adams, "Toward an Understanding of Inequity," *Journal of Abnormal and Social Psychology* 67 (1963): 422–36; R. T. Mowday, "Equity Theory Predictions of Behavior in Organizations," in *Motivation and Work Behavior,* ed. L. W. Porter and R. M. Steers, 5th ed. (New York: McGraw-Hill, 1991), 111–31; R. G. Cropanzano, J., "Progress in Organizational Justice: Tunneling through the Maze," in *International Review of Industrial and Organizational Psychology,* ed. C. L. Cooper and I. T. Robertson (New York: Wiley, 1997), 317–72; L. A. Powell, "Justice Judgments as Complex Psychocultural Constructions: An Equity-Based Heuristic for Mapping Two- and Three-Dimensional Fairness Representations in Perceptual Space," *Journal of Cross-Cultural Psychology* 36, no. 1 (January 2005): 48–73.

59. C. T. Kulik and M. L. Ambrose, "Personal and Situational Determinants of Referent Choice," *Academy of Management Review* 17 (1992): 212–37; G. Blau, "Testing the Effect of Level and Importance of Pay Referents on Pay Level Satisfaction," *Human Relations* 47 (1994): 1251–68.

60. K. S. Sauleya and A. G. Bedeian, "Equity Sensitivity: Construction of a Measure and Examination of Its Psychometric Properties," *Journal of Management* 26 (September 2000): 885–910; G. Blakely, M. Andrews, and R. Moorman, "The Moderating Effects of Equity Sensitivity on the Relationship between Organizational Justice and Organizational Citizenship Behaviors," *Journal of Business and Psychology* 20, no. 2 (2005): 259–73.

61. Y. Cohen-Charash and P. E. Spector, "The Role of Justice in Organizations: A Meta-Analysis," *Organizational Behavior and Human Decision Processes* 86 (November 2001): 278–321.

62. K. Jenkins et al., *The Anxious American Worker* (New Brunswick, NJ: John J. Heldrich Center for Workforce Development, Summer 2008).

63. M. Ezzamel and R. Watson, "Pay Comparability across and within UK Boards: An Empirical Analysis of the Cash Pay Awards to CEOs and Other Board Members," *Journal of Management Studies* 39, no. 2 (March 2002): 207–32; J. Fizel, A. C. Krautman, and L. Hadley, "Equity and Arbitration in Major League Baseball," *Managerial and Decision Economics* 23, no. 7 (October/November 2002): 427–35.

64. Greenberg and Lind, "The Pursuit of Organizational Justice"; K. Roberts and K. S. Markel, "Claiming in the Name of Fairness: Organizational Justice and the Decision to File for Workplace Injury Compensation," *Journal of Occupational Health Psychology* 6 (October 2001): 332–47; J. B. Olson-Buchanan and W. R. Boswell, "The Role of Employee Loyalty and Formality in Voicing Discontent," *Journal of Applied Psychology* 87, no. 6 (2002): 1167–74.

65. Canadian Press, "Pierre Berton, Canadian Cultural Icon, Enjoyed Long and Colourful Career," *Times Colonist* (Victoria, B.C.), November 30, 2004.

66. R. Hagey et al., "Immigrant Nurses' Experience of Racism," *Journal of Nursing Scholarship* 33 (Fourth Quarter 2001): 389–95; Roberts and Markel, "Claiming in the Name of Fairness"; D. A. Jones and D. P. Skarlicki, "The Effects of Overhearing Peers Discuss an Authority's Fairness Reputation on Reactions to Subsequent Treatment," *Journal of Applied Psychology* 90, no. 2 (2005): 363–72.

67. S. Zeller, "Good Calls," *Government Executive,* May 15, 2005; C. Bailor, "Checking the Pulse of the Contact Center," *Customer Relationship Management,* November 2007, 24–29.

68. A. Shin, "What Customers Say and How They Say It," *Washington Post,* October 18, 2006, D01; D. Ververidis and C. Kotropoulos, "Emotional Speech Recognition: Resources, Features, and Methods," *Speech Communication* 48, no. 9 (2006): 1162–81.

69. G. P. Latham, "Goal Setting: A Five-Step Approach to Behavior Change," *Organizational Dynamics* 32, no. 3 (2003): 309–18; E. A. Locke and G. P. Latham, *A Theory of Goal Setting and Task Performance* (Englewood Cliffs, NJ: Prentice Hall, 1990).

70. There are several variations of the SMARTER goal setting model; "achievable" is sometimes "acceptable," "reviewed" is sometimes "recorded," and "exciting" is sometimes "ethical." Based on the earlier SMART model, the SMARTER goal setting model seems to originate in British sports psychology writing around the mid 1990s. For early examples, see: P. Butler, *Performance Profiling* (Leeds, UK: The National Coaching Foundation, 1996), 36; R. C. Thelwell and I. A. Greenlees, "The Effects of a Mental Skills Training Program Package on Gymnasium Triathlon Performance," *The Sports Psychologist* 15, no. 2 (2001): 127–41.

71. S. P. Brown, S. Ganesan, and G. Challagalla, "Self-Efficacy as a Moderator of Information-Seeking Effectiveness," *Journal of Applied Psychology* 86, no. 5 (2001): 1043–51; P. A. Heslin and G. P. Latham, "The Effect of Upward Feedback on Managerial Behaviour," *Applied Psychology: An International Review* 53, no. 1 (2004): 23–37; D. Van-Dijk and A. N. Kluger, "Feedback Sign Effect on Motivation: Is It Moderated by Regulatory Focus?" *Applied Psychology: An International Review* 53, no. 1 (2004): 113–35; J. E. Bono and A. E. Colbert, "Understanding Responses to Multi-Source Feedback: The Role of Core Self-Evaluations," *Personnel Psychology* 58, no. 1 (Spring 2005): 171–203.

72. P. Drucker, *The Effective Executive* (Oxford, UK: Butterworth-Heinemann, 2007), 22. Drucker's emphasis on strengths was also noted in D. K. Whitney and A. Trosten-Bloom, *The Power of Appreciative Inquiry: A Practical Guide to Positive Change,* 2nd ed. (San Francisco: Berrett-Koehler Publishers, 2010), xii.

73. M. Buckingham, *Go Put Your Strengths to Work* (New York: Free Press, 2007); S. L. Orem, J. Binkert, and A. L. Clancy, *Appreciative Coaching: A Positive Process for Change* (San Francisco: Jossey-Bass, 2007); S. Gordon, "Appreciative Inquiry Coaching," *International Coaching Psychology Review* 3, no. 2 (March 2008): 19–31.

74. H. Aguinis, R. K. Gottfredson, and H. Joo, "Delivering Effective Performance Feedback: The Strengths-Based Approach," *Business Horizons* 55, no. 2 (2012): 105–11.

75. A. Terracciano, P. T. Costa, and R. R. McCrae, "Personality Plasticity after Age 30," *Personality and Social Psychology Bulletin* 32, no. 8 (August 2006): 999–1009; Leary, "Motivational and Emotional Aspects of the Self."

76. L. Hollman, "Seeing the Writing on the Wall," *Call Center* (August 2002): 37; S. E. Ante, "Giving the Boss the Big Picture," *BusinessWeek,* 13 February 13, 2006, 48.

77. F. P. Morgeson, T. V. Mumford, and M. A. Campion, "Coming Full Circle: Using Research and Practice to Address 27 Questions about 360–Degree Feedback Programs," *Consulting Psychology Journal* 57, no. 3 (2005): 196–209; J. W. Smither, M. London, and R. R. Reilly, "Does Performance Improve Following Multisource Feedback? A Theoretical

Model, Meta-Analysis, and Review of Empirical Findings," *Personnel Psychology* 58, no. 1 (2005): 33–66; L. E. Atwater, J. F. Brett, and A. C. Charles, "Multisource Feedback: Lessons Learned and Implications for Practice," *Human Resource Management* 46, no. 2 (Summer 2007): 285–307.

78. S. J. Ashford and G. B. Northcraft, "Conveying More (or Less) than We Realize: The Role of Impression Management in Feedback Seeking," *Organizational Behavior and Human Decision Processes* 53 (1992): 310–34; J. R. Williams et al., "Increasing Feedback Seeking in Public Contexts: It Takes Two (or More) to Tango," *Journal of Applied Psychology* 84 (December 1999): 969–76.

79. J. B. Miner, "The Rated Importance, Scientific Validity, and Practical Usefulness of Organizational Behavior Theories: A Quantitative Review," *Academy of Management Learning and Education* 2, no. 3 (2003): 250–68. Also see Pinder, *Work Motivation in Organizational Behavior,* 384.

80. P. M. Wright, "Goal Setting and Monetary Incentives: Motivational Tools That Can Work Too Well," *Compensation and Benefits Review* 26 (May- June 1994): 41–49; E. A. Locke and G. P. Latham, "Building a Practically Useful Theory of Goal Setting and Task Motivation: A 35–Year Odyssey," *American Psychologist* 57, no. 9 (2002): 705–17.

81. Latham, *Work Motivation,* 188.

82. J. R. Edwards, J. A. Scully, and M. D. Brtek, "The Nature and Outcomes of Work: A Replication and Extension of Interdisciplinary Work-Design Research," *Journal of Applied Psychology* 85, no. 6 (2000): 860–68; F. P. Morgeson and M. A. Campion, "Minimizing Tradeoffs When Redesigning Work: Evidence from a Longitudinal Quasi-Experiment," *Personnel Psychology* 55, no. 3 (Autumn 2002): 589–612.

83. Gallup Consulting, *The Gallup Q12–Employee Engagement Poll 2008 Results.*

84. S. Leroy, "Why Is It So Hard to Do My Work? The Challenge of Attention Residue When Switching between Work Tasks," *Organizational Behavior and Human Decision Processes* 109, no. 2 (2009): 168–81.

85. H. Fayol, *General and Industrial Management,* trans. C. Storrs (London: Pitman, 1949); Lawler III, *Motivation in Work Organizations,* Chap. 7; M. A. Campion, "Ability Requirement Implications of Job Design: An Interdisciplinary Perspective," *Personnel Psychology* 42 (1989): 1–24.

86. A. Smith, *An Inquiry into the Nature and Causes of the Wealth of Nations,* 5th ed. (London: Methuen and Co., 1904), 8–9.

87. F. W. Taylor, *The Principles of Scientific Management* (New York: Harper & Row, 1911); R. Kanigel, *The One Best Way: Frederick Winslow Taylor and the Enigma of Efficiency* (New York: Viking, 1997).

88. C. R. Walker and R. H. Guest, *The Man on the Assembly Line* (Cambridge, MA: Harvard University Press, 1952); W. F. Dowling, "Job Redesign on the Assembly Line: Farewell to Blue-Collar Blues?" *Organizational Dynamics* (Autumn 1973): 51–67; E. E. Lawler III, *High-Involvement Management* (San Francisco: Jossey-Bass, 1986).

89. M. Keller, *Rude Awakening* (New York: Harper Perennial, 1989), 128.

90. F. Herzberg, B. Mausner, and B. B. Snyderman, *The Motivation to Work* (New York: Wiley, 1959).

91. S. K. Parker, T. D. Wall, and J. L. Cordery, "Future Work Design Research and Practice: Towards an Elaborated Model of Work Design," *Journal of Occupational and Organizational Psychology* 74 (November 2001): 413–40. For a decisive critique of motivator-hygiene theory, see N. King, "Clarification and Evaluation of the Two Factor Theory of Job Satisfaction," *Psychological Bulletin* 74 (1970): 18–31.

92. J. R. Hackman and G. Oldham, *Work Redesign* (Reading, MA: Addison-Wesley, 1980).

93. C. Hosford, "Training Programs Benefit Rolls-Royce," *B to B,* July 16, 2007, 14/

94. J. E. Champoux, "A Multivariate Test of the Job Characteristics Theory of Work Motivation," *Journal of Organizational Behavior* 12, no. 5 (September 1991): 431–46; R. B. Tiegs, L. E. Tetrick, and Y. Fried, "Growth Need Strength and Context Satisfactions as Moderators of the Relations of the Job Characteristics Model," *Journal of Management* 18, no. 3 (September 1992): 575–93.

95. Data provided in several country-specific news releases from Kelly Services. For a white paper summary of the survey, see: Kelly Services, *Employee Loyalty Rises During Global Economic Recession, Kelly International Workforce Survey Finds* (Troy, MI: Kelly Services, March 8, 2010). Percentage of employees in India choosing higher salary/benefits and employees in China choosing meaningful responsibility are inferred (i.e., they were not stated in available sources but received a lower percentage than the other two identified categories).

96. "Region Positioned among Dcx Leaders in Advanced Manufacturing," *Toledo Business Journal,* August 2004, 1; M. Connelly, "Chrysler Wants to Put Team Assembly in All Plants," *Automotive News,* May 20, 2005, 53.

97. M. A. Campion and C. L. McClelland, "Follow-up and Extension of the Interdisciplinary Costs and Benefits of Enlarged Jobs," *Journal of Applied Psychology* 78 (1993): 339–51; N. G. Dodd and D. C. Ganster, "The Interactive Effects of Variety, Autonomy, and Feedback on Attitudes and Performance," *Journal of Organizational Behavior* 17 (1996): 329–47.

98. J. R. Hackman et al., "A New Strategy for Job Enrichment," *California Management Review* 17, no. 4 (1975): 57–71; R. W. Griffin, *Task Design: An Integrative Approach* (Glenview, IL: Scott Foresman, 1982).

99. E. Frauenheim, "Making the Call for Themselves," *Workforce Management,* August 2010, 16.

100. P. E. Spector and S. M. Jex, "Relations of Job Characteristics from Multiple Data Sources with Employee Affect, Absence, Turnover Intentions, and Health," *Journal of Applied Psychology* 76 (1991): 46–53; P. Osterman, "How Common Is Workplace Transformation and Who Adopts It?" *Industrial and Labor Relations Review* 47 (1994): 173–88; R. Saavedra and S. K. Kwun, "Affective States in Job Characteristics Theory," *Journal of Organizational Behavior* 21 (2000): 131–46.

101. Hackman and Oldham, *Work Redesign,* 137–138.

102. S. Wong, *"Open Communication Gives Better Connection," South China Morning Post (Hong Kong),* January 19, 2008, 4.

CHAPTER 6

1. S. Marchionne, "Fiat's Extreme Makeover," *Harvard Business Review* (December 2008): 45–48; "Marchionne's Weekend Warriors," *Automotive News,* June 22, 2009; D. Welch, D. Kiley, and C. Matlack, "Tough Love at Chrysler," *Businessweek,* August 24, 2009; B. Wernie and L. Ciferri, "Life under Marchionne: New Stars, Hasty Exits," *Automotive News,* October 12, 2009, 1, 42; "Marchionne Faces Tough Challenge to Match Ghosn's Success," *Automotive News,* April 28, 2010;

J. Reed, "High Stakes for Fiat's Sergio Marchionne," *Financial Times* (London), February 19, 2010; D. Kiley, "Imported from France," *Advertising Age,* 21 February 2011, 1; E. Mayne, "Chrysler-Fiat Merger under Consideration, Says CEO Marchionne," *Ward's Dealer Business,* March 2011, 12.

2. F. A. Shull Jr., A. L. Delbecq, and L. L. Cummings, *Organizational Decision Making* (New York: McGraw-Hill, 1970), 31.

3. R. E. Nisbett, *The Geography of Thought: How Asians and Westerners Think Differently—and Why* (New York: Free Press, 2003); R. Hanna, "Kant's Theory of Judgment" (Stanford Encyclopedia of Philosophy, 2004), accessed March 31, 2008, http://plato.stanford.edu/entries/kant-judgment/; D. Baltzly, "Stoicism" (Stanford Encyclopedia of Philosophy, 2008), accessed March 30, 2008, http://plato.stanford.edu/entries/stoicism/.

4. J. G. March and H. A. Simon, *Organizations* (New York: John Wiley & Sons, 1958).

5. This model is adapted from several sources, including H. A. Simon, *The New Science of Management Decision* (New York: Harper & Row, 1960); H. Mintzberg, D. Raisinghani, and A. Théorét, "The Structure of 'Unstructured' Decision Processes," *Administrative Science Quarterly* 21 (1976): 246–75; W. C. Wedley and R. H. G. Field, "A Predecision Support System," *Academy of Management Review* 9 (1984): 696–703.

6. P. F. Drucker, *The Practice of Management* (New York: Harper & Brothers, 1954), 353–57; B. M. Bass, *Organizational Decision Making* (Homewood, IL: Irwin, 1983), Chap. 3.

7. L. R. Beach and T. R. Mitchell, "A Contingency Model for the Selection of Decision Strategies," *Academy of Management Review* 3 (1978): 439–49; I. L. Janis, *Crucial Decisions* (New York: The Free Press, 1989), 35–37; W. Zhongtuo, "Meta-Decision Making: Concepts and Paradigm," *Systematic Practice and Action Research* 13, no. 1 (February 2000): 111–15.

8. N. Schwarz, "Social Judgment and Attitudes: Warmer, More Social, and Less Conscious," *European Journal of Social Psychology* 30 (2000): 149–76; N. M. Ashkanasy and C. E. J. Hartel, "Managing Emotions in Decision-Making," in *Managing Emotions in the Workplace,* ed. N. M. Ashkanasy, W. J. Zerbe, and C. E. J. Hartel (Armonk, NY: M. E. Sharpe, 2002); S. Maitlis and H. Ozcelik, "Toxic Decision Processes: A Study of Emotion and Organizational Decision Making," *Organization Science* 15, no. 4 (July/August 2004): 375–93.

9. A. Howard, "Opinion," *Computing* (July 8, 1999): 18.

10. For a recent discussion on problem finding in organizations, see: M. A. Roberto, *Know What You Don't Know: How Great Leaders Prevent Problems before They Happen* (Upper Saddle River, NJ: Wharton School Publishing, 2009).

11. T. K. Das and B. S. Teng, "Cognitive Biases and Strategic Decision Processes: An Integrative Perspective," *Journal Of Management Studies* 36, no. 6 (November 1999): 757–78; P. Bijttebier, H. Vertommen, and G. V. Steene, "Assessment of Cognitive Coping Styles: A Closer Look at Situation-Response Inventories," *Clinical Psychology Review* 21, no. 1 (2001): 85–104; P. C. Nutt, "Expanding the Search for Alternatives During Strategic Decision-Making," *Academy of Management Executive* 18, no. 4 (November 2004): 13–28.

12. J. Portman, "Harry Potter Was Almost a Yankee," *Vancouver Sun,* July 5, 2007.

13. W. Ocasio, "Toward an Attention-Based View of the Firm," *Strategic Management Journal* 18, no. S1 (1997): 187–206; S. Kaplan, "Framing Contests: Strategy Making under Uncertainty," *Organization Science* 19, no. 5 (September 2008): 729–52; J. S. McMullen, D. A. Shepherd, and H. Patzelt,

"Managerial (in)Attention to Competitive Threats," *Journal of Management Studies* 46, no. 2 (2009): 157–81.

14. P. C. Nutt, *Why Decisions Fail* (San Francisco, CA: Berrett-Koehler, 2002); S. Finkelstein, *Why Smart Executives Fail* (New York: Viking, 2003).

15. A. H. Maslow, *The Psychology of Science: A Reconnaissance* (Chapel Hill, NC: Maurice Bassett Publishing, 2002).

16. E. Witte, "Field Research on Complex Decision-Making Processes—the Phase Theorum," *International Studies of Management and Organization,* no. 56 (1972): 156–82; J. A. Bargh and T. L. Chartrand, "The Unbearable Automaticity of Being," *American Psychologist* 54, no. 7 (July 1999): 462–79.

17. J. Brandtstadter, A. Voss, and K. Rothermund, "Perception of Danger Signals: The Role of Control," *Experimental Psychology* 51, no. 1 (2004): 24–32; M. Hock and H. W. Krohne, "Coping with Threat and Memory for Ambiguous Information: Testing the Repressive Discontinuity Hypothesis," *Emotion* 4, no. 1 (2004): 65–86.

18. R. Rothenberg, "Ram Charan: The Thought Leader Interview," *strategy + business* (Fall 2004).

19. H. A. Simon, *Administrative Behavior,* 2d ed. (New York: The Free Press, 1957); H. A. Simon, "Rational Decision Making in Business Organizations," *American Economic Review* 69, no. 4 (September 1979): 493–513.

20. Simon, *Administrative Behavior,* xxv, 80–84.

21. S. Sacchi and M. Burigo, "Strategies in the Information Search Process: Interaction among Task Structure, Knowledge, and Source," *Journal of General Psychology* 135, no. 3 (2008): 252–70.

22. P. O. Soelberg, "Unprogrammed Decision Making," *Industrial Management Review* 8 (1967): 19–29; J. E. Russo, V. H. Medvec, and M. G. Meloy, "The Distortion of Information during Decisions," *Organizational Behavior & Human Decision Processes* 66 (1996): 102–10; K. H. Ehrhart and J. C. Ziegert, "Why Are Individuals Attracted to Organizations?" *Journal of Management* 31, no. 6 (December 2005): 901–19. This is consistent with the observations by Milton Rokeach, who famously stated, "Life is ipsative, because decisions in everyday life are inherently and phenomenologically ipsative decisions." M. Rokeach, "Inducing Changes and Stability in Belief Systems and Personality Structures," *Journal of Social Issues* 41, no. 1 (1985): 153–71.

23. A. L. Brownstein, "Biased Predecision Processing," *Psychological Bulletin* 129, no. 4 (2003): 545–68.

24. T. Gilovich, D. Griffin, and D. Kahneman, *Heuristics and Biases: The Psychology of Intuitive Judgment* (Cambridge: Cambridge University Press, 2002); D. Kahneman, "Maps of Bounded Rationality: Psychology for Behavioral Economics," *American Economic Review* 93, no. 5 (December 2003): 1449–75; F. L. Smith et al., "Decision-Making Biases and Affective States: Their Potential Impact on Best Practice Innovations," *Canadian Journal of Administrative Sciences/Revue Canadienne des Sciences de l'Administration* 27, no. 4 (2010): 277–91.

25. A. Tversky and D. Kahneman, "Judgment under Uncertainty: Heuristics and Biases," *Science* 185, no. 4157 (September 27, 1974): 1124–31; I. Ritov, "Anchoring in Simulated Competitive Market Negotiation," *Organizational Behavior and Human Decision Processes* 67, no. 1 (1996): 16; D. Ariely, G. Loewenstein, and A. Prelec, "Coherent Arbitrariness: Stable Demand Curves without Stable Preferences," *The Quarterly Journal of Economics* 118 (2003): 73; N. Epley and T. Gilovich, "Are Adjustments Insufficient?" *Personality and Social*

Psychology Bulletin 30, no. 4 (April 2004): 447–60; J. D. Jasper and S. D. Christman, "A Neuropsychological Dimension for Anchoring Effects," *Journal of Behavioral Decision Making* 18 (2005): 343–69; S. D. Bond et al., "Information Distortion in the Evaluation of a Single Option," *Organizational Behavior & Human Decision Processes* 102 (2007): 240–54.

26. A. Tversky and D. Kahneman, "Availability: A Heuristic for Judging Frequency and Probability," *Cognitive Psychology* 5 (1973): 207–32.

27. D. Kahneman and A. Tversky, "Subjective Probability: A Judgment of Representativeness," *Cognitive Psychology* 3, no. 3 (1972): 430; T. Gilovich, *How We Know What Isn't So: The Fallibility of Human Reason in Everyday Life* (New York: Free Press, 1991); B. D. Burns, "Heuristics as Beliefs and as Behaviors: The Adaptiveness of the 'Hot Hand'," *Cognitive Psychology* 48 (2004): 295–331; E. M. Altmann and B. D. Burns, "Streak Biases in Decision Making: Data and a Memory Model," *Cognitive Systems Research* 6, no. 1 (2005): 5.

28. H. A. Simon, "Rational Choice and the Structure of Environments," *Psychological Review* 63 (1956): 129–38.

29. S. S. Iyengar and M. R. Lepper, "When Choice Is Demotivating: Can One Desire Too Much of a Good Thing?" *Journal of Personality and Social Psychology* 79, no. 6 (2000): 995–1006; Iyengar, *The Art of Choosing,* 177–95.

30. S. Botti and S. S. Iyengar, "The Dark Side of Choice: When Choice Impairs Social Welfare," *Journal of Public Policy and Marketing* 25, no. 1 (2006): 24–38; K. D. Vohs et al., "Making Choices Impairs Subsequent Self-Control: A Limited-Resource Account of Decision Making, Self-Regulation, and Active Initiative," *Journal of Personality and Social Psychology* 94, no. 5 (2008): 883–98.

31. J. Beshears et al., "Simplification and Saving", 2006, http://ssrn.com/paper=1086462; J. Choi, D. Laibson, and B. Madrian, *Reducing the Complexity Costs of 401(K) Participation through Quick Enrollment(Tm)* (National Bureau of Economic Research, Inc, January 2006); S. Iyengar, *The Art of Choosing* (New York: Hachette, 2010), 194–200.

32. P. C. Nutt, "Search During Decision Making," *European Journal of Operational Research* 160 (2005): 851–76.

33. P. Winkielman et al., "Affective Influence on Judgments and Decisions: Moving towards Core Mechanisms," *Review of General Psychology* 11, no. 2 (2007): 179–92.

34. A. R. Damasio, *Descartes' Error: Emotion, Reason, and the Human Brain* (New York: Putnam Sons, 1994); P. Winkielman and K. C. Berridge, "Unconscious Emotion," *Current Directions in Psychological Science* 13, no. 3 (2004): 120–23; A. Bechara and A. R. Damasio, "The Somatic Marker Hypothesis: A Neural Theory of Economic Decision," *Games and Economic Behavior* 52, no. 2 (2005): 336–72.

35. J. P. Forgas and J. M. George, "Affective Influences on Judgments and Behavior in Organizations: An Information Processing Perspective," *Organizational Behavior and Human Decision Processes* 86 (September 2001): 3–34; G. Loewenstein and J. S. Lerner, "The Role of Affect in Decision Making," in *Handbook of Affective Sciences,* ed. R. J. Davidson, K. R. Scherer, and H. H. Goldsmith (New York: Oxford University Press, 2003), 619–42; M. T. Pham, "Emotion and Rationality: A Critical Review and Interpretation of Empirical Evidence," *Review of General Psychology* 11, no. 2 (2007): 155–78; J. P. Forgas, L. Goldenberg, and C. Unkelbach, "Can Bad Weather Improve Your Memory? An Unobtrusive Field Study of Natural Mood Effects on Real-Life Memory," *Journal of Experimental Social Psychology* 45 (2009): 254–57; H. J. M. Kooij-de Bode, D. Van Knippenberg, and W. P. Van Ginkel, "Good Effects of Bad Feelings: Negative Affectivity and Group Decision-Making," *British Journal of Management* 21, no. 2 (2010): 375–92.

36. D. Miller, *The Icarus Paradox* (New York: HarperBusiness, 1990); D. Miller, "What Happens after Success: The Perils of Excellence," *Journal of Management Studies* 31, no. 3 (1994): 325–68; A. C. Amason and A. C. Mooney, "The Icarus Paradox Revisited: How Strong Performance Sows the Seeds of Dysfunction in Future Strategic Decision-Making," *Strategic Organization* 6, no. 4 (November 2008): 407–34.

37. M. T. Pham, "The Logic of Feeling," *Journal of Consumer Psychology* 14 (September 2004): 360–69; N. Schwarz, "Metacognitive Experiences in Consumer Judgment and Decision Making," *Journal of Consumer Psychology* 14 (September 2004): 332–49.

38. L. Sjöberg, "Intuitive vs. Analytical Decision Making: Which Is Preferred?" *Scandinavian Journal of Management* 19 (2003): 17–29.

39. W. H. Agor, "The Logic of Intuition," *Organizational Dynamics* (Winter 1986): 5–18; H. A. Simon, "Making Management Decisions: The Role of Intuition and Emotion," *Academy of Management Executive* (February 1987): 57–64; O. Behling and N. L. Eckel, "Making Sense out of Intuition," *Academy of Management Executive* 5 (February 1991): 46–54. This process is also known as naturalistic decision making. For a discussion of research on naturalistic decision making, see the special issue in *Organization Studies:* R. Lipshitz, G. Klein, and J. S. Carroll, "Introduction to the Special Issue: Naturalistic Decision Making and Organizational Decision Making: Exploring the Intersections," *Organization Studies* 27, no. 7 (2006): 917–23.

40. D. Woods, "Managers Make Decisions About People Based on Gut Instinct Rather than Objective Data," *HR Magazine,* February 16, 2010.

41. M. D. Lieberman, "Intuition: A Social Cognitive Neuroscience Approach," *Psychological Bulletin* 126 (2000): 109–37; G. Klein, *Intuition at Work* (New York: Currency/Doubleday, 2003); E. Dane and M. G. Pratt, "Exploring Intuition and Its Role in Managerial Decision Making," *Academy of Management Review* 32, no. 1 (2007): 33–54.

42. Klein, *Intuition at Work*, 12–13, 16–17.

43. Y. Ganzach, A. H. Kluger, and N. Klayman, "Making Decisions from an Interview: Expert Measurement and Mechanical Combination," *Personnel Psychology* 53 (Spring 2000): 1–20; A. M. Hayashi, "When to Trust Your Gut," *Harvard Business Review* 79 (February 2001): 59–65. Evidence of high failure rates from quick decisions is reported in Nutt, *Why Decisions Fail;* Nutt, "Search during Decision Making"; P. C. Nutt, "Investigating the Success of Decision Making Processes," *Journal of Management Studies* 45, no. 2 (March 2008): 425–55.

44. P. Goodwin and G. Wright, "Enhancing Strategy Evaluation in Scenario Planning: A Role for Decision Analysis," *Journal of Management Studies* 38 (January 2001): 1–16; R. Bradfield et al., "The Origins and Evolution of Scenario Techniques in Long Range Business Planning," *Futures* 37, no. 8 (2005): 795–812; G. Wright, G. Cairns, and P. Goodwin, "Teaching Scenario Planning: Lessons from Practice in Academe and Business," *European Journal of Operational Research* 194, no. 1 (April 2009): 323–35.

45. J. Pfeffer and R. I. Sutton, "Knowing 'What' to Do Is Not Enough: Turning Knowledge into Action," *California Management Review* 42, no. 1 (Fall 1999): 83–108; R. Charan, C. Burke, and L. Bossidy, *Execution: The Discipline of Getting Things Done* (New York: Crown Business, 2002).

46. R. S. Nickerson, "Confirmation Bias: A Ubiquitous Phenomenon in Many Guises," *Review of General Psychology* 2, no. 2 (1998): 175–220; O. Svenson, I. Salo, and T. Lindholm, "Post-Decision Consolidation and Distortion of Facts," *Judgment and Decision Making* 4, no. 5 (2009): 397–407.

47. G. Whyte, "Escalating Commitment to a Course of Action: A Reinterpretation," *Academy of Management Review* 11 (1986): 311–21; J. Brockner, "The Escalation of Commitment to a Failing Course of Action: Toward Theoretical Progress," *Academy of Management Review* 17, no. 1 (January 1992): 39–61.

48. F. D. Schoorman and P. J. Holahan, "Psychological Antecedents of Escalation Behavior: Effects of Choice, Responsibility, and Decision Consequences," *Journal of Applied Psychology* 81 (1996): 786–93; N. Sivanathan et al., "The Promise and Peril of Self-Affirmation in De-Escalation of Commitment," *Organizational Behavior and Human Decision Processes* 107, no. 1 (2008): 1–14.

49. N. J. Roese and J. M. Olson, "Better, Stronger, Faster: Self-Serving Judgment, Affect Regulation, and the Optimal Vigilance Hypothesis," *Perspectives on Psychological Science* 2, no. 2 (2007): 124–41; C. L. Guenther and M. D. Alicke, "Deconstructing the Better-than-Average Effect," *Journal of Personality and Social Psychology* 99, no. 5 (2010): 755–70; S. Loughnan et al., "Universal Biases in Self-Perception: Better and More Human Than Average," *British Journal of Social Psychology* 49 (2010): 627–36.

50. P. Hall, *Great Planning Disasters* (New York: Penguin Books, 1980), Chap. 5; H. Drummond, *Escalation in Decision-Making: The Tragedy of Taurus* (Oxford: Oxford University Press, 1996); R. Montealagre and M. Keil, "De-Escalating Information Technology Projects: Lessons from the Denver International Airport," *MIS Quarterly* 24, no. 3 (September 2000): 417–47; I. Swanson, "Holyrood Firms Face Grilling over Costs," *Evening News* (Edinburgh), June 6, 2003, 2; Lord Fraser of Carmyllie QC, *The Holyrood Inquiry* (Edinborough: Scottish Parliamentary Corporate Body, 2004); P. Murray, *The Saga of Sydney Opera House* (London: Taylor & Francis, 2004); M. Sheehan, "Throwing Good Money after Bad," *Sunday Independent* (Dublin), October 9, 2005; D. Ferry, "Computer System Was Budgeted at Eur9m..It's Cost Eur170m..Now Health Chiefs Want a New One," *The Mirror* (London), July 7, 2007, 16.

51. M. Keil, G. Depledge, and A. Rai, "Escalation: The Role of Problem Recognition and Cognitive Bias," *Decision Sciences* 38, no. 3 (August 2007): 391–421.

52. G. Whyte, "Escalating Commitment in Individual and Group Decision Making: A Prospect Theory Approach," *Organizational Behavior and Human Decision Processes* 54 (1993): 430–55; D. Kahneman and J. Renshon, "Hawkish Biases," in *American Foreign Policy and the Politics of Fear: Threat Inflation since 9/11*, ed. T. Thrall and J. Cramer (New York: Routledge, 2009), 79–96.

53. J. D. Bragger et al., "When Success Breeds Failure: History, Hysteresis, and Delayed Exit Decisions," *Journal of Applied Psychology* 88, no. 1 (2003): 6–14. A second logical reason for escalation, called the Martingale strategy, is described in J. A. Aloysius, "Rational Escalation of Costs by Playing a Sequence of Unfavorable Gambles: The Martingale," *Journal of Economic Behavior & Organization* 51 (2003): 111–29.

54. I. Simonson and B. M. Staw, "De-Escalation Strategies: A Comparison of Techniques for Reducing Commitment to Losing Courses of Action," *Journal of Applied Psychology* 77 (1992): 419–26; W. Boulding, R. Morgan, and R. Staelin, "Pulling the Plug to Stop the New Product Drain," *Journal of Marketing Research,* no. 34 (1997): 164–76; B. M. Staw, K. W. Koput, and S. G. Barsade, "Escalation at the Credit Window: A Longitudinal Study of Bank Executives' Recognition and Write-Off of Problem Loans," *Journal of Applied Psychology,* no. 82 (1997): 130–42; M. Keil and D. Robey, "Turning around Troubled Software Projects: An Exploratory Study of the Deescalation of Commitment to Failing Courses of Action," *Journal of Management Information Systems* 15 (Spring 1999): 63–87; B. C. Gunia, N. Sivanathan, and A. D. Galinsky, "Vicarious Entrapment: Your Sunk Costs, My Escalation of Commitment," *Journal of Experimental Social Psychology* 45, no. 6 (2009): 1238–44.

55. D. Ghosh, "De-Escalation Strategies: Some Experimental Evidence," *Behavioral Research in Accounting,* no. 9 (1997): 88–112.

56. J. Zhou and C. E. Shalley, "Research on Employee Creativity: A Critical Review and Directions for Future Research," *Research in Personnel and Human Resources Management* 22 (2003): 165–217; M. A. Runco, "Creativity," *Annual Review of Psychology* 55 (2004): 657–87.

57. V. Khanna, "The Voice of Google," *Business Times Singapore,* January 12, 2008.

58. G. Wallas, *The Art of Thought* (London: Jonathan Cape, 1926). For recent applications of Wallas's classic model, see T. Kristensen, "The Physical Context of Creativity," *Creativity and Innovation Management* 13, no. 2 (June 2004): 89–96; U.-E. Haner, "Spaces for Creativity and Innovation in Two Established Organizations," *Creativity and Innovation Management* 14, no. 3 (2005): 288–98.

59. R. S. Nickerson, "Enhancing Creativity," in *Handbook of Creativity* ed. R. J. Sternberg (New York: Cambridge University Press, 1999), 392–430.

60. E. Oakes, *Notable Scientists: A to Z of STS Scientists* (New York: Facts on File, 2002), 207–9.

61. For a thorough discussion of illumination or insight, see R. J. Sternberg and J. E. Davidson, *The Nature of Insight* (Cambridge, MA: MIT Press, 1995).

62. R. J. Sternberg and L. A. O' Hara, "Creativity and Intelligence," in *Handbook of Creativity* ed. R. J. Sternberg (New York: Cambridge University Press, 1999), 251–72; S. Taggar, "Individual Creativity and Group Ability to Utilize Individual Creative Resources: A Multilevel Model," *Academy of Management Journal* 45 (April 2002): 315–30.

63. G. J. Feist, "The Influence of Personality on Artistic and Scientific Creativity," in *Handbook of Creativity,* ed. R. J. Sternberg (New York: Cambridge University Press, 1999), 273–96; R. I. Sutton, *Weird Ideas That Work* (New York: Free Press, 2002), 8–9, Chap. 10; T. Åsterbro, S. A. Jeffrey, and G. K. Adomdza, "Inventor Perseverance after Being Told to Quit: The Role of Cognitive Biases," *Journal of Behavioral Decision Making* 20 (2007): 253–72.

64. R. W. Weisberg, "Creativity and Knowledge: A Challenge to Theories," in *Handbook of Creativity,* ed. R. J. Sternberg (New York: Cambridge University Press, 1999), 226–50.

65. J. Ross, "Interactive Design," *North Shore Outlook* (North Vancouver), December 1, 2010; L. Sin, "Ideas, Passion Drive Inspired Designer," *Vancouver Province*, October 19, 2010.

66. Sutton, *Weird Ideas That Work,* 121, 153–54; E. Dane, "Reconsidering the Trade-Off between Expertise and Flexibility: A Cognitive Entrenchment Perspective," *Academy of Management Review* 35, no. 4 (2010): 579–603.

67. T. Koppell, *Powering the Future* (New York: Wiley, 1999), 15.

68. R. J. Sternberg and T. I. Lubart, *Defying the Crowd: Cultivating Creativity in a Culture of Conformity* (New York: Free Press, 1995); Feist, "The Influence of Personality on Artistic and Scientific Creativity"; S. J. Dollinger, K. K. Urban, and T. A. James, "Creativity and Openness to Experience: Validation of Two Creative Product Measures," *Creativity Research Journal* 16, no. 1 (2004): 35–47; C. E. Shalley, J. Zhou, and G. R. Oldham, "The Effects of Personal and Contextual Characteristics on Creativity: Where Should We Go from Here?" *Journal of Management* 30, no. 6 (2004): 933–58; T. S. Schweizer, "The Psychology of Novelty-Seeking, Creativity and Innovation: Neurocognitive Aspects within a Work-Psychological Perspective," *Creativity and Innovation Management* 15, no. 2 (2006): 164–72.

69. T. M. Amabile et al., "Leader Behaviors and the Work Environment for Creativity: Perceived Leader Support," *The Leadership Quarterly* 15, no. 1 (2004): 5–32; Shalley, Zhou, and Oldham, "The Effects of Personal and Contextual Characteristics on Creativity"; S. T. Hunter, K. E. Bedell, and M. D. Mumford, "Climate for Creativity: A Quantitative Review," *Creativity Research Journal* 19, no. 1 (2007): 69–90; T. C. DiLiello and J. D. Houghton, "Creative Potential and Practised Creativity: Identifying Untapped Creativity in Organizations," *Creativity and Innovation Management* 17, no. 1 (2008): 37–46.

70. R. Westwood and D. R. Low, "The Multicultural Muse: Culture, Creativity and Innovation," *International Journal of Cross Cultural Management* 3, no. 2 (2003): 235–59.

71. "Samsung CEO Yun Picks Google as New Role Model," *Korea Times*, October 1, 2007.

72. T. M. Amabile, "Motivating Creativity in Organizations: On Doing What You Love and Loving What You Do," *California Management Review* 40 (Fall 1997): 39–58; A. Cummings and G. R. Oldham, "Enhancing Creativity: Managing Work Contexts for the High Potential Employee," *California Management Review,* no. 40 (Fall 1997): 22–38; F. Coelho and M. Augusto, "Job Characteristics and the Creativity of Frontline Service Employees," *Journal of Service Research* 13, no. 4 (November 2010): 426–38.

73. T. M. Amabile, "Changes in the Work Environment for Creativity during Downsizing," *Academy of Management Journal* 42 (December 1999): 630–40.

74. J. Moultrie et al., "Innovation Spaces: Towards a Framework for Understanding the Role of the Physical Environment in Innovation," *Creativity & Innovation Management* 16, no. 1 (2007): 53–65.

75. J. M. Howell and K. Boies, "Champions of Technological Innovation: The Influence of Contextual Knowledge, Role Orientation, Idea Generation, and Idea Promotion on Champion Emergence," *The Leadership Quarterly* 15, no. 1 (2004): 123–43; Shalley, Zhou, and Oldham, "The Effects of Personal and Contextual Characteristics on Creativity"; S. Powell, "The Management and Consumption of Organisational Creativity," *Journal of Consumer Marketing* 25, no. 3 (2008): 158–66.

76. Innovation Tools, *2009 Creativity Survey,* (Milwaukee: InnovationTools.com, July 2009); *Working beyond Borders* (Somers, NY: IBM Institute for Business Value, September 2010); "Though 57% Say Innovation Is Key in 2011, Few Have Applied It to Drive Personal Growth." news release for FPC, May 25, 2011; *2010 Federal Employee Viewpoint Survey Results* (Washington, DC: 2011).

77. A. Hiam, "Obstacles to Creativity—and How You Can Remove Them," *Futurist* 32 (October 1998): 30–34.

78. M. A. West, *Developing Creativity in Organizations* (Leicester, UK: BPS Books, 1997), 33–35.

79. S. Hemsley, "Seeking the Source of Innovation," *Media Week,* August 16, 2005, 22.

80. A. Hargadon and R. I. Sutton, "Building an Innovation Factory," *Harvard Business Review* 78 (May/June 2000): 157–66; T. Kelley, *The Art of Innovation* (New York: Currency Doubleday, 2001), 158–62; P. F. Skilton and K. J. Dooley, "The Effects of Repeat Collaboration on Creative Abrasion," *Academy of Management Review* 35, no. 1 (2010): 118–34.

81. M. Burton, "Open Plan, Open Mind," *Director* (March 2005): 68–72; A. Benady, "Mothers of Invention," *The Independent* (London), November 27, 2006; B. Murray, "Agency Profile: Mother London," *Ihaveanidea,* January 28, 2007, www. ihaveanidea.org.

82. "John Collee-Biography," IMDb (Internet Movie Database), 2009, accessed April 27, 2009, http://www.imdb.com/name/nm0171722/bio.

83. N. Desai, "Management by Trust in a Democratic Enterprise: A Law Firm Shapes Organizational Behavior to Create Competitive Advantage," *Global Business and Organizational Excellence* 28, no. 6 (2009): 7–21.

84. M. Fenton-O'Creevy, "Employee Involvement and the Middle Manager: Saboteur or Scapegoat?" *Human Resource Management Journal,* no. 11 (2001): 24–40. Also see V. H. Vroom and A. G. Jago, *The New Leadership: Managing Participation in Organizations* (Englewood Cliffs, NJ: Prentice Hill, 1988).

85. Vroom and Jago, *The New Leadership.*

86. Some of the early OB writing on employee involvement includes C. Argyris, *Personality and Organization* (New York: Harper & Row, 1957); D. McGregor, *The Human Side of Enterprise* (New York: McGraw-Hill, 1960); R. Likert, *New Patterns of Management* (New York: McGraw-Hill, 1961).

87. A. G. Robinson and D. M. Schroeder, *Ideas Are Free* (San Francisco: Berrett-Koehler, 2004).

88. J. C. Barbieri and A. C. T. Álvares, "Innovation in Mature Industries: The Case of Brasilata S. A Metallic Packaging," paper presented at International conference on technology policy and innovation, Curitiba, Brazil, August 31, 2000; C. Heath and D. Heath, *Switch: How to Change Things When Change Is Hard* (New York: Broadway Books, 2010); "Simplification Project" (São Paulo, Brazil: Brasilata, 2011), accessed June 10, 2011, http://brasilata.jp/en/projeto_cronologia.php; "Brasilata Inventors Turned in 205,536 Innovative Suggestions in 2010" (São Paulo, Brazil: Brasilata, 2011), accessed June 10, 2011, http://brasilata.jp/en/noticias_detalhada.php?cd_noticia=264.

89. R. J. Ely and D. A. Thomas, "Cultural Diversity at Work: The Effects of Diversity Perspectives on Work Group Processes and Outcomes," *Administrative Science Quarterly* 46 (June 2001): 229–73; E. Mannix and M. A. Neale, "What Differences Make a Difference?: The Promise and Reality of Diverse Teams in Organizations," *Psychological Science in the Public Interest* 6, no. 2 (2005): 31–55.

90. D. Berend and J. Paroush, "When Is Condorcet's Jury Theorem Valid?" *Social Choice and Welfare* 15, no. 4 (1998): 481–88.

91. K. T. Dirks, L. L. Cummings, and J. L. Pierce, "Psychological Ownership in Organizations: Conditions under Which Individuals Promote and Resist Change," *Research in Organizational Change and Development,* no. 9 (1996): 1–23; J. P. Walsh and S.-F. Tseng, "The Effects of Job Characteristics on Active Effort at Work," *Work & Occupations,* no. 25 (February 1998):

74–96; B. Scott-Ladd and V. Marshall, "Participation in Decision Making: A Matter of Context?" *Leadership & Organization Development Journal* 25, no. 8 (2004): 646–62.

92. Vroom and Jago, *The New Leadership.*

CHAPTER 7

1. "Trends: Are Many Meetings a Waste of Time? Study Says So," MeetingsNet news release, November 1, 1998; "Teamwork and Collaboration Major Workplace Trends," *Ottawa Business Journal,* April 18, 2006; "Go Teams! Firms Can't Do without Them," (American Management Association, 2008), accessed april 21, 2010, http://amalearning.com.

2. S. Wuchty, B. F. Jones, and B. Uzzi, "The Increasing Dominance of Teams in Production of Knowledge," *Science* 316 (May 18, 2007): 1036–39.

3. M. E. Shaw, *Group Dynamics,* 3d ed. (New York: McGraw-Hill, 1981), 8; S. A. Mohrman, S. G. Cohen, and A. M. Mohrman Jr., *Designing Team-Based Organizations: New Forms for Knowledge Work* (San Francisco: Jossey-Bass, *1995*), 39–40; E. Sundstrom, "The Challenges of Supporting Work Team Effectiveness," in *Supporting Work Team Effectiveness,* ed. E. Sundstrom and Associates (San Francisco, CA: Jossey-Bass, 1999), 6–9.

4. R. A. Guzzo and M. W. Dickson, "Teams in Organizations: Recent Research on Performance and Effectiveness," *Annual Review of Psychology* 47 (1996): 307–38; D. A. Nadler, "From Ritual to Real Work: The Board as a Team," *Directors and Boards* 22 (Summer 1998): 28–31; L. R. Offerman and R. K. Spiros, "The Science and Practice of Team Development: Improving the Link," *Academy of Management Journal* 44 (April 2001): 376–92.

5. B. D. Pierce and R. White, "The Evolution of Social Structure: Why Biology Matters," *Academy of Management Review* 24 (October 1999): 843–53; P. R. Lawrence and N. Nohria, *Driven: How Human Nature Shapes Our Choices* (San Francisco: Jossey-Bass, 2002); J. R. Spoor and J. R. Kelly, "The Evolutionary Significance of Affect in Groups: Communication and Group Bonding," *Group Processes & Intergroup Relations* 7, no. 4 (2004): 398–412. For a critique of this view, see: G. Sewell, "What Goes around, Comes around," *Journal of Applied Behavioural Science* 37, no. 1 (March 2001): 70–91.

6. M. A. Hogg et al., "The Social Identity Perspective: Intergroup Relations, Self-Conception, and Small Groups," *Small Group Research* 35, no. 3 (June 2004): 246–76; N. Michinov, E. Michinov, and M. C. Toczek-Capelle, "Social Identity, Group Processes, and Performance in Synchronous Computer-Mediated Communication," *Group Dynamics: Theory, Research, and Practice* 8, no. 1 (2004): 27–39; M. Van Vugt and C. M. Hart, "Social Identity as Social Glue: The Origins of Group Loyalty," *Journal of Personality and Social Psychology* 86, no. 4 (2004): 585–98.

7. S. Schacter, *The Psychology of Affiliation* (Stanford, CA: Stanford University Press, 1959), 12–19; R. Eisler and D. S. Levine, "Nurture, Nature, and Caring: We Are Not Prisoners of Our Genes," *Brain and Mind* 3 (2002): 9–52; A. C. DeVries, E. R. Glasper, and C. E. Detillion, "Social Modulation of Stress Responses," *Physiology & Behavior* 79, no. 3 (August 2003): 399–407; S. Cohen, "The Pittsburgh Common Cold Studies: Psychosocial Predictors of Susceptibility to Respiratory Infectious Illness," *International Journal of Behavioral Medicine* 12, no. 3 (2005): 123–31.

8. Cohen, "The Pittsburgh Common Cold Studies: Psychosocial Predictors of Susceptibility to Respiratory Infectious Illness";

M. T. Hansen, M. L. Mors, and B. Løvås, "Knowledge Sharing in Organizations: Multiple Networks, Multiple Phases," *Academy of Management Journal* 48, no. 5 (2005): 776–93; R. Cross et al., "Using Social Network Analysis to Improve Communities of Practice," *California Management Review* 49, no. 1 (2006): 32–60; P. Balkundi et al., "Demographic Antecedents and Performance Consequences of Structural Holes in Work Teams," *Journal of Organizational Behavior* 28, no. 2 (2007): 241–60; W. Verbeke and S. Wuyts, "Moving in Social Circles: Social Circle Membership and Performance Implications," *Journal of Organizational Behavior* 28, no. 4 (2007): 357–79.

9. L. Buchanan, "2011 Top Small Company Workplaces: Core Values," *Inc.,* June 2011, 60–74.

10. M. Moldaschl and W. Weber, "The 'Three Waves' of Industrial Group Work: Historical Reflections on Current Research on Group Work," *Human Relations* 51 (March 1998): 347–88. Several popular books in the 1980s encouraged teamwork, based on the Japanese economic miracle. These books include W. Ouchi, *Theory Z: How American Management Can Meet the Japanese Challenge* (Reading, MA: Addison-Wesley, 1981); R. T. Pascale and A. G. Athos, *Art of Japanese Management* (New York: Simon and Schuster, 1982).

11. "Safe Hands a Boost for Blue Care," *Northern Miner* (Charters Towers, Queensland), July 11, 2008, 5; "Powerhouse Team Switched on by Pride," *The Australian,* August 23, 2008, 4; C. Walker, "Call Answered with Vigour," *Fraser Coast Chronicle* (Queensland), November 20, 2008, 7.

12. C. R. Emery and L. D. Fredenhall, "The Effect of Teams on Firm Profitability and Customer Satisfaction," *Journal of Service Research* 4 (February 2002): 217–29; G. S. Van der Vegt and O. Janssen, "Joint Impact of Interdependence and Group Diversity on Innovation," *Journal of Management* 29 (2003): 729–51.

13. R. E. Baumeister and M. R. Leary, "The Need to Belong: Desire for Interpersonal Attachments as a Fundamental Human Motivation," *Psychological Bulletin* 117 (1995): 497–529; S. Chen, H. C. Boucher, and M. P. Tapias, "The Relational Self Revealed: Integrative Conceptualization and Implications for Interpersonal Life," *Psychological Bulletin* 132, no. 2 (2006): 151–79; J. M. Feinberg and J. R. Aiello, "Social Facilitation: A Test of Competing Theories," *Journal of Applied Social Psychology* 36, no. 5 (2006): 1087–1109; A. M. Grant, "Relational Job Design and the Motivation to Make a Prosocial Difiference," *Academy of Management Review* 32, no. 2 (2007): 393–417; N. L. Kerr et al., "Psychological Mechanisms Underlying the Kohler Motivation Gain," *Personality & Social Psychology Bulletin* 33, no. 6 (2007): 828–41.

14. This information is from the Web sites of these companies. Credit Suisse statements are employee testimonials.

15. E. A. Locke et al, "The Importance of the Individual in an Age of Groupism," in *Groups at Work: Theory and Research,* ed. M. E. Turner (Mahwah, N J: Lawrence Erbaum Associates, 2001), 501–28; N. J. Allen and T. D. Hecht, "The 'Romance of Teams': Toward an Understanding of Its Psychological Underpinnings and Implications," *Journal of Occupational and Organizational Psychology* 77 (2004): 439–61.

16. I. D. Steiner, *Group Process and Productivity* (New York: Academic Press, 1972); N. L. Kerr and S. R. Tindale, "Group Performance and Decision Making," *Annual Review of Psychology* 55 (2004): 623–55.

17. D. Dunphy and B. Bryant, "Teams: Panaceas or Prescriptions for Improved Performance?," *Human Relations* 49 (1996): 677–99. For a discussion of Brooks's Law, see F. P. Brooks, ed., *The Mythical Man-Month: Essays on Software Engineering,* Second ed. (Reading, MA: Addison-Wesley, 1995).

18. S. J. Karau and K. D. Williams, "Social Loafing: A Meta-Analytic Review and Theoretical Integration," *Journal of Personality and Social Psychology* 65 (1993): 681–706; R. C. Liden et al., "Social Loafing: A Field Investigation," *Journal of Management* 30 (2004): 285–304; L. L. Chidambaram, "Is out of Sight, out of Mind? An Empirical Study of Social Loafing in Technology-Supported Groups," *Information Systems Research* 16, no. 2 (2005): 149–68; U.-C. Klehe and N. Anderson, "The Moderating Influence of Personality and Culture on Social Loafing in Typical Versus Maximum Performance Situations," *International Journal of Selection and Assessment* 15, no. 2 (2007): 250–62.

19. J. R. Engen, "Tough as Nails," *Bank Director,* July 2009, 24.

20. M. Erez and A. Somech, "Is Group Productivity Loss the Rule or the Exception? Effects of Culture and Group-Based Motivation," *Academy of Management Journal* 39 (1996): 1513–37; Kerr and Tindale, "Group Performance and Decision Making"; A. Jassawalla, H. Sashittal, and A. Malshe, "Students' Perceptions of Social Loafing: Its Antecedents and Consequences in Undergraduate Business Classroom Teams," *Academy of Management Learning and Education* 8, no. 1 (March 2009): 42–54.

21. G. P. Shea and R. A. Guzzo, "Group Effectiveness: What Really Matters?," *Sloan Management Review* 27 (1987): 33–46; J. R. Hackman et al., "Team Effectiveness in Theory and in Practice," in *Industrial and Organizational Psychology: Linking Theory with Practice,* ed. C. L. Cooper and E. A. Locke (Oxford, UK: Blackwell, 2000), 109–29.

22. M. A. West, C. S. Borrill, and K. L. Unsworth, "Team Effectiveness in Organizations," *International Review of Industrial and Organizational Psychology* 13 (1998): 1–48; R. Forrester and A. B. Drexler, "A Model for Team-Based Organization Performance," *Academy of Management Executive* 13 (August 1999): 36–49; J. E. McGrath, H. Arrow, and J. L. Berdahl, "The Study of Groups: Past, Present, and Future," *Personality & Social Psychology Review* 4, no. 1 (2000): 95–105; M. A. Marks, J. E. Mathieu, and S. J. Zaccaro, "A Temporally Based Framework and Taxonomy of Team Processes," *Academy of Management Review* 26, no. 3 (July 2001): 356–76.

23. J. S. DeMatteo, L. T. Eby, and E. Sundstrom, "Team-Based Rewards: Current Empirical Evidence and Directions for Future Research," *Research in Organizational Behavior* 20 (1998): 141–83; E. E. Lawler III, *Rewarding Excellence: Pay Strategies for the New Economy* (San Francisco: Jossey-Bass, 2000), 207–14; G. Hertel, S. Geister, and U. Konradt, "Managing Virtual Teams: A Review of Current Empirical Research," *Human Resource Management Review* 15 (2005): 69–95.

24. These and other environmental conditions for effective teams are discussed in R. Wageman, "Case Study: Critical Success Factors for Creating Superb Self-Managing Teams at Xerox," *Compensation and Benefits Review* 29 (September/October 1997): 31–41; Sundstrom, "The Challenges of Supporting Work Team Effectiveness"; J. N. Choi, "External Activities and Team Effectiveness: Review and Theoretical Development," *Small Group Research* 33 (April 2002): 181–208; T. L. Doolen, M. E. Hacker, and E. M. Van Aken, "The Impact of Organizational Context on Work Team Effectiveness: A Study of Production Team," *IEEE Transactions on Engineering Management* 50, no. 3 (August 2003): 285–96; S. D. Dionne et al., "Transformational Leadership and Team Performance," *Journal Of Organizational Change Management* 17, no. 2 (2004): 177–93; G. L. Stewart, "A Meta-Analytic Review of Relationships between Team Design Features and Team Performance," *Journal of Management* 32, no. 1 (February 2006): 29–54.

25. M. P. Grondahl, "Le Plan Re Ussite Du Patron De Psa," *Paris Match*, September 27, 2010; M. Assayas, "Les Médias Sont Ennuyés," *Enjeux Les Echos,* February 1, 2011, 46; PSA Peugeot Citroën, *2010 Sustainable Development and Annual Report*, (Paris: 2011).

26. M. A. Campion, E. M. Papper, and G. J. Medsker, "Relations between Work Team Characteristics and Effectiveness: A Replication and Extension," *Personnel Psychology* 49 (1996): 429–52; D. C. Man and S. S. K. Lam, "The Effects of Job Complexity and Autonomy on Cohesiveness in Collectivistic and Individualistic Work Groups: A Cross-Cultural Analysis," *Journal of Organizational Behavior* 24 (2003): 979–1001.

27. G. S. Van der Vegt, J. M. Emans, and E. Van de Vliert, "Patterns of Interdependence in Work Teams: A Two-Level Investigation of the Relations with Job and Team Satisfaction," *Personnel Psychology* 54 (Spring 2001): 51–69; R. Wageman, "The Meaning of Interdependence," in *Groups at Work: Theory and Research* ed. M. E. Turner (Mahwah, N J: Lawrence Erlbaum Associates, 2001), 197–217; S. M. Gully et al., "A Meta-Analysis of Team-Efficacy, Potency, and Performance: Interdependence and Level of Analysis as Moderators of Observed Relationships," *Journal of Applied Psychology* 87, no. 5 (Oct 2002): 819–32; M. R. Barrick et al., "The Moderating Role of Top Management Team Interdependence: Implications for Real Teams and Working Groups," *Academy of Management Journal* 50, no. 3 (2007): 544–57.

28. J. O'Toole, "The Power of Many: Building a High-Performance Management Team," March 2003, http://ceoforum.com.au.

29. A. Deutschman, "Inside the Mind of Jeff Bezos," *Fast Company,* August 2004, 52–58; L. Gratton and T. J. Erickson, "Ways to Build Collaborative Teams," *Harvard Business Review* (November 2007): 100–9.

30. G. Stasser, "Pooling of Unshared Information during Group Discussion," in *Group Process and Productivity,* ed. S. Worchel, W. Wood, and J. A. Simpson (Newbury Park, CA: Sage, 1992); J. R. Katzenbach and D. K. Smith, *The Wisdom of Teams: Creating the High-Performance Organization* (Boston: Harvard University Press, 1993), 45–47.

31. C. Fishman, "The Anarchist's Cookbook," *Fast Company,* July 2004, 70.

32. P. Wise, "How Shell Finds Student World's Brightest Sparks," *Financial Times* (London), January 8, 2004, 12; S. Ganesan, "Talent Quest," *Malaysia Star,* January 28, 2007.

33. F. P. Morgenson, M. H. Reider, and M. A. Campion, "Selecting Individuals in Team Setting: The Importance of Social Skills, Personality Characteristics, and Teamwork Knowledge," *Personnel Psychology* 58, no. 3 (2005): 583–611; V. Rousseau, C. Aubé, and A. Savoie, "Teamwork Behaviors: A Review and an Integration of Frameworks," *Small Group Research* 37, no. 5 (2006): 540–70. For a detailed examination of the characteristics of effective team members, see M. L. Loughry, M. W. Ohland, and D. D. Moore, "Development of a Theory-Based Assessment of Team Member Effectiveness," *Educational and Psychological Measurement* 67, no. 3 (June 2007): 505–24.

34. C. O. L. H. Porter et al., "Backing up Behaviors in Teams: The Role of Personality and Legitimacy of Need," *Journal of Applied Psychology* 88, no. 3 (2003): 391–403; C. E. Hårtel and D. Panipucci, "How 'Bad Apples' Spoil the Bunch: Faultlines, Emotional Levers, and Exclusion in the Workplace," *Research on Emotion in Organizations* 3 (2007): 287–310. The bad apple phenomenon is also identified in executive team "derailers." See: R. Wageman et al., *Senior Leadership Teams* (Boston: Harvard Business School Press, 2008), 97–102.

35. D. van Knippenberg, C. K. W. De Dreu, and A. C. Homan, "Work Group Diversity and Group Performance: An Integrative Model and Research Agenda," *Journal of Applied Psychology* 89, no. 6 (2004): 1008–22; E. Mannix and M. A. Neale, "What Differences Make a Difference? The Promise and Reality of Diverse Teams in Organizations," *Psychological Science in the Public Interest* 6, no. 2 (2005): 31–55. For a positive view of team diversity, see: G. K. Stahl et al., "A Look at the Bright Side of Multicultural Team Diversity," *Scandinavian Journal of Management* 26, no. 4 (2010): 439–47.

36. D. C. Lau and J. K. Murnighan, "Interactions within Groups and Subgroups: The Effects of Demographic Faultlines," *Academy of Management Journal* 48, no. 4 (August 2005): 645–59; R. Rico et al., "The Effects of Diversity Faultlines and Team Task Autonomy on Decision Quality and Social Integration," *Journal of Management* 33, no. 1 (February 2007): 111–32.

37. B. W. Tuckman and M. A. C. Jensen, "Stages of Small-Group Development Revisited," *Group and Organization Studies* 2 (1977): 419–42; B. W. Tuckman, "Developmental Sequence in Small Groups," *Group Facilitation* (Spring 2001): 66–81.

38. G. R. Bushe and G. H. Coetzer, "Group Development and Team Effectiveness: Using Cognitive Representations to Measure Group Development and Predict Task Performance and Group Viability," *Journal of Applied Behavioral Science* 43, no. 2 (June 2007): 184–212.

39. J. E. Mathieu and G. F. Goodwin, "The Influence of Shared Mental Models on Team Process and Performance," *Journal of Applied Psychology* 85 (April 2000): 273–84; J. Langan-Fox and J. Anglim, "Mental Models, Team Mental Models, and Performance: Process, Development, and Future Directions," *Human Factors and Ergonomics in Manufacturing* 14, no. 4 (2004): 331–52; B.-C. Lim and K. J. Klein, "Team Mental Models and Team Performance: A Field Study of the Effects of Team Mental Model Similarity and Accuracy," *Journal of Organizational Behavior* 27 (2006): 403–18; R. Rico, M. Sánchez-Manzanares, and C. Gibson, "Team Implicit Coordination Processes: A Team Knowledge-Based Approach," *Academy of Management Review* 33, no. 1 (2008): 163–84.

40. L. A. DeChurch and J. R. Mesmer-Magnus, "The Cognitive Underpinnings of Effective Teamwork: A Meta-Analysis," *Journal of Applied Psychology* 95, no. 1 (2010): 32–53.

41. A. P. Hare, "Types of Roles in Small Groups: A Bit of History and a Current Perspective," *Small Group Research* 25 (1994): 443–448; A. Aritzeta, S. Swailes, and B. Senior, "Belbin's Team Role Model: Development, Validity and Applications for Team Building," *Journal of Management Studies* 44, no. 1 (Jan. 2007): 96–118.

42. S. H. N. Leung, J. W. K. Chan, and W. B. Lee, "The Dynamic Team Role Behavior: The Approaches of Investigation," *Team Performance Management* 9 (2003): 84–90; G. L. Stewart, I. S. Fulmer, and M. R. Barrick, "An Exploration of Member Roles as a Multilevel Linking Mechanism for Individual Traits and Team Outcomes," *Personnel Psychology* 58, no. 2 (2005): 343–65.

43. W. G. Dyer, *Team Building: Current Issues and New Alternatives,* 3d ed. (Reading, MA: Addison-Wesley, 1995); C. A. Beatty and B. A. Barker, *Building Smart Teams: Roadmap to High Performance* (Thousand Oaks, CA: Sage Publications, 2004).

44. Langan-Fox and Anglim, "Mental Models, Team Mental Models, and Performance"; J. E. Mathieu et al., "Scaling the Quality of Teammates' Mental Models: Equifinality and Normative Comparisons," *Journal of Organizational Behavior* 26 (2005): 37–56.

45. R. W. Woodman and J. J. Sherwood, "The Role of Team Development in Organizational Effectiveness: A Critical Review," *Psychological Bulletin* 88 (1980): 166–86.

46. "German Businesswoman Demands End to Fun at Work," *Reuters,* July 9, 2003.

47. A. Zayas, "A Search for Teamwork," *St. Petersburg Times* (Florida), June 29, 2008, 1F; "Team Nestlé Stride out in Gcc Walking Challenge," Nestlé UK, 2009), accessed April 23, 2010, www.nestle.co.uk; S. W. Leow, "Firms Whip up a Dash of Team Spirit," *Straits Times* (Singapore), December 4, 2009; D. Moss, "The Value of Giving," *HRMagainze,* December 2009, 22

48. L. Mealiea and R. Baltazar, "A Strategic Guide for Building Effective Teams," *Personnel Management* 34, no. 2 (Summer 2005): 141–60.

49. G. E. Huszczo, "Training for Team Building," *Training and Development Journal* 44 (February 1990): 37–43; P. McGraw, "Back from the Mountain: Outdoor Management Development Programs and How to Ensure the Transfer of Skills to the Workplace," *Asia Pacific Journal of Human Resources* 31 (Spring 1993): 52–61.

50. D. C. Feldman, "The Development and Enforcement of Group Norms," *Academy of Management Review* 9 (1984): 47–53; E. Fehr and U. Fischbacher, "Social Norms and Human Cooperation," *Trends in Cognitive Sciences* 8, no. 4 (2004): 185–90.

51. N. Ellemers and F. Rink, "Identity in Work Groups: The Beneficial and Detrimental Consequences of Multiple Identities and Group Norms for Collaboration and Group Performance," *Advances in Group Processes* 22 (2005): 1–41.

52. J. J. Dose and R. J. Klimoski, "The Diversity of Diversity: Work Values Effects on Formative Team Processes," *Human Resource Management Review* 9, no. 1 (Spring 1999): 83–108.

53. S. Taggar and R. Ellis, "The Role of Leaders in Shaping Formal Team Norms," *Leadership Quarterly* 18, no. 2 (2007): 105–20.

54. D. J. Beal et al., "Cohesion and Performance in Groups: A Meta-Analytic Clarification of Construct Relations," *Journal of Applied Psychology* 88, no. 6 (2003): 989–1004; S. W. J. Kozlowski and D. R. Ilgen, "Enhancing the Effectiveness of Work Groups and Teams," *Psychological Science in the Public Interest* 7, no. 3 (2006): 77–124.

55. R. M. Montoya, R. S. Horton, and J. Kirchner, "Is Actual Similarity Necessary for Attraction? A Meta-Analysis of Actual and Perceived Similarity," *Journal of Social and Personal Relationships* 25, no. 6 (December 1, 2008): 889–922; M. T. Rivera, S. B. Soderstrom, and B. Uzzi, "Dynamics of Dyads in Social Networks: Assortative, Relational, and Proximity Mechanisms," *Annual Review of Sociology* 36 (2010): 91–115.

56. K. A. Jehn, G. B. Northcraft, and M. A. Neale, "Why Differences Make a Difference: A Field Study of Diversity, Conflict, and Performance in Workgroups," *Administrative*

Science Quarterly 44, no. 4 (1999): 741–63; van Knippenberg, De Dreu, and Homan, "Work Group Diversity and Group Performance." For evidence that diversity/similarity does not always influence cohesion, see S. S. Webber and L. M. Donahue, "Impact of Highly and Less Job-Related Diversity on Work Group Cohesion and Performance: A Meta-Analysis," *Journal of Management* 27, no. 2 (2001): 141–62.

57. E. Aronson and J. Mills, "The Effects of Severity of Initiation on Liking for a Group," *Journal of Abnormal and Social Psychology* 59 (1959): 177–81; J. E. Hautaluoma and R. S. Enge, "Early Socialization into a Work Group: Severity of Initiations Revisited," *Journal of Social Behavior & Personality* 6 (1991): 725–48.

58. B. Mullen and C. Copper, "The Relation between Group Cohesiveness and Performance: An Integration," *Psychological Bulletin* 115 (1994): 210–27; C. J. Fullagar and D. O. Egleston, "Norming and Performing: Using Microworlds to Understand the Relationship between Team Cohesiveness and Performance," *Journal of Applied Social Psychology* 38, no. 10 (October 2008): 2574–93.

59. Wageman et al., *Senior Leadership Teams,* 69–70.

60. M. Rempel and R. J. Fisher, "Perceived Threat, Cohesion, and Group Problem Solving in Intergroup Conflict," *International Journal of Conflict Management* 8 (1997): 216–34; M. E. Turner and T. Horvitz, "The Dilemma of Threat: Group Effectiveness and Ineffectiveness under Adversity," in *Groups at Work: Theory and Research* ed. M. E. Turner (Mahwah, NJ: Lawrence Erlbaum Associates, 2001), 445–70.

61. W. Piper et al., "Cohesion as a Basic Bond in Groups," *Human Relations* 36 (1983): 93–108; C. A. O'Reilly, D. E. Caldwell, and W. P. Barnett, "Work Group Demography, Social Integration, and Turnover," *Administrative Science Quarterly* 34 (1989): 21–37.

62. Mullen and Copper, "The Relation between Group Cohesiveness and Performance"; A. V. Carron et al., "Cohesion and Performance in Sport: A Meta-Analysis," *Journal of Sport and Exercise Psychology* 24 (2002): 168–88; Beal et al., "Cohesion and Performance in Groups"; Fullagar and Egleston, "Norming and Performing: Using Microworlds to Understand the Relationship between Team Cohesiveness and Performance"; DeChurch and Mesmer-Magnus, "The Cognitive Underpinnings of Effective Teamwork: A Meta-Analysis."

63. Fullagar and Egleston, "Norming and Performing: Using Microworlds to Understand the Relationship between Team Cohesiveness and Performance."

64. C. Langfred, "Is Group Cohesiveness a Double-Edged Sword? An Investigation of the Effects of Cohesiveness on Performance," *Small Group Research* 29 (1998): 124–43; K. L. Gammage, A. V. Carron, and P. A. Estabrooks, "Team Cohesion and Individual Productivity: The Influence of the Norm for Productivity and the Identifiablity of Individual Effort," *Small Group Research* 32 (February 2001): 3–18; N. L. Jimmieson, M. Peach, and K. M. White, "Utilizing the Theory of Planned Behavior to Inform Change Management," *Journal of Applied Behavioral Science* 44, no. 2 (June 2008): 237–62. Concerns about existing research on cohesion-performance are discussed in: M. Casey-Campbell and M. L. Martens, "Sticking It All Together: A Critical Assessment of the Group Cohesion-Performance Literature," *International Journal of Management Reviews* 11, no. 2 (2009): 223–46.

65. S. L. Robinson, "Trust and Breach of the Psychological Contract," *Administrative Science Quarterly* 41 (1996): 574–99; D. M. Rousseau et al., "Not So Different after All: A

Cross-Discipline View of Trust," *Academy of Management Review* 23 (1998): 393–404; D. L. Duarte and N. T. Snyder, *Mastering Virtual Teams: Strategies, Tools, and Techniques That Succeed,* 2d ed. (San Francisco, CA: Jossey-Bass, 2000), 139–55. For the importance of trust in virtual teams, see: L. M. Peters and C. C. Manz, "Getting Virtual Teams Right the First Time," in *The Handbook of High-Performance Virtual Teams: A Toolkit for Collaborating across Boundaries,* ed. J. Nemiro and M. M. Beyerlein (San Francisco: Jossey Bass, 2008), 105–30.

66. Rousseau et al., "Not So Different after All: A Cross-Discipline View of Trust."

67. D. J. McAllister, "Affect- and Cognition-Based Trust as Foundations for Interpersonal Cooperation in Organizations," *Academy of Management Journal* 38, no. 1 (February 1995): 24–59; M. Williams, "In Whom We Trust: Group Membership as an Affective Context for Trust Development," *Academy of Management Review* 26, no. 3 (July 2001): 377–96.

68. O. E. Williamson, "Calculativeness, Trust, and Economic Organization," *Journal of Law and Economics* 36, no. 1 (1993): 453–86.

69. E. M. Whitener et al., "Managers as Initiators of Trust: An Exchange Relationship Framework for Understanding Managerial Trustworthy Behavior," *Academy of Management Review* 23 (July 1998): 513–30; J. M. Kouzes and B. Z. Posner, *The Leadership Challenge,* 3d ed. (San Francisco: Jossey-Bass, 2002), Chap. 2; T. Simons, "Behavioral Integrity: The Perceived Alignment between Managers' Words and Deeds as a Research Focus," *Organization Science* 13, no. 1 (January/February 2002): 18–35.

70. S. L. Jarvenpaa and D. E. Leidner, "Communication and Trust in Global Virtual Teams," *Organization Science* 10 (1999): 791–815; M. M. Pillutla, D. Malhotra, and J. Keith Murnighan, "Attributions of Trust and the Calculus of Reciprocity," *Journal of Experimental Social Psychology* 39, no. 5 (2003): 448–55.

71. B. Schlender, "The Lost Steve Jobs Tapes," *Fast Company,* May 2012. This quotation specifically refers to the bond that formed between Pixar Animation Studios and Disney.

72. K. T. Dirks and D. L. Ferrin, "The Role of Trust in Organizations," *Organization Science* 12, no. 4 (July/August 2004): 450–67.

73. Mohrman, Cohen, and Mohrman Jr., *Designing Team-Based Organizations: New Forms for Knowledge Work;* D. E. Yeatts and C. Hyten, *High-Performing Self-Managed Work Teams: A Comparison of Theory and Practice* (Thousand Oaks, CA: Sage, 1998); E. E. Lawler, *Organizing for High Performance* (San Francisco: Jossey-Bass, 2001); R. J. Torraco, "Work Design Theory: A Review and Critique with Implications for Human Resource Development," *Human Resource Development Quarterly* 16, no. 1 (Spring 2005): 85–109.

74. Fishman, "The Anarchist's Cookbook"; J. Mackey, "Open Book Company," *Newsweek,* November 28, 2005, 42; K. Zimbalist, "Green Giant," *Time,* April 24, 2006, 24.

75. P. Panchak, "Production Workers Can Be Your Competitive Edge," *Industry Week,* October 2004, 11; S. K. Muthusamy, J. V. Wheeler, and B. L. Simmons, "Self-Managing Work Teams: Enhancing Organizational Innovativeness," *Organization Development Journal* 23, no. 3 (Fall 2005): 53–66.

76. Emery and Fredenhall, "The Effect of Teams on Firm Profitability and Customer Satisfaction"; A. Krause and H. Dunckel, "Work Design and Customer Satisfaction: Effects of

the Implementation of Semi-Autonomous Group Work on Customer Satisfaction Considering Employee Satisfaction and Group Performance (translated abstract)," *Zeitschrift Fur Arbeits-Und Organisationspsychologie* 47, no. 4 (2003): 182–93; H. van Mierlo et al., "Self-Managing Teamwork and Psychological Well-Being: Review of a Multilevel Research Domain," *Group & Organization Management* 30, no. 2 (April 2005): 211–35.

77. Moldaschl and Weber, "The 'Three Waves' of Industrial Group Work: Historical Reflections on Current Research on Group Work"; W. Niepce and E. Molleman, "Work Design Issues in Lean Production from Sociotechnical System Perspective: Neo-Taylorism or the Next Step in Sociotechnical Design?," *Human Relations* 51, no. 3 (March 1998): 259–87; J. L. Cordery et al., "The Impact of Autonomy and Task Uncertainty on Team Performance: A Longitudinal Field Study," *Journal of Organizational Behavior* 31 (2010): 240–58.

78. E. Ulich and W. G. Weber, "Dimensions, Criteria, and Evaluation of Work Group Autonomy," in *Handbook of Work Group Psychology* ed. M. A. West (Chichester, UK: John Wiley and Sons, 1996), 247–82.

79. K. P. Carson and G. L. Stewart, "Job Analysis and the Sociotechnical Approach to Quality: A Critical Examination," *Journal of Quality Management* 1 (1996): 49–65; C. C. Manz and G. L. Stewart, "Attaining Flexible Stability by Integrating Total Quality Management and Socio-Technical Systems Theory," *Organization Science* 8 (1997): 59–70.

80. J. Lipnack and J. Stamps, *Virtual Teams: People Working across Boundaries with Technology* (New York: John Wiley and Sons, 2001); Hertel, Geister, and Konradt, "Managing Virtual Teams"; L. Schweitzer and L. Duxbury, "Conceptualizing and Measuring the Virtuality of Teams," *Information Systems Journal* 20, no. 3 (2010): 267–95.

81. "Absence Makes the Team Uneasy," OfficeTeam news release, March 6, 2008; "Go Teams! Firms Can't Do without Them"; N. Weil, "Global Team Management: Continental Divides," *CIO,* January 23, 2008.

82. "Virtual Teams Now a Reality." Institute for Corporate Productivity, news release for Institute for Corporate Productivity, September 4, 2008.

83. G. Gilder, *Telecosm: How Infinite Bandwidth Will Revolutionize Our World* (New York: Free Press, 2001); L. L. Martins, L. L. Gilson, and M. T. Maynard, "Virtual Teams: What Do We Know and Where Do We Go Form Here?," *Journal of Management* 30, no. 6 (2004): 805–35.

84. Martins, Gilson, and Maynard, "Virtual Teams"; G. Hertel, U. Konradt, and K. Voss, "Competencies for Virtual Teamwork: Development and Validation of a Web-Based Selection Tool for Members of Distributed Teams," *European Journal of Work and Organizational Psychology* 15, no. 4 (2006): 477–504; J. M. Wilson et al., "Perceived Proximity in Virtual Work: Explaining the Paradox of Far-but-Close," *Organization Studies* 29, no. 7 (July 1, 2008 2008): 979–1002.

85. G. G. Harwood, "Design Principles for Successful Virtual Teams," in *The Handbook of High-Performance Virtual Teams: A Toolkit for Collaborating across Boundaries,* ed. J. Nemiro and M. M. Beyerlein (San Francisco: Jossey-Bass, 2008), 59–84. Also see: H. Duckworth, "How TRW Automotive Helps Global Virtual Teams Perform at the Top of Their Game," *Global Business and Organizational Excellence* 28, no. 1 (2008): 6–16; L. Dubé and D. Robey, "Surviving the Paradoxes of Virtual Teamwork," *Information Systems Journal* 19, no. 1 (2009): 3–30.

86. Dubé and Robey, "Surviving the Paradoxes of Virtual Teamwork."

87. V. H. Vroom and A. G. Jago, *The New Leadership* (Englewood Cliffs, NJ: Prentice-Hall, 1988), 28–29.

88. M. Diehl and W. Stroebe, "Productivity Loss in Idea-Generating Groups: Tracking Down the Blocking Effects," *Journal of Personality and Social Psychology* 61 (1991): 392–403; R. B. Gallupe et al., "Blocking Electronic Brainstorms," *Journal of Applied Psychology* 79 (1994): 77–86; B. A. Nijstad, W. Stroebe, and H. F. M. Lodewijkx, "Production Blocking and Idea Generation: Does Blocking Interfere with Cognitive Processes?," *Journal of Experimental Social Psychology* 39, no. 6 (November 2003): 531–48; B. A. Nijstad and W. Stroebe, "How the Group Affects the Mind: A Cognitive Model of Idea Generation in Groups," *Personality & Social Psychology Review* 10, no. 3 (2006): 186–213.

89. B. E. Irmer, P. Bordia, and D. Abusah, "Evaluation Apprehension and Perceived Benefits in Interpersonal and Database Knowledge Sharing," *Academy of Management Proceedings* (2002): B1–B6.

90. I. L. Janis, *Groupthink: Psychological Studies of Policy Decisions and Fiascoes*, 2d ed. (Boston: Houghton Mifflin, 1982); J. K. Esser, "Alive and Well after 25 Years: A Review of Groupthink Research," *Organizational Behavior and Human Decision Processes* 73, no. 2–3 (1998): 116–41.

91. J. N. Choi and M. U. Kim, "The Organizational Application of Groupthink and Its Limitations in Organizations," *Journal of Applied Psychology* 84, no. 2 (April 1999): 297–306; W.-W. Park, "A Comprehensive Empirical Investigation of the Relationships among Variables of the Groupthink Model," *Journal of Organizational Behavior* 21, no. 8 (December 2000): 873–87; D. D. Henningsen et al., "Examining the Symptoms of Groupthink and Retrospective Sensemaking," *Small Group Research* 37, no. 1 (February 2006): 36–64.

92. D. Miller, *The Icarus Paradox: How Exceptional Companies Bring about Their Own Downfall* (New York: HarperBusiness, 1990); S. Finkelstein, *Why Smart Executives Fail* (New York: Viking, 2003); K. Tasa and G. Whyte, "Collective Efficacy and Vigilant Problem Solving in Group Decision Making: A Non-Linear Model," *Organizational Behavior and Human Decision Processes* 96, no. 2 (March 2005): 119–29.

93. Cited in F. Dearmond, *Executive Thinking and Action* (New York: McGraw-Hill, 1946). Also credited to Wrigley in a 1931 issue of *American Magazine.*

94. K. M. Eisenhardt, J. L. Kahwajy, and L. J. Bourgeois III, "Conflict and Strategic Choice: How Top Management Teams Disagree," *California Management Review* 39 (1997): 42–62; R. Sutton, *Weird Ideas That Work* (New York: Free Press, 2002); C. J. Nemeth et al., "The Liberating Role of Conflict in Group Creativity: A Study in Two Countries," *European Journal of Social Psychology* 34, no. 4 (2004): 365–74. For a discussion on how all conflict is potentially detrimental to teams, see C. K. W. De Dreu and L. R. Weingart, "Task Versus Relationship Conflict, Team Performance, and Team Member Satisfaction: A Meta-Analysis," *Journal of Applied Psychology* 88 (August 2003): 587–604; P. Hinds and D. E. Bailey, "Out of Sight, out of Sync: Understanding Conflict in Distributed Teams," *Organization Science* 14, no. 6 (2003): 615–32.

95. Advertising executive Alex Osborn (the "O" in BBDO, the largest creative agency owned by Omnicom) first described brainstorming in the little-known 1942 booklet *How to Think Up.* He originally called them "brain-storm suppers" (pg. 29) because the company initially held these events in the evening

after a meal in the company dining room. Osborn gave a fuller description of the brainstorming process in his popular 1948 (*Your Creative Power*) and 1953 (*Applied Imagination*) books. See: A. F. Osborn, *How to Think Up* (New York: McGraw-Hill, 1942), Chap. 4; A. F. Osborn, *Your Creative Power* (New York: Charles Scribner's Sons, 1948); A. F. Osborn, *Applied Imagination* (New York: Charles Scribner's Sons, 1953).

96. B. S. Benson, "Let's Toss This Idea Up," *Fortune*, October 1957, 145–46.

97. B. Mullen, C. Johnson, and E. Salas, "Productivity Loss in Brainstorming Groups: A Meta-Analytic Integration," *Basic and Applied Psychology* 12 (1991): 2–23.

98. R. I. Sutton and A. Hargadon, "Brainstorming Groups in Context: Effectiveness in a Product Design Firm," *Administrative Science Quarterly* 41 (1996): 685–718; T. Kelley, *The Art of Innovation* (New York: Currency Doubleday, 2001); V. R. Brown and P. B. Paulus, "Making Group Brainstorming More Effective: Recommendations from an Associative Memory Perspective," *Current Directions in Psychological Science* 11, no. 6 (2002): 208–12; K. Leggett Dugosh and P. B. Paulus, "Cognitive and Social Comparison Processes in Brainstorming," *Journal of Experimental Social Psychology* 41, no. 3 (2005): 313–20.

99. N. W. Kohn, P. B. Paulus, and Y. Choi, "Building on the Ideas of Others: An Examination of the Idea Combination Process," *Journal of Experimental Social Psychology* 47 (2011): 554–61.

100. R. B. Gallupe, L. M. Bastianutti, and W. H. Cooper, "Unblocking Brainstorms," *Journal of Applied Psychology* 76 (1991): 137–42; W. H. Cooper et al., "Some Liberating Effects of Anonymous Electronic Brainstorming," *Small Group Research* 29, no. 2 (April 1998): 147–78; A. R. Dennis, B. H. Wixom, and R. J. Vandenberg, "Understanding Fit and Appropriation Effects in Group Support Systems Via Meta-Analysis," *MIS Quarterly* 25, no. 2 (June 2001): 167–93; D. M. DeRosa, C. L. Smith, and D. A. Hantula, "The Medium Matters: Mining the Long-Promised Merit of Group Interaction in Creative Idea Generation Tasks in a Meta-Analysis of the Electronic Group Brainstorming Literature," *Computers in Human Behavior* 23, no. 3 (2007): 1549–81.

101. A. L. Delbecq, A. H. Van de Ven, and D. H. Gustafson, *Group Techniques for Program Planning: A Guide to Nominal Group and Delphi Processes* (Middleton, WI: Green Briar Press, 1986).

102. D. M. Spencer, "Facilitating Public Participation in Tourism Planning on American Indian Reservations: A Case Study Involving the Nominal Group Technique," *Tourism Management* 31, no. 5 (2011): 684–90.

103. S. Frankel, "NGT + MDS: An Adaptation of the Nominal Group Technique for Ill-Structured Problems," *Journal of Applied Behavioral Science* 23 (1987): 543–51; H. Barki and A. Pinsonneault, "Small Group Brainstorming and Idea Quality: Is Electronic Brainstorming the Most Effective Approach?," *Small Group Research* 32, no. 2 (April 2001): 158–205.

104. P. P. Lago et al., "Structuring Group Decision Making in a Web-Based Environment by Using the Nominal Group Technique," *Computers & Industrial Engineering* 52, no. 2 (2007): 277–95.

CHAPTER 8

1. "Atos Origin Abandoning Email," *Computerworld UK,* February 9, 2011; G. Nairn, "The Trouble with Office Email," *Financial Times* (London), February 17, 2011.

2. A. H. Van de Ven, A. L. Delbecq, and R. Koenig Jr., "Determinants of Coordination Modes within Organizations," *American Sociological Review* 41, no. 2 (1976): 322–38; R. Foy et al., "Meta-Analysis: Effect of Interactive Communication between Collaborating Primary Care Physicians and Specialists," *Annals of Internal Medicine* 152, no. 4 (February 16, 2010): 247–58; J. H. Gittell, R. Seidner, and J. Wimbush, "A Relational Model of How High-Performance Work Systems Work," *Organization Science* 21, no. 2 (March 2010): 490–506.

3. C. Barnard, *The Functions of the Executive* (Cambridge, MA: Harvard University Press, 1938), 82. Barnard's entire statement also refers to the other features of organizations that we describe in Chapter 1, namely that (a) people are willing to contribute their effort to the organization and (b) they have a common purpose.

4. M. T. Hansen, M. L. Mors, and B. Løvås, "Knowledge Sharing in Organizations: Multiple Networks, Multiple Phases," *Academy of Management Journal* 48, no. 5 (2005): 776–93; S. R. Murray and J. Peyrefitte, "Knowledge Type and Communication Media Choice in the Knowledge Transfer Process," *Journal of Managerial Issues* 19, no. 1 (Spring 2007): 111–33; S. L. Hoe and S. L. McShane, "Structural and Informal Knowledge Acquisition and Dissemination in Organizational Learning: An Exploratory Analysis," *Learning Organization* 17, no. 4 (2010): 364–86.

5. J. O'Toole and W. Bennis, "What's Needed Next: A Culture of Candor," *Harvard Business Review* 87, no. 6 (2009): 54–61.

6. N. Ellemers, R. Spears, and B. Doosje, "Self and Social Identity," *Annual Review of Psychology* 53 (2002): 161–86; S. A. Haslam and S. Reicher, "Stressing the Group: Social Identity and the Unfolding Dynamics of Responses to Stress," *Journal of Applied Psychology* 91, no. 5 (2006): 1037–52; M. T. Gailliot and R. F. Baumeister, "Self-Esteem, Belongingness, and Worldview Validation: Does Belongingness Exert a Unique Influence Upon Self-Esteem?" *Journal of Research in Personality* 41, no. 2 (2007): 327–45.

7. A. M. Saks, K. L. Uggerslev, and N. E. Fassina, "Socialization Tactics and Newcomer Adjustment: A Meta-Analytic Review and Test of a Model," *Journal of Vocational Behavior* 70, no. 3 (2007): 413–46.

8. S. Cohen, "The Pittsburgh Common Cold Studies: Psychosocial Predictors of Susceptibility to Respiratory Infectious Illness," *International Journal of Behavioral Medicine* 12, no. 3 (2005): 123–31; B. N. Uchino, "Social Support and Health: A Review of Physiological Processes Potentially Underlying Links to Disease Outcomes," *Journal of Behavioral Medicine* 29, no. 4 (2006): 377–87.

9. C. E. Shannon and W. Weaver, *The Mathematical Theory of Communication* (Urbana, IL: University of Illinois Press, 1949); R. M. Krauss and S. R. Fussell, "Social Psychological Models of Interpersonal Communication," in *Social Psychology: Handbook of Basic Principles,* ed. E. T. Higgins and A. Kruglanski (New York: Guilford Press, 1996), 655–701.

10. J. R. Carlson and R. W. Zmud, "Channel Expansion Theory and the Experiential Nature of Media Richness Perceptions," *Academy of Management Journal* 42 (April 1999): 153–70.

11. P. Shachaf and N. Hara, "Behavioral Complexity Theory of Media Selection: A Proposed Theory for Global Virtual Teams," *Journal of Information Science* 33 (2007): 63–75.

12. M. Wolf et al., *How Real-Time Communications and Video Are Transforming the Workplace* (San Jose, CA: Skype and Giga Omni Media, February 26, 2011).

13. M. Hauben and R. Hauben, "Netizens: On the History and Impact of Usenet and the Internet," *First Monday* 3, no. 8 (August 1998); J. Abbate, (Cambridge, MA: MIT Press, 1999).

14. N. B. Ducheneaut and L. A. Watts, "In Search of Coherence: A Review of E-Mail Research," *Human-Computer Interaction* 20, no. 1–2 (2005): 11–48.

15. W. Lucas, "Effects of E-Mail on the Organization," *European Management Journal* 16, no. 1 (February 1998): 18–30; D. A. Owens, M. A. Neale, and R. I. Sutton, "Technologies of Status Management Status Dynamics in E-Mail Communications," *Research on Managing Groups and Teams* 3 (2000): 205–30; N. B. Ducheneaut, "Ceci N'est Pas Un Objet? Talking about Objects in E-Mail," *Human-Computer Interaction* 18, no. 1–2 (2003): 85–110.

16. N. B. Ducheneaut, "The Social Impacts of Electronic Mail in Organizations: A Case Study of Electronic Power Games Using Communication Genres," *Information, Communication, & Society* 5, no. 2 (2002): 153–88; N. Panteli, "Richness, Power Cues and Email Text," *Information & Management* 40, no. 2 (2002): 75–86.

17. N. Epley and J. Kruger, "When What You Type Isn't What They Read: The Perseverance of Stereotypes and Expectancies over E-Mail," *Journal of Experimental Social Psychology* 41, no. 4 (2005): 414–22.

18. J. Kruger et al., "Egocentrism over E-Mail: Can We Communicate as Well as We Think?" *Journal of Personality and Social Psychology* 89, no. 6 (2005): 925–36.

19. J. B. Walther, "Language and Communication Technology: Introduction to the Special Issue," *Journal of Language and Social Psychology* 23, no. 4 (December 2004): 384–96; J. B. Walther, T. Loh, and L. Granka, "Let Me Count the Ways: The Interchange of Verbal and Nonverbal Cues in Computer-Mediated and Face-to-Face Affinity," *Journal of Language and Social Psychology* 24, no. 1 (March 2005): 36–65; K. Byron, "Carrying Too Heavy a Load? The Communication and Miscommunication of Emotion by Email," *Academy of Management Review* 33, no. 2 (2008): 309–27; J. M. Whalen, P. M. Pexman, and A. J. Gill, "'Should Be Fun—Not!': Incidence and Marking of Nonliteral Language in E-Mail," *Journal of Language and Social Psychology* 28, no. 3 (September 2009): 263–80.

20. Byron, "Carrying Too Heavy a Load?"

21. G. Hertel, S. Geister, and U. Konradt, "Managing Virtual Teams: A Review of Current Empirical Research," *Human Resource Management Review* 15 (2005): 69–95; H. Lee, "Behavioral Strategies for Dealing with Flaming in an Online Forum," *The Sociological Quarterly* 46, no. 2 (2005): 385–403.

22. D. D. Dawley and W. P. Anthony, "User Perceptions of E-Mail at Work," *Journal of Business and Technical Communication* 17, no. 2 (April 2003): 170–200; G. F. Thomas and C. L. King, "Reconceptualizing E-Mail Overload," *Journal of Business and Technical Communication* 20, no. 3 (July 2006): 252–87; S. Carr, "Email Overload Menace Growing," *Silicon.com,* July 12, 2007.

23. R. D. Waters et al., "Engaging Stakeholders through Social Networking: How Nonprofit Organizations Are Using Facebook," *Public Relations Review* 35, no. 2 (2009): 102–6; J. Cunningham, "New Workers, New Workplace? Getting the Balance Right," *Strategic Direction* 26, no. 1 (2010): 5; A. M. Kaplan and M. Haenlein, "Users of the World, Unite! The Challenges and Opportunities of Social Media," *Business Horizons* 53, no. 1 (2010): 59–68.

24. J. H. Kietzmann et al., "Social Media? Get Serious! Understanding the Functional Building Blocks of Social Media," *Business Horizons* 54, no. 3 (2011): 241–51.

25. J. Champy, *What I Learned from Peter Drucker* (Boston: New Word City, 2010), Chap. 4.

26. S. Holtz, "Open the Door," *Communication World,* September 2010, 26.

27. Towers Watson, *Capitalizing on Effective Communication,* (New York: Towers Watson, February 4, 2010).

28. L. Z. Tiedens and A. R. Fragale, "Power Moves: Complementarity in Dominant and Submissive Nonverbal Behavior," *Journal of Personality and Social Psychology* 84, no. 3 (2003): 558–68.

29. P. Ekman and E. Rosenberg, *What the Face Reveals: Basic and Applied Studies of Spontaneous Expression Using the Facial Action Coding System* (Oxford, England: Oxford University Press, 1997); P. Winkielman and K. C. Berridge, "Unconscious Emotion," *Current Directions in Psychological Science* 13, no. 3 (2004): 120–23.

30. W. J. Becker and R. Cropanzano, "Organizational Neuroscience: The Promise and Prospects of an Emerging Discipline," *Journal of Organizational Behavior* 31, no. 7 (2010): 1055–59.

31. "Body Language in the Job Interview," CareerBuilder news release for CareerBuilder, August 23, 2011. The sample size of this survey was not stated, but is likely quite large. The same survey the previous year in the United States had a sample size of 2,500 employers. Results of the U.S. survey were similar to the more recent UK results reported here.

32. E. Hatfield, J. T. Cacioppo, and R. L. Rapson, *Emotional Contagion* (Cambridge, UK: Cambridge University Press, 1993); S. G. Barsade, "The Ripple Effect: Emotional Contagion and Its Influence on Group Behavior," *Administrative Science Quarterly* 47 (December 2002): 644–75; M. Sonnby-Borgstrom, P. Jonsson, and O. Svensson, "Emotional Empathy as Related to Mimicry Reactions at Different Levels of Information Processing," *Journal of Nonverbal Behavior* 27 (Spring 2003): 3–23; S. G. Barsade and D. E. Gibson, "Why Does Affect Matter in Organizations?" *Academy of Management Perspectives* (February 2007): 36–59; S. K. Johnson, "I Second That Emotion: Effects of Emotional Contagion and Affect at Work on Leader and Follower Outcomes," *Leadership Quarterly* 19, no. 1 (2008): 1–19.

33. J. R. Kelly and S. G. Barsade, "Mood and Emotions in Small Groups and Work Teams," *Organizational Behavior and Human Decision Processes* 86 (September 2001): 99–130.

34. J. Fulk, "Social Construction of Communication Technology," *Academy of Management Journal* 36, no. 5 (1993): 921–50; L. K. Treviño, J. Webster, and E. W. Stein, "Making Connections: Complementary Influences on Communication Media Choices, Attitudes, and Use," *Organization Science* 11, no. 2 (2000): 163–82; B. van den Hooff, J. Groot, and S. de Jonge, "Situational Influences on the Use of Communication Technologies," *Journal of Business Communication* 42, no. 1 (January 1, 2005): 4–27; J. W. Turner et al., "Exploring the Dominant Media: How Does Media Use Reflect Organizational Norms and Affect Performance?" *Journal of Business Communication* 43, no. 3 (July 2006): 220–50; M. B. Watson-Manheim and F. Bélanger, "Communication Media Repertoires: Dealing with the Multiplicity of Media Choices," *MIS Quarterly* 31, no. 2 (2007): 267–93.

35. Z. Lee and Y. Lee, "Emailing the Boss: Cultural Implications of Media Choice," *IEEE Transactions on Professional Communication* 52, no. 1 (March 2009): 61–74.

36. R. C. King, "Media Appropriateness: Effects of Experience on Communication Media Choice," *Decision Sciences* 28, no. 4 (1997): 877–910.

37. M. Madden and S. Jones, *Networked Workers,* Pew Internet & American Life Project (Washington, D.C.: Pew Research Center, September 24, 2008).

38. K. Griffiths, "KPMG Sacks 670 Employees by E-Mail," *The Independent* (London), November 5, 2002, 19; "Shop Worker Sacked by Text Message," *The Post* (Claremont/Nedlands, Western Australia), July 28, 2007, 1, 78.

39. R. L. Daft and R. H. Lengel, "Information Richness: A New Approach to Managerial Behavior and Organization Design," *Research in Organizational Behavior* 6 (1984): 191–233; R. H. Lengel and R. L. Daft, "The Selection of Communication Media as an Executive Skill," *Academy of Management Executive* 2 (1988): 225–32.

40. R. E. Rice, "Task Analyzability, Use of New Media, and Effectiveness: A Multi-Site Exploration of Media Richness," *Organization Science* 3 (1992): 475–500.

41. J. W. Turner and N. L. Reinsch Jr, "The Business Communicator as Presence Allocator," *Journal of Business Communication* 44, no. 1 (2007): 36–58; N. L. Reinsch Jr., J. W. Turner, and C. H. Tinsley, "Multicommunicating: A Practice Whose Time Has Come?" *Academy of Management Review* 33, no. 2 (2008): 391–403.

42. Carlson and Zmud, "Channel Expansion Theory and the Experiential Nature of Media Richness Perceptions"; N. Kock, "Media Richness or Media Naturalness? The Evolution of Our Biological Communication Apparatus and Its Influence on Our Behavior toward E-Communication Tools," *IEEE Transactions on Professional Communication* 48, no. 2 (June 2005): 117–30.

43. V. W. Kupritz and E. Cowell, "Productive Management Communication: Online and Face-to-Face," *Journal of Business Communication* 48, no. 1 (January 2011): 54–82.

44. D. Muller, T. Atzeni, and F. Butera, "Coaction and Upward Social Comparison Reduce the Illusory Conjunction Effect: Support for Distraction-Conflict Theory," *Journal of Experimental Social Psychology* 40, no. 5 (2004): 659–65; L. P. Robert and A. R. Dennis, "Paradox of Richness: A Cognitive Model of Media Choice," *IEEE Transactions on Professional Communication* 48, no. 1 (2005): 10–21.

45. E. V. Wilson, "Perceived Effectiveness of Interpersonal Persuasion Strategies in Computer-Mediated Communication," *Computers in Human Behavior* 19, no. 5 (2003): 537–52; K. Sassenberg, M. Boos, and S. Rabung, "Attitude Change in Face-to-Face and Computer-Mediated Communication: Private Self-Awareness Ad Mediator and Moderator," *European Journal of Social Psychology* 35 (2005): 361–74; P. Di Blasio and L. Milani, "Computer-Mediated Communication and Persuasion: Peripheral vs. Central Route to Opinion Shift," *Computers in Human Behavior* 24, no. 3 (2008): 798–815.

46. Kruger et al., "Egocentrism over E-Mail: Can We Communicate as Well as We Think?"

47. R. M. Krauss, "The Psychology of Verbal Communication," in *International Encyclopedia of the Social and Behavioral Sciences,* ed. N. Smelser and P. Baltes (London: Elsevier, 2002), 16161–16165.

48. H. Tsoukas, "The Missing Link: A Transformational View of Metaphors in Organizational Science," *The Academy of Management review* 16, no. 3 (1991): 566–85; G. Morgan, *Images of Organization,* 2d ed. (Thousand Oaks, CA: Sage, 1997); J. Amernic, R. Craig, and D. Tourish, "The Transformational Leader as Pedagogue, Physician, Architect, Commander, and Saint: Five Root Metaphors in Jack Welch's Letters to Stockholders of General Electric," *Human Relations* 60, no. 12 (December 2007): 1839–72.

49. M. Rubini and H. Sigall, "Taking the Edge Off of Disagreement: Linguistic Abstractness and Self-Presentation to a Heterogeneous Audience," *European Journal of Social Psychology* 32 (2002): 343–51.

50. T. Walsh, "Nardelli Brags on Vip Recruits, Game Plan," *Detroit Free Press,* September 8, 2007.

51. D. Goleman, R. Boyatzis, and A. McKee, *Primal Leaders* (Boston: Harvard Business School Press, 2002), 92–95.

52. O'Toole and Bennis, "What's Needed Next: A Culture of Candor."

53. T. Koski, "Reflections on Information Glut and Other Issues in Knowledge Productivity," *Futures* 33 (August 2001): 483–95.

54. A. G. Schick, L. A. Gordon, and S. Haka, "Information Overload: A Temporal Approach," *Accounting, Organizations & Society* 15 (1990): 199–220; A. Edmunds and A. Morris, "The Problem of Information Overload in Business Organisations: A Review of the Literature," *International Journal of Information Management* 20 (2000): 17–28; R. Pennington, "The Effects of Information Overload on Software Project Risk Assessment," *Decision Sciences* 38, no. 3 (August 2007): 489–526.

55. D. C. Thomas and K. Inkson, *Cultural Intelligence: People Skills for Global Business* (San Francisco: Berrett-Koehler, 2004), Chap. 6; D. Welch, L. Welch, and R. Piekkari, "Speaking in Tongues," *International Studies of Management & Organization* 35, no. 1 (Spring 2005): 10–27.

56. D. Woodruff, "Crossing Culture Divide Early Clears Merger Paths," *Asian Wall Street Journal,* May 28, 2001, 9; "Different Strokes," *Personnel Today,* November 25, 2008, 190.

57. S. Ohtaki, T. Ohtaki, and M. D. Fetters, "Doctor-Patient Communication: A Comparison of the USA and Japan," *Family Practice* 20 (June 2003): 276–82; M. Fujio, "Silence during Intercultural Communication: A Case Study," *Corporate Communications* 9, no. 4 (2004): 331–39.

58. T. Hasegawa and W. B. Gudykunst, "Silence in Japan and the United States," *Journal of Cross-Cultural Psychology* 29, no. 5 (September 1998): 668–84.

59. D. C. Barnlund, *Communication Styles of Japanese and Americans: Images and Realities* (Belmont, CA: Wadsworth, 1988); H. Yamada, *American and Japanese Business Discourse: A Comparison of Interaction Styles* (Norwood, NJ: Ablex, 1992), Chap. 2.

60. P. Harris and R. Moran, *Managing Cultural Differences* (Houston: Gulf, 1987); H. Blagg, "A Just Measure of Shame?" *British Journal of Criminology* 37 (Autumn 1997): 481–501; R. E. Axtell, *Gestures: The Do's and Taboos of Body Language around the World,* revised ed. (New York: Wiley, 1998).

61. D. Tannen, *You Just Don't Understand: Men and Women in Conversation* (New York: Ballentine Books, 1990); D. Tannen, *Talking from 9 to 5* (New York: Avon, 1994); M. Crawford, *Talking Difference: On Gender and Language* (Thousand Oaks, CA: Sage, 1995), 41–44; L. L. Namy, L. C. Nygaard, and D. Sauerteig, "Gender Differences in Vocal Accommodation: The Role of Perception," *Journal of Language and Social Psychology* 21, no. 4 (December 2002): 422–32; H. Itakura and A. B. M. Tsui, "Gender and Conversational Dominance in Japanese Conversation," *Language in Society* 33, no. 2 (2004): 223–48.

62. A. Mulac et al., "Uh-Huh. What's That All About?' Differing Interpretations of Conversational Backchannels and Questions as Sources of Miscommunication across Gender Boundaries," *Communication Research* 25 (December 1998): 641–68; N. M. Sussman and D. H. Tyson, "Sex and Power: Gender Differences in Computer-Mediated Interactions," *Computers in*

Human Behavior 16 (2000): 381–94; D. R. Caruso and P. Salovey, *The Emotionally Intelligent Manager* (San Francisco: Jossey-Bass, 2004), 23; D. Fallows, *How Women and Men Use the Internet,* (Washington, DC: Pew Internet and American Life Project, December 28, 2005).

63. Amernic, Craig, and Tourish, "The Transformational Leader as Pedagogue, Physician, Architect, Commander, and Saint: Five Root Metaphors in Jack Welch's Letters to Stockholders of General Electric."

64. This quotation is varied slightly from the original translations by: E. Carter, *All the Works of Epictetus, Which Are Now Extant,* 3rd ed., 2 vols., vol. 2 (London: J. and F. Rivington, 1768), 333; T. W. Higginson, *The Works of Epictetus* (Boston: Little, Brown, and Company, 1866), 428.

65. The three components of listening discussed here are based on several recent studies in the field of marketing, including: S. B. Castleberry, C. D. Shepherd, and R. Ridnour, "Effective Interpersonal Listening in the Personal Selling Environment: Conceptualization, Measurement, and Nomological Validity," *Journal of Marketing Theory and Practice* 7 (Winter 1999): 30–38; L. B. Comer and T. Drollinger, "Active Empathetic Listening and Selling Success: A Conceptual Framework," *Journal of Personal Selling & Sales Management* 19 (Winter 1999): 15–29; K. de Ruyter and M. G. M. Wetzels, "The Impact of Perceived Listening Behavior in Voice-to-Voice Service Encounters," *Journal of Service Research* 2 (February 2000): 276–84.

66. "The Shrinking Cubicle," *Chicago Tribune,* February 9, 2011; K. Shevory, "Office Work Space Is Shrinking, but That's Not All Bad," *New York Times,* January 19, 2011, 8.

67. A. Leaman and B. Bordass, "Productivity in Buildings: The Killer Variables," *Building Research & Information* 27, no. 1 (1999): 4–19; T. J. Allen, "Architecture and Communication among Product Development Engineers," *California Management Review* 49, no. 2 (Winter 2007): 23–41; F. Becker, "Organizational Ecology and Knowledge Networks," *California Management Review* 49, no. 2 (Winter 2007): 42–61

68. G. Evans and D. Johnson, "Stress and Open-Office Noise," *Journal of Applied Psychology* 85 (2000): 779–83; F. Russo, "My Kingdom for a Door," *Time Magazine,* October 23, 2000, B1.

69. D. Bracken, "Open Office Plans Make 'Mine' a Thing of the Past," *News & Observer* (Raleigh, NC), March 13, 2011.

70. D. Waisberg, "Quiet Please! . . . We're Working," *National Post,* May 30, 2007.

71. S. P. Means, "Playing at Pixar," *Salt Lake Tribune* (Utah), May 30, 2003, D1; G. Whipp, "Swimming against the Tide," *Daily News of Los Angeles,* May 30, 2003, U6.

72. Byron, "Carrying Too Heavy a Load?"; T. Hsieh, "How Twitter Can Make You a Better (and Happier) Person" (Las Vegas 2009), accessed March 17, 2011, http://blogs.zappos.com/blogs/ceo-and-coo-blog; J. Vijayan, "Staying on Message," *Computerworld,* October 19, 2009; "Social Media Training Programs: Different Approaches, Common Goals," *PR News,* January 4, 2010; A. Bryant, "On a Scale of 1 to 10, How Weird Are You?" *New York Times,* January 10, 2010; E. Ridgeway, "Zappos CEO on Getting Employees to 'Live the Brand'," *CNN,* March 23, 2011.

73. C. Wagner and A. Majchrzak, "Enabling Customer-Centricity Using Wikis and the Wiki Way," *Journal of Management Information Systems* 23, no. 3 (2006): 17–43; R. B. Ferguson, "Build a Web 2.0 Platform and Employees Will Use It," *eWeek,* June 20, 2007; C. Karena, "Working the Wiki Way," *Sydney Morning Herald,* March 6, 2007.

74. R. LaHood, "Dot Employees Give Department a Thumbs-Up," *Welcome to the Fastlane: the Official Blog of the U.S. Secretary of Transportation,* July 12, 2010, http://fastlane.dot.gov/2010/07/dot-employees-give-department-a-thumbsup.html.

75. T. Fenton, "Inside the Worldblu List: 1–800-Got-Junk?'s CEO on Why 'Being Democratic Is Extremely Important to Maintaining Our Competitive Advantage'" (Atlanta: WorldBlu, January 3, 2008). The original term is "management by *wandering* around," but this has been replaced with "walking around" over the years. See: W. Ouchi, *Theory Z* (New York: Avon Books, 1981), 176–77; T. Peters and R. Waterman, *In Search of Excellence* (New York: Harper and Row, 1982), 122.

76. J. B. Aloy and G. Leach, *The Communication Imperative: Dialoguing with Employees in Anxious Times,* (Toronto: Ipsos Reid, March 28, 2009).

77. R. Rousos, "Trust in Leaders Lacking at Utility," *The Ledger* (Lakeland, Fl), July 29, 2003, B1; B. Whitworth and B. Riccomini, "Management Communication: Unlocking Higher Employee Performance," *Communication World,* March/April 2005, 18–21.

78. K. Davis, "Management Communication and the Grapevine," *Harvard Business Review* 31 (September/October 1953): 43–49; W. L. Davis and J. R. O'Connor, "Serial Transmission of Information: A Study of the Grapevine," *Journal of Applied Communication Research* 5 (1977): 61–72.

79. H. Mintzberg, *The Structuring of Organizations* (Englewood Cliffs, NJ: Prentice Hall, 1979), 46–53; D. Krackhardt and J. R. Hanson, "Informal Networks: The Company Behind the Chart," *Harvard Business Review* 71 (July/August 1993): 104–11.

80. C. J. Walker and C. A. Beckerle, "The Effect of State Anxiety on Rumor Transmission," *Journal of Social Behaviour & Personality* 2 (August 1987): 353–60; R. L. Rosnow, "Inside Rumor: A Personal Journey," *American Psychologist* 46 (May 1991): 484–96; M. Noon and R. Delbridge, "News from behind My Hand: Gossip in Organizations," *Organization Studies* 14 (1993): 23–36.

81. N. Nicholson, "Evolutionary Psychology: Toward a New View of Human Nature and Organizational Society," *Human Relations* 50 (September 1997): 1053–78; R. F. Baumeister, L. Zhang, and K. D. Vohs, "Gossip as Cultural Learning," *Review of General Psychology* 8, no. 2 (2004): 111–21; E. K. Foster, "Research on Gossip: Taxonomy, Methods, and Future Directions," *Review of General Psychology* 8, no. 2 (2004): 78–99.

CHAPTER 9

1. D. A. Brown, *A Matter of Trust* (Ottawa: Government of Canada, June 15, 2007); N. Greenaway, "Ex-RCMP Boss Showed 'Lack of Leadership'," *Ottawa Citizen,* December 11, 2007; D. LeBlanc and C. Freeze, "Elliott Ousts Popular Deputy Commissioner in RCMP Regime Change," *Globe & Mail,* November 5, 2010, A9; T. MacCharles and R. J. Brennan, "Iconic Mountie Takes Aim at Bureaucrat Boss," *Toronto Star,* February 9, 2011.

2. J. R. P. French and B. Raven, "The Bases of Social Power," in *Studies in Social Power,* ed. D. Cartwright (Ann Arbor: University of Michigan Press, 1959), 150–67; A. D. Galinsky et al., "Power and Perspectives Not Taken," *Psychological Science* 17, no. 12 (2006): 1068–74. Also see: H. Mintzberg, *Power in and around Organizations* (Englewood Cliffs, NJ: Prentice Hall, 1983), Chap. 1; J. Pfeffer, *Managing with Power* (Boston: Harvard Business University Press, 1992), 17, 30; A. Guinote and T. K. Vescio, "Introduction: Power in Social Psychology," in

The Social Psychology of Power, ed. A. Guinote and T. K. Vescio (New York: Guilford Press, 2010), 1–18.

3. R. A. Dahl, "The Concept of Power," *Behavioral Science* 2 (1957): 201–18; R. M. Emerson, "Power-Dependence Relations," *American Sociological Review* 27 (1962): 31–41; A. M. Pettigrew, *The Politics of Organizational Decision-Making* (London: Tavistock, 1973).

4. G. A. Van Kleef et al., "Breaking the Rules to Rise to Power: How Norm Violators Gain Power in the Eyes of Others," *Social Psychological and Personality Science* 2, no. 5 (2011): 500–7.

5. J. Pfeffer and G. R. Salancik, *The External Control of Organizations* (New York: Harper & Row, 1978), 52–54; R. Gulati and M. Sytch, "Dependence Asymmetry and Joint Dependence in Interorganizational Relationships: Effects of Embeddedness on a Manufacturer's Performance in Procurement Relationships," *Administrative Science Quarterly* 52, no. 1 (2007): 32–69.

6. French and Raven, "The Bases of Social Power"; P. Podsakoff and C. Schreisheim, "Field Studies of French and Raven's Bases of Power: Critique, Analysis, and Suggestions for Future Research," *Psychological Bulletin* 97 (1985): 387–411; P. P. Carson and K. D. Carson, "Social Power Bases: A Meta-Analytic Examination of Interrelationships and Outcomes," *Journal of Applied Social Psychology* 23 (1993): 1150–69. The alternative models of power bases are reviewed in a recent dissertation by Heinemann, who points out that most of them parallel French and Raven's list. See: P. Heinemann, *Power Bases and Informational Influence Strategies: A Behavioral Study on the Use of Management Accounting Information* (Wiesbaden, DE: Deutscher Universitäts-Verlag, 2008). Raven subsequently proposed information power as a sixth source of power. We present this later as a derivation of the five sources of power rather than as a distinct sixth power base.

7. J. Renn, R. Schulmann, and S. Smith, *Albert Einstein/Mileva Maric-the Love Letters* (Princeton, NJ: Princeton University Press, 1992), xix.

8. C. Barnard, *The Function of the Executive* (Cambridge, MA: Harvard University Press, 1938), 167–70; C. Hardy and S. R. Clegg, "Some Dare Call It Power," in *Handbook of Organization Studies,* ed. S. R. Clegg, C. Hardy, and W. R. Nord (London: Sage, 1996), 622–41.

9. B. Crumley, "Game of Death: France's Shocking TV Experiment," *Time,* March 17, 2010; R. L. Parry, "Contestants Turn Torturers in French TV Experiment," *Yahoo! News,* March 16, 2010.

10. A. I. Shahin and P. L. Wright, "Leadership in the Context of Culture: An Egyptian Perspective," *Leadership & Organization Development Journal* 25, no. 5/6 (2004): 499–511; Y. J. Huo et al., "Leadership and the Management of Conflicts in Diverse Groups: Why Acknowledging versus Neglecting Subgroup Identity Matters," *European Journal of Social Psychology* 35, no. 2 (2005): 237–54.

11. B. H. Raven, "Kurt Lewin Address: Influence, Power, Religion, and the Mechanisms of Social Control," *Journal of Social Issues* 55 (Spring 1999): 161–86.

12. A. W. Gouldner, "The Norm of Reciprocity: A Preliminary Statement," *American Sociological Review* 25 (1960): 161–78.

13. G. Yukl and C. M. Falbe, "Importance of Different Power Sources in Downward and Lateral Relations," *Journal of Applied Psychology* 76 (1991): 416–23; Raven, "Kurt Lewin Address: Influence, Power, Religion, and the Mechanisms of Social Control."

14. P. L. Dawes, D. Y. Lee, and G. R. Dowling, "Information Control and Influence in Emergent Buying Centers," *Journal Of Marketing* 62, no. 3 (July 1998): 55–68; D. Willer, "Power-at-a-Distance," *Social Forces* 81, no. 4 (2003): 1295–1334; D. J. Brass et al., "Taking Stock of Networks and Organizations: A Multilevel Perspective," *Academy of Management Journal* 47, no. 6 (December 2004): 795–817.

15. L. S. Sya, "Flying to Greater Heights," *New Sunday Times* (Kuala Lumpur*),* July 31, 2005, 14; M. Bolch, "Rewarding the Team," *HRMagazine,* February 2007, 91–93.

16. J. M. Peiro and J. L. Melia, "Formal and Informal Interpersonal Power in Organisations: Testing a Bifactorial Model of Power in Role-Sets," *Applied Psychology* 52, no. 1 (2003): 14–35.

17. C. R. Hinings et al., "Structural Conditions of Intraorganizational Power," *Administrative Science Quarterly* 19 (1974): 22–44. Also see: C. S. Saunders, "The Strategic Contingency Theory of Power: Multiple Perspectives," *The Journal of Management Studies* 27 (1990): 1–21.

18. R. B. Cialdini and N. J. Goldstein, "Social Influence: Compliance and Conformity," *Annual Review of Psychology* 55 (2004): 591–621.

19. C. K. Hofling et al., "An Experimental Study in Nurse-Physician Relationships," *Journal of Nervous and Mental Disease* 143, no. 2 (1966): 171–77.

20. C. Perkel, "It's Not Csi," *Canadian Press,* November 10, 2007; "Dr. Charles Smith: The Man behind the Public Inquiry," *CBC News* (Toronto), August 10, 2010. Evidence-based management writers also warn against blindly following the advice of management gurus. See: J. Pfeffer and R. I. Sutton, *Hard Facts, Dangerous Half-Truths, and Total Nonsense* (Boston: Harvard Business School Press, 2006), 45–46.

21. K. Miyahara, "Charisma: From Weber to Contemporary Sociology," *Sociological Inquiry* 53, no. 4 (Fall 1983): 368–88; J. D. Kudisch and M. L. Poteet, "Expert Power, Referent Power, and Charisma: Toward the Resolution of a Theoretical Debate," *Journal of Business & Psychology* 10 (Winter 1995): 177–95; D. Ladkin, "The Enchantment of the Charismatic Leader: Charisma Reconsidered as Aesthetic Encounter," *Leadership* 2, no. 2 (May 2006): 165–79.

22. D. J. Hickson et al., "A Strategic Contingencies' Theory of Intraorganizational Power," *Administrative Science Quarterly* 16 (1971): 216–27; Hinings et al., "Structural Conditions of Intraorganizational Power"; R. M. Kanter, "Power Failure in Management Circuits," *Harvard Business Review* (July/August 1979): 65–75.

23. A. Bryant, "The Right Job? It's Much Like the Right Spouse," *New York Times,* May 22, 2011, 2. The "DNA" acronym is from: M. D. Johnson, *Brand Me. Make Your Mark: Turn Passion into Profit* (Blacklick, OH: Ambassador Press, 2008).

24. Hickson et al., "A Strategic Contingencies' Theory of Intraorganizational Power"; J. D. Hackman, "Power and Centrality in the Allocation of Resources in Colleges and Universities," *Administrative Science Quarterly* 30 (1985): 61–77; D. J. Brass and M. E. Burkhardt, "Potential Power and Power Use: An Investigation of Structure and Behavior," *Academy of Management Journal* 36 (1993): 441–70.

25. S. D. Harrington and B. Ivry, "For Commuters, a Day to Adapt," *The Record* (Bergen, N.J.), December 21, 2005, A1; S. McCarthy, "Transit Strike Cripples New York," *Globe & Mail (Toronto),* December 21, 2005, A17.

26. M. Kennett, "Remote Control," *Management Today,* March 1, 2011, 46.

27. R. Madell, "Ground Floor," *Pharmaceutical Executive* (Women in Pharma Supplement), June 2000, 24–31.

28. Kanter, "Power Failure in Management Circuits"; B. E. Ashforth, "The Experience of Powerlessness in Organizations," *Organizational Behavior and Human Decision Processes* 43 (1989): 207–42; L. Holden, "European Managers: HRM and an Evolving Role," *European Business Review* 12 (2000).

29. D. C. Hambrick and E. Abrahamson, "Assessing Managerial Discretion across Industries: A Multimethod Approach," *Academy of Management journal* 38, no. 5 (1995): 1427–41; M. A. Carpenter and B. R. Golden, "Perceived Managerial Discretion: A Study of Cause and Effect," *Strategic Management Journal* 18, no. 3 (1997): 187–206.

30. S. Wasserman and K. Faust, *Social Network Analysis: Methods and Applications, Structural Analysis in the Social Sciences* (Cambridge, UK: Cambridge University Press, 1994), Chap. 1; Brass et al., "Taking Stock of Networks and Organizations: A Multilevel Perspective."

31. M. Grossetti, "Where Do Social Relations Come From? A Study of Personal Networks in the Toulouse Area of France," *Social Networks* 27, no. 4 (2005): 289–300.

32. Y. Fan, "Questioning Guanxi: Definition, Classification, and Implications," *International Business Review* 11 (2002): 543–61; W. R. Vanhonacker, "When Good Guanxi Turns Bad," *Harvard Business Review* 82, no. 4 (April 2004): 18–19; R. J. Taormina and J. H. Gao, "A Research Model for Guanxi Behavior: Antecedents, Measures, and Outcomes of Chinese Social Networking," *Social Science Research* 39, no. 6 (November 2010): 1195–1212.

33. D. Krackhardt and J. R. Hanson, "Informal Networks: The Company behind the Chart," *Harvard Business Review* 71 (July/August 1993): 104–11; A. Portes, "Social Capital: Its Origins and Applications in Modern Society," *Annual Review of Sociology* 24 (1998): 1–24.

34. P. S. Adler and S. W. Kwon, "Social Capital: Prospects for a New Concept," *Academy of Management Review* 27, no. 1 (2002): 17–40.

35. R. F. Chisholm, *Developing Network Organizations: Learning from Practice and Theory* (Reading, MA: Addison Wesley Longman, 1998); W. S. Chow and L. S. Chan, "Social Network, Social Trust and Shared Goals in Organizational Knowledge Sharing," *Information & Management* 45, no. 7 (2008): 458–65.

36. R. S. Burt, *Structural Holes: The Social Structure of Competition* (Cambridge, MA: Harvard University Press, 1992).

37. M. T. Rivera, S. B. Soderstrom, and B. IUzzi, "Dynamics of Dyads in Social Networks: Assortative, Relational, and Proximity Mechanisms," *Annual Review of Sociology* 36 (2010): 91–115.

38. "It Still Comes Down to Who You Know," Hudson, New York, news release, February 21, 2007; "Monstercollege Survey Shows Grads Are Optimistic, but Expect a Long Haul," *Marketing Weekly News,* May 8, 2010.

39. R. Cross and R. J. Thomas, *Driving Results through Social Networks: How Top Organizations Leverage Networks for Performance and Growth* (San Francisco: Jossey-Bass, 2009); R. McDermott and D. Archibald, "Harnessing Your Staff's Informal Networks," *Harvard Business Review* 88, no. 3 (2010): 82–89.

40. M. Kilduff and D. Krackhardt, *Interpersonal Networks in Organizations: Cognition, Personality, Dynamics, and Culture* (New York: Cambridge University Press, 2008).

41. S. Humphries, "Companies Warm Up to Social Networks," *Christian Science Monitor,* September 8, 2008, 13.

42. Y. Amichai-Hamburger, G. Wainapel, and S. Fox, "'On the Internet No One Knows I'm an Introvert': Extroversion, Neuroticism, and Internet Interaction," *CyberPsychology & Behavior* 5, no. 2 (2002): 125–28; K. Brooks, "Networking 101 for Introverts," *Psychology Today* (October 31, 2010); D. Zack, *Networking for People Who Hate Networking* (San Francisco: Berret-Koehler, 2010).

43. N. B. Ellison, C. Steinfield, and C. Lampe, "The Benefits of Facebook 'Friends': Social Capital and College Students' Use of Online Social Network Sites," *Journal of Computer-Mediated Communication* 12, no. 4 (2007): 1143–68.

44. M. S. Granovetter, "The Strength of Weak Ties," *American Journal of Sociology* 78 (1973): 1360–80; B. Erickson, "Social Networks," in *The Blackwell Companion to Sociology,* ed. J. R. Blau (Malden, MA: Blackwell Publishing, 2004), 314–26.

45. B. Uzzi and S. Dunlap, "How to Build Your Network," *Harvard Business Review* 83, no. 12 (2005): 53–60.

46. S. C. de Janasz and M. L. Forret, "Learning the Art of Networking: A Critical Skill for Enhancing Social Capital and Career Success," *Journal of Management Education* 32, no. 5 (October 2008): 629–50.

47. A. Mehra, M. Kilduff, and D. J. Brass, "The Social Networks of High and Low Self-Monitors: Implications for Workplace Performance," *Administrative Science Quarterly* 46 (March 2001): 121–46.

48. Burt, *Structural Holes: The Social Structure of Competition.*

49. B. R. Ragins and E. Sundstrom, "Gender and Power in Organizations: A Longitudinal Perspective," *Psychological Bulletin* 105 (1989): 51–88; M. Linehan, "Barriers to Women's Participation in International Management," *European Business Review* 13 (2001).

50. A. DeFelice, "Climbing to the Top," *Accounting Technology* 24, no. 1 (2008): 12–18.

51. D. M. McCracken, "Winning the Talent War for Women: Sometimes It Takes a Revolution," *Harvard Business Review* (November/December 2000): 159–67.

52. J. Lammers, J. I. Stoker, and D. A. Stapel, "Differentiating Social and Personal Power: Opposite Effects on Stereotyping, but Parallel Effects on Behavioral Approach Tendencies," *Psychological Science* 20, no. 12 (2009): 1543–49.

53. D. Keltner, D. H. Gruenfeld, and C. Anderson, "Power, Approach, and Inhibition," *Psychological Review* 110, no. 2 (2003): 265–84; B. Simpson and C. Borch, "Does Power Affect Perception in Social Networks? Two Arguments and an Experimental Test," *Social Psychology Quarterly* 68, no. 3 (2005): 278–87; Galinsky et al., "Power and Perspectives Not Taken."

54. K. Atuahene-Gima and H. Li, "Marketing's Influence Tactics in New Product Development: A Study of High Technology Firms in China," *Journal of Product Innovation Management* 17 (2000): 451–70; A. Somech and A. Drach-Zahavy, "Relative Power and Influence Strategy: The Effects of Agent/Target Organizational Power on Superiors' Choices of Influence Strategies," *Journal of Organizational Behavior* 23 (2002): 167–79.

55. D. Kipnis, S. M. Schmidt, and I. Wilkinson, "Intraorganizational Influence Tactics: Explorations in Getting One's Way," *Journal of Applied Psychology* 65 (1980): 440–52; A. Rao and

K. Hashimoto, "Universal and Culturally Specific Aspects of Managerial Influence: A Study of Japanese Managers," *Leadership Quarterly* 8 (1997): 295–312; L. A. McFarland, A. M. Ryan, and S. D. Kriska, "Field Study Investigation of Applicant Use of Influence Tactics in a Selection Interview," *Journal of Psychology* 136 (July 2002): 383–98.

56. C. De Gaulle, *The Edge of the Sword (Le Fil De L'epée),* trans. G. Hopkins (London: Faber, 1960), 59.

57. Cialdini and Goldstein, "Social Influence: Compliance and Conformity."

58. Rao and Hashimoto, "Universal and Culturally Specific Aspects of Managerial Influence." Silent authority as an influence tactic in non-Western cultures is also discussed in: S. F. Pasa, "Leadership Influence in a High Power Distance and Collectivist Culture," *Leadership & Organization Development Journal* 21 (2000): 414–26.

59. J. Crichton, *Between Sandra Mccullough and Otago Sheetmetal and Engineering Limited,* CA 153/08 (Dunedin, NZ: Employment Relations Authority Christchurch, October 14, 2008).

60. "Be Part of the Team If You Want to Catch the Eye," *Birmingham Post* (UK), August 31, 2000, 14; S. Maitlis, "Taking It from the Top: How CEOs Influence (and Fail to Influence) Their Boards," *Organization Studies* 25, no. 8 (2004): 1275–1311.

61. J. J. Gabarro and J. P. Kotter, "Managing Your Boss," *Harvard Business Review* 58, no. 1 (1980): 92–100; Gabarro and Kotter, "Managing Your Boss"; P. Lencioni, "How to Manage Your Boss," *Wall Street Journal,* January 3, 2009; J. Baldoni, *Lead Your Boss: The Subtle Art of Managing Up* (New York: AMACOM, 2010); J. Espinoza, "Culture Change Is the Final Frontier," *Wall Street Journal,* February 23, 2010; B. Tulgan, *It's Okay to Manage Your Boss* (San Francisco: Jossey-Bass, 2010); R. C. Matuson, *Suddenly in Charge: Managing up, Managing down, Succeeding All Around* (Boston: Nicholas Brealey, 2011).

62. A. T. Cobb, "Toward the Study of Organizational Coalitions: Participant Concerns and Activities in a Simulated Organizational Setting," *Human Relations* 44 (1991): 1057–79; E. A. Mannix, "Organizations as Resource Dilemmas: The Effects of Power Balance on Coalition Formation in Small Groups," *Organizational Behavior and Human Decision Processes* 55 (1993): 1–22; D. J. Terry, M. A. Hogg, and K. M. White, "The Theory of Planned Behavior: Self-Identity, Social Identity and Group Norms," *British Journal of Social Psychology* 38 (September 1999): 225–44.

63. "One-in-Four Workers Have Felt Bullied in the Workplace, Careerbuilder Study Finds," PR Newswire news release for CareerBuilder, April 20, 2011; "Monster Global Poll Reveals Workplace Bullying Is Endemic," *OnRec: Online Recruitment Magazine,* June 10, 2011; "UK's Bully Bosses," *Daily Mirror* (London), January 9, 2012, 2; E. Weinbren, "Pharmacists Facing Employer Intimidation," *Chemist & Druggist,* May 19, 2012, 12.

64. A. P. Brief, *Attitudes in and around Organizations* (Thousand Oaks, CA: Sage, 1998), 69–84; D. J. O'Keefe, *Persuasion: Theory and Research* (Thousand Oaks, CA: Sage, 2002).

65. These and other features of message content in persuasion are detailed in: R. Petty and J. Cacioppo, *Attitudes and Persuasion: Classic and Contemporary Approaches* (Dubuque, IA: W. C. Brown, 1981); M. Pfau, E. A. Szabo, and J. Anderson, "The Role and Impact of Affect in the Process of Resistance to Persuasion," *Human Communication Research* 27 (April 2001): 216–52; O'Keefe, *Persuasion: Theory and Research,* Chap. 9; R. Buck et al., "Emotion and Reason in Persuasion: Applying the Ari Model and the Casc Scale," *Journal of Business Research* 57, no. 6 (2004): 647–56; W. D. Crano and R. Prislin, "Attitudes and Persuasion," *Annual Review of Psychology* 57 (2006): 345–74.

66. N. Rhodes and W. Wood, "Self-Esteem and Intelligence Affect Influenceability: The Mediating Role of Message Reception," *Psychological Bulletin* 111, no. 1 (1992): 156–71.

67. D. Strutton and L. E. Pelton, "Effects of Ingratiation on Lateral Relationship Quality within Sales Team Settings," *Journal of Business Research* 43 (1998): 1–12; R. Vonk, "Self-Serving Interpretations of Flattery: Why Ingratiation Works," *Journal of Personality and Social Psychology* 82 (2002): 515–26.

68. C. A. Higgins, T. A. Judge, and G. R. Ferris, "Influence Tactics and Work Outcomes: A Meta-Analysis," *Journal of Organizational Behavior* 24 (2003): 90–106.

69. D. Strutton, L. E. Pelton, and J. Tanner, J. F., "Shall We Gather in the Garden: The Effect of Ingratiatory Behaviors on Buyer Trust in Salespeople," *Industrial Marketing Management* 25 (1996): 151–62; J. O' Neil, "An Investigation of the Sources of Influence of Corporate Public Relations Practitioners," *Public Relations Review* 29 (June 2003): 159–69.

70. M. C. Bolino and W. H. Tunley, "More Than One Way to Make an Impression: Exploring Profiles of Impression Management," *Journal of Management* 29 (2003): 141–60.

71. T. Peters, "The Brand Called You," *Fast Company,* August 1997, http://www.fastcompany.com/magazine/10/brandyou.html; J. Sills, "Becoming Your Own Brand," *Psychology Today* 41, no. 1 (February 2008): 62–63.

72. J. S. Wilson, "Personal Branding in Today's Economy," *Atlanta Journa-Constitution,* May 29, 2011, D1

73. J. Foster, "Here Are Best Answers to Job Interview Questions," *The Herald* (Rock Hill, SC), April 4, 2010.

74. S. L. McShane, "Applicant Misrepresentations in Résumés and Interviews in Canada," *Labor Law Journal* (January 1994): 15–24; S. Romero and M. Richtel, "Second Chance," *New York Times,* 5 March 2001, C1; P. Sabatini, "Fibs on Résumés Commonplace," *Pittsburgh Post-Gazette,* February 24, 2006.

75. J. Laucius, "Internet Guru's Credentials a True Work of Fiction," *Ottawa Citizen,* June 12, 2001.

76. C. M. Falbe and G. Yukl, "Consequences for Managers of Using Single Influence Tactics and Combinations of Tactics," *Academy of Management Journal* 35 (1992): 638–52.

77. R. C. Ringer and R. W. Boss, "Hospital Professionals' Use of upward Influence Tactics," *Journal of Managerial Issues* 12 (2000): 92–108.

78. G. Blickle, "Do Work Values Predict the Use of Intraorganizational Influence Strategies?," *Journal of Applied Social Psychology* 30, no. 1 (January 2000): 196–205; P. P. Fu et al., "The Impact of Societal Cultural Values and Individual Social Beliefs on the Perceived Effectiveness of Managerial Influence Strategies: A Meso Approach," *Journal Of International Business Studies* 35, no. 4 (July 2004): 284–305.

79. "The 2008 Wasting Time at Work Survey Reveals a Record Number of People Waste Time at Work," Salary.com news release, 2008; "When It Comes to Red Tape, Many Canadian Employers Might Just Need to Cut It: RBC Study," CNW news release for RBC, January 23, 2008; "Survey: More than One-Quarter of Employees Have Had Ideas Stolen at Work," PR Newswire news release for OfficeTeam, October 8, 2009;

"Survey: Majority of Employees Have Had Ideas Stolen at Work," Canada NewsWire news release for OfficeTeam, November 10, 2009; J. Gifford et al., *The Management Agenda 2009,* (Horsham, UK: Roffey Park Institute, January 13, 2009).

80. This has become the generally agreed definition of organizational politics over the past two decades. See: G. R. Ferris and K. M. Kacmar, "Perceptions of Organizational Politics," *Journal of Management* 18 (1992): 93–116; R. Cropanzano et al., "The Relationship of Organizational Politics and Support to Work Behaviors, Attitudes, and Stress," *Journal of Organizational Behavior* 18 (1997): 159–80; E. Vigoda, "Stress-Related Aftermaths to Workplace Politics: The Relationships among Politics, Job Distress, and Aggressive Behavior in Organizations," *Journal of Organizational Behavior* 23 (2002): 571–91. However, organizational politics was previously viewed as influence tactics outside the formal role that could be either selfish or altruistic. This older definition is less common now, possibly because it is incongruent with popular views of politics and because its meaning is too ambiguous. For the older perspective of organizational politics, see: J. Pfeffer, *Power in Organizations* (Boston: Pitman, 1981); Mintzberg, *Power in and around Organizations.*

81. K. M. Kacmar and R. A. Baron, "Organizational Politics: The State of the Field, Links to Related Processes, and an Agenda for Future Research," in *Research in Personnel and Human Resources Management,* ed. G. R. Ferris (Greenwich, CT: JAI Press, 1999), 1–39; Vigoda, "Stress-Related Aftermaths to Workplace Politics"; C.-H. Chang, C. C. Rosen, and P. E. Levy, "The Relationship between Perceptions of Organizational Politics and Employee Attitudes, Strain, and Behavior: A Meta-Analytic Examination," *Academy of Management Journal* 52, no. 4 (2009): 779–801.

82. This famous quotation is attributed to both Niccolò Machiavelli and Sun-Tzu. None of Machiavelli's five main books (translated) has any statement close to this quotation. Sun-Tzu's Art of War book (translated) does not have this quotation, either, but he makes a similar statement about spies: "Hence it is that with none in the whole army are more intimate relations to be maintained than with spies." See: Sun-Tzu, *The Art of War,* trans. L. Giles (Mineola, NY: Dover, 2002), 98.

83. C. Hardy, *Strategies for Retrenchment and Turnaround: The Politics of Survival* (Berlin, DE: Walter de Gruyter, 1990), Chap. 14; G. R. Ferris et al., "Perceptions of Organizational Politics: Prediction, Stress-Related Implications, and Outcomes," *Human Relations* 49 (1996): 233–63; M. C. Andrews and K. M. Kacmar, "Discriminating among Organizational Politics, Justice, and Support," *Journal of Organizational Behavior* 22 (2001): 347–66.

84. S. Blazejewski and W. Dorow, "Managing Organizational Politics for Radical Change: The Case of Beiersdorf-Lechia S.A., Poznan," *Journal of World Business* 38 (August 2003): 204–23.

85. L. W. Porter, R. W. Allen, and H. L. Angle, "The Politics of Upward Influence in Organizations," *Research in Organizational Behavior* 3 (1981): 120–22; R. J. House, "Power and Personality in Complex Organizations," *Research in Organizational Behavior* 10 (1988): 305–57.

86. R. Christie and F. Geis, *Studies in Machiavellianism* (New York: Academic Press, 1970); S. M. Farmer et al., "Putting Upward Influence Strategies in Context," *Journal of Organizational Behavior* 18 (1997): 17–42; K. S. Sauleya and A. G. Bedeian, "Equity Sensitivity: Construction of a Measure and Examination of Its Psychometric Properties," *Journal of Management* 26 (September 2000): 885–910.

CHAPTER 10

1. D. Senor and S. Singer, *Start-Up Nation: The Story of Israel's Economic Miracle* (New York: Hachette Book Group, 2009).

2. D. Tjosvold, *Working Together to Get Things Done* (Lexington, MA: Lexington, 1986), 114–15; J. A. Wall and R. R. Callister, "Conflict and Its Management," *Journal of Management,* 21 (1995): 515–58; D. Tjosvold, "Defining Conflict and Making Choices about Its Management," *International Journal of Conflict Management* 17, no. 2 (2006): 87–95; M. A. Rahim, *Managing Conflict in Organizations,* 4th ed. (New Brunswick, NJ: Transaction Publishers, 2011), 15–17.

3. For example, see: L. Urwick, *The Elements of Administration,* 2d ed. (London: Pitman, 1947); C. Argyris, "The Individual and Organization: Some Problems of Mutual Adjustment," *Administrative Science Quarterly* 2, no. 1 (1957): 1–24; K. E. Boulding, "Organization and Conflict," *Conflict Resolution* 1, no. 2 (June 1957): 122–34; R. R. Blake, H. A. Shepard, and J. S. Mouton, *Managing Intergroup Conflict in Industry* (Houston: Gulf Publishing, 1964).

4. Rahim, *Managing Conflict in Organizations.*

5. *Workplace Conflict and How Businesses Can Harness It to Thrive,* CPP Global Human Capital Report (Mountain View, CA: CPP, Inc, July 2008).

6. J. Dewey, *Human Nature and Conduct: An Introduction to Social Psychology* (New York: Holt, 1922), 300.

7. C. K. W. De Dreu and L. R. Weingart, "A Contingency Theory of Task Conflict and Performance in Groups and Organizational Teams," in *International Handbook of Organizational Teamwork and Cooperative Working,* ed. M. A. West, D. Tjosvold, and K. G. Smith (Chicester, UK: John Wiley & Sons, 2003), 151–66; K. A. Jehn and C. Bendersky, "Intragroup Conflict in Organizations: A Contingency Perspective on the Conflict-Outcome Relationship," *Research In Organizational Behavior* 25 (2003): 187–242.

8. *Workplace Conflict and How Businesses Can Harness It to Thrive.*

9. Rahim, *Managing Conflict in Organizations,* 6–7.

10. M. P. Follett, "Constructive Conflict," in *Dynamic Administration: The Collected Papers of Mary Parker Follett,* ed. H. C. Metcalf and L. Urwick (Bath, UK: Management Publications Trust, 1941), 30–49.

11. M. A. Rahim, "Toward a Theory of Managing Organizational Conflict," *International Journal of Conflict Management* 13, no. 3 (2002): 206–35; M. Duarte and G. Davies, "Testing the Conflict-Performance Assumption in Business-to-Business Relationships," *Industrial Marketing Management* 32 (2003): 91–99. Although the 1970s marked a point when the benefits conflict became widely acknowledged, this view was expressed earlier by some writers. See: L. A. Coser, *The Functions of Social Conflict* (New York: Free Press, 1956); J. A. Litterer, "Conflict in Organization: A Re-Examination," *Academy of Management Journal* 9 (1966): 178–86; H. Assael, "Constructive Role of Interorganizational Conflict," *Administrative Science Quarterly* 14, no. 4 (1969): 573–82.

12. P. J. Carnevale, "Creativity in the Outcomes of Conflict," in *The Handbook of Conflict Resolution: Theory and Practice,* ed. M. Deutsch, P. T. Coleman, and E. C. Marcus, 2d ed. (San Francisco: Jossey-Bass, 2006), 414–35.

13. K. M. Eisenhardt, J. L. Kahwajy, and L. J. Bourgeois III, "How Management Teams Can Have a Good Fight," *Harvard Business Review* (July/August 1997): 77–85; K. M. Eisenhardt, J. L.

Kahwajy, and L. J. Bourgeois III, "Conflict and Strategic Choice: How Top Management Teams Disagree," *California Management Review* 39 (Winter 1997): 42–62; T. Greitemeyer et al., "Information Sampling and Group Decision Making: The Effects of an Advocacy Decision Procedure and Task Experience," *Journal of Experimental Psychology-Applied* 12, no. 1 (March 2006): 31–42; U. Klocke, "How to Improve Decision Making in Small Groups: Effects of Dissent and Training Interventions," *Small Group Research* 38, no. 3 (June 2007): 437–68.

14. H. Guetzkow and J. Gyr, "An Analysis of Conflict in Decision-Making Groups," *Human Relations* 7, no. 3 (Aug. 1954): 367–82; L. H. Pelled, K. M. Eisenhardt, and K. R. Xin, "Exploring the Black Box: An Analysis of Work Group Diversity, Conflict, and Performance," *Administrative Science Quarterly* 44 (March 1999): 1–28; Jehn and Bendersky, "Intragroup Conflict in Organizations." The notion of two types of conflict dates back to Georg Simmel, who described two types of conflict: one with a personal and subjective goal, the other which has an impersonal and objective quality. See: Coser, *The Functions of Social Conflict,* 112. Contemporary scholars use various labels for constructive and relationship conflict. We have avoided the "cognitive" and "affective" conflict labels because cognitions and emotions are interconnected processes in all human activity.

15. C. K. W. De Dreu, "When Too Little or Too Much Hurts: Evidence for a Curvilinear Relationship between Task Conflict and Innovation in Teams," *Journal of Management* 32, no. 1 (February 2006): 83–107.

16. R. S. Lau and A. T. Cobb, "Understanding the Connections between Relationship Conflict and Performance: The Intervening Roles of Trust and Exchange," *Journal of Organizational Behavior* 31, no. 6 (2010): 898–917.

17. C. K. W. De Dreu and L. R. Weingart, "Task versus Relationship Conflict, Team Performance, and Team Member Satisfaction: A Meta-Analysis," *Journal of Applied Psychology* 88 (August 2003): 587–604; A. C. Mooney, P. J. Holahan, and A. C. Amason, "Don't Take It Personally: Exploring Cognitive Conflict as a Mediator of Affective Conflict," *Journal of Management Studies* 44, no. 5 (2007): 733–58.

18. J. Yang and K. W. Mossholder, "Decoupling Task and Relationship Conflict: The Role of Intergroup Emotional Processing," *Journal of Organizational Behavior* 25 (2004): 589–605.

19. A. C. Amason and H. J. Sapienza, "The Effects of Top Management Team Size and Interaction Norms on Cognitive and Affective Conflict," *Journal of Management* 23, no. 4 (1997): 495–516.

20. L. Pondy, "Organizational Conflict: Concepts and Models," *Administrative Science Quarterly* 2 (1967): 296–320; K. W. Thomas, "Conflict and Negotiation Processes in Organizations," in *Handbook of Industrial and Organizational Psychology,* ed. M. D. Dunnette and L. M. Hough, 2nd ed. (Palo Alto, CA: Consulting Psychologists Press, 1992), 651–718.

21. H. Barki and J. Hartwick, "Conceptualizing the Construct of Interpersonal Conflict," *International Journal of Conflict Management* 15, no. 3 (2004): 216–44.

22. M. A. Von Glinow, D. L. Shapiro, and J. M. Brett, "Can We Talk, and Should We? Managing Emotional Conflict in Multicultural Teams," *Academy of Management Review* 29, no. 4 (2004): 578–92.

23. G. E. Martin and T. J. Bergman, "The Dynamics of Behavioral Response to Conflict in the Workplace," *Journal of Occupational & Organizational Psychology* 69 (December 1996): 377–87; J. M. Brett, D. L. Shapiro, and A. L. Lytle, "Breaking the Bonds

of Reciprocity in Negotiations," *Academy of Management Journal* 41 (August 1998): 410–24.

24. Although this quotation is widely attributed to Thomas Jefferson, scholars suggest that the third U.S. president and a founding father of the nation did not make this statement. However, Jefferson did write that young people should bring about change. According to one source, the popular quotation is a derivation of Jefferson's statement in a letter to Colonel William S. Smith on November 13, 1787: "God forbid we should ever be 20 years without such a rebellion," in T. Jefferson, *Memoir, Correspondence, and Miscellanies, from the Papers of Thomas Jefferson,* 2d ed. (Boston: Gray and Bowen, 1830), 267. See: http://wiki.monticello.org.

25. R. E. Walton and J. M. Dutton, "The Management of Conflict: A Model and Review," *Administrative Science Quarterly* 14 (1969): 73–84; S. M. Schmidt and T. A. Kochan, "Conflict: Toward Conceptual Clarity," *Administrative Science Quarterly* 17, no. 3 (September 1972): 359–70.

26. J. A. McMullin, T. Duerden Comeau, and E. Jovic, "Generational Affinities and Discourses of Difference: A Case Study of Highly Skilled Information Technology Workers," *British Journal of Sociology* 58, no. 2 (2007): 297–316.

27. Data are from the 2009 Kelly Global Workforce Index, based on information published in news releases in each country by Kelly Services in September 2009.

28. R. Wageman and G. Baker, "Incentives and Cooperation: The Joint Effects of Task and Reward Interdependence on Group Performance," *Journal of Organizational Behavior* 18, no. 2 (1997): 139–58; G. S. van der Vegt, B. J. M. Emans, and E. van der Vliert, "Patterns of Interdependence in Work Teams: A Two-Level Investigation of the Relations with Job and Team Satisfaction," *Personnel Psychology* 54, no. 1 (2001): 51–69.

29. P. C. Earley and G. B. Northcraft, "Goal Setting, Resource Interdependence, and Conflict Management," in *Managing Conflict: An Interdisciplinary Approach,* ed. M. A. Rahim (New York: Praeger, 1989), 161–70; K. Jehn, "A Multimethod Examination of the Benefits and Detriments of Intragroup Conflict," *Administrative Science Quarterly* 40 (1995): 245–82.

30. A. Risberg, "Employee Experiences of Acquisition Processes," *Journal of World Business* 36 (March 2001): 58–84.

31. Jehn and Bendersky, "Intragroup Conflict in Organizations."

32. M. Hewstone, M. Rubin, and H. Willis, "Intergroup Bias," *Annual Review of Psychology* 53 (2002): 575–604; J. Jetten, R. Spears, and T. Postmes, "Intergroup Distinctiveness and Differentiation: A Meta-Analytic Integration," *Journal of Personality and Social Psychology* 86, no. 6 (2004): 862–79.

33. E. Knowles, *Little Oxford Dictionary of Proverbs* (Oxford, UK: Oxford University Press, 2009), 21.

34. Follett, "Constructive Conflict"; Blake, Shepard, and Mouton, *Managing Intergroup Conflict in Industry;* T. Ruble and K. Thomas, "Support for a Two-Dimensional Model of Conflict Behavior," *Organizaiotnal Behavior and Human Performance* 16 (1976): 143–55; C. K. W. De Dreu et al., "A Theory-Based Measure of Conflict Management Strategies in the Workplace," *Journal of Organizational Behavior* 22 (2001): 645–68; Rahim, "Toward a Theory of Managing Organizational Conflict."

35. Jehn, "A Multimethod Examination of the Benefits and Detriments of Intragroup Conflict."

36. A. Bryant, "We're Family, So We Can Disagree," *New York Times,* February 21, 2010, 1.

37. D. W. Johnson et al., "Effects of Cooperative, Competitive, and Individualistic Goal Structures on Achievement: A Meta-Analysis,"

Psychological Bulletin 89 (1981): 47–62; Rahim, "Toward a Theory of Managing Organizational Conflict"; G. A. Callanan, C. D. Benzing, and D. F. Perri, "Choice of Conflict-Handling Strategy: A Matter of Context," *Journal of Psychology* 140, no. 3 (2006): 269–88.

38. R. A. Friedman et al., "What Goes around Comes around: The Impact of Personal Conflict Style on Work Conflict and Stress," *International Journal of Conflict Management* 11, no. 1 (2000): 32–55; X. M. Song, J. Xile, and B. Dyer, "Antecedents and Consequences of Marketing Managers' Conflict-Handling Behaviors," *Journal of Marketing* 64 (January 2000): 50–66; M. Song, B. Dyer, and R. J. Thieme, "Conflict Management and Innovation Performance: An Integrated Contingency Perspective," *Academy of Marketing Science* 34, no. 3 (2006): 341–56; L. A. DeChurch, K. L. Hamilton, and C. Haas, "Effects of Conflict Management Strategies on Perceptions of Intragroup Conflict," *Group Dynamics* 11, no. 1 (2007): 66–78.

39. G. A. Chung-Yan and C. Moeller, "The Psychosocial Costs of Conflict Management Styles," *International Journal of Conflict Management* 21, no. 4 (2010): 382–99.

40. C. K. W. De Dreu and A. E. M. Van Vianen, "Managing Relationship Conflict and the Effectiveness of Organizational Teams," *Journal of Organizational Behavior* 22 (2001): 309–28; R. J. Lewicki et al., *Negotiation,* 4th ed. (New York: McGraw-Hill/Irwin, 2003), 35–36.

41. J. Simms, "Blood in the Boardroom," *Director* 2009, 48.

42. *Workplace Conflict and How Businesses Can Harness It to Thrive.*

43. M. W. Morris and H.-Y. Fu, "How Does Culture Influence Conflict Resolution? Dynamic Constructivist Analysis," *Social Cognition* 19 (June 2001): 324–49; C. H. Tinsley, "How Negotiators Get to Yes: Predicting the Constellation of Strategies Used across Cultures to Negotiate Conflict," *Journal of Applied Psychology* 86, no. 4 (2001): 583–93; J. L. Holt and C. J. DeVore, "Culture, Gender, Organizational Role, and Styles of Conflict Resolution: A Meta-Analysis," *International Journal of Intercultural Relations* 29, no. 2 (2005): 165–96.

44. D. A. Cai and E. L. Fink, "Conflict Style Differences between Individualists and Collectivists," *Communication Monographs* 69 (March 2002): 67–87; C. H. Tinsley and E. Weldon, "Responses to a Normative Conflict among American and Chinese Managers," *International Journal of Conflict Management* 3, no. 2 (2003): 183–94; F. P. Brew and D. R. Cairns, "Styles of Managing Interpersonal Workplace Conflict in Relation to Status and Face Concern: A Study with Anglos and Chinese," *International Journal of Conflict Management* 15, no. 1 (2004): 27–57.

45. Holt and DeVore, "Culture, Gender, Organizational Role, and Styles of Conflict Resolution"; M. Davis, S. Capobianco, and L. Kraus, "Gender Differences in Responding to Conflict in the Workplace: Evidence from a Large Sample of Working Adults," *Sex Roles* 63, no. 7 (2010): 500–14.

46. K. Lewin, *Resolving Social Conflicts* (New York: Harper, 1948).

47. J. D. Hunger and L. W. Stern, "An Assessment of the Functionality of the Superordinate Goal in Reducing Conflict," *Academy of Management Journal* 19, no. 4 (1976): 591–605; M. Sherif, "Superordinate Goals in the Reduction of Intergroup Conflict," *The American Journal of Sociology* 63, no. 4 (1958): 349–56.

48. Sherif, "Superordinate Goals in the Reduction of Intergroup Conflict"; Eisenhardt, Kahwajy, and Bourgeois III, "How Management Teams Can Have a Good Fight"; Song, Xile, and Dyer, "Antecedents and Consequences of Marketing Managers'

Conflict-Handling Behaviors"; O. Doucet, J. Poitras, and D. Chenevert, "The Impacts of Leadership on Workplace Conflicts," *International Journal of Conflict Management* 20, no. 4 (2009): 340–54.

49. Lau and Cobb, "Understanding the Connections between Relationship Conflict and Performance: The Intervening Roles of Trust and Exchange."

50. H. C. Triandis, "The Future of Workforce Diversity in International Organisations: A Commentary," *Applied Psychology: An International Journal* 52, no. 3 (2003): 486–95.

51. "Can the New CEO End a Culture Clash after a Merger?," *Financial Times,* September 10, 2008, 16.

52. T. F. Pettigrew, "Intergroup Contact Theory," *Annual Review of Psychology* 49 (1998): 65–85; S. Brickson, "The Impact of Identity Orientation on Individual and Organizational Outcomes in Demographically Diverse Settings," *Academy of Management Review* 25 (January 2000): 82–101; J. Dixon and K. Durrheim, "Contact and the Ecology of Racial Division: Some Varieties of Informal Segregation," *British Journal of Social Psychology* 42 (March 2003): 1–23.

53. Variations of this action plan are described in several sources, including: A. Jay, P. Smith, and H. Barlcay, *From "No" to "Yes": The Constructive Route to Agreement* (London: Video Arts, 1988); D. Stone, B. Patton, and S. Heen, *Difficult Conversations: How to Discuss What Matters Most* (New York: Penguin, 1999); K. Patterson et al., *Crucial Conversations: Tools for Talking Whem Stakes Are High* (New York: McGraw-Hill, 2002).

54. Triandis, "The Future of Workforce Diversity in International Organisations."

55. Von Glinow, Shapiro, and Brett, "Can We Talk, and Should We?"

56. D. Nebenzahl, "Managing the Generation Gap," *Montreal Gazette,* February 28, 2009, G1; D. Deveau, "L'oréAl Canada Discovers the Beauty of Motivation," *Postmedia News* (Toronto), January 24, 2011.

57. E. Horwitt, "Knowledge, Knowledge, Who's Got the Knowledge," *Computerworld* (April 8 1996): 80, 81, 84.

58. L. L. Putnam, "Beyond Third Party Role: Disputes and Managerial Intervention," *Employee Responsibilities and Rights Journal* 7 (1994): 23–36; A. R. Elangovan, "The Manager as the Third Party: Deciding How to Intervene in Employee Disputes," in *Negotiation: Readings, Exercises, and Cases,* ed. R. J. Lewicki, J. A. Litterer, and D. Saunders, 3d ed. (New York: McGraw-Hill, 1999), 458–69. For a somewhat different taxonomy of managerial conflict intervention, see: P. G. Irving and J. P. Meyer, "A Multidimensional Scaling Analysis of Managerial Third-Party Conflict Intervention Strategies," *Canadian Journal Of Behavioural Science* 29, no. 1 (January 1997): 7–18. A recent review describes 10 species of third-party intervention, but these consist of variations of the three types described here. See: D. E. Conlon et al., "Third Party Interventions across Cultures: No 'One Best Choice,'" in *Research in Personnel and Human Resources Management* 26 (2007), 309–49.

59. B. H. Sheppard, "Managers as Inquisitors: Lessons from the Law," in *Bargaining inside Organizations,* ed. M. H. Bazerman and R. J. Lewicki (Beverly Hills, CA: Sage, 1983); N. H. Kim, D. W. Sohn, and J. A. Wall, "Korean Leaders' (and Subordinates') Conflict Management," *International Journal Of Conflict Management* 10, no. 2 (April 1999): 130–53; D. J. Moberg, "Managers as Judges in Employee Disputes: An Occasion for Moral Imagination," *Business Ethics Quarterly* 13, no. 4 (2003): 453–77.

60. R. Karambayya and J. M. Brett, "Managers Handling Disputes: Third Party Roles and Perceptions of Fairness," *Academy of Management Journal* 32 (1989): 687–704; R. Cropanzano et al., "Disputant Reactions to Managerial Conflict Resolution Tactics," *Group & Organization Management* 24 (June 1999): 124–53.

61. A. R. Elangovan, "Managerial Intervention in Organizational Disputes: Testing a Prescriptive Model of Strategy Selection," *International Journal of Conflict Management* 4 (1998): 301–35; P. S. Nugent, "Managing Conflict: Third-Party Interventions for Managers," *Academy Of Management Executive* 16, no. 1 (February 2002): 139–54.

62. J. P. Meyer, J. M. Gemmell, and P. G. Irving, "Evaluating the Management of Interpersonal Conflict in Organizations: A Factor-Analytic Study of Outcome Criteria," *Canadian Journal of Administrative Sciences* 14 (1997): 1–13; L. B. Bingham, "Employment Dispute Resolution: The Case for Mediation," *Conflict Resolution Quarterly* 22, no. 1–2 (2004): 145–74; M. Hyde et al., "Workplace Conflict Resolution and the Health of Employees in the Swedish and Finnish Units of an Industrial Company," *Social Science & Medicine* 63, no. 8 (2006): 2218–27.

63. W. H. Ross and D. E. Conlon, "Hybrid Forms of Third-Party Dispute Resolution: Theoretical Implications of Combining Mediation and Arbitration," *Academy of Management Review* 25, no. 2 (2000): 416–27; W. H. Ross, C. Brantmeier, and T. Ciriacks, "The Impact of Hybrid Dispute-Resolution Procedures on Constituent Fairness Judgments," *Journal of Applied Social Psychology* 32, no. 6 (June 2002): 1151–88.

64. R. Stagner and H. Rosen, *Psychology of Union—Management Relations* (Belmont, CA: Wadsworth, 1965), 95–96, 108–10; R. E. Walton and R. B. McKersie, *A Behavioral Theory of Labor Negotiations: An Analysis of a Social Interaction System* (New York: McGraw-Hill, 1965), 41–46; L. Thompson, *The Mind and Heart of the Negotiator* (Upper Saddle River, NJ: Prentice-Hall, 1998), Chap. 2.

65. K. G. Allred, "Distinguishing Best and Strategic Practices: A Framework for Managing the Dilemma between Creating and Claiming Value," *Negotiation Journal* 16 (2000): 287–397.

66. S. Doctoroff, "Reengineering Negotiations," *Sloan Management Review* 39 (March 1998): 63–71; D. C. Zetik and A. F. Stuhlmacher, "Goal Setting and Negotiation Performance: A Meta-Analysis," *Group Processes & Intergroup Relations* 5 (January 2002): 35–52.

67. B. McRae, *The Seven Strategies of Master Negotiators* (Toronto: McGraw-Hill Ryerson, 2002), 7–11.

68. A. F. Stuhlmacher, T. L. Gillespie, and M. V. Champagne, "The Impact of Time Pressure in Negotiation: A Meta-Analysis," *International Journal of Conflict Management* 9, no. 2 (April 1998): 97–116; C. K. W. De Dreu, "Time Pressure and Closing of the Mind in Negotiation," *Organizational Behavior and Human Decision Processes* 91 (July 2003): 280–95. However, one recent study reported that speeding up these concessions leads to better negotiated outcomes. See: D. A. Moore, "Myopic Prediction, Self-Destructive Secrecy, and the Unexpected Benefits of Revealing Final Deadlines in Negotiation," *Organizational Behavior and Human Decision Processes* 94, no. 2 (2004): 125–39.

69. R. J. Robertson, "Defusing the Exploding Offer: The Farpoint Gambit," *Negotiation Journal* 11, no. 3 (1995): 277–85.

70. A. Tversky and D. Kahneman, "Judgment under Uncertainty: Heuristics and Biases," *Science* 185, no. 4157 (September 27, 1974): 1124–31; J. D. Jasper and S. D. Christman, "A Neuropsychological Dimension for Anchoring Effects," *Journal of Behavioral Decision Making* 18 (2005): 343–69.

71. Lewicki et al., *Negotiation,* 90–96; S. Kwon and L. R. Weingart, "Unilateral Concessions from the Other Party: Concession Behavior, Attributions, and Negotiation Judgments," *Journal of Applied Psychology* 89, no. 2 (2004): 263–78.

72. D. Malhotra, "The Fine Art of Making Concessions," *Negotiation* (January 2006): 3–5.

73. J. Z. Rubin and B. R. Brown, *The Social Psychology of Bargaining and Negotiation* (New York: Academic Press, 1976), Chap. 9.

74. For a critical view of the problem solving style in negotiation, see: J. M. Brett, "Managing Organizational Conflict," *Professional Psychology: Research and Practice* 15 (1984): 664–78.

75. L. L. Thompson, "Information Exchange in Negotiation," *Journal of Experimental Social Psychology* 27 (1991): 161–79.

76. S. R. Covey, *The 7 Habits of Highly Effective People* (New York: Free Press, 1989), 235–60.

77. Lewicki et al., *Negotiation,* 95; M. Olekalns and P. L. Smith, "Testing the Relationships among Negotiators' Motivational Orientations, Strategy Choices, and Outcomes," *Journal of Experimental Social Psychology* 39, no. 2 (March 2003): 101–17.

78. M. Olekalns and P. L. Smith, "Moments in Time: Metacognition, Trust, and Outcomes in Dyadic Negotiations," *Personality and Social Psychology Bulletin* 31, no. 12 (December 2005): 1696–1707.

79. D. W. Choi, "Shared Metacognition in Integrative Negotiation," *International Journal of Conflict Management* 21, no. 3 (2010): 309–33.

80. J. M. Brett et al., "Sticks and Stones: Language, Face, and Online Dispute Resolution," *Academy of Management Journal* 50, no. 1 (February 2007): 85–99; D. Druckman and M. Olekalns, "Emotions in Negotiation," *Group Decision and Negotiation* 17, no. 1 (2008): 1–11; D. Pietroni et al., "Emotions as Strategic Information: Effects of Other's Emotional Expressions on Fixed-Pie Perception, Demands, and Integrative Behavior in Negotiation," *Journal of Experimental Social Psychology* 44, no. 6 (2008): 1444–54; M. J. Boland and W. H. Ross, "Emotional Intelligence and Dispute Mediation in Escalating and De-Escalating Situations," *Journal of Applied Social Psychology* 40, no. 12 (2010): 3059–3105.

81. P. J. Carnevale and A. M. Isen, "The Influence of Positive Affect and Visual Access on the Discovery of Integrative Solutions in Bilateral Negotiation," *Organizational Behavior and Human Decision Processes* 37 (1986): 1–13; Thompson, *The Mind and Heart of the Negotiator.*

82. J. W. Salacuse and J. Z. Rubin, "Your Place or Mine? Site Location and Negotiation," *Negotiation Journal* 6 (January 1990): 5–10; J. Mayfield et al., "How Location Impacts International Business Negotiations," *Review of Business* 19 (December 1998): 21–24.

83. J. Margo, "The Persuaders," *Boss Magazine,* December 29, 2000, 38. For a full discussion of the advantages and disadvantages of face-to-face and alternative negotiations situations, see: M. H. Bazerman et al., "Negotiation," *Annual Review of Psychology* 51 (2000): 279–314.

84. Lewicki et al., *Negotiation,* 298–322.

CHAPTER 11

1. Most of these statistics were collected in July 2012. Library of Congress data were collected in 2010.

2. Many of these perspectives are summarized in R. N. Kanungo, "Leadership in Organizations: Looking Ahead to the 21st Century," *Canadian Psychology* 39 (Spring 1998): 71–82; G. A. Yukl, *Leadership in Organizations,* 7th ed. (Upper Saddle River, NJ: Pearson Education, 2010).

3. R. House, M. Javidan, and P. Dorfman, "Project GLOBE: An Introduction," *Applied Psychology: An International Review* 50 (2001): 489–505; R. House et al., "Understanding Cultures and Implicit Leadership Theories across the Globe: An Introduction to Project GLOBE," *Journal of World Business* 37 (2002): 3–10.

4. J. E. Garten, *The Mind of the C.E.O.* (New York: Perseus Press, 2001).

5. S. Marchionne, "Fiat's Extreme Makeover," *Harvard Business Review* (December 2008): 45–48.

6. "Powered by Frontline People," *Employee Engagement Today,* September 2007; C. Hosford, "Flying High," *Incentive* 181, no. 12 (December 2007): 14–20.

7. J. A. Raelin, "We the Leaders: In Order to Form a Leaderful Organization," *Journal of Leadership & Organizational Studies* 12, no. 2 (2005): 18–30; C. L. Pearce, J. A. Conger, and E. A. Locke, "Shared Leadership Theory," *Leadership Quarterly* 19, no. 5 (2008): 622–28; E. Engel Small and J. R. Rentsch, "Shared Leadership in Teams: A Matter of Distribution," *Journal of Personnel Psychology* 9, no. 4 (2010): 203–11.

8. J. A. Raelin, *Creating Leaderful Organizations: How to Bring out Leadership in Everyone* (San Francisco: Berret-Koehler, 2003).

9. J. W. Gardner, *On Leadership* (New York: Free Press, 1990), 138–55.

10. C. A. Beatty, "Implementing Advanced Manufacturing Technologies: Rules of the Road," *Sloan Management Review* (Summer 1992): 49–60; J. M. Howell, "The Right Stuff: Identifying and Developing Effective Champions of Innovation," *The Academy of Management Executive* 19, no. 2 (2005): 108–19; J. M. Howell and C. M. Shea, "Effects of Champion Behavior, Team Potency, and External Communication Activities on Predicting Team Performance," *Group & Organization Management* 31, no. 2 (April 2006): 180–211.

11. The history of the trait perspective of leadership, as well as current research on this topic, is nicely summarized in S. J. Zaccaro, C. Kemp, and P. Bader, "Leader Traits and Attributes," in *The Nature of Leadership,* ed. J. Antonakis, A. T. Cianciolo, and R. J. Sternberg (Thousand Oaks, CA: Sage, 2004), 101–24.

12. R. M. Stogdill, *Handbook of Leadership* (New York: The Free Press, 1974), Chap. 5.

13. J. Intagliata, D. Ulrich, and N. Smallwood, "Leveraging Leadership Competencies to Produce Leadership Brand: Creating Distinctiveness by Focusing on Strategy and Results," *Human Resources Planning* 23, no. 4 (2000): 12–23; J. A. Conger and D. A. Ready, "Rethinking Leadership Competencies," *Leader to Leader* (Spring 2004): 41–47; Zaccaro, Kemp, and Bader, "Leader Traits and Attributes." For a recent discussion on leadership traits and evolutionary psychology, see: T. A. Judge, R. F. Piccolo, and T. Kosalka, "The Bright and Dark Sides of Leader Traits: A Review and Theoretical Extension of the Leader Trait Paradigm," *Leadership Quarterly* 20 (2009): 855–75.

14. This list is based on S. A. Kirkpatrick and E. A. Locke, "Leadership: Do Traits Matter?," *Academy of Management Executive* 5 (May 1991): 48–60; R. M. Aditya, R. J. House, and S. Kerr, "Theory and Practice of Leadership: Into the New Millennium," in *Industrial and Organizational Psychology: Linking Theory with Practice,* ed. C. L. Cooper and E. A. Locke (Oxford, UK: Blackwell, 2000), 130–65; D. Goleman, R. Boyatzis, and A. McKee, *Primal Leaders* (Boston: Harvard Business School Press, 2002); T. A. Judge et al., "Personality and Leadership: A Qualitative and Quantitative Review," *Journal Of Applied Psychology* 87, no. 4 (August 2002): 765–80; T. A. Judge, A. E. Colbert, and R. Ilies, "Intelligence and Leadership: A Quantitative Review and Test of Theoretical Propositions," *Journal Of Applied Psychology* 89, no. 3 (June 2004): 542–52; Zaccaro, Kemp, and Bader, "Leader Traits and Attributes."

15. M. Popper et al., "The Capacity to Lead: Major Psychological Differences between Leaders and Nonleaders," *Military Psychology* 16, no. 4 (2004): 245–63; R. G. Lord and R. J. Hall, "Identity, Deep Structure and the Development of Leadership Skill," *Leadership Quarterly* 16, no. 4 (August 2005): 591–615; D. V. Day, M. M. Harrison, and S. M. Halpin, *An Integrative Approach to Leader Development: Connecting Adult Development, Identity, and Expertise* (New York: Routledge, 2009); D. S. DeRue and S. J. Ashford, "Who Will Lead and Who Will Follow? A Social Process of Leadership Identity Construction in Organizations," *Academy of Management Review* 35, no. 4 (2010): 627–47.

16. The large-scale studies are reported in C. Savoye, "Workers Say Honesty Is Best Company Policy," *Christian Science Monitor,* June 15, 2000; J. M. Kouzes and B. Z. Posner, *The Leadership Challenge,* 3d ed. (San Francisco: Jossey-Bass, 2002), Chap. 2; J. Schettler, "Leadership in Corporate America," *Training & Development,* September 2002, 66–73.

17. BlessingWhite, *The State of Employee Engagement 2008: Asia Pacific Overview,* (Princeton, NJ: BlessingWhite, March 3, 2008).

18. R. Davidovitz et al., "Leaders as Attachment Figures: Leaders' Attachment Orientations Predict Leadership-Related Mental Representations and Followers' Performance and Mental Health," *Journal of Personality and Social Psychology* 93, no. 4 (2007): 632–50.

19. J. B. Miner, "Twenty Years of Research on Role Motivation Theory of Managerial Effectiveness," *Personnel Psychology* 31 (1978): 739–60; R. J. House and R. N. Aditya, "The Social Scientific Study of Leadership: Quo Vadis?," *Journal of Management* 23 (1997): 409–73.

20. J. Hedlund et al., "Identifying and Assessing Tacit Knowledge: Understanding the Practical Intelligence of Military Leaders," *Leadership Quarterly* 14, no. 2 (2003): 117–40; R. J. Sternberg, "A Systems Model of Leadership: WICS," *American Psychologist* 62, no. 1 (2007): 34–42.

21. J. George, "Emotions and Leadership: The Role of Emotional Intelligence," *Human Relations* 53 (August 2000): 1027–55; Goleman, Boyatzis, and McKee, *Primal Leaders;* Lord and Hall, "Identity, Deep Structure and the Development of Leadership Skill"; C. Skinner and P. Spurgeon, "Valuing Empathy and Emotional Intelligence in Health Leadership: A Study of Empathy, Leadership Behaviour and Outcome Effectiveness," *Health Services Management Research* 18, no. 1 (February 2005): 1–12.

22. B. George, *Authentic Leadership* (San Francisco: Jossey-Bass, 2004); W. L. Gardner et al., "'Can You See the Real Me?' A Self-Based Model of Authentic Leader and Follower

Development," *Leadership Quarterly* 16 (2005): 343–72; B. George, *True North* (San Francisco: Jossey-Bass, 2007), Chap. 4; M. E. Palanski and F. J. Yammarino, "Integrity and Leadership: Clearing the Conceptual Confusion," *European Management Journal* 25, no. 3 (2007): 171–84; F. O. Walumbwa et al., "Authentic Leadership: Development and Validation of a Theory-Based Measure," *Journal of Management* 34, no. 1 (February 2008): 89–126.

23. G. Kohlrieser, "Herna Verhagen, Managing Director Tnt Group HR: "Live Your Dream; Success Is Built on Passion," *States News Service,* April 13, 2010.

24. R. Jacobs, "Using Human Resource Functions to Enhance Emotional Intelligence," in *The Emotionally Intelligent Workplace,* ed. C. Cherniss and D. Goleman (San Francisco: Jossey-Bass, 2001), 161–63; Conger and Ready, "Rethinking Leadership Competencies."

25. R. G. Lord and D. J. Brown, *Leadership Processes and Self-Identity: A Follower-Centered Approach to Leadership* (Mahwah, NJ: Lawrence Erlbaum Associates, 2004); R. Bolden and J. Gosling, "Leadership Competencies: Time to Change the Tune?," *Leadership* 2, no. 2 (May 2006): 147–63.

26. V. Garrow and E. Stirling, *The Management Agenda 2007: Overview of Findings* (West Sussex, UK: Roffey Park, 2007); S. Stern, "Lofty View from Davos Could Just Be a Mirage," *Finaicial Times,* January 28, 2008, 14; "Over Half of Employees Say Their Managers Are Ineffective," i4cp news release, May 11, 2009; B. Watt, "Fuel for the Leadership Fire," *Recruitment Extra,* October 2011, 34.

27. E. A. Fleishman, "The Description of Supervisory Behavior," *Journal of Applied Psychology* 37, no. 1 (1953): 1–6. For discussion on methodological problems with the development of these people versus task-oriented leadership constructs, see: C. A. Schriesheim, R. J. House, and S. Kerr, "Leader Initiating Structure: A Reconciliation of Discrepant Research Results and Some Empirical Tests," *Organizational Behavior and Human Performance* 15, no. 2 (1976): 297–321; L. Tracy, "Consideration and Initiating Structure: Are They Basic Dimensions of Leader Behavior?," *Social Behavior and Personality* 15, no. 1 (1987): 21–33.

28. A. K. Korman, "Consideration, Initiating Structure, and Organizational Criteria—a Review," *Personnel Psychology* 19 (1966): 349–62; E. A. Fleishman, "Twenty Years of Consideration and Structure," in *Current Developments in the Study of Leadership,* ed. F. A. Fleishman and J. C. Hunt (Carbondale: Southern Illinois University Press, 1973), 1–40; T. A. Judge, R. F. Piccolo, and R. Ilies, "The Forgotten Ones?: The Validity of Consideration and Initiating Structure in Leadership Research," *Journal of Applied Psychology* 89, no. 1 (2004): 36–51; Yukl, *Leadership in Organizations,* pp. 62–75; D. S. Derue et al., "Trait and Behavioral Theories of Leadership: An Integration and Meta-Analytic Test of Their Relative Validity," *Personnel Psychology* 64, no. 1 (2011): 7–52.

29. V. V. Baba, "Serendipity in Leadership: Initiating Structure and Consideration in the Classroom," *Human Relations* 42 (1989): 509–25.

30. B. A. Scott et al., "A Daily Investigation of the Role of Manager Empathy on Employee Well-Being," *Organizational Behavior and Human Decision Processes* 113, no. 2 (2010): 127–40.

31. S. Kerr et al., "Towards a Contingency Theory of Leadership Based upon the Consideration and Initiating Structure Literature," *Organizational Behavior and Human Performance* 12 (1974): 62–82; L. L. Larson, J. G. Hunt, and R. N. Osbom, "The Great Hi—Hi Leader Behavior Myth: A Lesson from Occam's Razor," *Academy of Management Journal* 19 (1976): 628–41.

32. R. K. Greenleaf, *Servant Leadership: A Journey into the Nature of Lergitimate Power & Greatness* (Mahwah, NJ: Paulist Press, 1977; 2002); D. van Dierendonck and K. Patterson, "Servant Leadership: An Introduction," in *Servant Leadership: Developments in Theory and Research,* ed. D. van Dierendonck and K. Patterson (Houndmills, UK: Palgrave Macmillan, 2010), 3–11.

33. Greenleaf, *Servant Leadership,* 27.

34. J. E. Barbuto Jr. and D. W. Wheeler, "Scale Development and Construct Clarification of Servant Leadership," *Group & Organization Management* 31, no. 3 (June 2006): 300–26; R. C. Liden et al., "Servant Leadership: Development of a Multidimensional Measure and Multi-Level Assessment," *Leadership Quarterly* 19, no. 2 (2008): 161–77; S. Sendjaya, J. C. Sarros, and J. C. Santora, "Defining and Measuring Servant Leadership Behaviour in Organizations," *Journal of Management Studies* 45, no. 2 (2008): 402–24; K.-Y. Ng and C. S.-K. Koh, "Motivation to Serve: Understanding the Heart of the Servant-Leader and Servant Leadership Behaviours," in *Servant Leadership: Developments in Theory and Research,* ed. D. van Dierendonck and K. Patterson (Houndmills UK: Palgrave Macmillan, 2010), 90–104.

35. R. Tannenbaum and W. H. Schmidt, "How to Choose a Leadership Pattern," *Harvard Business Review* (May/June 1973): 162–80.

36. R. P. Vecchio, J. E. Justin, and C. L. Pearce, "The Utility of Transactional and Transformational Leadership for Predicting Performance and Satisfaction within a Path–Goal Theory Framework," *Journal of Occupational and Organizational Psychology* 81 (2008): 71–82.

37. For a thorough study of how expectancy theory of motivation relates to leadership, see R. G. Isaac, W. J. Zerbe, and D. C. Pitt, "Leadership and Motivation: The Effective Application of Expectancy Theory," *Journal of Managerial Issues* 13 (Summer 2001): 212–26.

38. R. J. House, "A Path-Goal Theory of Leader Effectiveness," *Administrative Science Quarterly* 16 (1971): 321–38; M. G. Evans, "Extensions of a Path-Goal Theory of Motivation," *Journal of Applied Psychology* 59 (1974): 172–78; R. J. House and T. R. Mitchell, "Path-Goal Theory of Leadership," *Journal of Contemporary Business* (Autumn 1974): 81–97; M. G. Evans, "Path Goal Theory of Leadership," in *Leadership,* ed. L. L. Neider and C. A. Schriesheim (Greenwich, CT: Information Age Publishing, 2002), 115–38.

39. R. J. House, "Path-Goal Theory of Leadership: Lessons, Legacy, and a Reformulated Theory," *Leadership Quarterly* 7 (1996): 323–52.

40. J. Indvik, "Path–Goal Theory of Leadership: A Meta-Analysis," *Academy of Management Proceedings* (1986): 189–92; J. C. Wofford and L. Z. Liska, "Path-Goal Theories of Leadership: A Meta-Analysis," *Journal of Management* 19 (1993): 857–76.

41. J. D. Houghton and S. K. Yoho, "Toward a Contingency Model of Leadership and Psychological Empowerment: When Should Self-Leadership Be Encouraged?," *Journal of Leadership & Organizational Studies* 11, no. 4 (2005): 65–83.

42. "Driving the Engine," *Broadcasting & Cable* 133, no. 16 (April 21, 2003): 6A; S. Pappu, "The Queen of Tween," *Atlantic Monthly,* November 2004, 118–25; A. Becker, "The Wonderful World of Sweeney," *Broadcasting & Cable,* February 25, 2008, 19; J. R. Littlejohn, "Distinguished Vanguard Award for Leadership," *Multichannel News,* May 19, 2008.

43. R. T. Keller, "A Test of the Path-Goal Theory of Leadership with Need for Clarity as a Moderator in Research and Development Organizations," *Journal of Applied Psychology* 74 (1989): 208–12.

44. C. A. Schriesheim and L. L. Neider, "Path-Goal Leadership Theory: The Long and Winding Road," *Leadership Quarterly* 7 (1996): 317–21.

45. Current information about situational leadership is from the company's Web site: http://www.situational.com. The 1997 figure is reported in: K. Blanchard and B. Nelson, "Recognition and Reward," *Executive Excellence,* April 1997, 15.

46. P. Hersey and K. H. Blanchard, *Management of Organizational Behavior: Utilizing Human Resources,* 5th ed. (Englewood Cliffs, NJ: Prentice Hall, 1988).

47. R. P. Vecchio, "Situational Leadership Theory: An Examination of a Prescriptive Theory," *Journal of Applied Psychology* 72 (1987): 444–51; W. Blank, J. R. Weitzel, and S. G. Green, "A Test of the Situational Leadership Theory," *Personnel Psychology* 43 (1990): 579–97; C. L. Graeff, "Evolution of Situational Leadership Theory: A Critical Review," *Leadership Quarterly* 8 (1997): 153–70; G. Thompson and R. P. Vecchio, "Situational Leadership Theory: A Test of Three Versions," *Leadership Quarterly* 20, no. 5 (2009): 837–48.

48. F. E. Fiedler, *A Theory of Leadership Effectiveness* (New York: McGraw-Hill, 1967); F. E. Fiedler and M. M. Chemers, *Leadership and Effective Management* (Glenview, IL.: Scott, Foresman, 1974).

49. F. E. Fiedler, "Engineer the Job to Fit the Manager," *Harvard Business Review* 43, no. 5 (1965): 115–22.

50. For a summary of criticisms, see Yukl, *Leadership in Organizations,* 217–18.

51. Judge, Piccolo, and Ilies, "The Forgotten Ones?" Judge, Piccolo, and Kosalka, "The Bright and Dark Sides of Leader Traits."

52. N. Nicholson, *Executive Instinct* (New York: Crown, 2000).

53. This observation has also been made by C. A. Schriesheim, "Substitutes-for-Leadership Theory: Development and Basic Concepts," *Leadership Quarterly* 8 (1997): 103–08.

54. D. F. Elloy and A. Randolph, "The Effect of Superleader Behavior on Autonomous Work Groups in a Government Operated Railway Service," *Public Personnel Management* 26 (Summer 1997): 257–72; C. C. Manz and H. Sims Jr., *The New SuperLeadership: Leading Others to Lead Themselves* (San Francisco: Berrett-Koehler, 2001).

55. M. L. Loughry, "Coworkers Are Watching: Performance Implications of Peer Monitoring," *Academy of Management Proceedings* (2002): O1–06.

56. P. M. Podsakoff and S. B. MacKenzie, "Kerr and Jermier's Substitutes for Leadership Model: Background, Empirical Assessment, and Suggestions for Future Research," *Leadership Quarterly* 8 (1997): 117–32; S. D. Dionne et al., "Neutralizing Substitutes for Leadership Theory: Leadership Effects and Common-Source Bias," *Journal of Applied Psychology* 87, no. 3 (June 2002): 454–64; J. R. Villa et al., "Problems with Detecting Moderators in Leadership Research Using Moderated Multiple Regression," *Leadership Quarterly* 14, no. 1 (February 2003): 3–23; S. D. Dionne et al., "Substitutes for Leadership, or Not," *Leadership Quarterly* 16, no. 1 (2005): 169–93.

57. J. M. Burns, *Leadership* (New York: Harper & Row, 1978); B. J. Avolio and F. J. Yammarino, eds., *Transformational and Charismatic Leadership: The Road Ahead* (Greenwich, CT: JAI Press, 2002); B. M. Bass and R. E. Riggio, *Transformational Leadership,* 2d ed. (Mahwah, NJ: Lawrence Erlbaum Associates, 2006).

58. V. L. Goodwin, J. C. Wofford, and J. L. Whittington "A Theoretical and Empirical Extension to the Transformational Leadership Construct," *Journal of Organisational Behavior,* 22 (November 2001), 759–74.

59. Burns, *Leadership,* 19–20. Burns also describes transactional and "transforming leadership" in his more recent book, J. M. Burns, *Transforming Leadership* (New York: Grove Press, 2004). In both books, Burns describes both leadership concepts in complex and occasionally confounding ways.

60. For Burns's discussion on the ethics of transactional leadership, see: Burns, *Transforming Leadership,* 28. Regarding transactional leadership and appealing to needs, justice, and morality, see: Burns, *Leadership,* 258.

61. A. Zaleznik, "Managers and Leaders: Are They Different?," *Harvard Business Review* 55, no. 5 (1977): 67–78; Bennis and Nanus, *Leaders.* For a recent discussion regarding managing versus leading, see G. Yukl and R. Lepsinger, "Why Integrating the Leading and Managing Roles Is Essential for Organizational Effectiveness," *Organizational Dynamics* 34, no. 4 (2005): 361–75.

62. W. Bennis and B. Nanus, *Leaders: The Strategies for Taking Charge* (New York: Harper & Row, 1985), 20. Peter Drucker is also widely cited as the source of this quotation. The closest passage we could find, however, is in the first two pages of *The Effective Executive* (1966) where Drucker states that effective executives "get the right things done." On the next page, he states that manual workers only need efficiency, "that is, the ability to do things right rather than the ability to get the right things done." See: P. F. Drucker, *The Effective Executive* (New York: Harper Business, 1966), 1–2.

63. B. M. Bass et al., "Predicting Unit Performance by Assessing Transformational and Transactional Leadership," *Journal of Applied Psychology* 88 (April 2003): 207–18; Yukl and Lepsinger, "Why Integrating the Leading and Managing Roles Is Essential for Organizational Effectiveness."

64. For a discussion on the tendency to slide from transformational to transactional leadership, see W. Bennis, *An Invented Life: Reflections on Leadership and Change* (Reading, MA: Addison-Wesley, 1993).

65. R. J. House, "A 1976 Theory of Charismatic Leadership," in *Leadership: The Cutting Edge,* ed. J. G. Hunt and L. L. Larson (Carbondale: Southern Illinois University Press, 1977), 189–207; J. A. Conger, "Charismatic Leadership," in *The Sage Handbook of Leadership,* ed. A. Bryman et al. (London: Sage, 2011), 86–102.

66. J. E. Barbuto Jr., "Taking the Charisma out of Transformational Leadership," *Journal of Social Behavior & Personality* 12 (September 1997): 689–97; Y. A. Nur, "Charisma and Managerial Leadership: The Gift That Never Was," *Business Horizons* 41 (July 1998): 19–26; M. D. Mumford and J. R. Van Doorn, "The Leadership of Pragmatism—Reconsidering Franklin in the Age of Charisma," *Leadership Quarterly* 12, no. 3 (Fall 2001): 279–309; A. Fanelli, "Bringing Out Charisma: CEO Charisma and External Stakeholders," *The Academy of Management Review* 31, no. 4 (2006): 1049–61; M. J. Platow et al., "A Special Gift We Bestow on You for Being Representative of Us: Considering Leader Charisma from a Self-Categorization Perspective," *British Journal of Social Psychology* 45, no. 2 (2006): 303–20.

67. L. Greenfeld, "Reflections on Two Charismas," *British Journal of Sociology* 36, no. 1 (1985): 117–32.

68. B. Shamir et al., "Correlates of Charismatic Leader Behavior in Military Units: Subordinates' Attitudes, Unit Characteristics, and Superiors' Appraisals of Leader Performance," *Academy of Management Journal* 41, no. 4 (1998): 387–409; R. E. De Vries, R. A. Roe, and T. C. B. Taillieu, "On Charisma and Need for Leadership," *European Journal of Work and Organizational Psychology* 8 (1999): 109–33; R. Khurana, *Searching for a Corporate Savior: The Irrational Quest for Charismatic CEOs* (Princeton, NJ: Princeton University Press, 2002). The effect of charismatic leadership on follower dependence was also noted earlier by noted U.S. government leader John Gardner. See: Gardner, *On Leadership,* 34–36.

69. J. Lipman-Blumen, "A Pox on Charisma: Why Connective Leadership and Character Count," in *The Drucker Difference: What the World's Greatest Management Thinker Means to Today's Business Leaders,* ed. C. L. Pearce, J. A. Maciariello, and H. Yamawaki (New York: McGraw-Hill, 2010), 149–74.

70. N. Augustine, *Augustine's Laws,* 3d ed. (New York: Viking, 1986), 32.

71. Y. Berson et al., "The Relationship between Vision Strength, Leadership Style, and Context," *The Leadership Quarterly* 12, no. 1 (2001): 53–73. Strategic collective vision has been identified as a key factor in leadership since Chester Barnard's seminal book in organizational behavior. See: C. Barnard, *The Functions of the Executive* (Cambridge, MA: Harvard University Press, 1938), 86–89.

72. Bennis and Nanus, *Leaders,* 27–33, 89; I. M. Levin, "Vision Revisited," *Journal of Applied Behavioral Science* 36 (March 2000): 91–107; R. E. Quinn, *Building the Bridge as You Walk on It: A Guide for Leading Change* (San Francisco: Jossey-Bass, 2004), Chap. 11; J. M. Strange and M. D. Mumford, "The Origins of Vision: Effects of Reflection, Models, and Analysis," *Leadership Quarterly* 16, no. 1 (2005): 121–48; D. Ulrich and W. Ulrich, *The Why of Work: How Great Leaders Build Abundant Organizations That Win* (New York: McGraw-Hill, 2010), Chap. 1.

73. J. R. Baum, E. A. Locke, and S. A. Kirkpatrick, "A Longitudinal Study of the Relation of Vision and Vision Communication to Venture Growth in Entrepreneurial Firms," *Journal of Applied Psychology* 83 (1998): 43–54; S. L. Hoe and S. L. McShane, "Leadership Antecedents of Informal Knowledge Acquisition and Dissemination," *International Journal of Organisational Behaviour* 5 (2002): 282–91.

74. Data from Towers Perrin and Towers Watson global reports and news releases in selected years, such as: Towers Perrin, *Working Today: Understanding What Drives Employee Engagement* (Stamford, CT: 2003); "Senior Leaders Improve Their Communication with Employees, Towers Perrin Consortium Finds," Business Wire news release for Towers Perrin, September 7, 2005.

75. "Canadian CEOs Give Themselves Top Marks for Leadership!," *Canada NewsWire,* September 9, 1999; L. Manfield, "Creating a Safety Culture from Top to Bottom," *WorkSafe Magazine,* February 2005, 8–9.

76. J. A. Conger, "Inspiring Others: The Language of Leadership," *Academy of Management Executive* 5 (February 1991): 31–45; G. T. Fairhurst and R. A. Sarr, *The Art of Framing: Managing the Language of Leadership* (San Francisco, CA: Jossey-Bass, 1996); A. E. Rafferty and M. A. Griffin, "Dimensions of Transformational Leadership: Conceptual and Empirical Extensions," *Leadership Quarterly* 15, no. 3 (2004): 329–54; D. A. Waldman, P. A. Balthazard, and S. J. Peterson, "Leadership and Neuroscience: Can We Revolutionize the Way That Inspirational Leaders Are Identified and Developed?," *Academy of Mnagement Perspectives* 25, no. 1 (2011): 60–74.

77. D. E. Berlew, "Leadership and Organizational Excitement," *California Management Review* 17, no. 2 (Winter 1974): 21–30; Bennis and Nanus, *Leaders,* 43–55; T. Simons, "Behavioral Integrity: The Perceived Alignment between Managers' Words and Deeds as a Research Focus," *Organization Science* 13, no. 1 (Jan-Feb 2002): 18–35.

78. K. Tyler, "Evaluating Values," *HRMagazine,* April 2011, 57.

79. M. Webb, "Executive Profile: Peter C. Farrell," *San Diego Business Journal,* March 24, 2003, 32; P. Benesh, "He Likes Them Breathing Easy," *Investor's Business Daily,* September 13, 2005, A04. For a discussion of trust in leadership, see C. S. Burke et al., "Trust in Leadership: A Multi-Level Review and Integration," *Leadership Quarterly* 18, no. 6 (2007): 606–32. The survey on leading by example is reported in J. C. Maxwell, "People Do What People See," *BusinessWeek,* November 19, 2007, 32.

80. C. Hymowitz, "Today's Bosses Find Mentoring Isn't Worth the Time and Risks," *Wall Street Journal,* March 13, 2006, B1.

81. A. Mackey, "The Effect of CEOs on Firm Performance," *Strategic Management Journal* 29, no. 12 (2008): 1357–67.

82. J. Barling, T. Weber, and E. K. Kelloway, "Effects of Transformational Leadership Training on Attitudinal and Financial Outcomes: A Field Experiment," *Journal of Applied Psychology* 81 (1996): 827–32.

83. A. Bryman, "Leadership in Organizations," in *Handbook of Organization Studies,* ed. S. R. Clegg, C. Hardy, and W. R. Nord (Thousand Oaks, CA: Sage, 1996), 276–92.

84. B. S. Pawar and K. K. Eastman, "The Nature and Implications of Contextual Influences on Transformational Leadership: A Conceptual Examination," *Academy of Management Review* 22 (1997): 80–109; C. P. Egri and S. Herman, "Leadership in the North American Environmental Sector: Values, Leadership Styles, and Contexts of Environmental Leaders and Their Organizations," *Academy of Management Journal* 43, no. 4 (2000): 571–604.

85. J. R. Meindl, "On Leadership: An Alternative to the Conventional Wisdom," *Research in Organizational Behavior* 12 (1990): 159–203; L. R. Offermann, J. J. K. Kennedy, and P. W. Wirtz, "Implicit Leadership Theories: Content, Structure, and Generalizability," *Leadership Quarterly* 5, no. 1 (1994): 43–58; R. J. Hall and R. G. Lord, "Multi-Level Information Processing Explanations of Followers' Leadership Perceptions," *Leadership Quarterly* 6 (1995): 265–87; O. Epitropaki and R. Martin, "Implicit Leadership Theories in Applied Settings: Factor Structure, Generalizability, and Stability over Time," *Journal of Applied Psychology* 89, no. 2 (2004): 293–310. For a broader discussion of the social construction of leadership, see: G. T. Fairhurst and D. Grant, "The Social Construction of Leadership: A Sailing Guide," *Management Communication Quarterly* 24, no. 2 (May 2010): 171–210.

86. L. M. Fisher, "Ricardo Semler Won't Take Control," *strategy+business,* no. 41 (Winter 2005): 1–11.

87. R. G. Lord et al., "Contextual Constraints on Prototype Generation and Their Multilevel Consequences for Leadership Perceptions," *Leadership Quarterly* 12, no. 3 (2001): 311–38; K. A. Scott and D. J. Brown, "Female First, Leader Second? Gender Bias in the Encoding of Leadership Behavior," *Organizational Behavior and Human Decision Processes* 101 (2006): 230–42; S. J. Shondrick, J. E. Dinh, and R. G. Lord, "Developments in Implicit Leadership Theory and Cognitive Science: Applications to Improving Measurement and Understanding Alternatives to Hierarchical Leadership," *Leadership Quarterly* 21, no. 6 (2010): 959–78.

88. R. Ilies, M. W. Gerhardt, and H. Le, "Individual Differences in Leadership Emergence: Integrating Meta-Analytic Findings and Behavioral Genetics Estimates," *International Journal of Selection and Assessment* 12, no. 3 (September 2004): 207–19.

89. S. F. Cronshaw and R. G. Lord, "Effects of Categorization, Attribution, and Encoding Processes on Leadership Perceptions," *Journal of Applied Psychology* 72 (1987): 97–106; J. L. Nye and D. R. Forsyth, "The Effects of Prototype-Based Biases on Leadership Appraisals: A Test of Leadership Categorization Theory," *Small Group Research* 22 (1991): 360–79.

90. Meindl, "On Leadership: An Alternative to the Conventional Wisdom"; J. Felfe and L.-E. Petersen, "Romance of Leadership and Management Decision Making," *European Journal of Work and Organizational Psychology* 16, no. 1 (2007): 1–24; B. Schyns, J. R. Meindl, and M. A. Croon, "The Romance of Leadership Scale: Cross-Cultural Testing and Refinement," *Leadership* 3, no. 1 (February 2007): 29–46.

91. J. Pfeffer, "The Ambiguity of Leadership," *Academy of Management Review* 2 (1977): 102–12.

92. R. Weber et al., "The Illusion of Leadership: Misattribution of Cause in Coordination Games," *Organization Science* 12, no. 5 (2001): 582–98; N. Ensari and S. E. Murphy, "Cross-Cultural Variations in Leadership Perceptions and Attribution of Charisma to the Leader," *Organizational Behavior and Human Decision Processes* 92 (2003): 52–66; M. L. A. Hayward, V. P. Rindova, and T. G. Pollock, "Believing One's Own Press: The Causes and Consequences of CEO Celebrity," *Strategic Management Journal* 25, no. 7 (July 2004): 637–53.

93. Six of the Project GLOBE clusters are described in a special issue of the *Journal of World Business,* 37 (2000). For an overview of Project GLOBE, see House, Javidan, and Dorfman, "Project GLOBE: An Introduction"; House et al., "Understanding Cultures and Implicit Leadership Theories across the Globe: An Introduction to Project GLOBE."

94. J. C. Jesiuno, "Latin Europe Cluster: From South to North," *Journal of World Business* 37 (2002): 88. Another GLOBE study, of Iranian managers, also reported that "charismatic visionary" stands out as a primary leadership dimension. See A. Dastmalchian, M. Javidan, and K. Alam, "Effective Leadership and Culture in Iran: An Empirical Study," *Applied Psychology: An International Review* 50 (2001): 532–58.

95. D. N. Den Hartog et al., "Culture Specific and Cross-Cultural Generalizable Implicit Leadership Theories: Are Attributes of Charismatic/Transformational Leadership Universally Endorsed?," *Leadership Quarterly* 10 (1999): 219–56; F. C. Brodbeck et al., "Cultural Variation of Leadership Prototypes across 22 European Countries," *Journal of Occupational and Organizational Psychology* 73 (2000): 1–29; E. Szabo et al., "The Europe Cluster: Where Employees Have a Voice," *Journal of World Business* 37 (2002): 55–68. The Mexican study is reported in C. E. Nicholls, H. W. Lane, and M. B. Brechu, "Taking Self-Managed Teams to Mexico," *Academy of Management Executive* 13 (August 1999): 15–25.

96. G. N. Powell, "One More Time: Do Female and Male Managers Differ?," *Academy of Management Executive* 4 (1990): 68–75; M. L. van Engen and T. M. Willemsen, "Sex and Leadership Styles: A Meta-Analysis of Research Published in the 1990s," *Psychological Reports* 94, no. 1 (February 2004): 3–18.

97. R. Sharpe, "As Leaders, Women Rule," *BusinessWeek,* November 20, 2000, 74; M. Sappenfield, "Women, It Seems, Are Better Bosses," *Christian Science Monitor,* January 16, 2001; A. H. Eagly and L. L. Carli, "The Female Leadership Advantage: An Evaluation of the Evidence," *The Leadership Quarterly* 14, no. 6 (December 2003): 807–34; A. H. Eagly, M. C. Johannesen-Schmidt, and M. L. van Engen, "Transformational, Transactional, and Laissez-Faire Leadership Styles: A Meta-Analysis Comparing Women and Men," *Psychological Bulletin* 129 (July 2003): 569–91.

98. A. H. Eagly, S. J. Karau, and M. G. Makhijani, "Gender and the Effectiveness of Leaders: A Meta-Analysis," *Psychological Bulletin* 117 (1995): 125–45; J. G. Oakley, "Gender-Based Barriers to Senior Management Positions: Understanding the Scarcity of Female CEOs," *Journal of Business Ethics* 27 (2000): 821–34; N. Z. Stelter, "Gender Differences in Leadership: Current Social Issues and Future Organizational Implications," *Journal of Leadership Studies* 8 (2002): 88–99; M. E. Heilman et al., "Penalties for Success: Reactions to Women Who Succeed at Male Gender-Typed Tasks," *Journal of Applied Psychology* 89, no. 3 (2004): 416–27; A. H. Eagly, "Achieving Relational Authenticity in Leadership: Does Gender Matter?," *The Leadership Quarterly* 16, no. 3 (June 2005): 459–74.

CHAPTER 12

1. P. Lavoie, "TAXI," *Campaign,* October 12, 2007, 15; L. Sylvain, "Taxi Deconstructed," *Strategy,* June 2007, 50; S. Vranica, "For Small Agency, a Battle to Shed 'Boutique Stigma'," *Wall Street Journal,* August 8, 2007, B2D; E. Wexler, "There's No Stopping TAXI," *Strategy,* January 2011, 40–42. Although it was recently acquired by WPP, the world's largest creative holding company, TAXI will apparently remain an autonomous business and use WPP's resources for European and further international expansion.

2. H. Mintzberg, *The Structuring of Organizations* (Englewood Cliffs, NJ: Prentice Hall, 1979), 2–3.

3. E. E. Lawler III, *Motivation in Work Organizations* (Monterey, CA: Brooks/Cole, 1973); M. A. Campion, "Ability Requirement Implications of Job Design: An Interdisciplinary Perspective," *Personnel Psychology* 42 (1989): 1–24.

4. G. S. Becker and K. M. Murphy, "The Division-of-Labor, Coordination Costs and Knowledge," *Quarterly Journal of Economics* 107, no. 4 (November 1992): 1137–60; L. Borghans and B. Weel, "The Division of Labour, Worker Organisation, and Technological Change," *The Economic Journal* 116, no. 509 (2006): F45–F72.

5. Mintzberg, *The Structuring of Organizations* Chap. 1; D. A. Nadler and M. L. Tushman, *Competing by Design: The Power of Organizational Architecture* (New York: Oxford University Press, 1997), Chap. 6; J. R. Galbraith, *Designing Organizations: An Executive Guide to Strategy, Structure, and Process* (San Francisco: Jossey-Bass, 2002), Chap. 4.

6. J. Stephenson Jr., "Making Humanitarian Relief Networks More Effective: Operational Coordination, Trust and Sense Making," *Disasters* 29, no. 4 (2005): 337.

7. A. Willem, M. Buelens, and H. Scarbrough, "The Role of Inter-Unit Coordination Mechanisms in Knowledge Sharing: A Case Study of a British MNC," *Journal of Information Science* 32, no. 6 (2006): 539–61; R. R. Gulati, "Silo Busting," *Harvard Business Review* 85, no. 5 (2007): 98–108.

8. Borghans and Weel, "The Division of Labour, Worker Organisation, and Technological Change."

9. For a discussion of the role of brand manager at Proctor & Gamble, see C. Peale, "Branded for Success," *Cincinnati Enquirer* (May 20, 2001): A1. Details about how to design integrator roles in organizational structures are presented in Galbraith, *Designing Organizations,* 66–72.

10. M. Villano, "The Control Freak in the Corner Office," *New York Times,* May 28, 2006, 10; "One-Third of Employees Feel Micromanaged by Boss," BlessingWhite news release for BlessingWhite, October 27, 2008; "Lack of Communication with Staff Most Damaging to Morale, Survey Finds," news release for Accountemps, November 20, 2008; T. Gould, "How Employees Really Feel about Their Bosses," *HR Morning,* July 7, 2011; Kelly Services, *Effective Employers: The Evolving Workforce,* Kelly Global Workforce Index (Troy, MI: Kelly Services, November 2011).

11. M. Hoque, M. Akter, and Y. Monden, "Concurrent Engineering: A Compromise Approach to Develop a Feasible and Customer-Pleasing Product," *International Journal of Production Research* 43, no. 8 (2005): 1607–24; S. M. Sapuan, M. R. Osman, and Y. Nukman, "State of the Art of the Concurrent Engineering Technique in the Automotive Industry," *Journal of Engineering Design* 17, no. 2 (2006): 143–57; D. H. Kincade, C. Regan, and F. Y. Gibson, "Concurrent Engineering for Product Development in Mass Customization for the Apparel Industry," *International Journal of Operations & Production Management* 27, no. 6 (2007): 627–49.

12. A. H. Van De Ven, A. L. Delbecq, and R. J. Koenig Jr., "Determinants of Coordination Modes within Organizations," *American Sociological Review* 41, no. 2 (1976): 322–38.

13. Y. M. Hsieh and A. Tien-Hsieh, "Enhancement of Service Quality with Job Standardisation," *Service Industries Journal* 21 (July 2001): 147–66.

14. For recent discussion of span of control, see N. A. Theobald and S. Nicholson-Crotty, "The Many Faces of Span of Control: Organizational Structure across Multiple Goals," *Administration Society* 36, no. 6 (January 2005): 648–60; R. M. Meyer, "Span of Management: Concept Analysis," *Journal of Advanced Nursing* 63, no. 1 (2008): 104–12.

15. H. Fayol, *General and Industrial Management,* trans. C. Storrs (London: Pitman, 1949); D. D. Van Fleet and A. G. Bedeian, "A History of the Span of Management," *Academy of Management Review* 2 (1977): 356–72; D. A. Wren, A. G. Bedeian, and J. D. Breeze, "The Foundations of Henri Fayol's Administrative Theory"; *Management Decision* 40, no. 9 (2002): 906–18.

16. D. Drickhamer, "Lessons from the Leading Edge," *Industry Week,* February 21, 2000, 23–26.

17. G. Anders, "Overseeing More Employees—with Fewer Managers—Consultants Are Urging Companies to Loosen Their Supervising Views," *Wall Street Journal,* March 24, 2008, B6.

18. D. D. Van Fleet and A. G. Bedeian, "A History of the Span of Management," *Academy of Management Review* 2 (July 1977): 356–72; B. Davison, "Management Span of Control: How Wide Is Too Wide?," *Journal of Business Strategy* 24, no. 4 (2003): 22–29; S. Nix et al., *Span of Control in City Government Increases Overall* (Seattle, WA: Office of City Auditor, City of Seattle, September 19, 2005); "FedEx 2008 Shareowners Meeting" (Memphis, TN: FedEx, September 29, 2008); State of Iowa, "Results Iowa: Operational Scan," February 1, 2008, accessed May 23, 2010; J. McLellan, *Administrative Review: An Agenda for Business Improvement,* (Portland, OR: Multnomah County, May 19, 2009); D. Thompson, "More on the Span of Control Issue," *Statesman Journal Blog (Oregon),* May 16, 2011.

19. J. Greenwald, "Ward Compares the Best with the Rest," *Business Insurance,* August 26, 2002, 16.

20. J. H. Gittell, "Supervisory Span, Relational Coordination and Flight Departure Performance: A Reassessment of Postbureaucracy Theory," *Organization Science* 12, no. 4 (July/August 2001): 468–83.

21. J. Denby, "Leaders in African Electricity," *African Business Review,* May 11, 2010.

22. T. D. Wall, J. L. Cordery, and C. W. Clegg, "Empowerment, Performance, and Operational Uncertainty: A Theoretical Integration," *Applied Psychology: An International Review* 51 (2002): 146–69.

23. J. Morris, J. Hassard, and L. McCann, "New Organizational Forms, Human Resource Management and Structural Convergence? A Study of Japanese Organizations," *Organization Studies* 27, no. 10 (2006): 1485–1511.

24. "BASF Culling Saves (GBP) 4m," *Personnel Today,* February 19, 2002, 3; S. Marchionne, "Navigating the New Automotive Epoch," *Vital Speeches of the Day* (March 2010): 134–37.

25. S. Wetlaufer, "The Business Case against Revolution: An Interview with Nestlé's Peter Brabeck," *Harvard Business Review* 79, no. 2 (February 2001): 112–19; H. A. Richardson et al., "Does Decentralization Make a Difference for the Organization? An Examination of the Boundary Conditions Circumscribing Decentralized Decision-Making and Organizational Financial Performance," *Journal of Management* 28, no. 2 (2002): 217–44; G. Masada, "To Centralize or Decentralize?," *Optimize,* May 2005, 58–61.

26. J. G. Kelley, "Slurpees and Sausages: 7–Eleven Holds School," *Richmond* (Va.) *Times-Dispatch,* March 12, 2004, C1; S. Marling, "The 24–Hour Supply Chain," *InformationWeek,* January 26, 2004, 43.

27. Mintzberg, *The Structuring of Organizations,* Chap. 5.

28. J. Kersnar, "Forget What You Think You Know," *CFO Magazine,* January/February 2011, 29–33.

29. W. Dessein and T. Santos, "Adaptive Organizations," *Journal of Political Economy* 114, no. 5 (2006): 956–95; A. A. M. Nasurdin et al., "Organizational Structure and Organizational Climate as Potential Predictors of Job Stress: Evidence from Malaysia," *International Journal of Commerce and Management* 16, no. 2 (2006): 116–29; C.-J. Chen and J.-W. Huang, "How Organizational Climate and Structure Affect Knowledge Management—the Social Interaction Perspective," *International Journal of Information Management* 27, no. 2 (2007): 104–18.

30. "Royal Bank Survey Finds Canadian Workplaces Buoyed by Optimism and High Level of Satisfaction," Canada NewsWire news release for R. B. o. Canada, October 8. 1998; "When It Comes to Red Tape, Many Canadian Employers Might Just Need to Cut It: RBC Study," CNW news release for RBC, January 23, 2008.

31. T. Burns and G. Stalker, *The Management of Innovation* (London: Tavistock: 1961).

32. J. Tata, S. Prasad, and R. Thom, "The Influence of Organizational Structure on the Effectiveness of TQM Programs," *Journal of Managerial Issues* 11, no. 4 (Winter 1999): 440–53; A. Lam, "Tacit Knowledge, Organizational Learning and Societal Institutions: An Integrated Framework," *Organization Studies* 21 (May 2000): 487–513.

33. W. D. Sine, H. Mitsuhashi, and D. A. Kirsch, "Revisiting Burns and Stalker: Formal Structure and New Venture Performance in Emerging Economic Sectors," *Academy of Management Journal* 49, no. 1 (2006): 121–32.

34. Mintzberg, *The Structuring of Organizations,* 106.

35. Mintzberg, *The Structuring of Organizations,* Chap. 17.

36. Galbraith, *Designing Organizations,* 23–25.

37. E. E. Lawler III, *Rewarding Excellence: Pay Strategies for the New Economy* (San Francisco: Jossey-Bass, 2000), 31–34.

38. These structures were identified from corporate Web sites and annual reports. These organizations typically rely on a mixture of other structures, so the charts shown have been adapted for learning purposes.

39. M. Goold and A. Campbell, "Do You Have a Well-Designed Organization?," *Harvard Business Review* 80 (March 2002): 117–24.

40. J. R. Galbraith, "Structuring Global Organizations," in *Tomorrow's Organization*, ed. S. A. Mohrman et al. (San Francisco: Jossey-Bass, 1998), 103–29; C. Homburg, J. P. Workman Jr., and O. Jensen, "Fundamental Changes in Marketing Organization: The Movement toward a Corganizational Structure," *Academy of Marketing Science. Journal* 28 (Fall 2000): 459–78; T. H. Davenport, J. G. Harris, and A. K. Kohli, "How Do They Know Their Customers So Well?," *Sloan Management Review* 42 (Winter 2001): 63–73; J. R. Galbraith, "Organizing to Deliver Solutions," *Organizational Dynamics* 31 (2002): 194–207.

41. Palmisano, "The Globally Integrated Enterprise." *Foreign Affairs* 85, no. 3 (May/June 2006): 127–36; S. Palmisano, "The Globally Integrated Enterprise," *Vital Speeches of the Day* 73, no. 10 (2007): 449–53.

42. S. J. Palmisano, "The Globally Integrated Enterprise."

43. "IBM Moves Engineering Vp to China as Part of Global Focus," *Manufacturing Business Technology*, September 2007, 13; J. Bonasia, "Globalization: Learning to Close the Continental Divide," *Investor's Business Daily*, September 7, 2007.

44. A. Deutschman, "The Fabric of Creativity," *Fast Company*, December 2004, 54–60; P. J. Kiger, "Power to the Individual," *Workforce Management*, February 27, 2006, 1–7; G. Hamel, *The Future of Management* (Boston: Harvard Business School Press, 2007), Chap. 5.

45. J. R. Galbraith, E. E. Lawler III, and Associates, *Organizing for the Future: The New Logic for Managing Complex Organizations* (San Francisco, CA: Jossey-Bass, 1993); R. Bettis and M. Hitt, "The New Competitive Landscape," *Strategic Management Journal* 16 (1995): 7–19.

46. P. C. Ensign, "Interdependence, Coordination, and Structure in Complex Organizations: Implications for Organization Design," *Mid-Atlantic Journal of Business* 34 (March 1998): 5–22.

47. M. M. Fanning, "A Circular Organization Chart Promotes a Hospital-Wide Focus on Teams," *Hospital & Health Services Administration* 42 (June 1997): 243–54; L. Y. Chan and B. E. Lynn, "Operating in Turbulent Times: How Ontario's Hospitals Are Meeting the Current Funding Crisis," *Health Care Management Review* 23 (June 1998): 7–18.

48. R. Cross, "Looking before You Leap: Assessing the Jump to Teams in Knowledge-Based Work," *Business Horizons* (September 2000); M. Fenton-O'Creevy, "Employee Involvement and the Middle Manager: Saboteur or Scapegoat?," *Human Resource Management Journal* 11 (2001): 24–40; G. Garda, K. Lindstrom, and M. Dallnera, "Towards a Learning Organization: The Introduction of a Client-Centered Team-Based Organization in Administrative Surveying Work," *Applied Ergonomics* 34 (2003): 97–105; C. Douglas and W. L. Gardner, "Transition to Self-Directed Work Teams: Implications of Transition Time and Self-Monitoring for Managers' Use of Influence Tactics," *Journal of Organizational Behavior* 25 (2004): 47–65.

49. R. Muzyka and G. Zeschuk, "Managing Multiple Projects," *Game Developer*, March 2003, 34–42; M. Saltzman, "The Ex-Doctors Are In," *National Post*, March 24, 2004, AL4; R. McConnell, "For Edmonton's Bioware, Today's the Big Day," *Edmonton Journal*, April 14, 2005, C1; D. Gladstone and S. Molloy, "Doctors & Dragons," *Computer Gaming World*, December 2006.

50. R. C. Ford and W. A. Randolph, "Cross-Functional Structures: A Review and Integration of Matrix Organization and Project Management," *Journal of Management* 18 (1992): 267–94.

51. Nestlé's geographic and product structure is somewhat more complex than is described here, and its matrix is not as balanced as described. For discussion of these variations, see: J. R. Galbraith, *Designing Matrix Organizations That Actually Work* (San Francisco: Jossey-Bass, 2009).

52. G. Calabrese, "Communication and Co-Operation in Product Development: A Case Study of a European Car Producer," *R & D Management* 27 (July 1997): 239–52; T. Sy and L. S. D'Annunzio, "Challenges and Strategies of Matrix Organizations: Top-Level and Mid-Level Managers' Perspectives," *Human Resource Planning* 28, no. 1 (2005): 39–48.

53. D. Enrich, "Citigroup Will Revamp Capital-Markets Group," *Wall Street Journal*, August 23, 2008, B7.

54. Nadler and Tushman, *Competing by Design*, Chap. 6; M. Goold and A. Campbell, "Structured Networks: Towards the Well-Designed Matrix," *Long Range Planning* 36, no. 5 (October 2003): 427–39.

55. D. Ciampa and M. Watkins, "Rx for New CEOs," *Chief Executive*, January 2008.

56. L. Donaldson, *The Contingency Theory of Organizations* (Thousand Oaks, CA: Sage, 2001); J. Birkenshaw, R. Nobel, and J. Ridderstrâle, "Knowledge as a Contingency Variable: Do the Characteristics of Knowledge Predict Organizational Structure?," *Organization Science* 13, no. 3 (May/June 2002): 274–89.

57. P. R. Lawrence and J. W. Lorsch, *Organization and Environment* (Homewood, IL: Irwin, 1967); Mintzberg, *The Structuring of Organizations*, Chap. 15.

58. Burns and Stalker, *The Management of Innovation*; Lawrence and Lorsch, *Organization and Environment*.

59. Mintzberg, *The Structuring of Organizations*, 282.

60. D. S. Pugh and C. R. Hinings, *Organizational Structure: Extensions and Replications* (Farnborough, UK: Lexington Books, 1976); Mintzberg, *The Structuring of Organizations*, Chap. 13.

61. Galbraith, *Designing Organizations*, 52–55; G. Hertel, S. Geister, and U. Konradt, "Managing Virtual Teams: A Review of Current Empirical Research," *Human Resource Management Review* 15 (2005): 69–95.

62. C. Perrow, "A Framework for the Comparative Analysis of Organizations," *American Sociological Review* 32 (1967): 194–208; D. Gerwin, "The Comparative Analysis of Structure and Technology: A Critical Appraisal," *Academy of Management Review* 4, no. 1 (1979): 41–51; C. C. Miller et al., "Understanding Technology-Structure Relationships: Theory Development and Meta-Analytic Theory Testing," *Academy of Management Journal* 34, no. 2 (1991): 370–99.

63. R. H. Kilmann, *Beyond the Quick Fix* (San Francisco: Jossey-Bass, 1984), 38.

64. A. D. Chandler, *Strategy and Structure* (Cambridge, MA: MIT Press, 1962).

65. D. Miller, "Configurations of Strategy and Structure," *Strategic Management Journal* 7 (1986): 233–49.

CHAPTER 13

1. "Nomura's Corporate Culture Still Flawed," *The Daily Yomiuri* (Tokyo), July 1, 2012, 3.

2. M. Shustack, "Volunteerism a Longtime Byproduct of Dannon's Corporate Culture," *Westchester County Business Journal*, June 25, 2012, 33.

3. "Whistleblower: 'The Culture Ultimately Comes from the Top'," *The Independent* (London), July 7, 2012.

4. The terms *organizational culture* and *corporate culture* were popularized in 1982 in: T. E. Deal and A. A. Kennedy, *Corporate Cultures* (Reading, MA: Addison-Wesley, 1982); T. J. Peters and R. H. Waternam, *In Search of Excellence: Lessons from America's Best-Run Companies* (New York: Warner, 1982). However, there are a few early references to an organization's culture, including: N. Margulies, "Organizational Culture and Psychological Growth," *The Journal of Applied Behavioral Science* 5, no. 4 (December 1, 1969): 491–508; S. Silverzweig and R. F. Allen, "Changing the Corporate Culture," *Sloan Management Review* 17, no. 3 (1976): 33.

5. A. Williams, P. Dobson, and M. Walters, *Changing Culture: New Organizational Approaches* (London: Institute of Personnel Management, 1989); E. H. Schein, "What Is Culture?," in *Reframing Organizational Culture*, ed. P. J. Frost et al. (Newbury Park, CA: Sage, 1991), 243–53.

6. M. Johnson and C. Roebuck, "Nurturing a New Kind of Capital," *Financial Executive*, July 2008, 32; Hay Group. "Hay Group Study Finds CEOs Target Employee Performance to Achieve Bullish Growth in 2011," news release for H. Group, 2011; Deloitte Touche Tohmatsu, *Core Beliefs and Culture* (New York: Deloitte Touche Tohmatsu, 2012).

7. B. M. Meglino and E. C. Ravlin, "Individual Values in Organizations: Concepts, Controversies, and Research," *Journal of Management* 24, no. 3 (1998): 351–89; B. R. Agle and C. B. Caldwell, "Understanding Research on Values in Business," *Business and Society* 38, no. 3 (September 1999): 326–87; S. Hitlin and J. A. Pilavin, "Values: Reviving a Dormant Concept," *Annual Review of Sociology* 30 (2004): 359–93.

8. N. M. Ashkanasy, "The Case for Culture," in *Debating Organization*, ed. R. Westwood and S. Clegg (Malden, MA: Blackwell, 2003), 300–10.

9. M. Lagace, "Gerstner: Changing Culture at IBM," *HBS Working Knowledge*, September 12, 2002.

10. T. Hsieh, *Delivering Happiness: A Path to Profits, Passion, and Purpose* (New York: Business Plus, 2010); K. Ladendorf, "For Facebook Workers, It's Not Just a Job," *Austin American-Statesman*, May 1, 2011, E1.

11. B. Kabanoff and J. Daly, "Espoused Values in Organisations," *Australian Journal of Management* 27, Special issue (2002): 89–104.

12. "Norway Criticizes BP, Smedvig over Safety," *Energy Compass*, January 3, 2003; "Norway Criticizes BP, Smedvig over Safety"; J. A. Lozano, "BP Refinery Had History of Dangerous Releases, Report Finds," *Associated Press*, October 28, 2005; S. McNulty, "A Corroded Culture?," *Financial Times* (London), December 18, 2006, 17; U.S. Chemical Safety and Hazard Invistigation Board, *Investigation Report: Refinery Explosion and Fire (BP, Texas City, Texas, March 23, 2005)* (Washington, DC: U.S. Chemical Safety Board, March 2007); S. Greenhouse, "BP Faces Record Fine for '05 Refinery Explosion," *New York Times*, October 30, 2009; L. C. Steffy, *Drowning in Oil: BP and the Reckless Pursuit of Profit* (New York: McGraw-Hill, 2011).

13. C. A. O'Reilly III, J. Chatman, and D. F. Caldwell, "People and Organizational Culture: A Profile Comparison Approach to Assessing Person–Organization Fit," *Academy of Management Journal* 34 (1991): 487–516; J. J. van Muijen, "Organizational Culture," in *A Handbook of Work and Organizational Psychology: Organizational Psychology*, ed. P. J. D. Drenth, H. Thierry, and C. J. de Wolff, 2d ed. (East Sussex, UK: Psychology Press, 1998), 113–32; P. A. Balthazard, R. A. Cooke, and R. E. Potter, "Dysfunctional Culture, Dysfunctional Organization: Capturing the Behavioral Norms That Form Organizational Culture and Drive Performance," *Journal of Managerial Psychology* 21, no. 8 (2006): 709–32; C. Helfrich et al., "Assessing an Organizational Culture Instrument Based on the Competing Values Framework: Exploratory and Confirmatory Factor Analyses," *Implementation Science* 2, no. 1 (2007): 13. For recent reviews of organizational culture survey instruments, see T. Scott et al., "The Quantitative Measurement of Organizational Culture in Health Care: A Review of the Available Instruments," *Health Services Research* 38, no. 3 (2003): 923–45; D. E. Leidner and T. Kayworth, "A Review of Culture in Information Systems Research: Toward a Theory of Information Technology Culture Conflict," *MIS Quarterly* 30, no. 2 (2006): 357–99; C. A. Hartnell, A. Y. Ou, and A. Kinicki, "Organizational Culture and Organizational Effectiveness: A Meta-Analytic Investigation of the Competing Values Framework's Theoretical Suppositions," *Journal of Applied Psychology* 96, no. 4 (2011): 677–94.

14. J. Martin, P. J. Frost, and O. A. O'Neill, "Organizational Culture: Beyond Struggles for Intellectual Dominance," in *Handbook of Organization Studies*, ed. S. Clegg et al., 2d ed. (London: Sage, 2006), 725–53; N. E. Fenton and S. Inglis, "A Critical Perspective on Organizational Values," *Nonprofit Management and Leadership* 17, no. 3 (2007): 335–47; K. Haukelid, "Theories of (Safety) Culture Revisited—an Anthropological Approach," *Safety Science* 46, no. 3 (2008): 413–26.

15. J. Martin and C. Siehl, "Organizational Culture and Counterculture: An Uneasy Symbiosis," *Organizational Dynamics* (Autumn 1983): 52–64; G. Hofstede, "Identifying Organizational Subcultures: An Empirical Approach," *Journal of Management Studies* 35, no. 1 (1990): 1–12; E. Ogbonna and L. C. Harris, "Organisational Culture in the Age of the Internet: An Exploratory Study," *New Technology, Work and Employment* 21, no. 2 (2006): 162–75.

16. H. Silver, "Does a University Have a Culture?," *Studies in Higher Education* 28, no. 2 (2003): 157–69.

17. A. Sinclair, "Approaches to Organizational Culture and Ethics," *Journal of Business Ethics* 12 (1993); T. E. Deal and A. A. Kennedy, *The New Corporate Cultures* (Cambridge, MA: Perseus Books, 1999), Chap. 10; A. Boisnier and J. Chatman, "The Role of Subcultures in Agile Organizations," in *Leading and Managing People in Dynamic Organizations*, ed. R. Petersen and E. Mannix (Mahwah, NJ: Lawrence Erlbaum Associates, 2003), 87–112; C. Morrill, M. N. Zald, and H. Rao, "Covert Political Conflict in Organizations: Challenges from Below," *Annual Review of Sociology* 29, no. 1 (2003): 391–415.

18. J. S. Ott, *The Organizational Culture Perspective* (Pacific Grove, CA: Brooks/Cole, 1989), Chap. 2; J. S. Pederson and J. S. Sorensen, *Organizational Cultures in Theory and Practice* (Aldershot, UK: Gower, 1989), 27–29; M. O. Jones, *Studying Organizational Symbolism: What, How, Why?* (Thousand Oaks, CA: Sage, 1996).

19. E. H. Schein, "Organizational Culture," *American Psychologist* (February 1990): 109–19; A. Furnham and B. Gunter, "Corporate Culture: Definition, Diagnosis, and Change," *International Review of Industrial and Organizational Psychology* 8 (1993):

233–61; E. H. Schein, *The Corporate Culture Survival Guide* (San Francisco: Jossey-Bass, 1999), Chap. 4.

20. M. Doehrman, "Anthropologists—Deep in the Corporate Bush," *Daily Record* (Kansas City, MO), July 19, 2005, 1.

21. Deal and Kennedy, *Corporate Cultures,* Chap. 5; C. J. Boudens, "The Story of Work: A Narrative Analysis of Workplace Emotion," *Organization Studies* 26, no. 9 (2005): 1285–1306; S. Denning, *The Leader's Guide to Storytelling* (San Francisco: Jossey-Bass, 2005).

22. A. L. Wilkins, "Organizational Stories as Symbols Which Control the Organization," in *Organizational Symbolism*, ed. L. R. Pondy et al. (Greenwich, CT: JAI Press, 1984), 81–92; R. Zemke, "Storytelling: Back to a Basic," *Training* 27 (March 1990): 44–50; J. C. Meyer, "Tell Me a Story: Eliciting Organizational Values from Narratives," *Communication Quarterly* 43 (1995): 210–224; W. Swap et al., "Using Mentoring and Storytelling to Transfer Knowledge in the Workplace," *Journal of Management Information Systems* 18 (Summer 2001): 95–114.

23. A. C. T. Smith and B. Stewart, "Organizational Rituals: Features, Functions and Mechanisms," *International Journal of Management Reviews* (2011): in press.

24. K. Roman, "The House That Ogilvy Built," *strategy+business* (April 29, 2009): 1–5.

25. A. Gostick and C. Elton, *The Orange Revolution* (New York: Free Press, 2010), 214–16; A. Powers, "Zappos Tours Showcase Company's Quirks," *Los Angeles Times*, April 29, 2011.

26. "The Ultimate Chairman," *Business Times Singapore*, September 3, 2005.

27. D. Roth, "My Job at the Container Store," *Fortune* (January 10, 2000): 74–78.

28. R. E. Quinn and N. T. Snyder, "Advance Change Theory: Culture Change at Whirlpool Corporation," in *The Leader's Change Handbook* ed. J. A. Conger, G. M. Spreitzer, and E. E. Lawler III (San Francisco: Jossey-Bass, 1999), 162–93.

29. G. Turner and J. Myerson, *New Workspace New Culture: Office Design as a Catalyst for Change* (Aldershot, UK: Gower, 1998).

30. P. Roberts, "The Empire Strikes Back," *Fast Company*, no. 22 (February/March 1999): 122–31; H. Nguyen, "Oakley Shades for Her Eyes Only," *Orange County Register* (Santa Ana, CA), May 11, 2006. Details and photos are also found at: www.oakley.com; and americahurrah.com/Oakley/Entry.htm.

31. Churchill apparently made this statement on October 28, 1943, in the British House of Commons, when London, damaged by bombings in World War II, was about to be rebuilt.

32. K. D. Elsbach and B. A. Bechky, "It's More than a Desk: Working Smarter through Leveraged Office Design," *California Management Review* 49, no. 2 (Winter 2007): 80–101.

33. M. Burton, "Open Plan, Open Mind," *Director* (March 2005): 68–72; B. Murray, "Agency Profile: Mother London," *Ihaveanidea*, January 28, 2007, www.ihaveanidea.org.

34. A. Krishnan, "CEOs from the Best Provide Insights Gained from Hewitt Best Employers Study," *the Edge* (Malaysia), July 21, 2008.

35. J. C. Collins and J. I. Porras, *Built to Last: Successful Habits of Visionary Companies* (London: Century, 1994); Deal and Kennedy, *The New Corporate Cultures;* R. Barrett, *Building a Values-Driven Organization: A Whole System Approach to Cultural Transformation* (Burlington, MA: Butterworth-Heinemann, 2006); J. M. Kouzes and B. Z. Posner, *The Leadership Challenge*, 4th ed. (San Francisco: Jossey-Bass, 2007), Chap. 3.

36. C. Siehl and J. Martin, "Organizational Culture: A Key to Financial Performance?," in *Organizational Climate and Culture*, ed. B. Schneider (San Francisco, CA: Jossey-Bass, 1990), 241–81; G. G. Gordon and N. DiTomasco, "Predicting Corporate Performance from Organizational Culture," *Journal of Management Studies* 29 (1992): 783–98; J. P. Kotter and J. L. Heskett, *Corporate Culture and Performance* (New York: Free Press, 1992); C. P. M. Wilderom, U. Glunk, and R. Maslowski, "Organizational Culture as a Predictor of Organizational Performance," in *Handbook of Organizational Culture and Climate*, ed. N. M. Ashkanasy, C. P. M. Wilderom, and M. F. Peterson (Thousand Oaks, CA: Sage, 2000), 193–210; A. Carmeli and A. Tishler, "The Relationships between Intangible Organizational Elements and Organizational Performance," *Strategic Management Journal* 25 (2004): 1257–78; S. Teerikangas and P. Very, "The Culture-Performance Relationship in M&A: From Yes/No to How," *British Journal of Management* 17, no. S1 (2006): S31–S48.

37. L. Carapiet, "NAB's John Stewart Knows His Abcs," *Australian Banking & Finance*, December 2007, 6; J. H. Want, *Corporate Culture: Key Strategies of High-Performing Business Cultures* (New York: St. Martin's Press, 2007), 38.

38. J. C. Helms Mills and A. J. Mills, "Rules, Sensemaking, Formative Contexts, and Discourse in the Gendering of Organizational Culture," in *International Handbook of Organizational Climate and Culture*, ed. N. Ashkanasy, C. Wilderom, and M. Peterson (Thousand Oaks, CA: Sage, 2000), 55–70; J. A. Chatman and S. E. Cha, "Leading by Leveraging Culture," *California Management Review* 45 (Summer 2003): 20–34.

39. B. Ashforth and F. Mael, "Social Identity Theory and the Organization," *Academy of Management Review* 14 (1989): 20–39.

40. Heidrick & Struggles, *Leadership Challenges Emerge as Asia Pacific Companies Go Global* (Melbourne: Heidrick & Struggles, August 2008).

41. M. R. Louis, "Surprise and Sensemaking: What Newcomers Experience in Entering Unfamiliar Organizational Settings," *Administrative Science Quarterly* 25 (1980): 226–51; S. G. Harris, "Organizational Culture and Individual Sensemaking: A Schema-Based Perspective," *Organization Science* 5 (1994): 309–21.

42. J. W. Barnes et al., "The Role of Culture Strength in Shaping Sales Force Outcomes," *Journal of Personal Selling & Sales Management* 26, no. 3 (Summer 2006): 255–70.

43. N. Byrnes, P. Burrows, and L. Lee, "Dark Days at Dell," *BusinessWeek*, September 4, 2006, 26; S. Lohr, "Can Michael Dell Refocus His Namesake?," *New York Times*, September 9, 2007, 1.

44. C. A. O'Reilly III and J. A. Chatman, "Culture as Social Control: Corporations, Cults, and Commitment," *Research in Organizational Behavior* 18 (1996): 157–200; B. Spector and H. Lane, "Exploring the Distinctions between a High Performance Culture and a Cult," *Strategy & Leadership* 35, no. 3 (2007): 18–24.

45. Kotter and Heskett, *Corporate Culture and Performance*; J. P. Kotter, "Cultures and Coalitions," *Executive Excellence* 15 (March 1998): 14–15; B. M. Bass and R. E. Riggio, *Transformational Leadership*, 2d ed. (New York: Routledge, 2006), Chap. 7. The term *adaptive culture* has a different meaning in organizational behavior than it has in cultural anthropology, where it refers to nonmaterial cultural conditions (such as ways of thinking) that lag the material culture (physical artifacts). For the anthropological perspective, see

W. Griswold, *Cultures and Societies in a Changing World*, 3d ed. (Thousand Oaks, CA: Pine Forge Press (Sage), 2008), 66.

46. T. Krisher and D.-A. Durbin, "General Motors CEO Akerson Leads Comeback from Bankruptcy by Ruffling Company's Bureaucracy," *Associated Press Newswires*, December 17, 2011.

47. W. E. Baker and J. M. Sinkula, "The Synergistic Effect of Market Orientation and Learning Orientation on Organizational Performance," *Academy of Marketing Science Journal* 27, no. 4 (Fall 1999): 411–27; Z. Emden, A. Yaprak, and S. T. Cavusgil, "Learning from Experience in International Alliances: Antecedents and Firm Performance Implications," *Journal of Business Research* 58, no. 7 (2005): 883–92.

48. T. Braithwaite and T. Alloway, "Silence Is No Longer Goldman," *Financial Times*, March 14, 2012; G. Smith, "Why I Am Leaving Goldman Sachs," *New York Times*, March 14, 2012; H. Touryalai, "The Real Problem at Goldman Sachs? Yuo, the Muppet Client," *Forbes*, March 14, 2012.

49. M. L. Sirower, *The Synergy Trap: How Companies Lose the Acquisition Game* (New York: The Free Press, 1997); C. Cook and D. Spitzer, *World Class Transactions*, (London: KPMG, 2001); J. P. Daly et al., "The Effects of Initial Differences in Firms' Espoused Values on Their Postmerger Performance," *Journal of Applied Behavioral Science* 40, no. 3 (2004): 323–43; J. Krug, *Mergers and Acquisitions: Turmoil in Top Management Teams* (Williston, VT: Business Expert Press, 2009).

50. M. L. Marks, "Adding Cultural Fit to Your Diligence Checklist," *Mergers & Acquisitions* 34, no. 3 (November/December 1999): 14–20; Schein, *The Corporate Culture Survival Guide* Chap. 8; M. L. Marks, "Mixed Signals," *Across the Board* (May 2000): 21–26.

51. Teerikangas and Very, "The Culture-Performance Relationship in M&A: From Yes/No to How"; G. K. Stahl and A. Voigt, "Do Cultural Differences Matter in Mergers and Acquisitions? A Tentative Model and Examination," *Organization Science* 19, no. 1 (January 2008): 160–76.

52. R. Smith and D. Fitzpatrick, "Cultures Clash as Merrill Herd Meets 'Wal-Mart of Banking'," *Wall Street Journal*, November 14, 2008, C1; "Bank of America-Merrill Lynch: A $50 Billion Deal from Hell," *Deal Journal* (Wall Street Journal Blog), January 22, 2009; M. Read, "Wall Street's Entitlement Culture Hard to Shake," *Associated Press*, January 23, 2009; D. Sarch, "Merrill Lynch: Culture Change or Just the Latest Innovation?," *Investment News*, May 27, 2010.

53. Sirower, *The Synergy Trap: How Companies Lose the Acquisition Game;* "KPMG Identifies Six Key Factors for Successful Mergers and Acquisitions," PR Newswire news release for KPMG, November 29, 1999; Cook and Spitzer, *World Class Transactions;* D. Henry, "Mergers: Why Most Big Deals Don't Pay Off," *BusinessWeek*, October 14, 2002; Krug, *Mergers and Acquisitions: Turmoil in Top Management Teams.*

54. C. A. Schorg, C. A. Raiborn, and M. F. Massoud, "Using a 'Cultural Audit' to Pick M&A Winners," *Journal of Corporate Accounting & Finance* (May/June 2004): 47–55; W. Locke, "Higher Education Mergers: Integrating Organisational Cultures and Developing Appropriate Management Styles," *Higher Education Quarterly* 61, no. 1 (2007): 83–102.

55. A. R. Malekazedeh and A. Nahavandi, "Making Mergers Work by Managing Cultures," *Journal of Business Strategy* (May/June 1990): 55–57; K. W. Smith, "A Brand-New Culture for the Merged Firm," *Mergers and Acquisitions* 35 (June 2000): 45–50.

56. M. Joyce, "Airtran Employees Getting New Culture," *Dallas Business Journal*, July 8, 2011.

57. E. Frauenheim, "Jungle Survival," *Workforce Management*, September 14, 2009, 19; B. Lennox and W. Nie, "The Case Study: Creating a Distinct Corporate Culture," *Financial Times* (London), February 17, 2011, 14.

58. Hewitt Associates, "Mergers and Acquisitions May Be Driven by Business Strategy—but Often Stumble over People and Culture Issues," PR Newswire news release, August 3, 1998.

59. J. Martin, "Can Organizational Culture Be Managed?," in *Organizational Culture*, ed. P. J. Frost et al. (Beverly Hills, CA: Sage, 1985), 95–98.

60. M. De Pree, *Leadership Jazz: The Essential Elements of a Great Leader*, 2d ed. (New York: Broadway Business, 2008).

61. E. H. Schein, "The Role of the Founder in Creating Organizational Culture," *Organizational Dynamics* 12, no. 1 (Summer 1983): 13–28; R. House, M. Javidan, and P. Dorfman, "Project GLOBE: An Introduction," *Applied Psychology: An International Review* 50 (2001): 489–505; R. House et al., "Understanding Cultures and Implicit Leadership Theories across the Globe: An Introduction to Project GLOBE," *Journal of World Business* 37 (2002): 3–10.

62. Deloitte, "Core Beliefs and Culture: Chairman's Survey Findings," 2012, accessed July 26, 2012, http://www.deloitte.com/print/en_US/us/About/Leadership/1fe8be4ad25e7310Vgn VCM1000001956f00aRCRD.htm.

63. A. S. Tsui et al., "Unpacking the Relationship between CEO Leadership Behavior and Organizational Culture," *Leadership Quarterly* 17 (2006): 113–37; Y. Berson, S. Oreg, and T. Dvir, "CEO Values, Organizational Culture and Firm Outcomes," *Journal of Organizational Behavior* 29, no. 5 (July 2008): 615–33.

64. M. De Pree, *Leadership Is an Art* (East Lansing: Michigan State University Press, 1987).

65. J. Kerr and J. W. Slocum Jr., "Managing Corporate Culture through Reward Systems," *Academy of Management Executive* 1 (May 1987): 99–107; J. M. Higgins et al., "Using Cultural Artifacts to Change and Perpetuate Strategy," *Journal of Change Management* 6, no. 4 (2006): 397–415.

66. R. Charan, "Home Depot's Blueprint for Culture Change," *Harvard Business Review* (April 2006): 61–70.

67. B. Schneider, "The People Make the Place," *Personnel Psychology* 40, no. 3 (1987): 437–53; B. Schneider et al., "Personality and Organizations: A Test of the Homogeneity of Personality Hypothesis," *Journal of Applied Psychology* 83, no. 3 (June 1998): 462–70; T. R. Giberson, C. J. Resick, and M. W. Dickson, "Embedding Leader Characteristics: An Examination of Homogeneity of Personality and Values in Organizations," *Journal of Applied Psychology* 90, no. 5 (2005): 1002–10.

68. T. A. Judge and D. M. Cable, "Applicant Personality, Organizational Culture, and Organization Attraction," *Personnel Psychology* 50, no. 2 (1997): 359–94; D. S. Chapman et al., "Applicant Attraction to Organizations and Job Choice: A Meta-Analytic Review of the Correlates of Recruiting Outcomes," *Journal of Applied Psychology* 90, no. 5 (2005): 928–44; A. L. Kristof-Brown, R. D. Zimmerman, and E. C. Johnson, "Consequences of Individuals' Fit at Work: A Meta-Analysis of Person-Job, Person-Organization, Person-Group, and Person-Supervisor Fit," *Personnel Psychology* 58, no. 2 (2005): 281–342; C. Hu, H.-C. Su, and C.-I. B. Chen, "The Effect of Person-Organization Fit Feedback Via Recruitment Web Sites on Applicant Attraction," *Computers in Human Behavior* 23, no. 5 (2007): 2509–23.

69. P. Nunes and T. Breene, "Reinvent Your Business before It's Too Late," *Harvard Business Review* 89, no. 1/2 (2011): 80–87.

70. A. Kristof-Brown, "Perceived Applicant Fit: Distinguishing between Recruiters' Perceptions of Person-Job and Person-Organization Fit," *Personnel Psychology* 53, no. 3 (Autumn 2000): 643–71; A. E. M. Van Vianen, "Person-Organization Fit: The Match between Newcomers' and Recruiters' Preferences for Organizational Cultures," *Personnel Psychology* 53 (Spring 2000): 113–49.

71. S. Cruz, "Park Place Lexus Mission Viejo Seeing Improvements," *Orange County Business Journal*, May 12, 2008, 15; C. Hall, "'Emotional Intelligence' Counts in Job Hires," *Dallas Morning News*, August 20, 2008.

72. D. M. Cable and J. R. Edwards, "Complementary and Supplementary Fit: A Theoretical and Empirical Integration," *Journal of Applied Psychology* 89, no. 5 (2004): 822–34.

73. Y. Lermusi, "The No. 1 Frustration of Your Job Candidates," August 15, 2006, accessed June 2, 2010, www.ere.net; S. Singleton, "Starbucks, Goodlife Fitness among Most Admired Companies," *Money.Canoe.ca* (Toronto), November 12, 2009; Taleo Research, "Talent Management Processes," 2010, accessed June 2, 2010, www.taleo.com; "Survey: 37% Use Social Media to Check Candidates," *Workforce*, April 18, 2012; Kelly Services, *Acquisition and Retention in the War for Talent*, Kelly Global Workforce Index (Troy, MI: Kelly Services, April 2012).

74. J. Van Maanen, "Breaking In: Socialization to Work," in *Handbook of Work, Organization, and Society*, ed. R. Dubin (Chicago: Rand McNally, 1976).

75. S. L. McShane, G. O'Neill, and T. Travaglione, "Managing Employee Values in Values-Driven Organizations: Contradiction, Façade, and Illusions" in *21st Annual ANZAM Conference*, (Sydney, Australia, December, 2007); S. L. McShane, G. O'Neill, and T. Travaglione, "Rethinking the Values-Driven Organization Process: From Values Engineering to Behavioral Domain Training," paper presented at Academy of Management 2008 Annual Meeting, Anaheim, CA, August 2008.

76. D. G. Allen, "Do Organizational Socialization Tactics Influence Newcomer Embeddedness and Turnover?," *Journal of Management* 32, no. 2 (April 2006): 237–56; A. M. Saks, K. L. Uggerslev, and N. E. Fassina, "Socialization Tactics and Newcomer Adjustment: A Meta-Analytic Review and Test of a Model," *Journal of Vocational Behavior* 70, no. 3 (2007): 413–46.

77. G. T. Chao et al., "Organizational Socialization: Its Content and Consequences," *Journal of Applied Psychology* 79 (1994): 450–63; H. D. Cooper-Thomas and N. Anderson, "Organizational Socialization: A Field Study into Socialization Success and Rate," *International Journal of Selection and Assessment* 13, no. 2 (2005): 116–28.

78. N. Nicholson, "A Theory of Work Role Transitions," *Administrative Science Quarterly* 29 (1984): 172–91; B. E. Ashforth, D. M. Sluss, and A. M. Saks, "Socialization Tactics, Proactive Behavior, and Newcomer Learning: Integrating Socialization Models," *Journal of Vocational Behavior* 70, no. 3 (2007): 447–62; T. N. Bauer, "Newcomer Adjustment during Organizational Socialization: A Meta-Analytic Review of Antecedents, Outcomes, and Methods," *Journal of Applied Psychology* 92, no. 3 (2007): 707–21; A. Elfering et al., "First Years in Job: A Three-Wave Analysis of Work Experiences," *Journal of Vocational Behavior* 70, no. 1 (2007): 97–115.

79. J. M. Beyer and D. R. Hannah, "Building on the Past: Enacting Established Personal Identities in a New Work Setting," *Organization Science* 13 (November/December 2002): 636–52; H. D. C. Thomas and N. Anderson, "Newcomer Adjustment: The Relationship between Organizational Socialization Tactics, Information Acquisition and Attitudes," *Journal of Occupational and Organizational Psychology* 75 (December 2002): 423–37.

80. S. L. Robinson and E. Wolfe Morrison, "The Development of Psychological Contract Breach and Violation: A Longitudinal Study," Journal of Organizational Behavior 21, no. 5 (2000): 525–46; K. J. McInnis, J. P. Meyer, and S. Feldman, "Psychological Contracts and Their Implications for Commitment: A Feature-Based Approach," *Journal of Vocational Behavior* 74, no. 2 (2009): 165–80; M.-È. Lapalme, G. Simard, and M. Tremblay, "The Influence of Psychological Contract Breach on Temporary Workers' Commitment and Behaviors: A Multiple Agency Perspective," *Journal of Business and Psychology* (2011): in press.

81. S. L. Robinson and D. M. Rousseau, "Violating the Psychological Contract: Not the Exception but the Norm," *Journal of Organizational Behavior* 15 (1994): 245–59; E. W. Morrison and S. L. Robinson, "When Employees Feel Betrayed: A Model of How Psychological Contract Violation Develops," *Academy of Management Review* 22 (1997): 226–56; S. D. Montes and P. G. Irving, "Disentangling the Effects of Promised and Delivered Inducements: Relational and Transactional Contract Elements and the Mediating Role of Trust," *Journal of Applied Psychology* 93, no. 6 (2008): 1367–81.

82. L. W. Porter, E. E. Lawler III, and J. R. Hackman, *Behavior in Organizations* (New York: McGraw-Hill, 1975), 163–67; Van Maanen, "Breaking In: Socialization to Work"; D. C. Feldman, "The Multiple Socialization of Organization Members," *Academy of Management Review* 6 (1981): 309–18.

83. B. E. Ashforth and A. M. Saks, "Socialization Tactics: Longitudinal Effects on Newcomer Adjustment," *Academy of Management Journal* 39 (1996): 149–78; J. D. Kammeyer-Mueller and C. R. Wanberg, "Unwrapping the Organizational Entry Process: Disentangling Multiple Antecedents and Their Pathways to Adjustment," *Journal of Applied Psychology* 88, no. 5 (2003): 779–94.

84. Porter, Lawler III, and Hackman, *Behavior in Organizations*, Chap. 5.

85. Louis, "Surprise and Sensemaking: What Newcomers Experience in Entering Unfamiliar Organizational Settings."

86. Robinson and Rousseau, "Violating the Psychological Contract: Not the Exception but the Norm."

87. D. L. Nelson, "Organizational Socialization: A Stress Perspective," *Journal of Occupational Behavior* 8 (1987): 311–24; Elfering et al., "First Years in Job."

88. J. P. Wanous, *Organizational Entry* (Reading, MA: Addison-Wesley, 1992); J. A. Breaugh and M. Starke, "Research on Employee Recruitment: So Many Studies, So Many Remaining Questions," *Journal of Management* 26, no. 3 (2000): 405–34.

89. J. M. Phillips, "Effects of Realistic Job Previews on Multiple Organizational Outcomes: A Meta-Analysis," *Academy of Management Journal* 41 (December 1998): 673–90.

90. Y. Ganzach et al., "Social Exchange and Organizational Commitment: Decision-Making Training for Job Choice as an Alternative to the Realistic Job Preview," *Personnel Psychology* 55 (Autumn 2002): 613–37.

91. H. Blodget, "Mark Zuckerberg, Moving Fast and Breaking Things," *Business Insider*, October 14, 2010; Ladendorf, "For Facebook Workers, It's Not Just a Job"; K. Raghav, "'We Paint the Walls'," *LiveMint*, June 10, 2011; M. Swift, "Facebook

Landing Team Transports Company Culture," *San Jose Mercury News* (California), March 25, 2011.

92. C. Ostroff and S. W. J. Koslowski, "Organizational Socialization as a Learning Process: The Role of Information Acquisition," *Personnel Psychology* 45 (1992): 849–74; Cooper-Thomas and Anderson, "Organizational Socialization: A Field Study into Socialization Success and Rate"; A. Baber and L. Waymon, "Uncovering the Unconnected Employee," *T&D* (May 2008): 60–66.

93. L. Buchanan et al., "That's Chief Entertainment Officer," *Inc.* 29, no. 8 (August 2007): 86–94; P. Burkes Erickson, "Welcoming Employees: Making That First Day a Great Experience," *Daily Oklahoman*, July 15, 2007.

CHAPTER 14

1. S. Lohr, "Even a Giant Can Learn to Run," *New York Times*, January 1, 2012, 3.

2. D. Howes, "Future Hinges on Global Teams," *Detroit News*, December 21, 1998.

3. M. Haid et al., *Ready, Get Set. . . Change!: The Impact of Change on Workforce Productivity and Engagement*, Leadership Insights (Philadelphia: Right Management, 2009).

4. J. Welch, *Jack: Straight from the Heart* (New York: Warner Business books, 2001), 432.

5. K. Lewin, *Field Theory in Social Science* (New York: Harper & Row, 1951).

6. D. Coghlan and T. Brannick, "Kurt Lewin: The 'Practical Theorist' for the 21st Century," *Irish Journal of Management* 24, no. 2 (2003): 31–37; B. Burnes, "Kurt Lewin and the Planned Approach to Change: A Re-Appraisal," *Journal of Management Studies* 41, no. 6 (September 2004): 977–1002.

7. "Ogilvy & Mather Corporate Culture," 2011, accessed May 17, 2011, http://www.ogilvy.com/About/Our-History/Corporate-Culture.aspx.

8. D. Howell, "Nardelli Nears Five-Year Mark with Riveting Record," *DSN Retailing Today*, May 9, 2005, 1, 38; R. Charan, "Home Depot's Blueprint for Culture Change," *Harvard Business Review* (April 2006): 61–70; R. DeGross, "Five Years of Change: Home Depot's Results Mixed under Nardelli," *Atlanta Journal-Constitution*, January 1, 2006, F1; B. Grow, D. Brady, and M. Arndt, "Renovating Home Depot," *BusinessWeek*, March 6, 2006, 50–57.

9. N. Machiavelli, *The Prince and Other Writings*, trans. W. A. Rebhorn, *Barnes & Noble Classics* (New York: Barnes & Noble, 2003), 25.

10. Some experts suggest that resistance to change should be re-stated in a more positive way by its opposite: readiness for change. See: M. Choi and W. E. A. Ruona, "Individual Readiness for Organizational Change and Its Implications for Human Resource and Organization Development," *Human Resource Development Review* 10, no. 1 (March 2011): 46–73.

11. S. Chreim, "Postscript to Change: Survivors' Retrospective Views of Organizational Changes," *Personnel Review* 35, no. 3 (2006): 315–35.

12. M. Johnson-Cramer, S. Parise, and R. Cross, "Managing Change through Networks and Values," *California Management Review* 49, no. 3 (Spring 2007): 85–109.

13. B. J. Tepper et al., "Subordinates' Resistance and Managers' Evaluations of Subordinates' Performance," *Journal of Management* 32, no. 2 (April 2006): 185–209; J. D. Ford, L. W. Ford, and A. D'Amelio, "Resistance to Change: The Rest

of the Story," *Academy of Management Review* 33, no. 2 (2008): 362–77.

14. E. B. Dent and S. G. Goldberg, "Challenging 'Resistance to Change'," *Journal of Applied Behavioral Science* 35 (March 1999): 25–41; D. B. Fedor, S. Caldwell, and D. M. Herold, "The Effects of Organizational Changes on Employee Commitment: A Multilevel Investigation," *Personnel Psychology* 59, no. 1 (2006): 1–29.

15. J. K. Galbraith, *Economics, Peace, and Laughter* (Boston: Houghton Mifflin, 1971), 50.

16. S. Oreg et al., "Dispositional Resistance to Change: Measurement Equivalence and the Link to Personal Values across 17 Nations," *Journal of Applied Psychology* 93, no. 4 (2008): 935–44.

17. R. R. Sharma, *Change Management: Concepts and Applications* (New Delhi, IN: Tata McGraw-Hill, 2007), Chap. 4; A. A. Armenakis and S. G. Harris, "Reflections: Our Journey in Organizational Change Research and Practice," *Journal of Change Management* 9, no. 2 (2009): 127–42; I. Cinite, L. E. Duxbury, and C. Higgins, "Measurement of Perceived Organizational Readiness for Change in the Public Sector," *British Journal of Management* 20, no. 2 (2009): 265–77; S. Jaros, "Commitment to Organizational Change: A Critical Review," *Journal of Change Management* 10, no. 1 (March 2010): 79–108.

18. C. O. Longenecker, D. J. Dwyer, and T. C. Stansfield, "Barriers and Gateways to Workforce Productivity," *Industrial Management*, March/April 1998, 21–28; D. Miller, "Building Commitment to Major Change—What 1700 Change Agents Told Us Really Works," *Developing HR Strategy*, no. 22 (September 2008): 5–8; W. Immen, "When Leaders Become Glory Hounds," *Globe & Mail* (Toronto), March 5, 2010, B15; Towers Watson, *Capitalizing on Effective Communication* (New York: Towers Watson, February 4, 2010).

19. D. A. Nadler, "The Effective Management of Organizational Change," in *Handbook of Organizational Behavior*, ed. J. W. Lorsch (Englewood Cliffs, NJ: Prentice Hall, 1987), 358–69; R. Maurer, *Beyond the Wall of Resistance: Unconventional Strategies to Build Support for Change* (Austin, TX: Bard Books, 1996); P. Strebel, "Why Do Employees Resist Change?," *Harvard Business Review* (May/June 1996): 86–92; D. A. Nadler, *Champions of Change* (San Francisco, CA: Jossey-Bass, 1998).

20. V. Newman, "The Psychology of Managing for Innovation," *KM Review* 9, no. 6 (2007): 10–15.

21. *Bosses Want Change but Workers Want More of the Same!* (Sydney: Talent2, June 29, 2005).

22. C. Ressler and J. Thompson, *Why Work Sucks and How to Fix It* (New York: Portfolio, 2008), Chapter 2.

23. R. Davis, *Leading for Growth: How Umpqua Bank Got Cool and Created a Culture of Greatness* (San Francisco: Jossey-Bass, 2007), 40.

24. T. G. Cummings, "The Role and Limits of Change Leadership," in *The Leader's Change Handbook*, ed. J. A. Conger, G. M. Spreitzer, and E. E. Lawler III (San Francisco: Jossey-Bass, 1999), 301–20; J. P. Kotter and D. S. Cohen, *The Heart of Change* (Boston: Harvard Business School Press, 2002), 15–36; J. P. Kotter, *A Sense of Urgency* (Boston: Harvard Business School Press, 2008).

25. C. Lawton and J. Lublin, "Nokia Names Microsoft's Stephen Elop as New CEO, Kallasvuo Ousted," *Wall Street Journal*, September 11, 2010; C. Ziegler, "Nokia CEO Stephen Elop

Rallies Troops in Brutally Honest 'Burning Platform' Memo? (Update: It's Real!)," *Engadget*, 8 (February 2011).

26. L. D. Goodstein and H. R. Butz, "Customer Value: The Linchpin of Organizational Change," *Organizational Dynamics* 27 (June 1998): 21–35.

27. D. Miller, *The Icarus Paradox: How Exceptional Companies Bring about Their Own Downfall* (New York: HarperBusiness, 1990); S. Finkelstein, *Why Smart Executives Fail* (New York: Viking, 2003); A. C. Amason and A. C. Mooney, "The Icarus Paradox Revisited: How Strong Performance Sows the Seeds of Dysfunction in Future Strategic Decision-Making," *Strategic Organization* 6, no. 4 (November 1, 2008): 407–34.

28. "Sustaining High Performance (Richard Goyder: Wesfarmers)," *CEOForum*, September 2006.

29. D. Darlin, "Growing Tomorrow," *Business 2.0*, May 2005, 126.

30. T. F. Cawsey and G. Deszca, *Toolkit for Organizational Change* (Los Angeles: Sage, 2007), 104.

31. J. P. Kotter and L. A. Schlesinger, "Choosing Strategies for Change," *Harvard Business Review* (March/April 1979): 106–14.

32. M. Meaney and C. Pung, "Creating Organizational Transformations: Mckinsey Global Survey Results," *McKinsey Quarterly*, July 2008, 1–7.

33. B. Nanus and S. M. Dobbs, *Leaders Who Make a Difference* (San Francisco: Jossey-Bass, 1999); Kotter and Cohen, *The Heart of Change*, 83–98; J. Allen et al., "Uncertainty during Organizational Change: Managing Perceptions through Communication," *Journal of Change Management* 7, no. 2 (2007): 187–210; T. L. Russ, "Communicating Change: A Review and Critical Analysis of Programmatic and Participatory Implementation Approaches," *Journal of Change Management* 8, no. 3 (2008): 199–211.

34. G. Jones, "Chemical Reaction," *Smart Business Pittsburgh*, February 2011, 10.

35. Towers Watson, *Capitalizing on Effective Communication*.

36. "A Cornerstone for Learning," *T&D* (October 2008): 66–89.

37. K. T. Dirks, L. L. Cummings, and J. L. Pierce, "Psychological Ownership in Organizations: Conditions under Which Individuals Promote and Resist Change," *Research in Organizational Change and Development* 9 (1996): 1–23; A. Cox, S. Zagelmeyer, and M. Marchington, "Embedding Employee Involvement and Participation at Work," *Human Resource Management Journal* 16, no. 3 (2006): 250–67; E. A. Lofquist, "Doomed to Fail: A Case Study of Change Implementation Collapse in the Norwegian Civil Aviation Industry," *Journal of Change Management* 11, no. 2 (2011/07/08 2011): 223–43.

38. N. T. Tan, "Maximising Human Resource Potential in the Midst of Organisational Change," *Singapore Management Review* 27, no. 2 (2005): 25–35.

39. M. McHugh, "The Stress Factor: Another Item for the Change Management Agenda?," *Journal of Organizational Change Management* 10 (1997): 345–62; D. Buchanan, T. Claydon, and M. Doyle, "Organisation Development and Change: The Legacy of the Nineties," *Human Resource Management Journal* 9 (1999): 20–37.

40. T. Wakefield, "No Pain, No Gain," *Canadian Business*, January 1993, 50–54; M. Cash, "Standardaero Back on the Sale Block," *Winnipeg Free Press*, December 14, 2010.

41. D. Nicolini and M. B. Meznar, "The Social Construction of Organizational Learning: Conceptual and Practical Issues in the Field," *Human Relations* 48 (1995): 727–46.

42. E. E. Lawler III, "Pay Can Be a Change Agent," *Compensation & Benefits Management* 16 (Summer 2000): 23–26; Kotter and Cohen, *The Heart of Change*, 161–77; M. A. Roberto and L. C. Levesque, "The Art of Making Change Initiatives Stick," *MIT Sloan Management Review* 46, no. 4 (Summer 2005): 53–60.

43. Lawler III, "Pay Can Be a Change Agent."

44. Goodstein and Butz, "Customer Value: The Linchpin of Organizational Change"; R. H. Miles, "Leading Corporate Transformation: Are You up to the Task?," in *The Leader's Change Handbook*, ed. J. A. Conger, G. M. Spreitzer, and E. E. Lawler III (San Francisco: Jossey-Bass, 1999), 221–67.

45. R. E. Quinn, *Building the Bridge as You Walk on It: A Guide for Leading Change* (San Francisco: Jossey-Bass, 2004), Chap. 11; D. M. Herold et al., "The Effects of Transformational and Change Leadership on Employees' Commitment to a Change: A Multilevel Study," *Journal of Applied Psychology* 93, no. 2 (2008): 346–57.

46. M. S. Cole, S. G. Harris, and J. B. Bernerth, "Exploring the Implications of Vision, Appropriateness, and Execution of Organizational Change," *Leadership & Organization Development Journal* 27, no. 5 (2006): 352–67.

47. Kotter and Cohen, *The Heart of Change*, 61–82; D. S. Cohen and J. P. Kotter, *The Heart of Change Field Guide* (Boston: Harvard Business School Press, 2005).

48. J. P. Kotter, "Leading Change: Why Transformation Efforts Fail," *Harvard Business Review* (March/April 1995): 59–67.

49. J. B. Cunningham and S. K. James, "Implementing Change in Public Sector Organizations," *Management Decision* 47, no. 2 (2009): 330.

50. S. Keller and C. Aiken, *The Inconvenient Truth about Change: Why It Isn't Working and What to Do about It* (New York: McKinsey & Company, 2008).

51. N. Edwards, *Using a Viral Communication Approach for Engaging Pfizer's Field Workforce in Realising Its Vision* (London: Pfizer, May 19, 2008); K. Dyer, "Changing Perceptions Virally at Novo Nordisk," *Strategic Communication Management* 13, no. 2 (2009): 24–27; Herrero, *Homo Imitans*.

52. A. De Bruyn and G. L. Lilien, "A Multi-Stage Model of Word-of-Mouth Influence through Viral Marketing," *International Journal of Research in Marketing* 25, no. 3 (2008): 151–63; J. Y. C. Ho and M. Dempsey, "Viral Marketing: Motivations to Forward Online Content," *Journal of Business Research* 63, no. 9–10 (2010): 1000–6; M. Williams and F. Buttle, "The Eight Pillars of Wom Management: Lessons from a Multiple Case Study," *Australasian Marketing Journal* 19, no. 2 (2011): 85–92.

53. L. Herrero, *Homo Imitans* (Beaconsfield Bucks, UK: meeting-minds, 2011).

54. J. Thottam, "Reworking Work," *Time*, July 25, 2005, 50; Ressler and Thompson, *Why Work Sucks and How to Fix It*, 20, 45–48.

55. M. Beer, R. A. Eisenstat, and B. Spector, *The Critical Path to Corporate Renewal* (Boston: Harvard Business School Press, 1990).

56. R. E. Walton, "Successful Strategies for Diffusing Work Innovations," *Journal of Contemporary Business* (Spring 1977): 1–22; R. E. Walton, *Innovating to Compete: Lessons for Diffusing and Managing Change in the Workplace* (San francisco: Jossey-Bass, 1987); Beer, Eisenstat, and Spector, *The Critical Path to Corporate Renewal*, Chap. 5.

57. E. M. Rogers, *Diffusion of Innovations*, 4th ed. (New York: Free Pree, 1995).

58. P. Reason and H. Bradbury, *Handbook of Action Research* (London: Sage: 2001); Coghlan and Brannick, "Kurt Lewin: The 'Practical Theorist' for the 21st Century"; C. Huxham and S. Vangen, "Researching Organizational Practice through Action Research: Case Studies and Design Choices," *Organizational Research Methods* 6 (July 2003): 383–403.

59. V. J. Marsick and M. A. Gephart, "Action Research: Building the Capacity for Learning and Change," *Human Resource Planning* 26 (2003): 14–18.

60. L. Dickens and K. Watkins, "Action Research: Rethinking Lewin," *Management Learning* 30 (June 1999): 127–40; J. Heron and P. Reason, "The Practice of Co-Operative Inquiry: Research 'with' Rather than 'on' People," in *Handbook of Action Research*, ed. P. Reason and H. Bradbury (Thousand Oaks, CA: Sage, 2001), 179–88.

61. D. A. Nadler, "Organizational Frame Bending: Types of Change in the Complex Organization," in *Corporate Transformation: Revitalizing Organizations for a Competitive World*, ed. R. H. Kilmann, T. J. Covin, and Associates (San Francisco: Jossey-Bass, 1988), 66–83; K. E. Weick and R. E. Quinn, "Organizational Change and Development," *Annual Review of Psychology* 50 (1999): 361–86.

62. T. M. Egan and C. M. Lancaster, "Comparing Appreciative Inquiry to Action Research: OD Practitioner Perspectives," *Organization Development Journal* 23, no. 2 (Summer 2005): 29–49.

63. "How I Spy Marketing Used the Strengths Approach to Embed a Culture of Success," 2011, accessed July 20, 2011, www.thestrengthsfoundation.org.

64. F. F. Luthans, "Positive Organizational Behavior: Developing and Managing Psychological Strengths," *The Academy of Management Executive* 16, no. 1 (2002): 57–72; N. Turner, J. Barling, and A. Zacharatos, "Positive Psychology at Work," in *Handbook of Positive Psychology*, ed. C. R. Snyder and S. Lopez (Oxford: Oxford University Press, 2002), 715–30; K. Cameron, J. E. Dutton, and R. E. Quinn, eds., *Positive Organizational Scholarship: Foundation of a New Discipline* (San Francisco: Berrett-Koehler Publishers, 2003); J. I. Krueger and D. C. Funder, "Towards a Balanced Social Psychology: Causes, Consequences, and Cures for the Problem-Seeking Approach to Social Behavior and Cognition," *Behavioral and Brain Sciences* 27, no. 3 (June 2004): 313–27; S. L. Gable and J. Haidt, "What (and Why) Is Positive Psychology?," *Review of General Psychology* 9, no. 2 (2005): 103–10; M. E. P. Seligman et al., "Positive Psychology Progress: Empirical Validation of Interventions," *American Psychologist* 60, no. 5 (2005): 410–21.

65. D. K. Whitney and D. L. Cooperrider, "The Appreciative Inquiry Summit: Overview and Applications," *Employment Relations Today* 25 (Summer 1998): 17–28; J. M. Watkins and B. J. Mohr, *Appreciative Inquiry: Change at the Speed of Imagination* (San Francisco: Jossey-Bass, 2001).

66. D. L. Cooperrider and D. K. Whitney, *Appreciative Inquiry: A Positive Revolution in Change* (San Francisco: Berrett-Koehler, 2005) Recent writing has extended this list to eight principles.

See: D. K. Whitney and A. Trosten-Bloom, *The Power of Appreciative Inquiry: A Practical Guide to Positive Change*, 2d ed. (San Francisco: Berrett-Koehler Publishers, 2010).

67. F. J. Barrett and D. L. Cooperrider, "Generative Metaphor Intervention: A New Approach for Working with Systems Divided by Conflict and Caught in Defensive Perception," *Journal of Applied Behavioral Science* 26 (1990): 219–39; Whitney and Cooperrider, "The Appreciative Inquiry Summit: Overview and Applications"; Watkins and Mohr, *Appreciative Inquiry: Change at the Speed of Imagination*, 15–21.

68. M. Schiller, "Case Study: Avon Mexico," in *Appreciative Inquiry: Change at the Speed of Imagination,* ed. J. M. Watkins and B. J. Mohr (San Francisco: Jossey-Bass, 2001), 123–26; P. Babcock, "Seeing a Brighter Future," *HRMagazine* 50, no. 9 (September 2005): 48; D. S. Bright, D. L. Cooperrider, and W. B. Galloway, "Appreciative Inquiry in the Office of Research and Development: Improving the Collaborative Capacity of Organization," *Public Performance & Management Review* 29, no. 3 (2006): 285; D. Gilmour and A. Radford, "Using OD to Enhance Shareholder Value: Delivering Business Results in BP Castrol Marine," *Organization Development Journal* 25, no. 3 (2007): P97–P102; Whitney and Trosten-Bloom, *The Power of Appreciative Inquiry.*

69. T. F. Yaeger, P. F. Sorensen, and U. Bengtsson, "Assessment of the State of Appreciative Inquiry: Past, Present, and Future," *Research in Organizational Change and Development* 15 (2004): 297–319; G. R. Bushe and A. F. Kassam, "When Is Appreciative Inquiry Transformational? A Meta-Case Analysis," *Journal of Applied Behavioral Science* 41, no. 2 (June 2005): 161–81.

70. G. R. Bushe, "Five Theories of Change Embedded in Appreciative Inquiry" in *18th Annual World Congress of Organization Development* (Dublin, Ireland, July 14–18, 1998).

71. T. C. Head and P. F. Sorenson, "Cultural Values and Organizational Development: A Seven-Country Study," *Leadership and Organization Development Journal* 14 (1993): 3–7; R. J. Marshak, "Lewin Meets Confucius: A Review of the OD Model of Change," *Journal of Applied Behavioral Science* 29 (1993): 395–415; C.-M. Lau, "A Culture-Based Perspective of Organization Development Implementation," *Research in Organizational Change and Development* 9 (1996): 49–79; C. M. Lau and H. Y. Ngo, "Organization Development and Firm Performance: A Comparison of Multinational and Local Firms," *Journal of International Business Studies* 32, no. 1 (2001): 95–114.

72. M. McKendall, "The Tyranny of Change: Organizational Development Revisited," *Journal of Business Ethics* 12 (February 1993): 93–104; C. M. D. Deaner, "A Model of Organization Development Ethics," *Public Administration Quarterly* 17 (1994): 435–46.

73. G. A. Walter, "Organization Development and Individual Rights," *Journal of Applied Behavioral Science* 20 (1984): 423–39.

74. The source of this often-cited quotation was not found. It does not appear, even in rough form, in the books that Andrew Carnegie wrote (such as *Gospel of Wealth,* 1900; *Empire of Business,* 1902; and *Autobiography,* 1920). However, Carnegie may have stated these words (or similar ones) in other places. He gave a multitude of speeches and wrote many articles, and his words are reported by numerous other authors.

Photo Credits

CHAPTER 1

Opener: Georgette Douwma/Getty Images RF
Page 4 Digital Vision/Getty Images RF
Page 5 HBS Archives Photograph Collection: Faculty and Staff. Baker Library Historical Collections. Harvard Business School
Page 6 Brand X Pictures/Jupiterimages RF
Page 7 ZUMA Wire Service/Alamy
Page 9 Courtesy of Brasilata
Page 11 Pixtal/age fotostock RF
Page 13 Courtesy of MTN
Page 14 Siede Preis/Getty Images RF
Page 15 Ingram Publishing RF
Page 16 Jon Feingersh/Blend Images/age fotostock RF
Page 19 Jon Feingersh/Blend Images LLC RF
Page 21 BloomImage/Getty Images RF

CHAPTER 2

Opener: Caroline Purser/Digital Vision/Getty Images RF
Page 25 mmaxer/Shutterstock Images LLC RF
Page 27 Photo by Amit Bhargava/Bloomberg via Getty Images
Page 28 Logo Courtesy of LinkedIn Corporation © 2012 (left), Logo Courtesy of Facebook © 2012 (center), Courtesy of Twitter © 2012 (right)
Page 29 Big Cheese Photo/Jupiterimages RF
Page 31 Jetta Productions/Walter Hodges/Getty Images RF
Page 32 ASSOCIATED PRESS RF
Page 33 Christin Gilbert/age fotostock
Page 36 Image Source/Getty Images RF
Page 37 2007 Getty Images, Inc. RF
Page 40 Photodisc Collection/Getty Images RF
Page 42 Image Source/Getty Images RF
Page 43 BloomImage/Getty Images RF

CHAPTER 3

Opener: Stockbyte/Getty Images RF
Page 46 Design Pics/Don Hammond RF
Page 47 Hamza Turkkol/iStockphoto RF
Page 48 Photo by Bob Hammerstrom/Nashua Telegraph
Page 50 Spark Studio/Getty Images RF
Page 51 Dave and Les Jacobs/Blend Images LLC RF
Page 54 Design Pics/Don Hammond RF
Page 55 Aluma Images/Photographer's Choice RF/Getty Images RF
Page 57 Image Source/Getty Images RF
Page 58 Manchan/Getty Images RF
Page 59 Imageegami/iStockphoto RF
Page 61 JGI/Blend Images LLC RF
Page 62 © Jake Lyell/Alamy
Page 63 BloomImage/Getty Images RF

CHAPTER 4

Opener: ASSOCIATED PRESS RF
Page 66 Richard Nelson/Cutcaster RF
Page 69 AP Photo/Atlanta Journal Constitution, Hyosub Shin
Page 70 Ingram Publishing RF
Page 71 Courtesy of Malaysia Airlines
Page 73 Jose Luis Pelaez Inc/Blend Images LLC RF
Page 75 Ingram Publishing/age fotostock RF
Page 79 Wu Tao/OJO Images/Getty Images
Page 81 Image Source/Corbis
Page 82 Corbis/PunchStock RF
Page 84 ASSOCIATED PRESS RF
Page 85 BloomImage/Getty Images RF

CHAPTER 5

Opener: Comstock/Jupiterimages RF
Page 88 K-PHOTOS/Alamy
Page 89 Blend Images/the Agency Collection/Getty Images RF

Page 91 Jiri Mouck Illustrations/Alamy RF
Page 92 Si Barber
Page 93 Design Pics/Kelly Redinger RF
Page 98 Tim Teebken/Photodisc/Jupiterimages RF
Page 99 Stockbyte/Getty Images RF
Page 102 Blend Images/Alamy RF
Page 105 Alex Maloney/Corbis RF
Page 106 Courtesy of Rolls-Royce plc
Page 109 BloomImage/Getty Images RF

CHAPTER 6

Opener: STOCK4B Creative/Getty Images RF
Page 112 Image Source/Getty Images RF
Page 114 WARNER BROS. PICTURES/Album/Newscom
Page 115 C Squared Studios/Getty Images RF
Page 117 Jonathan Evans/Photodisc/Getty Images RF
Page 118 bobhdeering/Alamy
Page 119 Brand X Pictures RF
Page 120 diego cervo/iStockphoto RF
Page 121 ASSOCIATED PRESS RF
Page 123 Brand X Pictures RF
Page 125 Copyright © Rob Newell, 2010
Page 126 Alamy Creativity/Alamy RF
Page 128 Courtesy of Brasilata
Page 129 BloomImage/Getty Images RF

CHAPTER 7

Opener: Getty Images/Digital Vision RF
Page 132 Andresr/Shutterstock Images LLC RF
Page 134 Courtesy of Ergon Energy
Page 135 PM Images/Getty Images
Page 137 PSA Peugeot Citroen Media Library
Page 138 Design Pics/Kristy-Anne Glubish RF
Page 140 Keith Brofsky/Getty Images RF
Page 143 Image Source/Getty Images RF
Page 145 Rubberball/Mark Andersen/Getty Images RF
Page 146 Courtesy of Whole Foods Market. "Whole Foods Market" is a registered trademark of Whole Food Market IP, LP
Page 148 Lane Oatey/Getty Images RF
Page 150 Image Source/Getty Images RF
Page 151 BloomImage/Getty Images RF

CHAPTER 8

Opener: ASSOCIATED PRESS RF
Page 155 Jorg Greuel/Getty Images RF
Page 157 Design Pics/Darren Greenwood RF
Page 159 Jose Luis Pelaez Inc/Blend Images LLC RF
Page 162 Jose Luis PelaezInc/Blend Images LLC RF
Page 164 Steve Cole/Getty Images RF
Page 166 Lane Oatey/Getty Images RF
Page 167 Vadym Drobot/Shutterstock Images LLC RF
Page 168 Flying Colours Ltd/Getty Images RF
Page 169 Courtesy of Zappos
Page 170 Comstock/PunchStock RF
Page 171 BloomImage/Getty Images RF

CHAPTER 9

Opener: © Douglas Schwartz/Corbis RF
Page 174 Comstock/Jupiterimages RF
Page 176 © Yami 2 (left), JGI/Jamie Grill/Blend Images LLC RF (right)
Page 177 Comstock Images/Jupiterimages RF
Page 178 Photo by Anysley Floyd, Courtesy of Leaders Magazine and Deloitte
Page 179 © CJ Burton/Corbis
Page 184 © Jon Feingersh/Blend Images LLC RF
Page 185 © John Lund/Matt Holmes/Blend Images LLC RF
Page 186 © Image 100/CORBIS RF

index

Note: page numbers followed by *n* indicate material found in footnotes or source notes.

A

A-B-C Model, 96–97
Abdoulah, Colleen, 33–34
Ability
  communication and, 155–156, 162, 166, 200
  defined, 25, 282
  EI and, 72
  global mindset and, 61–62
  HPWP and, 11
  human capital and, 9
  leadership and, 223, 224
  MARS Model of Individual Behavior and, 24, 25–26, 27
  motivation and, 88
  organizational change and, 275, 282, 283
  organizational structure and, 244
  personality and, 31
  self-efficacy and, 48
Absenteeism, 28, 105, 108, 219
Absorption, 177
Absorptive capacity, 124
Accountability, 246, 247, 277
Accountemps, 59*n*
Achievable goals, 101, 102
Achievement
  communication and, 202
  leadership and, 216
  motivation and, 90, 91, 92, 98, 108, 124
  self-fulfilling prophecy and, 58
  values and, 34, 35
Achievement-nurturing orientation, 42
Achievement orientation, 41, 42
Achievement-oriented leadership style, 221, 222
Action orientation, 283
Action research approach, 283–284
Action scripts, 120
Active listening, 57, 167
Active thinking, 196
Adaptive culture, 260
Adaptivity, 8
Adjourning stage, 140, 141
Adjustment, 266, 267
Advanced Research Projects Agency Network (ARPANET), 157
Advisory teams, 133
Affective commitment, 77–78, 89. *See also* Organizational commitment
Affiliation
  creativity and, 125
  motivation and, 91
  teams and, 132
Agilent Technologies, 18
Agreeableness, 31, 32, 33, 34, 223
AirAsia, 177
AirTran, 262

Akerson, Dan, 260
Alarm reaction stage, 80
Allied Signal, 121
Alvares, Antonio Carlos Teixeira, 9
Amazon, 138, 213, 263
Ambiguity, 42, 115, 163–164, 191, 200, 222, 223, 245
Ambiguous rules, 200
American Express, 108, 286
AMP Capital Investors, 6
Amtrak, 33
Analysis anchor of OB, 20
Analyzability, 248
Anchoring and adjustment heuristic, 117
Anderson, Dave, 227
Antecedents, 97
Anticipatory principle, 285
A123 Systems, 134
Apple Inc., 3, 8, 277, 284
Appreciative coaching, 102. *See also* Strengths-based coaching
Appreciative inquiry approach, 284–286
Aptitudes, 25, 104, 138, 216
Arbitration, 206, 207
Armstrong World Industries, Inc., 206
ARPANET. *See* Advanced Research Projects Agency Network (ARPANET)
Artifacts
  aligning, 264
  defined, 256
  legends as, 256
  organizational culture and, 252, 253, 256–259
  organizational language as, 257
  physical structures and symbols as, 257–258
  rituals and ceremonies as, 256–257
  stories as, 256
Asahi Breweries Ltd., 69
ASA theory. *See* Attraction-selection-attrition (ASA) theory
Assertiveness, 184, 185, 187, 189, 201
Assimilation strategy, 262
Associative play, 126
Assumptions, 252–259, 263, 264, 267, 286
Asymmetric dependence, 174
Atos Origin, 153
ATP, 69
Attitude(s)
  behavior and, 67–70
  Chick-fil-A and, 23
  communication and, 163, 171
  defined, 67
  emotions and, 66, 67–70
  global mindset and, 62
  influence and, 183, 186
  job satisfaction as (*See* Job satisfaction)
  MARS Model of Individual Behavior and, 24
  model of, 68

  motivation and, 97
  at OhioHealth, 65
  organizational change and, 277, 279, 282
  organizational commitment as (*See* Organizational commitment)
  personality and, 30, 70
  power and, 174, 183, 184, 186
  self-concept and, 46, 60
  stereotyping and, 54
Attitude object, 67, 68
Attraction, 265
Attraction-selection-attrition (ASA) theory, 264–265
Attribution errors, 55–56, 229
Attribution process, 55
Attribution rules, 55, 56
Attribution theory, 55–56
Attrition, 265
Aubé, C., 139*n*
Audience characteristics, 210–211
Augustine, Norman, 226
Authenticity, 217
Authentic leadership, 217–218
Autonomy, 106, 107, 108, 146
Availability heuristic, 117
Avoiding style, 202, 203, 204, 205
AVON Mexico, 286
Awareness training, 60

B

Baby Boomers, 15, 16
Baiocco, Maja, 14
Balance
  four-drive theory and, 94
  work/life, 15, 17–18, 83, 143, 282
Baldur's Gate, 245
Ballard, Geoffrey, 125
Ballard Power Systems, 125
Ballmer, Steve, 103
Bandura, Albert, 98
Bank of America (BofA), 261
Barclays, 252, 261
Bargaining zone of negotiations, 207–208, 209
Barnard, Chester, 6, 154
Barrett, F. J., 286*n*
Barrick Gold Corporation, 242*n*, 243
BASF, 239
Bass, Carl, 228
BATNA. *See* Best alternative to a negotiated agreement (BATNA)
Behavior(s)
  attitudes and, 67–70
  Chick-fil-A and, 23
  communication and, 154, 159–160
  conflict and, 205
  counterproductive work, 27, 28

defined, 67–69
EI and, 74
emotions and, 66, 67–70
ethical, 39–40
ethical values and, 37–40
individual (*See* Individual behavior)
influence and, 183, 185, 186
job satisfaction and, 75–76, 76
leadership and, 217–221, 225, 226, 228–230
MARS Model of Individual, 23–27, 48, 68, 89, 282
mindless, 39
model of, 68
motivation and, 88, 94, 95, 96, 97, 101, 102
organizational (*See* Organizational behavior (OB))
organizational change and, 273, 276, 277, 280, 281, 282, 284
organizational citizenship, 27–28, 77, 78, 100, 266
organizational culture and, 253, 255, 256, 260, 261, 265, 266
organizational politics and, 190, 191
organizational structure and, 240
personality and, 29, 30, 31, 32, 33, 70
power and, 174, 176, 183, 184, 186
preferred, 26
self-concept and, 46–47, 61
stereotyping and, 54
task performance, 27
teams and, 142, 143, 147
Behavioral intentions, 68
Behavioral modeling, 98
Behavioral perspective of leadership, 219–220, 225, 228
Behaviorism, 96
Beim, Alex, 125
Beliefs
  attitudes and, 67, 68, 69, 70
  behavior and, 67, 68, 69, 70
  communication and, 154, 163, 164
  emotions and, 67, 68, 70
  global mindset and, 62
  influence and, 183
  motivation and, 100
  organizational culture and, 253
  self-concept and, 60
Belongingness/love needs, 90
Benevolence, 34, 35, 223
Bennett, Steve, 278
Bennis, Warren, 225
Best alternative to a negotiated agreement (BATNA), 208–209
Best Buy, 83, 88, 276, 282
Betweenness, 182
BHP Billiton, 272
Bias. *See also* Stereotyping
  confirmation, 51–52, 121, 122
  perceptual, 51, 55, 58, 59–60
  self-serving, 56
  stereotype, 157

Bicultural audit, 261–262
Big Five personality dimensions, 30, 32, 33, 125, 216. *See also* Five-factor model (FFM) of personality
Bigler, Nathan, 227
Billing, Sean, 40
BioWare ULC, 245, 246
Bird, Brad, 75
Blake, R. R., 201*n*
"Blame game," 286
Blanchard, Ken, 223
Blogs, 33, 158, 169
Blom, David, 65
Blumer, Jason, 45
BMW, 257
Boehnke, K., 35*n*
BofA. *See* Bank of America (BofA)
Bonaparte, Napoleon, 237, 237*n*
Bootlegging, 133
Bossidy, Larry, 121
Boston Consulting Group, 69
Bounded rationality, 115
BP. *See* British Petroleum (BP)
B&Q, 92
Brainstorming, 150–151
Branson, Richard, 77
Brasilata, 9, 128
Breton, Thierry, 153
Britain's National Health System, 180
British Broadcasting Corporation, 286
British Gas New Energy, 179
British Petroleum (BP), 253, 254
Brooks's law, 135
Brown, S. P., 77*n*
Buckman Laboratories International Inc., 72
"Buddy system," 268
Buffering/buffers, 165, 206
Built to Last, 258
Bullying, 184, 185
Burning-platform strategy, 278
Burns, George, 71
Burns, James McGregor, 225
Burns, Ursula, 202
Burton, Pierre, 101
Business ethics, 77, 260–261
Business Objects, 204

C

Calcraft, Stef, 127
Calculus-based trust, 144–145, 197
Caldwell, D. F., 254*n*
Calgon Carbon Corporation, 279
Camp Fully Involved, 48
Canadian Tire, 286
Career development, 33, 122, 182
Carnegie, Andrew, 287
Castrol Marine, 286
Categorical thinking, 52, 53, 55
Categorization, 54
Centrality, 175, 179, 182–183

Centralization, 239, 240, 241, 248
Ceremonies, 256–257
CERN (European Organization for Nuclear Research), 52
Chain of command, 236, 241
Chanel, 125
Charisma, 178
Charismatic leadership, 226, 229
Charismatic visionary, 230
Chatman, J., 254*n*
Cherniss, C., 72*n*
Chick-fil-A, 23
Child care support, 83
Chrysler, 108, 164, 239
Chrysler Corp., 239
Chrysler Group LLC, 111
Churchill, Winston, 257
Circular logic, 228
Cisco Systems, 18
Citigroup, Inc., 246
City Telecom, 109
Claim value, 208–209
Clarity, 46–47
Client–consultant relationship, 284
Client divisional structure, 243
Client relationships, 109
Closed systems perspective, 7
Closeness, 182
Close ties, 182
Closing costs, 122
Cluster chain, 170
Clustering illusion, 117
Coaching, 57, 73, 74, 102–103, 231, 238
Coalition formation, 184–185, 189
Coalitions, 132, 187, 281–283
Coca-Cola Company, 187, 243, 244
Codebooks, 155–156, 163, 164
Code of ethical conduct, 39
Coercion, 278, 279, 280
Coercive power, 175, 177, 183, 184
Cognition, 66
Cognitive dissonance, 69–70
Cognitive intelligence, 124, 216, 217
Cognitive reasoning, 68
Collectivism, 40–41
Collee, John, 127
Colocation, 146
Comforting, 139
Command-and-control management, 12
Command-and-control workplaces, 31
Commitment
  affective, 77–78, 89 (*See also* Organizational commitment)
  continuance, 77–78
  decision, 128, 129
  escalation of, 121–122
  leadership and, 223, 228
  organizational (*See* Organizational commitment)
  organizational change and, 281
Communicating, 139

Communication
  at Atos Origin, 153
  conflict and, 164, 196, 199, 200, 205
  creativity and, 125
  cross-cultural, 165–166
  defined, 154
  direct, 169, 205, 236
  face-to-face, 157, 162, 168, 235
  gender, 165–166
  through "grapevine," 169–171
  importance of, 154
  improving, 168–169
  informal, 235–236, 237, 240, 241, 248
  Internet-based, 157
  Internet-based organizational, 168–169
  interpersonal, 20, 138, 166–167
  model of, 154–156
  motivation and, 101
  nonverbal (See Nonverbal communication)
  organizational change and, 278, 279,
      280, 281
  organizational learning perspective and, 14
  power and, 177, 181, 182
  through social media, 158–159, 166
  teams and, 132, 138, 147, 154–169
  verbal, 159
  written, 157, 159, 163
  at Zappos, 169
Communication barriers, 163–165. See also
      Noise
Communication channels, 155–163
Communication proficiency, 162
Communication technology, 156
Communities of practice, 133
Commuting time, 83
Competencies, 25–26, 48, 216
Competency development, 11
Competency perspective of leadership,
      215–219, 228
Competitors, 247
Complex environments, 247
Complexity, in self-concept, 46–47
Compliance, 189, 240
Compromising style, 202, 203, 204
Confirmation bias, 51–52, 121, 122
Conflict
  communication and, 164, 196, 199,
      200, 205
  consequences of, 194–198
  constructive, 149–150, 196–198
  contingency anchor and, 20
  defined, 194
  globalization and, 15
  Intel and, 193–194
  intergenerational, 199
  interpersonal, 201–204
  meaning of, 194–198
  negotiation and, 207–211
  open-systems perspective and, 14
  organizational change and, 275, 277, 286
  organizational culture and, 260, 265,
      267, 268
  organizational structure and, 245, 246, 247
  relationship, 196–198, 202, 205
  resolving, 206–211
  risk of, 128, 129

  socioemotional, 197 (See also Relationship
      conflict)
  sources of, 198–200
  task-related, 197 (See also Constructive
      conflict)
  workforce diversity and, 17
Conflict episodes, 198
Conflict handling styles, 201–204
"Conflict-is-bad" perspective, 195
Conflict management, 204–206
Conflict process model, 198
Conflict resolution, 206–211
Conflict resolving, 139
Conformity, 34, 35, 151
Confucius, 5
Connellan, T. K., 97n
Connelly, Anne, 61
Conscientiousness, 30–31, 139, 216, 223
Consensus, 55–56
Consequences
  of affective commitment, 77–78
  of change, 275
  of conflict, 194–198
  of continuance commitment, 77–78
  control stress, 84
  defined, 97
  of distress, 80–81
  of diversity, 16–17
  of influence tactics, 189–190
  of job dissatisfaction, 75
  of power, 183
  of team cohesion, 144
Consequential principle, 37
Conservation, 34, 35
Consistency, in self-concept, 46–47, 55–56
Constructionist principle, 285
Constructive conflict, 149–150, 196–198
Constructive confrontation, 194
Contact hypothesis, 61, 205
Container Store, The, 257
Contingencies
  of employee involvement, 128–129
  of organizational culture, 258, 259–260
  of organizational design, 247–249
  of power, 175, 178–180, 182
  of self-fulfilling prophecy, 58
Contingency anchor of OB, 20
Contingency perspective of leadership,
      220–224, 225, 228
Continuance commitment, 77–78
Control
  communication and, 206–207
  information, 176–177, 184, 185,
      187, 189
  locus of, 48–49, 83, 216, 218, 222
  situational, 223
  social, 259
  span of, 237–239, 240, 241, 244
  task, 82
Control system, 259
Convergent thinking, 124
Converse, 125
Coon, H. M., 41n
Cooperating, 139
Cooperrider, D. L., 285n, 286n
Coordinating, 139

Coordination
  through formal hierarchy, 235, 236
  through informal communication, 235–236
  through micromanagement, 236
  through standardization, 235, 236–237
  of work activities, 234–237
Cornerstone Research, 237
Corporate boards, 55
Corporate cults, 259–260
Corporate social responsibility (CSR),
      13–14, 251
Countercultures, 255
Counterproductive work behaviors (CWBs),
      27, 28
Countervailing power, 174
Covey, Stephen, 209
Create value, 208, 209–210
Creative process model, 123–124
Creative thinking, 125, 126
Creative workplaces, 125
Creativity
  activities encouraging, 126–127
  brainstorming and, 151
  conflict and, 196
  decision making and, 111–112, 122–127
  defined, 122
  Marchionne and, 111
  organizational conditions supporting,
      125–126
  organizational learning perspective and, 14
Credible feedback, 102
Credit Suisse, 134
Critical thinking, 149, 150
Cross-cultural communication, 165–166
Cross-cultural issues, 230–231, 286–287
Cross-cultural knowledge, 42–43
Cross-cultural research, 42–43
Cross-cultural values, 23, 40–41
Cross-functional teams, 245
Cross-pollination, 126–127
CSC, 279
CSR. See Corporate social responsibility (CSR)
Cultural differences, 204, 262
Cultural diversity, 42, 165
Cultural values
  conflict and, 207
  defined, 34
  globalization and, 15
  job satisfaction and, 75
  organizational culture and, 262, 263, 264
Culture(s)
  achievement-nurturing orientation and, 42
  adaptive, 260
  collectivism and, 40–41
  communication and, 159, 161, 165–166
  conflict and, 205
  cross-cultural knowledge and, 42–43
  dominant, 255, 256, 259, 260
  emotional display norms across, 71
  immersion in, 62
  individualism and, 40–41
  influence and, 184
  leadership and, 228, 229, 230
  nonverbal differences across, 165
  organizational (See Organizational culture)
  power and, 180

power distance and, 41–42
uncertainty avoidance and, 42
values across, 40–43
Customer satisfaction, 76–77, 146
Customer service, 134, 195
Customer surveys, 103
CWBs. *See* Counterproductive work
behaviors (CWBs)
Cxtec, 269
Cycle time, 104
Cynicism, 81

D

Daft, R., 161*n*
Daily Yomiuri, The, 251
Dannon Company, The, 251
Davis, Ray, 276
Dearth, Randall, 279
Debate, 197–198
Decentralization, 239, 247
Decision commitment, 128, 129
Decision heuristics, 117
Decision knowledge, 128–129
Decision making
alternatives in, 112, 115–121
communication and, 154, 157
creativity and, 111–112, 122–127
defined, 112
effective, 112, 120–121, 122
emotions and, 113–114, 118–119, 122
employee involvement in, 113, 127–129
evaluating decision outcomes in, 121–122
evaluating opportunities in, 118
goals and, 113, 115, 116, 129
implementing decisions in, 121
information processing and, 116–117
intuition and, 119–120
Marchionne and, 111
maximization in, 115, 117–118
opportunities in, 114–115
organizational change and, 279
organizational learning perspective and, 14
organizational structure and, 240, 245
problems in, 114–115
rational choice paradigm of, 112–118
self-concept and, 50, 121
stakeholders perspective and, 14
team, 147–151
Decisions
Chick-fil-A and, 23
emotions and, 66
leadership and, 221
motivation and, 94
nonprogrammed, 113, 128
organizational culture and, 253
organizational design and, 248
personality and, 30
programmed, 113, 128
self-concept and, 46
Decision structure, 128
Decisive leadership, 114–115
Decoding, 155–156, 166
Deculturation strategy, 262
de Dreu, C. K. W., 201*n*
Deep acting, 72

Deep-level diversity, 15, 16
de Gaulle, Charles, 184
Degree (number) centrality, 182
"Delayering," 239
Delegating leadership style, 223
Delivering stage, 286
Dell, Inc., 3, 101, 259
Deloitte LLP, 18
Deloitte Touche Tohmatsu, 178, 183
Departmentalization
divisional structure as, 242–244
forms of, 241–247
functional structure as, 241–242
matrix structure as, 245–247
simple structure as, 241
team-based structure as, 244–245
Departmental teams, 133
Depersonalization, 81
de Pree, Max, 263, 264
Descartes, 112
Designing stage, 286
Desportes, Marc-Henri, 153
Destiny stage, 286
Dewey, John, 195, 196
Diener, E., 67*n*
Differentiation, 54, 199, 204–205
Diffusion of change, 282–283
Direct communication, 169, 205, 236
Direct costs of change, 276
Direction, 24–25, 96
Directive leadership style, 221, 222, 223, 224
Direct supervision, 236, 237, 238, 240, 241, 242, 244
DIS AG, 69
Disclosure, 61
Discovery stage, 286
Discretion, 175, 180
Discrimination
intentional, 54, 55
perceptual biases and, 60
unintentional (systemic), 54
Dismissals, 280
Disney, Roy, 13
Disney/ABC Television Group, 222
Disney Media Networks, 222
Display rules, 70–71
Distinctiveness, 55–56
Distress, 80–81
Distributive justice, 37–38, 98, 101
Divergent thinking, 124
Diverse environments, 247–248
Diversity
consequences of, 16–17
cultural, 42, 165
deep-level, 15, 16
globalization and, 15
occupational, 16
organizational culture and, 254
organizational design and, 248
perceptual biases and, 60
self-concept, 47
surface-level, 15
team, 139–140
workforce, 15–17, 18
Diversity awareness training, 60
Diversity training, 62

"Divine discontent," 273
Divisional structure, 242–244, 246, 248
Division of labor, 234–237, 248
Dixon Schwabl, 69
Dominant culture, 255, 256, 259, 260
domino-world TM, 69
Doyle, Arthur Conan, 52
Dreaming stage, 286
Drives. *See also* Needs
defined, 89
employee (*See* Employee drives
and needs)
influencing employee motivation, 93
leadership and, 216
Drive to acquire, 92, 93
Drive to bond, 92, 93
Drive to comprehend, 92, 93
Drive to defend, 92, 93
Driving forces, 273, 277, 278
Drucker, Peter, 102, 159, 225, 226
Dynamic environments, 247

E

EAPs. *See* Employee assistance programs
(EAPs)
Eastern Idaho Regional Medical Center, 227
eBay, 168
Edward Jones, 49, 69
Effectiveness
leadership and, 223, 227, 229
motivation and, 106
organizational (*See* Organizational
effectiveness)
organizational change and, 272, 282, 284
of organizational culture, 259–260
Efficiency
leadership and, 225
motivation and, 104–105
organizational, 8 (*See also* Productivity)
organizational change and, 281
organizational structure and, 240
Effort
motivation and, 94, 95, 96
teams and, 135
Effort-to-performance (E-to-P) expectancy,
94, 95
EI. *See* Emotional intelligence (EI)
Einstein, Albert, 114, 123, 176
Electronic Arts, 246
Electronic brainstorming, 151
Elica, 69
Elop, Stephen, 277
Email
Atos Origin and, 153
"grapevine" and, 169, 171
information overload and, 164, 165
media richness and, 162
persuasion and, 162, 163
problems with, 157–158
social acceptance and, 161, 162
EMC, 69
Emotional contagion, 159–160
Emotional display norms, 71
Emotional dissonance, 71–72
Emotional exhaustion, 81

Emotional intelligence (EI)
  assessing, 73–74
  conflict and, 197, 210
  decision making and, 119
  defined, 72
  developing, 73–74
  dimensions of, 72
  globalization and, 15
  improving, 74
  leadership and, 216, 217, 220
  teams and, 147
Emotional labor, 70, 71
Emotional markers, 51, 68, 93, 119
Emotional stability, 31, 70, 83
Emotion detection software, 101
Emotions. *See also* Moods
  attitudes and, 66, 67–70
  behavior and, 67–70
  cognitive dissonance, 69–70
  communication and, 157, 159
  conflict and, 197, 198, 201, 208, 210
  decision making, 113–114, 118–119, 122
  defined, 66
  email and, 157
  job satisfaction and, 75, 76
  leadership and, 227
  Malaysia Airlines and, 71
  managing, 70–72
  MARS Model of Individual Behavior and, 24
  model of, 68
  motivation and, 89, 92, 93, 96, 97, 100
  negative, 67, 69, 70, 83, 97
  at OhioHealth, 65
  organizational culture and, 256
  personality and, 70
  positive, 67, 69, 70
  stress and, 83
  teams and, 149
  types of, 66–67
Empathy, 61, 62, 72, 84, 165, 181, 219
Employee assistance programs (EAPs), 84
Employee development opportunities, 89
Employee drives and needs
  defined, 89
  four-drive theory and, 92–94
  learned needs theory and, 91–92
  Maslow's needs hierarchy theory and, 90–91
Employee engagement, 88–89
Employee involvement
  benefits of, 127–128
  contingencies of, 128–129
  in decision making, 113, 127–129
  HPWP and, 11
  motivation and, 89
  organizational change and, 278, 279, 280
  organizational commitment and, 79
  organizational learning perspective and, 14
Employee involvement model, 128
Employee motivation. *See* Motivation
Employee turnover, 28
Employment relationships, 17–18
Enacted values, 36–37, 253, 254
Encoding, 155–156, 166
Encounter stage, 266, 267–268
Enron, 39
Epictetus, 167

Equality principle, 99
Equipment gauges, 103
Equity principle, 99
Equity sensitivity, 100
Equity theory, 98–101
Ergon Energy, 134
Ernst & Young, 62
Escalation of commitment, 121–122
Espoused–enacted value congruence, 36–37
Espoused values, 36–37, 253, 254
Esteem needs, 90
Ethical behavior, 39–40
Ethical conduct, 39–40, 260
Ethical issues, 286–287
Ethical misconduct, 39–40
Ethical principles, 37–38
Ethical sensitivity, 38–39
Ethical standards, 39
Ethical values, 23, 37–40, 260
Ethics
  business, 77
  defined, 13, 37
  stakeholders perspective and, 14
Ethics audits, 40
Ethics codes, 39
Ethics training, 39
E-to-P expectancy. *See* Effort-to-performance
    (E-to-P) expectancy
Eustress, 80
Evaluating, 167
Evaluation apprehension, 148, 149, 150
Evidence-based management, 19
EVLN model. *See* Exit-voice-loyalty-neglect
    (EVLN) model
Exactech Inc., 73
Exchange, 183, 185, 188–189
Executive dashboards, 103
Exercise, 84
Exhaustion stage, 80
Exit, job satisfaction and, 75, 76
Exit-voice-loyalty-neglect (EVLN)
    model, 75–76
Expectancy theory of motivation, 94–96, 220
Experience(s), 67, 124, 143, 222, 224
Expert power, 175, 177–178, 180, 183
External attributions, 55, 56, 57
External environment, 247–248, 259, 260,
    263, 273, 277, 286
External factors, 55, 56
External forces, 279
Extinction, 97
Extraversion, 31, 32, 33, 83, 139
Extraverts, 83
Extroversion, 216, 218
Extroverts, 181
E-zines, 168, 169

F

Facebook
  organizational culture and, 253, 258, 268
  personality and, 33
  power and, 176, 182
  social media and, 28
  team dynamics and, 133, 153, 158,
    159, 166

Face-to-face communication, 157, 162,
    168, 235
Fairmont Hotels, 40
False-consensus effect, 58–59
Families and Work Institute, 82
"Fault lines" in teams, 139–140
Fayol, Henri, 194, 237, 237n
Fear of unknown, 276, 279, 280
Feedback
  in communication, 155, 158, 159, 160,
    162, 163, 167
  credible, 102
  decision making and, 121, 122
  defined, 102
  evaluating, 103
  goal setting and, 101–103
  job, 107, 109
  Johari Window and, 61
  leadership and, 217
  motivation and, 101–103, 107, 109
  multisource (360-degree), 103, 149, 177
  nonsocial sources of, 103
  organizational change and, 281
  organizational structure and, 238
  relevant, 102
  social sources of, 103
  sources of, 103
  specific, 102
  strengths-based, 102
  through strengths-based coaching, 102–103
  sufficiently frequent, 102
  teams and, 141
  timely, 102
Feelings, 32, 67, 68, 69, 70, 76, 89, 154, 183
Fernandes, Tony, 177
FFM. *See* Five-factor model (FFM) of personality
Fiat S.p.A., 111
Fiedler, Fred, 223
Fiedler's contingency model, 223
"Fight-or-flight" response, 66, 81, 85, 92
Filtering, 164
Firing, 280
First impressions, 59
Five C's model, 138–139
Five-factor model (FFM) of personality, 30–32.
    See also Big Five personality dimensions
Flaming, 158
Flat structures, 238–239
Flattery, 210
"Flypaper" approach, 267
Follett, Mary Parker, 6, 196, 201
Forcing style, 201, 202, 203, 204
Ford, 103, 273
Forecasting, 177
Formal hierarchy, 235, 236, 237
Formalization, 239–240, 241, 244, 248
Forming stage, 140, 141
Fortune 500 companies, 39
Fortune magazine, 3
4C Corporate Culture Clash and Chemistry, 261
Four-D model of appreciative inquiry, 286
Four-drive theory, 92–94
Franklin, Benjamin, 38
French, John, 175
Friedman, Milton, 14
Frohman, Dov, 194

Frost, Harriet, 126
Functional structure, 241–242, 244, 246
Functional units, 243
Fundamental attribution error, 55–56

G

Galbraith, J., 235n
Galbraith, John Kenneth, 275
Gardner, John, 215
GE Aircraft Engines, 244
Gender communication, 165–166
Gender differences, 204
Gender issues, 230–231
Gendreau, Kyle, 239
General adaptation syndrome, 80
General Electric, 273, 274
General Motors, 260
Generation X, 15, 16
Generation Y, 15
Generation Z, 16, 16n
Geographic divisional structure,
    242–243, 248
Gerstner, Louis V., Jr., 253, 271
GlaxoSmithKline, 168
GLBC. See Great Little Box Company Ltd.
    (GLBC)
Globalization
    communication and, 165
    defined, 14–15
    employment relationships and, 17, 18
    stress and, 82
    teams and, 147
    values and, 37, 42
Globally integrated enterprise, 243
Global mindset, 61–63
Goal attainment perspective, 7
Goal incompatibility, 199
Goals
    achievable, 101, 102
    conflict and, 194, 198, 199, 200, 204,
        207, 208, 210
    decision making and, 113, 115, 116, 129
    leadership and, 216, 220, 221, 224
    measurable, 101, 102
    motivation and, 24–25, 88, 91, 94, 98
    organizational change and, 281
    organizational culture and, 264
    organizational structure and, 234,
        236, 249
    personality and, 31
    relevant, 101, 102
    role perceptions and, 26
    specific, 101, 102
    superordinate, 204
    teams and, 132, 134, 135, 138, 141,
        143, 149
Goal setting
    coaching and, 57
    defined, 101
    evaluating, 103
    feedback and, 101–103
    leadership and, 227
    motivation and, 89, 101–103, 105
    self-concept and, 57
    stress and, 84

Goddard, Mike, 62
Goldman Sachs, 261
Goleman, D., 72n
Good fit, 8
Goodnight, Jim, 9
Google (Brazil), 69
Google, Inc., 3, 13, 69, 123, 125,
    213, 277
Google Japan Inc., 69
Google Maps, 123
Google News, 123
Google Scholar, 213
Goyder, Richard, 278
"Grapevine," 169–171
Great Little Box Company Ltd.
    (GLBC), 87
Green Mountain Coffee Roasters, 286
Grievances, 219
Groupthink, 148, 149
Guanxi, 180
Guiding coalition, 281

H

Hackman, J. R., 106n
Halo effect, 58
Hamaberg, Bob, 280
Happy Feet, 127
Harassment, 81, 83
Hard influence tactics, 183, 189, 201
Hassell, Jim, 138
HCL Technologies, 76
Hedonism, 34, 35
Herman Miller Inc., 263, 264
Hersey, Paul, 223
Herzberg, Frederick, 105
Heskett, J. I., 77n
Hewlett-Packard, 169, 247
Hierarchy, formal, 235, 236, 237
High-expectancy employees, 57
High-performance work practices (HPWP)
        perspective
    connecting the dots with, 14
    defined, 11
    organizational effectiveness and, 7,
        11, 12, 14
    stakeholders perspective and, 12–14
Hiring, 118, 126, 256, 264, 265
Hofstede, G., 41n
Home Depot, 164, 264, 273–274, 280
Homogenization, 54
Honeywell, 121
Hostile environments, 248
Hostile work environment harassment, 81
HPWP perspective. See High-performance work
        practices (HPWP) perspective
Hsieh, Tony, 12, 13, 169, 263
Huddles, 169
Hudson's Bay Co., 14
Human capital, 9, 11
Human relations, 5
Human rights, 37
Humor, 84, 198, 210
Hunter Douglas, 286
Hurd, Mark, 247
Hygienes, 105

I

IAT. See Implicit Association Test (IAT)
IBM, 18, 25, 43, 62–63, 81, 82, 147, 168,
    169, 243, 253, 271–272
Ideal self, 45
Identification-based trust, 145
IHG. See Intercontinental Hotels Group (IHG)
Illumination, 123, 124
Implicit Association Test (IAT), 60
Implicit favorite, 116–117
Implicit leadership perspective/theory, 228–230
Impression management, 183, 185,
    187–188, 189
Incentives, 105
Incivility, 81
Incremental change, 284
Incubation, 123–124
Independent, The, 251
Independent imagination, 125
Individual behavior
    Chick-fil-A and, 23
    MARS Model of, 23, 24–27, 48, 68, 89, 282
    types of, 27–29
    values and, 35–36
    work attendance and, 29
Individualism, 40–41
Individual-level analysis, 20
Individual-level topics, 14
Individual rights, 37
Inequity tension, 100
Influence. See also Power
    defined, 183
    leadership and, 183, 223
    open-systems perspective and, 14
    organizational change and, 281, 282
    organizational politics and, 190–191
    persuasion and, 183, 185, 186–189
    at RCMP, 173
    self-concept and, 50
    strategies for, 189–190
    types of, 183–185
Influence tactics, 183–185, 186, 189–190
Informal communication, 235–236, 237, 240,
    241, 248
Informal groups, 132–133
Information control, 176–177, 184, 185,
    187, 189
Information load, 164
Information overload, 158, 266
Information processing, 115, 116–117
Information processing capacity, 164
Information systems, 284
Infosys, 259
Ingram, Harry, 60
Ingratiation, 183, 185, 187–188, 189
Initial offer point, 208, 209
Injustice, 101
Innovation, 8–9, 283
Inoculation effect, 187
Inquisition, 206, 207
Inquisitiveness, 216
Insight, 124. See also Illumination
Instant messages, 158
Instrumental values, 34

Integrated environments, 247–248
"Integration" perspective, 254
Integration strategy, 262–263
Integrator roles, 235
Integrators, 206
Integrity, 216
Intel, 168, 193–194, 197
Intel Israel, 194
Intellectual capital, 9–10
Intensity
  decision making and, 119
  moral, 38–39
  motivation and, 24–25, 88, 96, 101
Intentional discrimination, 54, 55. *See also*
    Prejudice
Intercontinental Hotels Group (IHG), 50
Interdependence, 137–138, 199–200, 206,
    207, 238, 281
Intergenerational conflict, 199
Internal attributions, 55, 56, 57
Internal factors, 55, 56
Internal self-concept, 49. *See also* Personal
    identity
Internal subsystems effectiveness, 8–9
Internet-based communication, 157
Internet-based organizational communication,
    168–169
Interpersonal communication, 20, 138,
    166–167
Interpersonal conflict handling styles, 201–204
Intervention, 284
Intranets, 103
Introversion, 31, 32, 34
Introverts, 83, 181
Intuit, 278
Intuition, 32, 119–120
iPad, 45
I Spy Marketing, 284–285
Israeli Defense Force, 58

J

Jargon, 164
JCPenney, 88
Jefferson, Thomas, 199
Job, defined, 104
Job autonomy, 11
Job burnout, 81
Job characteristics model, 105–107, 106
Job design
  defined, 104
  efficiency and, 104–105
  motivation and, 103–109
  open-systems perspective and, 14
Job design practices, 103–109
Job dissatisfaction, 28, 219
Job enlargement, 108
Job enrichment, 108–109
Job feedback, 107, 109
Job hunting, 181, 182
Job interviews, 188
Job redesign, 108
Job rotation, 108
Job satisfaction
  business ethics and, 77
  conflict and, 195

customer satisfaction and, 76–77
  defined, 74
  at LeasePlan USA, 69
  motivation and, 76, 105–106, 108
  organizational commitment and, 74, 79
  organizational culture and, 265
  organizational politics and, 190
  performance and, 76
  power and, 183
  in selected countries, 74
  teams and, 146
  work behavior and, 75–76
Job security, 29, 125, 280
Job sharing, 83
Job specialization, 104–105, 234, 248
Jobs, Steve, 5, 145
Johari Window, 60–61, 205
Johnson & Johnson, 50
Jones, Nick, 284
Jones, T. J., 38n
Jong-yong, Yun, 125
Jordan, P. J., 72n
Judging, 32
Judgments, 67
Jung, Carl, 32–33
Jungian personality theory, 32–33
Justice, 78, 89, 90–101, 275

K

Kahneman, Daniel, 117
Kanfer, R., 67n
Kelleher, Herb, 258
Kelly Services, 78n
Kemmelmeier, M., 41n
KenGen, 238
Key performance indicators (KPIs), 101
Kietzmann, J. H., 158n
Kimberly Clark, 69
Kirn, S. P., 77n
Klasko, Dean Stephen, 73
Klimoski, R. J., 67n
Knowledge
  communication and, 154, 156, 168
  creativity and, 124
  cross-cultural, 42–43
  decision, 128–129
  decision making and, 123
  globalization and, 15
  HPWP and, 11
  human capital and, 9
  leadership and, 216, 217
  MARS Model of Individual Behavior and,
    25, 26
  motivation and, 98, 99, 102
  organizational, 9–10
  organizational behavior (*See* Organizational
    behavior knowledge)
  organizational change and, 275, 276, 279,
    280, 282
  organizational culture and, 265, 266
  organizational structure and, 241, 244
  perception and, 57
  power and, 177, 179
  teams and, 135, 137
Knowledge acquisition, 10

Knowledge-based trust, 144–145
Knowledge management, 9. *See also*
    Organizational learning perspective
Knowledge of results, 107
Knowledge sharing, 10, 245, 246
Knowledge storage, 10
Knowledge use, 10
Kotter, J. P., 278n
KPIs. *See* Key performance indicators (KPIs)
KPMG, 165
Kreitner, R., 97n

L

LaHood, Ray, 169
Lam, S. K., 77n
Larson, J., 67n
Lavoie, Paul, 233
Lawrence, Paul, 92, 93n
Lawrence, P. R., 278n
Lawrence, S. A., 72n
Leader–member relations, 223
Leaders
  most important attribute of, 37
  self-fulfilling prophecy and, 58
Leadership
  authentic, 217–218
  behavioral perspective of, 219–220, 225, 228
  charismatic, 226, 229
  competency perspective of, 215–219, 228
  contingency anchor and, 20
  contingency perspective of, 220–224,
    225, 228
  cross-cultural issues in, 230–231
  decision making and, 114–115
  decisive, 114–115
  defined, 214–215
  gender issues in, 230–231
  globalization and, 15
  implicit leadership perspective in, 218,
    228–230
  influence and, 183, 223
  managerial, 225
  MBTI and, 33
  motivation and, 89, 91, 216, 217, 220,
    223, 226, 227
  open-systems perspective and, 14
  organizational change and, 230, 277,
    281–283
  organizational culture and, 264
  path–goal theory of, 220–222, 223, 224
  people-oriented, 219, 221, 223, 224, 230
  popularity of, 213–214
  romance of, 229–230
  self-concept and, 47, 50, 60, 216, 217,
    218, 227
  servant, 219–220
  shared, 215
  task-oriented, 219, 221, 223, 224, 230
  transactional, 225
  transformational perspective of, 220,
    225–228, 281, 286
Leadership motivation, 217
Leadership prototypes, 229, 230
Leadership styles, 221, 222, 223, 224,
    230, 231

Leadership substitutes, 224
Lean media, 162
Learned capabilities, 25
Learned needs theory, 91–92
Learning
    ability and, 25
    motivation and, 97
    organizational, 147, 154
    organizational change and, 278, 279, 280
    organizational socialization as, 266, 267
Learning behavior outcomes, 98
Learning needs, 92
Learning orientation, 125, 215, 260
LeasePlan USA, 69
Lee Kum Kee Health Products
        Company, Ltd., 258
Legitimate power, 175–177, 183, 184
Lengel, R., 161n
Lewin, Kurt, 273, 281, 283
Lewin's force field analysis model, 272–273,
        277, 281, 286
L'Express (magazine), 71
Liaison roles, 235
LinkedIn, 28, 133, 153, 182
Lochhead, Christopher, 82
Locus of control, 48–49, 83, 216, 218, 222
Logic
    circular, 228
    decision making and, 119
Logical linear sequence, 286
Logical thinking, 66, 113
Lombardi, Vince, 89
London Stock Exchange, 121
Lord, R. G., 67n
L'Oreal Canada, 205
Loughry, M. L., 139n
Low-expectancy employee, 57
Lowry, Frank, 210
Loyalty
    affective commitment and, 77–78
    employee involvement and, 79
    job satisfaction and, 75, 76, 77
    motivation and, 98
    organizational culture and, 268
    trust and, 79
Lucas, R. E., 67n
Lucent Technologies, 187–188
Luft, Joseph, 60, 60n
Luthans, F., 97n

M

Machiavelli, Niccolò, 191, 274
Machiavellian values, 191
Mackey, John, 146
Malaysia Airlines, 71
Malekzedeh, A. R., 262n
Management by walking around (MBWA), 169
Managerial leadership, 225
Marchionne, Sergio, 111, 112, 215, 239
Marks & Spencer, 88
MARS Model of Individual Behavior, 23,
        24–27, 48, 68, 89, 282
Maslow, Abraham, 90, 90n, 93, 115
Maslow's needs hierarchy theory, 90–91
Master and Commander, 127

Maternity leave, 83
Matrix structure, 245–247
Maturity, 73, 74
Mayo, Elton, 5, 6, 194
Mayo Clinic, 256
MBTI. See Myers-Briggs Type Indicator (MBTI)
MBWA. See Management by walking around
        (MBWA)
McCarthy, I. P., 158n
McClelland, David, 91
McDonald's, 240, 243, 244
McGuire, Lauren, 23
McKinsey & Company, 134
Meaningful interaction, 59, 61
Meaningfulness, 107
Measurable goals, 101, 102
Mechanistic structure, 240, 247, 248
Médecins San Frontières (Doctors Without
        Borders), 61
Media richness, 160, 161–162
Mediation, 206, 207
Medicare, 215
Meditation, 84
Meggy, Robert, 87
Member interaction, 144
Member similarity, 143
Men
    communication and, 165–166
    conflict and, 204
    leadership and, 230–231
Mencius, 104
Menlo Innovations, 133
Mental models, 53, 114, 141, 241, 260
Mental skill set, 93
Mentoring, 183
Merck, 3
Meridian Technology Center, 268
Merrill Lynch, 261
Mestral, Georges de, 124
Meta-decision, 113
Metropolitan Transit Authority, 179
M-form structure, 242. See also Divisional
        structure
Micromanagement, 236
Microsoft Co. Ltd., 69, 103, 257
Millennials, 15, 16, 16n
Mindless behavior, 39
Mindlessness, 38–39
Mintzberg, H., 235n
Modeling, 98, 228
Molson Coors, 39
Moods, 66, 76, 119, 149, 210. See also
        Emotions
Moore, D. D., 139n
Morale, 75, 76, 77, 108, 135, 169
Moral intensity, 38–39
Morphological analysis, 126
Mother, 126–127
Motivation
    affective commitment and, 77, 79
    communication and, 200
    creativity and, 124, 125
    decision making and, 128
    defined, 24, 88
    employee drives and needs and (See
        Employee drives and needs)

employee engagement and, 88–89
    expectancy theory of, 94–96, 220
    GLBC and, 87
    HPWP perspective and, 14
    job design practices and, 103–109
    job satisfaction and, 76, 105–106, 108
    leadership and, 89, 91, 216, 217, 220,
        223, 226, 227
    MARS Model of Individual Behavior and,
        24–25, 27
    OB Mod and, 96–97
    organizational change and, 275, 277, 278,
        280, 283
    organizational culture and, 263
    organizational justice and, 98–101
    organizational politics and, 190, 191
    organizational structure and, 244
    power and, 90, 91, 183
    self-concept and, 48, 50, 90, 92, 94
    social cognitive theory and, 96, 97–98
    teams and, 134, 135, 139, 141
Motivator-hygiene theory, 105
Motivators, 105
Mouton, J. S., 201n
MTN Group, 13
Multi-communicate, 162
Multiculturalism, 42
Multidisciplinary anchor, 19–20
Multidivisional structure, 242. See also
        Divisional structure
Multiple selves, 46–47
Multi-skilling, 108
Multisource (360-degree) feedback, 103,
        149, 177
Munificent environments, 248
Murdoch, Rupert, 222
Mutual understanding, 205
Muzyka, Ray, 245
Myers-Briggs Type Indicator (MBTI),
        32–33, 119

N

nAch. See Need for achievement (nAch)
Nadler, D. A., 235n
nAff. See Need for affiliation (nAff)
Nahavandi, A., 262n
Nardelli, Robert, 164, 264, 273, 280
Nasser, Jacques, 273
Natural grouping approach, 109
Nature, 30
NDA. See Nishith Desai Associates (NDA)
Need for achievement (nAch), 91, 124,
        202, 216
Need for affiliation (nAff), 91
Need for power (nPow), 91–92
Need principle, 99
Needs. See also Drives
    defined, 89
    employee (See Employee drives and needs)
    esteem, 90
    influence and, 183
    organizational change and, 278
    organizational culture and, 268
    physiological, 90
    primary, 89, 90

Negative emotions, 67, 69, 70, 83, 97
Negative reinforcement, 97
Neglect, job satisfaction and, 75, 76
Negotiation
    bargaining zone of, 207–208, 209
    conflict and, 207–211
    defined, 207
    organizational change and, 278, 279, 280
Nestlé, 239, 243, 246
Nestlé UK, 142
Nestlé Waters, 246
Networking, 181
Networks, 62
Neuroticism, 31, 33, 70, 83
News Corporation, 222
Ng, Ellis, 109
Ngure, Simon, 238
Nilekani, Nandan, 259
Nin, Anais, 51
Nishith Desai Associates (NDA), 127
Nohria, Nitin, 92, 93n
Noise, 155, 163–165, 167, 168
Nokia Corporation, 8, 277
Nominal group technique, 151
Nomura Securities Company, 251, 261
Nonprogrammed decisions, 113, 128
Nonsocial sources of feedback, 103
Nonverbal communication
    conflict and, 209
    across cultures, 165
    defined, 159
    emotions and, 159–160
    globalization and, 15
    motivation and, 103
    persuasion and, 163
Nordstrom chain, 8
Norming stage, 140, 141
Norm of reciprocity, 176
Norms
    conflict and, 204
    influence and, 185
    team, 140, 142–143, 149, 198,
        266, 276, 284
"Not-invented-here" syndrome, 276
Novo Nordisk, 282
nPow. See Need for power (nPow)
Nucor, 177
Nurture, 30

O

Oakley, Inc., 257
OB. See Organizational behavior (OB)
OB Mod. See Organizational behavior
    modification (OB Mod)
OCBs. See Organizational citizenship
    behaviors (OCBs)
Occupational diversity, 16
Office politics, 190
Ogilvy, David, 256
Ogilvy & Mather, 273
OhioHealth, 65
Ohland, M. W., 139n
Oldham, G., 106n
OMD, 126
Omitting, 165

1-800-Got-Junk?, 169
Openness to change, 34, 35, 125
Openness to experience, 31, 32, 33, 125
Open-systems perspective, 7–9, 11, 12, 14,
    260, 284
Opportunity
    communication and, 200
    defined, 113
    evaluating, 118
"Optimal conflict" perspective, 196
Optimer Pharmaceuticals, 35
Oracle, 247
O'Reilly, C. A., III, 254n
Organic structure, 240, 244, 247, 248, 249
Organizational behavior (OB)
    benefits of studying, 6
    conflict and, 194
    continuing journey in, 287
    defined, 5
    field of, 4–6
    historical foundations of, 5–6
    HPWP perspective and (See
        High-performance work
        practices (HPWP) perspective)
    importance of, 6
    introduction to, 2–21
    organizational effectiveness and (See
        Organizational effectiveness)
    positive, 58, 91, 285
    self-concept and, 48, 50
Organizational behavior discipline, 72
Organizational behavior knowledge
    analysis anchor and, 20
    multidisciplinary anchor and, 19–20
    systematic research anchor and, 18–19
    value of, 6
Organizational behavior modification (OB Mod),
    96–97
Organizational boundaries, 266
Organizational capital, 9
Organizational change
    approaches to, 283–286
    coalitions and, 281–283
    cross-cultural issues in, 286–287
    diffusion of, 282–283
    effectiveness of, 272, 282, 284
    ethical issues in, 286–287
    IBM and, 271–272
    leadership and, 230, 277, 281–283
    Lewin's force field analysis model and,
        272–273, 277
    open-systems perspective and, 14
    organizational culture and, 262, 264, 284
    organizational politics and, 190–191
    pilot projects and, 281–283
    refreezing in, 277–281
    resistance to (See Resistance to change)
    unfreezing in, 277–281
    urgency for, 277–278
Organizational charts, 241
Organizational citizenship, 190
Organizational citizenship behaviors (OCBs),
    27–28, 77, 78, 100, 266
Organizational commitment, 50
    building, 78–79
    defined, 77

job satisfaction and, 74, 79
    organizational politics and, 190
    power and, 183
Organizational comprehension, 79, 89
Organizational culture
    through artifacts (See Artifacts)
    Barclays and, 252
    business ethics and, 260–261
    changing, 263–265
    content of, 254–255
    contingencies of, 258, 259–260
    Dannon Company and, 251
    defined, 252
    effectiveness of, 259–260
    elements of, 252–255
    during hiring process, 265
    importance of, 258–261
    merging, 261–263
    Nomura Securities Company and, 251
    organizational change and, 262, 264, 284
    organizational socialization and (See
        Organizational socialization)
    stakeholders perspective and, 14
    strengthening, 263–265
Organizational design
    contingencies of, 247–249
    external environment and, 247–248
    organizational size and, 248
    organizational strategy and, 248–249
    technology and, 248
Organizational diagnosis, 284
Organizational effectiveness
    defined, 7
    HPWP perspective and, 7, 11, 12, 14
    MARS Model of Individual Behavior and, 26
    open-systems perspective of, 7–9
    organizational culture and, 258, 259, 260
    organizational learning perspective and (See
        Organizational learning perspective)
    perspectives of, 7–11, 14
Organizational efficiency, 8. See also
    Productivity
Organizational justice, 78, 89, 98–101, 275
Organizational knowledge, 9–10
Organizational language, 257
Organizational learning, 147, 154
Organizational learning perspective
    connecting the dots with, 14
    defined, 9
    intellectual capital and, 9–10
    organizational knowledge and, 9–10
    organizational learning processes and, 10
    organizational memory in, 10–11
    in survival/success of organizations, 14
    unlearning in, 10–11
Organizational learning processes, 10, 147
Organizational legends, 256
Organizational memory, 10–11
Organizational performance, 11
Organizational politics, 20, 190–191, 195
Organizational productivity, 8
Organizational size, 238, 248, 249
Organizational socialization
    defined, 265
    improving, 268–269
    as learning and adjustment process, 266, 267

psychological contracts and, 266
stages of, 266–268
Organizational stories, 256, 264
Organizational strategy, 248–249
Organizational structure
coordination and (*See* Coordination)
defined, 234
departmentalization and (*See* Departmentalization)
designing, 233–249
division of labor and, 234–237
elements of, 237–240
globalization and, 15
open-systems perspective and, 14
organizational design and (*See* Organizational design)
requirements of, 234
TAXI Canada and, 233–234, 235
Organizational subcultures, 255, 260
Organizational systems, 276–277
Organizational values, 34
Organization-community values congruence, 37
Organization-environment fit, 8
Organization-level analysis, 20
Organizations
challenges for, 14–18
defined, 5, 234
features of, 5
joining/staying with, 27, 28
perceptions in (*See* Perception(s))
personality in, 29–33 (*See also* Personality)
personality testing in, 33
Osborn, Alex, 150
Otago Sheetmetal, 184
Outcome/input ratio, 99, 100
Outcome valences, 94, 95, 96
Overconfidence, 149
Overreward inequity, 99–100
Overt resistance, 274
Oyserman, D., 41*n*

P

Palmisano, Sam, 243, 271, 272
Park Place Dealerships, 265
Participative leadership style, 221, 222, 223, 230
Participative management, 127. *See also* Employee involvement
Paternity leave, 83
Path–goal theory of leadership, 220–222, 223, 224
People-oriented leadership, 219, 221, 223, 224, 230
Perceived self, 45
Perceiving, 32
Perception(s). *See also* Self-concept
about accountants, 45, 54
across borders, 61–63
conflict and, 194, 196, 197, 198, 200, 201, 205
defined, 50
emotions and, 66
global mindset and, 61–63
improving, 59–61

leadership and, 229, 230
MARS Model of Individual Behavior and, 24, 25–26
motivation and, 100, 101
organizational change and, 275
organizational culture and, 253, 259, 266
organizational politics and, 190
power and, 174
role, 24, 25–26, 27, 48, 221, 283
self-concept and, 45–53, 59–61, 61–63
social, 45
Perceptual biases, 51, 55, 58, 59–60
Perceptual defense, 115
Perceptual grouping, 52–53
Perceptual organization and interpretation, 52–53
Perceptual processes/problems/effects
attribution theory as, 55–56
false-consensus effect as, 58–59
halo effect as, 58
model of, 51
primacy effect as, 59
recency effect as, 59
self-fulfilling prophecy as, 56–58
stereotyping as, 53–55
Performance
conflict and, 195, 200
continuance commitment and, 78
EI and, 73
HPWP and, 11
improving, 101
influence and, 184
job satisfaction and, 76
leadership and, 216, 217, 219, 220, 221, 222, 224, 228
MARS model of individual behavior and, 24–26, 27
MBTI and, 33
motivation and, 88, 94, 95, 96, 101, 103–105, 107, 108
organizational, 11
organizational commitment and, 77
organizational culture and, 255, 260, 264, 268
organizational structure and, 238
personality and, 32
power and, 183
self-concept and, 46, 47, 50, 57, 61
task, 27, 190
teams and, 134, 135, 136, 140, 141, 144, 149
Performance-to-outcome (P-to-O) expectancy, 94, 95–96, 98
Performing stage, 140, 141
Persistence
creativity and, 124
motivation and, 24–25, 88, 101
Personal brand, 178
Personal characteristics, 216, 218
Personal identity, 49–50
Personality
Chick-fil-A and, 23
communication and, 161
creativity and, 125
defined, 29
emotions and, 70

Facebook, 33
FFM of, 30–32
job satisfaction and, 76
leadership and, 216, 223–224, 229
MARS Model of Individual Behavior and, 24, 25
MBTI and, 32–33
motivation and, 90, 94, 103
nature versus nurture in, 30
organizational change and, 275
organizational culture and, 264
in organizations, 29–33
stress and, 32, 83
teams and, 141
work attendance and, 28
Personality determinants, 30
Personality test, 29
Personality testing, 33
Personality theory, 29, 30
Personality traits, 30, 31, 34, 73, 176, 181
Personalized power, 92, 217
Personal leave, 83
Personal networks, 181
Personal values
defined, 34
individual behavior and, 35–36
motivation and, 90, 93
organizational culture and, 253, 262, 265
self-concept and, 50
Person–job matching strategy, 26
Person–organization value congruence, 35
Persuasion
communication channels and, 163
conflict and, 206
defined, 186–187
effectiveness of, 186, 187
exchange and, 188–189
impression management and, 187–188
influence and, 183, 185, 186–189
ingratiation and, 187–188
Peter, Laurence J., 116
Peters, Tom, 237*n*
Pfizer, 282
P&G. *See* Procter & Gamble (P&G)
Philips, 242*n*, 243, 244
Physiological needs, 90
Pilot projects, 281–283
Pivot, Laurence, 71
Pixar Animation Studios, 10, 75, 168
Plan.Do.See Inc., 69
Plato, 5, 51, 104, 112
Poetic principle, 285
Poincaré, 123
Politics
office, 190
organizational, 20, 190–191, 195
Pooled interdependence, 137, 200
Position power, 223
Positive emotions, 67, 69, 70
Positive organizational behavior, 58, 91, 285
Positive principle, 285
Positive reinforcement, 97, 98
Post-decisional justification, 121

Power. *See also* Influence
  coercive, 175, 177, 183, 184
  conflict and, 208–209
  consequences of, 183
  contingencies of, 175, 178–180, 182
  contingency anchor and, 20
  countervailing, 174
  defined, 174
  expert, 175, 177–178, 180, 183
  leadership and, 217, 220, 223, 226
  legitimate, 175–177, 183, 184
  meaning of, 174–175
  motivation and, 90, 91, 183
  open-systems perspective and, 14
  organizational change and, 282, 286
  organizational politics and, 191
  organizational structure and, 236, 238–239,
    245, 246
  personalized, 92, 217
  of personal networks for job hunting, 181
  position, 223
  at RCMP, 173
  referent, 175, 178, 180, 183, 206,
    226, 282
  reward, 175, 177, 183
  socialized, 92, 217
  of social networks, 180–183
  sources of, 175–178, 180–181
  values and, 34, 35, 41–42, 176
Power dependence model, 175
Power distance, 41–42, 176, 207, 230
"Power Point culture," 257
Practical intelligence, 124, 216, 217
Preemployment socialization stage,
    266–267
Preferred behaviors, 26
Prejudice, 54, 60. *See also* Intentional
    discrimination
Preparation, 123
Presenteeism, 28–29
Pressure to conform, 148, 149
Prevention, 177
PricewaterhouseCoopers LLP, 14
Primacy effect, 59
Primary needs, 89, 90. *See also* Drives
Prince, The (Machiavelli), 191
Priority of tasks, 26
Privacy rights, 286
Problem, defined, 113
Problem identification, 114–115
Problem solving style, 201, 202, 203, 204,
    209, 210
Procedural justice, 98, 101, 207, 275
Process losses, 135
Procter & Gamble (P&G), 27, 62, 235, 246
Production blocking, 148, 150
Production/service/leadership teams, 133
Productivity. *See also* Organizational
    efficiency
  at Brasilata, 9
  conflict and, 199
  defined, 8
  motivation and, 105, 108, 109
  organizational, 8
  teams and, 146
  virtual work and, 18

  work attendance and, 29
  workforce diversity and, 17
Product/service divisional structure, 243
Programmed decisions, 113, 128
Project GLOBE, 230
Proquest, 213
Prospect theory effect, 122
PSA Peugeot Citroën, 137
Psychological contracts, 266, 268
Psychological harassment, 81
P-to-O expectancy. *See* Performance-to-outcome
    (P-to-O) expectancy
Public images, 187
Punishment, 97

Q

Quala, 69
Quantum change, 284
Quid pro quo harassment, 81
Quinn, R. T., 77*n*

R

Rackspace Hosting, 139
Rahim, M. A., 201*n*
Rapport talk, 166
Ratatouille, 75
Rational choice paradigm, 112–114, 115,
    116, 117, 118
Raven, Bertrand, 175
Razer, 69
RCMP. *See* Royal Canadian Mounted Police
    (RCMP)
Realistic job preview (RJP), 268
Reality shock, 267, 268
Recency effect, 59
Reciprocal interdependence,
    137–138, 200
Reckitt-Benckiser, 146, 265
Recognition, 47, 76
Reduced personal accomplishment, 81
Reed, Scott, 23
Referent power, 175, 178, 180, 183, 206,
    226, 282
Refreezing, 273, 277–281, 284
Relational psychological contracts, 266
Relationship capital, 10
Relationship conflict, 196–198, 202, 205
Relationships
  client, 109
  client–consultant, 284
  communication and, 159, 166
  conflict and, 204, 210
  employment, 17–18
  global mindset and, 62
  leadership and, 218
  motivation and, 92, 109
  power and, 181
  teams and, 141
Relevant feedback, 102
Relevant goals, 101, 102
Reliance Industries, 11
Renault-Sofasa, 69
Report talk, 166
Representativeness heuristic, 117

Research
  on communication, 154, 166, 170
  on confirmation bias, 52
  on conflict, 197, 198, 204, 207
  cross-cultural, 42–43
  on decision making, 119
  on "grapevine," 170
  on leadership, 216, 219, 220, 222, 224,
    229, 231
  on motivation, 89, 92, 93
  on organizational change, 280, 284, 286
  on organizational culture, 258, 259, 261,
    265, 266
  on organizational politics, 191
  on power, 183
  on teams, 139, 147
Research orientation, 283
Resistance, 189
Resistance point, 208, 209
Resistance stage, 80
Resistance to change
  driving force and, 273
  at Home Depot, 273–274, 280
  reasons for, 275–277
  restraining force and, 273
  strategies for minimizing, 278–280
  success and, 278
  understanding, 273–277
Resources
  conflict and, 199, 200, 206
  leadership and, 214
  motivation and, 88, 89
  organizational structure and, 241, 244,
    245, 246, 247
Responding, 167
Responsibility, 107, 109
Restraining forces, 273, 277, 278–280
Results-only work environment (ROWE), 83,
    276, 282
Retention, 76
Reuters, Thomson, 181
Reward power, 175, 177, 183
Rewards
  leadership and, 214, 220, 221, 225
  motivation and, 94–96, 103
  organizational change and, 275, 276, 281,
    282, 284
  organizational culture and, 264
Rich media, 162
Risk-aversion, 278
Risk of conflict, 128, 129
Rituals, 256–257
RJP. *See* Realistic job preview (RJP)
Robert Half, 59*n*
Roethlisberger, Fritz, 5, 6
Rokeach, Milton, 34
Role clarity, 26, 31, 88, 275
Role management stage, 266, 267, 268
Role perceptions, 24, 25–26, 27, 48,
    221, 283
Roles, team, 141
Rolls Royce, 106
Rolls-Royce Engine Services, 215
Rompré, Marjolaine, 205
Rousseau, V., 139*n*
Roving Coach, 57

ROWE. *See* Results-only work environment (ROWE)
Royal Canadian Mounted Police (RCMP), 173
Royal Dutch/Shell, 138
Ruble, T. L., 201*n*
Rucci, A. J., 77*n*
Rules, conflict and, 199, 200, 206
Russell, J. A., 67*n*

S

Safety needs, 90
Sage Software, 183
Salzberg, Barry, 178
Samsonite, 239
Samsung Electronics, 125
San Jorge Children's Hospital, 83
SAP, 204–205
SAS Institute Inc., 9, 69
Satisfaction
  decision making and, 112, 128
  job (*See* Job satisfaction)
  teams and, 136
Satisficing, 117–118
Saving face, 276, 279
Savoie, A., 139*n*
Scarlet, CJ, 57
Scenario planning, 120–121
Schau, C., 286*n*
Schlesinger, L. A., 77*n*, 278*n*
Schnitzer, Ken, 265
Schrage, Michael, 35
Schwalm, Cynthia, 35
Schwartz, Shalom, 34, 35, 35*n*
Schwarz, John, 204
Scientific management, 104–105
Scudamore, Brian, 169
SDTs. *See* Self-directed teams (SDTs)
Security, 34, 35
Seidenberg, Ivan, 15
Selection, 265
Selective attention, 50–51, 53
Self-actualization needs, 90, 91, 92
Self-awareness
  conflict and, 205
  leadership and, 217
  MBTI and, 33
  self-concept and, 59, 60–61, 62
Self-concept. *See also* Perception(s)
  characteristics of, 46–47
  conflict and, 197, 200
  decision making and, 50, 121
  defined, 45, 46
  four processes shaping, 46, 47–50
  individualism/collectivism and, 41
  internal, 49 (*See also* Personal identity)
  job satisfaction and, 75, 76
  leadership and, 47, 50, 60, 216, 217, 218, 227
  MARS Model of Individual Behavior and, 24
  motivation and, 48, 50, 90, 92, 94
  OB and, 50
  organizational change and, 281
  perceptions and, 45–53, 59–61, 61–63

perceptual processes/problems and (*See* Perceptual processes/problems/effects)
  personality and, 30
  power and, 180
  self-enhancement and, 46, 47, 48, 49, 54
  self-evaluation and, 46, 47, 48–49
  self-verification and, 46, 47, 48
  social self and, 46, 47, 49–50
  stereotyping and, 53–55, 60
    (*See also* Bias)
  stress and, 83, 84
  teams and, 132, 140, 143, 145
Self-confidence, 84, 98, 218
Self-directed teams (SDTs), 11, 133, 145, 146, 147, 237, 244
Self-direction, 34, 35, 90, 125
Self-discipline, 218
Self-efficacy, 48, 83, 88, 98, 102, 103, 216, 218, 226
Self-enhancement, 35, 46, 47, 48, 49, 54, 102, 149
Self-enhancement effect, 121–122
Self-esteem, 48, 83, 103, 121, 124, 149, 216, 218, 280, 286
Self-evaluation, 46, 47, 48–49, 84, 216, 217, 218
Self-fulfilling prophecy, 56–58
Self-fulfilling prophecy awareness training, 60
Self-fulfilling prophecy cycle, 57
Self-justification effect, 121, 122
Self-presentation, 149
Self-reflection, 74, 217
Self-regulation, 98
Self-reinforcement, 84
Self-serving bias, 56
Self-transcendence, 35
Self-verification, 46, 47, 48
Self-worth, 154
Selling leadership style, 223
Selye, Hans, 80
Semco SA, 215, 229
Semler, Ricardo, 229
Sense making, 259
Sensing, 32, 167
Separation strategy, 262, 263
Sequential interdependence, 137
Sequential interdependence work relationships, 200
Servant leadership, 219–220
Service profit chain model, 76–77
7-Eleven, 239
Sexual harassment, 81
Shadbolt, Lucy, 179
Shalom Schwartz, 93
Shared assumptions, 252, 253, 254, 256, 263
Shared leadership, 215
Shared values, 12, 34, 78–79, 252, 253, 254, 256, 263
Shattered Steel, 245
Shaw, George Bernard, 163
Shell, 246
Shepard, H. A., 201*n*
Sheridan, Richard, 133

Siemens, 142, 165
Silence, 165
Silent authority, 183–184, 185, 187, 189
"Silents," 16
Silvestre, B. S., 158*n*
Similar-to-me effect, 58. *See also* False-consensus effect
Simon, Herbert, 115, 118
Simple environments, 247
Simple structure, 241
Simultaneity principle, 285
Singer, Isaac Bashevis, 29
Sitel, 101
Situational barriers, 102
Situational control, 223
Situational factors
  MARS Model of Individual Behavior and, 24, 25, 26, 27
  organizational change and, 283
  self-concept and, 48
  for unethical conduct, 39
Situational influences, 38–39, 210–211
Situational leadership theory (SLT), 223
Situation favorableness, 223
"Skill-and-will" model of performance, 24
Skills
  ability and, 25
  conflict and, 200, 208
  decision making and, 123
  globalization and, 15
  HPWP and, 11
  human capital and, 9
  leadership and, 214, 216, 222, 224
  MARS Model of Individual Behavior and, 25
  motivation and, 98, 99, 102, 104
  organizational change and, 275, 276, 279, 282
  organizational culture and, 266, 268
  organizational structure and, 234, 236, 237, 242
  perception and, 57
  power and, 177, 179
  social, 31
  standardized, 236, 237
  teams and, 135, 137, 138, 139, 147, 150
Skill variety, 106, 107, 108
Skunkworks, 132, 133
Skype, 45, 161
SLT. *See* Situational leadership theory (SLT)
"Sludge," 276
SMARTER, 101, 102
Smith, Adam, 5, 104
Smith, K. W., 262*n*
Smith, Nina, 183
Social acceptance, 160, 161
Social capital, 180–181
Social cognitive theory, 96, 97–98
Social control, 259
"Social glue," 259
Social identity
  communication and, 154
  conflict and, 197, 204
  organizational culture and, 259, 265, 266
  perception and, 49–50, 54, 59
  power and, 185
  teams and, 134, 149

Social identity theory, 49, 132
Socialization agents, 268–269
Socialized power, 92, 217
Social loafing, 135
Social media
  communication through, 158–159, 166
  functions of, 158
  recruitment and, 28
Social network centrality, 182–183
Social networks, 133, 157, 171, 180–183,
      184, 269, 281–282
Social network sites, 33
Social perception, 45
Social presence effects, 162
Social responsibility, 251
Social responsibility missions, 62
Social self, 46, 47, 49–50
Social skills, 31
Social sources of feedback, 103
Social support, 84–85
Socioemotional conflict, 197. *See also*
      Relationship conflict
Soft influence tactics, 183, 187, 189
Solution-focused problem
      identification, 115
Sony Europe, 73
Southwest Airlines, 33, 258, 262
Span of control, 237–239, 240, 241, 244
Span of management, 237. *See also* Span of
      control
Specific feedback, 102
Specific goals, 101, 102
Stable environments, 247
Stakeholder framing, 114
Stakeholders
  defined, 12
  emotions and, 72
  ethical principles and, 37
  organizational structure and, 247
Stakeholders perspective, 7, 12–14
StandardAero, 280
Standardization, 235, 236–237,
      240, 248
Standardized outputs, 236
Standardized processes, 236
Standardized skills, 236, 237
Stanley Milgram, 176
Stanley, Morgan, 27
Stereotype biases, 157
Stereotypes, 183, 196, 197, 200, 205,
      230, 231
Stereotyping, 53–55, 60, 183. *See
      also* Bias
Stimulation, 34, 35, 90, 125
Storming stage, 140, 141
Strategic Investments, 135
Strengths-based coaching, 102–103
Strengths-based feedback, 102
Stress
  causes of, 81–82
  communication and, 164
  defined, 79
  distress and, 80–81
  general adaptation syndrome
      and, 80
  individual differences in, 82–83

leadership and, 224
managing, 79–85
MARS Model of Individual Behavior
      and, 24
motivation and, 107
organizational culture and, 259, 267
organizational politics and, 190
organizational structure and, 245
personality and, 32, 83
teams and, 133, 149
telecommuting and, 83
work-related, 17, 18, 28, 79–85
Stress consequences, 84
Stress management, 278, 279, 280
Stressors, 81–85, 280
Strong ties, 182
Structural approaches to conflict
      management
  clarifying rules and procedures as, 206
  emphasizing superordinate goals
      as, 204
  increasing resources as, 206
  reducing differentiation as, 204–205
  reducing interdependence as, 206
Structural capital, 9, 11
Structural hole, 183
Study in Scarlet, A (Doyle), 52
Subjective expected utility, 112–113, 117
Substitutability, 175, 178–179
Subtle resistance, 274
Sufficiently frequent feedback, 102
Summarizing, 165
Sun-Tzu, 190
Superordinate goals, 204
Support, 78
Supportive leadership style, 221,
      222, 223
Surface acting, 71
Surface-level diversity, 15
Sweeney, Anne, 222
Swift trust, 145
Swinfard, Ronald, 73
Sydney Opera House, 121
Systematic research anchor, 18–19, 20
Systemic discrimination. *See* Unintentional
      (systemic) discrimination

T

Tall structures, 238–239
Tangible Interaction Design, 125
Target point, 208
Task characteristics, 137–138
Task control, 82
Task force (project) teams, 133
Task identity, 106, 107, 109
Task interdependence, 137–138,
      199–200, 206
Task-oriented leadership, 219, 221, 223,
      224, 230
Task performance, 27, 190
Task performance behaviors, 27
Task-related conflict, 197. *See also*
      Constructive conflict
Task significance, 106, 107, 109
Task structure, 222, 223

TAXI Canada, 233–234, 235
Taylor, Frederick Winslow, 5, 104, 105
Team-based organizational structure,
      244–245
Team building, 141–142
Team characteristics, 137–138
Team cohesion, 143–144, 149, 151, 196,
      197, 222
Team competence, 141
Team composition, 138–139
Team decision making, 147–151
Team design elements, 136, 137–140
Team development, 140–142, 143
Team diversity, 139–140
Team dynamics
  brainstorming and, 150
  conflict and, 196
  contingency anchor and, 20
  decision making and, 129
  HPWP perspective and, 14
  leadership and, 222
  organizational change and, 276,
      281, 283
  organizational structure and, 245
  polls involving, 131
  self-concept and, 50
Team effectiveness model, 135,
      136, 145
Team identity, 140
Team-level analysis, 20
Team mental models, 141
Team norms, 140, 142–143, 149, 198,
      266, 276, 284
Team processes, 136, 140–145
Team roles, 141
Teams
  advantages of, 133–135
  advisory, 133
  Atos Origin and, 153
  challenges of, 135
  communication barriers and, 163–165
      (*See also* Noise)
  communication channels and, 155–163
  communities of practice as, 133
  cross-cultural communication and,
      165–166
  cross-functional, 245
  defined, 132
  departmental, 133
  disadvantages of, 133–135
  gender communication and, 165–166
  "grapevine" and, 169–171
  importance of communication to, 154
  improving communication on, 168–169
  informal groups and, 132–133
  interpersonal communication and,
      166–167
  leadership and, 215
  MBTI and, 33
  model of communication and, 154–156
  organizational structure and, 235–236, 238,
      241, 246
  production/service/leadership, 133
  self-directed, 11, 133, 145, 146, 147,
      237, 244
  skunkworks as, 132, 133

task force (project), 133
types of, 132, 133
virtual, 133, 145, 146–147
workforce diversity and, 17
Team size, 138, 143
Team success, 144
Team trust, 140, 144–145
Teamwork
  globalization and, 15
  leadership and, 231
  organizational design and, 247
  organizations and, 134
  virtual, 243
Technology
  communication, 156
  creativity and, 123
  defined, 248
  human capital and, 9
  organizational design and, 248, 249
  power and, 178
  stress and, 82
  teams and, 147
Telecommuting, 18, 83
Telefónica, 69
Telework, 18, 83
Telling leadership style, 223
"Tend and befriend" response, 85
Tension, 100, 210, 286
Terminal values, 34
Testing theory, 283
Texas Instruments, 39
Text messages, 161
Third-party conflict resolution, 206–207
Thomas, K., 201n
3M, 176
360-degree feedback. See Multisource
    (360-degree) feedback
Timberland Co., 142
Time constraints, 148–149
Timely feedback, 102
TNT, 218
Toyota Motor Company, 136
Tradition, 34, 35
Training
  awareness, 60
  on brainstorming, 151
  diversity, 62
  diversity awareness, 60
  EI and, 73, 74
  ethics, 39
  MARS Model of Individual Behavior
      and, 26
  motivation and, 92, 105
  organizational structure and, 236, 245
  perceptual biases and, 60
  self-fulfilling prophecy and, 58, 60
  stereotyping and, 55
Transactional leadership, 225
Transactional psychological
    contracts, 266
Transformational perspective of leadership,
    220, 225–228, 281, 286
Trosten-Bloom, A., 285n
Trust
  calculus-based, 144–145, 197
  conflict and, 197, 202, 208, 209, 210

defined, 79, 144
  identification-based, 145
  knowledge-based, 144–145
  leadership and, 226, 228
  organizational change and, 278,
      280, 282
  power and, 175, 176
  swift, 145
  team, 140, 144–145
Tunmore, Neil, 168
Turnover, 28, 76–77, 105, 108, 128, 195,
    219, 268
Tushman, M. L., 235n
Tversky, Amos, 117
21 Days of Y'ello Care program, 13
Twitter, 28, 45, 153, 157, 158, 161, 166,
    169, 171

U

Ulrich, Dave, 81, 82
Umpqua Bank, 276
Uncertainty avoidance, 41, 42
Underreward inequity, 99–100
Unfreezing, 273, 277–281
Unintentional (systemic) discrimination, 54
U.S. Air Force (USAF), 73
U.S. Department of Transportation, 169
U.S. Internal Revenue Service,
    242n, 243
U.S. Library of Congress catalogue, 213
Universalism, 34, 35
Unlearning, 10–11, 280
Upward appeal, 185, 187, 189
Urwick, Lindall, 237n
USAF. See U.S. Air Force (USAF)
Usenet, 157
Utilitarianism, 37
Utility, 112, 113, 117

V

Valences, 94, 95, 96
Value-expressive function, 101
Values
  Chick-fil-A and, 23
  communication and, 164
  conflict and, 204, 210
  creativity and, 125
  cross-cultural, 23, 40–41
  cultural (See Cultural values)
  across cultures, 40–43
  defined, 12–14, 34, 253
  enacted, 36–37, 253, 254
  espoused, 36–37, 253, 254
  ethical, 23, 37–40, 260
  global mindset and, 62
  individual behavior and, 35–36
  influence and, 189
  instrumental, 34
  job satisfaction and, 76
  leadership and, 216, 218, 220,
      223–224, 230
  Machiavellian, 191
  MARS Model of Individual Behavior and,
      24, 25

organizational, 34
  organizational change and, 275, 278, 279,
      281, 284, 286
  organizational commitment and, 78–79
  organizational culture and, 252–265, 268
  personal (See Personal values)
  personality and, 34
  power and, 34, 35, 41–42, 176
  self-concept and, 60
  shared, 12, 34, 78–79, 252, 253, 254,
      256, 263
  stakeholders perspective and, 14
  teams and, 132, 141, 143
  terminal, 34
  types of, 34–35
  work attendance and, 28
  in workplace, 33–37
Values congruence, 23, 36–37
Value system, 34
Vancouver Olympics, 125
van Gogh, Vincent, 66
Variability, 248
Variable ratio schedule, 97
Varin, Philippe, 137
Veolia Environnement, 134
Verbal communication, 159
Verhagen, Herna, 218
Verification, 123, 124
Verizon Communications, 15, 17
Verizon Wireless, 142
Viewpoints, 194
Viral change, 281–282
Virtual teams, 133, 145, 146–147
Virtual teamwork, 243
Virtual work, 18
Visibility, 175, 179, 180
Vision
  in leadership, 226–228
  organizational change and, 281
Vocal authority, 184
Vodafone, 40
Voice, job satisfaction and, 75, 76, 101
Volunteerism, 251
von Helmholtz, Hermann, 123
vos Savant, Marilyn, 102

W

"Walking the talk," 227–228
Wallas, Graham, 123, 124
Walmart, 40
Watson, Thomas J., Jr., 25, 272
Weak ties, 182
Weber, Max, 5, 194
Wegmans Food Markets, 69, 76
Welch, Jack, 10, 214, 273
Well-being
  motivation and, 91, 98
  self-concept and, 46–47, 50
Wellness programs, 84
Westchester County Business Journal, 251
Westfarmers, 278
Westfield Group, 210
Whirlpool, 257
Whitney, D. K., 285n, 286n
Whole Foods Market, 134, 138, 146

Wide Open West, 34
WikiCentral, 169
Wikipedia, 169
Wikis, 158, 159, 169
Wilson, Jerry, 187
Win–lose orientation, 201, 210
Win–win orientation, 201
W. L. Gore & Associates, 215, 244
Women
    communication and, 165–166
    conflict and, 204
    leadership and, 230–231
    power and, 183
    self-concept and, 48, 55, 57
    workforce diversity and, 15
Work addict, 83

Workaholic, 83
Work attendance, 27, 28–29
Workforce diversity, 15–17, 18
Work/life balance, 15, 17–18, 83,
    143, 282
Work overload, 81–82, 143
Workplace injustice, 101
Work-related stress, 17, 18,
    28, 79–85
WorkSafeBC, 227
Works Applications Co. Ltd., 69
Workspace design, 168
Wrigley, William Jr., 149
Written communication, 157,
    159, 163
Wyman, Jess, 48

X

Xerox, 202

Y

Yielding style, 202, 203

Z

Zappos, 13, 169, 253, 257, 263
Zebro, David, 135
Zeschuk, Greg, 245
Zollinger, Cindy, 237
Zone of indifference, 176
Zou, Melody, 104

SUMMARY

LO1 **Define organizational behavior and organizations, and discuss the importance of this field of inquiry.**

Organizational behavior (OB) is the study of what people think, feel, and do in and around organizations. Organizations are groups of people who work interdependently toward some purpose. OB theories help people to (a) make sense of the workplace, (b) question and rebuild their personal mental models, and (c) get things done in organizations. OB knowledge is for everyone, not just managers. OB knowledge is just as important for the organization's financial health.

LO2 **Compare and contrast the four current perspectives of organizational effectiveness as well as the early goal attainment perspective.**

The goal attainment perspective, which states that organizations are effective if they achieve their stated objectives, is no longer accepted because (a) the goals set may be too easy, (b) goals may be too abstract to determine their accomplishment, and (c) achievement of some goals may threaten the company's survival.

The open systems perspective views organizations as complex organisms that "live" within an external environment. They depend on the external environment for resources, then use organizational subsystems to transform those resources into outputs which are returned to the environment. Organizations receive feedback from the external environment to maintain a good "fit" with that environment. Fit occurs by adapting to the environment, managing the environment, or moving to another environment. According to the organizational learning perspective, organizational effectiveness depends on the organization's capacity to acquire, share, use, and store valuable knowledge. Intellectual capital consists of human capital, structural capital, and relationship capital. Knowledge is retained in the organizational memory; companies also selectively unlearn.

The high-performance work practices (HPWP) perspective identifies a bundle of systems and structures to leverage workforce potential. The most widely identified HPWPs are employee involvement, job autonomy, developing employee competencies, and performance/skill-based rewards. HPWPs improve organizational effectiveness by building human capital, increasing adaptability, and strengthening employee motivation and attitudes. The stakeholder perspective states that leaders manage the interests of diverse stakeholders by relying on their personal and organizational values for guidance. Ethics and corporate social responsibility (CSR) are natural variations of values-based organizations because they rely on values to guide the most appropriate decisions involving stakeholders. CSR consists of organizational activities intended to benefit society and the environment beyond the firm's immediate financial interests or legal obligations.

LO3 **Debate the organizational opportunities and challenges of globalization, workforce diversity, and emerging employment relationships.**

Globalization, which refers to various forms of connectivity with people in other parts of the world, has several economic and social benefits, but it may also be responsible for work intensification, and reduced job security and work/life balance. Workforce diversity is apparent at both the surface level (observable demographic and other overt differences in

KEY TERMS

corporate social responsibility (CSR) Organizational activities intended to benefit society and the environment beyond the firm's immediate financial interests or legal obligations.

deep-level diversity Differences in the psychological characteristics of employees, including personalities, beliefs, values, and attitudes.

ethics The study of moral principles or values that determine whether actions are right or wrong and outcomes are good or bad.

evidence-based management The practice of making decisions and taking actions based on research evidence.

globalization Economic, social, and cultural connectivity with people in other parts of the world.

high-performance work practices (HPWP) A perspective that holds that effective organizations incorporate several workplace practices that leverage the potential of human capital.

human capital The stock of knowledge, skills, and abilities among employees that provide economic value to the organization.

intellectual capital A company's stock of knowledge, including human capital, structural capital, and relationship capital.

open systems A perspective that holds that organizations depend on the external environment for resources, affect that environment through their output, and consist of internal subsystems that transform inputs to outputs.

organizational behavior (OB) The study of what people think, feel, and do in and around organizations.

organizational effectiveness A broad concept represented by several perspectives, including the organization's fit with the external environment, internal subsystems configuration for high performance, emphasis on organizational learning, and ability to satisfy the needs of key stakeholders.

organizational efficiency The amount of outputs relative to inputs in the organization's transformation process.

organizational learning A perspective that holds that organizational effectiveness depends on the organization's capacity to acquire, share, use, and store valuable knowledge.

organizations Groups of people who work interdependently toward some purpose.

relationship capital The value derived from an organization's relationships with customers, suppliers, and others.

stakeholders Individuals, organizations, or other entities that affect, or are affected by, the organization's objectives and actions.

structural capital Knowledge embedded in an organization's systems and structures.

surface-level diversity The observable demographic or physiological differences in people, such as their race, ethnicity, gender, age, and physical disabilities.

values Relatively stable, evaluative beliefs that guide a person's preferences for outcomes or courses of action in a variety of situations.

virtual work Work performed away from the traditional physical workplace by using information technology.

work–life balance The degree to which a person minimizes conflict between work and nonwork demands.

people) and deep level (differences in personalities, beliefs, values, and attitudes). There is some evidence of deep-level diversity across generational cohorts. Diversity may be a competitive advantage by improving decision making and team performance on complex tasks, yet it also brings numerous challenges such as team "faultlines," slower team performance, and interpersonal conflict. One emerging employment relationship trend is the call for more work/life balance (minimizing conflict between work and nonwork demands). Another employment trend is virtual work, particularly working from home. Working from home potentially increases employee productivity and reduces employee stress, but it may also lead to social isolation, reduced promotion opportunities, and tension in family relations.

● ● **LO4 Discuss the anchors on which organizational behavior knowledge is based.**

The multidisciplinary anchor states that the field should develop from knowledge in other disciplines (e.g., psychology, sociology, economics), not just from its own isolated research base. The systematic research anchor states that OB knowledge should be based on systematic research, which is consistent with evidence-based management. The contingency anchor states that OB theories generally need to consider that there will be different consequences in different situations. The multiple levels of analysis anchor states that OB topics may be viewed from the individual, team, and organization levels of analysis.

SUMMARY

●● **LO1** **Describe the four factors that directly influence individual behavior and performance.**

Four variables—motivation, ability, role perceptions, and situational factors—that are represented by the acronym MARS—directly influence individual behavior and performance. Motivation represents the forces within a person that affect his or her direction, intensity, and persistence of voluntary behavior; ability includes both the natural aptitudes and the learned capabilities required to successfully complete a task; role perceptions are the extent to which people understand the job duties (roles) assigned to them or expected of them; situational factors include conditions beyond the employee's immediate control that constrain or facilitate behavior and performance.

●● **LO2** **Summarize the five types of individual behavior in organizations.**

There are five main types of workplace behavior. Task performance refers to goal-directed behaviors under the individual's control that support organizational objectives. Organizational citizenship behaviors consist of various forms of cooperation and helpfulness to others that support the organization's social and psychological context. Counterproductive work behaviors are voluntary behaviors that have the potential to directly or indirectly harm the organization. Joining and staying with the organization refers to agreeing to become an organizational member and remaining with the organization. Maintaining work attendance includes minimizing absenteeism when capable of working and avoiding scheduled work when not fit (i.e., low presenteeism).

●● **LO3** **Describe personality and discuss how the "Big Five" personality dimensions and four MBTI types relate to individual behavior in organizations.**

Personality is the relatively enduring pattern of thoughts, emotions, and behaviors that characterize a person, along with the psychological processes behind those characteristics. Personality traits are broad concepts about people that allow us to label and understand individual differences. Personality is developed through hereditary origins (nature) as well as socialization (nurture). The "Big Five" personality dimensions include conscientiousness, agreeableness, neuroticism, openness to experience, and extroversion. Conscientiousness and emotional stability (low neuroticism) predict individual performance in most job groups. Extraversion is associated with performance in sales and management jobs, whereas agreeableness is associated with performance in jobs requiring cooperation and openness to experience and is associated with performance in creative jobs.

Based on Jungian personality theory, the Myers-Briggs Type Indicator (MBTI) identifies competing orientations for getting energy (extraversion versus introversion), perceiving information (sensing versus intuiting), processing information and making decisions (thinking versus feeling), and orienting to the external world (judging versus perceiving). The MBTI improves self-awareness for career development and mutual understanding but is more popular than valid. It is useful to understanding an individual's personality, but testing for personality in organizations raises a few concerns.

●● **LO4** **Summarize Schwartz's model of individual values and discuss the conditions under which values influence behavior.**

Values are stable, evaluative beliefs that guide our preferences for outcomes or courses of action in a variety of situations. Compared to personality traits, values are evaluative

KEY TERMS

ability The natural aptitudes and learned capabilities required to successfully complete a task.

achievement–nurturing orientation A cross-cultural value describing the degree to which people in a culture emphasize competitive versus cooperative relations with other people.

collectivism A cross-cultural value describing the degree to which people in a culture emphasize duty to groups to which they belong and to group harmony.

competencies Skills, knowledge, aptitudes, and other personal characteristics that lead to superior performance.

conscientiousness A personality dimension describing people who are careful, dependable, and self-disciplined.

counterproductive work behaviors (CWBs) Voluntary behaviors that have the potential to directly or indirectly harm the organization.

ethical sensitivity A personal characteristic that enables people to recognize the presence of an ethical issue and determine its relative importance.

extraversion A personality dimension describing people who are outgoing, talkative, sociable, and assertive.

five-factor model (FFM) The five abstract dimensions representing most personality traits: conscientiousness, agreeableness, neuroticism, openness to experience, and extroversion.

individualism A cross-cultural value describing the degree to which people in a culture emphasize independence and personal uniqueness.

moral intensity The degree to which an issue demands the application of ethical principles.

motivation The forces within a person that affect his or her direction, intensity, and persistence of voluntary behavior.

Myers-Briggs Type Indicator (MBTI) An instrument designed to measure the elements of Jungian personality theory, particularly preferences regarding perceiving and judging information.

neuroticism A personality dimension describing people with high levels of anxiety, hostility, depression, and self-consciousness.

organizational citizenship behaviors (OCBs) Various forms of cooperation and helpfulness to others that support the organization's social and psychological context.

personality The relatively enduring pattern of thoughts, emotions, and behaviors that characterize a person, along with the psychological processes behind those characteristics.

power distance A cross-cultural value describing the degree to which people in a culture accept unequal distribution of power in a society.

presenteeism Attending scheduled work when one's capacity to perform is significantly diminished by illness or other factors.

role perceptions The extent to which a person accurately understands the job duties (roles) assigned to or expected of him or her.

uncertainty avoidance A cross-cultural value describing the degree to which people in a culture tolerate ambiguity (low uncertainty avoidance) or feel threatened by ambiguity and uncertainty (high uncertainty avoidance).

(rather than descriptive), more likely to conflict with each other, and are formed more from socialization than heredity. Schwartz's model organizes 57 values into a circumplex of 10 dimensions along 2 bipolar dimensions: openness to change to conservation and self-enhancement to self-transcendence. Values influence behavior under three conditions: (1) we can think of specific reasons for doing so, (2) when the situation supports those values, and (3) when we actively think about them. Values congruence refers to how similar a person's values hierarchy is to the values hierarchy of another source (organization, person, etc.).

● ● **LO5** **Describe three ethical principles and discuss four factors that influence ethical behavior.**

Ethics refers to the study of moral principles or values that determine whether actions are right or wrong and outcomes are good or bad. Three ethical principles are utilitarianism, individual rights, and distributive justice. Ethical behavior is influenced by the degree to which an issue demands the application of ethical principles (moral intensity), the individual's ability to recognize the presence and relative importance of an ethical issue (ethical sensitivity), situational forces, and the extent to which people actively evaluate their decisions and actions against ethical and personal values (i.e., mindfulness). Ethical conduct at work is supported by codes of ethical conduct, ethics training, mechanisms for communicating ethical violations, the organization's culture, and the leader's behavior.

● ● **LO6** **Review five values commonly studied across cultures.**

Five values that are often studied across cultures are individualism (valuing independence and personal uniqueness); collectivism (valuing duty to in-groups and to group harmony); power distance (valuing unequal distribution of power); uncertainty avoidance (tolerating or feeling threatened by ambiguity and uncertainty); and achievement–nurturing orientation (valuing competition versus cooperation). Although cross-cultural knowledge is valuable, we need to be concerned that some of this knowledge is based on nonrepresentative samples, old information, and lack of sensitivity to cultural differences within countries.

SUMMARY

●● LO1 Describe the elements of self-concept and explain how they affect an individual's behavior and well-being.

Self-concept includes an individual's self-beliefs and self-evaluations. It has three structural dimensions: complexity, consistency, and clarity, all of which influence employee well-being, behavior, and performance. People are inherently motivated to promote and protect their self-concept (self-enhancement) and to verify and maintain their existing self-concept (self-verification). Self-evaluation consists of self-esteem, self-efficacy, and locus of control. Self-concept also consists of both personality identity and social identity. Social identity theory explains how people define themselves in terms of the groups to which they belong or have an emotional attachment.

●● LO2 Outline the perceptual process and discuss the effects of categorical thinking and mental models in that process.

Perception involves selecting, organizing, and interpreting information to make sense of the world around us. Perceptual organization engages categorical thinking—the mostly nonconscious process of organizing people and objects into preconceived categories that are stored in our long-term memory. Mental models—internal representations of the external world—also help us to make sense of incoming stimuli.

●● LO3 Discuss how stereotyping, attribution, self-fulfilling prophecy, halo, false-consensus primacy, and recency influence the perceptual process.

Stereotyping occurs when people assign traits to others based on their membership in a social category. This economizes mental effort, fills in missing information, and enhances our self-concept, but it also lays the foundation for prejudice and systemic discrimination. The attribution process involves deciding whether an observed behavior or event is caused mainly by the person (internal factors) or the environment (external factors). Attributions are decided by perceptions of the consistency, distinctiveness, and consensus of the behavior. This process is subject to fundamental attribution error and self-serving bias. Self-fulfilling prophecy occurs when our expectations about another person cause that person to act in a way that is consistent with those expectations. This effect is stronger when employees first join the work unit, when several people hold these expectations, and when the employee has a history of low achievement. Four other perceptual errors commonly noted in organizations are the halo effect, false-consensus effect, primacy effect, and recency effect.

●● LO4 Discuss three ways to improve perceptions, with specific application to organizational situations.

One way to minimize perceptual biases is to become more aware of their existence. Awareness of these biases makes people more mindful of their thoughts and actions, but this training sometimes reinforces rather than reduces reliance on stereotypes and tends to be ineffective for people with deeply held prejudices. A second strategy is to become more aware of biases in our own decisions and behavior. Self-awareness increases through formal tests such as the AIT and by applying the Johari Window, which is a process in which others provide feedback to you about your behavior and you offer disclosure to them about yourself. The third strategy is meaningful interaction, which applies the contact hypothesis that people who interact with each other will be less

KEY TERMS

attribution process The perceptual process of deciding whether an observed behavior or event is caused largely by internal or external factors.

categorical thinking Organizing people and objects into preconceived categories stored in our long-term memory.

confirmation bias The process of screening out information that is contrary to our values and assumptions and more readily accepting confirming information.

contact hypothesis A theory stating that the more we interact with someone, the less prejudiced or perceptually biased we will be against that person.

empathy A person's understanding of and sensitivity to the feelings, thoughts, and situations of others.

false-consensus effect A perceptual error in which we overestimate the extent to which others have beliefs and characteristics similar to our own.

fundamental attribution error The tendency to see the person rather than the situation as the main cause of that person's behavior.

global mindset An individual's ability to perceive, appreciate, and empathize with people from other cultures, and to process complex cross-cultural information.

halo effect A perceptual error whereby our general impression of a person, usually based on one prominent characteristic, colors our perception of that person's other characteristics.

Johari Window A model of mutual understanding that encourages disclosure and feedback to increase our own open area and reduce the blind, hidden, and unknown areas.

locus of control A person's general belief about the amount of control he or she has over personal life events.

mental models Visual or relational images in our mind representing the external world.

perception The process of receiving information about and making sense of the world around us.

positive organizational behavior A philosophy that suggests focusing on the positive rather than negative aspects of life will improve organizational success and individual well-being.

primacy effect A perspective of organizational behavior that focuses on building positive qualities and traits within individuals or institutions as opposed to focusing on what is wrong with them.

recency effect A perceptual error in which the most recent information dominates our perception of others.

selective attention The process of attending to some information received by our senses and ignoring other information.

self-concept An individual's self-beliefs and self-evaluations.

self-efficacy A person's belief that he or she has the ability, motivation, correct role perceptions, and favorable situation to complete a task successfully.

self-enhancement A person's inherent motivation to have a positive self-concept (and to have others perceive him/her favorably), such as being competent, attractive, lucky, ethical, and important.

self-fulfilling prophecy The perceptual process in which our expectations about another person cause that person to act more consistently with those expectations.

self-serving bias The tendency to attribute our favorable outcomes to internal factors and our failures to external factors.

self-verification A person's inherent motivation to confirm and maintain his/her existing self-concept.

social identity theory A theory stating that people define themselves by the groups to which they belong or have an emotional attachment.

stereotyping The process of assigning traits to people based on their membership in a social category.

prejudiced or perceptually biased against each other. Meaningful interaction is strongest when people work closely and frequently with each other in relatively equal status on a shared meaningful task that requires cooperation and reliance on each other. Meaningful interaction helps to improve empathy, which is a person's understanding and sensitivity to the feelings, thoughts, and situations of others.

LO5 Outline the main features of a global mindset and justify its usefulness to employees and organizations.

A global mindset is a multidimensional competency that includes the individual's ability to perceive, know about, and process information across cultures. This includes (a) an awareness of, openness to, and respect for other views and practices in the world, (b) the capacity to empathize and act effectively across cultures, (c) the ability to process complex information about novel environments, and (d) the ability to comprehend and reconcile intercultural matters with multiple levels of thinking. A global mindset enables people to develop better cross-cultural relationships, to digest huge volumes of cross-cultural information, and to identify and respond more quickly to emerging global opportunities. Employees develop a global mindset through self-awareness, opportunities to compare their own mental models with people from other cultures, through formal cross-cultural training, and through immersion in other cultures.

SUMMARY

●● LO1 Explain how emotions and cognition (logical thinking) influence attitudes and behavior.

Emotions are physiological, behavioral, and psychological episodes experienced toward an object, person, or event that create a state of readiness. Emotions differ from attitudes, which represent a cluster of beliefs, feelings, and behavioral intentions toward a person, object, or event. Beliefs are a person's established perceptions about the attitude object. Feelings are positive or negative evaluations of the attitude object. Behavioral intentions represent a motivation to engage in a particular behavior toward the target.

Attitudes have traditionally been described as a purely rational process in which beliefs predict feelings, which predict behavioral intentions, which predict behavior. We now know that emotions have an influence on behavior that is equal to or greater than that of cognition. This dual process is apparent when we internally experience a conflict between what logically seems good or bad and what we emotionally feel is good or bad in a situation. Emotions also affect behavior directly. Behavior sometimes influences our subsequent attitudes through cognitive dissonance.

●● LO2 Discuss the dynamics of emotional labor and the role of emotional intelligence in the workplace.

Emotional labor consists of the effort, planning, and control needed to express organizationally desired emotions during interpersonal transactions. It is more common in jobs requiring a variety of emotions and more intense emotions, as well as in jobs where interaction with clients is frequent and has a long duration. Cultures also differ on the norms of displaying or concealing a person's true emotions. Emotional dissonance occurs when required and true emotions are incompatible with each other. Deep acting can minimize this dissonance, as can the practice of hiring people with a natural tendency to display desired emotions.

Emotional intelligence is the ability to perceive and express emotion, assimilate emotion in thought, understand and reason with emotion, and regulate emotion in oneself and others. This concept includes four components arranged in a hierarchy: self-awareness, self-management, awareness of others' emotions, and management of others' emotions. Emotional intelligence can be learned to some extent, particularly through personal coaching.

●● LO3 Summarize the consequences of job dissatisfaction as well as strategies to increase organizational (affective) commitment.

Job satisfaction represents a person's evaluation of his or her job and work context. Four types of job dissatisfaction consequences are quitting or otherwise getting away from the dissatisfying situation (exit), attempting to change the dissatisfying situation (voice), patiently waiting for the problem to sort itself out (loyalty), and reducing work effort and performance (neglect). Job satisfaction has a moderate relationship with job performance and with customer satisfaction. Affective organizational commitment (loyalty) is the employee's emotional attachment to, identification with, and involvement in a particular organization. This contrasts with continuance commitment, which is a calculative bond with the organization. Companies build loyalty through justice and support, shared values, trust, organizational comprehension, and employee involvement.

KEY TERMS

attitudes The cluster of beliefs, assessed feelings, and behavioral intentions toward a person, object, or event (called an attitude object).

cognitive dissonance Condition that occurs when we perceive an inconsistency between our beliefs, feelings, and behavior.

continuance commitment An employee's calculative attachment to the organization, whereby an employee is motivated to stay only because leaving would be costly.

emotional intelligence (EI) A set of abilities to perceive and express emotion, assimilate emotion in thought, understand and reason with emotion, and regulate emotion in oneself and others.

emotional labor The effort, planning, and control needed to express organizationally desired emotions during interpersonal transactions.

emotions Physiological, behavioral, and psychological episodes experienced toward an object, person, or event that create a state of readiness.

exit–voice–loyalty–neglect (EVLN) model The four ways, as indicated in the name, that employees respond to job dissatisfaction.

general adaptation syndrome A model of the stress experience that consists of three stages: alarm reaction, resistance, and exhaustion.

job burnout The process of emotional exhaustion, cynicism, and reduced personal accomplishment resulting from prolonged exposure to stressors.

job satisfaction A person's evaluation of his or her job and work context.

organizational (affective) commitment The employee's emotional attachment to, identification with, and involvement in a particular organization.

psychological harassment Repeated and hostile or unwanted conduct, verbal comments, actions, or gestures that affect an employee's dignity or psychological or physical integrity and that result in a harmful work environment for the employee.

service profit chain model A theory explaining how employees' job satisfaction influences company profitability indirectly through service quality, customer loyalty, and related factors.

sexual harassment Unwelcome conduct of a sexual nature that detrimentally affects the work environment or leads to adverse job-related consequences for its victims.

stress An adaptive response to a situation perceived as challenging or threatening to the person's well-being.

stressors Any environmental condition that places a physical or emotional demand on the person.

trust Positive expectations one person has toward another person in situations involving risk.

workaholic A person who is highly involved in work, feels compelled to work, and has a low enjoyment of work.

● ● **LO4** **Describe the stress experience and review three major stressors.**

Stress is an adaptive response to a situation that is perceived as challenging or threatening to a person's well-being. The stress experience, called the general adaptation syndrome, involves moving through three stages: alarm, resistance, and exhaustion. Stressors are the causes of stress and include any environmental conditions that place a physical or emotional demand on a person. Three stressors that have received considerable attention are harassment and incivility, work overload, and low task control.

● ● **LO5** **Identify five ways to manage workplace stress.**

Many interventions are available to manage work-related stress, including removing the stressor, withdrawing from the stressor, changing stress perceptions, controlling stress consequences, and receiving social support.

SUMMARY

LO1 Define employee engagement.

Employee engagement is defined as an individual's emotional and cognitive (rational) motivation, particularly a focused, intense, persistent, and purposive effort toward work-related goals. It is emotional involvement in, commitment to, and satisfaction with the work, as well as a high level of absorption in the work and sense of self-efficacy about performing the work.

LO2 Explain how drives and emotions influence employee motivation, and summarize Maslow's needs hierarchy, McClelland's learned needs theory, and four-drive theory.

Motivation consists of the forces within a person that affect his or her direction, intensity, and persistence of voluntary behavior in the workplace. Drives (also called primary needs) are the "prime movers" of behavior; they energize individuals to correct deficiencies or maintain an internal equilibrium. Needs—goal-directed forces that people experience—are shaped by the individual's self-concept (including personality and values), social norms, and past experience.

Maslow's needs hierarchy groups needs into a hierarchy of five levels and states that the lowest needs are initially most important, but higher needs become more important as the lower ones are satisfied. Although very popular, the theory lacks research support because it wrongly assumes that everyone has the same hierarchy. The emerging evidence suggests that needs hierarchies vary from one person to the next according to their personal values.

McClelland's learned needs theory argues that needs can be strengthened through learning. The three needs studied in this respect have been need for achievement, need for power, and need for affiliation. Four-drive theory states that everyone has four innate drives—the drives to acquire, bond, comprehend, and defend. These drives activate emotions that people regulate through a skill set that considers social norms, past experience, and personal values. The main recommendation from four-drive theory is to ensure that individual jobs and workplaces provide a balanced opportunity to fulfill the four drives.

LO3 Apply the expectancy theory model to explain employee motivation.

Expectancy theory states that work effort is determined by the perception that effort will result in a particular level of performance (E-to-P expectancy), the perception that a specific behavior or performance level will lead to specific outcomes (P-to-O expectancy), and the valences that the person feels for those outcomes. The E-to-P expectancy increases by improving the employee's ability and confidence to perform the job. The P-to-O expectancy increases by measuring performance accurately, distributing higher rewards to better performers, and showing employees that rewards are performance based. Outcome valences increase by finding out what employees want and using these resources as rewards.

LO4 Outline organizational behavior modification (OB Mod) and social cognitive theory and explain their relevance to employee motivation.

Organizational behavior modification takes the behaviorist view that the environment teaches people to alter their behavior so they maximize positive consequences and minimize adverse consequences. Antecedents are environmental stimuli that provoke (not necessarily cause) behavior. Consequences are events following behavior that

KEY TERMS

autonomy The degree to which a job gives employees the freedom, independence, and discretion to schedule their work and determine the procedures used in completing it.

distributive justice Perceived fairness in the individual's ratio of outcomes to contributions compared with another's ratio of outcomes to contributions.

drives Hardwired characteristics of the brain that correct deficiencies or maintain an internal equilibrium by producing emotions to energize individuals.

employee engagement Individual's emotional and cognitive motivation, particularly a focused, intense, persistent, and purposive effort toward work-related goals.

equity theory A theory explaining how people develop perceptions of fairness in the distribution and exchange of resources.

expectancy theory A motivation theory based on the idea that work effort is directed toward behaviors people believe will lead to desired outcomes.

four-drive theory A motivation theory based on the innate drives to acquire, bond, learn, and defend that incorporates both emotions and rationality.

goal setting The process of motivating employees and clarifying their role perceptions by establishing performance objectives.

job characteristics model A job design model that relates the motivational properties of jobs to specific personal and organizational consequences of those properties.

job design The process of assigning tasks to a job, including the interdependency of those tasks with other jobs.

job enlargement The practice of adding more tasks to an existing job.

job enrichment The practice of giving employees more responsibility for scheduling, coordinating, and planning their own work.

job rotation The practice of moving employees from one job to another.

job specialization The result of division of labor in which work is subdivided into separate jobs assigned to different people.

Maslow's needs hierarchy theory A motivation theory of needs arranged in a hierarchy, whereby people are motivated to fulfill a higher need as a lower one becomes gratified.

motivation Forces within a person that affect the direction, intensity, and persistence of voluntary behavior.

motivator-hygiene theory Herzberg's theory stating that employees are primarily motivated by growth and esteem needs, not by lower-level needs.

need for achievement (nAch) A learned need in which people want to accomplish reasonably challenging goals and desire unambiguous feedback and recognition for their success.

need for affiliation (nAff) A learned need in which people seek approval from others, conform to their wishes and expectations, and avoid conflict and confrontation.

need for power (nPow) A learned need in which people want to control environment, including people and material resources, to benefit either themselves (personalized power) or others (socialized power).

needs Goal-directed forces that people experience.

organizational behavior modification A theory that explains employee behavior in terms of the antecedent conditions and consequences of that behavior.

procedural justice Perceived fairness of the procedures used to decide the distribution of resources.

scientific management The practice of systematically partitioning work into its smallest elements and standardizing tasks to achieve maximum efficiency.

self-reinforcement Reinforcement that occurs when an employee has control over a reinforcer but doesn't "take" it until completing a self-set goal.

skill variety The extent to which employees must use different skills and talents to perform tasks within their jobs.

social cognitive theory A theory that explains how learning and motivation occur by observing and modeling others as well as by anticipating the consequences of our behavior.

strengths-based coaching A positive organizational behavior approach to coaching and feedback that focuses on building and leveraging the employee's strengths rather than trying to correct his or her weaknesses.

task identity The degree to which a job requires completion of a whole or an identifiable piece of work.

task significance The degree to which a job has a substantial impact on the organization and/or larger society.

influence its future occurrence. Consequences include positive reinforcement, punishment, negative reinforcement, and extinction. The schedules of reinforcement also influence behavior.

Social cognitive theory states that much learning and motivation occur by observing and modeling others as well as by anticipating the consequences of our behavior. It suggests that people typically infer (rather than only directly experience) cause–effect relationships, anticipate the consequences of their actions, develop self-efficacy in performing behavior, exercise personal control over their behavior, and reflect on their direct experiences. The theory emphasizes self-regulation of individual behavior, including self-reinforcement, which is the tendency of people to reward and punish themselves as a consequence of their actions.

●● LO5 Summarize equity theory and describe ways to improve procedural justice.

Organizational justice consists of distributive justice (perceived fairness in the outcomes we receive relative to our contributions and the outcomes and contributions of others) and procedural justice (fairness of the procedures used to decide the distribution of resources). Equity theory has four elements: outcome/input ratio, comparison other, equity evaluation, and consequences of inequity. The theory also explains what people are motivated to do when they feel inequitably treated. Companies need to consider not only equity of the distribution of resources but also fairness in the process of making resource allocation decisions.

●● LO6 Describe the characteristics of effective goal setting and feedback.

Goal setting is the process of motivating employees and clarifying their role perceptions by establishing performance objectives. Goals are more effective when they are SMARTER (specific, measurable, achievable, relevant, time framed, exciting, and reviewed). Effective feedback is specific, relevant, timely, credible, and sufficiently frequent. Strengths-based coaching (also known as appreciative coaching) maximizes employee potential by focusing on their strengths rather than weaknesses. Employees usually prefer nonsocial feedback sources to learn about their progress toward goal accomplishment.

●● LO7 List the advantages and disadvantages of job specialization, and describe three ways to improve employee motivation through job design.

Job design is the process of assigning tasks to a job, including the interdependency of those tasks with other jobs. Job specialization subdivides work into separate jobs for different people. This increases work efficiency because employees master the tasks quickly, spend less time changing tasks, require less training, and can be matched more closely with the jobs best suited to their skills. However, job specialization may reduce work motivation; create mental health problems; lower product or service quality; and increase costs through discontentment, absenteeism, and turnover.

The job characteristics model is a template for motivating employees through job redesign. The model's five core job dimensions are skill variety, task identity, task significance, autonomy, and job feedback. These produce psychological states, leading to motivation. Contemporary job design strategies try to motivate employees through job rotation, job enlargement, and job enrichment. Organizations introduce job rotation to reduce job boredom, develop a more flexible workforce, and reduce the incidence of repetitive strain injuries. Job enlargement involves increasing the number of tasks within the job. Two ways to enrich jobs are clustering tasks into natural groups and establishing client relationships.

SUMMARY

●● LO1 Describe the rational choice paradigm in decision making.

Decision making is a conscious process of making choices among one or more alternatives with the intention of moving toward some desired state of affairs. The rational choice paradigm relies on subjective expected utility to identify the best choice. It also follows the logical process of identifying problems and opportunities, choosing the best decision style, developing alternative solutions, choosing the best solution, implementing the selected alternative, and evaluating decision outcomes.

●● LO2 Explain why people differ from the rational choice paradigm when identifying problems/opportunities, evaluating/choosing alternatives, and evaluating decision outcomes.

Stakeholder framing, perceptual defense, mental models, decisive leadership, and solution-oriented focus affect our ability to objectively identify problems and opportunities. We can minimize these challenges by being aware of the human limitations and discussing the situation with colleagues.

Evaluating and choosing alternatives is often challenging because organizational goals are ambiguous or in conflict, human information processing is incomplete and subjective, and people tend to satisfice rather than maximize. Decision makers also short-circuit the evaluation process when faced with an opportunity rather than a problem. People generally make better choices by systematically evaluating alternatives. Scenario planning can help to make future decisions without the pressure and emotions that occur during real emergencies.

Confirmation bias and escalation of commitment make it difficult to accurately evaluate decision outcomes. Escalation is mainly caused by self-justification, self-enhancement effect, the prospect theory effect, and closing costs. These problems are minimized by separating decision choosers from decision evaluators, establishing a preset level at which the decision is abandoned or reevaluated, relying on more systematic and clear feedback about the project's success, and involving several people in decision making.

●● LO3 Discuss the roles of emotions and intuition in decision making.

Emotions shape our preferences for alternatives and the process we follow to evaluate alternatives. We also listen in to our emotions for guidance when making decisions. This latter activity relates to intuition—the ability to know when a problem or opportunity exists and to select the best course of action without conscious reasoning. Intuition is both an emotional experience and a rapid unconscious analytic process that involves both pattern matching and action scripts.

●● LO4 Describe employee characteristics, workplace conditions, and specific activities that support creativity.

Creativity is the development of original ideas that make a socially recognized contribution. The four creativity stages are preparation, incubation, insight, and verification. Incubation assists divergent thinking, which involves reframing the problem in a unique way and generating different approaches to the issue.

Four of the main features of creative people are intelligence, persistence, expertise, and independent imagination. Creativity is also strengthened for everyone when the work environment supports a learning orientation; the job has high intrinsic motivation; the organization provides a reasonable level of job security; and project leaders provide

KEY TERMS

anchoring and adjustment heuristic A natural tendency for people to be influenced by an initial anchor point such that they do not sufficiently move away from that point as new information is provided.

availability heuristic A natural tendency to assign higher probabilities to objects or events that are easier to recall from memory, even though ease of recall is also affected by nonprobability factors (e.g., emotional response, recent events).

bounded rationality The view that people are bounded in their decision-making capabilities, including access to limited information, limited information processing, and tendency toward satisficing rather than maximizing when making choices.

creativity The development of original ideas that make a socially recognized contribution.

decision making The conscious process of making choices among alternatives with the intention of moving toward some desired state of affairs.

divergent thinking Reframing a problem in a unique way and generating different approaches to the issue.

employee involvement The degree to which employees influence how their work is organized and carried out.

escalation of commitment The tendency to repeat an apparently bad decision or allocate more resources to a failing course of action.

implicit favorite A preferred alternative that the decision maker uses repeatedly as a comparison with other choices.

intuition The ability to know when a problem or opportunity exists and to select the best course of action without conscious reasoning.

prospect theory effect A natural tendency to feel more dissatisfaction from losing a particular amount than satisfaction from gaining an equal amount.

rational choice paradigm The view in decision making that people should—and typically do—use logic and all available information to choose the alternative with the highest value.

representativeness heuristic
A natural tendency to evaluate probabilities of events or objects by the degree to which they resemble (are representative of) other events or objects rather than on objective probability information.

satisficing Selecting an alternative that is satisfactory or "good enough," rather than the alternative with the highest value (maximization).

scenario planning A systematic process of thinking about alternative futures and what the organization should do to anticipate and react to those environments.

subjective expected utility The probability (expectation) of satisfaction (utility) resulting from choosing a specific alternative in a decision.

appropriate goals, time pressure, and resources. Three types of activities that encourage creativity are redefining the problem, associative play, and cross-pollination.

LO5 Describe the benefits of employee involvement and identify four contingencies that affect the optimal level of employee involvement.

Employee involvement refers to the degree that employees influence how their work is organized and carried out. The level of participation may range from an employee providing specific information to management without knowing the problem or issue, to complete involvement in all phases of the decision process. Employee involvement may lead to higher decision quality and commitment, but several contingencies need to be considered, including the decision structure, source of decision knowledge, decision commitment, and risk of conflict.

SUMMARY

●● **LO1** **Explain why employees join informal groups and discuss the benefits and limitations of teams.**

Teams are groups of two or more people who interact and influence each other, are mutually accountable for achieving common goals associated with organizational objectives, and perceive themselves as a social entity within an organization. All teams are groups because they consist of people with a unifying relationship; not all groups are teams because some groups do not exist to serve organizational objectives.

People join informal groups (and are motivated to be on formal teams) for four reasons: (1) people have an innate drive to bond, (2) group membership is an inherent ingredient in a person's self-concept, (3) some personal goals are accomplished better in groups, and (4) individuals are comforted in stressful situations by the mere presence of other people. Teams have become popular because they tend to make better decisions, support the knowledge management process, and provide superior customer service. People also tend to be more motivated working in teams. However, teams are not always as effective as individuals working alone. Process losses and social loafing are two particular concerns that drag down team performance.

●● **LO2** **Outline the team effectiveness model and discuss how task characteristics, team size, and team composition influence team effectiveness.**

Team effectiveness includes the team's ability to achieve its objectives, fulfill its members' needs, and maintain its survival. The model of team effectiveness considers the team and organizational environment, team design, and team processes. Three team design elements are task characteristics, team size, and team composition. Teams tend to be better suited for situations in which the work is complex and the tasks among employees have high interdependence. Teams should be large enough to perform the work yet small enough for efficient coordination and meaningful involvement. Effective teams are composed of people with the competencies and motivation to perform tasks in a team environment. Team member diversity has advantages and disadvantages for team performance.

●● **LO3** **Discuss how the four team processes—team development, norms, cohesion, and trust—influence team effectiveness.**

Teams develop through the stages of forming, storming, norming, performing, and eventually adjourning. Within these stages are two distinct team development processes: developing team identity and developing team competence. Team development can be accelerated through team building—any formal activity intended to improve the development and functioning of a work team. Teams develop norms to regulate and guide member behavior. These norms may be influenced by initial experiences, critical events, and the values and experiences that team members bring to the group.

Team cohesion—the degree of attraction people feel toward the team and their motivation to remain members—increases with member similarity, smaller team size, higher degree of interaction, somewhat difficult entry, team success, and external challenges. Cohesion increases team performance when the team's norms are congruent with organizational goals. Trust is a psychological state comprising the intention to accept vulnerability on the basis of positive expectations of another person's intent or behavior. People trust others on the basis of three foundations: calculus, knowledge, and identification.

KEY TERMS

brainstorming A freewheeling, face-to-face meeting where team members aren't allowed to criticize but are encouraged to speak freely, generate as many ideas as possible, and build on the ideas of others.

Brooks's law The principle that adding more people to a late software project only makes it later. Also called the mythical man-month.

constructive conflict A type of conflict in which people focus their discussion on the issue while maintaining respect for people having other points of view.

electronic brainstorming A form of brainstorming that relies on networked computers for submitting and sharing creative ideas.

evaluation apprehension A limitation of team decisions whereby individuals are reluctant to mention ideas that seem silly because they believe (often correctly) that other team members are silently evaluating them.

groupthink The tendency of highly cohesive groups to value consensus at the price of decision quality.

nominal group technique A variation of brainstorming consisting of three stages: Participants (1) silently and independently document their ideas, (2) collectively describe these ideas to the other team members without critique, and then (3) silently and independently evaluate the ideas presented.

norms The informal rules and shared expectations that groups establish to regulate the behavior of their members.

process losses Resources (including time and energy) expended toward team development and maintenance rather than the task.

production blocking A time constraint in team decision making due to the procedural requirement that only one person may speak at a time.

role A set of behaviors people are expected to perform because of the positions they hold in a team and organization.

self-directed teams (SDTs) Cross-functional work groups that are organized around work processes, complete an entire piece of work requiring several interdependent tasks, and have substantial autonomy over the execution of those tasks.

social loafing The problem that occurs when people exert less effort (and usually perform at a lower level) when working in teams than when working alone.

task interdependence The extent to which team members must share materials, information, or expertise in order to perform their jobs.

team building A process that consists of formal activities intended to improve the development and functioning of a work team.

team cohesion The degree of attraction people feel toward the team and their motivation to remain members.

teams Groups of two or more people who interact with and influence each other, are mutually accountable for achieving common goals associated with organizational objectives, and perceive themselves as a social entity within an organization.

trust Positive expectations one person has toward another person in situations involving risk.

virtual teams Teams whose members operate across space, time, and organizational boundaries and are linked through information technologies to achieve organizational tasks.

● ● **LO4** Discuss the characteristics and factors required for success of self-directed teams and virtual teams.

Self-directed teams (SDTs) complete an entire piece of work requiring several interdependent tasks, and they have substantial autonomy over the execution of their tasks. Members of virtual teams operate across space, time, and organizational boundaries and are linked through information technologies to achieve organizational tasks. Virtual teams are more effective when the team members have certain competencies, the team has the freedom to choose the preferred communication channels, and the members meet face-to-face fairly early in the team development process.

● ● **LO5** Identify four constraints on team decision making and discuss the advantages and disadvantages of four structures aimed at improving team decision making.

Team decisions are impeded by time constraints, evaluation apprehension, conformity to peer pressure, and groupthink (specifically overconfidence). Four structures potentially improve decision making in team settings: constructive conflict, brainstorming, electronic brainstorming, and nominal group technique.

SUMMARY

●●● LO1 Explain why communication is important in organizations and discuss four influences on effective communication encoding and decoding.

Communication refers to the process by which information is transmitted and understood between two or more people. Communication supports work coordination, organizational learning, decision making, changing others' behavior, and employee well-being. The communication process involves forming, encoding, and transmitting the intended message to a receiver, who then decodes the message and provides feedback to the sender. Effective communication occurs when the sender's thoughts are transmitted to and understood by the intended receiver. Four ways to improve this process is for both sender and receiver to be proficient with the communication channel, have similar codebooks, have shared common mental models of the communication context, and for the sender to be experienced at sending that message.

●●● LO2 Compare and contrast the advantages of and problems with electronic mail, other verbal communication media, and nonverbal communication.

The two main types of communication channels are verbal and nonverbal. Various forms of Internet-based communication are widely used in organizations, with email the most popular. Although efficient and a useful filing cabinet, email is relatively poor at communicating emotions; it tends to reduce politeness and respect; it is an inefficient medium for communicating in ambiguous, complex, and novel situations; and it contributes to information overload. Facebook-like Web sites, wikis, virtual reality platforms, and other forms of social media are gaining popularity in the workplace. Social media include Internet-based tools (Web sites, applications, etc) that allow users to generate and exchange information. They serve several functions, including presenting the individual's identity, enabling conversations, sharing information, sensing the presence of others in the virtual space, maintaining relationships, revealing reputation or status, and supporting communities. Nonverbal communication includes facial gestures, voice intonation, physical distance, and even silence. Unlike verbal communication, nonverbal communication is less rule bound and is mostly automatic and nonconscious. Some nonverbal communication is automatic through a process called emotional contagion.

●●● LO3 Explain how social acceptance and media richness influence the preferred communication channel.

The most appropriate communication medium partly depends on its social acceptance and media richness. Social acceptance refers to how well the communication medium is approved and supported by the organization, teams, and individuals. This contingency includes organization and team norms, individual preferences for specific communication channels, and the symbolic meaning of a channel. A communication medium should also be chosen for its data-carrying capacity (media richness). Nonroutine and ambiguous situations require rich media. However, technology-based lean media might be almost as effective as rich media for transferring information. This particularly occurs where users can multicommunicate and have high proficiency with that technology, and where social distractions of high media richness channels reduce the efficient processing of information through those channels. These contingencies are also considered when selecting the best channels for persuasion.

KEY TERMS

communication The process by which information is transmitted and understood between two or more people.

emotional contagion The nonconscious process of "catching" or sharing another person's emotions by mimicking that person's facial expressions and other nonverbal behavior.

grapevine An unstructured and informal communication network founded on social relationships rather than organizational charts or job descriptions.

information overload A condition in which the volume of information received exceeds the person's capacity to process it.

management by walking around persuasion (MBWA) A communication practice in which executives get out of their offices and learn from others in the organization through face-to-face dialogue.

media richness A medium's data-carrying capacity, that is, the volume and variety of information that can be transmitted during a specific time.

persuasion Changing another person's beliefs and attitudes.

● ● **LO4** **Discuss various barriers (noise) to effective communication, including cross-cultural and gender-based differences in communication.**

Several barriers create noise in the communication process. People misinterpret messages because of misaligned codebooks due to different languages, jargon, and use of ambiguous phrases. Filtering messages and information overload are two other communication barriers. These problems are often amplified in cross-cultural settings where the above problems occur along with differences in meaning of nonverbal cues, silence, and conversational overlaps. There are also some communication differences between men and women, such as the tendency for men to exert status and engage in report talk in conversations, whereas women use more rapport talk and are more sensitive than are men to nonverbal cues.

● ● **LO5** **Explain how to get your message across more effectively, and summarize the elements of active listening.**

To get a message across, the sender must learn to empathize with the receiver, repeat the message, choose an appropriate time for the conversation, and be descriptive rather than evaluative. Listening includes sensing, evaluating, and responding. Active listeners support these processes by postponing evaluation, avoiding interruptions, maintaining interest, empathizing, organizing information, showing interest, and clarifying the message.

● ● **LO6** **Summarize effective communication strategies in organizational hierarchies, and review the role and relevance of the organizational grapevine.**

Some companies try to encourage communication through workspace design, as well as through Internet-based communication channels. Some executives also meet directly with employees, such as through management by walking around (MBWA) and town-hall meetings, to facilitate communication across the organization.

In any organization, employees rely on the grapevine, particularly during times of uncertainty. The grapevine is an unstructured and informal network founded on social relationships rather than organizational charts or job descriptions. Although early research identified several unique features of the grapevine, some of these features may be changing as the Internet plays an increasing role in grapevine communication.

SUMMARY

● ● **LO1** Describe the dependence model of power and describe the five sources of power in organizations.

Power is the capacity to influence others. It exists when one party perceives that he or she is dependent on the other for something of value. However, the dependent person must also have countervailing power—some power over the dominant party—to maintain the relationship and the parties must have some level of trust.

There are five power bases. Legitimate power is an agreement among organizational members that people in certain roles can request certain behaviors of others. This power has restrictions represented by the target person's zone of indifference. It also includes the norm of reciprocity (a feeling of obligation to help someone who has helped you) as well as control over the flow of information to others. Reward power is derived from the ability to control the allocation of rewards valued by others and to remove negative sanctions. Coercive power is the ability to apply punishment. Expert power is the capacity to influence others by possessing knowledge or skills they value. An important form of expert power is the (perceived) ability to manage uncertainties in the business environment. People have referent power when others identify with them, like them, or otherwise respect them.

● ● **LO2** Discuss the four contingencies of power.

Four contingencies determine whether these power bases translate into real power. Individuals and work units are more powerful when they are nonsubstitutable, that is, there is a lack of alternatives. Employees, work units, and organizations reduce substitutability by controlling tasks, knowledge, and labor, and by differentiating themselves from competitors. A second contingency is centrality. People have more power when they have high centrality—that is, the number of people affected is large and people are quickly affected by their actions. The third contingency, visibility, refers to the idea that power increases to the extent that a person's or work unit's competencies are known to others. Discretion, the fourth contingency of power, refers to the freedom to exercise judgment. Power increases when people have freedom to use their power.

● ● **LO3** Explain how people and work units gain power through social networks.

Social networks are social structures of individuals or social units (e.g., departments, organizations) that are connected to each other through one or more forms of interdependence. People receive power in social networks through social capital, which is the goodwill and resulting resources shared among members in a social network. Three main resources from social networks are information, visibility, and referent power.

Employees gain social capital through their relationship in the social network. Social capital tends to increase with the number of network ties. Strong ties (close-knit relationships) can also increase social capital because these connections offer more resources and offer them more quickly. However, having weak ties with people from diverse networks can be more valuable than having strong ties with people in similar networks. Weak ties provide more resources that we do not already possess. Another influence on social capital is the person's centrality in the network. Network centrality is determined in several ways, including the extent to which you are located between others in the network (betweenness), how many direct ties you have (degree), and the closeness of these ties. People also gain power by bridging structural holes—linking two or more clusters of people in a network.

KEY TERMS

centrality A contingency of power pertaining to the degree and nature of interdependence between the power holder and others.

charisma A personal characteristic or special "gift" that serves as a form of interpersonal attraction and referent power over others.

coalition A group that attempts to influence people outside the group by pooling the resources and power of its members.

countervailing power The capacity of a person, team, or organization to keep a more powerful person or group in the exchange relationship.

impression management The practice of actively shaping our public images.

influence Any behavior that attempts to alter someone's attitudes or behavior.

ingratiation Any attempt to increase liking by, or perceived similarity to, some targeted person.

inoculation effect A persuasive communication strategy of warning listeners that others will try to influence them in the future and that they should be wary about the opponent's arguments.

legitimate power An agreement among organizational members that people in certain roles can request certain behaviors of others.

Machiavellian values The beliefs that deceit is a natural and acceptable way to influence others and that getting more than one deserves is acceptable.

norm of reciprocity A felt obligation and social expectation of helping or otherwise giving something of value to someone who has already helped or given something of value to you.

organizational politics Behaviors that others perceive as self-serving tactics at the expense of other people and possibly the organization.

persuasion Presenting facts, logical arguments, and emotional appeals to change another person's attitudes and behavior.

power The capacity of a person, team, or organization to influence others.

referent power The capacity to influence others on the basis of an identification with and respect for the power holder.

social capital The knowledge and other resources available to people or social units (teams, organizations) from a durable network that connects them to others.

social networks Social structures of individuals or social units that are connected to each other through one or more forms of interdependence.

structural hole An area between two or more dense social network areas that lacks network ties.

substitutability A contingency of power pertaining to the availability of alternatives.

upward appeal A type of influence in which someone with higher authority or expertise is called on in reality or symbolically to support the influencer's position.

●● **LO4** **Describe eight types of influence tactics, three consequences of influencing others, and three contingencies to consider when choosing an influence tactic.**

Influence refers to any behavior that attempts to alter someone's attitudes or behavior. The most widely studied influence tactics are silent authority, assertiveness, information control, coalition formation, upward appeal, ingratiation and impression management, persuasion, and exchange. "Soft" influence tactics such as friendly persuasion and subtle ingratiation are more acceptable than "hard" tactics such as upward appeal and assertiveness. However, the most appropriate influence tactic also depends on the influencer's power base; whether the person being influenced is higher, lower, or at the same level in the organization; and personal, organizational, and cultural values regarding influence behavior.

●● **LO5** **Identify the organizational conditions and personal characteristics that support organizational politics, as well as ways to minimize organizational politics.**

Organizational politics refers to influence tactics that others perceive to be self-serving behaviors at the expense of others and sometimes contrary to the interests of the organization. It is more common when ambiguous decisions allocate scarce resources and when the organization tolerates or rewards political behavior. Individuals with a high need for personal power and strong Machiavellian values have a higher propensity to use political tactics. Organizational politics can be minimized by providing clear rules for resource allocation, establishing a free flow of information, using education and involvement during organizational change, supporting team norms and a corporate culture that discourage dysfunctional politics, and having leaders who role model organizational citizenship rather than political savvy.

SUMMARY

●●● LO1 Define conflict and debate its positive and negative consequences in the workplace.

Conflict is the process in which one party perceives that its interests are being opposed or negatively affected by another party. The earliest view of conflict was that it was dysfunctional for organizations. Even today, we recognize that conflict sometimes or to some degree consumes productive time, increases stress and job dissatisfaction, discourages coordination and resource sharing, undermines customer service, fuels organizational politics, and undermines team cohesion. But conflict can also be beneficial. It is known to motivate more active thinking about problems and possible solutions, encourage more active monitoring of the organization in its environment, and improve team cohesion (where the conflict source is external).

●●● LO2 Distinguish constructive from relationship conflict and describe three strategies to minimize relationship conflict during constructive conflict episodes.

Constructive conflict occurs when people focus their discussion around the issue while showing respect for people with other points of view. Relationship conflict exists when people view each other, rather than the issue, as the source of conflict. It is apparent when people attack each other's credibility and display aggression towards the other party. It is difficult to separate constructive from relationship conflict. However, three strategies or conditions that minimize relationship conflict during constructive debate are: (1) emotional intelligence of the participants, (2) team cohesion, and (3) supportive team norms.

●●● LO3 Diagram the conflict process model and describe six structural sources of conflict in organizations.

The conflict process model begins with the five structural sources of conflict: incompatible goals, differentiation (different values and beliefs), interdependence, scarce resources, ambiguous rules, and communication problems. These sources lead one or more parties to perceive a conflict and to experience conflict emotions. This, in turn, produces manifest conflict, such as behaviors toward the other side. The conflict process often escalates through a series of episodes.

●●● LO4 Outline the five conflict handling styles and discuss the circumstances in which each would be most appropriate.

There are five known conflict handling styles: problem solving, forcing, avoiding, yielding, and compromising. People who use problem solving have a win–win orientation. Others, particularly forcing, assume a win–lose orientation. In general, people gravitate toward one or two preferred conflict handling styles that match their personality, personal and cultural values, and past experience.

The best style depends on the situation. Problem solving is best when interests are not perfectly opposing, the parties trust each other, and the issues are complex. Forcing works best when you strongly believe in your position, the dispute requires quick action, and the other party would take advantage of a cooperative style. Avoiding is preferred when the conflict has become emotional or the cost of resolution is higher than its benefits. Yielding works well when the other party has substantially more power, the issue is less important to you, and you are not confident in the logical soundness of your position. Compromising is preferred when the parties have equal power, they are under time pressure, and they lack trust.

KEY TERMS

best alternative to a negotiated agreement (BATNA) The best outcome you might achieve through some other course of action if you abandon the current negotiation.

conflict A process in which one party perceives that his or her interests are being opposed or negatively affected by another party.

constructive conflict A type of conflict in which people focus their discussion around the issue while showing respect for people with other points of view.

negotiation The process whereby two or more conflicting parties attempt to resolve their divergent goals by redefining the terms of their interdependence.

relationship conflict A type of conflict in which people focus on characteristics of other individuals, rather than on the issues, as the source of conflict.

superordinate goals Goals that the conflicting parties value and whose attainment requires those parties' joint resources and effort.

third-party conflict resolution Any attempt by a relatively neutral person to help conflicting parties resolve their differences.

win–lose orientation The belief that conflicting parties are drawing from a fixed pie, so the more one party receives, the less the other party will receive.

win–win orientation The belief that conflicting parties will find a mutually beneficial solution to their disagreement.

LO5 Apply the six structural approaches to conflict management and describe the three types of third-party dispute resolution.

Structural approaches to conflict management include emphasizing superordinate goals, reducing differentiation, improving communication and understanding, reducing interdependence, increasing resources, and clarifying rules and procedures.

Third-party conflict resolution is any attempt by a relatively neutral person to help the parties resolve their differences. The three main forms of third-party dispute resolution are mediation, arbitration, and inquisition. Managers tend to use an inquisition approach, although mediation and arbitration are more appropriate, depending on the situation.

LO6 Describe the bargaining zone model and outline strategies skilled negotiators use to claim value and create value in negotiations.

Negotiation occurs whenever two or more conflicting parties attempt to resolve their divergent goals by redefining the terms of their interdependence. The bargaining zone model identifies three strategic positions for each party (initial, target, resistance) and shows how each party moves along a continuum in opposite directions with an area of potential overlap. All negotiations consist of two divergent objectives: claiming value (getting the best personal outcome) and creating value (discover ways to achieve mutually satisfactory outcomes for both parties). Skilled negotiators claim more value by preparing and setting goals, knowing their best alternatives to a negotiated agreement (BATNA), managing time to their advantage, and managing first offers and concessions. Skilled negotiators create more value by gathering information, using offers and concessions to discover issue priorities, and building relationships with the other party. The situation is also an important consideration in negotiations, including location, physical setting, and audience characteristics.

SUMMARY

●● LO1 Define *leadership* and *shared leadership.*

Leadership is defined as the ability to influence, motivate, and enable others to contribute toward the effectiveness and success of the organizations of which they are members. Leaders use influence to motivate followers and arrange the work environment so they do the job more effectively. Shared leadership views leadership as a role rather than a formal position, so employees throughout the organization act informally as leaders as the occasion arises. These situations include serving as champions for specific ideas or changes as well as filling leadership roles where it is needed.

●● LO2 Identify eight competencies associated with effective leaders and describe authentic leadership.

The competency perspective tries to identify the characteristics of effective leaders. Recent writing suggests that leaders have specific personality characteristics, positive self-concept, drive, integrity, leadership motivation, knowledge of the business, cognitive and practical intelligence, and emotional intelligence. Authentic leadership refers to how well leaders are aware of, feel comfortable with, and act consistently with their self-concept. This concept consists mainly of two parts: self-awareness and engaging in behavior that is consistent with one's self-concept.

●● LO3 Describe the key features of task oriented, people oriented, and servant leadership, and discuss their effects on followers.

The behavioral perspective of leadership identifies two clusters of leader behavior: people-oriented and task-oriented. People-oriented behaviors include showing mutual trust and respect for subordinates, demonstrating a genuine concern for their needs, and having a desire to look out for their welfare. Task-oriented behaviors include assigning employees to specific tasks, clarifying their work duties and procedures, ensuring they follow company rules, and pushing them to reach their performance capacity.

Servant leadership defines leadership as serving others toward their need fulfillment and personal development and growth. Servant leaders have a natural desire or "calling" to serve others. They maintain a relationship with others that is humble, egalitarian, and accepting. Servant leaders also anchor their decisions and actions in ethical principles and practices.

●● LO4 Discuss the key elements of path–goal theory, Fiedler's contingency model, and leadership substitutes.

The contingency perspective of leadership takes the view that effective leaders diagnose the situation and adapt their style to fit that situation. The path–goal model is the prominent contingency theory that identifies four leadership styles—directive, supportive, participative, and achievement-oriented—and several contingencies relating to the characteristics of the employee and of the situation.

Two other contingency leadership theories include the situational leadership theory and Fiedler's contingency theory. Research support is quite weak for both theories. However, a lasting element of Fiedler's theory is the idea that leaders have natural styles and, consequently, companies need to change the leaders' environments to suit their style. Leadership substitutes theory identifies contingencies that either limit the leader's ability to influence subordinates or make a particular leadership style unnecessary.

KEY TERMS

authentic leadership The view that effective leaders need to be aware of, feel comfortable with, and act consistently with their values, personality, and self-concept.

Fiedler's contingency model Developed by Fred Fiedler, an early contingency leadership model that suggests that leader effectiveness depends on whether the person's natural leadership style is appropriately matched to the situation.

implicit leadership theory A theory stating that people evaluate a leader's effectiveness in terms of how well that person fits preconceived beliefs about the features and behaviors of effective leaders (leadership prototypes) and that people tend to inflate the influence of leaders on organizational events.

leadership Influencing, motivating, and enabling others to contribute toward the effectiveness and success of the organizations of which they are members.

leadership substitutes A theory identifying contingencies that either limit a leader's ability to influence subordinates or make a particular leadership style unnecessary.

managerial leadership A leadership perspective stating that effective leaders help employees improve their performance and well-being in the current situation.

path–goal leadership theory A contingency theory of leadership based on the expectancy theory of motivation that relates several leadership styles to specific employee and situational contingencies.

servant leadership The view that leaders serve followers, rather than vice versa; leaders help employees fulfill their needs and are coaches, stewards, and facilitators of employee development.

shared leadership The view that leadership is broadly distributed, rather than assigned to one person, so that people within the team and organization lead each other.

situational leadership theory A commercially popular but poorly supported leadership model stating that effective leaders vary their style (telling, selling, participating, delegating) with the "readiness" of followers.

● ● **LO5** **Describe the four elements of transformational leadership and distinguish this theory from transactional and charismatic leadership.**

Transformational leaders create a strategic vision, communicate that vision through framing and use of metaphors, model the vision by "walking the talk" and acting consistently, and build commitment toward the vision. This contrasts with transactional leadership, which has ambiguous meaning but is usually viewed as an exchange relationship with followers. Transformational leadership is also distinguished from managerial leadership, which relates to the contingency theories of leadership. Some transformational leadership theories view charismatic leadership as an essential ingredient of transformational leadership. However, this view is inconsistent with the meaning of charisma and at odds with research on the dynamics and outcomes of charisma in leader–follower relationships.

● ● **LO6** **Describe the implicit leadership perspective.**

According to the implicit leadership perspective, people have leadership prototypes, which they use to evaluate the leader's effectiveness. Furthermore, people form a romance of leadership; they want to believe that leaders make a difference, so they engage in fundamental attribution error and other perceptual distortions to support this belief in the leader's impact.

● ● **LO7** **Discuss cultural and gender similarities and differences in leadership.**

Cultural values also influence the leader's personal values, which in turn influence his or her leadership practices. Women generally do not differ from men in the degree of people-oriented or task-oriented leadership. However, female leaders more often adopt a participative style. Research also suggests that people evaluate female leaders on the basis of gender stereotypes, which may result in higher or lower ratings.

SUMMARY

● ● LO1 Describe three types of coordination in organizational structures.

Organizational structure is the division of labor, as well as the patterns of coordination, communication, workflow, and formal power that direct organizational activities. All organizational structures divide labor into distinct tasks and coordinate that labor to accomplish common goals. The primary means of coordination are informal communication, formal hierarchy, and standardization.

● ● LO2 Discuss the role and effects of span of control, centralization, and formalization, and relate these elements to organic and mechanistic organizational structures.

The four basic elements of organizational structure are span of control, centralization, formalization, and departmentalization. The optimal span of control—the number of people directly reporting to the next level in the hierarchy—depends on what coordinating mechanisms are present other than formal hierarchy, whether employees perform routine tasks, and how much interdependence there is among employees within the department.

Centralization occurs when a small group of people, typically senior executives, hold formal decision authority. Many companies decentralize as they become larger and more complex, but some sections of the company may remain centralized while other sections decentralize. Formalization is the degree to which organizations standardize behavior through rules, procedures, formal training, and related mechanisms. Companies become more formalized as they get older and larger. Formalization tends to reduce organizational flexibility, organizational learning, creativity, and job satisfaction.

Span of control, centralization, and formalization cluster into mechanistic and organic structures. Mechanistic structures are characterized by a narrow span of control and a high degree of formalization and centralization. Companies with an organic structure have the opposite characteristics.

● ● LO3 Identify and evaluate five types of departmentalization.

Departmentalization specifies how employees and their activities are grouped together. It establishes the chain of command, focuses people around common mental models, and encourages coordination through informal communication among people and subunits. A simple structure employs few people, has minimal hierarchy, and typically offers one distinct product or service. A functional structure organizes employees around specific knowledge or other resources. This structure fosters greater specialization and improves direct supervision, but it weakens the focus on serving clients or developing products.

A divisional structure groups employees around geographic areas, clients, or outputs. This structure accommodates growth and focuses employee attention on products or customers rather than tasks. However, this structure also duplicates resources and creates silos of knowledge. Team-based structures are very flat, with low formalization, and organize self-directed teams around work processes rather than functional specialties. The matrix structure combines two structures to leverage the benefits of both types. However, this approach requires more coordination than functional or pure divisional structures, may dilute accountability, and increases conflict.

KEY TERMS

centralization The degree to which formal decision authority is held by a small group of people, typically those at the top of the organizational hierarchy.

divisional structure An organizational structure in which employees are organized around geographic areas, outputs (products or services), or clients.

formalization The degree to which organizations standardize behavior through rules, procedures, formal training, and related mechanisms.

functional structure An organizational structure in which employees are organized around specific knowledge or other resources.

globally integrated enterprise An organizational structure in which work processes and executive functions are distributed around the world through global centers, rather than developed in a home country and replicated in satellite countries or regions.

matrix structure An organizational structure that overlays two structures (such as a geographic divisional and a functional structure) in order to leverage the benefits of both.

mechanistic structure An organizational structure with a narrow span of control and a high degree of formalization and centralization.

organic structure An organizational structure with a wide span of control, little formalization, and decentralized decision making.

organizational strategy The way the organization positions itself in its setting in relation to its stakeholders, given the organization's resources, capabilities, and mission.

organizational structure The division of labor as well as the patterns of coordination, communication, workflow, and formal power that direct organizational activities.

span of control The number of people directly reporting to the next level in the hierarchy.

team-based organizational structure An organizational structure built around self-directed teams that complete an entire piece of work.

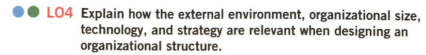

● ● **LO4** **Explain how the external environment, organizational size, technology, and strategy are relevant when designing an organizational structure.**

The best organizational structure depends on the firm's external environment, size, technology, and strategy. The optimal structure depends on whether the environment is dynamic or stable, complex or simple, diverse or integrated, and hostile or munificent. As organizations increase in size, they become more decentralized and more formalized. The work unit's technology—including variability of work and analyzability of problems—influences whether it should adopt an organic or mechanistic structure. These contingencies influence but do not necessarily determine structure. Instead, corporate leaders formulate and implement strategies that shape both the characteristics of these contingencies and the organization's resulting structure.

SUMMARY

● ● LO1 Describe the elements of organizational culture and discuss the importance of organizational subcultures.

Organizational culture consists of the values and assumptions shared within an organization. Shared assumptions are nonconscious, taken-for-granted perceptions or beliefs that have worked so well in the past they are considered the correct way to think and act toward problems and opportunities. Values are stable, evaluative beliefs that guide our preferences for outcomes or courses of action in a variety of situations.

Organizations differ in their cultural content—that is, the relative ordering of values. There are several classifications of organizational culture, but they tend to oversimplify the wide variety of cultures and completely ignore the underlying assumptions of culture. Organizations have subcultures as well as a dominant culture. Subcultures maintain the organization's standards of performance and ethical behavior. They are also the source of emerging values that replace aging core values.

● ● LO2 List four categories of artifacts through which corporate culture is deciphered.

Artifacts are the observable symbols and signs of an organization's culture. Four broad categories of artifacts are organizational stories and legends, rituals and ceremonies, language, and physical structures and symbols. Understanding an organization's culture requires assessment of many artifacts because they are subtle and often ambiguous.

● ● LO3 Discuss the importance of organizational culture and the conditions under which organizational culture strength improves organizational performance.

Organizational culture has three main functions: a form of social control, the "social glue" that bonds people together, and a way to help employees make sense of the workplace. Companies with strong cultures generally perform better than those with weak cultures, but only when the cultural content is appropriate for the organization's environment. Also, the culture should not be so strong that it drives out dissenting values, which may form emerging values for the future. Organizations should have adaptive cultures so employees support ongoing change in the organization and their own roles.

● ● LO4 Compare and contrast four strategies for merging organizational cultures.

Organizational culture clashes are common in mergers and acquisitions. This problem can be minimized by performing a bicultural audit to diagnose the compatibility of the organizational cultures. The four main strategies for merging different corporate cultures are integration, deculturation, assimilation, and separation.

● ● LO5 Identify four strategies for changing or strengthening an organization's culture, including the application of attraction–selection–attrition theory.

Organizational culture is very difficult to change, but cultural change is possible and sometimes necessary for a company's continued survival. Four strategies for changing and strengthening an organization's culture are the actions of founders and leaders; aligning artifacts with the desired culture; introducing culturally consistent rewards; and attracting, selecting, and socializing employees.

KEY TERMS

adaptive culture An organizational culture in which employees are receptive to change, including the ongoing alignment of the organization to its environment and continuous improvement of internal processes.

artifacts The observable symbols and signs of an organization's culture.

attraction–selection–attrition (ASA) theory A theory that states that organizations have a natural tendency to attract, select, and retain people with values and personality characteristics that are consistent with the organization's character, resulting in a more homogeneous organization and a stronger culture.

bicultural audit A process of diagnosing cultural relations between companies and determining the extent to which cultural clashes will likely occur.

ceremonies Planned displays of organizational culture, conducted specifically for the benefit of an audience.

organizational culture The values and assumptions shared within an organization.

organizational socialization The process by which individuals learn the values, expected behaviors, and social knowledge necessary to assume their roles in the organization.

psychological contract The individual's beliefs about the terms and conditions of a reciprocal exchange agreement between that person and another party (the employer in most work situations).

realistic job preview (RJP) A method of improving organizational socialization in which job applicants are given a balance of positive and negative information about the job and work context.

reality shock The stress that results when employees perceive discrepancies between their preemployment expectations and on-the-job reality.

rituals The programmed routines of daily organizational life that dramatize the organization's culture.

Attraction–selection–attrition (ASA) theory states that organizations have a natural tendency to attract, select, and retain people with values and personality characteristics that are consistent with the organization's character, resulting in a more homogeneous organization and a stronger culture. Organizational socialization is the process by which individuals learn the values, expected behaviors, and social knowledge necessary to assume their roles in the organization. It is a process of both learning about the work context and adjusting to new work roles, team norms, and behaviors.

● ● **LO6** **Describe the organizational socialization process and identify strategies to improve that process.**

Organizational socialization is the process by which individuals learn the values, expected behaviors, and social knowledge necessary to assume their roles in the organization. It is a process of both learning and adjustment. During this process, job applicants and newcomers develop and test their psychological contract—personal beliefs about the terms and conditions of a reciprocal exchange agreement between that person and another party (the employer).

Employees typically pass through three socialization stages: preemployment, encounter, and role management. To manage the socialization process, organizations should introduce realistic job previews (RJPs) and recognize the value of socialization agents in the process. RJPs give job applicants a realistic balance of positive and negative information about the job and work context. Socialization agents provide information and social support during the socialization process.

SUMMARY

●● ● LO1 Describe the elements of Lewin's force field analysis model.

Lewin's force field analysis model states that all systems have driving and restraining forces. Change occurs through the process of unfreezing, changing, and refreezing. Unfreezing produces disequilibrium between the driving and restraining forces. Refreezing realigns the organization's systems and structures with the desired behaviors.

●● ● LO2 Discuss the reasons people resist organizational change and how change agents should view this resistance.

Restraining forces are manifested as employee resistance to change. The main reasons people resist change are direct costs, saving face, fear of the unknown, breaking routines, incongruent team dynamics, and incongruent organizational systems. Resistance to change should be viewed as a resource, not an inherent obstacle to change. Employee resistance is a resource in three ways: (1) it is a signal that the conditions for effective change are not yet in place; (2) it is a form of constructive conflict; and (3) it is a form of voice, so it may improve procedural justice.

●● ● LO3 Outline six strategies for minimizing resistance to change, and debate ways to effectively create an urgency to change.

Organizational change requires employees to have an urgency for change. This typically occurs by informing them about driving forces in the external environment. Urgency to change also develops by putting employees in direct contact with customers. Leaders often need to create an urgency to change before the external pressures are felt, and this can occur through a vision of a more appealing future.

Resistance to change may be minimized by keeping employees informed about what to expect from the change effort (communicating); teaching employees valuable skills for the desired future (learning); involving them in the change process; helping employees cope with the stress of change; negotiating trade-offs with those who will clearly lose from the change effort; and using coercion (sparingly and as a last resort).

●● ● LO4 Discuss how leadership, coalitions, social networks, and pilot projects influence organizational change.

Every successful change also requires transformational leaders with a clear, well-articulated vision of the desired future state. They also need the assistance of several people (a guiding coalition) who are located throughout the organization. Change also occurs more informally through social networks. Viral change operates through social networks using influencers.

Many organizational change initiatives begin with a pilot project. The success of the pilot project is then diffused to other parts of the organization. This occurs by applying the MARS model, including motivating employees to adopt the pilot project's methods, training people to know how to adopt these practices, helping clarify how the pilot can be applied to different areas, and providing time and resources to support this diffusion.

●● ● LO5 Describe and compare action research and appreciative inquiry as formal approaches to organizational change.

Action research is a highly participative, open-systems approach to change management that combines an action orientation (changing attitudes and behavior) with a research orientation (testing theory). It is a data-based, problem-oriented process that diagnoses

KEY TERMS

action research A problem-focused change process that combines action orientation (changing attitudes and behavior) and research orientation (testing theory through data collection and analysis).

appreciative inquiry An organizational change strategy that directs the group's attention away from its own problems and focuses participants on the group's potential and positive elements.

force field analysis Kurt Lewin's model of systemwide change that helps change agents diagnose the forces that drive and restrain proposed organizational change.

refreezing The latter part of the change process in which systems and conditions are introduced that reinforce and maintain the desired behaviors.

unfreezing The first part of the change process in which the change agent produces disequilibrium between the driving and restraining forces.

the need for change, introduces the intervention, and then evaluates and stabilizes the desired changes.

Appreciative inquiry embraces the positive organizational behavior philosophy by focusing participants on the positive and possible. Along with this positive principle, this approach to change applies the constructionist, simultaneity, poetic, and anticipatory principles. The four stages of appreciative inquiry include discovery, dreaming, designing, and delivering.

Large-group interventions, such as future search conferences, are highly participative events that typically try to get the entire system into the room. Parallel learning structures rely on social structures developed alongside the formal hierarchy with the purpose of increasing the organization's learning. They are highly participative arrangements, composed of people from most levels of the organization who follow the action research model to produce meaningful organizational change.

● ● **LO6** **Discuss two cross-cultural and three ethical issues in organizational change.**

One significant concern is that organizational change theories developed with a Western cultural orientation potentially conflict with cultural values in some other countries. Also, organizational change practices can raise one or more ethical concerns, including increasing management's power over employees, threatening individual privacy rights, and undermining individual self-esteem.